ⁿᵇˡᵉ Winston S. Churchill.

				1900	
1443	15	-	May	24	By sale 200 Goldfields
1350	-				" " 200 East Rands
3623	2	6			" " 100 Rand Mine
54	16	10	June	30	" interest @ 3%
436	17	11	Oct	15	" " " "
1602	10	-		19	" Cash
782	10	-	Nov.	19	" "
1762	10	-	Dec.	3	" "
1002	10	-		13	" profit 250 Atchison
951	5	-		31	" 3% interest
2011	14	6	Feb.	19	" div.ᵈ 100 Central Lond
950	-	-			" sale $2000- Nor. Pac. P.L.
600	-	-			" " $3000- Atchison. 4%
400	-	-			" " 100 " Or
300	-	-			" div.ᵈ 100 " Pres
550	-	-	May	15	" Sale 100 " do
1000	-	-	June	30	" interest @ 4%
300	-	-	Aug.	22	" div.ᵈ £1000- Cent. Lons. Ry.
250	-	-	Oct	18	" cp.ʰ $15000- Atchison Ad
700	-	-	Nov.	26	" Cash
500	-	-	Dec.	31	" interest @ 3½%
300	-	-	Jan.	15	" int. Lire 55,000- Ital Med
750	-	-	Feb.	12	" div. £1000- Central Lond
			Jan.	16	" " £1000 Mex Cent.
			May	3	" sale Lire 55.000- Ital Med.
				27	" " £10,000- New Cong
			June	3	" " 1000 Cent Lond Ry.
				30	" interest @ 3½%
			July	19	" " £1000- Mex Cent Sec
			Oct.	16	" return applic.ⁿ £10000- Japa

No More Champagne

David Lough studied history at Oxford under Richard Cobb, Michael Howard and Theodore Zeldin. After a career in financial markets, he founded a business that advises families on looking after their investments, tax affairs and estates.

No More Champagne

Churchill and His Money

David Lough

First published in the UK in 2015 by Head of Zeus Ltd

3 5 7 9 10 8 6 4

A CIP catalogue record for this book is available from
the British Library.

ISBN (HB) 9781784081812
ISBN (E) 9781784081805

Typeset by
e-type, Aintree, Liverpool

Printed in Great Britain by
Clays Ltd, St Ives plc

Head of Zeus Ltd
Clerkenwell House
45–47 Clerkenwell Green
London EC1R 0HT

www.headofzeus.com

To my mother Mary,
who taught me to read and write

CONTENTS

ILLUSTRATIONS

1. Frances Vane, marchioness of Londonderry, Churchill's great-grandmother (National Portrait Gallery).
2. Leonard Jerome, Churchill's maternal grandfather (The Granger Collection/Topfoto).
3. The Jerome family mansion on Madison Avenue in Manhattan, New York (Library of Congress).
4. Lord and Lady Randolph Churchill, 1874 (Churchill Archives Centre, The Papers of Sir Winston Churchill).
5. Winston and Jack Churchill as teenagers, 1892 (BNPS).
6. Churchill reporting on the Boer War in southern Africa, 1900 (Library of Congress).
7. Sir Ernest Cassel, banker and financial adviser, 1906 (Timea/Wiki).
8. Edward Marsh, Churchill's private secretary and literary assistant (Topfoto).
9. Churchill and his fiancée, Clementine Hozier, 1908 (Getty Images).
10. Churchill, as home secretary, on his way to the coronation of George V, 1911 (Ullstein bild/Getty Images).
11. Churchill and David Lloyd George, political allies, circa 1910 (Buyenlarge/Getty Images).
12. Churchill, First Lord of the Admiralty, inspecting trainee sailors, 1912 (Hulton Archive/Getty Images).
13. Colonel Churchill and his second-in-command Major Sir Archibald Sinclair, Armentières, 1916 (Keystone/Getty Images).
14. Thornton Butterworth, London publisher, 1938 (Churchill Archives Centre, The Papers of Sir Winston Churchill).
15. Charles Scribner III, New York publisher (Princeton University Archive).
16. Newman Flower, chairman of London publishers Cassell & Co. (Alamy).

INTRODUCTION

'The only thing that worries me in life is money.'*
Winston Churchill, 1898

THIS BOOK OWES its genesis to a provocative history teacher and to a scandalized grandmother. The first tried to stimulate independent thought in his fourteen-year-old pupils by describing Winston Churchill as 'a romantic old windbag'; when I took his verdict home as my own, the second ordered my re-education by setting me to read each volume of Churchill's official biography on its publication.

The early volumes of this work reveal how money problems weighed heavily on the young Churchill's mind, but the trail becomes fainter in the later volumes as the public man takes centre stage. Only in 1998 when Churchill's youngest daughter Mary published a collection of her parents' private correspondence did it become clear that financial difficulties dogged him for most of his life.

Although Churchill's many biographers have covered almost every imaginable angle of his life, none has tackled the story of his finances. Surprisingly most of the material needed to piece together the story survives and is open to researchers. One of Churchill's endearing characteristics is that he happily left his own bank statements, bills, investment records and tax demands in his archive, despite the fact that they reveal evidence of debts, gambling losses and last-minute rescues. Some of his financial benefactors partially

---

* Letter from Winston Churchill to his brother Jack, 16 February 1898 (CHAR 28/152/148, Churchill Archives Centre).

covered the trail by weeding out evidence from their own papers or by ordering their destruction, but it has been possible to fill most of the gaps. For example, Lady Soames kindly gave me permission, before her recent death, to examine those of her father's bank statements which survive in his bank's archive, although not in his own papers.

There are many reasons why the tale of Churchill and his money deserves to be told. It adds undeniable colour to a tapestry already rich in detail. It offers a human story of survival against the odds, although many of his difficulties were self-inflicted. It captures a time in British life when wealth was passing from a privileged few families of the landed aristocracy to a new class of entrepreneurs who were forging fortunes in businesses as varied as the railways, mining, newspapers and finance – the 'plutocrats', as they were known in their day. Unusually, Churchill had a foot in both camps: a grandson of the 7th duke of Marlborough, he was born a member of the aristocracy and enjoyed its trappings of expensive clothes, fine food, personal servants and the delayed payment of bills; yet he was equally at home among the new breed of entrepreneurs, many of whom were friends of his parents, especially of his talented and attractive American mother.

Churchill's financial trials also had an impact on his politics. When his father Lord Randolph Churchill died aged forty-five, he left no immediate allowance for his children in his will and the twenty-year-old Churchill had to rely on his own talents. Within five years he had built up a capital sum equivalent to a million pounds today. This meant that he could make an early start in politics, but it also gave him a greater affinity with the attitudes of 'new' money rather than 'old' when party politics demanded he choose between them. His early defection from the Tory Party of his aristocratic friends to the Liberal Party of enterprise is explained at least as well by his personal experiences of the decade following his father's death as it is by any abstract, ideological preference for 'free trade' over 'protection'. A lasting sense of betrayal at this defection among many Tories contributed to Churchill's loss of political office in 1915: his head was part of the price demanded by Tory leaders before they would join a wartime National Government.

Churchill's Liberal colleagues, in contrast, suspected that he remained a Tory at heart. Their suspicions were confirmed when, some twenty years later, he rejoined the Conservative benches. Biographers variously attribute Churchill's behaviour to a concern over social disorder following the war or to sheer political ambition, but there is a third possibility: Churchill had recently inherited his great-grandmother's Irish estate, transforming the erstwhile entrepreneur into a propertied landlord for the first time in his life – a *rentier*, as his wife Clementine put it.

To her intense disappointment, Churchill consumed the entire inheritance within a decade – by underestimating the cost of converting his new country home at Chartwell, by gambling more than he ever let on and by losing heavily in the Wall Street Crash of 1929, an episode curiously omitted from his official biography.

These losses caused another financial impact on his political career in the 1930s: Churchill resigned from the Conservative front bench not just because he was out of sympathy with the party's policy on future independence for India, but to devote sufficient time to writing books and churning out newspaper columns to keep the bank at bay. In return for his high fees as a journalist, Churchill's friends among the press proprietors expected colourful copy that ran against the conventional political wisdom. Churchill delivered it, but the trenchant journalism made his political rehabilitation more difficult.

Several times during the decade he held his journalist's pen in check while ministerial changes were in the air, but neither Prime Minister Stanley Baldwin nor his successor Neville Chamberlain was tempted to invite such an awkward talent back to the cabinet table at a time when the electorate preferred peace to adventure.

A common thread of exceptional risk-taking unites Churchill's financial dealings and his political career. This was never more clearly on display than in the 1930s, when he was a married man in his fifties with four dependent children and already borrowing today's equivalent of more than £2.5 million ($3.75 million). Yet, during the decade, he gambled heavily enough on his holidays to lose an average of £40,000 each year in today's money.

I have never encountered risk-taking on Churchill's scale during my career of advising people about their finances, including such natural risk-takers as entrepreneurs and politicians. I have sought an explanation for it in the growing body of literature that analyses Churchill's mind. However, this is inconclusive as to whether his appetite was simply a facet of a wonderfully extravagant personality or whether it pointed to a more complicated state of mind. Churchill himself referred to periods when the 'black dog' of anxiety or depression struck him; this book tells of contrasting phases during which he gambled or traded shares and currencies with such intensity that he appeared to be on a 'high' – devoid of inhibition, full of self-confidence and energy, but prone to 'risky behaviours'. The truth is that we will never know whether Churchill's addiction to risk was a matter of personality or state of mind; by today's standards of diagnosis, a psychiatrist would require a long, first-hand conversation with his subject before reaching a conclusion – and sadly Churchill is not available.

Whatever the driving force behind the risks he took, Churchill left behind him a trail of financial failures that required numerous rescues by family, friends and acquaintances, the story of which I tell in these pages. One rescuer alone wrote out two cheques, together worth more than £1 million ($1.5 million) today. He did so only because he admired Churchill's political courage, another testament to the links between Churchill's political career and his finances.

Throughout the Second World War many of those around Churchill worked hard to tame his risk-taking, their success ultimately evidenced by his willingness to delay the Allied invasion of Normandy until the summer of 1944. Churchill's attitude to his own finances underwent a similar conversion over the course of the war, during which he devoted more time to his private affairs than is often realized. Having begun the war with substantial debts, he finished it with today's equivalent of £4 million ($6 million) in his bank account. The secret of this turnaround lay not in books, as is often supposed, but in films.

The remarkable story of Churchill and his money only makes the man himself more fascinating. In an age when we demand that our politicians are paragons of financial virtue it is salutary to discover that one of the most successful political figures of the twentieth century ran up huge personal debts, gambled heavily, lost large amounts on the stock exchange, avoided tax with great success and paid his bills late.

NOTES TO THE READER

Biographical footnotes: biographical footnotes are given in the main text only if the person continues to play a role in Churchill's financial life. Notes on those people who feature in Churchill's public life are on page 432, before the Reference Notes.

'*Conservative and Unionist*' *Party*: the Tory group in British politics became known officially as the Conservative Party after 1845, although many people still used the term 'Tories' as a form of shorthand. Between 1895 and 1905 the Conservative Party formed governments with the help of Liberal Unionists; from 1909 it changed its name to the Conservative and Unionist Party. Until after 1922, when the Irish Free State came into existence, party members were most often known as Unionists. For simplicity, they are called Conservatives in this book – or Tories for short.

Monetary values: all amounts are quoted in the currency and the value of their day, as Churchill encountered them. A simple formula appears at the beginning of each chapter (and abbreviated at the top of each page) to help convert these amounts to an *approximate* value today.

This value can only be very approximate. Statistical techniques have changed over the period concerned, which exceeds 150 years. The conversion factors given in this book are also 'rounded' so as to help with quick mental arithmetic (rounded to the nearest 10 down to x50, to the nearest 5 down to x25, then to the nearest whole figure). Moreover no single multiple can cover the different rates at which different items of spending inflate in price: generally, manufactured goods have risen in price by less than the inflation multiple given, while the value of land, housing and wages has risen by more than the inflation multiple shown. Nevertheless, the conversion factors will give the reader a framework within which to appreciate the size of the sums Churchill earned, inherited, lost or spent.

Thus, in chapter 11, an American reader who wishes to convert Churchill's gambling losses in 1923 – £2,000 – should use the chapter's exchange rate ($5 = £1) to convert the sum to $10,000; then multiply by the chapter's US inflation factor (x 15) to reach $150,000 as today's approximate equivalent.

Likewise, in chapter 13, a British reader who wishes to convert Churchill's losses in the Wall Street Crash of 1929 – $75,000 – should use the chapter's exchange rate (also $5 = £1) to convert the sum to £15,000: then multiply by the chapter's UK inflation factor (x 50) to reach £750,000 as the modern equivalent.*

---

* The conversion factors are derived from statistics published by the United Kingdom Office of National Statistics (Composite Price Index, 1750–2003, Economic Trends 604; 2004); by the Bank of England (Three Centuries of Data, 2010); and by the United States Bureau of Labour Statistics (Historical Statistics of the United States, volume 3, Consumer Price Indexes 1774–2003, Bilateral Exchange Rates in Europe 1913–99; 2006).

PRELUDE

———

CHURCHILL TOOK OFFICE as prime minister on 10 May 1940, the same day that German forces invaded Holland, Belgium and Luxembourg. Within a week his French counterpart Paul Reynaud told him that France's battle was lost, while Britain's professional army faced encirclement on the country's northeast coast. Shuttling back and forth across the Channel in an attempt to persuade the French to fight on, Churchill had to confront another unpleasant truth closer to home: he was running out of money to pay his household bills or his tax or the interest on his large overdraft, which was due at the end of the month.

He asked Lloyds Bank for a special statement of his account and gave it to the young magazine publisher Brendan Bracken, asking his fixer to arrange a rescue as discreet as the one he had managed two years earlier, just as Hitler had launched his *Anschluss* against Austria. Bracken took it to the same man who had helped then, the Austrian-born banker and businessman Sir Henry Strakosch, who had asked for nothing in return and had kept the secret. On 18 June, the day after 4,000 British troops lost their lives when their ship sank off the French coast in the worst maritime loss in British history, Sir Henry wrote out a cheque for £5,000 (equivalent to £250,000 today). He disguised the trail by entering Brendan Bracken's name as the payee, but Bracken endorsed it on to Britain's embattled prime minister.

The amount reached Churchill's account on 21 June. Thus fortified, he paid a clutch of overdue bills from shirt-makers, watch-repairers and wine merchants before he turned his attention back to the war.

1

'Very little money on either side'
The Churchills and Jeromes

Exchange rate: $5 = £1
Inflation multiples (1850): US x 30; UK x 100

I T WAS IN August 1873, at an afternoon ball on board the HMS
Ariadne, then at anchor off the Isle of Wight for Cowes Week,
that two families from very different worlds collided. Lord
Randolph Churchill, the younger son of the 7th duke of
Marlborough, had been a natural choice on the guest list of the
prince and princess of Wales to meet Grand Duke Cesarevitch of
Russia and his duchess. More surprising was the inclusion of Mrs
Clara Jerome, the American wife of a colourful Wall Street
entrepreneur. It was true that she had featured at the Parisian
court of Napoleon III, until the self-styled emperor had been
driven from the capital three years earlier, but Mrs Jerome's place
on the royal guest list probably owed more to a shortage of suitable
young females. Staying with her for the season in a rented house at
Cowes were her three daughters Clarita, Jeannette and Leonie, the
first two over eighteen and therefore eligible to attend.

It was Jeannette, better known as Jennie, who caught the eye of
Lord Randolph Churchill across the ship's wardroom that afternoon. She was slim and dark, hinting at her mother's Indian
background; he was slight and narrow-shouldered with the pale,
almost translucent skin of a typical Churchill male. After one dance
together they spent the rest of the afternoon deep in conversation,
which came easily to Jennie, who had been educated in New York

and Paris, but which startled Lord Randolph, whose six sisters' education had been limited to the attentions of a governess inside the confines of the ducal home at Blenheim Palace, although he himself had read history and law at Oxford.

Over the next few days Jennie persuaded her mother to invite Lord Randolph to dinner twice and they managed two more unsupervised conversations. Before he left Cowes the duke's son proposed marriage and the equally impulsive daughter of Wall Street accepted.

'Mr Jerome is a gentleman who is obliged to live in New York to look after his business. I do not know what it is,' Lord Randolph hastily explained in a letter to his father, on whom he remained wholly reliant for the income he would need in order to marry. 'He is reputed to be very well-off and his daughters, I believe, have very good fortunes, but I do not know anything for certain.'[1] In fact, both families had seen better days. 'Very little money on either side' was the more accurate verdict, some sixty years later, of the couple's first son, Winston Churchill.[2]

Timothy Jerome had set sail for America from the Isle of Wight back in 1710, settling on arrival in Connecticut, before the family later moved up the east coast to the state of New York. Jennie's father Leonard was born in 1818, the fifth of eight sons and one daughter to Isaac Jerome, a doctor and descendant of Timothy's. His elder brothers attended the expensive College of New Jersey in Princeton, but Leonard, whose reputation was as a high-spirited nuisance, had to complete his studies elsewhere after family financial support melted away. He emerged, nevertheless, with high enough marks to join his brother Lawrence on the legal staff of his uncle, Judge Hiram K. Jerome, and each was to marry one of the two Hall sisters, whose parents had died early and left them comfortably off.

Clara's reserve contrasted with Leonard's charm and extroversion, while her family money helped the brothers buy a local newspaper, the *Rochester Daily American*, which they sold five years later after trebling its circulation. Leonard moved on to a telegraph company in New York, where he shared a home in Brooklyn with another brother, Addison, who persuaded him to change career and join him buying and selling shares on Wall Street. New York still boasted only nineteen millionaires at the time, but the number was clearly set to grow as the American population increased.

After the birth of their first daughter, Leonard put his business career briefly on hold to answer a call from President Fillmore, whom the brothers had supported as a state politician, to take up a consulship to a European city. Trieste, on the Adriatic coast, attracted the European aristocracy at play during the summer and, although Leonard stayed only eighteen months before he insisted on returning to sort out his affairs in New York, it proved long enough to leave Clara with a lifelong fascination for court life.

Their second daughter,* known as 'Jennie', was born in 1854, just before a fall in the share price of the Cleveland and Toledo Railroad Company, of which Leonard was a large shareholder. It was the first real check to his career. Unabashed, the brothers combined with a Maryland financier to start a new stockbroking business, Travers Jerome, exploiting their strong newspaper contacts by entertaining editors to excellent lunches where they planted share tips for publication, having first positioned their own portfolios appropriately. By the late 1850s Leonard was reputed to be worth $10 million on paper,[3] but progress was uneven and after one less successful episode he deemed it wise to retreat with the family for a few months to Paris, where they rented an apartment on the Champs-Elysées and found themselves, as wealthy Americans, fêted at the Imperial Court.

When they returned to New York in 1859 it was to a city that stretched no further north than 23rd Street[4] and remained the social domain of the 400 descendants of the Dutch settlers who could fit into the ballroom of the former Caroline Schermerhorn,

---

* A third, Camille, followed in 1855, but died in 1863; a fourth, Leonie, was born in 1859.

now Mrs William Astor.[5] Excluded from the chosen few, Leonard bought land next to their stronghold on the corner of Madison Avenue and 23rd Street, where he built a French-style mansion in red brick and white marble at a cost of $55,000. Its ballroom may have held a mere 300, but alongside it stood a theatre for 600 in which liveried servants led guests to their seats as Leonard hosted the city's leading musical talent, much of it female.

Leonard Jerome's fortune was to reach its peak during the American Civil War (1861–5), in the course of which he offered strong support to Abraham Lincoln and the North's anti-slavery cause through the pages of *The New York Times*, where he and the family had built up the largest shareholding of almost 20 per cent.[6] Just as the American business magnate Cornelius Vanderbilt used his position as the government's shipping agent to expand his fortune during the war, Leonard took advantage of coded information passed from the battlefields by his own telegraph company to deal audaciously on the stock market. He had settled enough money on Clara to make her secure, but contemporaries spoke of an almost blind risk-taking, combined with a complete confidence in his own destiny: 'He used to paralyse his friends by the magnitude of his transactions,' wrote his biographer Anita Leslie. 'Clara said she did not think he himself knew how many millions he had made or lost. Too many other interests held his attention.'[7]

By the late 1860s, tiring of her husband's adventures and extramarital affairs, Clara used her financial independence to remove her daughters from Miss Lucy Green's boarding school on Fifth Avenue, where they had been taught French, and take them back to Paris, this time without their father. Jennie attended a *lycée* and studied piano to concert standard under a friend of Chopin's, while her mother established her own *salon* at their home on the Boulevard Malesherbes and re-inserted herself at the court of Emperor Napoleon III and the Empress Eugénie.

Soon afterwards her husband's fortunes began to falter in New York, where he suffered a serious theft of valuable bearer bonds from his office, followed by the failure of a new share issue that he had underwritten for the Pacific Mail Steamship Company in which he was the largest shareholder. His losses were said to have halved his fortune.[8] More widespread falls in share prices during 1869 reduced his wealth to little more than the value of his Madison Square mansion, which he let for $25,000 a year to the Union League Club, before leaving to join the family in Paris. He reached the French capital in January 1870, only to be greeted by rioters in the streets protesting against the excesses of the imperial regime. Leonard led his family to temporary sanctuary in Nice, but they were back in Paris – and he in New York – by the summer, when a desperate Napoleon III tried to shore up his crumbling support by declaring war on Prussia. It was a serious miscalculation: within weeks Otto von Bismarck's forces threatened the French capital, forcing Clara and her daughters to catch the last train to Deauville so that they could cross to safety in England.

Leonard arranged a suite of rooms for them all at Brown's Hotel off Piccadilly, but after Paris the family found London damp and polluted. Leonard crossed the Atlantic and took them for the summer of 1871 to enjoy the sea air of the Isle of Wight, where he knew the annual Cowes yachting festival would attract the English and European aristocracy that Clara missed. The expedition was such a success that it was repeated each summer, even after the women had returned to Paris. Leonard joined them in 1872, but a slide in share prices prevented him from leaving New York the following year. A telegram bringing news of the first falls had reached Leonard while he was dining with friends. He waited until the end of the meal before announcing its contents: 'Gentlemen, it is a message in which you are all interested. The bottom has fallen out of stocks and I am a ruined man. But your dinner is paid for and I did not want to disturb you while you were eating it.'[9] Clara and their daughters therefore arrived in Cowes on their own for the season of 1873.

Like the Jeromes', the Churchills' fortune had also been built within a generation, although it took longer to dissipate. Born in 1650, its chief creator John Churchill had grown up in the shadow of depri-vation after his father Winston was fined three times the annual income from his small estate, all because as a young captain in the king's army he had fought on the losing side during the English Civil War (1642–51). The experience shaped what his biographer and direct descendant Winston Churchill described as an 'iron parsimony and personal frugality, never relaxed in the blaze of fortune and abundance'.[10]

Following the Restoration in 1660, the sixteen-year-old John Churchill's elder sister managed to secure him an appointment as a page at the court of Charles II's younger brother James, duke of York, a Catholic. Within a year John had shrewdly learned to combine twin incomes from simultaneous court and military service by gaining a commission in the King's Own Company of the First Guards (later the Grenadier Guards). A third stream of earnings (some claim as the most lucrative) came from services provided in the bedroom of the king's former mistress Barbara Villiers; however, these ceased on his marriage to the sixteen-year-old Sarah Jennings, an attendant to the duke's younger daughter Princess Anne. Sarah came without dowry or family connections, but with an astuteness and independence of mind that never left her.

By the time their patron had succeeded his brother on the throne in 1685 as James II and Princess Anne had formed her own court on marriage, the newly ennobled Lord Churchill and his wife employed seven liveried servants at homes in London and the countryside. The smooth progress of their twin careers met its first serious challenge when Prince William of Orange, who was married to the king's elder daughter Mary, raised the standard of Protestant revolt against his Catholic father-in-law, presenting Churchill with a difficult choice. A committed Protestant himself, yet one of the king's most senior military officers, he waited to see which way the wind was blowing before switching allegiance on the battlefield, a manoeuvre that required his wife to escort Princess Anne from London at the same moment, for their safety.

After the Glorious Revolution (1688–9) pragmatism dictated that the victorious new joint monarchs William III and Mary II should offer Churchill an earldom, which he took in the name of Marlborough. They also awarded him the lucrative task of reviewing his fellow officers' fitness to retain their commissions. However, William and Mary never entirely trusted Marlborough, who kept lines open to the former king's exiled supporters in France, and Mary engineered his dismissal from all court and military appointments in 1692.

Marlborough's rehabilitation began after her death two years later, but it was not complete until Princess Anne came to the throne in 1702, when she showered the earl and countess of Marlborough with appointments. The countess earned £6,000 a year from combined positions as groom of the stole, mistress of the robes and keeper of the privy purse, while Marlborough became responsible for equipping and supplying Queen Anne's army as master of the ordnance, a post that no predecessor had left without becoming a great deal richer.

Their joint income, already estimated at £64,000 a year,[11] rose still further when Marlborough was given command of the combined armies of Britain, Holland and some German principalities that were to fight France in the long War of the Spanish Succession (1701–14). Marlborough not only earned a salary of £10,000 a year, but received a commission of 2½ per cent of the payroll of his combined armies; in theory this was intended to fund his headquarters and intelligence staff, but no detailed accounting was required.

Early military success, during which Marlborough outmanoeuvred the French Marshal Boufflers to capture Liège in the Low Countries, brought an offer from the queen of elevation from earl to duke. The countess advised against it, on account of the expense of a ducal lifestyle, but Marlborough accepted, after negotiating a lifetime pension of £5,000 a year from Post Office revenues. Parliament had refused Queen Anne's initial request that the pension should be extended in perpetuity to Churchill's heirs, but changed its mind after a clear military victory against

Franco-Bavarian forces at the Battle of Blenheim (13 August 1704) in Bavaria.

The queen marked this success by a grant of land at Woodstock, near Oxford, where Marlborough could build a commemorative palace at public expense. Marlborough continued his series of victories over French commanders at the battles of Ramillies (23 May 1706), Oudenarde (11 July 1708) and Malplaquet (11 September 1709), each of which expanded the list of his spoils from grateful European princes, but none was decisive enough to bring the campaign to an end. Eventually the political tide at home began to turn against proponents of the costly war, with the result that the duke and duchess of Marlborough found themselves mercilessly lampooned by Jonathan Swift and other satirists for 'profiteering' at the public expense.

The queen put a stop to the payment of bills at Blenheim, where construction had already cost £130,000, and parliament went further in 1712 by calling for Marlborough to reimburse more than £400,000 to the public purse. Taking refuge in Europe, where he was widely fêted, the duke carefully cultivated the support of the House of Hanover, to whom the British throne would pass on Queen Anne's death because none of her children had survived childhood. Although his health was too poor for a return to public life, Marlborough returned to London on the day after Anne died, as work resumed on his palace at Blenheim. He finally moved into part of the building three years before his death in 1722.

The dowager duchess had always considered the building a wasteful extravagance, but dutifully used the £50,000 set aside in her husband's will to complete it in his memory. Justifiably nervous that it would prove an expensive liability in the long term, she set about building up the surrounding land to strengthen the finances of the estate while she still remained its trustee and tenant for her remaining years.

As an additional precaution against profligate heirs, she arranged for the building itself, her husband's prizes inside (such as the paintings, jewellery and porcelain presented to him after his victories), and the core surrounding estate to be protected from sale in perpetuity by a special Act of Parliament. Although she outlived her husband by twenty-two years, during which her determination to secure the future of Blenheim never flagged, the estate reached no more than half the size of its conterparts owned by the longer-established dukes of Devonshire, Norfolk and Northumberland, each of whom owned more than 100,000 acres of land.[12]

In addition, her determination to maintain an iron control over the Blenheim estate proved ill-suited to the family unity required to consolidate its recent origins. Exceptionally, Parliament had allowed the Marlborough title to pass down the female line, after the Churchills' only son had died of smallpox aged seventeen. The dowager duchess, however, was not on speaking terms with her elder daughter Henrietta, who succeeded to the dukedom on her father's death. The dowager duchess disapproved equally strongly of her younger daughter Anne's son Charles Spencer, who became the next in line to take over the dukedom after Henrietta's only surviving son died in 1731.

Charles had already assumed the smaller Spencer family fortune before he became the 3rd duke of Marlborough in 1733. He could expect to inherit the further £60,000 a year which the Blenheim estate yielded until the dowager duchess died, but he unwisely paid little attention to her views on a suitable marriage partner or to her threats to disinherit him of her personal share of the estate unless he gave up an addiction to gambling. When she finally died in 1744, the dowager duchess was as good as her word: in the first fateful weakening of the Marlborough fortune, the twenty-sixth version of her will left almost half of the estate, the portion that she had accumulated and personally controlled, not to the 3rd duke but to his younger brother Johnny.[13]

During the fourteen years that he had left to run Blenheim, the 3rd duke economized sufficiently to pass on an estate producing an income of £45,000 a year, of which half was required to meet allowances for members of the family. The 4th duke, a man of charm and a great connoisseur, spent the first part of his sixty-year reign at Blenheim building up its collection of books and gems and remodelling its landscape with the help of the landscape architect Capability Brown, before he, too, was forced to economize by cutting the size of the household staff to seventy-five.

It was his son, the future 5th duke, who was to prove the main agent in the decline of the family fortunes. Forced to wait in the wings for several decades on an allowance of £2,000 a year, George Spencer-Churchill indulged himself in expensive passions for books, plants and women by borrowing ever greater sums against his eventual inheritance. When his father allowed the family trustees to buy him the 2,580-acre Whiteknights estate on his marriage, George was spurred into spending a further £25,000 on books and £50,000 on plants, which needed a team of fifty gardeners to look after them.[14]

Whiteknights had to be mortgaged to raise £45,000 to reduce his debts in 1815, two years before he announced his succession at Blenheim by redesigning its gardens with cash raised by the sale of land. Within three years Whiteknights was seized by its mortgagors and bailiffs arrived at Blenheim to claim any fittings not protected by the ancient Act of Parliament: the 5th duke hired replacements for the furniture they seized from a firm of Piccadilly upholsterers at a cost of £50 a year.[15] 'The family of the great Duke is gone sadly to decay and are but a disgrace to the illustrious name of Churchill,' the duke of Wellington's companion Mrs Arbuthnot wrote after visiting Blenheim. 'The Duke is overloaded with debt and very little better than a common swindler.'[16]

When he died in 1840 his successor the 6th duke was confronted by urgent repairs costing £80,000 on an estate reduced to an income of £10,000.[17] He had no option but to accelerate the sale of assets unprotected by the Act of Parliament and to start borrowing against whatever remained.[18] Confined to a wheelchair for the last years of his life, he parted with rare books, engravings, musical instruments, clocks, china and porcelain before leaving the stage in 1857 to Winston Churchill's grandfather.

While 'not rich for a Duke' (as Benjamin Disraeli drily observed to Queen Victoria),[19] the 7th duke made a determined effort to match expenditure to income. Eventually, however, he had to resort to more asset sales. First to go, in 1862, were peripheral estates in Wiltshire and Shropshire; next, in 1870, more books; early in 1873 it was the turn of the gemstones collected by his great-grandfather, which fetched 35,000 guineas.[20] By the time his younger son Lord Randolph announced his unexpected plans to marry an American, the duke was planning the sale of more land in Buckinghamshire, which Baron Ferdinand de Rothschild bought for £220,000. The Blenheim estate was reduced to 23,000 acres in Oxfordshire, well below the 30,000 acres that marked out Britain's top 250 landowning families.[21]

American heiresses had become increasingly attractive to the straitened aristocracy,* but in this case neither the duke nor the duchess approved of their son's match. After making early enquiries in London about the background of Jennie Jerome's family, the duke was not encouraging: 'From what you have told me & what I have heard,' he wrote to Randolph, 'this Mr J seems to be a sporting, and I should think, vulgar kind of man. It is evident he is of the class of speculators; he has been bankrupt once; and may be so again.'[22] Leonard Jerome, by contrast, initially approved, telling his wife to agree an allowance of £2,000 a year for their daughter, but changed his tune abruptly on hearing that the duke had extended the investigation of his family to America, using the help of the British Embassy in Washington.

Undeterred, Lord Randolph returned to Cowes where he managed to secure the approval of the prince of Wales for his choice of bride. It was a signal for his parents to concede that the

---

* By 1907 more than 500 'dollar princesses' are said to have married titled Europeans, taking some $220 million with them to their adopted continent. This trend led to the launch of a quarterly magazine, *Titled Americans: A List of American Ladies Who Have Married Foreigners of Rank*, which was published in America.

match should proceed if both parties wished it to do so after waiting for a full year. His father had always earmarked him for a career in politics and Lord Randolph managed to reduce the waiting time by half by agreeing to stand for what amounted to the family seat in Parliament at Woodstock, near Blenheim, when an unexpected election was called before the end of the year. His victory duly achieved, the duke and duchess agreed to visit Jennie in Paris, where her prowess in playing Beethoven sonatas on the piano and in discussing British politics led them to approve the start of formal negotiations between the two families for a marriage settlement, a form of legal agreement used in England at the time to set out each family's financial contributions to a marriage and to determine their distribution among future generations.

The duke's lawyers opened the bidding by suggesting that he would contribute an income of £1,000 a year, secured by a £20,000 charge against the Blenheim estate.[23] Leonard Jerome's team talked of contributing an income twice as high, $10,000 a year, backed by $200,000 of capital.[24] His enthusiasm for the match had been rekindled, as he told his daughter: 'Between you and I and the post – and your mother etc I am delighted more than I can tell. It is magnificent. The greatest match any American has made since the Duchess of Leeds.'[25]

When the duke's advisers held out for a capital sum of $250,000 – to be secured on Leonard's New York racetrack and remaining railroad shares, as well as his Manhattan mansion – the negotiations became more difficult. It was partly a matter of distance and partly of each family's fanciful ideas of the other's wealth. There was an added complication when Leonard made it clear that he expected to pay his allowance to his daughter and not to her husband. The Churchill solicitor warned Lord Randolph of the consequences: 'Miss Jerome is made quite independent of you in a pecuniary sort of way, which in my experience is most unusual.'[26]

The impasse continued until a week before the wedding, when Leonard suggested a compromise under which half his contribution went to each side, but he told the duke that he thought 'your

English custom of making the wife so utterly dependent upon the husband most unwise'.[27] The duke responded by agreeing to clear his son's debts and promising to provide £10,000 towards the couple's purchase of a London house.[28]

The settlement documents reached Paris for signing on the eve of the wedding at the chapel of the British Embassy on 15 April 1874. 'I am quite decided that Jennie will have to manage the money,' Lord Randolph told his father afterwards, 'and I am quite sure that she will keep everything straight, for she is clever, and like all Americans, has a sacred, and I should almost say, insane horror of buying anything she cannot pay for.'[29] It was a monumental misjudgement, a hint of which lay in the twenty-five gowns from leading Parisian couturiers that made up Jennie's trousseau.

2

'How I long for you to be back with sacks of gold'

Spendthrift Parents, 1875–94

Exchange rate: $5 = £1
Inflation multiples: US x 25; UK x 100

B Y THE END of their honeymoon (or earlier) the Churchills were expecting their first child. Before its arrival, they used the money given to them by the duke of Marlborough to buy a four-storey London home in Charles Street, near Berkeley Square, where they settled down to live off their joint income of more than £3,000 a year. This should have proved sufficient in mid-Victorian Britain, at a time when average earnings barely exceeded £50 a year, but difficulties soon emerged. Lord Randolph could not throw off the Churchill penchant for gambling, whether at cards, on the horses or in casinos around the coast of France.

Still less could his wife wean herself off Parisian couturiers when preparing her wardrobe for a summer season at London's dinner parties and country house weekends. To make certain they could entertain in the style expected of an ambitious politician, the Churchills employed a butler, French cook, footman, valet, lady's maid and a housemaid.

Once the season was over, Jennie withdrew to Blenheim where she gave birth to her first child unexpectedly early at the end of November 1874. He was christened Winston Leonard. Writing his father's biography some thirty years later, Churchill described how his parents soon resumed their life in London 'on a somewhat more generous scale than their income warranted'.[1] The problem was compounded by the fact that Leonard Jerome's allowance from New York sometimes arrived late or not at all. In 1876 they had to borrow £2,400 from Standard Insurance; early the following year, the Charles Street house was put on the market and Lady Randolph moved to Paris as an 'economy' measure, while her husband negotiated a further loan in London. 'I shall get 5000£,' he wrote to her. 'There is also a balance of 682£ out of the valuation & house money. This latter I shall bring with me to Paris to pay your bills and keep us until March.'[2]

The next blow was social rather than financial. Lord Randolph had rashly backed his elder brother in a dispute with the prince of Wales over a married woman and in retaliation the prince refused to visit any London home that still welcomed the Churchills. Prudently, they removed themselves to New York, where they stayed with a demoralized Leonard Jerome. The situation appeared to be intractable, until the duke of Marlborough agreed to the prime minister's suggestion that it would be best for all concerned if he became Queen Victoria's viceroy in Ireland and took Lord Randolph to Dublin as his private secretary. Officially Lord Randolph remained unpaid by the crown, so he could retain his seat as an MP at Westminster, but £800 a year of his father's £21,000 a year viceregal expense allowance found its way to his bank account.[3]

The family remained in Ireland for almost three years until William Gladstone and his Liberal colleagues replaced Disraeli's Tory administration in April 1880. It was long enough for Jennie to produce a second son, christened John (but always known as Jack), and for the couple to require a third loan. Lord Randolph warned her it was 'positively the last we shall be able to make'.[4] Having witnessed Irish poverty and famine, Lord Randolph's politics carried a keen edge that turned him into a leading advocate for 'Tory Democracy', a more progressive policy that encouraged Conservatives to adopt reforms popular with newly enfranchised voters instead of allowing the Liberal Party to pose as their sole champions. At the same time, however, a shortage of funds continued to restrain the couple's social life. 'I haven't been to many balls, as I simply cannot afford to get dresses and one can't wear always the same thing,' Lady Randolph reported to her mother. 'Money is such a hateful subject to me just now don't let us talk about it.'[5]

For all his growing political success, Lord Randolph was troubled by mounting health problems[*] which forced a leave of absence from Westminster. The Churchills returned to New York. Leonard Jerome could still not pay their allowance regularly, but after remortgaging his Manhattan mansion he handed over a capital sum which allowed them to buy a new London home on the northern, less fashionable side of Hyde Park.

Another change in Lord Randolph's fortunes arrived in July 1883 when the duke of Marlborough died suddenly of a heart attack. His eldest son George automatically became the 8th duke, inheriting Blenheim and its immediate estate, but the 7th duke's will awarded his personal estate, valued at £146,000, to his second son Lord Randolph after the dowager duchess's eventual death and after it had paid dowries of £10,000 on the marriage of each surviving daughter.[6] His inheritance prospects thus clarified, Lord Randolph was able to repay the loans he had accumulated from unofficial moneylenders and to borrow £31,000 in their place from Scottish Widows Insurance Company, at a lower rate.

He was powerless, however, to prevent his elder brother from raising much larger sums by selling off more of Blenheim's treasures. Lord Randolph's father the 7th duke had persuaded his political friends that the only way to save Blenheim was to amend the protective Act of Parliament and allow the sale of the 1st duke's possessions. The 7th duke had limited himself to selling off one of

---

[*] These may or may not have been related to the onset of syphilis, the latent period of which can continue for ten or twenty years before the final phase. Modern medical opinion suggests that syphilis may not have been the problem: Dr John Mather has suggested that Lord Randolph may have been suffering from a left-sided brain tumour; others have advanced the possibility of a genetic bipolar disorder. However, the illness was certainly treated as syphilis.

Europe's greatest private libraries for £57,000,[7] but the 8th duke now consigned Blenheim's collection of Old Masters paintings – including works by Raphael, Titian, Rubens, Van Dyck, Stubbs and Gainsborough[8] – to the National Gallery or auction rooms, where they fetched more than £400,000.*

Lord Randolph consoled himself by escaping to winter sunshine in India, a visit that paved the way for his appointment as secretary of state for the colony when the Conservative Party displaced Gladstone's Liberal government in the middle of 1885. The post brought a welcome ministerial salary of £5,000, the standard reward at the time for a secretary of state (and considerably higher in real terms than their salary today). However it lasted just six months because Gladstone temporarily recaptured power early in 1886. Within another six months the Liberals had been driven out of power again by a decisive Conservative campaign against home rule for Ireland, masterminded by Lord Randolph.

The new Tory prime minister Lord Salisbury rewarded the thirty-six-year-old Lord Randolph with the twin posts of chancellor of the exchequer and leader of the House of Commons. This time the salary would have lasted longer had Lord Randolph not overestimated the strength of his political capital: he tried to force cuts in military expenditure on colleagues who already resented his forays into their ministerial territory. The situation worsened and the prime minister calmly accepted Lord Randolph's impulsive letter of resignation.

This sudden loss of both position and salary came as a shock to Lord Randolph, but neither he nor Jennie made any serious attempt

---

* The 8th duke required more money to modernize Blenheim. He enlisted help in finding a rich American bride from Leonard Jerome, who suggested a thirty-three-year-old widow, Lily Hammersley. A native of Troy in the state of New York, Lily had inherited $5 million on the death of her first husband. After the wedding in 1888, she was affectionately known as 'Lily of Troy'. Leonard died in 1891; his wife Clara paid off his debts just before she died in 1895.

to curb their spending. Their marriage was under strain, and an increasingly ill Lord Randolph spent long periods abroad each winter, while for three successive summers they economized by renting out their London home and spending the season in a house rented by the dowager duchess near Newmarket racecourse. Here their young sons Winston and Jack would sell hens' eggs to supplement their pocket money, which was always in short supply.[9]

Racing produced one of Lord Randolph's rare financial successes: his mare L'Abbesse de Jouarre cost only £300 but during her career won prize money of more than £6,000.[10] More often, however, the Churchills' finances remained chaotic. 'I regained at baccarat all I lost at racing,' Lord Randolph told his wife in 1890. 'I am sorry your money affairs are in such confusion & have told Hemmerde [of the London and Westminister Bank] to put £500 in your account. In June you had £400 & £1500, but you only account for £1,477 leaving £400 + £300 overdrawn unaccounted for. . . You had better send me Rouff's [a French publisher] bills.'[11]

That autumn Lord Randolph turned down a salary of £2,000 a year to chair an American mining company; he was confident that he could find better-paid work in the City of London if he needed to. Since his schooldays he had remained a close friend of Nathaniel Rothschild, now Lord Rothschild and the head of a family that had led the City's move into funding the trade of luxury goods and precious metals.[12] Through The Exploration Company[13] the Rothschilds provided logistical and financial support to expeditions designed to expand gold-mining in southern Africa, a new frontier; the region accounted for only 1 per cent of the world's gold production in 1890, but would reach 15 per cent just two years later.[14] Alfred Beit, a mining expert close to the Rothschilds, was convinced they could mine down to deeper levels and he had already bought several properties in the Central Rand area to back his hunch.*

---

* Beit would float Deep Levels (his holding company for the individual deep-level mines in the Witwatersrand district) as the renamed Rand Mines

Leading such an expedition presented one of the few socially acceptable ways for the younger son of a duke to replenish the family coffers and by the spring of 1891 Lord Randolph had decided that this had become necessary.[15] He agreed to lead a party to explore further north in Mashonaland (a region which later became Rhodesia and is now in Zimbabwe), guided by a mining engineer and logistics expert found by the Rothschilds. Lord Randolph's bank lent him £1,000 of the £5,000 that he was to put into his syndicate; the remainder, which arrived late, came from a mysterious Mr Saunders. It was Lord Randolph, rather than the Rothschilds, who raised another £11,000 for the syndicate from 'family and friends',[16] while he secured a personal fee of £2,000 from his friends, the Borthwicks, to report on progress for their newspaper *The Morning Post.*[17]

By the time Lord Randolph had paid the Rothschilds' experts, £10,000 remained to meet the party's costs in Africa. Unfortunately, local supplies turned out to be twice as expensive as he had expected. 'The business affairs of my amalgamated syndicates out here are not altogether satisfactory,' Lord Randolph reported home. 'Very much more money has been spent than I or the people in London had any idea of and if their claims already acquired are not very valuable I shall have made a poor bargain.'[18]

After merging with two other expeditions to save money, the enlarged party made its way to Kimberley's diamond mines, its wagons pulled by ninety oxen, twelve mules, twelve donkeys and eight horses.[19] From there, they moved on to the recently discovered gold deposits near Johannesburg, where Lord Randolph asked his friend Oliver Borthwick to buy some 'Transvaal Silvers' and 'Nigels' shares in London,[20] while he invested the syndicate's temporarily surplus funds on the local stock exchange.[21]

The expedition's supplies for the six-week trek to Fort Salisbury

---

in 1893. He allowed his friends, such as the Rothschilds, Sir Ernest Cassel and Randolph Churchill, to buy shares privately before the flotation.

became the talk of the town: 'The wonderful thing was that they could never buy enough,' wrote the experienced African traveller Percy Fitzpatrick. 'They put in some supplementaries at Cape Town, and some "after-thoughts" at Kimberley, and etceteras at Johannesburg, and extras at Pretoria, and replenishments at Pietersburg, till they looked like the commissariat of a continental army.'[22]

On reaching Mashonaland, £5,000 remained for buying mining concessions, but the engineers found only one shaft that showed any promise. They bought it for £2,000.[23] After two weeks of excavation Lord Randolph wrote to tell Jennie that 'The Matchless', as they called it, looked good enough to be worth 'from quarter to half a million'. It then filled with water and had to be abandoned.[24]

Back at home, money remained an acute problem. Jennie had sold the Hyde Park home in order to economize, taking refuge with the children at the dowager duchess of Marlborough's house in Grosvenor Square.[25] 'How I long for you to be back with sacks of gold,' she wrote,[26] but her husband confessed that the expedition's only real success had been a £1,000 profit on the shares he had bought in Johannesburg; when final accounts were compiled, investors found they had lost their entire capital. (The Rothschilds debited the final shortfall of £370 to Lord Randolph's estate.)

'I shall cut politics & try to make a little money for the boys and ourselves,' Lord Randolph told Jennie as he set off for home, but he had, as it turned out, already taken the first vital steps to doing so.[27] The expedition had provided him with valuable intelligence about the gold fields of the Transvaal's Witwatersrand district, to which he had diverted his mining experts on their return journey. It was their favourable report that convinced him to spend £1,250 of his own money to take up an offer from Alfred Beit of 5,000 shares in his new private mining company Deep Levels, at five shillings per share, before he floated it publicly on a stock exchange. The rapidly rising value of these shares was to fund Lord Randolph's family for the remainder of his life and to form the cornerstone of his legacy.[28]

*

Winston Churchill made his first plea for more cash on his first day at school, when he lost his pocket money. The requests soon became more frequent. 'You do get through it in the most rapid manner,'[29] his mother told him.

It was the one subject on which he fell out with his nanny Mrs Everest, who once complained that Winston had asked for a second loan before even acknowledging the first: 'I am extremely sorry my dear Boy I cannot oblige you this time it is utterly impossible unless you wish me to starve,' she wrote. 'I do think you are awfully extravagant to have spent 15/- in a week. Some familys [*sic*] of 6 or 7 people have to live upon 12/- a week. You squander it away & the more you have the more you want to spend.'[30]

Jennie opened a bank account for Winston when he was fourteen, instructing the London & Westminster's manager to transfer twenty shillings into it each month from her own account. She tried her best to install a sense of financial discipline in him: 'The only thing you must avoid on all accounts is <u>not</u> to overdraw the money due to you.' Her credentials for offering such advice are dubious; in any event he ignored it.[31]

Winston was seventeen when Lord Randolph returned from Africa. When Winston won a fencing competition at his school, Harrow, Lord Randolph gave him two pounds to buy a present for his instructor. He lost his temper when Winston overspent and asked for more. 'If you were a millionaire you could not be more extravagant,' Lord Randolph wrote. 'I think you have got through about £10 this term. This cannot last & if you are not more careful should you get into the army six months of it will see you in the Bankruptcy Court.'[32]

Winston turned to female relations for help: Aunt Cornelia, one his father's sisters who had married into the wealthy Guest steel family, and Duchess Lily, the wealthy American heiress who had married the 8th duke of Marlborough, were special favourites. His mother could also be relied on to help, albeit only after a ritual dressing-down. 'Yr wants are many – & you seem a perfect sieve as regard money,' she wrote in answer to one such plea; nevertheless, she enclosed a thirty-shilling postal order.[33]

When Winston failed to pass the Royal Military Academy's entrance exam for his intended career as an army officer his increasingly unwell father was exasperated and threatened his son with a career 'in business' if he failed again. ('I could get him something very good with Natty [Nathaniel, Lord Rothschild] or Horace [Farquharson] or Cassel,'* Lord Randolph told the dowager duchess.)[34] Winston did fail a second time, but his improved placing (203rd out of 664 candidates) led to a rapid transfer into a London crammer that specialized in the entrance exam. Back at Harrow, Jack was left to settle his older brother's debts to fellow pupils. At his third attempt, Winston passed the exam, but he came too far down the list to qualify for the less expensive infantry and would therefore have to enter the cavalry. His increasingly irascible father was scathing:

> By accomplishing the astonishing feat of getting into the Cavalry, you imposed on me an extra charge of some £200 a year. . . Make this position indelibly impressed on your mind, that if your conduct and action at Sandhurst is similar to what it has been in the other establishments in which it has [been] sought vainly to impart to you some education, then that part of my responsibility for you is over. I shall leave you to depend on yourself giving you merely such assistance as may be necessary to permit of a respectable life.[35]

However, when he arrived at Sandhurst Winston was immediately elevated to the infantry. Admitting to some 'past extravagance', he

---

* Ernest Cassel (1852–1921), born to a Jewish family in Germany; arrived in Liverpool 1869; started his own banking business in London 1870; a City leader investing in railroad companies, sugar, diamond and gold mines by 1900; financial adviser to the prince of Wales (later Edward VII); retired following the king's death 1910. Knighted 1899.

appealed to his father for a fresh start to his finances: 'I should so much like to have an annual allowance – payable quarterly. Out of it, I would get my clothes, pay for my amusements – railway journeys – and sundries (cigarettes etc): in fact everything. . . I will promise to keep accounts of what I spend and send them to you regularly.'[36]

Lord Randolph, however, was not yet ready to cut the purse strings, as he explained to the dowager duchess: 'I thought he was somewhat precipitate in his ideas about an allowance & that his figures were too summary. I told him I would give him £10 a month out of which he would have to pay for small articles of clothing, & for other small necessities but that I will continue to pay his tailor and haberdasher.'[37]

His health deteriorating, Lord Randolph often forgot to send a cheque or sent it late, making his son late in paying his mess bills. 'It is no use me trying to explain to Papa,' Winston complained to his mother. 'I suppose I shall go on being treated as "that boy" until I am 50 years old.'[38] After a rare visit to Sandhurst in November, however, Lord Randolph was impressed by the change in his son. Flush after a recent share sale, he explained to the dowager duchess that he had relented:[39] 'I paid his mess bill for him £6 so that his next allowance might not be *"empiété"* upon.'[40]

Early in 1894 the thaw between father and son came to an abrupt end when the 7th duke's gold watch ended up at the bottom of a Sandhurst lake; the local fire brigade had to pump the lake dry to recover it. After being repaired, the watch was handed to Jack and Winston was told to buy his own replacement.[41] 'Oh! Winny, what a harum scarum fellow you are,' his mother commiserated the next day. 'I am sending you £2 with my love.'[42]

In April Lord Randolph's doctors advised him to retire completely from politics and to take a trip around the world, accompanied by his wife and a specialist. To fund the voyage he sold L'Abbesse de Jouarre for £8,000[43] and borrowed £3,000 against his remaining gold shares,[44] but he made no special provision to keep up his son's allowance at Sandhurst. A worried Winston used a new typewriter to ask his father for an increased sum of £15 to be sent each month to a new account that he had opened with the army's bankers, Cox & Co.[*]

Lord Randolph's cool reply – the last letter he would write to his son – dissected Winston's request, sentence by sentence:

> You write stupidly on what you call the 'subject of finance'. 'Since I had my allowance you have given me a little extra without which I should have been terribly hard up (elegant). If therefore (logical!) you could make a <u>deposit!!</u> of <u>*say*</u> (commercial & banking expression) £15 which I was to draw upon (rather frail security) without real necessity (very difficult to define) & which I was to account to you for as I drew it out (perhaps you would, you have to send your letter 10,000 miles) it would make things so much easier.' Would it? Perhaps. I do not comment on this letter so delicately expressed except to observe that Jack would have cut off his fingers rather than write such a very free-spoken letter to his father. . . Finally if you are going to write letters to me when I am travelling, type-written & so ridiculously expressed I would rather not receive them.[45]

Winston wrote to his parents while they travelled, but there was no reply. 'I never saw him again, except as a swiftly-fading shadow,' he later recalled.[46] His father's health declined so sharply after they reached Asia in November that Jennie and the doctor decided on an immediate return home. 'He is quite unfit for society,' she told her sister.[47] They reached London just in time for Christmas, but Lord Randolph had less than a month to live. He fell into a coma and died on 24 January 1895 aged forty-five.

---

[*] Cox & Co. had served British army officers since 1758, when Richard Cox became secretary to Lord Ligonier, Colonel of the Grenadier Guards. Among the tasks Ligonier delegated to Cox was the disbursement of pay to his officers and men. Cox was so efficient that by 1815 he had been asked to perform the same task for the Household Brigade, Royal Artillery and almost all cavalry and infantry regiments.

*

Writing almost forty years later, Winston Churchill claimed that his father had 'died at the moment when his new fortune almost exactly equalled his debts'.[48] This judgement has since been accepted by most historians: the gross value of Lord Randolph's estate was published as £75,971,[49] but he is said to have owed the Rothschilds' bank anything between £66,000 and £72,000, leaving almost no net balance. In reality, the Rothschild ledgers reveal that Lord Randolph owed the bank only £12,758 on 31 December 1894, less than a month before he died and after settling all the bills for his last voyage.[50] So, after deducting the amount still owed them, the Rothschilds sent Lord Randolph's executors two cheques totalling £54,237.[51]

A boom in southern African mining shares had made this result possible. The boom continued throughout 1894 and the early part of 1895, with the result that at least one firm of stockbrokers had been forced to employ separate shifts of day and night staff to cope with the volume of transactions. 'In clubs and trains, in drawing rooms and boudoirs, people are discussing "Rands" and "Modders"', one financial journalist reported.[52]

The boom was still under way in March 1895, but Lord Randolph's executors decided that they must sell his remaining 2,300 shares. It was believed that 'Rands' were too risky as a share to be owned by a trust for a widow with young children. The Rothschilds sold the remaining shares in two batches at an average price of over £28 each, more than 100 times what Lord Randolph had originally paid. Years later, Winston Churchill ruminated on what might have happened if the executors had held on for longer: 'Soon afterwards they rose to nearly fifty or sixty times this price; and had he lived another year he would have been possessed of a substantial fortune,' he claimed, but in fact prices quickly subsided six months later in October, after heavy sales from Paris.[53]

Drafted after the 7th duke's sudden death in 1883, Lord Randolph's will closely followed the paternal template. It left his widow a small cash legacy to meet immediate bills, then settled the rest into a trust, to be known as Lord Randolph Churchill's will trust. Although Jennie was not entitled to any capital, all the income earned by the trust's investments was to go to her; the children would take over the income after her death, but the capital was to remain protected in the trust.

There was, however, a twist: if Jennie remarried, Lord Randolph's trustees would be allowed to divert half of the trust's income to Winston and Jack, an important provision given the social code of the day, which linked their marriage prospects to their financial 'expectations'.[54] When Jennie did remarry six years later, nobody remembered this clause.

3

'We are damned poor'
Distant Army Duty, 1895–9

Exchange rate: $5 = £1
Inflation multiples: US x 30; UK x 100

W HEN HIS FATHER died Winston Churchill immediately transferred from the infantry to a cavalry regiment commanded by a family friend, Colonel John Brabazon. Subalterns in the 4th Hussars earned ten pounds a month,[1] but they were expected to equip themselves for hunting and polo. Duchess Lily helped by providing Winston with a 'charger' and his mother agreed to come up with the £500 a year allowance that Churchill told her he would need to 'maintain his position'.[2]

Widowed at the age of forty-one, Jennie had been left with almost £5,000 a year from the various Churchill and Jerome trusts;[3] it was a level of income enjoyed by only a few thousand people in Britain at the time.[4] However, Jennie was not supposed to touch the trusts' capital and had none of her own. The distinction between capital and income appeared to escape her anyway: she left for Paris, accompanied by her late husband's butler and her maid, establishing herself in an apartment near the Champs-Elysées, which was swiftly redecorated.

Jennie enjoyed friendships (or more) with the millionaire American lawyer Bourke Cockran, Hugh Warrender, William Waldorf Astor (the couple were briefly rumoured to be engaged) and the prince of Wales, who invited her aboard the Royal Yacht *Britannia*. Back in London for the autumn she bought a lease on a seven-storey house near Marble Arch, which she also redecorated 'from top to toe', installing electric light and hot water. Jennie remained a popular guest at country house weekends and stayed close to her husband's financial friends Ernest Cassel and Alfred and Natty Rothschild. Her children would benefit from her social network, but it came at a great cost in lavish spending on clothes and entertaining.

Winston Churchill's leisurely military year was divided into seven months of summer 'training' and five of winter 'social activities', during which officers were expected to take at least ten weeks of 'uninterrupted repose'.[5] Unable to afford his fellow officers' lifestyle of daily hunts, Churchill sought out a foreign adventure. His attention turned to the long drawn-out guerrilla campaign between Spanish occupiers and local rebels in Cuba and Sir Henry Wolff, an old political colleague of his late father's and now Britain's ambassador in Madrid, secured permission for a visit.

Churchill funded the expedition by badgering his mother into buying a transatlantic ticket for him and she also arranged for him to write a series of dispatches at five guineas each for the *Daily Graphic*, owned by one of her friends. With a colleague, Churchill sailed to New York, where another of his mother's friends, Bourke Cockran, introduced the pair to a world of luxury, cigars and top-level contacts at his Fifth Avenue apartment, before sending them on their way to Miami by private railway car. From Cuba Churchill described the experience of coming under fire for the first time. His report was vivid enough for T. Heath Joyce, the *Daily Graphic*'s editor, to compliment him handsomely, while enclosing a cheque for twenty-five guineas.

Churchill rejoined the 4th Hussars in the spring of 1896, six months before the regiment began a posting to Bangalore which was expected to last twelve years. Officers took the summer off to arrange their affairs, but Churchill concentrated on his polo, pressing his mother to lend him £200 to buy a 'really first class animal' to complement his 'five quite good ponies'. If she could not, he would borrow from his bankers at Cox & Co. with the help of her guarantee. 'It is not a question of spending the money,' he argued, 'but of putting it into stock – an investment in fact – which though not profitable would produce much pleasure. Our finance is indeed involved!! If I had not been so foolish as to pay a lot of bills I should have the money now.'[6]

As the summer wore on, the idea of moving to India palled. Casting around for an alternative, Churchill tried to persuade the *Daily Chronicle* to appoint him as its special correspondent in Crete. Next he begged his mother to engineer a transfer within the army. 'A few months in South Africa would earn me the S.A. Medal and in all probability the [British South Africa] company's Star,' he suggested. 'Thence hot foot it to Egypt – to return with two more decorations in a year or two – and beat my sword into an iron despatch box.'[7]

Lady Randolph's lobbying proved fruitless: her son sailed to India, where his time was soon occupied by polo, reading and Miss Pamela Plowden,* the daughter of the British resident in Hyderabad. In *My Early Life* (1930) Churchill described the financial pressures on a young cavalry subaltern in India:

> It was. . . better in a cavalry regiment in those days to supplement the generous rewards of the Queen-Empress by an allowance from home three or four times as great. Altogether we received for our services about fourteen shillings a day, with about £3 a month on which to keep two horses. This, together with £500 a year paid quarterly [Churchill's allowance from his mother] was my sole means of support: all the rest had to be borrowed at usurious rates of interest from the all-too-accommodating native bankers. Every officer was warned against these gentlemen: I always found them most agreeable: very fat, very urbane, quite honest and mercilessly rapacious.[8]

---

* Pamela Plowden (1874–1971), married the earl of Lytton, 1902 (later under-secretary of state for India 1920–2, governor of Bengal 1922–7).

Churchill and his mother wrote to each other weekly, but letters took at least a fortnight to arrive, confusing the correspondence. Lady Randolph meant to mark her son's twenty-second birthday in November with a cheque for £50: 'I know you are hard up, but so am I – lost cheque book – will follow.'[9] Half followed a week later and the rest just before Christmas, by which time she was also cheerfully paying off some of Churchill's outstanding London bills. 'I have communicated with Mr Richmond of Crouch Hill and it will be all right,' she reassured him. 'I also am paying the rest of the outfit bills, also a bill of yrs at R. Paynes [wine merchant] & one at Leaders.'[10] She was less pleased to be summoned to the bank in February to guarantee a cheque that her son had written on an empty account:

It is with unusual feelings that I sit down to write to you my weekly letter. … I went to Cox's this morning & find out not only have you anticipated the whole of yr quarter's allowance due this month but £45 besides – & now this cheque for £50 – & that you knew you had nothing at the bank. … I must say I think it is too bad of you – indeed it is hardly honourable knowing as you do that you are dependent on me & that I give you the biggest allowances I possibly can and more than I can afford. I am very hard up. . . I have told them at Cox's not to apply to me in future as you must manage yr own affairs. I am not responsible. If you cannot live on yr allowance from me & yr pay you will have to leave the Fourth Hussar. I cannot increase your allowance.[11]

She took up cudgels again the following week, before Churchill could reply:

What an extraordinary boy you are as regards your business affairs. Dearest this is the only subject on which we ever fall out. Out of £2,700 a year, £800 goes to you two boys, £410 for house rent and stables, which leaves me about £1,500 for everything – taxes, servants, stables, food, dress, travelling – & I now have to pay interest on money borrowed. I <u>really</u> fear for the future. . . I make out that you get about £200 pay, which makes yr income for the present £700 a year. Of course it is not <u>much</u> & I can quite understand that you will have to deny yourself many things if you mean to try & live within it. But the fact is that you have got to do more than try.[12]

'I am sorry that stupid Cox refused my cheque,' Churchill eventually replied, unabashed, but enclosing a cheque for £30. He asked his mother to forgive the balance until he next came home to take a more serious look at his finances: 'There are several bills in London unpaid that really will have to be paid soon,' he conceded. 'I shall have to borrow a certain sum on my life or effect a loan in some way or other.'[13] Already keen for a break from Bangalore, which he described as 'a third rate watering place, out of season & without the sea', he planned to be home for the Derby* in June.

He asked the family solicitor to arrange a loan for £3,000, secured against his future inheritance, but Lumley & Lumley could only persuade the Norwich Union insurance company to lend £2,300, of which £300 was to cover Lumley's fee (a charge that rankled with Churchill for years). The loan was still incomplete when Churchill met one of his father's Indian army friends, General Sir Bindon Blood, while staying for the weekend with Duchess Lily and her new husband Lord William Beresford. Encouraged by Beresford, the general promised to take the young subaltern on to his staff should he be given command of an Indian frontier expeditionary force.

A month later, at the Goodwood races, Churchill heard that Sir Bindon had taken charge of three brigades to quash a Pathian rebellion in the Swat Valley on the North West Frontier. Pausing only to cable the general and remind him of his promise, Churchill immediately set off for India. On reaching Bangalore in mid-August, he asked his mother to sign the loan documents for him: 'I am counting

---

* A valuable horse race held on the first Tuesday of June, traditionally marking the beginning of London's summer season.

on the money and have already written several cheques to pay the bills here,' he told her. 'Hustle Lumley & wire if there is a hitch.'[14]

There was no reply from Sir Bindon in Aden or on arrival at Bangalore, but a letter reached Churchill at the end of August: although the general's headquarters staff was full, Churchill would be fitted in 'on the first opportunity'[15] and could start as a war correspondent. Putting down the novel *Savrola* which he had started writing (he had reached the fifth chapter), Churchill set off on the five-day rail journey north, instructing his mother to arrange an urgent newspaper contract. She found that *The Times* had already made its appointment, but agreed terms with *The Daily Telegraph*: Churchill wanted 'not less than £10 per letter', published under his own name,[16] but Jennie settled for £5 and the by-line 'A Young Officer'.[17]

Churchill dispatched twelve letters to the newspaper over five weeks of daily skirmishes, during which he deliberately courted danger so that no onlooker could doubt his courage. Halfway through the fighting he was furious to find out his mother had agreed to the rate of £5: 'I mean to solace myself financially. I will not accept less than £10 a letter and I shall return any cheque for a less [sic] sum,' he told her. 'The £75 which the *D.T.* propose to give me will hardly pay my ticket for self & horses. . . As Dr Johnson says, "No one but a blockhead ever wrote except for money."'[18]

Churchill remained distracted by his finances while the fighting continued. 'I am perplexed and worried by a telegram wh. arrived from England and reached me two days ago saying "NO". Does this apply to the loan?' he asked Jennie. 'If so – I am indeed in a serious position. I have written £500 of cheques in settlement of debts and if they are dishonoured, I really do not know – or care to guess – what the consequences might be.'[19]

Jennie was equally in the dark: 'I wonder if you have heard from Lumley yet?. . . He is a very tiresome man. My own affairs are in a dreadful state – & I hope to get him to put them right. How it is to be done Heaven knows.'[20] She tried to atone for *The Daily Telegraph* disappointment by suggesting that Churchill publish his letters in book form, an idea that he immediately took up, dropping his novel again and asking her to find a publisher. He was bored by life in Bangalore, even polo, but at least 'financially my frontier affair has been good business as with my press money I have spent *nothing* for two months'.[21]

It took only a month before it became obvious that the Norwich Union loan had not solved the difficulty of Churchill's unpaid London bills. 'I find that my original estimate of my liabilities was considerably below the actual amount,' he wrote home in November 1897. 'All borrowed money and a good number of the most pressing bills have been paid – but nearly £500 – to people like Bernau, Tautz, Sowter etc will remain.'[22] Jennie was no better off. 'Personally I am going through a very serious crisis,' she told him. 'I will write to you the particulars once I have come to some tangible plan. Lumley is trying to devise something.'[23]

Churchill wrote for six hours a day, racing to beat *The Times*'s war correspondent in order to be the first to publish a book about the Malakand field force. He was so busy he missed the significance of his mother's mention of a possible financial scheme to reorganize her finances. Dispatching the book's manuscript to her on the last day of 1897, as he was about to set off for Calcutta to stay with the Viceroy Lord Elgin, he emphasized its urgency to his mother. 'Do not I beg you – lose one single day – in taking the MS to some publisher,' he implored her. 'As to price, I have no idea what the book is worth but do not throw it away. I don't think I ought to get less than £300 for the first edition with some royalty on each copy – but if the book hit the mark I might get much more.'[24]

Jennie's search led to Arthur Balfour's publishing 'broker' A. P. Watt,* who sold it within a fortnight to Longman Green.[25] Posting her son a copy of the contract, Jennie explained that Thomas Longman usually only published at the author's expense, but would

---

* A. P. Watt (1834–1914), bookseller and advertising agent, Edinburgh 1870s; first person to be called 'literary agent', 1881, representing Thomas Hardy, Arthur Conan Doyle and Rudyard Kipling.

be advancing him £50 and that his royalty would increase from 15 to 20 per cent after the sale of 3,000 copies.[26] 'If the book is a success – and I am sure it will be – you can command yr own price next time,' she suggested.[27]

Churchill realized that he could not dictate terms from so far away. 'All financial arrangements in connexion with it – I shall leave entirely in your hands, but please have no false scruples or modesty about bargaining,' he told her, five days after she had already settled. 'The publication of the book will certainly be the most noteworthy act of my life – up to date (of course). By its reception I shall measure the chances of my success in the world.'[28]

A proof copy of *The Story of the Malakand Field Force* did not reach Churchill in Bangalore until a week after the book's publication in London on 14 March 1898. It was too late to do anything about the many typesetting errors he found, so Churchill could only 'writhe' from a distance while the book sold 1,473 copies during its first three months on the market, followed by another 1,198 copies over the next year. Early in 1899 Churchill received his first literary royalty: the cheque for £46 (on top of his £50 advance) fell well short of his earlier expectations.[29]

Before the book's publication, Churchill had already turned his attention to his mother's efforts to secure him a transfer to the campaign in Egypt: 'Now do stir up your influence,' he wrote. 'Don't be afraid of every line of attack. So far I have done it all myself. You have so much more power.'[30] Jennie replied that no military advance was likely until the summer of 1898; she was considering her own trip to Egypt to work on the army commander General Kitchener 'at nearer quarters with more chance of success.'[31]

Meanwhile the family solicitor Theodore Lumley was about to share with Jennie his long-awaited scheme to reorganize her finances. 'He takes such a time to do anything,' she complained to her son. 'In time you will receive all the documents. If the arrangement I contemplate comes off I think it will be possible to find a few hundreds to settle those bills of yours. I will explain all to you later when the papers are ready.'[32]

Jennie had been staying at Chatsworth House in Derbyshire and returned to London to hear the details of Lumley's plan early in January 1899. However, when she reached London she realized that Lumley had already sent the legal documents to Churchill in India, without any proper explanation of a scheme that required her son's written approval, because it affected his inheritance. Grasping something of the sensitivities involved, she dashed off a note to Churchill intending to catch the same mail as Lumley's package:

> This £14,000 is in order to buy up all the loans I have made in different Insurance offices – with a margin enough to pay the interest for a couple of years & I think give you the few hundreds you require. Of course in helping you to do this you understand that you reduce yr portion after my death. . . Anyhow it is Hobson's choice. I can't give you an allowance or have anything to live on until this is done. So sign the papers & send them back by return. I will explain in next, post off.[33]

But Jennie missed the post. Lumley's legal papers reached Bangalore late in January 1897. The difficulty facing the solicitor was that Jennie had no capital of her own – only the income flowing from capital theoretically ring-fenced inside family trusts. Leonard Jerome had deliberately prevented the American settlement's future income from being pledged to secure any loans, but neither the English Settlement nor her husband's will trust (both drawn up by Lumley) had taken the same precaution. The solicitor had therefore persuaded the Norwich Union to lend £17,000* against their future flow of income, so long as her son consented,

---

* The loan was to be set at £17,000, but Jennie was only to benefit from £14,000; the balance of £3,000 was to repay Churchill's £2,300 Norwich Union loan and to leave him £700 to pay overdue bills.

on behalf of both himself and his under-age brother, to put his future inheritance at risk in this way. If any part of Jennie's loan was still outstanding when she died (which seemed practically inevitable), Churchill would have to forego that portion of his inheritance.

All this took time to sink in. His first reaction, sent on the same day that Lumley's package arrived, was relatively muted and complained only that Lumley's letter had been full of legal jargon:

> £17,000 is a great deal of money, about a quarter indeed of all we shall ever have in the world – under American settlement – Duke's will & Papa's property. . . I do not quite understand how the signing of these documents will affect my prospects. . . What I want to know – and that Lumley – if not a verbose fool – might easily have explained is – how much difference it will make. . . Speaking quite frankly on the subject – there is no doubt that we are both you & I equally thoughtless – spendthrift and extravagant. We both know what is good – and we like to have it. Arrangements for paying are left to the future. . . We shall very soon come to the end of our tether – unless a considerable change comes over our fortunes and dispositions. As long as I am dead sure & certain of an ultimate £1,000 a year* – I do not much care – as I could always make money on the press – and might marry. . . I sympathize with all your extravagances – even more than you do with mine – it seems just as suicidal to me when you spend £200 on a ball dress as it does to you when I purchase a new polo pony for £100. And yet I feel that you ought to have the dress & I the polo pony. The pinch of the whole matter is that we are damned poor.[34]

By the time Jennie's hurried note reached him forty-eight hours later, Churchill's reaction had hardened. Convinced now that he

---

* Churchill's reference is to a private income of £1,000 per annum, requiring capital of £20,000, according to the rule of thumb at the time.

was being asked to sign away almost half his inheritance[35] –
enough to damage his marriage prospects – he also suspected
(rightly as it turned out) that the cost of the scheme (nearly £1,400
a year in interest and life insurance charges)[36] would soon prevent
Jennie from keeping up the payment of his and Jack's allowances.
The only bait for him was a single contribution of £700 towards
his unpaid bills.

Churchill sent his mother a letter that would haunt him for
weeks:

> I have read all the papers very carefully and I understand that by
> signing, as you ask me to do, I deprive myself for ever of an
> income equal to the sum of Interest and premium necessary to
> borrow £14,000 or perhaps £17,000 upon an Insurance policy.
> Neither you – nor Lumley, in whom it is inexcusable – have
> informed me what this amount will be. Assuming that the rate
> is 5% (a moderate estimate) and that £14,000 is the sum bor-
> rowed (the minimum stated) – I learn that by signing I ultimately
> forego £700 per annum. As I understand it that if Jack lives I
> shall only have £1,800 a year – you will recognize that this is a
> very serious matter for me. Nor do I think that it should have
> been put before me in so sketchy and offhand a manner – as if it
> were a thing of no importance. I have written to Lumley on the
> subject.
>
> I have thought the whole matter over and have considered all
> the different influences. . . I do not intend to profit by this loan
> you are raising – or to confuse the matter by allowing you to
> think that I consent to deprive myself of half my property – for
> the sake of such a 'mess of pottage' as a few hundreds of pounds
> to pay my bills.
>
> I sign these papers – purely & solely out of affection for you.
> I write plainly that no other consideration would have induced
> me to sign them. As it is I sign them upon two conditions –
> which justice & prudence alike demand.

Churchill stipulated that his mother must switch his informal allowance into a binding legal commitment and that Jack must share the burden once he turned eighteen years old:

> I need not say how painful it is to me to have to write in so formal a strain – or to take such precautions. But I am bound to protect myself in the future – as I do not wish to be left – should I survive you – in poverty. In three years from my father's death you have spent a quarter of our entire fortune in the world. I have also been extravagant: but my extravagances are a very small matter besides yours. . . If this letter does not please you – you must balance your annoyance against my reluctance to be £700 a year poorer and then I think you will admit that my side of the account is the heavier.[37]

He wrote to Jack on the same day, asking him to promise to share the charge when he came of age: 'I am sure that you would not wish that in any way we should depart from our old principle – which Papa laid down in his will – that we should share all money we inherited equally.'[38]

4

'Fine sentiments and empty stomachs do not accord'

The World's Highest-Paid War Correspondent, 1899–1900

Exchange rate: $5 = £1
Inflation multiples: US x 30; UK x 100

CHURCHILL FELT GLOOMY about his financial prospects at the start of 1898. 'The only thing that worries me in life is – money,' he told Jack. 'Extravagant tastes, an expensive style of living – small and diminished resources – these are fertile sources of trouble.'[1] This despondent mood followed him to Camp Peshawar on India's northern border, where he found himself unexpectedly posted to the staff of Sir William Lockhart, a general commanding yet another border force. Jennie's allowance had failed to reach his London bank; he owed his Indian bankers more than £200; London tradesmen were pursuing him for bills totalling more than £500 and no bank in Peshawar would honour Cox & Co.'s cheques. 'These filthy money matters are the curse of my life and my only worry,' he complained to his mother. 'I shudder sometimes when I contemplate the abyss into which we are sinking. Personally I live simply – uncomfortably – squalidly. I eat bad food – I spend nothing on my clothes. There is no dissipation. We shall finish up stone broke.'[2]

Ten days later, when he was still unable to draw money and there was no word from his mother, he suspected his letter about her scheme was the reason:

I feel that you have probably taken amiss what I then wrote. I
think you will be wrong and unkind to do this. You must
remember that you never put the case before me in any clear
way. . . I have also to reckon on the possibility of your marrying
again – perhaps some man I did not like – or did not get on with
– and troubles springing up – which might lessen your affection
for me. . . I did not write without thinking and, much as I hated
it at the time, much as I have hated it since, I do not desire to
alter it.[3]

Jennie had in fact written, but from Aswan in Egypt. Her letter
reached Churchill as he left Peshawar and it simply asked him
never to mention money matters again. He feared a permanent rift,
but his mother had travelled to Egypt ostensibly to lobby for his
transfer to the Sudan. A rumour that she had been found at a Cairo
hotel in bed with one of her army lovers, Caryl Ramsden, suggested a broader agenda, but her friend Lady St Helier* proved a
more effective advocate of Churchill's cause. 'Soudan all right –
writing,' she cabled after tackling her powerful friend, the adjutant
general Sir Evelyn Wood.[4] Impatient to set off straight away,
Churchill had to wait in Bangalore when it became clear that no
action on the Nile was expected until August.

Only one letter from his mother arrived over the next five
weeks. Churchill assumed that their quarrel over her scheme
remained the reason, but she had written three times and sent
them all to Peshawar, where they languished in a field post office.
Her most recent catalogued her own financial difficulties, claiming
that she now had only £900 a year of her own to spend freely. 'The
situation as described in your letter is appalling. As you say, it is of
course impossible to live in London on such a pittance,' Churchill
at once replied, dropping his insistence on a legally binding

---

* Susan Stewart-Mackenzie (1845–1931), married Francis Jeune QC, judge
advocate-general, later Baron St Helier; Lady St Helier hosted the dinner
party at which Churchill met his future wife in 1908.

allowance. 'I hate the idea of your marrying – but that of course would be a solution.' For himself, he was becoming more confident of earning an independent living as a writer. 'This literary sphere of action may enable me in a few years to largely supplement my income,' he explained. He would finish his novel, write a life of Garibaldi or a history of the American Civil War and stay in the army until sure of a seat in Parliament.[5]

When his aunt Leonie questioned the wisdom of writing a novel, Churchill explained it simply:

> Il faut vivre. . . Finance! Ah I confess I shudder. I do not know whither we are descending. I felt a horrid sordid beast to do what I did, but I had to contemplate the possibility of Mama marrying – perhaps a poor man that I disliked. . . I have withdrawn the conditions now, but only because I have confidence in my ability to keep myself from squalor by journalism in the ultimate issue. . . Her silence always makes me pessimistic and forlorn. Indeed the future is very black. I can never afford to go into Politics after the properties are so reduced. Fancy <u>half</u> is spent. . . Am I extravagant? Perhaps, but consider the scale. £2,000 would pay every farthing I owe in the world and more. I neither race nor drink nor gamble, nor squander my money on concubines and I don't worry over accounts and small details and hence pay about twice as much as I need for the little pleasure there is in this cross-grained existence.[6]

By the time he dispatched the novel's first ten chapters to his mother in mid-May, Churchill's spirits had begun to recover. To save an agent's commission, he wanted Jennie to sell the book directly to Longman, although she was to accept nothing 'less than £100 down and all rights reserved'.[7] He planned to leave India in the middle of June, drop his 'native servant and campaigning kit' on the way in Cairo and spend three weeks in England, before setting off back to the Nile on 20 July. Before he left, he would settle his Indian debts by selling his polo ponies and reclaiming a loan that he had made to Hugo Baring. Baring had been forced to leave the Hussars because, as Churchill pointedly explained to his mother, 'his father only left him two hundred a year'.[8] Churchill's unpaid bills in London were now more than £1,000, but only two, he maintained, were 'pressing'. The rest would have to wait.*

The England to which Churchill returned was changing only slowly, especially the City where Jack had just started work as a private secretary to his grandmother's neighbour Sir Ernest Cassel. The stock exchange boasted a hat-rack one-eighth of a mile long to accommodate its 4,000 male members. A leading merchant bank, Kleinwort, had surrounded its sole female employee with a screen to placate a partner who had agreed to her employment only on condition that he never had to set eyes on her. Its rival, Schroder, had just installed its first telephone, on the condition that its number remained ex-directory, lest incoming calls distract the staff from their work.[9]

Outside London Churchill tested his political ambitions by addressing two public meetings, but he also spent time in the City dealing with the fall-out from his mother's financial difficulties. As he had feared, Lumley announced that Jennie would no longer be able to afford to pay either Winston's or Jack's allowances, suggesting instead that Winston should borrow against his future inheritances to fund their living expenses for the next three years. Life insurance companies, Lumley explained, made it their business to lend against 'reversionary' interests, such as his expectations from his grandfather's and father's estate once both his grandmother and mother had died; although they would insist that the risk of Winston dying before them was covered by life insurance on top of interest charges.

Lumley expected Churchill to be able to raise the full £3,500

---

* Churchill owed over £600 to E. Tautz & Sons (military tailors), A. F. Bernau (tailors) and Palmer & Co. (bootmakers). They waited until 1901 before they were paid.

that he needed to pay off all his bills and to fund three years' living expenses, but Norwich Union would not lend more than £2,000 without guarantors for the balance. Unenthusiastic about the loan, Churchill gladly abandoned his search for backers to deal with the unwelcome news that General Kitchener had reversed Churchill's appointment in the Sudan in favour of a rival correspondent.

Churchill was not to be beaten. He marshalled the combined forces of the prime minister Lord Salisbury, Lady St Helier and her friend the adjutant general, before the death of a subaltern allowed his supernumerary appointment to the 21st Lancers, one of the two British regiments attached to the force. 'It is understood that you will proceed at your own expense,' the War Office's letter stated, 'and that in the event of your being killed or wounded in the impending operations, or for any other reason, no charge of any kind will fall upon British army funds.'[10]

Churchill redrafted his will, arranged a series of war dispatches with *The Morning Post* at £10 a time[11] and instructed his mother to sell the resulting book to Longman. Then he set off three days later, handing his mother a script to use in case he was recalled:

> Arguments: 1. I have spent on the Egyptian business. Chargers 70 Telegrams 20 Ticket 20 Servant from India 20 Kit 30 Total 160. If forfeited – a heavy pecuniary fine. & poor. 2. Failing Egypt, you are <u>afraid</u> that I shall leave. I shall. . . [12]

The sea voyage between Marseilles and Cairo provided the time Churchill needed to resume his search for loan guarantors. Churchill explained the background of Jennie's scheme, to his cousin, the duke of Marlborough, in a letter, which he sent on arrival at Luxor.

> You are acquainted with the state of my mother's finances. . . The arrangement was based on the understanding that I should forth-with raise a fresh loan – sufficient to pay my own allowance of £500 per annum and an allowance of £200 to Jack – for three years;

> my mother's income being so much reduced by the interest and
> premium of her loan that she could no longer afford to make these
> payments. . . You ask 'why three years?' The idea is that in three
> years the Duchess* will perhaps have died and the funds accruing
> to my mother at her death will enable her to resume the payment
> of my allowance. The financial unsoundness of this arrangement
> – based as it is on an uncertainty – hardly a probability – will no
> doubt strike you.[13]

He also wrote to Jennie, complaining that she had failed to send the
promised money to await him in Cairo: 'I have to pay £40 for one
charger, £35 for the other & £20 subs to the mess. I am settling
these by cheque and I trust you will arrange that Cox & Co. meet
the amounts.'[14]

By mid-August Churchill's squadron was marching down the
west bank of the Nile towards Khartoum. 'Within the next ten
days there will be a general action – perhaps a very severe one,'
he warned his mother. 'I may be killed. I do not think so. . . '[15]
When battle was joined at Omdurman on 2 September, the 21st
Lancers lost twenty men, while fifty were wounded in a short
skirmish on the flank. It turned out to be the British cavalry's last
charge and was described by Churchill in a cable to *The Morning
Post*.

By the middle of October Churchill was back at Jennie's London
home, once more short of money. Only *The Morning Post*'s cheque
for his fifteen letters saved him from having to accept the loan
offered by his uncle. 'When I look ahead, I see difficulties and am
filled with apprehension, but more on my mother's account than
on my own,' he told his uncle Moreton Frewen. 'But I have not
extravagant tastes, only creature comforts, and I am v[er]y conscious of my ability to earn my bread if need be.'[16]

---

* The dowager duchess, Frances, grandmother of both Churchill and the
duke.

Jennie had failed to persuade Longman to pay an advance for Churchill's novel *Savrola* or his planned book about the Sudan campaign, so Churchill asked his old agent to do battle. A. P. Watt justified his commission by arranging *Savrola*'s serialization in *Macmillan's Magazine* for £100 before publication[17] and at least extracted a choice between an advance or higher royalty rates for the Sudan book:[18] confident of strong sales, Churchill chose in favour of higher royalties. 'The only point I should suggest being altered,' he told his agent, 'is that Mr Longman should give me 25% on all copies over 5,000 sold and should not worry about advancing me £100 on the day of publication.'[19] (Churchill's decision to decline an advance was not a good one: by the time *The River War* was published almost a year later, the Boer War had captured the public's attention. Sales only reached 3,000 in 1914.)

Breaking off from an outing with the Quorn Hunt early in November, Churchill completed his Norwich Union loan, transferring £1,100 to pay the first year or so of his and Jack's allowances into a new 'Separate Account' at Cox & Co.[20] He asked Sir Ernest Cassel to invest the rest, but this precarious arrangement forced a rethink about his future: writing had already earned him five times as much as the army. 'My allowance of £500 a year was not sufficient to meet the expenses of Polo and the Hussars,' he explained in *My Early Life*. 'I now saw that the only profession I had been taught would never yield me enough money to avoid getting into debt, let alone to dispense with my allowance and become completely independent as I desired.'

Churchill decided to return to India only for the duration of the army polo championships, then to resign his commission in order to write and find a parliamentary seat. He made a call to Conservative Party headquarters to ask after his prospects of finding a seat. When the party manager asked how much he would be able to donate to any constituency interested in selecting him, Churchill could promise no more than to meet his own expenses. His family's lack of money presented a serious obstacle to his career and neither his father's reputation nor his own military background could offset this disadvantage, the party manager explained, giving examples of 'cases where as much as a thousand pounds a year or more was paid by the member in subscriptions and charities in return for the honour of holding the seat. Risky seats could not afford to be so particular, and "forlorn hopes" were very cheap.'[21]

Despite rough seas in December, Churchill spent the voyage to India working on *The River War*. On his arrival in India, however, he was greeted by the usual money problems. He shared his fears with his mother:

> It is appalling. In three years, I can't think what will happen. God only knows. I detest business even more than you do. Years of trouble and squalor are before us. Poverty produced by thoughtlessness will rot your life of peace & happiness, mine of success.[22]

Before leaving for the polo tournament, he asked her to secure access to his father's papers so that he could one day write a biography. 'The time has not come yet but in six or seven years it will have arrived – and I shall insist on undertaking the work,' he told her. 'I have every right and can do it much better than anyone else. From a financial point of view alone – the biography would be worth £2,000.'[23]

After helping his regiment win the polo tournament by scoring three of his side's four goals in the final, Churchill paid his Indian bills and ended up with a small surplus. He sailed home without his girlfriend, Pamela Plowden, to whom he wrote sadly: 'My dear Miss Pamela, I have lived all my life seeing the most beautiful women London produces. Never have I seen one for whom I could forgo the business of life. Then I met you. . . Were I a dreamer of dreams, I would say. . . "Marry me – and I will conquer the world and lay it at your feet."' Marriage, however, required two conditions to be met. 'Money and the consent of both parties. One certainly, both probably are absent. And this is such an old story. . .'[24]

*

The growing drumbeat of war with the Boers of southern Africa's
Orange Free State and Transvaal greeted Churchill on his arrival
home in London in April. Nevertheless he left the army as planned
on 3 May and found that his plans for a political career moved
more quickly than he had expected. Elders in the constituency of
Oldham, near Manchester, had been showing an interest in adopting Churchill as their junior candidate at the next general election.
However, when their senior sitting member suddenly died and
their junior member resigned, Churchill found himself catapulted
into fighting his first by-election.

He lost narrowly, although he succeeded in attracting large
public audiences. Afterwards, Churchill carefully thanked the
owner of the new *Daily Mail* for his newspaper's support and for
providing his transport home. 'I am sorry that neither of our enterprises were successful in Oldham,' he told Alfred Harmsworth.*
'But I don't expect my career or your car will be seriously damaged.'[25]

War in southern Africa grew steadily more likely during the
summer, while Churchill worked at Blenheim on *The River War*.
He was distracted by visits from Pamela Plowden and by his mother's burgeoning relationship with an army officer almost half her
age. Jennie had met George Cornwallis-West the previous a year
while staying with her friend Daisy, Countess of Warwick. She had
always declared herself most unlikely to remarry, unless for serious
money: 'If a perfect darling with at least £40,000 a year wants me
very much, I might consider it,' she told Daisy.[26]

Cornwallis-West was certainly not in that league: his family had
once owned 60,000 acres in Shropshire and northern Wales, but a
dispute over his great-grandfather's will and agricultural depression

---

* Alfred Harmsworth (1865–1922), freelance reporter 1870; founded a
magazine business, later Amalgamated Press (with his brother Harold) 1887;
purchased *Evening News* 1894; founded *Daily Mail* 1896; purchased *Observer*
1905 (sold 1912), *The Times* 1908; knighted 1904; Baron Northcliffe 1905;
viscount 1917.

had produced division and decline. His parents had retreated to London, short of cash, after tenanting their one-sixth share of the estate, while George trod the well-worn path from Eton to Sandhurst and the Scots Guards. He had proposed to Jennie several times during the summer of 1899, undeterred by the opposition of his parents, his godfather the prince of Wales (whom some thought to be his natural father) and his regimental colonel, all of whom were shocked by the age difference. Churchill's reaction was essentially practical. 'Reflect most seriously on all the aspects of the question,' he warned his mother, unclear how the cash-strapped George could ever keep his mother in the style to which she was accustomed. 'Fine sentiments and empty stomachs do not accord.'[27]

By September war in the Transvaal seemed so likely that Churchill set aside *The River War* and sought a correspondent's post accompanying Britain's expeditionary force. The *Daily Mail's* interest strengthened his hand with *The Morning Post*, to which he offered first refusal, provided they did not quibble with his terms. These were reputed to be the highest ever conceded to a war correspondent: a salary of £1,000 for the first four months, followed by £200 a month (the time to be measured from shore to shore), all expenses paid and Churchill to retain copyright, so that he could convert his dispatches into another book, provisionally entitled *War in the Transvaal.** Bypassing his agent A. P. Watt, he hastily agreed terms with Longman, with whom he left the completed texts of *The River War* and *Savrola*, asking his mother to sign any paperwork.[28]

Churchill sailed three days after war was declared, accompanied by his father's old valet and aided by cash gifts from Lord Rothschild and Sir Ernest Cassel;[29] he was also protected by special life insurance[30] and sustained on the journey by six cases of wine and spirits.[31] After a three-week voyage that coincided with the publication of *The River War*,[32] Churchill disembarked at Cape Town to

---

* It was eventually called *London to Ladysmith via Pretoria*.

reach the war zone by train. Britain had underestimated the military prowess of its Boer opponents, who had succeeded during the early stages of the campaign in surrounding a large detachment of British troops at Ladysmith in Natal. Churchill sent Jack a private code by which he would pass on any military news likely to prove useful to his brother's City career,[33] and then set off for Estcourt, the closest point to the besieged British forces. Here he accepted a place on a probing mission towards Ladysmith commanded by a fellow North West Frontier officer, Captain Aylmer Haldane. However, their armoured train was attacked and derailed. Churchill helped to unblock the line while under fire, then went to direct the engine driver. He was confronted by a group of armed Boers and surrendered.

Churchill was well treated by his captors. He wrote to the Boer secretary of state for war demanding his release on the grounds that he was a non-combatant and had taken no part in the defence of the train, a claim which local Boer commanders rebutted. Before Churchill's offer of his *parole* to remain a non-combatant could be officially accepted, he had escaped. He eluded his captors in the darkness by happening to stumble on the one English home for miles around. The owners hid him down a mineshaft for five days at great personal risk, after which he was smuggled on to a freight train travelling to the neutral Portuguese enclave at Delagoa Bay; from there he moved on by boat to Lourenço Marques and then to Durban, where he was given a hero's welcome on Christmas Eve.

The publicity surrounding Churchill's capture and escape helped to make him a household name back home. He returned to the action, however, to cover the fierce fighting around Ladysmith. General Sir Redvers Buller then gave him an unpaid lieutenancy in the South African Light Horse, a mobile force living largely off the land. 'Meanwhile I dispatched a continual stream of letters and cables to *The Morning Post*,' he later wrote, 'and learned from them that I commanded a wide and influential public.'[34]

Returning to Cape Town when Ladysmith was relieved at the end of February, Churchill hoped for swift accreditation to the staff of the new commander-in-chief. However, neither Lord Roberts (his father's old friend from India) nor his deputy General Kitchener was keen for the young journalist to be posted anywhere near them. A recent article on army chaplains had upset Roberts, while General Kitchener was still smarting from Churchill's criticism in *The River War* of the British army's treatment of wounded dervishes in the Sudan.

While summoning support from two generals with whom he had served on the Indian frontier, Churchill spent his enforced leisure befriending the new duke of Westminster, one of three dukes to serve on Lord Roberts's staff (alongside the dukes of Norfolk and Marlborough). The twenty-year-old duke had only three months earlier inherited property in London which generated an income exceeding £250,000 a year. He also owned three estates in Scotland and 30,000 acres around the family seat in Cheshire, where his staff numbered more than 300 and house parties could accommodate sixty guests. It was the start of a long friendship, which proved a mixed blessing to Churchill: generous beyond measure in hospitality to his friends, the duke drew Churchill into a circle whose lifestyle required more money than he ever commanded.[35]

Lord Roberts finally gave way to Churchill's pleas to be allowed to move to Bloemfontein in the Orange Free State. He instructed his young military secretary, Neville Chamberlain, to hand on the pass with the message that it had been awarded only 'for your father's sake'.[36]

Churchill spent April switching between columns, observing the attempts of elderly commanders to adjust a ponderous British army to the Boers' light-footed, guerrilla tactics.

When Lord Roberts was finally ready to advance early in May, he dropped one of the dukes from his staff, giving Churchill the opportunity to persuade his cousin the duke of Marlborough to move fifty miles eastwards with him to join forces commanded by another friend from India, General Ian Hamilton.* 'We had an ox-wagon with four oxen and two good horses (the kind of animal that cost two hundred pounds),' Churchill told his doctor years later. 'The whole outfit cost *The Morning Post* a thousand pounds. The wagon was full of Fortnum and Mason groceries and of course liquor.'[37]

Back home Longman had taken advantage of Churchill's hour in the spotlight to publish *Savrola*. When it sold over 8,000 copies,[38] they pressed Churchill to write a quick foreword to his book about the current campaign, *London to Ladysmith via Pretoria*, so that its publication could be accelerated. Wisely, the editors cut this section: 'I had always designed to publish the letters in a book form at the end of the military operations; but I am shrewdly advised to seize the hour while the attention of the world is fixed on South Africa.'[39]

No one at home followed Churchill's exploits more closely than did his agent A. P. Watt, who heard on the literary grapevine that Churchill had dispensed with his services to deal with Longman directly. Watt decided to test the young author's mettle and passed on the news that he had a well-known London publisher willing to pay an advance of £1,000 for British rights to *London to Ladysmith* and that he expected to raise a similar sum in America.[40] Ruing his hasty deal with Longman, which contained no advance at all, Churchill instructed his mother to tackle the publisher as soon as she could: 'The book must be made worth at least £2,000 to me,' he told her.[41]

Soon afterwards he informed Jennie of another offer: a lecture tour of Britain that could earn him as much as £3,000. 'I do not relish lecturing in England,' he told her, 'but you must remember how much money means to me, and how much I need it for

---

* Ian Hamilton (1853–1947); army officer; served in India, Egypt, southern Africa, Burma 1871–1902; attached to the Japanese army 1904; general 1907; commanding officer, Allied Mediterranean Expeditionary Force, Dardanelles campaign March–October 1915; lieutenant of the Tower of London 1918–20.

political expense and other purposes. . . I do hope you will realize
the importance of making the very best terms you can for me, both
as writer and lecturer. The sinews of war are what I lack.'[42] Three
weeks later, he asked her to investigate a similar offer from Major J.
B. Pond's Lyceum Lecture Bureau in America. 'I would not go to the
United States unless guaranteed *at least* a thousand pounds a month
for three months and I should expect a great deal more', he told her.
'£5,000 is not too much for such a labour. . . I have so much need of
the money and we cannot afford to throw away a single shilling.'[43]

Although Jennie had her own problems (her latest venture, the
Nimrod Club, had 'gone smash' and she was 'trying to settle lots of
bills and horrors'), she dutifully obliged her son.[44] Longman sweetened the book's royalty rates slightly, so that Churchill would
achieve his £2,000 target if he sold 25,000 copies, a level that the
publisher declared 'pretty certain', while adding ominously that
'war books are not selling well'.[45] (This warning proved prophetic:
London to Ladysmith via Pretoria sold only 14,000 copies in its first
year.)[46]

Churchill left for home as soon as Pretoria was captured early
in June. The war was far from over, but 'politics, Pamela, finances
and books all need my attention', he told his mother. He planned to
lecture in Britain in the autumn, then move to America for three
months in December.[47] Years later, Churchill summed up the
impact of the Boer War on his finances and future career: 'If I had
not been caught, I could not have escaped, and my emprisonment
and escape provided me with enough materials for lectures and a
book which brought me in enough money to get into parliament
in 1900.'[48]

5

'Needlessly extravagant'

Bachelor, Author, MP, 1900–5

Exchange rate $5 = £1
Inflation multiples: US x 30; UK x 100

RUMOURS OF A general election in Britain reached the island of Madeira, where Churchill's ship had stopped on her way home from Cape Town. Within a week of his return to London in July 1900, Churchill was adopted as a Conservative candidate for Oldham. He was naturally pleased, but a pressing personal matter briefly diverted his attention from politics: his mother had accepted a renewed marriage proposal from George Cornwallis-West. The Churchills turned out for the occasion 'in a solid phalanx' of support, but Winston's hopes that the marriage might lead to a regular allowance quickly evaporated when George's family boycotted the ceremony and George was drummed out of his regiment. George took a pile of his new wife's unpaid bills on their protracted honeymoon, but he 'found it a bit thick when expected to pay for Lord Randolph Churchill's barouche purchased in the [eighteen] eighties'.[1]

Churchill was not too despondent about his own position. After all, he had already saved almost £4,000 of his earnings from books and journalism.[2] 'With judicious economy, I shall hope to make that carry me through the lean years,' he told his brother Jack. 'In November I am going to lecture in England, and I hope to make the best part of £2,000. December, January and February I shall be in the States, March, I shall be back in England

and hope to have made £5,000 or £6,000 and be able to write MP after my name.'[3]

He spent part of August and most of September campaigning in Oldham, the rest working on a second book of his Boer War dispatches, to be called *Ian Hamilton's March*. Longman again refused any advance on the book, citing *London to Ladysmith*'s disappointing sales and a general cooling of interest in the war. The publisher's judgement was vindicated: *Ian Hamilton's March* sold only half the number of *London to Ladysmith*'s copies and earned its author less than £400.[4]

On 1 October, after a close-fought contest, the voters of Oldham elected Churchill as their member of Parliament. He won by a margin of 222 votes and the next stage of his career plan fell into place.[5] Helpfully, the duke of Marlborough promised to pay a third of Churchill's election expenses.[6] The duke also solved the problem of accommodation in London by offering Churchill the last two years' lease of his bachelor rooms at 105 Mount Street (off Park Lane), which the duke no longer needed now that he was to marry a wealthy American heiress, Consuelo Vanderbilt. Churchill asked his aunt Leonie to help furnish the rooms as Jennie was still away on a prolonged honeymoon with her young husband: 'You cannot imagine how that kind of material arrangement irritates me,' he told his aunt. 'So long as my table is clear and there is plenty of paper, I do not worry about the rest.'[7]

Parliament was not due to sit for four months, giving its new member an ideal window for his lecture tours of Britain and the United States entitled 'The War as I Saw It'. Churchill began with a dry run at Harrow, his old school, where he covered just a quarter of his notes during ninety minutes.

The British lecture tour was organized by Gerald Christie's Lecture Agency. It attracted ticket sales of almost £4,000, but required Churchill to speak at thirty venues within a period of just over a month.[8] Before his appearance in Liverpool on 22 November

Churchill sat down to list his assets and liabilities. Adopting the optimistic outlook that came to characterize his financial arithmetic, Churchill calculated that his assets had now reached £8,000.[9] However, the liabilities column contained his loan of £3,500 and unpaid bills of £640, one of which had reached the hands of solicitors.[10] Churchill's constituents in Oldham were also pressing him to make the expected financial contributions in support of causes as diverse as the Oldham Deaf and Dumb Society, the Oldham branch of the Boys' Brigade and the Oldham & District Ornithological Society.[11] Nevertheless, Churchill felt confident enough about his finances at the end of the tour to join a series of exclusive London clubs, including the Carlton Club, a bastion of the Conservative Party.

Mark Twain was on hand to introduce Churchill at his first packed lecture in New York early in December, but as the tour progressed it became clear that the organizer J. B. Pond had greatly overestimated Churchill's drawing power. Churchill averaged only £50 a lecture, half the amount in Britain, despite travelling much greater distances each day.[12] Worse was to come in Toronto, Canada, where attendances were higher but (much to Churchill's outrage) Pond sub-contracted the events for a fixed fee, so Churchill received only 15 per cent of the takings.[13]

Christmas at the governor-general's house in Ottawa, with Pamela Plowden as a fellow guest, did not go well. Churchill refused to resume the lecture tour until Pond travelled to Canada and persuaded him to soldier on throughout January without a change of his terms. He was cheered instead by an investment success which he shared with his mother: 'Cassel made a speculation for me the other day which resulted in a profit of £187.10. He is v[er]y kind and his judgement is marvellously accurate. I hope, my dearest Mama, to be able to provide for myself in the future – at any rate until things are better for you.' The one bone of contention between them remained the loan that Churchill had taken out from Norwich Union to pay his own allowance – and Jack's. He wrote to Jennie:

If you can arrange to relieve me of this loan, with the interest of which I am heavily burdened – £300 per annum – I will not ask for any allowance whatever from you, until old Papa Wests decides to give you and George more to live on. Jack in a few years should be self-supporting too. But what a lucky thing it is that I did not remain in the army, for I could not have retained my commission under the circumstances. I am very proud that there is not one person in a million who at my age could have earned £10,000 without any capital in less than two years. But it is sometimes v[er]y unpleasant work. For instance, last week I arrived to lecture in an American town & found Pond had not arranged any public lecture but that I was hired out for £40 to perform at an evening party in a private house – like a conjurer. Several times I have harangued in local theatres to almost empty benches.[14]

Churchill headed home on the day after Queen Victoria's funeral. He was $6,000 better off, but exhausted, as he recalled in *My Early Life*:

For more than five months I had spoken for an hour or more almost every night except Sundays, and often twice a day, and had travelled without ceasing, usually by night, rarely sleeping twice in the same bed. But the results were substantial. I had in my possession nearly £10,000. I was entirely independent and had no need to worry about the future, or for many years to work at anything but politics. I sent my £10,000 to my Father's old friend, Sir Ernest Cassel, with the instruction 'Feed my sheep'. He fed the sheep with great prudence. They did not multiply fast, but they fattened steadily, and none of them ever died. Indeed from year to year they had a few lambs; but these were not numerous enough for me to live upon. I had every year to eat a sheep or two as well, so gradually my flock grew smaller, until in a few years it was almost entirely devoured.[15]

Not all of the cash was handed over to Sir Ernest. While still feeling flush, Churchill paid off a clutch of old bills from tailors, saddlers and stables, some of them dating back to 1895.[16] He also sent his mother a cheque for £300 on the day that he took his seat in the House of Commons. 'In a certain sense, it belongs to you,' he explained, 'for I could never have earned it had you not transmitted to me the wit and energy which are necessary.'[17]

The young bachelor MP's expenditure began to assume a pattern, dominated by fine clothing, footwear, books, wine, cigars, hotel meals and horses, for hunting and polo. A generation later, in *Edwardian Hey-Days* (1930), Jennie's second husband George Cornwallis-West claimed that 'a bachelor in London with a thousand a year was comparatively well-off':

> He could get a very good flat in Mayfair, to hold himself and his servant, for a hundred and fifty pounds per annum. Dinner at his club cost him about four shillings, and any good restaurant would have been prepared to provide an excellent dinner, if he chose to give one to his friends, at ten and sixpence a head. The best tailor in Savile Row would make a suit of evening clothes for eleven guineas, and a morning suit for about eight guineas; dress shirts could be bought for ten and sixpence.[18]

Churchill, on the other hand, spent nearer to £1,400 a year during his bachelor years, as we know from his secretary's analysis of his outlays during 1905.[19] Like his mother, Churchill patronized only the best suppliers: boots and shoes came from Palmer & Co., inventor of the waterproof boot; hats from Scotts Hatters, while J. W. Allen provided solid leather cases for them, lined with brown satin.[20] Frank Smythson added the suffix 'MP' to Churchill's calling cards,[21] while membership of the Bicester Hunt and the Ranelagh Club for polo set him back forty guineas a year between them, before stabling and equipment consumed a similar sum.[22] Weekends were spent moving between country houses and polo grounds, driven by his chauffeur-cum-servant Émile Violon, who was equipped for the purpose with a uniform of a blue serge jacket, 'vest' and trousers.

Oppressed by the weight of bills, invitations and correspondence, Churchill again turned to his mother for help: 'It is quite clear to me that unless I get a Secretary, I shall be pressed into my grave with all sorts of ridiculous things – which I have no need whatever to do.'[23] She lent him the part-time use of Annette Anning, her own secretary, but soon lost her completely to Churchill, who had embarked on a way of life that was to last another fifty years: a combination of politics and writing.

Pamela Plowden, to whom he had not written for eight weeks, felt seriously neglected and, when Churchill proposed to her at Warwick Castle during the summer of 1901, she declined. Jack learned that at least three other men considered themselves to be informally engaged to Pamela and soon afterwards she chose the earl of Lytton. 'I think Winston is quite right to have put off with dear little Pamela,' his military mentor Colonel Brabazon reassured Churchill's aunt. 'She ought to be a rich man's wife.'[24]

There was still no sign of Jennie repaying the loan that Churchill had taken on for the last three years to fund his allowance, despite the death of the dowager duchess in 1899, which had added the residuary estate of the 7th duke of Marlborough to Lord Randolph's will trust. Indeed, by the end of 1901 his mother's financial problems were once again coming to a head: Jennie had bowed to the inevitable and closed her society magazine, *The Anglo-Saxon Review*, which was still making losses after ten issues.* Her husband George, a stranger to the idea of earning a living, had continued with his life's main interests, which might be deduced from the chapter headings of his book *Edwardian Hey-Days*: Hunting, Racing, Deer-Stalking, Fishing, Golf, Cricket, Motoring and (not untruthfully) Unsuccessful Enterprises – that is, until Sir Ernest

---

* 'It's a guinea a number, too little by half, / For the crowned heads of Europe are all on the staff,' ran a contemporary satirical rhyme.

Cassel found him a directorship of an electrical company in far-off Glasgow. His modest salary might have mattered less if his wife's spending had been less extravagant. '[Jennie] dressed beautifully, and her taste, not only in clothes, but in everything, was of the best,' George observed ruefully. 'In money matters she was without any sense of proportion.'[25]

Aware of the tensions caused by Churchill's loan within the family, the duke of Marlborough chided Churchill for his 'needlessly extravagant' expenditure before meeting him to discuss the matter with their family solicitor at the end of 1901.[26] The duke left straight afterwards to winter in South Africa without giving any inkling of his intentions to Churchill, but he instructed Theodore Lumley to find a way that he could help his cousin as head of the family.[27] The solicitor 'considered' the problem in January 1902, then held a 'long meeting' with Churchill in February, followed by a 'long and private interview' in March with the duke, who finally decided to lend Churchill £3,500 interest-free to repay the Norwich Union loan.[28]

Unfortunately, the duke had forgotten this arrangement by the time the insurance company's six months' notice period had expired; Lumley's diplomatic reminders went unanswered, so Churchill himself visited the duke at Blenheim. They reached an agreement: the Churchill brothers' loan would remain interest-free until their mother's death, but they would provide security for its eventual repayment from what remained of their future inheritance.

At last, during the summer of 1902, his father's literary executors (Ernest Beckett, a banker, and Earl Howe, the husband of one of Lord Randolph's sisters) gave Churchill access to the papers and letters at Blenheim, so that he could begin work on a biography. 'There emerges from these dusty records a great and vivid drama,' he told his mother as he began sifting through them.[29]

He was soon distracted by an invitation to witness the opening of the Aswan dam in Egypt. It came from Sir Ernest Cassel, who had arranged the dam's financing after his rivals the Rothschilds turned down the opportunity. While he was away, Churchill ordered his newsagent to forward the usual six daily newspapers, as well as *The Spectator* and *Punch*. He also took with him the extra reading required for the political campaigns he was planning, one for reform of the army and another against 'tariff reform', the political issue which was to define Churchill's separation from the Conservative Party's mainstream.

Churchill's vision of imperialism was founded on the mutual progress towards liberalism and democracy of members of the empire, not on a shared economic self-interest. Although he was born into the landed class, which almost always identified with the Tory Party, Churchill had never owned an acre of land. His experience of having to earn his own living through personal enterprise led him to identify just as closely at this stage of his life with the new breed of 'plutocrats', many of whom were friends or friends of his parents: the bankers Nathaniel and Alfred Rothschild and Sir Ernest Cassel; the newspaper owners Alfred Harmsworth and Oliver Borthwick; the mining financier Abe Bailey.* Although keen to acquire many of the trappings of the aristocracy – a country home, a shoot, a stretch of river – many 'plutocrats' identified politically with the values of reform, enterprise and free trade, as championed by the Liberal Party.

Churchill was associated with a small group of Tories known as the 'Hooligans'** who nursed hopes of a realignment at the centre of British politics and kept in touch with leading Liberal Party figures. Many fellow politicians suspected the motives of the 'Hooligans' to owe more to ambition than to principle; however the issue of 'free trade' provided members of the group with the cover of principle. Within a month of the leading Conservative

---

* Abraham ('Abe') Bailey (1864–1940), born in southern Africa, educated in England; woolbroker 1879; goldmining in southern Africa 1881; mentored by Cecil Rhodes, stock-broking of mining shares; later owned his own mining properties; baronet 1919.
** Also known as the 'Hughligans', taking their name from a leader, Hugh Cecil MP.

Joseph Chamberlain announcing in May 1903 his conversion to a policy of trade tariffs loaded in favour of imports from Britain's colonies, Churchill signalled his opposition was sufficiently deep-seated to cause a break with the Tories and a move towards the Liberal Party.

By the middle of 1903 Churchill was so exhausted by his twin careers of writing and politics that he underwent a course of twenty-three 'Galvanic Medical Treatments',[30] a harbinger of growing medical expenditure during his late bachelor years. At least he had little tax to pay: the combined rate of direct and indirect taxes was still around 20 per cent for those on the highest or lowest incomes,[31] but Churchill was told that he should not have to pay more than £50 for either the 1902/3 or 1903/4 tax years* – he was still unpaid as an MP, and was allowed to spread his literary earnings over three successive years and to deduct all his bank interest and insurance payments.[32]

City markets had remained so depressed since the end of the Boer War – one commentator reported stockbrokers picking up cigarette ends in the street[33] – that two years of comparative peace on his mother's finances came to an end late in 1904, when Norwich Union took fright at the dwindling value of investments backing its £17,000 loan to the family trusts. Preoccupied at this time by politics as he prepared the ground for crossing the floor of the House from the Tory to the Liberal benches, Churchill asked his brother Jack to deal with the insurers. At the same time he reassured Jennie that Cornwallis-West family money would eventually come to their rescue: 'I have no doubt that when Papa G.** is at length gathered to Abraham, you will be able to renew your youth like the eagle.'[34] The duke chastised Churchill for not taking a closer personal interest in his mother's affairs, prompting him to set aside two days for what he called a 'Grand Inquisition'.

---

* In Britain the tax year runs from 6 April to 5 April of the following year.
** George Cornwallis-West's father.

Jennie welcomed the gesture. 'I am sure it will save you & Jack a lot of bother later on,' she wrote to him; 'it is really such a heavy, difficult estate to understand.'[35]

Churchill's 'Inquisition' failed to live up to the rigorous standards of its Spanish namesake; too many of his energies were bent on establishing a new political identity. His biography of Lord Randolph had also made little progress, but he gave it more of his attention during August when he stayed at Sir Ernest Cassel's mountain-top retreat above the Swiss village of Mörel. 'I divide [the days] into three parts,' he told his mother. 'The morning when I read and write: the afternoons when I walk – real long walks and climbs about these hills or across the glacier: the evenings, of course 4 rubbers of bridge – then bed.'[36]

Whenever he could during the autumn, Churchill continued writing, whether at a moated house near St Albans rented by the Cornwallis-Wests, at Blenheim Palace or in London, the location where politics and Jennie's finances proved most distracting. By March 1905 Churchill felt sufficiently confident about his biography to discuss terms with the publisher of his first five books. However, Thomas Longman's offer of a £4,000 advance fell so far short of the £8,000 or £10,000 that he had been told to expect that Churchill decided to look elsewhere once the book was more complete.[37]

Meanwhile his former colleagues in the Conservative Party were not making the task of finishing the book any easier. They forced his resignation from the Carlton Club and blackballed his application to the polo club at Hurlingham.[38] When Churchill dried up during a House of Commons speech in May, sympathy flowed from many quarters, but no one was as practical as his aunt Cornelia, who sent money. 'Now I know elections and Parliament in general all means a great deal of expense & so we want to enjoy the prerogative of standing in the relation of uncles and aunts to send a little present which we feel may be useful at any rate at the present time,' she wrote, unable to resist adding:

'When the heiress* is found, I think the good fortune will not only be on your side.'[39]

Despite the blackball at the Hurlingham, polo weighed heavily on Churchill's time and finances during the summer of 1905. He had sold two ponies for ten guineas each earlier in the year,[40] replacing them with four of a much higher pedigree, each costing at least £100.[41] Although Wembley Park Polo Club allowed MPs to play in the mornings for a reduced membership fee, housing each pony cost three shillings a day and moving them cost a minimum of nineteen shillings whenever he played elsewhere.

Lord Randolph's biography languished until Churchill spent another three weeks at Sir Ernest Cassel's Swiss villa in August, after which he reopened publishing negotiations. He had a new agent, Frank Harris, an author himself and former editor of the *Evening News*, *Fortnightly Review* and *Vanity Fair*.** Harris would earn commission only on any improvement he achieved on Longman's offer of £4,000. He sent details of *Lord Randolph Churchill* to several publishers, telling Churchill: 'Properly worked this book should bring you in £10,000 or I'm a Dutchman!'[42] Harris provided Churchill with a blow-by-blow account of negotiations: Heinemann was the first to decline; Methuen talked well, but 'is not rich enough to risk a sum like eight or ten thousand'; Cassell was the richest publisher, he thought, and ought to emerge victorious; but in the end it was Frederick Macmillan, one of the doyens of British publishing, who made the highest offer of £8,000 for combined British and American rights.[43]

Churchill immediately met Macmillan to make some final demands: he wanted £1,000 on signing, another £1,000 on delivery of the proofs and the remaining £6,000 on publication. Forty-eight hours later, impressed by Churchill's self-assurance, Macmillan

---

* The 'rich heiress' was a rare but much sought-after Victorian creature: she had wealthy parents, but no brothers and as few sisters as possible.
** Frank Harris (1856–1931); best known for his explicit memoirs, *My Life and Loves* (1922–7).

acquiesced: 'My partners and I have discussed the proposals you made to us on Saturday and I now write to confirm that we shall be glad to publish your *Lord Randolph Churchill* on the terms suggested by you.'[44]

There was no contract. 'The terms contained in your letter of this day are perfectly satisfactory to me,' Churchill simply wrote on Macmillan's office notepaper the same day,[45] before passing on details to his mother and his former publisher. Longman congratulated him on the 'splendid price', but told Macmillan privately that he had paid too much.[46]

This earned Churchill a stern rebuke from Macmillan: 'By the way, we do not propose to tell the world at large what our arrangement with you is. It always seems to me that gossip of this kind serves no good end and is a little bit undignified.'[47] Churchill claimed only to have told 'some of my relations and a few intimate friends',[48] but his generous advance soon became common knowledge in the book world. 'Winston Churchill is a bright young man and will make the most of his material but there is not much of vital interest in the subject,' was the lukewarm verdict of the London office of Charles Scribner's Sons.[49]

Manuscripts and proofs travelled between Churchill and his new publisher almost daily in November, although the cordial mood soured slightly when Churchill decided that Macmillan's proofreader was not up to the task and insisted that his agent Harris should act instead at his publisher's expense.[50] Meanwhile, Churchill prepared the ground among his newspaper friends: Sir Alfred Harmsworth 'has most kindly promised me to push the book by every means in his power', as long as he was sent five copies ten days in advance, he told his publisher.[51]

The publication date of the biography was set for January 1906 until Prime Minister Arthur Balfour resigned in the preceding December, having failed to resolve Tory differences over tariff reform. Although he did not ask the king to dissolve Parliament in case the Liberal leader Sir Henry Campbell-Bannerman was unable to form a government, the prospect of power rapidly united Sir

Henry's colleagues. Among those Sir Henry contacted about an appointment was Churchill himself, to whom he offered the choice of financial secretary at the Treasury (under Herbert Asquith as chancellor) or under-secretary for the colonies (under Lord Elgin, a former viceroy whom he had met in India). Churchill preferred the latter's scope to shine in the House of Commons.

Emboldened by the ease with which he had formed his administration, Prime Minister Campbell-Bannerman asked the king himself for a dissolution of Parliament and set the general election date for early in January, just as *Lord Randolph Churchill* was due to be published. Churchill wanted to delay the launch while he stood for the first time as a Liberal in northwest Manchester (and comfortably beat his Tory opponent),[52] but Macmillan pressed ahead, in the hope of capitalizing on a wave of political interest.

Lord Randolph Churchill was published as the first election results were declared. British sales reached almost 5,000 in January, before slowing down sharply.[53] Macmillan admitted disappointment, but felt that Churchill's expectations had always been too high.[54] *The Times* Book Club had just been established in an effort to restore the newspaper's flagging sales and Macmillan sold it 1,900 copies from surplus stock; he had not realized that the newspaper would then offer the book to its Book Club members at one fifth of its bookshop price.[55] 'I am very sorry to see by a cutting which has reached me that *The Times* have played you a shabby trick,' Churchill wrote to his publisher.[56] Nevertheless, Churchill had his generous advance and he told his tax adviser Theodore Lumley to submit a profit on the biography of £7,250 after expenses, easily the best profit of his writing career thus far.[57]

Before Churchill submerged himself under the cares of office, he earmarked £6,000 of the sum for investment by Sir Ernest Cassel and the balance for the lease of a larger London home, of the class expected of a rising young minister. It was Jennie who found the four-storey home at 12 Bolton Street in Mayfair, while the duke of Marlborough agreed over Christmas at Blenheim that Churchill

could leave Mount Street at short notice. With Jennie's help, alterations were agreed over the New Year – the architect's initial estimate
of less than £250 being revised to £850 after he had met Churchill
and his mother.[58]

Then there was the £750 cost of a library, which Churchill
wanted but could not afford until Sir Ernest Cassel offered to pay
for it – a fact that would emerge seventeen years later, during the
libel trial of Lord Alfred Douglas. Churchill set about filling the
bookshelves, spending more than £300 on hundreds of new and
secondhand volumes procured from the bookshops of Charing
Cross Road.[59]

He was discovering the cost of home ownership: Harrods' bill
alone was seven pages long, covering kitchen, bedroom and bathroom items ordered by his mother.[60] There was annual rent of £250
to pay to the freeholder, plus local property income taxes, and bills
for insurance and utilities.[61] Two male servants, a housekeeper,
cook and a housemaid looked after the new minister, although his
long-established laundress Mrs Thornley still collected his washing,
which she took to her emporium in Earlsfield for the not inconsid-
erable cost of £100 a year.[62]

6

No 'rich heiress'

Junior Minister and Marriage, 1906–8

Exchange rate $5 = £1
Inflation multiples: US x 25; UK x 100

THE NEW UNDER-SECRETARY for the colonies paid £5.10s. for his first red Moroccan-leather dispatch box.[1] Churchill's in-tray in December 1905 was dominated by southern Africa's continuing problems, particularly the need to devise a self-governing constitution for the Transvaal. In addition the Liberal Party's election manifesto had promised to bring to an end the local administration's controversial use of 50,000 Chinese labourers in the mines.

Despite these tasks, the new minister still found time to play polo, which Edward Marsh,* his new private secretary at the Colonial Office, charitably entered as 'equitation' in the ministerial diary. Marsh had been private secretary for Joseph Chamberlain, but he came personally recommended by the new Countess Lytton (formerly Pamela Plowden) and by Churchill's own aunt Leonie.

Public office failed to restrain Churchill's private spending, which reached £1,700 in 1906, well ahead of a junior minister's salary of £1,500 a year.[2] In order to secure an expanding overdraft at the bank, Cox & Co. required Churchill to transfer some of his investments for

---

* Edward Marsh (1872–1953), classical scholar; private secretary to Churchill in each of his ministerial posts 1905–29; knighted 1937. Marsh collected the paintings of British watercolourists and published the works of young poets in his *Georgian Poetry* anthologies.

registration under its name. On the way to observe German army summer manoeuvres, Churchill and his cousin Ivor Guest visited the Deauville casino, where his early successes might have helped reduce Churchill's debts; but his fortunes changed as they gambled every night until five in the morning. 'I have made a little money – had made a lot,' he told Marsh.[3] The eventual profit from his visits (£260) disappeared on a diversion to Paris, where it was split between four hundredweight of books bought for his new library and what Churchill coyly described to his brother Jack as 'other directions'.[4]

Left to hold the fort at home, Marsh asked innocently whether he should pay any of the minister's overdue private bills. Churchill explained his philosophy: 'They may as well wait a little longer, having already waited so long.' However, he did ask his brother to keep an eye on a couple of bills. 'I do not want to pay them now unless I am forced, in wh[ich] case I can find the money,' he told Jack. 'But I do not want them to take legal proceedings and I hope you will let me know before the matter becomes urgent.'[5]

The truth was that Churchill could only pay by increasing an overdraft limit that he had already raised once, or by selling more investments at what he considered a bad time. One of his stock-broking friends, Cecil Grenfell, had recommended 'Unions' shares to him earlier in the summer, but Churchill had missed an opportunity by selling them much too soon. He admitted to Jack (who was now a member of the stockbroking fraternity at Nelke Phillips & Co.) that Sir Ernest Cassel and Grenfell had criticized his habit of darting in and out of the market.[6]

Churchill's bank was no happier: Churchill had breached an increased overdraft limit and it now insisted that part of the arrangement was converted into a formal loan. 'It seems pre-destined that money is to avoid me,' Churchill complained to his mother, 'except in such driblets that it cannot be enjoyed without feelings of uncertainty & anxiety.'[7]

Mr and Mrs Cornwallis-West were not without their own difficulties. With a little help from Lord Rothschild, George had two years earlier formed a new City partnership, Wheater, Cornwallis-West & Co. The two principals hardly knew each other, but the north countryman Wheater was supposed to provide the brains, and George the London introductions. 'In the first year, merely operating in large lines of the shares in north-country steel and iron works controlled by the late Lord Furness, we made over twenty-three thousand pounds,' George recalled in his memoirs. However, the firm started to struggle when Wheater, 'a born gambler', reinvested their gains in a Spanish copper mine and an Australian cultured pearls project,[8] before a solicitor defrauded the business in the summer of 1906.

Left to find £8,000 in a hurry, George hid the difficulty from Jennie, but not from Churchill, who was one of those he approached to produce the balance that the bank would not lend. Churchill was in Vienna when a letter with a cheque for £3,000 arrived from Nairobi, sent by the duke of Westminster.[9] Bendor (as the duke was known to friends) was George's brother-in-law and, although his own marriage was in trouble, he made it clear that Churchill should use the cheque, rather than his own money, if George genuinely needed to be rescued. The duke's only condition was that George should not be able to trace its source.

Fittingly, George was stalking deer in Scotland when Churchill's letter reached Jennie, asking for private information on George's affairs. Things were a little slack in the City, she thought, but Wheater, Cornwallis-West & Co. had earned at least £12,000 over the previous three months, as far as she knew.[10] In fact, as she wrote, the Bank of England was pushing through two bank rate rises within ten days to try to stop gold draining away from London to New York.* Handing over the duke's money to George, Churchill hinted heavily that it had come from Sir Ernest Cassel, with whom he had just stayed in Switzerland. He explained to Bendor that he could not pretend that he had supplied the money himself, because George would never have believed him.

---

* From 4 to 5 per cent on 11 October 1906 and to 6 per cent on 19 October.

Churchill then had to put aside the Cornwallis-West's difficulties and turn to another branch of the family: his Londonderry cousins in Ireland. His great-grandmother Frances Vane, marchioness of Londonderry, had died forty-two years ago, leaving her money and land in Co. Antrim to her younger grandchildren, because her eldest grandson was to inherit the main Londonderry estate. To prevent her Garron Tower estate from being broken up, the marchioness's will established a strict order of precedence among her inheritors: first, her second grandson Lord Herbert Vane-Tempest and his heirs; failing whom, his brother Lord Henry Vane-Tempest; failing whom Lord Randolph Churchill, the son of her daughter Frances and the 7th duke of Marlborough. When Lord Herbert inherited the Garron Tower estate in 1864, its land, loans and investments had been valued at £72,874, even without one of its most attractive components, the marchioness's jewellery.[11]

The chances of Lord Randolph's heirs ever succeeding must at first have seemed remote, but now a letter had arrived from the Londonderry family's solicitors announcing that Churchill was the next in line: Lord Henry had just died childless in 1906, while Lord Herbert remained unmarried at the age of forty-four.

Worried at the increasing risk that the estate would eventually pass to the English branch of the family, the Londonderrys wished to buy their mother's jewellery out of the estate and now required Churchill's formal approval as the next in line. Churchill's solicitor suggested that the jewels should be independently valued (the Londonderrys' adviser had suggested a price of £4,420) and that Churchill should reserve the right to buy back the jewels later, a move unsurprisingly resisted by the Londonderrys, as it would have defeated the whole object of the exercise.[12]

Family harmony was tested again in the autumn when the duke of Marlborough asked for Churchill's help in bringing his six-year marriage to an end. Personally sympathetic towards Consuelo Vanderbilt (who had not only produced the necessary heir but also used a considerable slice of the Vanderbilt fortune to help modernize Blenheim), Churchill was exasperated by his cousin's obstinacy, which defied his attempts to broker an amicable separation.

Churchill's family relations survived this test, but there was a growing political estrangement. The Liberal government of which Churchill was a member had begun to put into practice its philosophy that the state should play a greater role in combating poverty among children, the sick and the elderly. On his holiday during the summer of 1906 Churchill read H. G. Wells's *A Modern Utopia* (1905), in whose parallel world the state owned all land and subsidized motherhood.[13] Churchill publicly declared his support for a radical programme in a speech at Glasgow soon after his holiday. 'The cause of the Liberal Party is the cause of the left-out millions,' he declared, adding: 'I should like to see the state embark on various novel and interesting experiments.'[14]

Churchill overcame his immediate ministerial challenges in southern Africa and, after helping to host a Colonies' Conference in London during April 1907, he decided to make a trip to eastern Africa. The plan, partly to inspect territories for which he was responsible and partly to travel for private pleasure, was approved by Lord Elgin, the secretary of state, who hoped that the absence of his hyperactive young minister might lead to a quieter Scottish summer. In order to forestall any possible suggestion of impropriety, Churchill offered to pay his own travel expenses and asked his former agent A. P. Watt to arrange a series of five articles with *The Strand Magazine* at £150 each to offset part of the cost.[15] For additional contributions Churchill asked his mother to let his house and find alternative employment for his secretary: 'I do rely upon you dear Mamma to help me in arranging these affairs; for wh[ich] I am not at all suited by disposition or temperament.'[16] Jennie could not understand why he had offered to pay his way: 'C'est magnifique, mais ce n'est pas la guerre,' she told him. 'And no one will thank you for it.'[17]

At Malta Churchill met his travelling party: his uncle by marriage, Colonel Gordon Wilson, his private secretary Edward Marsh and his manservant Scriving. They embarked on HMS *Venus*, a light cruiser detailed to carry them in style through the Suez Canal to Aden and then on to Mombasa in the British East Africa Protectorate. Jennie had failed to let the Mount Street home, but Jack reported success soon after taking over the task. 'Who do you think?' he asked. 'Mr Bob Scrivier!'[18] Seldom out of the newspapers, Scrivier was one of the racing world's rogues, recently banned from the sport for a spell. Churchill cabled home twice, protesting at the risk to his reputation,[19] but Jack held his ground, accusing his brother of double standards:

> You have made great friends with Frank Harris whose reputation in the City, where they have some experience and are fairly good judges – is only equalled by Scrivier's renown on the turf. . . You are always having fits of economical fervour but it all evaporates the moment there is any sign of any retrenchment, or of any of your luxuries being curtailed.[20]

As HMS *Venus* sailed down the east African coast, Jack sounded a note of triumphalism about a sudden crisis in New York's financial markets:

> It has been raging for three days and is not over. A year ago all the New York millionaires were telling us that they were the only people on the earth and that New York was the centre of the financial world. Well most of them are ruined today and money is 100% in New York while it remains 4½% here. I think the slow and sure system of Threadneedle Street has survived their jeers. . . Our finances are not looking their best. I fear we shall have to borrow when you come back.[21]

Churchill disembarked at Mombasa and proceeded in style up the new railway line to Nairobi: 'Everything moves on the smoothest of wheels for me – a special train with dining and sleeping cars was at my disposal all the way; wherever I wished to stop, it stopped,' he told his mother. 'We sat in front of the engine with our rifles & as soon as we saw anything to shoot at – a wave of the hand brought the train to a standstill.'[22]

A good deal of business had been transacted 'in the intervals of these field sports',[23] Churchill claimed, but it proved a challenge to apportion the unexpectedly high expenses for the trip between various governments and Churchill's private purse. The protectorate's bill for half the visitors' costs in Nairobi remained unpaid for six months; it was only cancelled when Marsh brokered a deal that Churchill would pay thirty shillings a day, while the other members of his party were treated as officials.[24] 'The Tour. . . originally was intended to be a pure sporting and private expedition,' Lord Elgin mused to his successor the following year, '& I really don't know how it drifted into an official progress.'[25]

The governor and his staff joined Churchill for the onward journey along the new railway line to Kisumu on Lake Victoria, from which the visitors crossed Uganda on a luxury steamer. While Churchill was there, a letter from Jack broke the news of his romance with Lady Gwendoline, the daughter of Lord and Lady Abingdon. The couple had decided six months earlier that marriage was impossible because of the Churchill family's shortage of money, but Goonie (as she was universally known) had changed her mind: 'She said that she would sacrifice anything for her love,' Jack wrote excitedly, 'that her ambition for riches and everything else had vanished and that she would wait for me until I could come and fetch her.' Jack had no savings of his own, but was going to try to arrange for a guarantee of £1,000 a year from his firm, Nelke Phillips, where he had just been made a partner. 'In moderate times I ought to get 2 thousand and in good times 3, 4 or even 5 thousand,' he explained to Churchill. 'It is just my luck that this should happen in a year which for financial disasters is a record in any living memory.'

He went on to share an unwelcome discovery that he had made during the course of researching his marriage prospects: it concerned their father's will. 'I am rather disturbed to hear that the

American property* and the English "Will"** are settled on our children and we have only a life interest in these things. The only thing which we absolutely have for our own are the "settlements"*** amounting in all to about £13,000.'[26]

Churchill did not react to this news, but encouraged Jack to tackle Goonie's father head-on and hold out the likelihood that he would earn more than his minimum of £1,000 a year: '£1,400 a year is quite enough for two sensible people who care about one another. Of course to go the London pace it is a wisp of straw.'[27]

Returning to England in mid-January 1908 Churchill found his mother's finances once again vying for attention next to a pile of ministerial papers. The family solicitors, Lumley & Lumley, had proved poor administrators of his father's will trust – unable to police Jennie's spending or to produce proper accounts for the trustees. Before Churchill left for Africa, George Curzon had tried to retire as a trustee, arguing that the two Churchill brothers were now old enough to act themselves, alongside their mother; but as a co-trustee, the duke of Marlborough wanted reassurance from an independent firm of solicitors that all was well before any change of trustees took place.

The solicitors employed for the purpose, Nicholl, Manisty & Co., advised that the Churchills should not take over as trustees until proper accounts had been prepared. The consequent delay prompted Curzon to refuse to sanction any further transactions, including the sale of the trust's main asset, the freehold of 12 St James's Square, which had fallen into the trust from the estate of the 7th duke of Marlborough after the dowager duchess's death.

---

* The Jerome family's contribution to Lord and Lady Randolph's marriage settlement.
** Lord Randolph Churchill's will trust, now supplemented by the 7th duke of Marlborough's personal estate after the death of his widow.
*** The Marlborough family's contribution to their parents' marriage settlement.

The property was let for £1,500 a year to a Mr Long, who had offered to buy the freehold for £37,500, comfortably above its professional valuation; but the sale had to wait while Nicholl Manisty prepared new accounts.

These accounts greeted Churchill on his return. Their contents were serious enough for the trust's lender, Norwich Union, to insist on the formal appointment of Edward Manisty as Receiver to the trust, charged with keeping future accounts and approving any movements of money from it. On these conditions, it approved the appointment of the Churchill brothers as trustees alongside their mother.[28]

Churchill rapidly made his presence felt, insisting that he would agree a price of nothing less than £45,000 for 12 St James's Square. A furious Mr Long took six weeks to raise his offer grudgingly to £39,500, but Churchill stood out for £42,000, offering to draft the lawyer's letter for them when they proved reluctant to accept his instruction; three weeks later Mr Long paid £41,000.[29] Churchill then caused further waves by rejecting Wheater, Cornwallis-West's ideas as to how best to invest the money; instead he awarded the business to his brother Jack's stockbroking firm Nelke Phillips.[30]

During Churchill's absence, Sir Henry Campbell-Bannerman's health had deteriorated to the point where he had temporarily given up his duties as prime minister. An attempt to return to work in February 1908 proved unsuccessful and Edward VII asked Herbert Asquith to start planning to take over in March, although Sir Henry did not resign until April. Churchill was offered promotion to the cabinet at either the Admiralty or the Local Government Board; he chose the latter, for he was reluctant to displace his uncle, Lord Tweedmouth, at the Admiralty. However, at the last minute Asquith made Churchill the president of the Board of Trade. It was a full cabinet position at the heart of his Liberal government's legislative programme, but the post held one distinct disadvantage for Churchill: for historical reasons, it paid only half of a secretary of state's £5,000 salary. Asquith promised to ask Parliament to address the anomaly, but it emerged that the present post-holder could not benefit from any change.

Churchill's appointment was announced on the same April weekend that he had asked his mother to invite to Salisbury Hall the twenty-three-year-old Miss Clementine Hozier. Clementine was the second of four children of the divorced Sir Henry Hozier and Lady Blanche Ogilvy, the eldest daughter of the earl of Airlie. After army service, Sir Henry had become secretary of Lloyd's Corporation in London, but he was not a rich man; and, although a grand Scottish family, the Airlies were not rich either.

The Hoziers' marriage had been unhappy since the start. Their first child, Kitty, had arrived after five years, followed by Clementine in 1885 and the twins Nellie and Bill in 1888. Lady Blanche was considered promiscuous by the standards of the day and it is generally accepted that Sir Henry was not the father of the twins, or probably Clementine, or possibly Kitty.*

Clementine's parents separated when she was seven and her mother took the children to live in a series of rented lodgings and eventually across the Channel to Dieppe, after Sir Henry began to default on the small allowance he was supposed to pay and threatened to claim custody of the elder children. Following Kitty's death from typhoid, they returned to live in Hertfordshire, where Clementine attended Berkhamsted High School for Girls, unsurprisingly winning the school French prize and supplementing her small allowance by giving language lessons for 2s.6d. an hour.

Churchill had first met Clementine at a London ball four years

---

* The alternative candidates were Bay Middleton, a dashing army officer killed in a riding accident in 1892 or Lady Blanche's brother-in-law Bertie Mitford, later Lord Redesdale. Wilfrid Scawen Blunt, a friend of Lady Blanche, recorded in his diary on 22 June 1892 that she had told him both Clementine and Kitty were Bay Middleton's children – see Elizabeth Longford, *A Pilgrimage of Passion: The Life of Wilfrid Scawen Blunt*, (Weidenfeld & Nicolson, London 1971), p. 271.

earlier. He had asked to be introduced, but then is supposed to have stared at her, struck speechless, without asking for a dance. Clementine had been engaged three times since then, twice secretly to Viscount Peel's third son Sidney, and once officially to Lionel Earle, a civil servant almost twice her age. Her sister Nellie had suggested that a file of 'Proposals to Clementine' should be kept, with subdivisions: 'Discussed', 'Answered' and 'Pending a decision'.[31]

Clementine met Churchill again two months after his return from Africa, at a dinner party organized by Lady St Helier, her great-aunt, who had invited her to make up the numbers at the last minute. Churchill arrived late to fill the gap next to Clementine only because his private secretary Eddie Marsh had persuaded him to honour an obligation to Lady St Helier, who had helped arrange Churchill's posting to the Sudan a decade earlier.

This time the conversation had flowed freely enough for Churchill to ask his mother to issue the weekend invitation to Salisbury Hall, before Clementine left for six weeks abroad with her mother. The couple met several times at social occasions, always with others present, during June and July, but agreed to meet more privately early in August.

A few days beforehand, Churchill was staying in a Rutland house rented by the Guest family when a fire broke out. It destroyed a whole wing early in the morning, but he escaped unharmed, earning a telegram of relief from Clementine who had read about the incident in the newspapers. Given the signal he needed, Churchill moved their planned meeting to Blenheim, ostensibly on the grounds that it was closer to Jack's wedding celebrations the next weekend.

Jennie had forecast that Churchill would 'pop off' in the wake of his brother's marriage and she was correct: just three days after Jack's wedding Churchill proposed to Clementine in the gardens at Blenheim. She accepted. He planned to carry on working at Blenheim the next day, sending Clementine to London with a letter from him to obtain her mother's blessing, but he changed his mind at the last minute and decided to go with Clementine.

'I am not rich nor powerfully established,' his letter read.[32] In 1900 Churchill had calculated his own net worth (the value of his assets less the amounts owed to the bank and tradesmen) at £4,000 and it remained of the same order in 1908, with the important difference that £2,000 was now sunk into the Bolton Street house's lease and fittings, reducing his 'free' assets (his net bank and investment balances) to the other £2,000.[33]

His future mother-in-law's blessing nonetheless obtained, Churchill visited the London offices in the Strand of the solicitors Nicholl, Manisty & Co., where he had three weeks earlier signed documents as a trustee of his brother's marriage settlement. This time it was to arrange his own. Marriage settlements were designed to provide wives and children with greater financial security in an era of limited life expectancy. Traditionally, they drew contributions from the parents of both the bride and the groom, but Churchill knew that his mother's situation meant that he was on his own. At least the Hoziers were not expected to set the bar too high: Clementine may have attracted other suitors, but emphatically she was not his aunt Cornelia's hoped-for rich heiress. 'Never talk rich, never talk poor; never talk money,' had been Lady Blanche's sound advice under the circumstances.[34]

Churchill accepted Nicholl, Manisty & Co.'s plan to leave the Garron Tower estate out of the equation, basing his contribution instead (as Jack had done) on the future inheritance of his mother's American settlement.[35] That, however, left a gap should he die before Jennie, who was still only in her early fifties. The solution (as in Jack's case) was for Churchill to pay for a life insurance policy, to be held in the settlement, which would pay out £10,000 on his death. Appointing his brother and cousin, the duke of Marlborough, as trustees, Churchill set a 'pin money' allowance for Clementine of £300 a year (for her personal spending) and instructed his lawyers to send their draft to Lady Blanche's solicitor Mr Humbert of Taylor & Humbert:

This gentleman – a Mr Humbert – is now in Scotland on his holidays, but I have telephoned to him this evening to ask him to London so as to be able to meet you in conference with me here at the Board of Trade on Saturday next at noon.[36] Mr Humbert proved understandably reluctant to break off his Scottish holiday. After a meeting at a more junior level, Churchill's solicitors reported the not unexpected news that Clementine would arrive at the altar 'absolutely entitled' only to a sum of £2,000 plus a further £20,000 on her mother's death.[37] Nevertheless, Churchill's own offer had to be improved when Humbert returned from Scotland: he asked for Churchill's life assurance policy to be trebled to more than £35,000, so that his widow could enjoy 'a clear income of £1,000' if he died first. It was left to Nicholl Manisty's senior partner to pay a visit to Mr Humbert to explain that £35,000 was 'out of the question'.[38]

Five days before the wedding, on 12 September, all parties agreed that the main life insurance policy would stay at £10,000, but that Churchill would arrange for a 'reverse annuity' policy; this would pay Clementine an extra £300 a year if Churchill died before his mother. On her death, Clementine would inherit at least this sum, and probably more, from Lord Randolph's will trust.[39]

Mr Humbert's bill of more than £350 for his fees and stamp duty came as an unwelcome surprise to the groom, but Nicholl, Manisty explained that it was quite usual for 'the Husband to pay the Lady's legal charges'.[40] The £50 fee for the marriage service at St Margaret's Church, Westminster, seems like good value by comparison. 'The bride was pale, as was the bridegroom,' Wilfrid Scawen Blunt noted in his diary. 'Winston's responses were clearly made in a pleasant voice, Clementine's inaudible.'[41] Beatrice Webb's assessment was more practical: Clementine was 'a charming lady, well bred and pretty and earnest withal – but not rich, by no means a good match, which is to Winston's credit'.[42]

The groom gave the bride a pair of Burmese rubies and a gold wedding ring, for which he finished paying three years later.[43] Their wedding presents included thirty items of jewellery and more than two hundred of silver, sixty of them duplicates, for

[$5 = £1 / US x 25; UK x 100]

which silversmiths offered a credit to be put towards a silver plate service to be engraved with the Marlborough crest. The same crest featured on the tip of the gold-capped Malacca cane presented by Edward VII. Sir Ernest Cassel gave them a more practical £500 in cash.

7

'The Pug is décassé'
The HMS *Enchantress* Years, 1909–14

Exchange rate $5 = £1
Inflation multiples: US x 25; UK x 90

C HURCHILL'S MOTHER REDECORATED 12 Bolton Street in late 1908 while the couple honeymooned in Italy, with results that pleased neither her daughter-in-law's taste nor her son's wallet. Churchill sold £500-worth of investments, but was still unable to pay for more than a proportion of his bills: Hatchard the bookseller, for example, received just £25 of the £88 he owed. Churchill asked his solicitor whether he might be able to borrow against his possible inheritance of the Garron Tower estate, but his solicitor's response was discouraging: 'I have received a quotation which in my view is too high,' he reported back.[1]

Nevertheless, there was still sufficient money to keep essentials such as wine and cigars flowing. Churchill calculated that he spent an average of £1,160 with the family's wine merchants each year between 1908 and 1914; part of the appeal of Randolph Payne & Sons was that they were happy to provide long-established account-holders such as the Churchills with almost as much credit as a bank – by 1914 the amount Churchill owed the firm was regularly over £500.[2] His cigar suppliers, J. Grunebaum & Sons, were almost as flexible: Churchill was smoking about a dozen cigars a day, costing more than £13 a month, but he had not paid one of Grunebaum's bills for five years.[3]

*

Soon their first child was on the way, and the Churchills realized they would have to move out of Mount Street before it arrived in the middle of 1909. Churchill was anxious to extract a premium for the remainder of the lease – 'It is absolutely necessary to the furnishing of another house,' he explained to his mother[4] – but by March, when Clementine was five months pregnant, no takers had emerged. Churchill had to hand over the lease to a local doctor without any payment while they stayed with Guest cousins until their new home in Pimlico was ready.

Churchill had considered buying 33 Eccleston Square for £2,000, but he decided to lease it instead after winning a rent reduction to £195 a year to help pay for bathroom improvements;[5] the economics looked less sound once the cost of the work required to panelling the front room and a library and extend the dining room rose to £475.[6] Clementine had to settle for reusing the Bolton Street curtains and carpets, and resorted to 'cheap linoleum' to finish the last servants' rooms.[7]

They moved in ten weeks before their first child Diana arrived on 11 July 1909. After the birth, Clementine recuperated at a small house on Wilfrid Scawen Blunt's Horsham estate, while Diana remained in London with her father and nanny. The couple were reunited for their first wedding anniversary, which they spent near Strasburg, observing German army manoeuvres.

On their return Clementine left her husband in London, taking the baby, her nanny and a maid to the Crest Hotel in Crowborough, Sussex, forty miles south. Churchill sent regular cheques and visited most weekends, but after paying bills for Diana's delivery and the building works, he had to report at the end of October that 'the Pug is *décassé* for the moment'.* Their cash position would improve, he assured an alarmed Clementine, once Hodder &

---

* 'The Pug' was Clementine's nickname for Churchill. *Décassé* was his term for 'out of funds'. 27 October 1909 WSC letter to CSC, SFT:35.

Stoughton had paid him a £150 advance for a book of his recent speeches that it was about to publish entitled *Liberalism and the Social Problem*.[8] Despite his cash shortage, Churchill visited the jewellers on Christmas Eve to buy Clementine a pair of pearl and diamond earrings costing £45, for which he paid three years later.[9]

During 1908 and 1909 Asquith's government had set out a programme of radical policies to lay the foundations of Britain's modern welfare state, some of which – such as the Coal Mines (Eight Hours) Bill, which improved the lot of miners – it fell to Churchill to guide through Parliament. In response to the economic setbacks of 1907–8, employers reduced wages, which led to strikes and lockouts – in January it was the shipwrights; in February the engineers; in May the shipyards on the Tyne, Merseyside and Clyde. All of which kept Churchill busy in 1909 as President of the Board of Trade.

Borrowing from Sidney and Beatrice Webb's ideas, Churchill introduced labour exchanges and laid the foundations for compulsory unemployment insurance and old age pensions, but the measures all cost money. In January 1909, Lord Rothschild predicted a 'predatory, certainly spiteful and very revengeful budget' to his Paris partners,[10] and when the chancellor, David Lloyd George, unveiled it at the end of April, he was quite clear that his objective was to redistribute money from the landed class toward those living in poverty and squalor. He raised tax on petrol, cars, alcohol and tobacco, while making concessions for those on modest incomes, especially married men with children. For the first time, 'unearned' investment income was to be taxed at a higher rate than 'earned' income (at 1s.2d. rather than 1s. in the pound), a new super-tax was introduced on incomes above £5,000 (at rates of up to 1s.9d. in the pound) and the top rates of death duty were almost doubled. Landowners faced a new duty on undeveloped acres, a 20 per cent charge on increases in land values and 10 per cent duty on increases in capital values at the end of leases. Lloyd George deployed all his rhetorical skills to win popular support: 'a fully-equipped duke cost as much to keep up as two Dreadnoughts,' he claimed in a well-publicized speech at Limehouse, 'and dukes are just as great a terror and last longer.'[11]

Grandson of a duke but strongly supportive of the measures, Churchill faced accusations of class treachery among his former Conservative and Unionist colleagues. Cartoons illustrated a radical cabinet minister hounding the landed class in Westminster before retiring to the luxury of Blenheim Palace for the weekend. Most people on middle-class incomes of up to £2,000 were hardly affected and then only by small changes in death duty, Churchill claimed in the House of Commons: 'The chief burden of the increase of taxation is placed upon the main body of wealthy classes in this country... and that is a class which, in opportunities of pleasure, in all the amenities of life, and in freedom from penalties, obligations, and dangers, is more fortunate than any other equally numerous class of citizens in any age or in any country.'[12]

Passions ran high as the House of Lords threatened to reject the 'People's Budget': Lord Revelstoke, senior partner of the merchant bank Baring, spoke for many in the City when he used the upper chamber to blame the government for an 'unparalleled depreciation in British credit and British stocks'. Investors in British government bonds had nearly quadrupled the real purchasing power of their money during almost a century of falling prices between the end of the Napoleonic wars and 1897, he claimed, but now 'Consols'* had fallen by 6 per cent and English railways by 10 per cent, 'a steady and hopeless depreciation of the securities in which the most conservative of us have been brought up to pin our faith.'[13] The House of Commons passed the measures by a comfortable majority, but they were defeated in the House of Lords. By asking the king to dissolve Parliament and test popular support at a general election in January, Asquith deprived Churchill of his usual New Year holiday.

The prospect of fresh election expenses was an unwelcome one,

---

* In 1754 the British government refinanced all its floating-rate debt and most of its 4 per cent annuities into a single issue of 3 per cent Consolidated Stock, which is never due to be repaid. Known as 'Consols', these remain the oldest public bond instruments still actively traded.

coming on top of bank borrowings that already stood at over £2,000 by early 1910.[14] It coincided with an approach that Churchill had just received from a Dundee constituent and philanthropist, James Caird,* who had made a fortune in the jute business, and now asked his MP how he might make a useful financial contribution to the cause of free trade. When Churchill suggested funding a programme of lectures on the subject up and down the country, Caird sent him a personal cheque for £10,000, and followed up with further contributions of £12,000 during 1910,[15] suggesting that the minister was much the better placed man to disburse the funds. Banking the funds in a separate 'C' account at Cox & Co., Churchill handed them out gradually during 1910, mainly through the Free Trade Union, which accounted meticulously for its expenditure until it slowed down its activity during 1911 and sent Churchill a cheque for the surplus in its accounts, taking his balance of Caird funds in his account back up to £1,500 on 1 April.[16] Despite the temptations of handling funds that dwarfed his own means, there is no sign that Churchill conflated any of Caird's money with his own at this stage and his calculations of his net worth during the period scrupulously excluded it.

Nevertheless Churchill's private office found it difficult to disentangle his ministerial from his electoral expenses during the campaign of January 1910 as the minister rushed between London, Sheffield, Manchester, Edinburgh, Dundee and the south, commandeering a special train from Dundee to Edinburgh and his own steamer from Southampton to the Isle of Wight. 'If a cheque is sent to [Mr Eason] for £11, and one for £4 sent to the Chief Whip, the Chief Whip's cheque for £7-8-1 can be paid into the Home Secretary's a/c at Cox & Co., and the whole thing is finished,' wrote one private secretary.[17] Churchill broke off his return journey

---

* James Caird (1837–1916), the owner and director of Caird (Dundee) Ltd, a textile manufacturers using modern technology to weave cloth from jute; a philanthropist, Caird donated £240,000 during his lifetime to charities, many in the Dundee region; he also helped to fund Shackleton's Antarctic expedition (1914–16); baronet, 1913.

to London for a shooting party at Warter Priory in Yorkshire, where he found his fellow guests 'puissant, presentable, radical in preponderance – a rare combination'.[18]* Clementine tried to encourage the habit of the Edwardian country house weekend but it was never a Churchill favourite, however hard he tried. The diary of Wilfrid Scawen Blunt describes him arriving for one that autumn, 'dressed in a little close-fitting, fur-lined jacket, tight leggings and gaiters, and a little round hat, which with his half-mischievous face, made him look, as Miss Lawrence said, the exact figure of Puck'.[19] Churchill preferred the meat of politics: 'How much more power and great business are to me than this kind of thing, pleasant tho' it seems by contrast to our humble modes of entertainment', he explained to Clementine.[20]

Churchill was re-elected, but with a reduced majority of fewer than 400 votes over his Labour opponent, part of a wider loss of ground by the Liberal Party, which ended with only two more seats than the Tories. Asquith remained in power with the help of Irish Nationalist and Labour votes and offered Churchill a move to the Irish Office as an alternative to staying at the Board of Trade. As tactfully as he could, Churchill declined both, suggesting either the Admiralty or the Home Office instead and slipping in a subtle reminder that for the last two years he had sacrificed the full pay of a secretary of state. Early in February, he became home secretary, paid a salary of £5,000 a year that took him for the first time into Lloyd George's new super-tax bracket, a privilege enjoyed in the tax's early years by only some 10,000 of the country's top taxpayers.[21]

As home secretary, Churchill's duties ranged across maintaining law and order, running the police service, prisons, courts and passing legislation on criminal justice: he was kept busy by a rash of strikes across the mining and railway industries that required careful decisions on the use of police (and potentially troops); by severe

---

* The party included Churchill's hosts Lord and Lady Nunburnholme, the earl of Granard, Earl Cowley, Viscount Chelsea, Lord Elcho, Lord Lovat, Lord Tweedmouth and The Mackintosh of Mackintosh. Churchill's shooting card shows that they killed 2,947 birds on the first day and 2,034 on the second.

over-crowding in Britain's prisons; and by hotly contested debate over the extensions of the vote to female property-owners. On the strength of the government's renewed electoral mandate, the new Parliament's upper chamber had passed the previous year's controversial budget, but a Parliament Bill that cautiously limited its future ability to amend Commons legislation was a step too far. The new king, George V, convened a constitutional conference of the main political parties, but its failure to reach agreement in November allowed Asquith to extract a secret pledge from the king to create as many peers as the bill's passage needed if the Liberals fought and won a fresh election. A second dissolution within a year forced Churchill to return to Dundee, but the outcome across the country was little different: the balance of power remained held by the Irish Nationalist and Labour MPs, but Asquith's government stayed in place.

Even the doubled salary of a full secretary of state proved insufficient to meet Churchill's personal spending, which reached £5,000 during the first year of his appointment, before either tax or election expenses.[22] He sold some shares late in 1910, but preferred to borrow in 1911 to reduce the amounts owed to his wine, cigar, shirt and saddle suppliers, in each case more than £200.[23] In return for the transfer of all his remaining share certificates, whether bought by Cassel, Grenfell or Nelke Phillips & Co., Cox & Co. agreed to triple his formal bank loan to £3,000, allowing him to pay Grunebaum in full for his cigars, while asking the rest to be content with half of the amounts he owed them.[24]

The Churchills spent another summer largely apart after the birth of their second child, Randolph, at the end of May 1911. This time, it was Churchill rather than Clementine who took himself off, first to the Oxfordshire Yeomanry's summer camp at Blenheim, then to stay with Sir Abe Bailey and American actress Maxine Elliott.[*] By the time he returned from the prince of Wales's

---

[*] Maxine Elliott (1871–1940), born as Jessie Dermot in Rockland, Maine; took the stage name Maxine Elliott at her début in *The Middleman* in New York 1890; first appeared as a 'star' in her own right in New York 1903; London 1905; opened her own New York theatre 1908.

investiture, Clementine had left London with the children, their nurse and nursery maid and her own personal maid for a respite on the English coast at Seaford. The summer apart continued when the German and French governments' confrontation at Agadir* prevented Churchill from joining her in the Alps.

Churchill consoled himself by buying a new fifteen-horse-power, four-cylinder Napier Landaulette,[25] intended to convey them both to Balmoral to stay with the new king and queen, but a misunderstanding over colours prevented the grand arrival. Churchill had ordered 'the Marlborough hue' without specifying its shade and it took Napier almost a week to find out. They were able to depart in style once Churchill had agreed to pay for a Napier engineer to travel from Euston to Balmoral to act as their chauffeur during a motor tour of Scotland that was designed to take in the Asquiths' home near North Berwick. There the prime minister invited his minister to take over as First Lord of the Admiralty, a post Churchill accepted with alacrity. It brought control of the world's most powerful military force and two coveted privileges: use of the Royal Navy's 4,000-ton yacht HMS *Enchantress* and of the fine eighteenth-century Admiralty House, overlooking Horse Guards Parade in central London. The official purpose of HMS *Enchantress* and her crew of 196 officers and ratings was to facilitate the First Lord's visits to inspect the fleet, but it was understood that he should be allowed to entertain personal guests as long as their out-of-pocket expenses were met: Churchill was to spend eight of the next thirty-three months aboard her, attracting the satirical attentions of *Punch* magazine.[26]

Admiralty House was a different proposition. The rent charged for some of London's finest rooms was only £500 a year, but the First Lord was expected to meet the wages of twelve servants, seven

---

* French troops occupied Fez, the Moroccan capital, to quell a rebellion against the country's sultan. Fearing imminent French annexation of the country, Germany despatched a gunboat to the port of Agadir. There were no hostilities, but the speed at which a serious confrontation developed caused widespread concern in Europe.

more than the Churchills employed at Eccleston Square. Making calculations on Admiralty notepaper, Churchill decided that he could not afford the move: as a married man with two children, his monthly salary was already fully committed before even paying for staples such as wine, cigars and clothes. His judgement remained unmoved by the arrival of another £11,500 from James Caird,[27] this time to encourage the cause of Home Rule for Ireland and Scotland. Caird limited himself to two early donations on this occasion, but it brought the amount that he had entrusted to Churchill's judgement (and bank account) up to £33,500 within two years, a multiple of more than eight times Churchill's own means at the time. For an ambitious young politician who could not match the easy means of many contemporaries, the ability to distribute largesse on this scale was extraordinary.

Churchill set up an extra account at Cox & Co., his 'D' account, to control the flow of Home Rule money, £6,000 of which he gave in two batches to the government's chief whip, the Master of Elibank, who was to emerge as one of the murkier protagonists in the following year's Marconi share scandal.[28] In September 1912, Churchill still had £4,000 of the Home Rule money and £1,500 of the free trade money lodged in his accounts, a situation that Caird happily accepted when Churchill sent him the bank passbooks to inspect.[29] What happened to the £5,500 left of Caird's money thereafter becomes less transparent. During November 1912, the chief whip's office asked for more funds in a letter marked 'Secret', claiming already to have spent over £8,000 (without giving details of how) although Churchill had only provided £6,000.[30]

All Churchill's bank statements for the remainder of 1912 and 1913, a period of great sensitivity over the personal finances of government ministers during the Marconi scandal, are missing from his archive. However, it seems likely that the chief whip did receive his extra £2,000 (or more), because the next report of Churchill's Caird deposits, in June 1915, put them at £3,320, exactly where one would expect if he had acceded to the chief whip's request in 1912 and then sat on the rest of the money during the

Marconi scandal.[31] Between June 1915 and August 1916, the balance fell from £3,320 to just £600;[32] Sir James Caird died in March 1916 and Churchill's finances were under stress at the time because his ministerial salary had been replaced by the pay of an army colonel, but it is impossible to be precise about whether he eventually used the balance of Caird's money because the records of his 'C' and 'D' accounts during 1915 and 1916 are simply missing. What we can say is that the money was never transferred to his or Clementine's main bank account and that he never included it in any forecasts of his own cash flow during the war.

He had also excluded Caird's money in 1912 when trying to work out whether he and his family could afford to move into the First Lord's official quarters at Admiralty House. It took eighteen months, until late in 1913, before a compromise was worked out: the grander rooms were mothballed, while the Churchills moved in to the rest with seven servants, not twelve.

Over that same period, the previously intimate political relationship between Churchill and Lloyd George had begun to change. The First Lord was now a spending minister, trying to extract funds to match an expanding German naval shipbuilding programme from a sceptical chancellor; but tensions were put aside in the summer of 1912 when long-standing Tory complaints at the corruption of Liberal politicians by newly acquired wealth suddenly erupted into the Marconi scandal. The allegations of personal gain from improper dealing in Marconi shares never touched Churchill, but did involve both the chancellor and chief whip.[33] Churchill came to his colleagues' aid by urging Lord Northcliffe* to restrain his newspapers' coverage of the affair and by persuading the two outstanding lawyers of the day, Sir Edward Carson and F. E. Smith (both Tories), to represent his fellow ministers in court.[34] 'I was so encouraged to hear from Winston that you took his view of my little worry,' Lloyd George wrote to Clementine. 'I am almost ill with worry over it.'[35]

---

* Formerly Alfred Harmsworth.

As the scandal subsided, Churchill's mother finally threw out her second husband. Their difficulties had become increasingly public since 1910, when they had rented a house in Cavendish Square while she put the finishing touches to a play that she was writing in a fresh attempt to earn money. Keen to secure the services of a well-known actress as the female lead, she had invited Mrs Patrick Campbell* for daytime visits to Cavendish Square, soon reciprocated by George's nocturnal trysts to her 'charming little house in Kensington Square',[36] a habit that outlasted the short run of *His Borrowed Plumes*'.

Churchill tried but failed to broker a financial settlement 'before any avoidable publicity is given to your rupture' and returned to the fray in 1911, after his mother summoned both brothers to a 'council of war'. Asking her to stay away from her husband, Churchill summoned 'George West' to a business interview, warning him that both he and his wife were treading dangerously: 'Your joint financial position must be considered in regard to the maintenance of credit, the sudden removal of which might be ruinous to both of you.'[37]

His mother waited another five months until September 1911 before she gave up any hope of their living together again: 'I could – but he will always hanker after the things he wants,' she told her son sadly. 'Of what use to chain him to me?. . . Tear this letter up and don't worry about me.'[38] Divorce discussions limped along during 1912, while George fought a demand to pay Jennie £2,000 a year, complaining to Jack of her 'ghastly and persistent extravagances'.[39] Jennie found a fresh solicitor, Wodehouse,** who suggested a scheme to raise funds by reshuffling insurance policies, but Churchill refused to play his part by providing her with a £2,000 guarantee. He told his mother:

---

* Beatrice Tanner (1865–1940), took her stage name from her first husband Patrick Campbell (who died in the Boer War); stage debuts in Liverpool 1888, London 1890, New York 1900; the inspiration for George Bernard Shaw's Eliza Doolittle in *Pygmalion*.
** H. Wodehouse, senior partner of Messrs Wodehouse & Davidson of St James Street, London.

Although there may be advantages in simplifying the control of your insurance policies, the real effect of the transaction is to secure you about £2,500 ready money, at the cost of perma- nently reducing your income by £300 a year. This is certainly not a good or wise arrangement, & only means a brief flutter followed by long deprivations.[40]

His mother's reply at the beginning of December was emotional:

Forgive me if I return to the 'charge' & ask you to reconsider yr. answer in respect to this Insurance Scheme. The risk to you is infinitesimal. . . My position is an untenable one, & apart from anything else I <u>must</u> find a guarantor instead of George. . . I know you would do anything for me and always have. . . I hate having to write all this, as I know how overworked you are, but I can't very well help it. . . Bless you – Mother.[41]

Churchill and his mother spent Christmas and the New Year together at the duke of Westminster's new hunting lodge near Bayonne in France, where Churchill acquiesced. Pre-occupied by cabinet battles with Lloyd George over the £3 million required to build four rather than two battleships, he decided against fighting on a second front with his mother. His change of mind unlocked the divorce negotiations: George was to keep the first £2,000 of his earnings, give her the next £1,000 and then share any more equally until he had paid her £2,000 a year. 'I am returning to you my engagement and wedding rings. I say goodbye – a long goodbye', Lady Randolph wrote as her decree nisi was granted on 16 April 1914.[42] The next day, her former husband married Mrs Patrick Campbell, busy playing Eliza Doolittle in Bernard Shaw's *Pygmalion*.

This episode finally opened the Churchill brothers' eyes to the true size of their mother's income over the last twenty years: she had always claimed it to be barely in four figures, but her solicitor's schedules showed that it had exceeded £5,000 a year. The problem was that two-fifths had disappeared in paying interest on £22,500-worth of 'official' loans, while another fifth had gone to unofficial moneylenders. In addition, Lady Randolph estimated her unpaid bills at £5,000,[43] a sum that her ex-husband claimed at his bankruptcy proceedings she had spent each year on clothes alone.

As her financial reorganization neared completion, what her solicitor called 'a very bad hitch' came to light. An alert lawyer acting for the Legal & General insurance company, which was due to provide her new loan, spotted the clause in Lord Randolph's will that had given its trustees the power to divert half its income to her children if his wife remarried; if this clause was ever to be exercised, the Legal & General would find its security halved. The only way out, her solicitor suggested, was to obtain a judgement from the Chancery Court that, as it stood, the clause was iniquitous and almost certainly not what Lord Randolph had intended. Theodore Lumley broke the news to Churchill as though his firm had made the discovery, glossing over the fact that the brothers could have been receiving a formal allowance for the last fourteen years. Churchill, however, was quick to pick up the point, summoning Lumley to appear at the Admiralty that same evening:

> I and my brother Mr John Churchill should surely have been informed by you at some period during the years which have passed of our rights under the Will. It appears to me extraordinary that we should have been left in ignorance of a matter of such consequence for the last 15 years.[44]

Nor did Jack conceal his shock from their mother:

> We had always thought that Papa was very wrong not making any provision for us during your life. We thought the Will left us in the possible position of being for many years without a penny while you were in receipt of over £5,000 a year. This did in fact happen & you were unable to give us any allowance... Winston and I are now both making our own living and as long as we do

so of course nothing will be claimed, although I believe that at
the present moment we could each demand about £600 a year."*....
We have begged you so often to live within your income – which
is not a very severe demand. Your income is larger than mine in
most years and you have nothing whatever to keep up. Unless
you are able to do so and if you start running up bills again –
there is nothing that can save you from a crash and bankruptcy.[45]

Agreeing to sell her home and buy a 'doll's house' as replacement,
Lady Randolph paid brief obeisance to her younger son's home
truths, while he juggled her increasingly litigious creditors. Her
elder son needed money almost as badly, having finished 1913 with
loans of £3,000, an overdraft of £2,740 and unpaid bills of at least
£2,000. He recognized that his mother's scheme, which still needed
his approval, might provide a bargaining chip: if the disputed
clause's exact meaning could be established, it might help him to
borrow more money to pay bills. 'Strictly confidentially', he asked
Lumley in mid-February to look into the prospects of borrowing
an extra £5,000 if the verdict went the right way.

The problem had become more urgent by April 1914: 'Our
finances are in a condition wh[ich] requires serious & prompt attention,' he confessed to Clementine, promising to divert himself from
ministerial duties for however long was required: 'The expense of
the 1st quarter of 1914 with our holiday trip is astonishing. Money
seems to flow away.'[46] Discreetly, he arranged an interview with the
chairman of his bank, Reginald Cox.** It was a long one, he told
Clementine afterwards, as a result of which he was to prepare a
'scheme' to pay off their debts: 'We shall have to pull in our horns.
The money simply drains away.'[47]

'Scheme' turned out to be rather a grand term for what Churchill

---

* Jack's calculation suggests the trust's income was £2,400 a year; using
the then customary assumption of an income of 5 per cent from trust
investments, this implies that the trust's capital value stood at c. £50,000.
** Reginald Cox (1865–1922), senior partner, Cox & Co.; agent to the British
army; baronet 1922.

had in mind: he asked to borrow an extra £4,000 to make a clean sweep of all his old, unpaid bills. He would provide security in the form of a charge over all his own and his wife's future inheritances under the various family settlements, once he had established legal certainty to his entitlement. Cox declared himself 'favourably inclined to entertain the matter'[48] but the bank's solicitors Fladgate & Co. wanted expensive extra security in the shape of life insurance: 'My business proposals do not go smoothly, for the reason that the insurance companies try to charge excessive premiums on my life – political strain, short-lived parentage & of course flying,' he told Clementine in June.[49]

Both Jennie and her sons now had an incentive to establish the precise meaning of Lord Randolph's will. Churchill preferred the privacy of an arbitration, but accepted that a formal trial was inevitable because the decision of an arbitrator would not be binding on his children (who had an interest as the ultimate beneficiaries of Lord Randolph's will trust). Wodehouse lodged papers in the case of *Churchill v. Churchill* which was heard behind the closed doors of the Chancery Division of the High Court on 18 June 1914. Helpfully for the brothers, the judge ruled that the trustees could make a lawful advance to them or their children without Lady Randolph's consent, because she was adequately safeguarded by her position as one of the trustees.[50] Churchill completed the paperwork for his new £4,000 loan the next day.

Cox & Co. lodged the money in his account ten days after Archduke Ferdinand's assassination in Sarajevo.[51] By the end of July, he had paid fifty tradesmen in full or in part, and only £200 remained in the account. His wine merchant was one beneficiary, but the flow of Churchill's orders continued unabated as Randolph Payne delivered twelve consignments of the familiar mix of Perrier-Jouët champagne, brandy and vermouth to his households at Admiralty House and their rented Norfolk holiday house in the five weeks that passed between the assassination and the outbreak of war.[52]

8

'The clouds are blacker and blacker'

The Legacy of War, 1914–18

Exchange rate $5 = £1
Inflation multiples: 1914 US x 25; UK x 90
1918 US x 15; UK x 45

EW IN BRITAIN even noticed Archduke Ferdinand's assassination on 28 June 1914. The Irish Question had dominated politics in Britain for most of 1914. Writing to his Paris partners soon after the Archduke's death, Lord Rothschild was more worried about the chancellor of the exchequer Lloyd George's demagoguery. Markets, he reported, were better than they had been all year, and 'all the new issues which were at a discount are now at a premium'.[1]

The mood among politicians and financiers began to darken in mid-July, however. European stock exchanges fell on Monday 20 July, and London reacted badly to news of Austria's ultimatum to Serbia on the following Friday. The next morning the London Stock Exchange experienced its worst fall since 1870. When Serbia rejected the ultimatum, commentators described the markets as chaotic: 'A DAY OF FORCED SALES' ran the headline in the *Financial Times*.

After spending a few days with his family on the coast of Norfolk, Churchill returned to London in time to approve the First Sea Lord Prince Louis of Battenburg's recommendation to delay the dispersal of Britain's fleet to its home ports following its gathering at Spithead for a review by the king. It passed without lights through the Dover

Strait to take up battle stations in the North Sea on the night of Wednesday 29 July; the very day when Austria-Hungary declared war on Serbia, prompting a steep drop in government bond prices across Europe.* The Bank of England raised the bank rate to 4 per cent on Thursday 30 July, doubled it to 8 per cent on Friday and raised it again to 10 per cent on Saturday 1 August, when the London Stock Exchange closed 'until further notice'.

Paying one of his last bills – for personal use of HMS *Enchantress* – Churchill described the scene in the capital to Clementine, who remained in Norfolk: 'The city has simply broken into chaos. The world's credit system is virtually suspended. You cannot sell stocks and shares. You cannot borrow. Quite soon it will not perhaps be possible to cash a cheque.'[2] Three days later, with the agreement of Prime Minister Asquith, he ordered the full mobilization of the British fleet; on the following day, Britain's ultimatum to Germany expired. Shortly before midnight Churchill authorized a signal to all ships: 'Commence hostilities at once with Germany.'[3]

Financiers and politicians alike were taken by surprise: Cassel was still on holiday in Switzerland; Paul Nelke, the senior partner of Jack's stockbroking firm, spoke for many when he told a stock exchange committee that 'he was a rich man on 1st July but what he was now he could not say'.[4] A complete financial collapse was prevented only by a government moratorium on all debts and emergency funding from the Bank of England.

Churchill warned Clementine that they would have to take 'rigorous measures' to reduce spending. However, his immediate difficulty sprang from his new life insurance policy's restrictions against using submarines or aeroplanes: he was forced to pay an extra £39 to cover 'aviation (including sea-planing)' for six months, while his insurers wanted £146 if he stepped on to a warship.[5]

---

* British Consols fell from 74 to 69.5 between 18 July and 1 August, before trading was suspended in most capitals; Russian government bond prices fell by 8.7 per cent; French bonds by 7.8 per cent; German bonds by 4 per cent. See Niall Ferguson, *The Rothschilds*, p. 963.

While Britain and Germany's navies began a game of cat-and-mouse at sea, the start of hostilities made little early impact in London itself. Churchill marked the birth of his third child Sarah, at Admiralty House on 7 October, with an order of a large number of fresh cigars and of wine which took the balance of his account at Randolph Payne back above £500.[6]

Only his earnings as an author slowed: Thomas Nelson & Sons offered £70 for the right to issue a new, cheap edition of *The Malakand Field Force*, but otherwise the literary field lay quiet.[7] Instead Churchill turned his mind to a means of breaking the dead-lock on the Western Front, backing a plan to use a combined army and navy assault to force a way through the Dardanelles straits to Constantinople. A successful thrust might not only remove the Ottoman Empire as an ally of Germany but encourage Bulgaria and Roumania to enter the war on the side of the Allies.

Churchill did not initiate the Dardanelles Campaign, but he was its most consistent and vigorous advocate. It started badly during the spring of 1915: the army reduced the number of troops it was prepared to commit and Turkish resistance proved stouter (and the British naval detachment's leadership poorer) than expected. This failure provoked a political crisis at home, sparked by the sudden resignation as First Sea Lord of the eccentric Admiral Fisher, whom Churchill had controversially recalled to duty in October 1914 in order to resume the vigorous leadership of the British fleet which he had previously demonstrated in the post (1903–10).

Once linked in the public mind to evident disarray at the top of the Admiralty, the poor start to the Dardanelles Campaign led to calls for a national wartime government that Prime Minister Asquith and his senior Liberal colleagues were unable to resist. As their price for joining, Tory elders demanded the head of Churchill as the First Lord of the Admiralty: they had not forgiven him for defecting to the Liberal Party a decade before or for supporting what they perceived as its assault on the landowning class to which he belonged.

Churchill was demoted from First Lord of the Admiralty to Chancellor of the Duchy of Lancaster, although he remained a member of the War Committee, now called the Dardanelles Committee. The duties of Chancellor of the Duchy of Lancaster proved little more arduous than the appointment of county magistrates. It normally paid a salary of only £2,000, but Churchill continued to earn £4,360 because the cabinet had decided to pool its pay and divide it equally for the duration of the war. It was the exclusion from the centre of power which hurt him: 'The hour is bitter: and idleness – torture,' he told his friend Archibald Sinclair,* already serving at the Front. 'Here I am in a fat sinecure v[er]y well received & treated by the new Cabinet. . . I cannot endure sitting here waiting for a turn of the political wind.'[8]

Conscious that his government salary might not last for long, Churchill reappraised his finances in the middle of June 1915. His overdraft stood at a relatively modest £444; his various investments added up to a net £2,500, and there was still £3,300 of James Caird's money in his deposit accounts.[9] He noted some small economies that he could make: resigning from four of his clubs would save £41 a year; and he asked Clementine to give up the Ladies' Athenaeum and Walton Heath Golf Club. Eccleston Square was still being rented to Sir Edward Grey, so he moved the family into the large house at 41 Cromwell Road that Jack had just bought with help from his father's will trust. The brothers had also jointly leased a fifteenth-century farmhouse near Godalming in Surrey for the summer of 1915, before it became clear that the war was going to last.

Hoe Farm provided a welcome respite from Churchill's political misery: 'It really is a delightful valley and the garden gleams with summer jewellery,' he told Jack, who had already left on army service. 'We live v[er]y simply – but with all the essentials of life

---

* Sir Archibald Sinclair, Bt. (1890–1970), son of an American mother and a Scottish landowner; first met Churchill at the home of actress Maxine Elliott; joined Life Guards 1910; personal military secretary to secretary of state for war (Churchill) 1919–21; private secretary to secretary of state for colonies (Churchill) 1921–2; MP 1922–45; secretary of state for Scotland 1931–2; Liberal Party leader 1935–45; secretary of state for air 1940–45; baronet 1912, Viscount Thurso 1952.

well understood and well provided for – hot baths, cold champagne, new peas, & old brandy'.[10] It was in the garden of Hoe Farm that Churchill first observed Jack's wife Goonie painting. When he tried it and found himself absorbed, Clementine rushed into the nearby town to buy artists' materials, relieved that her husband had found a distraction from his gloom. Once back in London, according to his secretary Eddie Marsh, Churchill 'bought up the entire contents of Robertson's colour-shop in Piccadilly – easels, palettes, brushes, tubes and canvasses'.[11]

A measure of political redemption beckoned during the summer of 1915 when Prime Minister Asquith asked Churchill to visit the Dardanelles task force and to report back to the cabinet. Churchill asked Cox & Co's chairman to arrange insurance cover under an oath of secrecy,[12] before preparing a letter summarizing his finances. It was marked 'To be sent to Mrs Churchill in the event of my death':

> Cox holds about £1,000 worth of securities of mine (chiefly Witbank Colliery). Jack has in his name about £1,000 worth of Pretoria Cement shares; & Cassel has American stocks of mine wh shd exceed in value my loans from him by about £1,000. I believe this will be found sufficient to pay my debts & overdraft... The insurance policies are all kept up and every contingency is covered. You will receive £10,000 and £300 a year in addition until you succeed my Mother.

He asked her to secure all his Admiralty papers:

> Masterton Smith* will help you secure all that is necessary for a complete record. There is no hurry: but some day I should like the truth to be known. Randolph will carry on the lamp.[13]

---

* James Masterton-Smith (1878–1938), joined the Admiralty 1901. Private secretary to the Second Sea Lord 1904–8, to the permanent secretary 1908–10 and to successive First Lords of the Admiralty 1910–17; he served Churchill again as permanent under-secretary of state for the colonies 1921–4.

A day before he was due to leave, however, senior Tories heard of Churchill's visit to the Dardanelles task force and vetoed it. It was a fresh humiliation. 'Mr Churchill asks me to say that he now finds he cannot go on the journey wh[ich] he discussed with you, & is staying in London,' Marsh had to inform Cox. 'In these circumstances, he hopes that if the insured premium has not been paid, it need not be; and that if it has, it can be recovered.'[14]

Despite this setback, Churchill did not resign. 'Naturally I have been thinking constantly of the possibility of escaping to simpler and more congenial tasks,' he told his friend Archibald Sinclair. 'But since we parted political events have laid hold of me, & I must abide their issue.'[15] Though he could not initiate policy, Churchill still sat on the Dardanelles Committee, where he and others openly questioned General Kitchener's competence at the head of the War Office. Churchill continued to nurse hopes of a return to the centre of the government's decision-making in any reorganization that followed the general's removal, although he forfeited the support of Asquith and Lloyd George by persistently advocating the reinforcement of the Allies' failing forces in the Dardanelles.

Asquith refused to dismiss the general and instead replaced the Dardanelles Committee with a five-man war cabinet at which there was no seat for Churchill. Churchill waited a week to see whether he would be offered another post, but resigned on 30 October when nothing came. Asquith asked him to stay his hand for a few days, during which time Churchill suggested he might take over as governor and commander-in-chief of British East Africa. Asquith declined to appoint him, so Churchill resigned for a second time on 11 November to join his regiment, the Queen's Own Oxfordshire Hussars on the Western Front.

Departure preparations were swift: within a week Churchill had arranged full war-risk insurance cover through Phoenix Assurance (at a cost of £472) and raised his second loan of £1,000 within five weeks from Cox & Co., both made possible only with the help of a guarantee from his cousin Captain Freddie Guest.[16] Churchill's loans from the bank had now reached £9,000: their annual interest would absorb all his new pay of £420 a year as an army major, leaving only his salary as an MP (of £400 a year)* to look after the family. They would clearly need more, so before leaving for St Omer on 18 November Churchill paid a last-minute visit to Sir Ernest Cassel who was still managing Churchill's remaining investments although he had all but retired five years earlier. Sir Ernest set Churchill's mind at rest by promising him an immediate advance of £1,000 and 'unlimited credit' thereafter, even if the balance on his account had been exhausted.[17]

Churchill's parting instructions certainly did not encourage thrift in the Cromwell Road household, which now consisted of two mothers, five young children, nine servants and his mother Jennie, who contributed £40 a month to the household's expenses.

> I really don't think you or Goonie should deny yourself any
> reasonable comfort or convenience. Keep a good table: keep suf
> ficient servants & yr maid: entertain with discrimination, have
> a little amusement from time to time. I don't see any reason for
> undue skimping. With about £140 a month there shd be suffi
> cient. Extra bills you must write to me about.[18]

As usual, Churchill's calculations turned out to be optimistic. Household expenses had been averaging £220 a month since the start of 1915, and while he was away he would end up transferring to Clementine twice his original monthly estimate. It didn't help that he sent regular orders from the front for extra food, drink and clothes. The day after arriving, Churchill asked for new riding trousers, a warm brown leather waistcoat ('with the utmost speed'), a pair of trench wading boots, a periscope and a sheepskin sleeping bag; three days later he requested a weekly 'small box of food to supplement the rations', containing 'sardines, chocolate, potted meats, and other things wh[ich] may strike your fancy'.[19]

---

* Payment of MPs was introduced in 1911.

So that Churchill could learn his military craft, his com-mander-in-chief Sir John French (an old friend) posted him to the Grenadier Guards, where, after a difficult start, he won over both officers and men. Sir John planned to give Churchill command of a brigade in the rank of major general.* Asquith, however, squashed the plan as soon as he heard of it. Clementine had to cancel the general's tunic that she had ordered, while her husband awaited new orders in a house full of Canadians, where he befriended Max Aitken.**

Sir John French was soon replaced by Sir Douglas Haig, who gave Churchill command of a badly depleted battalion of Royal Scots Fusiliers early in 1916. A young officer described Churchill's arrival: their new commanding officer was seated on a black charger and accompanied by Archie Sinclair as his second-in-command, plus two equally well-mounted grooms and a pile of luggage well above regulation weight, including 'a long bath and a boiler for heating the water'.[20] Churchill soon restored morale among the Scots Fusiliers, which held a thousand yards of front line near the village of Ploegsteert ('Plug Street', as it became known by British soldiers).

Clementine relayed to him the latest political gossip while Churchill waited for a suitable moment to return to Westminster life. His wife urged caution, but after a short spell of leave in January 1916, Churchill returned for a second visit in March, at the end of which he spoke in a House of Commons debate, attracting ridicule in the final moments of his speech by calling for Admiral Fisher's reinstatement at the head of the navy. *The Spectator* magazine mocked Churchill's 'restlessness of mind and instability of purpose, joined with the restless egotism of the political gambler, which would make him a most dangerous element'.[21] Chastened, Churchill

---

* A major general earned £1,000 a year; a colonel £500, a major £420.
** Max Aitken (1879–1964), born in Canada; MP 1910–16; minister of information and Chancellor of the Duchy of Lancaster 1918; acquired control of *Daily Express* 1916, later the *Sunday Express* and *Evening Standard*; minister for aircraft production 1940–41, supply 1941–2, war production 1942, Lord Privy Seal 1943–5; knighted 1911, Lord Beaverbrook 1917.

spent another two months at the Front before he stepped down from his command in May 1916 when his regiment was conveniently amalgamated with another whose commanding officer was more senior in rank.

There was to be no swift return for Churchill to front-line politics. From a financial point of view, this was fortunate. With only £123 left in his current account[22] and his MP's salary wholly devoured by interest payments, Churchill needed the time to resume his role as a journalist in order to support his growing family. In June he made use of his connection with the newspaper owner Lord Northcliffe (formerly Sir Alfred Harmsworth) to win four articles (at a fee of £250 each) for the family's new *Sunday Pictorial*.* In July came a commission from *The Strand Magazine* for six articles (also £250 each) to be published in 1916;[23] Lord Northcliffe's *The London Magazine* paid double the price (£500 each) for a series of six articles in August. By the time the *Sunday Pictorial* returned in November for a second series, Churchill had earned more in six months from journalism than he would have done in a year as a cabinet minister.

Literary success brought with it a new financial confidence. The *Sunday Pictorial* payments bolstered his threadbare bank account, but Churchill forwarded *The London Magazine*'s cheque to Abe Bailey for him to invest in South African mining shares. 'Money worries need not weigh with you,' he told his brother Jack, who was still based with the army in the eastern Mediterranean. 'I find myself able quite easily to earn ten or twelve thousand pounds in the next six months. So that Cromwell [Road] and all in it will be well supplied. Mind you let me know of anything that wants paying. I get 4 or 5 shillings a word for everything I write: and apparently even at this price the newspaper is the gainer.'[24]

---

* Founded in March 1915; Sunday newspapers started during the Boer War (1899–1900) as a response to the thirst for news of the war. The *Sunday Pictorial*'s circulation rose by 400,000 to 2,500,000 copies during Churchill's series.

By the autumn Churchill felt confident enough to start looking for the 'country seat' that he and Clementine coveted: she was after 'a little country basket';[25] he 'a place to end my days amid trees & upon grass of my own!' he told Archie Sinclair, who was the owner of more than 100,000 acres in Scotland. 'Freed from the penury of office these consolations become possible.'[26]

Estate agents suggested Lullenden Manor, near Lingfield. The half-timbered Elizabethan house, built of grey stone and surrounded by sixty-seven acres, lay at the end of a long lane, in a hollow among hills where the counties of Sussex, Surrey and Kent meet. Churchill fell for the far-flung views from the back of the house, closing his mind to the property's poor condition. Early in 1917 he followed Jack's example by funding the £5,500 cost of the main house through a loan from his father's will trust (which leased it back to Clementine at an annual rent equivalent to 5 per cent of its cost). He then emptied his own bank account to share with the trust the separate £1,750 cost of Lullenden's lodge.[27]

The British government's Commission of Inquiry into the Dardanelles began work in August 1916, but it would clearly need several months of work before it could report its findings. Churchill's political reputation therefore remained under its cloud when the failure of the Allies' offensive at the battle of the Somme brought long-simmering dissatisfaction over Britain's conduct of the war to a head in November. Conservatives in the House of Commons insisted on turning a vote on an obscure issue (the sale of enemy property in Nigeria) into a vote of confidence which the government only narrowly survived. Asquith's Liberal rival Lloyd George and the Conservative leader Bonar Law then plotted to restructure the Coalition. Asquith was forced out of office and Lloyd George became prime minister. Although Liberal members of the outgoing cabinet refused to serve under Lloyd George, Britain's new prime minister was able to form an administration by including the Labour Party and the previous coalition's Conservative members. Part of their price was that Churchill should be left out in the cold.

Churchill was bitterly disappointed, but it allowed him to continue his journalism. He might have used his earnings from another six articles for the *Sunday Pictorial* to reduce his debts or to establish a reserve to pay future tax (the Inland Revenue allowed writers and journalists to spread payments over three years).[28] Instead he used them to build up his shareholdings, which were worth £8,500 by the middle of 1917; he also asked his bank to make an extra loan to him of £2,000, so that he could invest in the new technology of smokeless coal. Cox & Co. refused to lend the full amount, but Churchill's loans reached a record level of £10,690.[29]

Churchill's only hope of servicing this debt lay in keeping up his earnings from journalism. However, in March 1917 the Dardanelles Commission's first report cleared Churchill of acting impetuously on his own, the most damaging of the charges levelled against him. Three months later Lloyd George offered him a chance to return to government as Chancellor of the Duchy of Lancaster, a post which Churchill declined. In July Lloyd George suggested the new post of minister of munitions while he and Churchill travelled together by train to Dundee. Churchill immediately accepted.

Churchill was in his element back at the centre of British politics, but his finances soon suffered. A ministerial salary of £4,000 failed to compensate for the loss of earnings as a journalist, just as his tax bill for the previous year became due.[30] He decided that Eccleston Square had to be sold if he was to hold on to Lullenden. As a result, on weekday nights Churchill stayed at his ministry's offices, the commandeered Hotel Metropole near Trafalgar Square, or 'perched' at the London homes of friends or family; the rest of the Churchill family stayed in the country.

Cox & Co. offered Churchill a breathing space by extending his four wartime loans until April 1919, but once again Churchill chose to act on a strong tip from Sir Abe Bailey that he should buy

1. Frances Vane, marchioness of Londonderry and Churchill's paternal great-grandmother, whose Garron Tower estate in Ireland he unexpectedly inherited in January 1921, almost sixty years after her death.

2. The 'fabulous' Leonard Jerome, Churchill's maternal grandfather and an early Wall Street adventurer, late in his life, circa 1880.

3. The Jerome family mansion on the corner of Madison Avenue and 26th Street, New York. It provided the security for Leonard Jerome's contribution to the marriage settlement of Churchill's parents.

4. Lord Randolph Churchill and Jennie Jerome, Churchill's parents, shortly before or after their wedding, 1874.

5. Winston (left, aged fifteen) and Jack Churchill (right, aged twelve) at Canford House, the home of their generous aunt Cornelia Spencer Churchill, Lady Wimborne, 1892.

6. Churchill outside *The Morning Post*'s tent, reporting for the newspaper on the Boer War while 'embedded' with the South African Light Horse, 1900.

7. Sir Ernest Cassel in 1906. An immigrant from Germany, next-door neighbour of the Churchills and leading City of London banker, Cassel acted as a financial adviser (and benefactor) to Edward VII and Churchill.

8. Edward Marsh, Churchill's long-serving private secretary, occasional literary ghost and frequent copy-editor. In his own right Marsh was a patron of artists and published anthologies of the 'Georgian poets'.

10. Churchill and his fiancée, Clementine Hozier, shortly before their wedding, September 1908.

9. Churchill, home secretary, riding to George V's coronation with his mother, Jennie, June 1911. Clementine was spared the coach journey because she had given birth to Randolph a month earlier.

11. Churchill, president of the board of trade, with David Lloyd George, chancellor of the exchequer, at the height of their political intimacy, circa 1910.

12. Churchill, First Lord of the Admiralty, inspecting bare-footed trainee sailors, 1912.

shares in Government Gold Mining Areas (Modderfontein) Consolidated. He hoped that his father's will trust would do the buying, but when Norwich Union objected that the shares were too risky Churchill arranged another personal bank loan for £2,000.[31]

The decision to buy more shares came at the expense of Lullenden, which needed serious money spent on it. Churchill had paid £400 to connect the house to the public water supply. He also commissioned a plan to develop the gardens and tennis court, but there is no evidence of any further spending once he resumed political office. Armed with wartime powers of inspection to enforce efficient food production, the local Godstone District War Agricultural Committee objected to what it saw as Churchill's neglect of Lullenden's farming potential: 'We found the property in a very poor and derelict state,' they reported after an inspection. 'We are informed that this neglect is due to lack of labour, but we should have thought that Mr Churchill would have been in a position to obtain all the labour required in the way of German prisoners.'[32]

Stung by the committee's criticism, Churchill claimed by the end of 1918 to have invested more than £1,000 by building a cowshed, a haystack, three pig sties and a manure heap; by enlarging the vegetable garden and sowing an acre of potatoes; and by buying a horse, a cart, two cows and seventeen bullocks. Six little pigs had even been sold at market for £12: 'See how scrupulous & God-fearing I am!' Clementine told Eddie Marsh. 'Instead of spending these cheques on paying household bills I send them to you for W's Cox account.'[33] Churchill was so happy at Lullenden, she told the visiting Wilfrid Blunt, that he planned to stay there for the rest of his life.

But the cost of renting Lullenden from his father's trust and the drop in his income were gradually squeezing Churchill's finances: including the Lullenden loan from his father's trust, he was paying almost £1,000 in interest each year. Within three months of asking for his last loan, Churchill returned to his new bank manager

William Bernau[*] for yet another £2,000 to pay urgent bills. This took his bank loans up to £14,690.[34] When Bernau politely asked for the transfer to the bank of £3,000-worth of 'South African' investments that Churchill mentioned during their meeting, it was left to Eddie Marsh to break the news to Bernau that they were actually worth only £2,000.[35]

Something had to give and Lullenden was the obvious candidate. Churchill covered three sheets of paper trying to work out whether he could buy the property from his trustees by selling £5,500 worth of investments and finding another £1,300 from the bank, but his arithmetic was flawed: he recorded his bank loans at £12,500 rather than £14,690, and even then he came up £3,000 short.[36]

Desperate to hold on to Lullenden if possible, he asked Nicholl, Manisty & Co. whether he could use his marriage settlement's life policy as additional security for a loan, but their reply was no. He asked Bernau whether the bank could lend against the security of Lullenden itself, but was told that the bank did not lend on mortgages. Time was running out. Soon he was due to make expensive life insurance payments underpinning £4,000 of wartime loans guaranteed by Freddie Guest. Churchill finally came up with the idea of reducing his loans by selling shares, but Bernau told him dustily that he had already pledged the proceeds from his shares to reducing his separate overdraft, which now stood at £2,276.[37]

Late in August 1918 another nasty shock came: Churchill was faced with a tax payment of £476 against his earnings from journalism in 1916 and 1917. He questioned the figure, only to be told that the amount was not only correct but already overdue. He had to ask Bernau to delay paying the insurance renewals until the insurers' thirty days' grace period had expired, a request that rang alarm bells at the bank. Bernau sent a summary of Churchill's £16,000 debts to his senior partner Reginald Cox and asked whether the facilities should be renewed. Cox knew that rumours

---

[*] William Bernau (1870–1937), banker; Churchill's manager at Cox & Co., then Lloyds Bank 1919–33.

about his bank's health were already circulating in government quarters, so he decided not to risk a battle: the bank would renew for twelve more months, provided Captain Guest would reconfirm his guarantee.[38] Three days later Eddie Marsh assured Sir Reginald that Churchill 'has seen Capt. Guest who is willing to undertake the responsibility which he discussed with you'.[39] It had been a close shave and the fate of Lullenden was still undecided as six weeks later the couple's fourth child Marigold was born.

When the war drew to a close in November 1918 Churchill was not alone in surveying the damage to his finances. The wartime suspension of the gold standard, which had fixed the value of sterling against gold since 1819, and the debts taken on to fund five years of fighting, had sapped Britain's pre-eminent position in the world's financial order. Jack had lost his job: his stockbroking firm had collapsed. Even the duke of Westminster looked at the grand houses on his Mayfair estate and wondered aloud whether the wealthy would ever again be able to afford them.

9

'It is like floating in a bath of cream'
A Timely Train Crash, 1918–21

Exchange rate $5 = £1
Inflation multiples: US x 13; UK x 40

THE AFTERMATH OF the Great War proved disorientating for many members of the Edwardian élite. 'Ladies who came to lunch with my mother deplored Modern Times,' Loelia, duchess of Westminster remembered. 'They said how crippling the taxes were, how dreadful the housing shortage, how expensive the shops, how high the wages, how spoilt the children.' Above all, they complained about the cost of servants: 'Cooks were offered £35 to £65 a year; Nannies round about £50. Actually we all continued to live with what now seems a vast quantity of servants. If one had a servant at all one did not even pull a curtain or open the front door when the bell rang.'[1]

Taxes had risen, but the Government had financed three-quarters of the cost of the war by borrowing.* The City lobbied for government spending cuts to balance the books and to allow for a return to the pre-war fixed parity between sterling and gold. However, politicians, including Churchill, worried more about deflation and its social consequences, ever conscious of the spread of Bolshevism to Britain's workers. Commitments to social welfare

---

* Britain's debt stood at 130 per cent of its pre-war gross national product, below its level at the end of the Napoleonic Wars, but far above the level in the United States (30 per cent), which took over Britain's mantle as the world's leading financial power.

spending could not easily be cut; meanwhile several million servicemen had to be fed and paid until they were demobilized, and a
million had been kept under arms to occupy the parts of Europe,
the Middle East and Africa that Britain had agreed to police in the
aftermath of war.

Demobilizing the army became Churchill's primary challenge when
in January 1919 he was appointed to the combined posts of secretary of state for war and air – 'of course there will be but one salary!'
Lloyd George had enjoyed adding to his letter when he made the
appointment.[2] Neither post carried a London residence, so Churchill
sold £400-worth of shares to furnish a house which he leased close
to the Houses of Parliament in Dean Trench Street. Despite the
burden of more than £20,000 borrowed from family trusts and the
bank, he resisted selling any more of his remaining £10,000-worth
of shares while the stock markets enjoyed a post-war boom.[3]

Although restored to its pre-war level of £5,000, Churchill's
ministerial salary still fell at least £300 short of his spending each
month.[4] As a result he found himself in breach of his £3,000 bank
overdraft limit by March 1919. He had to argue for an increase on
the strength of higher share prices. 'He is about to sell his Cassels
shares* to reduce overdraft but will wait for them to rise further,' his
bank manager William Bernau noted. 'Mr A. C. C[ox] agrees and
has marked yellow strip for £500.'[5]

Lullenden remained at the heart of Churchill's difficulties, as he
confessed to weekend visitors to the house, his old army friend
General Sir Ian Hamilton and his independently wealthy wife Jean. At
the time the Hamiltons were frustrated in their own search for a
country seat; a few days after their visit Sir Ian wrote to suggest that
they could rent the main house of Lullenden from Churchill for a
year, leaving the lodge and farm to the current owners. Churchill suggested a rent of £500 a year for three years, adding that he would

---

* These were 500 Cassel Coal Collieries shares worth £872 at the end of
February 1919.

complete the En-Tout-Cas tennis court (at a cost of £200) provided the Hamiltons rented the court for an additional £10 a year.[6] 'I love it and want it for my own, and would like to plunge in and buy it,' Lady Jean Hamilton recorded in her diary during April. 'It's the sort of romantic place I long to have – it's a snuggy place with rocks, pools, trees and streams such as my childish soul loved and still loves.'[7]

Churchill was busy at the time trying to persuade his cabinet colleagues to recognize the White Russian movement of General Kolchak,* but he realized that the scheme to split up the house from the lodge and the farm in this way was too complicated. Reluctantly, he decided that he would have to sell Lullenden in its entirety. The Hamiltons eased the pain of the decision by allowing the Churchills and their young family to enjoy one final summer at the property.

'The great pleasure Jean and I do feel at the idea of possessing Lullenden is very much tempered by our regret that you should have to leave it,' Sir Ian wrote. 'I simply hate the idea that you should loose [sic] this pleasure and Diana and Randolph, I am afraid, will never forgive us.'[8]

Churchill was lucky. Sir Ian left his wife to settle on a price for Lullenden and he was astonished to discover that she paid £10,000, adding a further £1,885 for what Churchill called 'commodities'.[9] 'The purchase of Lullenden by my wife from Mr Winston Churchill was entirely unbusinesslike and had no relation to any real value,' he wrote four years later. 'Had Lullenden belonged to anyone else but Mr Churchill or some of the two or three equally great friends I have, I would have waited for the auction and bought it, very likely, for £3,000.'[10]

Nicholl, Manisty & Co. relieved the pressure on Churchill's finances further by ruling that Lord Randolph's trust's £3,000 profit on the Lullenden sale could go to him, as he had carried out many of the

---

* Alexander Kolchak (1874–1920), Russian naval commander, Black Sea fleet 1916; ordered to leave Russia following 1917 Revolution; returned to establish Siberian Regional Government 1918; after initial success in 1919, captured and shot February 1920.

improvements.[11] They also agreed that the Churchills could look for a new London home using the £7,000 returned to the trust, while they 'perched' for the time being in another Guest family property near Richmond Park.

A London architect and developer, Frederick Foster, showed Churchill a four-storey house at Hyde Park Gate leased by the duke of Wellington's younger son Lord Gerald Wellesley. The lease was on offer for £2,300, a low price that might have given a more cautious buyer pause for thought. Churchill agreed to buy it on the spot, without asking for a survey or mentioning that his father's trust would be the buyer rather than himself. When the trust's lawyers insisted on a survey it revealed that expensive repairs were needed. Churchill immediately withdrew his bid, offering to reimburse any costs incurred by Lord Wellesley.

Lord Wellesley's lawyers wrote to Churchill to say that his lordship had been 'taken by surprise when he heard that Mr Winston Churchill was inclined to repudiate arrangements made by the correspondence which we are advised contains all the essential terms of an enforceable Contract'.[12] Churchill commissioned an expensive legal opinion as to whether the contract was binding, but it was not clear-cut in his favour. When Lord Wellesley signalled that he intended to press his point by switching to expensive London lawyers, Churchill made as graceful a retreat as possible to protect his reputation: he altered the draft of his lawyers' letter to remove a reference to 'financial reasons' as the motive for his original withdrawal.[13]

Lord Wellesley raised no objection to Churchill re-advertising the property before his purchase was due to complete at Christmas. Meanwhile, he still needed a suitable home. Foster suggested another tall house overlooking Hyde Park, this time on the less expensive north side. The architect had already bought 2 Sussex Square for development, but offered to sell it on to the Churchill trust for £4,750 on condition that his business carried out the modernization. Nicholl, Manisty also agreed that the trust could fund the renovation up to a limit of £2,250.[14]

*

By early October, post-war inflation had helped to increase the value of Churchill's South African shares by £4,500.[15] However, his overdraft had risen to £5,500, taking the total he owed his bank to more than £22,000. Anxious, nevertheless, not to miss out on the boom, Churchill asked Cox & Co. for another £2,000 to buy more shares. Bernau relayed three conditions from the bank: (1) that Churchill transfer all his share certificates to Cox & Co., (2) that he use the Lullenden money to reduce his overdraft, and (3) that he renew his promise to reduce his loan balance by the end of the year.[16] Churchill agreed, but two weeks later[17] when he produced the Lullenden money he diverted it to invest in more shares recommended by Sir Abe Bailey and his brother's new firm of London stockbrokers, Vickers da Costa.[18]

Halfway through December Churchill's solicitors suddenly reminded him that he had to pay Lord Gerald Wellesley £2,300 on Christmas Eve, because no replacement buyer for his house had come forward.[19] Churchill could not approach either his bank or his father's trust, having exhausted his credit with both of them. Still anxious not to sell any investments while the market was booming, he visited Sir Ernest Cassel at his Park Lane home. The ailing financier produced a cheque made out to Churchill, accompanied by a carefully worded note: 'My dear Winston: I enclose my cheque for £2,300 in payment for the lease of 2, Hyde Park Street, secured by you on my behalf.' Churchill was equally precise when he sent the cheque to his bank manager: 'Sir Ernest Cassel has now paid me the £2,300 I disbursed on his account for 2 Hyde Park Street.'[20]

The prime minister Lloyd George summoned Churchill and other British ministers in January 1920 to Versailles, where he was taking part in negotiations to establish a peace treaty between the Allied powers and Germany. As Lloyd George convened a series of emergency cabinet meetings to discuss a response to the military reverses suffered by White Russian forces at the hands of the Bolshevik army, share prices began to fall. Early in February Churchill worked out that his own port-folio of some £20,000[21] had dropped in value by 5 per cent, but he was too caught up in the Russian crisis to heed Bernau's warning about the dangers of remaining so fully invested on borrowed money.

Churchill remained pre-occupied for most of the summer with cabinet battles over policy towards Russia, Poland, Egypt and Ulster. He did get away for three weeks' holiday at the duke of Westminster's hunting lodge in France, but on his return to London in September he found a summons from Bernau. Further falls in share prices had left the bank distinctly unhappy with its security on his loans of £22,000.[22]

Churchill had to meet his bank manager twice on consecutive days. He had no more shares that he could offer to transfer into the bank's name, so Bernau asked him to take out additional life insur-ance. 'WSC seen 20/9/20 & 21/9/20. . . No more securities to come at present,' Bernau noted. He also recorded Churchill's insistence that more money was about to arrive in his account: '£1500 expected from trustees for Current a/c but £400 to be pd. for In. Tax + various other cheques say £1500 in all, leaving a/c about £2000 Dr [overdrawn].'[23]

Churchill had to change his tune the next day after remind-ing himself that the trustees would not be contributing so much as he expected towards the building works at Sussex Square, which had exceeded the trust's budget as early as April. Churchill had originally offered to fund the excess himself, but had taken fright in August after paying an extra £1,750 during June and July. He had asked Nicholl, Manisty whether the trust could cover all remaining bills, but the solicitors insisted on obtaining a professional opinion from a firm of surveyors. It recom-mended that the trust pay no more than an extra £500, leaving Churchill seriously short of the contribution which he had told the bank to expect.[24]

Unabashed, he suggested a different solution to Bernau: 'I expect now to receive from £400–600 for the reproduction of my articles in a book form, wh[ich] sh'd be received in a month or two,'[25] he wrote two days after their second meeting. 'If in these circumstances you wish to take up one of the £2000 policies please let me know, but I daresay you will not consider this necessary.'[26] Bernau went to the top for a decision. 'Advise him we will leave it for now,' Reginald Cox decided, still not keen on a confrontation between his weakened bank and a senior politician.[27]

More falls in mining shares followed in November 1920. However, Churchill was able to turn to his friend Sir Abe Bailey to save him from further embarrassment. Sir Abe offered a personal guarantee 'against any loss on all shares purchased on my advice'; this was immediately accepted by the bank.

Churchill recognized that he had to find a way of supplementing his ministerial earnings if he was to reduce his debts. Inspired by a conversation with General Rawlinson, his fellow veteran at Omdurman who had commanded British forces on the Somme, Churchill had started to think seriously of writing his own account of the Dardanelles campaign. In March he visited Sir Frederick Macmillan, the publisher of *Lord Randolph Churchill*. 'We shall be very pleased to put into type the Memoranda and Minutes written while you were away at the Admiralty which you wish to have ready for publication at some future time,' Sir Frederick wrote to him. 'I will see that it is printed in a satisfactory form and with all proper regard to secrecy.'[28]

By October 1920 a short book about the Dardanelles had grown into an ambitious history of the First World War that would be called *The World Crisis*. Rather than publish through Macmillan, Churchill decided to employ a literary agent. Frank Harris was now living in America, so Churchill drove a hard bargain with a new agency set up during the war by an American journalist in London called Albert Curtis Brown.* It was agreed that Curtis

---

* Albert Curtis Brown (1866–1945), born in United States; joined *Buffalo Express* 1884–94; *New York Press* Sunday editor 1894–8, London

Brown would earn his 10 per cent commission only if royalties exceeded £15,000. Churchill, for his part, undertook to produce the first volume of *The World Crisis* by the end of 1922 and the second a year later, while still holding down his position as secretary of state for war.[29]

Prompted by a review Churchill had written of one of its books, the publisher Thornton Butterworth* offered to publish any book that Churchill might care to write.[30] Curtis Brown immediately obtained a guaranteed advance of £5,000 for the British Empire rights, with £2,000 paid in cash on signature.[31] Newspaper serial rights seemed to sell just as easily.[32] *The Times* offered another £5,000, but before accepting Churchill wanted a commitment from H. Wickham Steed, the editor, that there would be no damaging Dardanelles editorial. 'I think you are entitled to assume that consideration for our own consistency, quite apart from the ingrained admiration we have always felt and have sometimes expressed for you, will be a guarantee that we shall not wilfully foul your and our nest,' Wickham Steed replied carefully.

Churchill wanted an absolute assurance and Wickham Steed had to write again: 'You may regard my letter as an undertaking that we shall not criticize you for having written the book... this without prejudice to our freedom of criticism in regard to the political aspects of any policies or political or military enterprises for which you may have been responsible.' Churchill filed away this second letter, marking it 'Keep secret'. He signed a contract with *The Times* four days later.[33]

When he met Cox & Co. for a promised 'end of year' review, Churchill first flourished his new contracts with Butterworth and *The Times*, then went on to mention more: 'American agents $50,000 (probably) for whole rights, South Asia and Continental

---

correspondent 1898–1910; founder and managing director International Publishing Bureau 1900–16; founder and managing director Curtis Brown Ltd. 1916–45.

* Thornton Butterworth publisher (of G. K. Chesterton and Margot Asquith among others); his business went into receivership in September 1940.

rights about £2000; Bernau noted afterwards.[34] The $50,000 figure came from a conversational aside by Butterworth rather than a forecast by Curtis Brown, who had always been more cautious about Churchill's prospects across the Atlantic.

When no offers had arrived by December, Butterworth approached Charles Scribner's Sons, the firm that had turned down *Lord Randolph Churchill* fifteen years earlier. The Scribners' London representative remained sceptical of Churchill, warning head office that he was 'frankly out for all the traffic will bear'.[35] However, before joining the family firm Charles Scribner II's son had fought on the Western Front and he was keen. 'Unlike Lloyd George, Churchill has the power – and the very great power of writing,' Butterworth urged. 'Do please, and here I place the greatest stress, make your royalty <u>as high as you can</u>'.[36]

The Scribners held their fire until the last minute, waiting while Curtis Brown recommended offers of $17,500 from a monthly magazine *Metropolitan* for the serial rights and $10,000 for the book from Duran & Co.; then they cabled Butterworth at the end of January: 'Offer for Churchill 20 per cent royalty, tax free, with $16,000 dollars advance.'[37] 'No better or more dignified publisher could have been found for the work in America,' enthused Curtis Brown.[38] (These generous sums were dwarfed by the £90,000 announced the following year for Lloyd George's memoirs, although that deal caused such controversy that the prime minister first declared he would give the money to charity and then had to abandon the project.)[39] Churchill went on to earn £25,000 from *The World Crisis*, but he avoided any public censure for profiting personally from his public position because his earnings expanded gradually as the book grew from first one to two, and eventually three volumes.[40]

Throughout 1920 relations between the prime minister and his secretary of state for war had been strained by policy differences over Russia. While they were both in the south of France in January 1921 for a New Year holiday, Lloyd George suggested that Churchill be transferred to the Colonial Office. The new post would keep Churchill clear of Russia or Eastern Europe, but it had just added responsibility for Britain's two post-war Middle Eastern mandates, Iraq and Palestine, to the rest of the empire.[41]

In the absence of formal government guidance on conflicts of interest for ministers, Churchill took it upon himself to ask Austen Chamberlain, the new chancellor of the exchequer, whether he should keep his mining shares, now that so much of Africa, including the south, was part of his new ministerial bailiwick. 'I chose this South African theatre for my investments as it seemed one of the very few into which Admiralty, Munitions or War Office business was unlikely to enter,' he claimed, with an element of hindsight.

> Now that I have undertaken to go to the Colonial Office, I must disclose my interest, and I should be glad to have your opinion as to whether I am bound to sell the Securities at their present low value. I do not myself think so, but no man is a good judge in his own case and you, as Chancellor of the Exchequer, seem to be in a special position to pronounce on such questions of Ministerial propriety.[42]

Chamberlain consulted the prime minister before replying:

> It is not easy for a man in public life, even with the most scrupulous care, so to invest his money that no one of his investments shall ever be affected or be capable of being affected by action of the British Government. There is, as far as I can see, no probability, or even possibility, that the holding of these investments in a Self-Governing Dominion can in any way conflict with your duty as a Minister of the Crown or embarrass you in the discharge of it.

Chamberlain added a rider that Churchill had not expected, but had to accept: 'I think that apart from any unforeseen change in political conditions or any over-riding private necessity, we ought to leave the investment unaltered during our tenure of Office.'[43]

'We must try to live within our income', Churchill urged Clementine on 27 January 1921, although he offered no advice on how to do this.[44] His usual strategy was to increase his income rather than to cut spending. True to form, he told her that he had accepted an invitation from *The Strand Magazine* to write two articles on his new hobby of painting for a fee of £1,000.[45]

Churchill sat down to write, unaware that his fortunes were about to change. On 26 January 1921 two trains collided on a length of single track between Welshpool and Newtown in Wales.[46] Among the victims was a fifty-one-year-old railway company director, Lord Herbert Vane-Tempest, Churchill's Londonderry cousin and the current beneficiary of the Garron Tower estate. Since Lord Herbert was unmarried and without an heir, his grandmother's will ordained that the whole estate should jump across to the eldest surviving Churchill male.

Winston had been next in line for more than a decade, but only occasionally concerned himself with the estate's affairs. In 1909 his solicitors had told him that its income amounted to £3,700 a year. In 1919 its capital value had stood at almost £90,000, the majority safely invested in Irish government bonds and stocks, following the trustees' sale of most of the estate's houses and the fire-damaged Garron Tower Hotel. The only remaining property was the local Carnlough Lime Works, its harbour and nearby tenements, whose rent hardly matched the costs of their collection.[47]

On the day after the accident Lord Herbert's lawyer visited Churchill's solicitor to notify him. He mentioned a likely annual income from the estate of £4,200 a year, but could not say how much estate duty would be owed. Whatever its level, the remainder would be sufficient to transform Churchill's finances.[48]

Churchill's first step on hearing the news was to arrange an immediate meeting to soothe the fears of his bank manager

William Bernau, with whom a crisis had been brewing since his loans and overdraft had now reached almost £28,000.[49] Clementine's priority was to attack their pile of unpaid bills. 'What would you really wish done about the Bills?' she asked her husband. 'In the first flush of the rosy news, you suggested paying them off & you said I was to send them all to you to have dealt with – it would be heavenly if this could be done, but I don't know if you really mean it.'[50]

The following day she was still absorbing the news. 'I can't describe the blessed feeling of relief that we need never never be worried about money again (except thro' our own fault of course!),' she told Churchill. 'It is like floating in a bath of cream.'[51] In her excitement, Clementine wrote daily for four days. 'We will have to pay our bills more regularly now that we are substantial people, shan't we?' she mused, before asking for an infusion of funds. 'Please may I have a little money now that you are what the French call a "*rentier*"?'* As regards his articles on painting for *The Strand Magazine*, she wondered if he could now afford to drop them as she felt they were bad for his image.

> I have a sort of feeling that the 'All Highest' [George Curzon, then foreign secretary] rejoices every time you write an Article & thinks it brings him nearer the Premiership, tho' I think that a man who has had to bolster himself up with two rich wives** to keep himself going is not so likely to keep the Empire going as you, who for 12 years have been a Cabinet Minister & have besides kept a fortuneless Cat and four hungry kittens.[52]

Clementine's only regret was that the jewels were no longer part of

---

* A person living on a financial return from property or investments.
** Curzon's two wives were Mary Leiter, daughter of Levi Leiter, co-founder of the Chicago department store Field & Leiter (later Marshall Field), whom he married in 1895. She died in 1906. After a long affair with the novelist Elinor Glyn, Curzon next married Grace Hands, a wealthy American widow, in 1917.

the Garron Tower estate. Sensing her disappointment, Churchill briefly considered an effort to recover them, but he told the marquess of Londonderry that he accepted their earlier arrangement. 'I am sorry you regret the jewels but I am not sure you need to do that,' his cousin responded, dispatching his butler to Sussex Square with what could be found of his great-grandmother's silver. 'The emeralds are nice, but now no one likes anything but the Cartier setting.'[53]

Churchill and Bernau hoped that most of the estate's investments could be transferred to Cox & Co. before the colonial secretary left for Cairo, where he was to chair an imperial conference on the Middle East. They had decided that Churchill should repay the £4,000 of his bank loans that his cousin had guaranteed, but keep the rest until the final size of his inheritance was known. 'I had a blow yesterday when I found that the Estate is about £7,000 less than I thought,' Churchill told Clementine. 'It now seems likely to work out at about £57,000 after duty. This would have been £85,000 pre-war. It will produce nearly 4000 a year from its present trustee securities: & I am being carefully advised as to rather more fruitful investments.'[54] Clementine was philosophical:

> I am so sorry my Dearest that you have had a deception as to the amount of the inheritance. It is certainly very disappointing after you had worked it out so carefully & thought about how to lay it out to the best advantage; but don't let a 'crumpled rose leaf' like this spoil the really glorious fact which rushed on us so suddenly a little time ago – that haunting care had vanished for ever from our lives. . . It's so delicious to be easy – I hope I shall never take it for granted but always feel like a cork bobbing on a sunny sea.

Could he not, she asked, 'take me in your waistcoat pocket to Egypt'?[55] Churchill said she could come, prompting a further question as to whether Bessie, Clementine's lady's maid, could travel too? Bessie made the journey – the Churchills' spending had moved up another step.*

---

* 'With such elaborate clothes a lady's maid was really a necessity. Skirts that trailed on the floor needed constant cleaning and mending. Zips were still in the distant future and bodices had intricate fastenings.' Loelia, duchess of Westminster, *Grace and Favour*, pp. 40–1.

10

***

'Our castle in the air'

A Country Seat at Last, 1921–2

Exchange rate $5 = £1
Inflation multiples: US x 14; UK x 45

THE CHURCHILLS JOURNEYED in style for six weeks – breaching ministerial travel guidelines by booking a luxury cabin for the sea journey – before returning in the spring of 1921 to find that the transfer of the Garron Tower estate had made little progress during their absence. The estate's value had turned out to be £64,000, reduced by estate duty to £56,000,[1] which was lower than hoped. Nevertheless, Churchill increased Clementine's monthly housekeeping allowance by a third. Proudly handing his bank manager a two-page list of investments he had inherited, Churchill invited William Bernau to select those he wished to use as security for a new consolidated loan of £30,000, which Churchill would use to replace all his old borrowing facilities.[2] He was going to use the windfall to enlarge his investment portfolio, rather than reduce his borrowings.

The reorganization of Churchill's finances was interrupted by two family tragedies in quick succession. First, Clementine's thirty-three-year-old brother Bill committed suicide in a French hotel room, unable to overcome his addiction to gambling. Just two months earlier Churchill had used £750 of his new funds to clear Bill Hozier's debts, and his brother-in-law had made a written undertaking 'not to engage in any form of gambling at cards, racing or game of chance'.[3]

Weeks later, Churchill's mother fell down some stairs and broke her ankle. Jennie had divorced George Cornwallis-West in 1914 and had married for the third time in 1918, once again a man younger than her son. Montagu Porch, a member of the British civil service in Nigeria, had not been dissuaded from marrying her by Churchill's warnings of murky financial trouble ahead[4] or by Jennie's refusal to move to Nigeria. The couple enjoyed a honeymoon in Europe that lasted for almost a year, until their money ran out and Porch returned to Nigeria.

Jennie then achieved the one real financial coup of her life. She borrowed money from Porch's family trusts to buy a property in Berkeley Square, London; she modernized it and sold it early in 1921 for a clear profit of £15,000.[5] After paying off five of her most insistent moneylenders, Jennie made a celebratory shopping trip to Florence, Rome and Naples, spending £1,000 on Italian antiques.[6] 'We ransacked all the curiosity shops and Jennie bought profusely,' recalled her companion Vittoria Colonna, duchess of Sermoneta. 'Her zest in spending money was one of her charms.'[7]

Now, however, Jennie's broken ankle had badly infected her leg, which had to be amputated above the knee. Churchill cabled reassuring messages to Porch in Nigeria, insisting that she was out of danger, but Jennie died of a sudden haemorrhage on 29 June 1921. She was sixty-seven and technically intestate, having failed to remake a will after remarrying. It made little difference: after several of society's most fashionable moneylenders had lodged their claims, Jennie's debts easily outstripped her assets.[8]

Churchill mourned his mother's loss, but her death completed the transformation of his finances. His half share of both his parents' trusts could be added to the money that he had recently inherited from his great-grandmother. Extracting the lump sum of $250,000 due from his grandfather Leonard Jerome's 'American settlement' proved difficult: New York's Manhattan Club had taken over the liability to make the payment after buying the Jerome mansion in 1913, but it did not have the funds available. Churchill was anxious to receive payment while the dollar's exchange rate to sterling remained strong, but the club took time to find a lender, who then insisted on seeing a copy of Jerome's original 1874 deed, which had gone missing.

The Churchill brothers hired an American lawyer to force the pace, but almost inevitably the sterling value of the dollar fell by 10 per cent during the time it all took.[9] When the dust had settled, Churchill's own share of all his parents' trusts produced another £54,000 of capital,[10] but its one big disadvantage compared to the Garron Tower inheritance was that it remained tied up in trusts to protect the next generation. He would earn investment income each year from the trusts, but could only touch their capital if the transaction was treated as a loan and he paid the trustees a market rate of interest.

The family tragedies made it difficult for Churchill to complete the reordering of his finances on which he had embarked during the spring. To complicate matters, his relationship with Lloyd George had reached a new low. The prime minister had appointed the less-experienced Robert Horne to replace Austen Chamberlain as chancellor of the exchequer, a position in which Churchill aspired to follow his father. Three days after his mother's funeral, amid press reports that he was plotting to unseat the prime minister, Churchill met Sir Reginald Cox, the senior partner of Cox & Co., to promise that he would produce a more detailed blueprint of his future financial arrangements once Parliament rose for its summer recess.[11]

'Dealing in round figures,' he wrote confidently to Sir Reginald in August, 'I owe the bank £15,000 on promissory notes, £7,000 on 4% loan against a life policy of £10,000, £11,000 overdraft on current account, & £2,000 overpaid on the Investment a/c, total £35,000.'[12]

In place of all these different facilities he suggested a single loan of £35,000 to be repaid slowly over eleven years. Sir Reginald baulked at this. 'Told him that an annual repayment, as it implies renewal from year to year, is not acceptable,' Bernau noted after a second meeting, held on the same day that the cabinet met to discuss Churchill's proposals for Britain's administration of its new mandates in Iraq and Palestine. Churchill's loan was restricted to £30,000, to be reduced 'substantially' in 1922, plus an overdraft of £3,000.[13]

During the parliamentary recess the Churchills decided to acquire some of the trappings associated with their new station in life: a country house, a smart car and a trust for their children. Churchill inspected Chartwell, a west Kent manor large enough for a family of nine children and with a domestic staff of thirteen, its seventy acres of land looked after by an outdoor team of twenty.[14]

Clementine preferred the idea of a house on its own: 'Personally "farming" rather frightens me after our experience at Lullenden which is now costing the Hamiltons dear,' she explained from the nearby estate of Fairlawne, where she was staying.[15] Her message was even clearer the next day: 'I want to lie in the sun & blink & wake up now & then to eat a mouse caught by some one else, & drink a little cream and doze off*. . . . Darling let us beware of risking our newly come fortune in operations which we do not understand & have not the time to learn & to practise what we have learnt'.[16]

However, she did agree to inspect Chartwell on her way home and this seems to have changed her mind: 'My darling, I can think of nothing but that heavenly tree-crowned Hill. It is rather like a view from an aeroplane up there.' The house was due to be auctioned and Clementine set out her ideas for change beforehand:

> Don't you think if the Estate would pay for it it would be wise to add at once a corresponding wing on the left side of the house.**
> My reasons for this are as follows: 1) We need a minimum of 12

---

* In the Churchills' private correspondence, Clementine often took on the persona of a cat (Churchill of a pig).
** The estate to which Clementine referred was the Garron Tower. She included a drawing corresponding closely to the west wing that the Churchills would add to Chartwell, at great cost, when they finally bought it.

bedrooms to accommodate the whole family & the servants [. . .]
If we put in 4 bathrooms that will leave 13 bedrooms if we do not
add a Wing, i.e. room for 1 guest only – I think you would like
to be able to put up 2 or 3 guests at least with 1 or 2 visiting servants.[17]

The caption at the foot of the letter, below her familiar drawing of
a cat, reads: 'Whiskers have grown 2 inches at the thought of our
castle in the Air.' A few days later, Chartwell failed to sell at auction,
but there is no record of whether the Churchills submitted a bid.[18]

The couple's decision to transfer £10,000 of their inheritance to
a new settlement for their children was not entirely altruistic.[19] As
trustees, they would still control how the money was spent and the
trust's own set of allowances would reduce the family's overall tax
burden, now that much higher rates for the better-off were clearly
to remain a permanent feature of the post-war tax landscape.
Churchill planned to borrow the full £10,000 straight back from the
trust for his own purposes. The cost of interest on the loan was
allowed to be subtracted from his own taxable income, thus reducing his own tax rate as well – a double tax benefit. Churchill held off
signing the legal papers, knowing it was a sensitive move. A recent
royal commission had recommended closing down abuses of the
trust system, but he went ahead early in 1922 when well-organized
lobbying resulted in many of the loopholes remaining open.[20]

The last item on Churchill's summer shopping list was a Rolls-
Royce Silver Ghost Cabriolet, costing £2,593, which he planned to
christen during a September motoring holiday around Scotland.[21]
Impatient for its arrival painted in the Marlborough blue, Churchill
persuaded the coachbuilders Barker & Co. to lend him a car of the
same model in London. Meanwhile, Clementine travelled to
Cheshire to play in the duke of Westminster's annual tennis tournament, leaving their children with a young French governess to
spend August by the sea in Kent.

What followed was yet another family tragedy. At the seaside
Marigold, their youngest child, who was not quite three years old,

developed a cold and a sore throat. It turned into tonsillitis. Alarmed at the child's deteriorating condition, an anxious landlady persuaded the young governess to summon Clementine, who rushed down to Kent from Cheshire. Her first letter to Churchill, written on 18 August, gave no hint of concern, but instead recorded her delight at the imminent arrival of the Rolls-Royce.[22] Four days later, Marigold died of septicaemia. Churchill arrived before the end came. 'She said: "So tired" and closed her eyes. And I thought that Clemmie would die in the violence of her grief. She screamed like an animal under torture,' Churchill told his private secretary almost forty years later.[23]

Churchill paid £146 for Marigold's small, satin-lined coffin and its sad journey to Kensal Green Cemetery.[24] After the funeral the family travelled by train to the duke of Westminster's Scottish home, where the Rolls-Royce awaited them. Clementine and the children returned to London a fortnight later for the new school year, leaving Churchill to drive the car northwards to a cabinet meeting in Inverness. On the way, near the Cromarty Firth, he collided with a car carrying a disabled man, to whom he sent an extra cheque for £500 along with £30 for repairs.[25] It was the end of the Rolls-Royce's short, ill-starred life with the Churchill family. The ever-obliging Aunt Cornelia took it over at a price only £150 less than its cost and Churchill hired a Daimler.

Churchill spent much of the autumn dealing with the future governance of Iraq and Ireland and negotiating his plans through the House of Commons. Shortly before Christmas he finally sat down at home to examine his finances. It had been an extraordinary year.

His own assets, he estimated, amounted to £65,000, but a net £30,000 after deducting his bank loans. His family trusts contained another £54,000 of assets, while Clementine's portion of their marriage settlement held £14,000, taking the family's entire net worth close to £100,000 (a level which it would not regain until the final stages of the Second World War). The annual balance between income and expenditure was not so healthy: income had stayed steady at £9,000–10,000 a year, but 'normal' family spending was still out-stripping it by at least £3,000 a year.

For the sake of his finances, Churchill would have to press on with *The World Crisis*, his book about the Great War.[26] In order to make progress on it during the parliamentary recess, he joined an exodus of British politicians to the French Riviera. He arrived on Boxing Day and planned to write by day and spend the evenings in the company of his colleagues. 'LG [Lloyd George] read two of my chapters in the train & was well content with the references to himself. . . And the pelf* will make us feel very comfortable,'[27] he wrote to Clementine. Back home, however, first Diana, then Randolph, then two maids and finally Clementine herself fell victim to a virulent strain of flu that was to kill more than 13,000 people in Britain.[28] Fortunately, everyone in the Churchill home recovered.

Churchill's next letter rather tactlessly let slip that he planned to meet Clementine's mother at a Monte Carlo casino: 'The Sporting Club people mentioned her name to me with the utmost appreciation & granted me my ticket of admission "*sans phrase*". Evidently she has taken possession of this gambling resort.'[29] It was not the sort of news that Clementine – ill and terrified by the damage gambling had done to her family – wanted to hear; she wrote an anguished reply, but followed it up with a cable asking Churchill not to open it. He received the letter the next day, as news of street violence in Ireland filtered down to the south of France, and he admitted to opening it: 'In law it was my property once it was delivered to me,' he explained, before sympathizing with her and then breaking his own news which concerned the casino: 'I must confess to you that I have lost some money here; though nothing like so much as last year.'

Churchill withdrew almost £700-worth of French francs in cash during his two-week stay, according to his bank statement.[30] On the most generous of estimates, a week's hotel bills (Churchill was the guest of the countess of Essex and Lord Beaverbrook** for the

---

* *Pelfre* is an Old French word for money of questionable source.
** Formerly Sir Max Aitken.

second week), car hire and tips would not have cost more than £200, leaving his probable gambling losses at some £500. 'It excites me so much to play – foolish moth,' he explained to Clementine. 'But I have earned many times what I have lost by the work that I have done here at my book; and also our shares at home have gone well. I am vexed with myself. Max highly disapproved on every ground. As I was punished by the Cat when I was not at fault, you must now pardon me when I am.'[31]

After Churchill returned home on 8 January he sanctioned a new flurry of stock exchange transactions over the next four months, despite his immersion in Parliament in the politics of Egypt and Ireland. Worth more than £250,000, these transactions were all conducted through Vickers da Costa, where his brother Jack was about to become a junior partner. They concentrated on fixed-interest stocks, which not only raised fewer conflicts of interest for ministers than company shares, but were also thriving as interest rates fell in the face of Britain's struggling post-war economy.[32]

After recording dealing profits of £2,850 in the year since his inheritance,[33] Churchill felt confident enough to send more money to Clementine, who was pregnant again and staying in southern France. 'I know what an economical cat it is,' he explained. 'But the Riviera is a frightfully expensive place.'[34]

Busier than ever at Westminster, Churchill now trusted Clementine with more of the housekeeping budget, although he still paid all their doctors' bills and for cars, trains, clubs, wine, cigars and his holidays. Clementine's monthly allowance was supposed to cover clothes, domestic staff, school fees, food, flowers, furnishings and her own holidays, but nevertheless during 1922 the 'economical cat' required transfers of an extra £10,000. By April 1922 Churchill's bank borrowings were already £6,000 higher than the sum he had agreed six months earlier and he had to take on an extra loan, raising his borrowings to £39,000.[35]

Confined to bed for a week after a nasty fall from a horse at
the start of the new polo season, Churchill realized that *The
World Crisis* was so far behind schedule he could not meet
Thornton Butterworth's publication timetable. He had learned
that the art of dealing with publishers is to break the bad news at
the start of the letter, but to provide a morsel of good news
towards the end. Butterworth was supposed to be cheered on this
occasion by the cabinet's recent decision to allow ministers to
quote from official documents in their memoirs, where they were
defending their conduct in office, the so-called 'vindicator clause'.
Churchill, who had been involved in so many of the war's contro-
versies, foresaw considerable new source material; Butterworth,
however, saw only the extra costs of paper, ink and binding which
would fall on the publisher.[36]

There was a whiff of decay around the Coalition government
during the summer of 1922, as ageing men of differing political
persuasions, some having been in office for almost two decades,
struggled to find common solutions to the problems of post-war
Europe.

Should his political fortunes decline, Churchill felt financially
strong enough to withstand the consequences. At the first signs of
economic recovery in June he had sold his entire bond portfolio
and repaid all his bank loans with the £46,500 raised. His current
account at the bank was in surplus for the first time in nearly
twenty years. It didn't last, however, for in a matter of days he had
reborrowed £15,000 and sent Vickers da Costa £25,000 to buy
more shares.[37] Clementine was allowed to spend a little of the
proceeds at Sussex Square: 'I think we are justified in making the
new bath room you wished for and I put in a plea for my parquet
[flooring for Churchill's study].'[38]

The governing Coalition's demise came a step closer when the
Ulster Unionists protested at the names included in June's official
honours list. There was nothing new about selling titles to fund
Britain's political parties, but Lloyd George had taken the art to a

new level by including on the list individuals convicted of tax evasion, fraud and trading with the enemy during wartime.*

Recognizing that his ministerial salary might soon come to an end, Churchill raised the subject of the timetable for *The World Crisis* with his agent Curtis Brown before he set off on his summer holiday. He could still finish the first volume by the end of the year, as required by his contract, but he would be able to improve the final result greatly, he told his agent, after leaving office. Churchill asked Curtis Brown to find out whether he might postpone publication for a year without triggering the need to return his advances. Churchill thought *The Times* would object, but it was the first to agree, allowing him to set off in good heart for a rendezvous with his friend Lord Beaverbrook at Deauville.

They spent time at the casino, as Clementine feared, but Churchill restricted his own losses by watching, fascinated, as the Shah of Persia gambled away his subjects' money, fed to him by his prime minister, packet by packet.[39] Clementine was more nervous of the casino at Biarritz, near to the duke of Westminster's hunting lodge, where Churchill was due to stay next. 'I hope my own Darling you are being wise & wary & not singeing your pork whiskers at the Tables,' she wrote from the English seaside at Frinton-on-Sea, where she had taken the children. 'Just think last year in one night you lost nearly the rent of this lovely house.'[40] Churchill lost £40 at the start of his visit, but recouped it all before leaving: 'So I said goodnight to Mephistopheles & came away, having neither lost nor won,'[41] he reported home proudly.

Clementine was enjoying the seaside home at Frinton ('I am so comfortable here – it's so comfortable and delicious,' she wrote), but Churchill had not given up hope of buying Chartwell and its land. When the estate agents Knight Frank & Rutley warned that the property was likely to return to auction in the autumn, he kept

---

* William Vestey, Joseph Robinson and John Drughorn, respectively. The honours tariff was supposed to stand at £10,000 for a knighthood, £30,000 for a baronetcy and from £50,000 upwards for a peerage. The Order of the British Empire was introduced to fill a gap below £5,000.

using his bank passbook to work out what he could afford to bid. A heavily pregnant Clementine had convinced herself that the house faced the wrong way and was too close to the road, and pushed the case for a seaside home: 'If you do let me buy a little house here (there is one with 10 bed-rooms & 2 baths on which I have cast covetous eyes which I think could be had for £4000),' she wrote from Frinton in mid-August, 'I would like to sell the gold pots and contribute. I could also sell my shares & then that would be more than half.'[42]

Churchill spent ten days with the family at Frinton towards the end of the month, but he remained unconvinced of its merits. On his return to London he learned that a rebel Turkish army was advancing on the demilitarized Dardanelles straits and Constantinople;[*] he was so engrossed at work that he ignored the two other house possibilities that Clementine suggested. Then, just as events in the Near East threatened to develop into a full-scale political crisis, Knight Frank & Rutley offered Churchill ten days in which to buy Chartwell at a pre-auction price of £5,500;[43] the letter arrived on the same day that he argued in cabinet for an extra division to reinforce Britain's army at Constantinople. It was also the day on which Clementine went into labour with their fifth child.

Without waiting to consult her, Churchill carried out some quick sums before replying with a lower offer of £4,800. 'The house will have to be very largely rebuilt and the presence of dry rot in the northern wing is I am advised a very serious adverse factor,' he explained.[44] Representing both buyer and seller, Knight Frank & Rutley's agent Norman Harding found himself summoned to the Colonial Office. He recalled that Churchill 'strode up and down, using every argument he could think of to lower the price. . .

---

* The post-war treaty of Sèvres had reduced Turkey's size and established a 'Neutral Zone of the Straits' on each side of the Dardanelles and Bosphorus straits and of the sea of Marmaris. The Allies dealt with a puppet government under the sultan in Constantinople; however, Mustafa Kemal, the hero of Gallipoli, set up a rival Turkish national government whose forces soon threatened the limited Allied forces policing the neutral zone.

Eventually, with a very bad grace, he gave way.'[45] In fact, Churchill only raised his price to £5,000. That weekend he looked after the elder children, while Clementine recovered from the birth of another daughter, Mary. Sarah Churchill later recalled:

> We clambered into an old Wolsey and with my father at the wheel off we went. He told us on the way that the purpose of this journey was to inspect a house that he thought of buying in Kent, and he wanted our opinion. . . Chartwell was wildly over-grown and untidy, and contained all the mystery of houses that had not been lived in for many years. . . 'Do you like it?' Did we like it? We were delirious. 'Oh, do buy it!' we exclaimed. 'Well, I'm not sure. . . ' He kept us in anxious suspense. . . Not until we reached Parliament Square did he divulge that he had already bought it.[46]

Still pre-occupied by the Turkish crisis, Churchill asked his brother Jack to help arrange funding for the purchase and mod-ernization of Chartwell until royalties started to arrive for *The World Crisis*. On 22 September, having decided to borrow £11,500 from a mixture of the bank and the marriage settlement, Churchill turned aside from a series of emergency ministerial meetings – called to discuss the encirclement of a small Anglo-French-Italian force at Chanak, south of the Dardanelles – to write to his bank manager. 'I shall have to rebuild to a large extent the house which is quite unworthy of the beautiful situation, and this is estimated to cost about £8,000,' he told William Bernau. He would borrow £3,500 from his marriage settlement trustees and asked for a loan of £8,000 from the bank, just until the arrival of his royalties, which he expected to amount to at least £25,000. 'It is from this fund that I propose to defray the bulk of the expense on Chartwell,' he concluded.[47]

Churchill told the bank that he expected 'no difficulty'[48] from his marriage settlement trustees, but he had reckoned without the duke of Marlborough. Against a background of falling property values, the duke insisted that the trustees could not lend more than half the property's cost. Churchill countered by claiming that, with its cottages, timber and land, Chartwell would be worth at least £15,000 by the time he had spent '£7,000 or £8,000' on it, to create 'a first-class medium size perfectly appointed modern house standing in its own park and grounds within 25 miles of London'.[49] Unwisely, he added that house price deflation was confined to the very largest houses (he stopped short of mentioning Blenheim), but his cousin stood his ground. 'The bottom has not yet been reached,' he insisted. 'You know that vast portions of the land of England are to-day unsaleable.'[50]

There was no time to make other plans before Churchill suffered what *The Times* reported as 'acute gastro-enteritis',[51] but which turned into full-scale appendicitis. Surgeons operated on 18 November, the day on which the Liberals lost an important by-election, in large part due to public disquiet at the apparent willingness of Lloyd George and Churchill to wage war over disputes in far-off lands. The Liberals' Coalition partners were unnerved. The Conservatives became convinced they should fight the next general election on their own. There was a meeting at the Carlton Club, during which the party's MPs and peers backed Stanley Baldwin and Andrew Bonar Law's calls for an immediate withdrawal from government.

Churchill was still in hospital when Lloyd George resigned and Bonar Law formed a minority Conservative government, before calling a general election. Churchill dictated his campaign manifesto from bed in a London nursing home. He sent Clementine north to Dundee with their six-week-old daughter to start campaigning until he was well enough to join her; meanwhile he tried to revise his funding plans for Chartwell.

The plan to borrow from the marriage settlement and to use book royalties was dropped. Instead, he would sell some investments and borrow a larger amount from his father's trust, where he expected that Jack would prove a more compliant trustee than his cousin. 'I propose to purchase it out of the Trust Fund under Lord

Randolph Churchill's Will, but up to the present I have not been, through illness and other preoccupations, [able] to make the arrangements I desired,' he explained to Bernau, asking the bank for a smaller, bridging loan of £4,500.[52]

Churchill's doctor allowed him to join Clementine for the last days of the general election campaign, but in disadvantaged Dundee the political ground had shifted to the left and they faced noisy crowds. A 15,000 majority evaporated in the face of co-oper-ation between his Labour and Prohibitionist opponents, who defeated both Churchill and his fellow Liberal candidate in the two-member constituency – Churchill came fourth in the poll. Nationally, the Conservatives won a clear majority and the Labour Party increased its vote to four million. Churchill found himself with a new country home, but 'without an office, without a seat, without a party and without an appendix'.[53]

11

'What about the 50,000 quid
Cassel gave you?'
Out of Office, 1923–4

Exchange rate $5 = £1; (1923) francs 80 = £1
Inflation multiples: US x 14; UK x 50

EXHAUSTED BY FIVE years in power, at the end of 1922 Churchill followed the advice given to him by one of his former advisers at the Colonial Office, Colonel T. E. Lawrence: 'Rest a little – six months perhaps. There is that book of memoirs* to be made not merely worth £30,000, but of permanent value.'[1] Making plans for a spell in the south of France with Clementine, he arranged an extra £2,000 of overdraft to pay their staff while they were away, let Sussex Square and rented a car and a villa near Cannes.[2]

To help fund the visit Churchill took out a large 'bear' position against the French franc, betting that it would weaken over the months they were there. Jack tried to explain the risks, but Churchill was confident of his analysis: in contrast to Britain's much heavier use of taxation, France had financed its war effort almost entirely through borrowing, so was now saddled with a public debt almost twice the size of its gross national product. In addition, hopes were fading of substantial German reparation payments.

Churchill made three short visits home to deal with building works at Chartwell. Within a fortnight of buying the house (and

---

* Lawrence referred to *The World Crisis*, as yet unfinished.

disregarding more experienced candidates) he had appointed the thirty-four-year-old Philip Tilden as his architect, a decision made in haste and repented at leisure. Tilden belonged to a set of fashionable young artists and writers in London, but had spent the war on a Dartmoor farm, where he met the daughter of the wealthy art historian Sir Martin Conway. Sir Martin asked Tilden to oversee the restoration of his family seat,* before introducing him to Sir Louis Mallet, Britain's wartime ambassador in Constantinople. Sir Louis taught Tilden the use of tempera paint for interior decoration and in turn introduced Sir Philip Sassoon, who gave Tilden the task of completing Port Lympne, the grandiose home on the Romney marshes that he had started before the war. Tilden installed a Moorish courtyard at Port Lympne, complete with green marble floor and white marble pillars, a domed octagonal library and a staircase flanked by columns of blue and mauve, all of which clearly appealed to Churchill, a frequent visitor, although an appalled Lady Honor Guinness described it as resembling a Spanish brothel.[3]

Tilden's other notable credential was that he had just built a home for Lloyd George in Surrey, reputedly funded by Lloyd George's and Churchill's mutual friend, George Riddell, owner of the *News of the World*.[4] Whatever the route to his appointment, Tilden relished the challenge of Chartwell, which he described in his memoirs as:

> A dreary house perched on the edge of the hillside, very close to the road, but banked on its western side by a cascade of full-grown rhododendrons... So embowering were the giant trees, so encroaching was the verdure that the red bricks of the house were slimed with green... only the kernel of the old manor, floored and raftered with solid oak, had withstood the ravages of wet; the rest was weary of its own ugliness so that the walls ran with moisture, and creeping fungus tracked down the cracks and crevices.[5]

---

* Allington Castle in Kent.

Tilden soon discovered that Churchill wanted to be much more closely involved in the project than Lloyd George had been. Accepting the normal architects' fee scale,* Churchill explained that he and his wife wished to have larger bedrooms, new bathrooms and kitchen, a library, a large study and a room for entertaining. However, they had not agreed any detailed plan or estimate of costs before Tilden pressed for an early decision on the addition of a south-facing wing, which would not only provide the extra rooms but create the effect of turning the main frontage of the house away from the road towards its majestic views of the Kentish Weald below.[6]

Architect and client began to set a pattern of piecemeal arrangements without any master scheme: Tilden engaged brothers Alec and Harold Brown as principal builders, while Churchill engaged his own local joiner, William Wallace, whom he directed himself on smaller jobs in order to save money. Proper plans only arrived just before the Churchills left for France: the new wing was to be ready by the end of March 1923, the rest of the house by August. Tilden expected to exceed Churchill's target cost of £8,000 by only £500.

In France Churchill concentrated on finishing the first two volumes of *The World Crisis* and on his investments by day, the casino by night. His publisher had become impatient at the manuscript's delays. He had bid aggressively back in 1920, Thornton Butterworth explained, because he had been trying to win his publishing spurs at the time: 'The éclat of publishing such a book as yours was then of such moment to me that I was willing to offer terms which could, in the most favourable circumstances, only cover my outlay, but short of this, would inevitably entail a loss.'[7]

Churchill, however, was more concerned by Curtis Brown's failure to sell the American newspaper rights at all, let alone for the price he had forecast to his bankers: 'We have been hoping to make

---

* This was 6 per cent on new building work, 7½ per cent on alterations.

two or three thousand from this source,' he reported back to Clementine late in January from his temporary London base, The Ritz Hotel.[8]

Extracts from *The World Crisis* did start to appear in *The Times* in February 1923, but Churchill found himself forced on the defensive when they led to questions in Parliament and the Tory home secretary William Bridgeman referred in a speech to politicians enriching themselves using information gained through their public duties. In a long letter to the new prime minister Bonar Law, Churchill argued that many other politicians and soldiers had already published quotations from official documents, and it was unfair to expect a minister who held responsibility for such matters to be the only person prevented from doing so. He added in a postscript:

> The contracts on which my book is based were made before a word of it was written and leave me entirely free as to what is published. There is no obligation on me to publish any official document, and I derive no financial advantage from doing so. Whether the book succeeds or fails and whatever its contents, I am equally secured.[9]

No longer a minister and freed from any concerns about conflicts of interest, Churchill relished his return to the daily excitement of the world's stock markets. 'I am wondering whether you have got rid of the London & Rhod[esian],' he wrote to his brother Jack. 'There seems to be a good many transactions in them at 5/10½. Do exactly what you think fit. 6/- is better than 5/10. . . Why has Rezende jumped so much? A whole pound in a month? What about Courtaulds. I thought perhaps you could have nipped out at 66/-.' He pointed out that the French franc had weakened from 63 to 77 against sterling over the six weeks since he had laid his bet:

> Here again I leave it entirely to you. If there is a steady gradual fall I should hold on. If there is a sudden drop of four or five points it might be well to get out and come back in again for the

recovery. . . If there is a slow recovery, I should hope you could
get at not worse than 68. I am strongly of the opinion that the
Rühr business* will turn out ill for France.[10]

Success with speculation against the French franc made it tempting
to try the Deutschmark: 'What about selling a bear in marks?' he
asked Jack. 'France has got them by the balls. Write me a proposition; or if it is urgent sell £2,000 for the end of April. Act as you
think fit.'[11] He spent time at Jack's office on a visit at the end of
January, 'settling up a lot of business here and reconsidering most
of my investments', then returned to France, where he started
giving the trading orders himself: 'I should like you to sell the
Coats and buy me another 1,000 City Lights. For this purpose you
might take the balance from the February franc money wh[ich]
perhaps you can discount for me, as Vickers suggested. . . Wd you
advise my getting another 500 Mexican Eagles? If so sell enough of
the Imps** (there is a good profit on them) to cover the purchase.'[12]

Days later he was disconcerted to read in *The Times* of Cox &
Co.'s sudden collapse and rescue by Lloyds Bank. 'It makes me
shiver to think what we may have escaped,' he wrote immediately
to Jack. 'Fancy if they had impounded or embezzled my overdraft!
It is disconcerting to see how uncertain the ground is under one's
feet.'[13] He might have been even more concerned had he known
that a report commissioned by Lloyds revealed errors in almost a
quarter of Cox & Co.'s investment accounts, including three of
Churchill's holdings.[14]

Weakened by its clients' financial difficulties during the war, Cox
& Co. had compounded its problem by expensively rebuilding its
offices in Pall Mall and Gracechurch Street. When rumours of its

---

* France and Belgium occupied Germany's Rühr Valley in January 1923 in
response to the Weimar Republic's failure to continue reparation payments
due as a result of the First World War.
** Coats (J. & P. Coats), is a British textile company; City Lights an American
utility company; Mexican Eagles an American oil company; and Imps
(Imperial Tobacco) a British tobacco company.

difficulties surfaced during the summer of 1918, the bank had drawn on its strong political connections to ward off the Bank of England's inquiries.[15] The sale of its French arm in 1921 and a review of its Indian activities in 1922 signalled continuing problems. The end came suddenly in February 1923 when the Bank of England engineered an emergency rescue by Lloyds Bank, whose general manager insisted, for the record, that Lloyds acted only 'through a sense of public duty, and with marked lack of enthusiasm'.[16]

Churchill sympathized with his bank manager, but William Bernau made light of the change: 'As far as our customers are concerned, the only difference there will be is the further security of Lloyds' enormous funds. The same men will attend to them and the same facilities will be given to them. You can always write to me and look to me to carry on exactly as in the past.'[17]

Churchill's night-time activities in France centred on the Casino de Cannes and proved to be expensive. On 4 January he was up 25,000 francs, thanks to 'playing quite low', as he told Jack. The next day he still claimed to be ahead. Victor Cazalet recorded: 'Winston has taken to gambling with great earnestness. He plays twice daily and is now 20,000 up after a month's play. He does not play very high.'[18] Churchill's bank account records twenty-nine cash withdrawals at the casino during his stay, starting at 5,000 francs each, but mounting to 10,000 francs and finally to 20,000 francs by the time he left; in all, he withdrew 164,000 francs, the equivalent of £2,350.[19] Churchill made only one withdrawal of £300 elsewhere,* so perhaps the casino was the most convenient place to draw cash for everyday expenses. However, his own records of his spending in Cannes show an average of £75 a week, implying approximately £1,000 for his stay of three months; this leaves his casino losses at more than £1,500.[20]

Churchill's gambling was 'a source of deep anxiety' to Clementine. As their daughter Mary recalled: 'To her it was a senseless, almost wicked waste of money, and yet it was her fate in

---

* At the Cannes branch of Barclays Overseas Bank.

life to be surrounded by those who were drawn to it: her mother, her brother, her sister and, now, her husband were all, to varying degrees, gamblers.'[21]

The Churchills returned to London in time for the launch of the first volume of *The World Crisis*. Beforehand, Butterworth tried to reduce the author's advance, because the book had overrun in length. 'Let me put it this way,' he explained. 'If you placed a contract for twelve 20" guns for a battleship and subsequently decided to have 25" guns, you would not expect the original contract to stand.' Churchill batted away the suggestion and pointed to Butterworth's own strong sales predictions: 30,000–40,000 in Britain and 15,000 in America.

Publisher and author were to be disappointed. After four months, British sales of *The World Crisis* barely topped 10,000 copies.[22] Fortunately, Churchill had already persuaded his publishers to pay for a third volume, albeit on reduced terms.

Churchill had asked *The Times* for another £2,500 for the serialization rights, but the newspaper was not convinced. 'You will forgive me. . . in being quite frank in expressing the view that the sum of £2,500 you mention seems rather high in the face of what we have already paid, considering that when the negotiations were opened we thought we were to get the whole of your War memoirs,' came the reply, suggesting a reduced fee of £2,000.[23] As usual, Churchill suggested they split the difference.

The extra £250 counted because the bills for building work at Chartwell had started to arrive. Alarm bells ought to have begun ringing when Tilden's January account used a final cost of £12,000, not the £8,500 expected, to calculate his fee, but Churchill kept paying promptly until March, when the kitchen ceiling was found to be only nine feet high. 'Some other plans will have to be made or the cook will be unable to carry on under such conditions,' Churchill insisted in his first serious quarrel with the architect.[24] By July he had already paid £8,000, but Tilden had still to produce an estimate for the new south wing on which work had not yet started. 'I was hoping. . . that a sum of £1,500 would have completed the new wing, but my not very satisfactory interview with the builders yesterday. . . has disappointed me in this,'[25] Tilden confessed in August. Churchill used a figure of £2,000 for the wing in hurried calculations on the back of Tilden's letter to see whether he could afford to go ahead. Reluctantly he did so, calculating that the final cost had now risen to £11,700, excluding Tilden's fees. A week later, when the solution to the problem of the kitchen ceiling turned out to be another extra wing, it had risen to almost £13,000.[26]

In July 1923 Churchill suffered the indignity of having his finances publicly aired in court. Lord Alfred Douglas, the notorious son of the marquess of Queensbury and erstwhile lover of Oscar Wilde, had brought a libel suit against *The Morning Post*, which had accused Douglas of 'vile insults against the Jews' in his anti-Semitic magazine *Plain English*. Douglas claimed that Churchill and a 'clique of rich Jews' had conspired to enrich themselves after the Battle of Jutland in 1916. He maintained that these Jewish financiers (among them the late Sir Ernest Cassel, who had died in 1921) had bought shares heavily after sharp price falls in New York, when the press initially presented the battle as a serious British defeat. Douglas claimed that they had then sold these shares when prices rose sharply after Churchill, having been briefed by the Admiralty, drafted a public statement giving a more favourable outcome of the battle.

At the trial in July *The Morning Post*'s barrister put it to Douglas that he had written in relation to Churchill:

It is true that by most subtle means and by never allowing him more than a pony ahead, this ambitious and brilliant man, short of money and eager for power, was trapped by the Jews. After the Jutland business his house was furnished for him by Sir Ernest Cassel.

He asked whether Douglas had meant to imply that Churchill was financially indebted to the Jews?

'Yes, certainly,' Douglas replied.

'Who were the Jews in whose clutches he was?'

'Chiefly Cassel.'

Asked for his evidence, Douglas quoted a London surgeon Sir Alfred Fripp, who had told him that 'Cassel had given Mr Churchill £40,000 in one cheque'. However, Sir Ernest Cassel's former private secretary W. D. Geddes refuted the claim, testifying that Sir Ernest had neither bought nor sold any shares for months either side of the battle.[27]

The jury found that *The Morning Post* had technically committed a libel but awarded Douglas token damages of a farthing. After instructing a barrister to keep a watching brief on his behalf, Churchill was landed with a legal bill of £182.[28]

It was not the end of the saga. Angry that his barrister had not cross-examined Churchill, Douglas went on to repeat the libel deliberately in public and was arrested. Churchill was spared a much larger bill at the second trial when the attorney general ruled that the government should pay his legal costs (£650), as he had been carrying out work for the government at the time.

Examining him first for the Crown, Sir Douglas Hogg led Churchill through a series of pre-emptive disclosures: he admitted to a close friendship with Sir Ernest Cassel, a friend of his parents; to the fact that Sir Ernest had not charged him for looking after his investments; that he had often been a guest at Sir Ernest's Swiss villa; and that he had received £500 cash from Sir Ernest as a wedding present.

'Did Sir Ernest Cassel give you any furniture?' Sir Douglas asked.

'The foundation for that was that in 1905 I took a small house in South Bolton Street and Sir Ernest asked Lady Randolph whether he could furnish a library for me,' Churchill replied. 'She consented.'[29]

By the time Douglas's less-experienced counsel started his own cross-examination, there was little to come out: Churchill happily agreed with counsel's suggestion that *The World Crisis* had earned him £15,000 and managed to avoid any reference to Sir Ernest Cassel coming to his rescue in 1921, when he stepped in to buy Lord Gerald Wellesley's lease in Hyde Park.[30]

While Churchill's finances were being discussed in court, two British oil companies approached him with a business opportunity. Shell Transport & Trading and Burmah Oil wanted him to lobby ministers to allow them to purchase the government's controlling stake in the Anglo-Persian Oil Company. Anglo-Persian had been acquired during Churchill's watch at the Admiralty in order to secure fuel supplies for a fleet that was increasingly powered by oil rather than coal. The oil companies suggested a fee for Churchill of £5,000. Steeped in the Gladstonian notion that a politician ought to be 'disinterested' in making a personal gain from his public duty, Churchill sought clearance from Stanley Baldwin, the new Conservative prime minister, before accepting. Baldwin indicated general support for the plan, but Churchill did not tell him 'at this preliminary & non-committal stage' of his own possible employment by the oil companies. 'It is a question of how to arrange it so as to leave no just ground of criticism,' Churchill told Clementine in a letter marked 'secret'.[31]

Churchill had already begun to make a contribution to the project by the time he left a fortnight later to spend time in the southwest of France on the duke of Westminster's four-masted yacht, *The Flying Cloud*, which had a crew of forty. Afterwards, he warned the duke that he might not be able to return as planned for a second visit, this time to the duke's hunting lodge nearby at Mimizan, on account of 'important business (oleaginous)'.[32] In the event he did make the return trip at the beginning of October, just as the oil companies sent their cheque for £5,000 to his brother Jack's address.[33]

The money went straight into Churchill's account at Vickers da Costa, rather than his bank. It was used to back Churchill's underwriting, for a fee of 2 per cent, of £50,000 of a new bond issued by

The Daily Mail and General Trust, in which the sponsors* had been asked to reserve him space.

The duke's lodge lay within reach of the Mons Detrimont Casino at Biarritz, to which Churchill made a return visit for a celebration of his fee. He was less successful than on the first holiday with the duke in September, when he had won almost 30,000 francs (and the duke more than half a million).[34] This time he withdrew 85,000 francs in cash at the casino window, but deposited only 6,224 francs at his bank on return to London. The loss took the cumulative cost of Churchill's forays into gambling during 1923 well above £2,000 – more than the price quoted for Chartwell's new wing.[35]

As a result, Clementine began to question her husband's stewardship of his inheritance, which had been supposed to banish their money worries for ever. Passing over his losses, Churchill bridled at her suggestion that it was being frittered away: 'The estate at the moment is at least as large as it was when I succeeded, but part is invested in Chartwell instead of in shares.' It was an 'economically self-contained' home that they could keep for many years before handing it on to Randolph: 'It will have cost us £20,000 and will be worth at least £15,000 apart from a fancy price [i.e. unless someone was so keen on the house they paid a special premium price].'

Royalties from *The World Crisis* would pay enough to finish it, he argued, and would keep them going for another six or seven months:[36] 'I have already planned out the third volume & anticipate no difficulty in completing it by April. It is really quite reasonable to count on £6,000 from this – perhaps £8,000.'[37] They would need £10,000 a year to meet their living costs, he calculated. This was no mean sum: in the mid 1920s only 1,300 people in Britain enjoyed an after-tax income of more than £10,000 a year. For each of the first three years of the 1920s, Churchill himself had declared a pre-tax income of just under £10,000 to the Inland Revenue, and had been left with an average of £6,500 after tax.[38] He did his best to reassure Clementine:

---

* British, Foreign & Colonial Corporation Ltd. Churchill earned £1,000 from the underwriting. See CHAR 1/170/21.

Add to this my darling yr courage & goodwill and I am certain
that we can make ourselves a good, permanent resting place,
so far as the money side of this uncertain & transitory world
is concerned. But if you set yourself against Chartwell, or lose
heart, or bite your bread & butter & yr pig then it only means
further instability, recasting of plans & further expense &
worry.[39]

Back in Britain, during the second half of October 1923, Churchill
resumed work on the oil merger, convinced it would strengthen the
security of the British fleet's oil supplies. However, he swiftly dis-
tanced himself from the deal shortly afterwards when Stanley
Baldwin surprised him (and everyone else) by calling a general
election at the end of November. Carefully filing his version of
events in case he should face accusations of impropriety later,
Churchill transferred £4,000 of his fee from his stockbrokers[40] back
to his bank and resumed campaigning.

Baldwin pledged to reintroduce tariffs to fight high levels of
unemployment, but this put strains on the unity of the Conservatives
while at the same time providing common cause in opposition to
both wings of the Liberal Party and to Labour. Still unable to
embrace the idea of introducing tariffs, Churchill stood for the last
time as a Liberal candidate, but signalled his rapprochement with
the right on other matters of policy by choosing to fight in Leicester
West, a Labour stronghold where he hoped that the Conservatives
might allow him a free run.

It proved the most uncomfortable election of his career, as he
told Brendan Bracken,* his new, twenty-three-year-old aide.

---

* Brendan Bracken (1901–58), born in Ireland; introduced to Churchill by
J. L. Garvin, editor of the *Observer*, 1923; started work at publisher Eyre &
Spottiswoode 1923, relaunching its *Illustrated Review* as *English Life* 1924;
launched *The Banker* 1926; acquired half-share of *The Economist* with Sir
Henry Strakosch 1928; MP 1929–51; parliamentary private secretary to prime
minister 1940–1; minister of information 1941–5; First Lord of the Admiralty
1945; chairman, *Financial Times* 1945–1958; viscount 1952.

Bracken recorded 'a travelling crowd of socialist rowdies' that disrupted his meetings, 'howling a series of monotonous chants such as "What about the Dardan-eels?" "What about Gally-Polly?" "What about the fifty thousand quid Cassel gave you?"'[41]

Just before polling day, Churchill bet Lord Beaverbrook that Asquith, the Liberal leader, would return as prime minister and that the Labour Party would not form a government. He was wrong on both counts: the Tories remained the largest party with 258 seats nationally, but failed to secure a Commons majority; Labour gained 191 seats and the Liberal Party trailed in third position with only 157. It was a hung parliament.

Churchill was comfortably beaten by the Labour Party candidate in Leicester and could only look on as Labour's leader Ramsay MacDonald formed a minority government. For the second time in his life Churchill began to prepare for a switch of allegiance. Twenty years earlier, when he had no land and little money, he had left the Tories, the party of the landed gentry, to join the Liberals, the party of enterprise and new money. Now with some modest land and much more money he prepared for a return journey back to the Tories.

Meanwhile, the Chartwell building project remained fraught with difficulties. Early in 1924 an account from the architect Philip Tilden showed that its costs had reached almost £18,000,[42] but the work was far from finished. Churchill decided not to share the news with Clementine that Knight Frank & Rutley had just valued the property at only £12,000 on completion.[43]

'Yesterday we motored to Biarritz & raided the Casino,' he told her instead from Mimizan, where he had returned for the New Year. 'Play was meagre, but after some vicissitudes I collected five *milles* [5,000 francs] & levanted with them.'[44] 17,000 francs was deposited in Churchill's bank account.

Once home, he concentrated on churning out newspaper articles to repair his finances. In February the Tory leader Stanley Baldwin announced that he would drop his support for tariff reform, which eased Churchill's passage towards the Tories. Invited by the Liberals to fight a by-election in Bristol, Churchill declined. Instead he stood as an 'anti-socialist independent' at another by-election in the Abbey division of Westminster but his hopes of remaining unopposed by an official Conservative candidate were dashed. He was encouraged by Baldwin's tacit encouragement and by the support of both the Rothermere and Beaverbrook newspapers, although the official Conservative candidate narrowly won. Churchill described the experience as 'incomparably the most exciting, stirring, sensational election I have ever fought'.[45]

This burst of political activity put paid to any chance of the final volume of *The World Crisis* appearing that October. Having first secured the agreement of *The Times*, Churchill told his publisher that the book would have to be postponed until March 1925. Butterworth allowed Churchill to hold on to the first advance which had been paid on signature of his contract, but the postponement of the second advance which was due on publication left an awkward gap in his cash flow. Churchill's agent Curtis Brown suggested that he could plug this gap with a volume of autobiography which he could conjure up by assembling some of his old articles. 'Butterworth doesn't like the idea of this book coming out ahead of the third volume, but my surmise is that Mr Churchill may insist upon it for the sake of quick cash,'[46] Curtis Brown confided to the American publisher Charles Scribner. However, Churchill kept this idea in reserve for another day.

He certainly needed money. He had to pay not only Chartwell's escalating costs, but various tax bills of almost £5,000 would also fall due in the next two years.[47] At least the Churchill family was finally able to move in to part of the remodelled Chartwell during April 1924, although Clementine was pointedly absent visiting her mother in Dieppe. 'You will be pleased with the result. It is majestic,' Churchill wrote to her. 'Only one thing lack these banks of green – The Pussy Cat who is their Queen.'[48]

The following month, however, relations between Churchill and his architect reached breaking point. Churchill learned that

Tilden had charged for the costs of correcting his own mistakes, ignoring the cap on fees that they had agreed. Churchill commissioned an independent investigation by John Leaning & Sons, a firm of London surveyors. To brief them, he produced a history of events covering six pages: 'Mr Churchill pressed Mr Tilden for personal assurances that the cost would not exceed £7,000,' it read in part, 'and Mr Tilden freely and repeatedly gave these assurances both to Mr Churchill and in the presence of others.'

Churchill claimed Tilden had kept to this figure until May 1923, at which point he had announced that the roof alone had cost an extra £1,000; next Churchill had had to insist on an extra tower because Tilden's original plan 'would not be satisfactory or even presentable'. The thus revised cost of £8,700 soon emerged to be 'illusory': 'The estimates were raised week after week, and it soon became certain that £11,000 or even £12,000 would not see the completion of the work,' Churchill continued. To add insult to injury, 'the walls of the nursery wing were found to be defective. The water poured through the roof and gable at this end of the house and defaced all the plaster work which had been done.' He concluded that the final cost now looked more like £18,000.[49]

The accounts became hopelessly tangled, the more so because Churchill now insisted on paying the contractors directly rather than through Tilden, as had originally been the case. For his part Tilden refused to co-operate with Churchill's investigating surveyors and declared that any discussion of his own fees was off-limits.[50]

To Churchill's disappointment, his own surveyors largely endorsed Tilden's version of the costs incurred to date, at £17,500 before taking into account the architect's fees. As a result, they found that Churchill still owed the builders a final payment of £1,183. Grudgingly, he offered 1,000 guineas (equivalent to £1,050).

In all, Churchill's bank accounts reveal that he made payments of more than £23,000 to cover the first two years of alterations to Chartwell. Adding in the purchase price, the Chartwell dream had cost him close to £30,000 – almost three-fifths of his Garron Tower inheritance. Some consolation came when Sir Howard Frank confirmed to Churchill's lawyers that Lord Randolph's will trust could justifiably lend £7,000 against a mortgage on Chartwell, rather than £4,000. Churchill increased his loan from the trust by the difference, while insuring the property for £20,000.[51]

Late in September 1924 Ramsay MacDonald's minority Labour government lost support in the House of Commons. Churchill inched closer to the Conservative Party, telling a meeting of its Scottish followers that no great 'gulf of principle' existed between Liberals and Conservatives when it was compared to the threat from socialism. Days before Parliament's dissolution early in October, Epping's Conservative Association adopted Churchill as its 'Constitutionalist' candidate.

In the general election that followed Churchill gained a large majority. Nationally, the Tories won 419 seats to Labour's 151, while the Liberals fell to 42. The Conservatives were back in power. The new prime minister Stanley Baldwin summoned Churchill to see him in London and asked whether he would serve 'as chancellor'.

'Of the duchy?' Churchill asked.

'No, of the exchequer.'[52]

12

'No more champagne is to be bought'
Chancellor under Pressure, 1925–8

Exchange rate $5 = £1
Inflation multiples: US x 14; UK x 50

C HURCHILL WAS CONSCIOUS that as chancellor of the exchequer his financial habits would have to change. As soon as he was appointed in November 1924, he wrote to William Bernau, his bank manager, announcing that he planned to repay all his £22,000 of loans and overdraft.[1] He instructed his brother Jack to sell enough shares to produce the necessary funds, leaving £7,000-worth of holdings in case he needed to secure a fresh overdraft in the future.

A few days later Churchill was disconcerted to hear that Jack's sales had left him at least £10,000 short of his target. Embarrassed, Churchill had to borrow an extra £1,300 from his father's trust. He also had to persuade Bernau not only to keep his overdraft in place, but to lend him extra money temporarily until three magazines had paid their fees of £1,500 for articles he had recently written.[2]

Sussex Square was sold for £10,750, thanks to the Churchills' entitlement to an official residence in Downing Street; however, most of the proceeds from the sale had to go back to the family trust which had made the purchase; the rest was required to furnish the Churchills' new home.[3]

All in all, it was an inauspicious start for the chancellor. His new post brought a salary of £5,000 a year, but Churchill entered office

164

with an overdraft of £6,000; he was borrowing £15,000 from family trusts; bills were still arriving for yet more work at Chartwell; and Eric Nonweiler, his tax adviser at Lloyds Bank, warned him that he faced tax bills of £16,000 over the next three years.[4]

The moment he became chancellor, Churchill told his publishers that the final volume of *The World Crisis* would have to 'remain in its box until the skies are clearer'.[5] Even before then, Nonweiler had been suggesting temporary retirement as an author as a possible way to reduce his bills, because any payments arriving after 'cessation' would be treated as capital receipts rather than income and therefore left untaxed.

Churchill understood that it was a delicate matter for a chancellor of the exchequer to exploit what his adviser clearly labelled a 'loophole',[6] so on 5 December, shortly after taking office, he summoned the chairman of the Inland Revenue Sir Richard Hopkins* for a private discussion. Six years younger than his political master, Hopkins was nonetheless experienced enough to understand the sensitivities involved and asked two senior officials to advise him how he might best respond after a second meeting with Churchill inside three days. Sir Richard drafted his response several times before writing it in his own hand on unofficial notepaper, which he headed 'Private & Confidential':

> As I understand the matter, you feel yourself precluded by the responsibilities of your office from continuing to exercise the profession of author or indeed to write for profit in any way & you intend merely to complete certain minor outstanding engagements entered into before joining the Government and another more important engagement – the remaining volume of your current work – which you find you could not cancel with justice to the interests of your publisher. You intend

---

* R. N. V. Hopkins (1880–1955), joined the Inland Revenue, Britain's tax-collecting agency, 1902; chairman 1922–7; joined HM Treasury 1927, permanent secretary 1942–5; knighted 1920.

further, I understand, to assign on sale* any royalties to which you may be entitled.

Upon the assumption that before the 6th April 1926, you have completed the outstanding contracts & received payment therefore, and given full effect to your other intentions, & thus definitively ceased as [an] author, it is in my judgement (reached after taking careful advice) quite clear that, under the law, you will not be liable to assessment to Income Tax for the year 1926/7 in respect of profits from the profession of author.[7]

Nonweiler told Churchill that the immediate benefit of this manoeuvre would be to halve his next income tax payment to £2,000.[8] Churchill carried on writing for the press right up to the deadline of 5 April: 'I have just polished off two more articles to help pay the Income tax,' he told Clementine in mid-March. 'Perhaps I may get another one out of myself this afternoon or tomorrow morning.'[9]

As Churchill prepared for his first Budget, Chartwell continued to be an unwelcome distraction. Water streamed into the building on a February site meeting that he attended, but nobody could agree who was liable to pay for the repair. 'According to your view, the Architect is apparently responsible for nothing,' Churchill complained to Philip Tilden. 'If this is your doctrine, it appears to me very extraordinary – so extraordinary that it ought to be tested.'[10]

Churchill's first Budget was dominated by one political issue: whether or not Britain should rejoin the gold standard at sterling's pre-war rate of exchange. Most opinion in the Treasury and City supported the orthodox view that the move was essential to restore Britain's pre-eminence in the world of finance. However,

---

* As part of his 'retirement' as an author, Churchill was to 'assign' any royalties still to be earned by the books he had already written. He planned to sign them over to a new trust for his youngest daughter Mary, who was not a beneficiary of Churchill's Elder Children's Settlement (she had not been born when the trust was formed early in 1922).

a clutch of economists led by J. M. Keynes warned that the result would be depression and unemployment. Churchill agonized over the decision, before accepting the Treasury orthodoxy. He later admitted it was one of his greatest mistakes: 'I had no special comprehension of the currency problem and therefore fell into the hands of the experts, as I never did later where military matters were concerned.'[11]

Churchill was on more familiar territory dealing with changes to Britain's personal tax regime. He aimed to 'stabilize' society by reducing taxes on 'active' wealth at the expense of 'inherited' wealth. 'The doctor, engineer and lawyer earning 3 or 4 thousand a year and with no capital will get the greatest relief,' he told Parliament. 'The possessor of unearned income derived from a capital estate of 2 or 3 hundred thousands, the smallest relief; while the millionaire will remain substantially liable to the existing scales of high taxation.'[12]

By the summer of 1925 the chancellor's salary was proving wholly inadequate to cope with the constant stream of bills emanating from Chartwell. The pace of Churchill's official duties slackened after the Budget, but his 'cessation' as an author prohibited him from finishing *The World Crisis*, the most obvious way of reducing his overdraft, which was again over its limit.[13] As a stop-gap Churchill borrowed another £4,400 from family trusts, confessing to Jack that the days of plenty of 1921 already seemed like a distant memory: 'We are having a great economy rush here and putting down things in all directions.'[14] Clubs, cows and polo ponies all found themselves in the firing line,[15] but this first economy drive made little difference. If by the end of 1925 Churchill's overdraft was below the (raised) £7,000 limit, it was because he had sold more of his few remaining shares.

Christmas at Chartwell revealed more leaks in the roof, forcing the children to leave the nursery whenever it rained. 'All the three rooms, the Butler's, the Cook's and the Housemaid's are dripping wet,' Churchill complained to his surveyor. He had reached the end of his tether and finally called in his lawyers.[16] In response, Philip Tilden briefed his own surveyors:

> Mrs Churchill, who has great influence over Mr Churchill, has given it as her opinion that the house is falling down. I want you professionally and independently to make an examination of this concrete, as I will not be played about with over this house, which has been excellently built.[17]

With Jack's agreement as co-trustee, Churchill borrowed another £2,200 from his father's trust while these arguments continued, taking the trust's loan up to £10,000.

Clementine took the children to the French coast and from Downing Street a Churchill burdened by money worries wrote to her: 'How I wish I was with you all – reviving in Riviera brightness, with just an occasional flutter at *trente et quarante*, in the evenings or even the afternoon as soon as they open.'[18]

In March 1926 Churchill revived himself with the help of an 'Arnold Alpine Sun Lamp'[19] as another Budget approached. It was followed in May by the General Strike when workers downed tools in key industries such as the railways, the docks, and electricity and gas supply. The government enlisted volunteers to maintain some semblance of normality and, in the absence of normal newspapers due to striking printers, Churchill oversaw production of the government's short-lived substitute, the *British Gazette*.

By the time the strike came to an end ten days later, Churchill's overdraft had risen above £6,000.[20] There was tax to pay, as well as a pile of bills from Chartwell. His credit exhausted with both Lloyds Bank and his father's trust, Churchill realized that something had to give. The only realistic solution was to abandon his eighteen-month-old 'cessation' as an author so that he could complete *The World Crisis*.

The challenge was to do this without re-triggering the tax bill that he had so recently avoided by retiring and which he was in no position to pay. On 9 June, while Jack negotiated a fourth emergency loan from his father's trust's lawyers,[21] Churchill discussed the difficulty with Sir Richard Hopkins, the Inland Revenue's chairman. Sir Richard recorded Churchill's request in a handwritten note, which he stored in a special file marked 'Semi-official correspondence to be kept by the Private Secretary':[22]

> In December 1924 he made a definite decision to cease all [writing] activities and took immediate steps to do so. He had no intention of resuming until he left office. He then understood that any other course was barred by government policy. He now finds that publication of books by the Prime Minister and Lord Birkenhead* introduce a new factor: he has now ascertained that mere publication of a book is not barred.
>
> The two books he proposes to publish were mainly complete when he ceased. They can be completed in spare time in his vacation and in subsequent week-ends. I told him that I would consult....[23]

After a second meeting with Churchill, which he recorded in a note marked 'Secret', Sir Richard sent to his chancellor a handwritten draft of 'the sort of letter which I suggest you might write to me'. Churchill left the chairman's opening paragraph untouched:

> At the time when I took office, as Chancellor of the Exchequer, understanding that by the very fact of holding such an office I was precluded from continuing in any way my previous profession as a journalist and author, I took immediate steps to wind my profession up. I ceased all journalistic work & although I had entered into contracts to publish the books both of which were nearly completed I cancelled the contracts, forgoing both serial rights & royalties.

---

* In 1926 Prime Minister Stanley Baldwin published *On England*; Lord Birkenhead published *Famous Trials of History*.

Hopkins suggested that Churchill should limit himself to just completing *The World Crisis*, but Churchill was satisfied that this draft letter left him greater flexibility to do more if needed, especially where it said: 'I have no other work of authorship (or journalism) in view, except that possibly I may give permission for re-publication of some old articles (the copyright of which I had treated as worthless) & receive some *honorarium* therefore.' He removed from Hopkins's draft any suggestion that he would not pursue a newspaper serialization.

The letter's real rub came in its final paragraph, which Hopkins had drafted as: 'I assume that if I take this course that my past liability will not be altered, but I will be glad if you let me know authoritatively on this subject so that I may know just where I stand.' Churchill changed the final phrase, substituting 'what my position is under the law & the existing practice'.[24]

On receipt of Churchill's amended letter, Hopkins again consulted his senior staff. A Mr Shaw summed up the prevailing mood: 'Granted a cessation, subsequent events cannot transform the cessation into a continuance.'[25] This was the conclusion for which Hopkins and Churchill had hoped: the tax Churchill had saved when he retired as an author just over a year earlier would not have to be repaid now that he was taking up the profession once more. Accordingly, Hopkins wrote to Churchill again, privately and on unheaded notepaper:

> Dear Chancellor, The question of your liability to Income Tax is in law, as you are of course aware, a matter for determination by the appropriate body of Income Tax Commissioners. I have however consulted our experts as to your case (as set forth in your letter of the 20 inst) in relation to the relevant law & practice. In their opinion, which we as a Board share, there was a cessation and the past liability would not be altered by the circumstances now contemplated.[26]

Churchill found it more difficult to accelerate the cash advances due from his publishers for the third volume of *The World Crisis*, which the contracts stipulated to be payable on publication, but which he now needed to be paid straightaway. Scribner's Sons would pay only on publication[27] and Butterworth told Churchill's agent that he would charge interest if he had to pay earlier. '£2,000 is of course a small matter to Mr Churchill, but to me the loss of its use is a big matter,' he claimed, seriously misjudging Churchill's situation.[28]

Churchill was forced to take on another emergency bank loan in July. This took his borrowings from bank and family trusts above £30,000.[29] Cornered, he abandoned his earlier assurances to Butterworth that he would not sell the newspaper serialization rights. The editor of *The Times* agreed to revive its fee of £2,500, but then Churchill had to go to the prime minister, somewhat warily, for permission. Stanley Baldwin's agreement proved the easiest step of all. 'I had some conversation with the Prime Minister and found he considered it perfectly proper for me to publish the book in serial form,' he was able to tell Butterworth.[30]

Writing was not going to be enough on its own, so Churchill used the parliamentary break of summer 1926 to devise a second, more stringent economy drive at Chartwell. This time all the cattle, chickens, pigs and ponies (bar one in foal) were to be sold; the family was to spend Christmas in London and from the New Year Chartwell was be let. Monthly household expenses (which covered food, wages, maintenance and cars, running at nearly £480 a month), were to be halved. 'The following should be tried at once,' he proposed to Clementine:

> a. No more champagne is to be bought. Unless special directions are given only white or red wine, or whisky and soda will be offered at luncheon, or dinner. The Wine Book to be shown to me every week. No more port is to be opened without special instructions.*

---

* The cost of wine and spirits 'paid for' at Chartwell during 1926 came to £309, but Churchill's secretary underlined the distinction between 'paid for' and 'consumed'. CHAR 1/192/14.

b. Cigars must be reduced to four a day. None should be put on
the table; but only produced out of my case . . .

There was to be no fish course when the Churchills ate by themselves, which would be most of the time, because visitors were to
be invited 'very rarely, if at all'. The secretaries should choose the
most urgent £1,500 of bills for payment, but the rest would have to
wait. 'Every new bill as it occurs is to be shown to me,' Churchill
announced to his wife. 'Nothing expensive is to be bought, by
either of us, without talking it over.'[31] Since the move to Chartwell
two years earlier, Clementine had requested transfers of no less
than £13,000 to her account, over and above her normal allowances, which suggested that she was not such an 'economical cat'.
Wisely, however, she made no written reply to Churchill's suggestions, but took herself off on a shooting holiday in Scotland, where
she waited for this new regime to unravel as quickly as the first.

The cattle and ponies were sold and the groom was sacked, but
Chartwell was never let. According to Churchill's daughter Mary, just
four at the time, there appeared to be no shortage of food or drink,
either. Her father did forego his usual summer holiday in France:
instead he confined himself to writing, painting and laying some
bricks at Chartwell. 'The output was colossal,' recalled Churchill's new
parliamentary secretary Robert Boothby, after a visit to Chartwell
that summer. 'Yet he always found time, plenty of time, to talk.'[32] By
the end of October the third volume of *The World Crisis* had grown
to a longer than expected 230,000 words.[33]

Early in 1927 Churchill went on a European journey with his fif-
teen-year-old son Randolph. He took the proofs of *The World
Crisis* with him for a final polish, then dispatched the corrections
from Genoa before setting off on a cruise around the Mediterranean.
'Thank God the book is finished,' he told Clementine. 'It is now off
my hands for good or ill for ever. It will I hope secure us an easy
two years without having to derange our Chartwell plans: & by that
time I will think of something else.'[34]

Clementine might have been more reassured had the trip not included the detour on the way home of a pig-hunt in Normandy with the duke of Westminster and his new girlfriend Coco Chanel. Nearby at Dieppe was the Casino R. Ferrand, where Churchill proceeded to lose an estimated £350.[35] 'The Sherwoods [Sherwood Starr shares] have lost over £1,000 since we last parted,' Churchill wrote home, 'so do not fret about my peccadillos [*sic*] at the Casino.' Overall, he argued, their finances were 'by no means in an unsatisfactory state. Indeed I am hoping that with care & prudence we may have a couple of peaceful years, & consolidate our position at Chartwell.'[36]

When he returned, *The Times* began printing extracts from *The World Crisis* and judged this final volume to be the strongest of the three. This view was endorsed by the book-buying public. Sales were strong in Britain from the outset, reaching 12,000 by the middle of the year.[37] They started slowly in America, but soon picked up. Churchill instructed his tax adviser to include profits of more than £9,000 in his tax return.[38]

Chancellor Churchill's 1927 Budget was dominated by the £30 million hole left in the government's finances by the previous year's General Strike. Senior Treasury officials advised Churchill to borrow the whole amount, but Churchill won Prime Minister Baldwin's agreement to a cut in government and defence spending, while he also raised taxes on tyres, wines and tobacco. Baldwin greeted Churchill's Budget speech as 'a masterpiece of cleverness and ingenuity', but Churchill doubted whether he had really helped to drag the economy out of its post-war malaise. 'This debt and taxation lie like a vast wet blanket across the whole process of creating new wealth by new enterprise,' he told a senior aide.[39] It went against his instincts, and in the summer he supported a large cut in local taxes or rates paid by factories and farmers, the 'de-rating scheme' suggested by a young Conservative MP, Harold Macmillan.

Meanwhile, the chancellor's own finances were in need of a boost before the holiday season began. It came in part from Bernau, who conceded a temporary increase in Churchill's overdraft limit (now up to £9,000), and in part from Butterworth, who agreed to accelerate Churchill's next royalty payment, otherwise not due until October.[40] Final bills remained at Chartwell, where Philip Tilden suspected further allegations of falling plaster from the ceilings were in fact a tactic to delay payment; when dry rot was discovered Tilden blamed Churchill's carpenter for using soft woods. He then abruptly declared his own role at Chartwell to be 'closed'. There were renewed threats of legal action on both sides, but the financial trail disappears at this point because Churchill's bank accounts for the last part of 1927 and 1928 are missing from his archive. Already, however, Chartwell and its furnishings had cost at least £40,000 – three times Churchill's original estimate.[41]

Churchill urgently needed to find a new way to supplement his ministerial salary. Without using his agent, he approached Butterworth and *The Times* in November, proposing an extra book in *The World Crisis* series to cover the aftermath of the war: their response was enthusiastic. A rather demotivated Curtis Brown was left to approach Charles Scribner for the American rights:

> Doubtless you have heard that the Rt. Hon. Winston Churchill is at work on a book called *Aftermath* that serves as a conclusion to his *World Crisis* series. He thinks he is going to keep it down to 100,000 words, but I doubt that. You know how keen he is on advances, and will understand why it is that I have to ask £1,000 advance on 20% on this new book.[42]

Butterworth and *The Times*[43] accepted Churchill's proposed completion date of 1928, but soon afterwards a more lucrative offer of £6,000 arrived from Ray Long,* the head of William

---

* Ray Long (1878–1935), reporter *Indianapolis News* 1900; editor-in-chief International Magazine Company 1919–31, publisher 1931–5; bankrupt 1933; committed suicide 1935.

Hearst's* International Magazine Company stable. He wanted a series of twelve articles to publish in their magazines on both sides of the Atlantic.[44] Churchill decided to postpone *The Aftermath* until September 1929, leaving him time to finish the articles. 'The General Election will almost certainly be over by then,' he explained to Butterworth, anxious not to return the advance on signature, 'and if I were out of office a great deal more freedom could be used in the telling of the tale.'[45]

Backed up by *The Times*, Butterworth called the chancellor at the Treasury to change his mind – and he knew just how to do it: he offered an extra £1,500 in cash if Churchill stuck to the original 1928 deadline for *The Aftermath*. Churchill persuaded Ray Long to accept a first batch of only four articles, and on subjects that required minimal research ('Eminent personages'); he then accepted Butterworth's money:

> After careful reflection, I am prepared to try to work to the timetable you suggested in your long letter. I cannot however give any binding guarantee other than a provision for the return of the advance if publication has to stand over till 1929. But this is a fairly good spur, you will have to be content with it. Now let me have the contract.[46]

Churchill still needed yet another loan in March 1927 from Lord Randolph's trust, but Butterworth's first cheque for *The Aftermath* arrived just in time to help pay some pressing bills, even if these did not include Churchill's super-tax bill which was already overdue by four months.[47] 'Everything is v[er]y comfortable in the house and seems to go with the utmost smoothness,' he reported happily to Clementine. 'Butterworth has sent the extra £1,500 advance on *The*

---

* William Randolph Hearst (1863–1951), president *San Francisco Examiner* (owned by his father); introduced banner headlines 1887; controlled twenty daily, eleven Sunday newspapers (in thirteen US cities), magazine and film interests by late 1920s; fortunes declined during the Depression until a court-enforced reordering in 1937.

Aftermath: & I have sent my first 2 articles (£1,000) to America – so that we can jog along. But August, Sept & Oct will be months of hard work at the book.'[48]

After a fourth Budget that concentrated on implementing Macmillan's de-rating scheme, Churchill spent the summer of 1928 reining in military spending, based on an assumption (to be tested each year) that Britain would not be engaged 'in any great war in the next decade'. Afterwards he settled down at Chartwell for a busy holiday season spent writing, in preparation for which he had secured help from extra secretaries and from a team of researchers led by Brigadier General Edmonds, the army's senior historian.[49] Edmonds had, in turn, recruited Owen O'Malley, a former Foreign Office official, who had been suspended for speculating on the French franc – not a serious crime in the eyes of his new employer.

Churchill gave O'Malley a list of official documents relevant to *The Aftermath* and O'Malley asked his former employer at the Foreign Office to send over copies. However, the list of documents was reduced considerably, apparently on the direct orders of Sir Austen Chamberlain, the foreign secretary. As reported to O'Malley, Sir Austen also insisted that Churchill submit his manuscript 'for careful scrutiny' by the Foreign Office's historical adviser before publication.

Regarding this as a serious threat to his future literary livelihood, Churchill crafted a response for his secretary to sign, making it clear that he was quite capable of deciding for himself, as a minister, whether a passage was contentious or not. Foreign Office mandarins beat a temporary retreat, but later asked for proofs of the book when its launch date was announced in the press. This time, Churchill intervened personally with Sir Austen, agreeing that the Foreign Office should see the text in advance, but that any disputed passages would be ironed out in private between them.[50]

'The beginning is the difficult part of a book,' Churchill told Clementine after completing 3,000 words early in August.[51] By the end of the month, he had reached 35,000 of the 100,000 words required, but was already worried about the timetable. A September visitor, James Scrymgeour-Wedderburn, described the Chartwell holiday routine:

> [Churchill] works at bricklaying four hours a day, and lays 90 bricks an hour which is a very high output. He also spends a considerable time on a history of post-war Europe which he is writing. His ministerial work comes down from the Treasury every day, and he has to give some more hours to that. It is a marvel how much time he gives to his guests, talking sometimes for an hour after lunch and much longer after dinner.[52]

Although he reached 70,000 words by the end of September, Churchill knew that there would be no time for 'polishing' even if he did complete his quota by the October deadline. He therefore set about securing a postponement from Butterworth without losing his bonus for completion: he could of course meet the deadline if absolutely necessary, he told his publisher, but they would both gain if he took a little longer to add the extra 30,000 words that would justify a higher cover price. 'Pray turn these matters over carefully in your mind,' he urged. 'Meanwhile I am forging ahead.'[53] He snatched odd moments at the book during the autumn parliamentary season, then told the editor of *The Times* that he would have most of the text ten days after Christmas and the rest a week later.[54]

Increasingly convinced that the Conservatives would lose the 1929 general election, Churchill spent part of the autumn lining up future writing contracts to compensate for the loss of his ministerial salary. His own preference was for an 'autobiographical book', but his agent Curtis Brown suggested a fortnightly newspaper column written for worldwide syndication that could make '£300 to £400 per article. . . providing the subjects were of international interest, and providing you had, meanwhile, made a visit to America.'[55] Then Churchill's former agent A. P. Watt suggested a subject that had long interested Churchill: a biography of his ancestor John Churchill, 1st duke of Marlborough.*

Watt unveiled a joint offer of £8,000 in advances, made by Hodder & Stoughton in Britain and Longman Green in America. 'No doubt better terms can be obtained,'[56] Churchill told Clementine, knowing that Butterworth had yet to make an offer. 'You do drive a hard bargain,' Butterworth complained, before matching his rivals' bids and pointing out that his would not involve any commission.[57] Hodder responded straightaway with a higher offer, but Churchill told both early in January 1929 that because Parliament had resumed he was too busy to decide for the time being.

Weeks later, as he prepared his fifth Budget, two more offers arrived. The first, £10,000 for British Empire rights alone, came from a textbook publisher, George Harrap,** who was keen to break into the publishing mainstream.[58] The second offer, from Ferris Greenslet at the American publishers Houghton Mifflin, was $12,500 for the US rights on their own.[59]

Once the Budget was out of the way, Churchill summoned Harrap to Chartwell to set out his terms: he wanted a single contract worth at least £15,000 to cover both the US and British markets. Pointing Harrap confidently towards Houghton Mifflin as a willing American partner, he left to campaign in the general election, which had been called for May.

It was a surprise to Churchill and Harrap when Greenslet returned to Boston, refusing to pay a dollar more. Undeterred, Harrap asked Churchill for a month in which to find a replacement in New York. Churchill insisted on receiving a firm proposal from him for the British market first and Harrap responded by adding a generous five-year period for the work to be written.[60] Still on the

---

* First suggested in 1898 by a small publisher, Nisbet & Co.; revived in 1924, but ruled out by Churchill's appointment as chancellor of the exchequer.
** George Harrap (1867–1938), managing director, George G. Harrap & Co. 1901; launched *Harrap's Standard French Dictionary*; regarded as 'a bit of a rough diamond' by Britain's gentlemanly publishing fraternity. See D. Flower, *Fellows in Foolscap*, p. 147.

campaign trail, Churchill warned his old publisher Butterworth, who was in New York looking for his own US partner, that he was minded to settle with Harrap and deal with America separately after the election. Butterworth pleaded for a few days' grace, but the cable that reached Churchill shortly afterwards came from Charles Scribner, not Butterworth. Acting independently for the first time, Scribner offered $25,000 for the US rights, double Houghton Mifflin's price. Realizing that Harrap and Scribner together would take him to his £15,000 target, Churchill dismissed Butterworth, his publisher for more than a decade with little ceremony: 'Am now in possession of an offer from Scribner's for America and Harrap's for English book rights which together are markedly superior to what you now kindly offer. Am therefore accepting both these offers.'[61]

13

'*Friends and former millionaires*'

Making – and Losing – a New World
Fortune, 1928–9

Exchange rate: $5 = £1
Inflation multiples: US x 14; UK x 50

ELECTORAL DEFEAT DULY arrived at the end of May 1929. Churchill's personal majority in Epping fell to fewer than 5,000 votes, while the Labour Party's 288 seats across the country outstripped the Conservatives' 260 and the Liberals' 59. Stanley Baldwin resigned as prime minister and was replaced by Ramsay MacDonald at the head of a minority Labour government dependent on Liberal support.

Churchill was well prepared for the loss of his ministerial salary and official home. Still using Treasury notepaper, he sketched out his financial prospects:[1] he needed to pay £5,250 of overdue bills and find £3,750 for living expenses over the rest of the year. On the other hand, he expected to earn £12,700, mostly from writing. Nearly all the contracts for *Marlborough: His Life and Times* fell satisfactorily into place soon after the election, although Churchill had to concede a small reduction to Scribner after he found that he had awarded Canadian rights to both publishers. The only disappointment was that *The Times*, which had serialized each volume of *The World Crisis*, opted out of *Marlborough*, claiming that the subject was too dated for its readers. Fortunately, Lord Camrose,*

---

* William Berry (1879–1954), journalist, founder *Advertising World* 1901, *The War Illustrated* 1914; with his brother Gomer, purchased inter alia *The*

another press owner whom Churchill had courted, was happy for his new purchase *The Daily Telegraph*[2] to step into the breach.

When he lost office, Churchill still had eight articles to finish for Hearst's International Magazine Company, then another twelve to write (at £500 each) for Hearst's London rival, *The Strand Magazine*.[3] Not content with this order book, he had agreed, just before the election, to meet Paul Reynolds,[*] a leading New York agent, who had spoken of the need to visit America to build up his readership. Churchill heard nothing more from him until June, when Reynolds suddenly produced an offer for six articles at $2,000 each from an upmarket magazine called *Collier's Weekly*, edited by William Chenery.[4] Churchill accepted, but declared that he could not start for at least a year while he completed his other commitments; a startled Reynolds could only repeat his advice to travel to America and meet Chenery face to face.

As it happened, Reynolds was pushing at an open door: Churchill already planned to mark his loss of office by taking a break from Britain, just as he had done in 1922, and Curtis Brown had also suggested visiting America rather than Europe. The idea looked even more appealing when Williams College offered to pay Churchill $1,500 plus $500 travel expenses to lecture in Massachusetts. This invitation came through the good offices of an American friend, Bernard Baruch,[**] whom Churchill had first

---

Sunday Times 1915, the *Financial Times* 1919, established Allied Newspapers Ltd. 1924, purchased *The Daily Telegraph* 1927, *The Morning Post* 1937; knighted 1921, Lord Camrose 1929, viscount 1941.

[*] Paul Reynolds (1905–83), joined his father's Paul R. Reynolds literary agency 1926; retired 1978.

[**] Bernard Baruch (1870–1965), clerk, partner A. A. Housman & Co, stockbrokers 1891–5, making his first financial coup in sugar; purchased seat, New York Stock Exchange 1897; adviser, Guggenheim family from 1903, earned an estimated $7–9 million in the stock of Texas Gulf Sulphur Company (see J. Grant, *Bernard Baruch*, p. 140); chairman, War Industries Board 1918; US delegate, Versailles Peace Conference 1919; US representative, United Nations Atomic Energy Commission 1946–7.

encountered when he was munitions minister at the end of the
Great War. Baruch had made his fortune in the American business
world long before the war, chiefly by financing the extraction of
mineral resources, and had then been appointed to head the
American end of Allied munitions procurement after his country
entered the conflict. He had shown an unusual level of trust in his
British opposite number even before they met, but their friendship had blossomed in Paris during the Versailles peace
negotiations. Baruch had gone on to become a very well-con-
nected Wall Street investor: his personal dealing profits in 1925
had exceeded $2.6 million.[5]

Serious plans were soon underway for a Churchill family visit
to Canada and the United States. The party was to include
Churchill's brother Jack and his son John, as well as Clementine
and Randolph, and they were to sail westwards late in July, then
cross Canada by train and move down the US West Coast to
California, before returning eastwards by train to New York. In the
best tradition of the British aristocracy's younger sons, Churchill
mobilized friends and acquaintances to fix free hospitality along
the route, while he told Curtis Brown to syndicate newspaper articles in which he would write of his impressions.[6]

He leaned heavily on Bernard Baruch to suggest American hosts
along the way: 'I want to see the country and to meet the leaders of
its fortunes,' he explained. 'I have no political mission and no axe to
grind.'[7] Baruch sketched out possible candidates on the margin of
Churchill's letter: Van Antwerp* in San Francisco, Hearst in Los
Angeles, Mellon** in Pittsburgh and McClure*** in Chicago.[8]

---

* William Van Antwerp (1868–1938), night city editor, *The New York Times*
1899; purchased seat, New York Stock Exchange 1900; stockbroker, E. F.
Hutton 1927; collector of rare English books; author *The Stock Exchange
Within* (1913).
** Richard Mellon (1858–1933), banker and philanthropist; president,
Mellon Bank, Pittsburgh 1921–33; brother of Andrew, secretary of US
Treasury 1921–32.
*** Samuel McClure (1857–1949), born in Ireland; established the first US
newspaper syndicate 1884; founder *McClure's Magazine* 1897; co-founder,

Churchill asked his cousin Freddie Guest to try his steel industry contacts for a free railcar carriage back to the East Coast, but this plan made little progress. Churchill then remembered Charles Schwab, the chairman of Bethlehem Steel. In 1914 Schwab had travelled straight to see Churchill at the Admiralty after witnessing the sinking of a British warship HMS *Audacious* while en route to London and he had promised his factories' help in building submarines for the British.* 'We got on very well and settled everything on the dead level quite easily in an hour or two,' Churchill told Baruch, as he sent a late request for help to Schwab.[9] Baruch promised to stand by to help: 'Tell me what you want done and it will be done at once,' he insisted. 'If you have a private [rail]car OK, if not I will get you one.'[10]

Before leaving, Churchill realized that he needed to bolster his finances. The income that he had so confidently forecast six weeks before was taking longer than expected to arrive. Meanwhile, deferred tax bills on his earnings from *The World Crisis* (which he had long ago spent) now loomed large. In response to feelers, Lord Inchcape offered to appoint Churchill as a director of two of his private companies, paying fees of £500 a year each without any risk of publicity, but Churchill filed the letter until his return in a box marked 'Private'; he realized that he could not take on the directorships shortly before spending three months abroad.

More than £5,000 tax was due within a year, of which £872 was already overdue. How did he propose to pay it? his tax adviser at Lloyds Bank asked. It was a good question: Churchill's current account was nearly £8,000 overdrawn.[11] He could have used his *Marlborough* signing fees (due in July), but he had mentally earmarked these for a return to the world's booming stock markets, from which he had taken temporary leave of absence while

---

Doubleday & McClure 1897; introduced investigative ('muckraking') journalism.
* The submarines were taken across the Canadian border for assembly, to circumvent American neutrality.

serving as chancellor. A short burst of trading before Churchill sailed, funded by instructing both Harrap and Scribner to send their *Marlborough* cheques to his stockbroker rather than to his bank, produced a profit of £1,000. Churchill used it to meet the overdue tax.[12]

Flushed with his success on the markets, Churchill decided to leave the *Marlborough* advances with Vickers da Costa, ready to fund more trading once he reached North America. He asked his bank manager Bernau to increase his overdraft and to extend it until his return to Britain in November, while professing confidence that another £6,000 of income would reach his account while he was away. 'I have accepted a contract to write ten articles on my impressions of the United States at £250 each, for British and American rights; other Continental rights being estimated at £50–100 each, but say, £3,000, less commission, £2,700,' he explained.[13] It was as well that Bernau did not make further enquiries, because Curtis Brown had just reported that negotiations were not going well: Hearst and *The New York Times* had both turned down Churchill, while the Canadian papers had contrasted the $200 demanded for each Churchill column with the $20 that they paid Lloyd George and Mussolini.[14]

In the end Clementine had to stay in Britain after a minor operation, so the 'troupe' of two fathers and their sons left Southampton early in August. They boarded *The Empress of Australia*, a Canadian Pacific ship whose owners had offered Churchill a free Atlantic passage and a private railway carriage across Canada in return for four speeches along the route. The brothers sailed in a relaxed frame of mind: in the absence of any reply from Charles Schwab, the only gap left in their arrangements was rail transport back from America's West Coast, Churchill told Clementine:

> It is a wonderful thing to have all these contracts satisfactorily settled, and to feel that two or three years' agreeable work is mapped out and, if completed, will certainly be rewarded... I

have written an article on John Morley... When it is paid for everything will be provided satisfactorily up to the end of October, when the big payments for *The Aftermath* come in.[15]

Regular stock market bulletins from Jack's partner Cecil Vickers* reached *The Empress of Australia*'s new wireless. 'His news has so far been entirely satisfactory,' Churchill reassured Clementine before arrival in Quebec, where Charles Schwab's personal assistant unexpectedly greeted the party.[16] 'Mr Schwab places his [rail] car at our disposal during the whole of our tour in the United States! This solves all problems,' Churchill wrote home excitedly. 'We timidly suggested paying the haulage, but this was brushed aside with pained looks.' Even better, Canadian Pacific had agreed to supply a shorthand typist for their private railcar, Mont Royal, over which he enthused:

> The car is a wonderful habitation. Jack and I have large cabins with big double beds and private bathrooms. Randolph and Johnnie have something like an ordinary sleeping car compartment. There is a fine parlour with an observation room at the end and a large dining room which I use as the office. . . The car has a splendid wireless installation, refrigerators, fans, etc.[17]

There was soon another reason to be cheerful: after failing to sell any articles before Churchill arrived in Canada, Curtis Brown reported offers from two newspaper chains within a week, one from Britain's *Daily Telegraph* and the other from America's Bell Syndicate, which fed the *Washington Post*, *Los Angeles Times* and New York's *The World*.[18] Better still, Churchill found that he could sell plenty of copies of *The World Crisis* to the crowds that flocked to his speeches. 'Montreal bought 600 copies of my *W/C* and with

---

* Horace Cecil Vickers (1882–1944), founding partner, Vickers da Costa 1917; Vickers' previous firm, Nelke & Phillips, had closed when the Stock Exchange banned Paul Nelke on account of his German origins.

my rights I get pd cash,' he told Clementine excitedly. 'If this keeps up we shall make an unexpected profit.'[19]

Across Canada Churchill found himself intoxicated by the country's money-making opportunities, especially in exploration for oil and gas. Gripped by investment fever as he reached the Prairies, he asked Butterworth to pay his next set of royalties early and to Vickers da Costa, not to the bank, explaining: 'I see various opportunities of profitable investment of the money in this country which may not be open by the time I return.'[20] To head off any protests from Clementine, he set out the successes of the trip so far:

> I have written one article for *Nash*'s & one for *Answers* for £750, have sold 1,200 extra copies of *The Aftermath* so far, (in Canada £250), have made another £250 with Vickers in London: & £2,000 wh[ich] Sir H. McGowan* made for me by investing in Electric shares & have contracted to write 10 articles in Canada & the US @ $250–300 each. I hope to make some successful investments here & in US; & am glad to be able to find a little capital for that purpose. So you do not need to worry about money. The more we can save the better, but there is enough for all of us.'[21]

At Winnipeg Churchill began to put his plan into action. He instructed Vickers da Costa to transfer £2,000 to an account he had opened with James Richardson,** a local commodity trader and a director of the Canadian Pacific Railway. Before the money had

---

* Harry McGowan (1874–1961), office boy, Nobel's Explosives Co. 1889; instrumental in consolidation of the British explosives industry during First World War, dealing with Churchill as munitions minister; chairman Explosives Trades Ltd. 1918 (renamed Nobel Explosives Ltd. 1920); merged to form Imperial Chemical Industries (ICI) 1926; chairman ICI 1930–50; knighted 1928, baron 1937.
** James Richardson (1885–1939), employed by his father's Wheat Export Company 1906–18; president, James Richardson & Sons, investment bankers 1919.

even arrived Churchill found himself the proud owner of stakes in two small exploration companies, Baltac Oil and Hargal Oil.[22]

The excitement continued as the party moved on to Alberta's oilfields – 'dotted with structures shaped like the Eiffel Tower, 120 feet high', as he described them to Clementine. 'I am thinking of buying a thousand pound share in one of these companies if all my enquiries are satisfactory.'[23] He mentioned the cautionary tale of Lord Cowdray, who had turned down a stake in an oilfield, which would have cost him $80,000, only for the field to turn out to be worth $80 million. By writing and investing, Churchill had earned nearly £6,000 since leaving London, he confided to Clementine, yet he had paid for virtually nothing.

> I am greatly attracted to this country. Immense developments are going forward. There are fortunes to be made in many directions. The tide is flowing strongly. I have made up my mind that if N. Ch. [Neville Chamberlain] is made leader of the C.P. [Conservative Party] or anyone else of that kind, I clear out of politics and see if I cannot make you & the kittens a little more comfortable before I die.[24]

As soon as the party reached Vancouver, Churchill committed another $2,000 to Structure Oil, a Calgary exploration venture promoted by the fast talking Fred A. Schultz. 'Now, Mr Churchill,' wrote Schultz, 'to be quite frank with you I liked your manner of fast action in accepting our proposition, showing that we Britishers can make up our mind in a hurry as well as any Yankees can.'[25] Structure Oil was to be put into administration two years later, without finding any significant oil.

Before he left Canada Churchill's final move was to open an extra account with James Richardson for dealing in American shares, so that he could buy $26,400-worth of stock in American Rolling Mills. In all, Churchill had transferred £3,000 of cash from London to Richardson in order to back £7,000 of investments made through him. Richardson wanted another £500 contribution transferred, so that he was lending Churchill no more than half, but Churchill preferred not to do so. 'I do not expect to hold these shares for more than a few weeks,' he explained.[26]

Early in September the Churchills reached America, where they endured a less comfortable night on a public train from Seattle down the western coast. 'I am lying on the top berth of our compartment,' Randolph confided to his diary. 'Papa is unpacking and swearing down below. We miss the Mount Royal.'[27] The party transferred early to cars for the remainder of the journey to San Francisco, where they stayed with the banker William H. Crocker.* Next they moved on to William Randolph Hearst's mansion and ranch at San Simeon, where host and guest circled each other warily before the ice broke. Churchill described his impressions in a letter home to Clementine:

> A vast income always overspent: ceaseless building & collecting not v[er]y discriminating works of art: two magnificent establishments, two charming wives;** complete indifference to public opinion, a strong liberal and democratic outlook, a 15 million daily circulation, oriental hospitalities, extreme personal courtesy (to us at any rate) & the appearance of a Quaker elder – or perhaps better Mormon elder.[28]

At San Simeon Churchill encountered one of the other names on Baruch's list: William Van Antwerp. His senior by ten years, the anglophile collected early editions of books by English authors, but doubled as a San Francisco partner of the major American securities firm E. F. Hutton. Conversation between the pair clearly concentrated on stocks rather than books, because within days

---

* William Crocker (1861–1937), president, Crocker National Bank, which was bought for him (as Woolworth National Bank) by his father Charles, a founder of the Central Pacific Railroad.
** Mrs Millicent Hearst and Marion Davies, Hearst's mistress and a Hollywood actress.

Churchill had opened a new investment account with Van Antwerp's firm. A letter to Clementine, marked 'All v[er]y secret', explained how Churchill's appetite for investment had been whetted again by a bulletin from Sir Henry McGowan.

> Now my darling I must tell you that v[er]y g[reat]t & extraordinary good fortune has attended me lately in finances. Sir Harry McGowan asked me – rather earnestly – before I sailed whether he might if an opportunity came buy shares on my account without previous consultation. I replied that I could always find 2 or 3,000£. I meant this as an investment limit. He evidently took it as the limit to wh[ich] I was prepared to go in a speculative purchase on margin. Thus he operated on about ten times my usual scale, & as I told you made a profit on our joint account of £2,000 in Electric Bonds & Shares. With my approval he reinvested this in Columbia Gas & Electric & sold at a further profit of £3,000. He thus has £5,000 in hand on my account, & as he has profound mines of information about this vast American market, something else may crop up.

Churchill listed £22,000 of 'earnings' that had now 'come to hand' since leaving office, although in truth much of it was due for books or articles still to be written or investment profits still to be realized. 'So here we have really recovered in a few weeks a small fortune,' he wrote to Clementine. 'I am trying to keep £20,000 fluid for investment & speculation with Vickers da Costa & McGowan. This 'mass of manoeuvre' is of the utmost importance and must not be frittered away.[29]

In between late-night parties with the Hollywood élite and daytime studio tours, Churchill set about arranging his new reserve: half was to be kept in London and the other half invested in North America. He held on to his new Canadian oil exploration companies, but transferred the rest of his cash in Winnipeg and at Vickers da Costa to E. F. Hutton's San Francisco office, eager to join in America's share boom.[30]

Four days later, after lunch with Charlie Chaplin on the set of *City Lights*, Churchill reported his first success: 'Since my last letter from Santa Barbara, I have made another £1,000 by speculating in a stock called Simmons. It is a domestic furniture business. They say "You can't go wrong on a Simmons mattress". He had taken his profit while on board Hearst's yacht, but failed to mention to Clementine that he had sold only half of the $70,000 which he had originally invested in the company (five times the amount of cash in his E. F. Hutton account). As far as Churchill was concerned, Van Antwerp had already earned his spurs. 'I think he is a very good man,' he wrote home. 'This powerful firm watch my small interests like a cat and mouse. There is a stock exchange in every big hotel. You go and sit and watch the figures being marked up on slates every few minutes.'[31]

Emboldened, Churchill abandoned his new strategy and moved more than half of his funds to America. Selling some London stocks, he bought shares in another two of Van Antwerp's recommendations: American Smelting and Montgomery Ward, a large department store.[32] Then, after meeting Van Antwerp's wife, Churchill handed his new friend full dealing authority over his share account during his eastward journey by rail. 'His firm has the best information about the American Market,' he told Clementine. 'He will manipulate it with the best possible chances of success. All this looks very confiding – but I am sure it will prove wise.'[33]

Van Antwerp's telegrams followed Churchill's progress eastwards in Schwab's railcar. The second cable of 1 October, which intercepted Churchill's train at Damille, might perhaps have sounded a warning note: 'Market heavy. Liquidating becoming more urgent. Will await your telephone from Wellington. Your bank still losing gold & there are rumours of increase in bank rate.'[34]

*

A lull in dealings followed until Churchill reached New York, where he was put up in the Savoy Plaza Hotel at Bernard Baruch's expense.[35] Neither the long train journey nor Van Antwerp's warning had permanently dampened Churchill's enthusiasm to rejoin the trading action. Baruch, one of the biggest participants in the Wall Street market, provided Churchill with a desk and an introduction to his East Coast brokers. On Tuesday 8 October Churchill signalled to Van Antwerp that he was once again ready 'to take command'.[36] Over the next four days Churchill's turnover with E. F. Hutton reached $200,000, mostly quick trades in and out of Simmons. 'Have sent you some reinforcements,' he cabled to Van Antwerp, after sending on his fee for a New York speech (arranged by Baruch) in response to a call for more cash.[37]

Nor did Churchill neglect his London-based holdings. 'Delighted Sherwood. Shall I get a few thousand more?' he cabled to Sir Abe Bailey.[38] A positive reply brought an instruction to Vickers to spend another £2,500,[39] which Bernau refused to lend, so Vickers had to fund. At this stage, Churchill began to lose track of his positions, which were now spread across at least three different brokers, markets and time zones. He complicated matters by telling Vickers (instead of Hutton) to buy extra Simmons shares in London rather than San Francisco, while asking the London firm to send certificates for a share that he had sold in New York.[40]

Undeterred by the confusion, Churchill increased his turnover during the week between Monday 14 and Friday 18 October to $420,000.[41] He also managed to make time for the long-awaited meeting at *Collier's Weekly*. He convinced the editor, William Chenery, to squeeze in six articles before his *Strand* series started appearing the following spring. When Curtis Brown won another series of six from the *Saturday Evening Post*, Churchill was able to tell Clementine that his trip had brought twenty-two writing assignments, worth nearly £10,000,[42] on top of his investment successes.

*

On Saturday 19 October Baruch took the Churchills on a four-day trip to Virginia's Civil War battlefields. Only occasional brokers' calls punctuated the pilgrimage until on 22 October, a day before their return, Churchill asked his brokers by telephone to prepare a list of all his shareholdings, their original cost, latest price and the location of their certificates, ready for his return. He found himself confused: E. F. Hutton no longer listed any Simmons shares, for example, yet Churchill thought he had at least 100 in San Francisco and 200 in London.

By the time he arrived back in New York on Wednesday 23 October storm clouds were gathering as traders followed the tortuous passage of the Smoot–Hawley Tariff bill through Congress:* the price of two of Churchill's shareholdings had already fallen appreciably – 'Smelters' (the American Smelting and Refining Company) from 116 to 106 and Silica Gel from 36½ to 32. Churchill made two sales that day, but bought other stock, as did Baruch. At the opening bell in the New York Stock Exchange on Thursday 24 October prices fell by an average of 11 per cent. However, leading Wall Street bankers stemmed the panic by authorizing the Exchange's vice president to bid for large blocks of leading shares, just as they had done in 1907. The Dow Jones Industrial Average index closed only 2 per cent down at the end of the day.

That evening Churchill asked Van Antwerp for advice on what he should do about his remaining Simmons and Montgomery Ward shares. 'I believe yesterday's debacle laid the foundation for a constructive advance which will probably extend well into next year,' his broker replied. 'My best judgement is that you should buy two hundred additional shares each [of] the stocks you name.'[43] While prices continued tumbling the next morning, Friday 25 October, Churchill followed Van Antwerp's advice, investing an

---

* Sponsored by Reed Smoot, Republican senator from Utah, and Wills Hawley, Republican representative from Oregon, the bill was designed to raise import tariffs on more than 20,000 imported goods; a version of the bill was signed into law as The Tariff Act 1930 on 17 June 1930.

extra $26,500 in five more batches of Simmons shares: the first cost $120 each, the last $100.*

Churchill was only slightly concerned that Friday evening, when he cabled Sir Henry McGowan: 'Trust gale damage not irreparable. Returning *Berengaria*. Regards Winston.'[44] The weekend was spent trying to close his American accounts and transfer their contents to London, before they all sailed home on the Monday evening.

The first inkling of serious losses did not come until Monday morning, when Churchill tried to make sense of Hutton's valuation based on prices at the close of business the previous Friday evening. Headed 'Cash equity' the bottom figure was only $25,097, where Churchill had expected at least $35,000. He cabled Hutton urgently to ask whether there had been a mistake. No, came the reply.

Share prices continued to fall on Monday and showed no sign of stopping. The Dow Jones index ended the day down by a record 13 per cent. Bernard Baruch had arranged a dinner that evening for New York's financial élite to bid Churchill farewell. His guests were stoic and Churchill's parting toast was to 'Friends and former millionaires.'[45]

The full extent of his own losses did not begin to sink in until the following day, Tuesday 29 October, while Churchill crossed the Atlantic. He used prices from the ship's ticker tape to recalculate his fortunes. The Dow Jones index had lost another 12 per cent: over two trading days $30 billion of the market's $80 billion value had disappeared. That evening the ticker tape did not stop recording its litany of losses until 7:45 p.m.** Churchill's loss on Simmons alone, now down to $85 a share, had cost him $32,000; Montgomery Ward, its price now less than half of what he paid, had cost him another $12,000.[46]

*

---

* Churchill sold the Simmons shares on 11 November for $73, an average loss of $37 per share.
** After a brief recovery on 30 October (when it regained its losses of the previous day), the market continued to fall until the middle of November.

The mood on the way home was a far cry from the optimism of the outward voyage. Churchill always told friends that his losses in the Wall Street Crash of 1929 amounted to $50,000. W. Averell Harriman, who first met him at Baruch's farewell dinner, recalled: 'He told me on a number of occasions he had this money and he saw Baruch speculating and calling on the telephone and he thought he'd do the same thing and he succeeded in losing all the fifty thousand dollars.'[47]

But this was only part of the story. The $50,000 figure only accounts for Churchill's losses on shares that he bought through E. F. Hutton. He was lucky to escape damage on those he had purchased via Bernard Baruch's brokers, because his friend felt partially responsible and could afford to be generous (despite severe losses, Baruch's tax return shows earnings for 1929 of almost $2 million).[48] 'Oh boy Montgomery 66 Simmons 82 Bethlehem 95 Steel 185 Miss you',[49] Baruch cabled two days after Churchill had left, while transferring to his friend the $7,200 personal profit he had made for himself on a big Montgomery Ward trade. 'This nearly evens the Rolling Mills and Smelts miss I took over for you.'[50]

Even with Baruch's compensation, however, Churchill's losses almost certainly exceeded $75,000, taking into account the falls in other shares kept with Richardson, McGowan and Vickers. Churchill decided to wait until he met Clementine on the station platform in London before telling her the grim news that he had lost the equivalent of all his advances for the *Marlborough* book before having written a single word of it.

Nevertheless, in a newspaper column written a month after his return, Churchill showed that the trauma of the Crash had not dislodged his sense that America remained a testing ground for a new way of life:

> Under my very window a gentleman cast himself down fifteen storeys and was dashed to pieces. No one could doubt that this financial disaster, huge as it is, cruel as it is to thousands, is only

a passing episode in the march of a valiant and serviceable people who by fierce experiment are hewing new paths for man, and showing to all nations much that they should attempt and much that they should avoid.[51]

Churchill's abiding impression of America's strength and vitality would help shape his wartime strategy a decade later, and would ultimately lead to a transformation in his finances.

14

'He is writing all over the place'
A Strategy for Survival, 1930–1

Exchange rate: $5 = £1; francs 125 = £1
Inflation multiples: US x 15; UK x 60

CHURCHILL HAD TO explain his severe losses not only to Clementine but to his bank manager. He prepared for the encounter in November 1929 by listing the £16,500-worth of new writing commissions he had been awarded while in America. However, a sceptical William Bernau was more interested in the income that Churchill had promised would arrive in the autumn but failed to appear. As a result, he told Churchill, the bank was owed £13,700, but its security was barely worth £14,000.

Churchill was still drafting a request for increased short-term facilities when Bernau forwarded a letter from his head office, warning that the bank's overdraft arrangement had only two days left to run and would have to be renewed at a lower, not a higher, figure.[1] However, Bernau, an insurance specialist, then offered to work personally with Churchill's lawyers to persuade an insurance company to lend more money to him, in place of Lloyds Bank. Bernau suggested that the future income flow from Churchill's marriage settlement, which was yet not pledged elsewhere, could provide the necessary security.

A relieved Churchill deemed it wise not to tell Bernau that one of the fixtures of his income for the next few months now looked uncertain. George Blake, *The Strand*'s editor, had caught wind of

Churchill's American magazine deals and was threatening to cut his contract on the grounds that it would now be almost impossible to resell his own Churchill series on the other side of the Atlantic. Churchill invited the editor and his proprietor, Lord Riddell, to lunch at Chartwell, proposing that business talk should be saved until after the meal. He was confident that his relationship with Riddell would carry the day. Afterwards, however, Blake still halved the number of articles commissioned and also the magazine's fee for each article, thereby slashing Churchill's income from £6,000 to £1,500.[2]

Chartwell was 'dust-sheeted' for the winter. Only the study was left as it was so that Churchill could write there at weekends. Strapped for cash, he narrowly escaped the indignity of accepting an emergency loan from Lord Beaverbrook when Bernau coaxed a loan of £5,000 out of the Commercial Union. However, it came at a steep cost of more than 10 per cent a year.[3]

Churchill promised Bernau that part of the money, at least, would be used to reduce his overdraft, but then a message from Bernard Baruch in America made him rethink. It said, simply: 'Financial storm definitely passed.'[4] Churchill instructed that the whole £5,000 should be sent to Vickers da Costa, so that he could restart trading.[5] By Christmas Churchill was buying Montgomery Ward again.[6] In January and February he kept adding more Simmons shares to his list, despite the fact that its price fell to the point where Cecil Vickers, the senior partner, felt compelled to advise Churchill to stop dealing in what he called little more than a 'gambling stock'.[7] Vickers da Costa recorded Churchill's activity in four different accounts, making it difficult to track the overall results, but by the middle of 1930 Churchill had lost an additional £7,000 on the stock market.[8]

No number of newspaper or magazine articles could replenish his losses. Instead Churchill tried to persuade his publishers to make cash advances for new books that he could quickly conjure up from past articles. At the same time he reassured George Harrap that *Marlborough* was still on course. He invited Harrap to lunch at

Blenheim and gave him a tour of the archive. Still new to Churchill's ways, Harrap may not have grasped the full meaning of the letter that followed: 'This is a work which will gain by not being hurried,' Churchill wrote, 'and I do not propose in all probability to begin the actual writing until I am saturated with the subject and have formed all the large views of Marlborough's personality and of the period.'[9]

In reality, he would not begin writing until several other books were complete. While writing an article for *Collier's* magazine about the Battle of Tannenburg (26–30 August 1914), he realized that the story of the Eastern Front was almost unknown and worth a book in itself. He suggested it to Thornton Butterworth, dropping a broad hint that he might find time to fit it into his busy schedule if offered a generous enough advance. Keen to win back his author, Butterworth obliged with an advance of £2,500 for *The Eastern Front*, £1,500 of it payable on signature.[10] The editor of *The Times*, however, was less enthusiastic and would offer only £500. 'Churchill's stock is not very high at the moment,' he observed. 'He is writing all over the place.'[11]

In America Charles Scribner agreed to come in on some deal, but he preferred his own idea of an abridged version of *The World Crisis*. His firm would edit it, he explained, therefore providing Churchill with 'a financial return out of proportion to the time and labour that would be entailed'.[12] Butterworth was sceptical, but in the end supported the idea. A third book was then conjured out of thin air when Churchill proposed adding 50,000 fresh words about his early life to the 50,000 he had already written in various articles, together making an autobiographical book worth a guinea. Butterworth and Scribner liked the idea and quickly signed up to *My Early Life*.[13] Suddenly, Churchill's cash flow looked rosier: stock exchange losses aside, he now expected to generate a surplus in 1930.[14]

However, Churchill was now obliged to do almost nothing but write, and his remorseless schedule took its toll, forcing him to restrict his political activity. He had committed himself to the completion of three books and and would write more than forty articles for newspapers and magazines, many of them American, before 1930 was finished.

The challenge of juggling so many commitments without the help of a researcher proved formidable. William Chenery wanted changes to both of Churchill's first two articles for *Collier's*; the Bell Syndicate threatened to cut short its series because, it alleged, Churchill kept recycling the same material in different columns; then the *Saturday Evening Post* cancelled his final four articles (worth $10,000) when it saw that Churchill was writing for *Collier's*, although neither Churchill nor his agent had realized the two publications were rivals. Finally *Collier's* rubbed salt into the wound by refusing to renew Churchill's commission for 1931; as a result he was forced to accept a much lower fee from the only real alternative, Hearst Newspapers.

Only the arrival of proofs for *My Early Life* in April relieved the gloom. The publishers' enthusiasm prompted its promotion from third to second in the order of publication, once Butterworth agreed that he would not reclaim Churchill's signing advance for *The Eastern Front* as a result. By June it had jumped to the top of the list with publication in October. The abridged *World Crisis* would follow in February 1931, then *The Eastern Front* in September. Whatever the order, it was clear that *Marlborough: His Life and Times* had been sidelined.

All of these extra book deals did not immediately improve Churchill's dire finances after his investment losses. In March 1930 Cecil Vickers had asked for an extra £2,000 cash,[15] but Churchill had only been able to find half of the money, so that Jack had to write a cheque for the balance until funds arrived from a New York royalty account.[16] By mid-summer 1930 Churchill faced a series of what he called 'inescapable payments', together adding up to £4,300. His secretaries' list of unpaid bills at Chartwell ran to two pages, interest was due to the bank at the end of June and large life insurance payments loomed in September.[17]

Churchill drafted a letter to Bernau setting out his difficulties, but in the end decided on a face-to-face meeting, using his draft as an aide-memoire. It lists more than £5,000-worth of fees due for articles already written, plus an additional £12,000 now contracted for 'no fewer than three books' over the coming months. Finally it reminds Bernau of a separate £14,000 due for *Marlborough* in 1932. His difficulties were therefore temporary, Churchill stressed, although he did need to borrow another £2,000 as a result of timing problems and would need to delay the reduction in his overdraft until the end of the year.[18]

Before Lloyds Bank would agree to come to his aid, Churchill had to promise to reduce his borrowings by £3,000 before the end of the year. His cousin Captain Guest also had to guarantee the temporary new loan of £2,000, while Sir Abe Bailey was asked to reconfirm his personal guarantee of the value of Churchill's Sherwood Starr shareholding. Churchill's lawyers found a puzzled Sir Abe in Harrogate, where he was on holiday. 'I thought I paid you off £2,000,' he told Churchill. 'At any rate whatever you wish me to do I will gladly do for you.'[19] Yet another crisis had been averted.

Throughout his summer holiday in France, Churchill's writing commitments had to vie for attention with the world's stock markets. He asked Cecil Vickers to send him a daily cable of prices, led by three American railway companies whose shares Churchill had sold short. He cut the first position too soon after losing his nerve, but managed to hold on and sell the other two at a profit, when Bernard Baruch cabled from America to forecast a turn for the better in the market.[20] Even on holiday, Churchill's journalistic instincts remained alert and he took advantage of Lloyd George's illness and then of the crash of a British airship to win commissions for two special articles. A third followed when the *Sunday Chronicle* bashfully asked whether he would lead on a new series it was planning about biblical figures; it all came down to price, he told the paper.[21] It was on this holiday, too, that Churchill first suggested to

Butterworth that 'the fifteen or twenty articles I have already written on eminent personages could be easily harnessed' into a book, the idea that was to turn into *Great Contemporaries*.[22]

On Churchill's return, extracts from *My Early Life* started appearing in the *Daily News*[23] before the full edition was published in October. 'I am hopeful that the book will do more than it was originally written to do, namely, to pay the Tax collector,' Churchill told Stanley Baldwin. 'There may even be a small surplus to nourish the author and his family.'[24] It was not to be: the 9,000 copies sold in Britain left royalties still short of Churchill's advance at the end of the year and the picture was similar in America.[25] Churchill realized that writing alone would not be sufficient to pay off his debts.

Obligingly, Lord Inchcape was happy to resuscitate the plan for two of his private subsidiaries to appoint Churchill a director at a fee of £500 each. Churchill remained a director of both Mann George Depots and R. & J. H. Rea until 1939; neither turned out to hold many meetings of their directors, and, when they did, the meetings were often arranged at too short notice for Churchill to attend. The other plan that Churchill had considered and now put into action was a lecture tour of America. Possible promoters were asked to guarantee payment of $50,000 net of expenses and penalty-free cancellation if Churchill regained office or faced a general election. Louis Alber's Affiliated Lecture & Concert Association accepted the terms and dispatched a contract, but Churchill had not yet signed it when he was distracted in December by a second call for extra cash from Cecil Vickers: Churchill's investment account had suffered fresh losses and Vickers wanted him to inject £2,000 into it.[26] Churchill was supposed to be reducing his bank loans, not increasing them, so he arranged to borrow the extra £2,000 from the Commercial Union, a more expensive source. The move took his combined loans from bank and insurance companies up to £22,000; he was also paying market rates of interest on loans of only a little less from his family trusts.[27]

Worse was to come in the following month, January 1931, when Churchill lost a further £3,000 trading in and out of Montgomery

Ward's shares.[28] To cover the loss, he tried to borrow from his daughter Mary's Settlement, only for the lawyers to rule that he could offer insufficient security; as a result, Churchill asked his friend Sir Howard Frank* to put Chartwell on the market. The estate agent was unconvinced about the price Churchill wanted: 'I do not think anyone will ever give you £30,000, but, of course, if you are quite happy to continue living there on the chance of the right person coming along one day and giving you a fancy price, all well and good.'[29]

Churchill's only other option in the short term was a second appeal to his brother. Jack could hardly refuse, given that he was a partner in the firm to which money was owed. Just before the stock exchange closed its fortnightly account on 14 January, Jack produced a cheque for £2,000,[30] whereupon the senior partner Cecil Vickers suggested Churchill take a rest from the market. 'I think your policy should be, at the present time, one of masterly inaction, waiting for the rise which will come,' he advised.[31]

There was no New Year holiday on the French Riviera for Churchill at the start of 1931. He remained at home, making what he described to George Harrap as 'good headway with *Marlborough*', before he turned his attention back to *The Eastern Front* and his list of unwritten articles which he valued at £7,500.[32]

A decade earlier Churchill's journalism had found easy targets in Lenin, Bolshevism and the trade unions: he enjoyed good support on each subject among both his political peers and press proprietors. Now, however, his strong opposition to Indian independence and his emerging concern at the rise in Germany of National Socialism (the Nazi Party led by Adolf Hitler had won six million votes in the country's most recent election) proved more isolated pre-occupations. Indian self-government threatened the security of Britain's eastern Empire, Churchill believed,

---

* Howard Frank (1871–1932), senior partner Knight Frank & Rutley & Co (London), Walton & Lee (Edinburgh); president, the Institute of Estate Agents 1912-14; adviser, Ministry of Munitions 1916–22; knighted 1914, baronet 1922.

but each of Britain's main political parties had supported the call by Britain's viceroy in India, Lord Irwin, for a conference to discuss the country's possible dominion status. Isolated and short of time for all the writing required to keep his finances afloat, Churchill resigned from the Conservative Business Committee in the House of Commons (which would now be known as the shadow cabinet).

Little was going Churchill's way in the early part of 1931: the Indian constitutional conference had endorsed the principle of self-government; the abridged *World Crisis* was selling very slowly;[33] and for his annual article previewing the Budget, he reluctantly accepted a lower rate of £200, rather than his usual £500.[34] Moreover his American lecture contract had raised numerous tax complications. Louis Alber had agreed to pay any US charges, but it was the possibility of being charged tax in Britain that worried Churchill. Unconvinced by the cautious assurances of experts that he should be safe,[35] he resorted to his usual tactic of consulting directly the chairman of the Inland Revenue, P. J. Grigg, who had been Churchill's private secretary at the Treasury. Agreeing to refer to his former minister only by the initials 'A.B.' throughout their correspondence, Grigg consulted his '*alguazils*',* as Churchill called them, and then confirmed his fears: lecturing was too similar to his profession as an author for him to escape taxation: '[A.B.] is merely addressing hearers orally instead of delivering his message by means of the printed word.' Churchill contested their conclusion:

> The art of delivering a lecture is not literary but histrionic in its character. It is a physical and psychic exertion of which most literary men or journalists would be incapable, a certain standard of quality being essential. . . In the circumstances I think A.B. would be ill advised to undertake the lectures as. . . he would receive little more than two-fifths himself.[36]

---

* In Spain, an 'inferior officer of justice'.

Churchill left the contract for his lecture tour unsigned while he continued to search for projects that might generate immediate cash but did not require immediate work. He came back to an idea he had discussed with Charles Scribner at a Yale football match two years earlier: a book about the history of the relationship between Britain and America's 'English-speaking peoples'. Scribner heard no more until June 1931, when a cable suddenly arrived out of the blue from the London publisher Eyre & Spottiswoode, asking for best bids and claiming to hold exclusive 'world rights'.[37] Scribner was still waiting for the first chapter of *Marlborough*, for which he had paid a substantial advance, so he asked his London office to investigate. *Marlborough* being virtually finished, their report ran, Eyre & Spottiswoode was merely reacting to Churchill's request for bids of at least £30,000 for a subsequent book.

Scribner wrote Churchill a long letter, reminding his author that he had forecast that the English-speaking peoples book would require at least 'three or four years after the *Marlborough*' when they first discussed it; his only possible conclusion therefore was that Churchill must be short of money, but Scribner would rather lend him cash than bid for another book.[38] Churchill quietly put the project on ice.

Similar complications were inevitable as Churchill continued to pitch articles and book extracts to magazines and newspapers, usually dispensing with the services of an agent in order to save commission. In June 1931 *The Strand* sold to *Liberty* the American rights to one of Churchill's articles, with Churchill's blessing but without William Hearst's permission, as was contractually required. To avoid litigation Churchill had to fall back on his personal relationship with Hearst. He won few friends at Hearst's headquarters, however, and his attempts to renew his column for the following year went ignored. Then the sale to *The Sunday Times* of newspaper rights for *The Eastern Front* fell through, because Churchill could not get the newspaper to agree dates with the book publishers. To top it all, Curtis Brown had to cancel its European sale of the newspaper rights when Brendan Bracken announced out of the blue that he had sold the world rights to the London General Press Agency, a contract reached in haste and later to cause a lengthy lawsuit.[39] Curtis Brown advised Churchill to let him take charge of everything to avoid similar problems in the future; he offered to do it for half the normal agency's rate, but Churchill could not afford the luxury.

He had been writing non-stop, yet during the first half of 1931 Churchill had brought in to his bank account £5,000 less than he had spent.[40] Undaunted, he left for his usual August holiday with the duke of Westminster, as soon as he had handed over the finished *The Eastern Front* to his publishers. 'Thank God it is finished,' he told Eddie Marsh. 'I am longing to get on to *Marlborough*.'

At Mimizan Churchill found his fellow guests pre-occupied by the global markets. 'Everybody I meet seems vaguely alarmed that something terrible is going to happen financially,'[41] he confided to Marsh. Austria's Creditanstalt bank had sparked a run on its deposits after announcing a large loss in May, and the contagion had spread through Eastern Europe after Austria's severance of its currency's link with gold.

Warnings from Bernard Baruch had prompted Churchill to cut back his stock exchange positions during June and July. Once he had finished his book in August, however, he returned to trading. He incurred more losses when the shock waves reached London: the Bank of England was forced into borrowing from the US Federal Reserve Bank and from the Banque de France to stop gold leaving the City. Just as Vickers da Costa asked Churchill for another £3,000 of cash to meet his fresh losses on the share markets, the crisis produced an unlikely insurance windfall.

Because of his money worries, Churchill had decided during the summer that he would have to go ahead with his American lecture tour, whatever the tax position. However, he had insured himself against the cost of having to cancel for political or medical reasons and having to pay a cancellation penalty. Quotes had been as high as 40 per cent of the sum assured, until Thornton Butterworth produced a contact at the Excess Insurance Company, who were prepared to quote only 5 per cent.[42] Churchill immediately took out a policy for £5,000, for which he paid on 13 August,[43] a week before the Labour government announced an emergency package of measures to save sterling's link to gold. This package combined spending cuts and higher taxes in equal measure, but Conservative leaders told Prime Minister Ramsay MacDonald that they would support only one quarter of the total coming from taxes; several Labour ministers resigned in sympathy with the trade unions, which opposed any spending cuts.

MacDonald handed in his resignation as prime minister on 23 August 1931, but was asked by the king to stay on to lead a National Government to meet the immediate economic emergency. MacDonald invited four senior Conservatives to join his new cabinet, but Churchill was not one of them, so no claim was triggered on his insurance policy. However, an autumn election now looked a distinct possibility and this would trigger a full payout of the policy. Merrick-Taylor, Excess Insurance's managing director, decided to cut his likely losses and to unwind his company's policy at almost any cost less than the £5,000 covered. Bernau, an insurance specialist, led Churchill's side of the negotiations, Churchill appearing only at the end of the talks to seal the 'highly confidential' deal under which the insurer would pay him £3,750[44] in return for a promised Churchill oil painting. The windfall was all the more valuable because it was untaxed, and because Churchill faced no corresponding penalty to pay Alber, whose lecturing contract lay still unsigned on his desk. Only once the insurance cheque had been safely banked did Churchill cable the promoter with the news that he was postponing his lecture tour.[45]

Churchill used £2,000 of the windfall money to repay his brother's loan from earlier in the year. He returned to Mimizan increasingly optimistic that he could earn enough to meet the following year's expenditure, which he estimated at £12,000.[46] That forecast was still based on his standard figure for household bills of £500 a month, although a look at Churchill's bank account would have revealed the real cost to be running at almost double that amount. Nor did

Churchill's estimates ever include his losses at casinos, which became a regular feature of his holidays in France during the 1930s.[47] In 1931 the poor summer weather in southern France helped drive Churchill towards the casinos in both Biarritz and Cannes, where he withdrew 72,000 francs in cash. On return to London, he deposited only 10,000 francs, a loss of approximately £500.[48]

More happily, Brendan Bracken rang Churchill during his holiday with some good news: Esmond Harmsworth,* son of Lord Rothermere, was taking a more prominent role at the ailing *Daily Mail* and on Bracken's suggestion he had decided to liven up the newspaper by carrying a weekly column from Churchill at £150 a column; the contract would be worth up to £7,800 a year. Churchill was delighted, but then began to impose conditions from afar, despite Bracken's warning that some old hands at the *Daily Mail* were resistant to the idea. In the end, Harmsworth scaled back his offer to thirteen columns a year, worth a much reduced £1,950.

A disappointed Churchill returned to England just as the new National Government prepared for Britain's final break with gold. He told Harrap that he was at last about to turn his attention towards *Marlborough*.[49] In truth, he was still distracted by the need for immediate cash. He sent Butterworth twenty old articles on 'eminent personages', which he planned to put together into two fresh books, one to be called *Great Contemporaries* and the other *Thoughts and Adventures*.[50] Butterworth and Scribner quickly signed up.[51] Then, in October 1931 a general election was announced and *Marlborough* was shelved once more.

The election campaign produced an unexpected family complication. Earlier that year Churchill's son Randolph, now twenty years old, had returned from his own American lecture tour saddled with debts of $2,000.[52] Work as a journalist on both

---

* Esmond Harmsworth (1898–1978), MP 1919–29; chairman, Associated Newspapers 1932–71; chairman, Daily Mail & General Trust 1932–78; 2nd Viscount Rothermere 1940.

Rothermere and Beaverbrook newspapers had done little to ease the situation. Recklessly, Randolph then bet just under £400 that the National Government would win the general election by a majority of fewer than 150 seats; on the other hand, the higher the National Government's majority climbed above that number, the more he would lose.

By the middle of the campaign period, the National Government appeared to be heading for a landslide victory and an exasperated Churchill had to call in his brother Jack to deal with a serious threat (the National Government's final victory by a majority of 493 seats would have cost Randolph approximately £600 in addition to the loss of his initial stake). Coolly deploying £1,000 from Churchill's account at Vickers da Costa, Jack closed off Randolph's bets and took out a much larger bet on a high majority in his father's name. The tactic proved so successful that Churchill emerged with a profit of almost £900, once he had reallocated just enough of his winnings to limit Randolph's loss to £100.[53] Churchill's letter to his son carries echoes of those his father had sent him at Sandhurst forty years earlier:

> If you feel yourself able to keep a magnificent motor car & chauffeur at a rate which must be £700 or £800 a year, you are surely able to pay yr debts of honour yrself. Unless & until you give proof of yr need by ridding yrself of this gross extravagance you have no right to look for aid from me: nor I to bestow it.[54]

While the election results were still emerging, *The Eastern Front* hit London's and New York's bookshelves. Sales were disappointing. Butterworth attributed this to the general economic malaise, but Churchill's own researcher, Maurice Ashley,* had a different

---

* Maurice Ashley (1907–94), literary assistant to Churchill 1929–33; leader writer *Manchester Guardian* 1933–7; sub-editor *The Times* 1937–9; editor *Britain Today* 1939–40; Intelligence Corps 1940–5; deputy editor, editor (from 1958) *The Listener* 1945–68; author *Churchill as Historian* 1968.

explanation: 'I received the impression that *The Eastern Front* was written primarily to earn money,' he wrote years later.[55] Financially, the book was a disappointment: more than half of Churchill's final £1,000 advance had been eaten up by bills for author's corrections and for the inclusion of sixty-nine maps.[56]

Ramsay MacDonald remained at the head of the National Government, although the number of Labour Party seats had collapsed from 288 to just 52 after the election. Meanwhile, Churchill had doubled his personal majority at Epping. His victory was part of a strong national showing by the Conservatives, whose leader Stanley Baldwin emerged as the new government's real master. Baldwin asked eleven Conservatives to take up the majority of cabinet positions, but Churchill was again overlooked. An isolated objector to Indian self-government, Churchill remained outside the Party's mainstream and was reconciled to yet another period on the backbenches. At least this meant he could tell Alber that he was now free to lecture in the United States between December and February. Chartwell's ground floor was dust-sheeted and Churchill sailed in early December for New York, accompanied by Clementine, their daughter Diana and a bodyguard.

On the evening of their arrival in New York Churchill gave the first of forty lectures, before the family spent a quiet weekend. On the Sunday evening Bernard Baruch invited Churchill to meet two old colleagues from the War Industries Board at his apartment. Dispensing with his bodyguard, Churchill hailed a cab, but forgot to take with him Baruch's address. After a fruitless hour trying to find the building, he climbed out of the cab to examine the street from the other side of the road and was promptly hit by a car.

15

'Poor Marlborough has been shunted'
Trading Futures, 1932–3

Exchange rate: $5 = £1; (1933) francs 100 = £1
Inflation multiples: US x 18; UK x 60

THE INJURIES TO Churchill's head and legs were serious enough to keep him in hospital for over a week in December 1931, running up a bill. It would have been higher if the New York Telephone Company's president had not provided the 'princely courtesy' of free telegrams from Churchill's bedside.[1]

Churchill's second insurance policy from Phoenix Assurance did not cover medical bills, but it would pay compensation of £60 a week if he was 'totally disabled'.[2] So Churchill cabled William Bernau on the morning after the accident: 'Notify insurance that accident will entail at least four weeks total disablement.'[3]

Within days of the accident he had recovered sufficiently to appreciate its journalistic potential. 'Have complete recollection of whole event & believe can produce literary gem about 2,400 words,' he cabled Esmond Harmsworth. 'Am of course marketing here & will synchronize publication.'[4] The resulting article – sold to the *Sunday Star* in Washington and the *Los Angeles Times* – fetched more than £600 worldwide. 'I received a great price for it,' Churchill told his son, 'but find it very dearly bought.'[5]

Unfortunately the *Daily Mail* printed Churchill's article in Britain on the same day that Bernau notified Phoenix Assurance of the doctors' ruling that Churchill should remain out of action for a month. A phone call followed from a manager at the insurance company, who 'pointed out that as you were well enough to follow your "profession or occupation" of writing you were no longer totally disabled and the weekly allowance would, of course, cease'. Bernau enjoyed telling Churchill how he had dealt with the objections: 'I pointed out that you did not write the articles yourself but merely dictated them, and from my knowledge of you I told him there was no more exertion to you in giving off these remarks than there would be for him to write to his brother describing an accident he had been through.'[6] Phoenix Assurance relented and continued to pay.

From his hospital bed Churchill managed to tie up final arrangements for another six articles with *Collier's Weekly*, then opened a dollar bank account with the National City Bank of New York, ready to receive his lecture and writing fees. The bank's vice president George Duis explained to Churchill how he could take advantage of the dollar's rise of almost a third against sterling in the four months since Britain had abandoned the gold standard, by buying sterling in advance of being paid in dollars, using the 'forward' currency market. Impressed by the bank's professionalism (its statements were machine-produced, while Lloyds Bank's were still handwritten), Churchill committed half of his fees to buy £6,000 forward for the end of March.[7]

The next day he sailed to convalesce in the Bahamas, where his party stayed at Nassau's expensive Polly Leach Hotel, until a newly arrived governor invited them to move into Government House. Churchill was suffering, however. 'Last night he was very sad,' Clementine told Randolph, 'and said that he had now in the last 2 years had 3 very heavy blows. First the loss of all that money in the crash, then the loss of his political position in the Conservative Party and now this terrible physical injury.'[8]

Expecting his accident to cost him half the lecture tour's profits,[9] Churchill forced himself to start lecturing again at the end of January, usually speaking each day and travelling by night. The first results surpassed expectations. 'Very fine meetings and very fat profits,' he reported a week later to his former parliamentary aide, Bob Boothby,[10] after being paid for early engagements in New York, Hartford and St Louis. Then the cheque for his lecture in Cleveland bounced, the first of three to do so, forcing Churchill to waive his daily expense allowance as part of a renegotiation with Alber. An increasingly exhausted Churchill continued lecturing and travelling almost daily until 10 March, taking only one weekend off at Bernard Baruch's waterside home in the Carolinas. Churchill had fallen behind with his *Daily Mail* columns. 'I have not the margin of life and strength to do them while travelling and speaking so many nights in succession,' he confessed to Esmond Harmsworth.[11]

In the end Churchill's lecture tour earned him profits of $23,000[12] rather than $50,000, but another $9,000 was expected from *Collier's*. Churchill consulted Cecil Vickers, Baruch and Duis about what to do with the dollars that he had not already committed to buying sterling. Vickers offered little practical help from London: 'Market wild uncontrolled. Opinion immediate future impossible advise.'[13] Duis, on the other hand, gave Churchill a second master-class on hedging, prompting his pupil to commit all of his surplus dollars to buying more sterling 'forward'. The last to reply, Baruch urged Churchill to buy US government bonds. Unable to resist, although all his dollars were theoretically committed, Churchill emptied his New York bank account to follow this advice, ending up 'short' of $15,000, rather than hedged as Duis had advised.[14]

Business complete, Churchill sailed home first class at Alber's expense* to be greeted at London's Paddington station by a new Daimler, a gift worth £2,000 from a group of English and American friends. 'There was some controversy as to whether you would prefer a Rolls-Royce, a Daimler or a Bentley,' its organizer Brendan Bracken explained to Churchill. 'The controversy was solved by fixing on the car which is least expensive to maintain.'[15]

---

* The party's fares cost $755. As a result of losses incurred on Churchill's tour, Alber's business was forced to merge with a competitor in 1932.

*

There had been no time to dabble on the stock market in America, but Churchill returned home to find that his remaining shares were worth only £4,900 while he owed Vickers da Costa £5,700 in funding. The deficit widened as prices fell further during March, at the end of which his brokers asked for another cheque.

Churchill decided on a complete change of approach: he asked for a list of large American companies whose share prices had fallen to low levels. He planned to buy them and to hold on for two or three years until the economy recovered. Cecil Vickers sent a list, but advised him against buying what amounted to 'gambling' stocks. 'I am very much afraid of missing the bus,' Churchill had to explain to an equally sceptical Jack. 'I do not think America is going to smash. On the contrary I believe that they will quite soon recover.'[16]

A compromise was reached: 'If and when the market goes weak,' Vickers summarized, 'we shall buy a certain number of low priced shares. . . with the intention of selling them at say anywhere between 70% to 100% profit and then wait for another fall.'[17] Jack still disapproved, but Churchill possessed the broader view of the politician:

> Undoubtedly the whole force of the Republican Party will be to make a better market before the election, and give the appearance the corner has turned. The risk of investments in America now is incomparably less than it was a year ago when I sometimes had as much as twenty thousand pounds of steak [sic].[18]

Churchill made his move in late July and early August, when he sold the US Treasury bonds he had bought in March, emptied his New York bank account and used the $12,000 thus raised to buy $20,000-worth of shares (he borrowed the balance from brokers).[19] An anxious Churchill tracked the shares' prices closely each day using a copy of the New York Herald specially delivered to Chartwell by train and taxi. 'There seemed a good many telephone calls to Baruch in New York and some sense of financial botherations,' recalled the Oxford historian Keith Feiling, who was staying at Chartwell before embarking with Churchill on a study trip to Marlborough's battlefields.[20]

The new investment policy lasted a month before Churchill abandoned it: he sold three of his new shares for gains of up to 50 per cent, then bought and sold Western Union shares four times within a fortnight. Meanwhile, Vickers da Costa had swung its market view behind Churchill's, suggesting to all of its clients in a mid-August letter that the market had reached a major turning point: 'The establishment of British credit,' it argued, 'and the reliquefication of the American banking position, due to the activities of the Federal Reserve Board, have re-established confidence in the survival power of the capitalist system.'[21]

Churchill accelerated his switch towards the North American market, spending another $30,000 on buying shares in Otis Elevators, Texas Gulf and his old favourite Montgomery Ward, which he traded sixteen times within four days. Dealing commission alone cost £300 and most of the money was borrowed,[22] but Cecil Vickers was moved to describe his client's investment style as 'very cosmopolitan' when he enclosed separate accounts for London, American and Canadian holdings.[23]

Churchill's surge of interest in trading and investment that summer did not slow down his literary progress. Looking through his old articles convinced him there was enough material for three short books, rather than two: 'The first *Thoughts and Adventures* requires no new writing at all,' he told Butterworth. 'The second *American Impressions* (or some better title) still wants four articles I have to do for *Collier's* this year. The third, *Notable Contemporaries*, will require anything from 16,000 to 20,000 words of new composition.'[24] The recently retired Eddie Marsh agreed to edit each book for the same £20 *honorarium* that he had just earned for drafting Churchill's *Daily Mail* article about the Royal Academy's Summer Exhibition:[25] a literary ghost was in the making.

Churchill managed to settle two important newspaper

contracts for 1933. His mention to Esmond Harmsworth of 'approaches' from other newspapers had the intended effect of producing a longer contract with the *Daily Mail*.[26] Harmsworth was relieved that Churchill had begun to turn the column's focus from India to Germany, in particular the new German chancellor's call for reduced war reparations, which his columnist had described as nothing more than 'mush, slush and gush'.[27]

Churchill's *Daily Mail* contract ruled out writing a political column for any other British newspaper, but his old friend George Riddell (now Lord Riddell) overcame this problem by suggesting a non-political series for the *News of the World*, which boasted 3.5 million readers on each Sunday. Riddell invited Churchill to name his own price if he would retell popular stories, such as *Ben-Hur* and *Uncle Tom's Cabin*, in his own words.[28] Naming as high a price as he dared, of £2,000 for six stories, Churchill also proposed an 'unlet space' in his programme during the spring of 1933. To his delight, Riddell not only accepted the fee but offered an extra £500 if Churchill delivered the stories before the end of 1932.[29] Churchill accepted Riddell's terms, but only after he had secured Eddie Marsh's agreement to produce a 'foundation' of each story at £25 a time. 'If you would like writing more on any of them, all the better,' Churchill added.[30]

Meanwhile, Curtis Brown's Nancy Pearn* had managed to resurrect interest in the plan for a 'history of the English-speaking peoples'. It came from Newman Flower,** chairman and now the main owner of publishers Cassell & Co., which he aimed to reposition from its niche in publishing reference works to the industry's mainstream. Flower had heard from Charles Scribner of Churchill's high asking price, but he felt that Churchill would be a worthy prize for Cassell and merited a premium price.

---

* Nancy Pearn (1950), literary agent; joined Curtis Brown 1922; left with two colleagues to found Pearn, Pollinger & Higham 1935.
** Walter Newman Flower (1879–1964), magazine publisher, Cassell & Co 1906; bought Cassell's book business from Amalagamated Press 1927; author *George Frideric Handel* 1923, *Franz Schubert* 1928; knighted 1938.

Instead of the traditional licence and royalty, Flower proposed an outright purchase of the copyright, which would provide Churchill with tax advantages: it would be treated as a capital transaction and the British government did not tax capital sums. As the main publisher, Cassell would bear the risks of selling on the newspaper and book rights to its counterparts overseas. Churchill provisionally agreed to Pearn's suggested price of £20,000 late in July, but he wanted a face-to-face meeting with Flower to settle the final details.

First, however, came a long-planned research trip to Marlborough's battlefields.[31] When he and his team left on 27 August, Churchill took along the proofs of the first four *Marlborough* chapters, printed in his favoured format of three pages alongside each other on a single sheet. 'This enables the structure to be much more easily shaped,' he told his new publisher. 'You must not however suppose that I attach any finality to the proofs because they are printed. I always knock them about a great deal and incorporate the criticisms of many who read them.'[32] It was an expensive method, but Churchill was prepared to pay the author's usual contribution towards the cost of corrections.

While they were away, Churchill had arranged for his stockbrokers to send a daily cable of New York share prices in a pre-ordained sequence, but otherwise he left the journey's logistics to his researcher, Colonel Pakenham-Walsh. The party crossed the Channel on an 'autocarrier boat', so that Churchill could continue to Brussels in a Rolls-Royce belonging to his friend Frederick Lindemann,* a professor of physics at Oxford University. Churchill had given Pakenham-Walsh prior guidance

---

* Frederick Lindemann (1886–1957), known as 'the prof'; professor of experimental philosophy (physics) Oxford University 1919–56; fellow of the Royal Society 1920; member, government sub-committee on air defence research 1935–6; personal assistant to Churchill, head of statistical section, Admiralty 1939–40; chief government scientific adviser 1939-45; paymaster-general 1942–5; paymaster-general 1951–3; Baron Cherwell 1941, Viscount Cherwell 1956; a teetotaler, non-smoker and vegetarian, but a close friend of Churchill (and his scientific adviser) after meeting him in 1921.

on the accommodation standards he expected in Brussels: 'My wife and I, two rooms and two bathrooms adjoining and a sitting room, my daughter, Sarah, one room and a bathroom preferred. Professor Lindemann a good room and a bathroom, not necessarily en suite, but as near as possible.'[33]

As the party toured Ramillies, Oudenarde and Blenheim, Marlborough's heroics had to vie for Churchill's attention with contemporary events in Germany and on the American stock market. In recent elections, Adolf Hitler's National Socialist Party had attracted 13.5 million votes and 230 Reichstag seats, just short of a majority. Initially excluded from government, Hitler stepped up attacks on his political opponents and on Jewish property until he was offered the vice-chancellorship – he turned it down. Churchill followed these developments from each staging point of his battle-field tour, during which Cecil Vickers also sent two warnings that share prices in New York had reached levels that were 'impossible to justify'. By the time the second message reached Churchill, he was unable to reply: he had contracted typhoid, which required ten days' of expensive treatment at a Salzburg sanatorium.[34]

Churchill's illness delayed the launch of *Thoughts and Adventures*, which was ready at the printers but missing an author's preface. Eddie Marsh was persuaded to ghost one which Churchill described as 'delightful' and Marsh himself thought 'rather a good pastiche!'[35] Churchill next suffered a relapse in his recovery at Chartwell and moved for several weeks to a London nursing home which was conveniently close to Buck's Club, allowing the regular delivery of oysters and champagne at lunchtime. Churchill's unac-customed leisure allowed him to advance *Marlborough* by 20,000 words, but his ancestor's progress through his career failed to keep pace. As a result Churchill suggested to Harrap that they should split the book into two volumes: since the author had not asked for any extra money, Harrap readily agreed.

Churchill's illness twice delayed the meeting with Newman Flower to discuss *A History of the English-Speaking Peoples*, but his series of stories for the *News of the World* series made good progress once Eddie Marsh had mastered the technique of story-telling. Churchill had to return Marsh's first effort at *The Count of Monte Cristo*: 'We are not writing great stories <u>summarized</u>,' he explained from his bed, 'but great stories <u>retold</u>.'[36] Unusually, three tales were delivered to the newspaper at the end of October, ahead of schedule. The decision by the *News of the World* to start using them straightaway then caused a problem: Churchill had sold the series for $1,000 per tale to the *Chicago Tribune*, which expected to publish simultaneously with the *News of the World*. Accordingly the *Chicago Tribune* had cleared a space in its schedule for January 1933 and was unwilling to move. Churchill had to intervene personally with Riddell, first to secure a postponement by the *News of the World* and then to persuade him to yield the Canadian rights that the *Chicago Tribune* insisted must be theirs.

Nevertheless, each tale earned Churchill almost £700 worldwide, before Marsh collected his £25 *honorarium*. 'I trust that we may continue in the field of journalism, or shall we say literature, that collaboration which has become so famous in politics,' a delighted Churchill wrote to Marsh.[37] Three weeks later the *News of the World* offered a second series: 'They like them so much that they have ordered another half-dozen,'[38] Churchill told Marsh, asking him at the same time to edit the latest batch of his drafts for *Collier's*. 'They are awful stuff I fear, but it is what they like and what they pay for,' he added, enclosing a draft of *Land of Corn and Lobsters*. 'They help to pay the American debt – with a vengeance.'[39]

It was the end of October 1932 before Newman Flower visited Chartwell and the two men met face to face. Churchill had recovered sufficiently to run rings around the publisher. While he was ready to accept Cassell & Co.'s offer of £20,000 'in broad principle', he wrote to Flower afterwards, some last-minute details still needed settling. He would 'require three years from April 1934 to complete the work, together with a right if substantial progress should be made of a further two years' – in other words almost seven years in total. Nor did he feel that he should have to pay Curtis Brown's commission of £2,000. Although it was true that

Nancy Pearn had introduced them, 'the plan of this book and various negotiations were very far advanced before Curtis Brown came into it in any way', a point that Churchill drove home by enclosing a copy of Eyre & Spottiswoode's first offer. He was in no hurry and was quite prepared to take longer to make his own arrangements. 'Nevertheless,' he continued, 'I should be willing to discuss the contract in detail with you upon the basis that I received a net £20,000 as a lump sum. . . and that you arrange with Curtis Brown what commission they are to receive and defray it, relieving me of all charge.'[40]

Flower asked for a second meeting before he put final terms to his board of directors, but he was told that that was not the way Churchill did business. Churchill would make a decision only when he had a firm offer and then it would be a quick one. Predictably, the battle of wills went Churchill's way: Cassell absorbed all of Curtis Brown's commission, extended the book's deadline to April 1939 and agreed to pay Churchill £1,000 on signature with another £1,000 a year later. Another £3,000 would follow 'during the writing of the work' and a final £15,000 would be split between delivery of the manuscript and publication.

Churchill's illness did not put a halt to his stock market activity. Ignoring Cecil Vickers' warning, he made more purchases in September 1932, beating a retreat only on advice from Bernard Baruch a month later. 'Got completely out of market just below top. Am now waiting for re-entry. How good your judgement was,' he cabled from his nursing home.[41]

For much of his convalescence, Churchill was keen to reinvest in shares in order to back his hunch that the American presidential election would prove a turning point for the country's sick economy. When Baruch advised him to stay clear he turned to the currency markets instead. Agreeing the codename 'Winch' with his American bankers, he bought $20,000 forward for delivery in January 1933, then took modest profits a fortnight later.[42]

*

Once he was able to leave the nursing home, the Churchills moved into Morpeth Mansions, a four-bedroomed flat in Westminster, which they had leased the previous winter.[43] Enlarging Morpeth Mansions' entertaining room and creating a large study on the top floor had taken almost a year. The full cost of running two households had yet to emerge when the couple began to consider how best to provide a dowry for the wedding of their eldest daughter Diana. She was to marry the son of one of Churchill's benefactors, the South African mining financier Sir Abe Bailey. Unfortunately, years of economic depression had left him only able – or willing – to contribute assets providing an income of £600 a year to the marriage settlement.

'I am going thro' the worst time of my life,' Sir Abe explained to Churchill. 'However I expect with ordinary luck to get through without having to sell valuable assets – I hear on all sides of very rich people losing everything.'[44]

Churchill managed to contribute £200 a year by transferring to his daughter a one-fifth share of his father's will trust; at the same time advancing two-fifths to Randolph earlier than planned to help him clear fresh debts. Churchill's own income did not drop, because the lawyers had presciently worded the Elder Children's Trust in 1921 so that he would be able to claw back money from it if he used his parents' trusts to pass money to the children.[45]

The dowry was neatly negotiated, but 1932 had proved a difficult year: Churchill's bank overdraft had now swollen to £7,000. It was not that his earnings were low: at over £15,000 gross during the tax year that had ended in April 1932, he remained placed among the country's top 10,000 income earners, just as he had been before the Great War. The problem was that his spending during the year had reached a record £30,000, including £6,000 needed to cover investment losses.[46]

Churchill escaped to the south of France as the New Year guest of the duke of Westminster. The duke had rented a chateau, partly for its hunting and partly for the modest journey required to reach the nearby Casino G. Du Chaulier. There Churchill withdrew 75,000 francs in cash, but returned home with only 3,250 francs. It was not the best prelude to his first meeting with his new bank manager at Lloyds.[47]

An ailing William Bernau had been replaced by Stanley Williams, who came from a different school of banking. He formally requested 'the favour of early attention' to Churchill's overdraft, which had already exceeded its limit before the casino losses. Churchill asked Williams to be patient and to wait until Cassell's first advance for *A History of the English-Speaking Peoples* arrived. However, the advance failed to come before the February housekeeping allowance was due to be sent to Clementine. Anxious not to have to explain the reasons for its non-appearance, Churchill pleaded with Williams for a few days' grace. It was granted, but the scare did trigger a third Chartwell economy drive.[48]

Franklin D. Roosevelt, the new American president, had been elected in November 1932 on a platform of economic reform to fight the Depression. Churchill watched America anxiously, convinced that the stock markets were about to reverse four years of falling prices and help him break the cycle of debt that he could not escape through writing alone.

Reshuffling his holdings during January and early February of 1933, Churchill left his brokers instructions to take profits once each holding had reached the expected gains of 10 per cent. But prices continued to fall. Halfway through February Churchill finally admitted defeat. He sold all his shares in New York and repatriated the proceeds of £2,500 to bring his London overdraft back under its limit.[49] Just two weeks later, on the announcement of Anglo-American monetary talks, Vickers da Costa predicted that the markets were about to turn – and this time it was right. In no mood to listen, Churchill missed out on March's strong share rally.

On 5 April 1933 Roosevelt announced the end of the US dollar's link to gold. He gave American citizens four weeks to surrender all but nominal quantities of their gold to the US Treasury at a discount of more than 40 per cent to the new price set by the government.* Roosevelt had 'drawn a coach and horses through the sanctity of contract', Brendan Bracken complained,[50] but Churchill was quick to appreciate the significance of the moment which he had long been predicting: for good or ill, it would now be politicians rather than central bankers who called the tune on economic policy.

Churchill turned first to the currency futures market, which required no capital in order to participate. He sold dollars in the expectation that the currency would weaken against sterling, which had broken its own link to gold three years earlier. Adding a bet against the French franc for good measure, Churchill carried on selling dollars as the exchange rate weakened from $3.52 to each £ to $4.20 in June.[51] Having made profits of more than £800 from his early contracts, he added a bet against the Canadian dollar, so that by July he was 'short' of three different currencies against the pound.[52]

In May Churchill managed to make arrangements to return to trading shares: Vicker da Costa's associate Frazier Jelke would lend three-quarters of each purchase in New York while Vickers would make up the balance of one-quarter in London: every dollar that Churchill invested was borrowed. His loan from Frazier Jelke peaked at $52,000 in mid-June, before falling back by the end of the month to $16,000.[53] Wholly dependent on borrowed money, Churchill did not dare expose himself to the markets for long, so he traded in and out of a few selected shares, where he thought he understood the usual price ranges. It was an investment approach ill-suited to a time when many share prices doubled within six weeks.

---

* President Roosevelt's executive order required American citizens to transfer their gold to the US Treasury within four weeks, in exchange for $20.67 per troy ounce. Any future transactions would take place at $35 per ounce, a devaluation of the dollar by more than 40 per cent. The US government used the Treasury's profits on these transactions to create an Exchange Stabilization Fund to use for intervention in currency markets.

In any case, Churchill found it difficult to keep track of his results. To help him, Vickers prepared a loose-leaf book with a page for each share; 'closed' positions were indicated in black or red ink and 'open' holdings in pencil. This book reveals that Churchill earned profits of only £935 during the stock market's main recovery between April and July 1933, and that was before taking into account the cost of borrowing from his brokers.[54] In August both shares and currencies reversed direction, so Vickers da Costa had to ask Churchill for a fresh cash injection of £1,850.[55] Churchill's remaining shares in London and New York combined were worth only £625.[56]

Churchill had been trying to minimize the distractions of journalism all summer so that he could finish the first volume of *Marlborough* in time for its autumn launch. The most effective method, he discovered, was to set himself a tariff of £100 per 1,000 words for any fresh assignments, although the need for cash sometimes took precedence. He accepted, for example, *The Strand's* offer of only £200 to retell a Shakespeare play in 4,000 words – on the express condition that he was allowed to choose *Julius Caesar*, because he knew it well.[57]

Fleet Street proprietors knew the value of trenchant copy from a well-known name. Lord Riddell, for one, was happy to meet Churchill's self-imposed tariff. Not content with just 'Great Stories Retold' in the *News of the World*, Riddell commissioned an illustrated version of *The World Crisis* to be sold in weekly episodes alongside his Sunday newspaper. An unexpected success, it averaged sales of 35,000 copies a week and earned Churchill royalties of more than £4,000.[58]

A successful literary year was crowned when the first volume of *Marlborough: His Life and Times* finally reached British bookshops on 6 October, the day on which Hitler withdrew from the Geneva Disarmament Conference. Greeted by critical and public acclaim, the book's sales reached 8,500 in Britain within a week.[59]

'I sometimes look at that row of volumes in my little library, and

I cannot think how you have found the spare time to have got through the physical labour alone of writing them,' Stanley Baldwin wrote to Churchill. 'This last book would mean years of work even for a man whose sole occupation was writing history. Well, there is the miracle and let it remain. But I don't understand it.'[60]

Churchill celebrated *Marlborough*'s success by borrowing \$25,000 from Vickers da Costa to buy a New York share strongly recommended by Bernard Baruch. 'I bought seven hundred Brooklyn Manhattan Transit around [\$]30, sold four hundred around [\$]35 and am now sitting on three hundred. Many thanks for the fruitful suggestion,' Churchill cabled in mid-October.[61] Brooklyn Manhattan Transit – or 'BMTs' as they soon became known around Chartwell – featured strongly for several years, as Baruch (who still owned \$500,000-worth himself) was sure that consolidation of New York's railway system was bound to come and had a well-informed source within the boardroom, some of whose intelligence found its way to London.[62]

For the time being, Churchill's *Marlborough* money and his last Sherwood Starrs shares (sold with the help of Sir Abe Bailey's price guarantee)[63] brought his overdraft down to respectable levels during the autumn. However, it rose again when the special commissioners of the Inland Revenue demanded that a long overdue sur-tax bill of £3,000 was paid before the end of December.[64] Churchill's borrowings from his bank, brokers, insurers and family trusts finished 1933 at a total of £45,000.[65]

It was not his income that was the problem, because the £15,500 earnings from his writing that year put him among Britain's best-paid men. But Churchill had lost nearly half this amount at the casino or on the stock market.[66]

16

'The work piles up ahead'

Summoning More Ghosts, 1934–5

Exchange rates: $5 = £1; francs 76 = £1
Inflation multiples: US x 17; UK x 60

CHURCHILL WAS IN great demand as a writer in 1934. *Collier's*, the *News of the World* and *Daily Mail* had all renewed their commitments for the new year. They were joined by the *Sunday Dispatch*, whose veteran editor, William Blackwood, Churchill had known in his days as a Manchester MP. Blackwood wanted 'second serial' rights to Churchill's old material, which one of his jobbing journalists, Adam Marshall Diston,* would rework; Churchill would be expected to write only one fresh piece in four.[1]

Six articles under Churchill's name appeared in the press during January, the first of a total of fifty during the year.[2] Each one had to be typed, retyped and dispatched by Violet Pearman, Churchill's senior secretary at Chartwell, or her assistant, Grace Hamblin, who told an audience many years later:

> In the wilderness years [Churchill] worked like a tiger to keep up his literary output. It was his living, and he wasn't terribly well off. He would start at about ten o'clock in the evening,

---

* Adam Marshall Diston (1893–1956), journalist, Amalgamated Press 1919; assistant editor, acting editor *Answers* 1934; an official of the National Union of Journalists.

after dinner, and the secretaries (during those years there were only two of us, Mrs Pearman and myself) worked alternately. The one who went home early went at seven, and the one who was on late duty had dinner there and waited until he was ready. He would keep on and on and on until he'd gone as far as he wanted to.

Newspaper articles, she observed, 'were very exciting because they were done in one evening, quickly put out and sent off usually the next day. He got his money very quickly, which he liked too.'[3]

Following the first volume's British success, Churchill suggested splitting *Marlborough* once again to produce a third volume, but this time with an extra reward for the author. He first put the case to George Harrap: 'Our original contract was for two hundred thousand words. I shall now in any case write four hundred thousand at the same price, but if I am to make a third volume, the whole amounting to six hundred thousand words, a new arrangement would be necessary.' He mentioned that he already had a valuable deal from Cassell to keep him going beyond 1935, but made it clear that the 'lucrative' commitment could be postponed if Harrap offered him £3,000 and fellow publishers followed suit.[4] Harrap agreed by return, but Charles Scribner flatly declined on the grounds that he had never made any money from a single Churchill book. Even Lord Camrose at *The Daily Telegraph* baulked at the extra £1,250 that he was asked to produce, but at the next dinner of The Other Club,* to which Camrose had been elected, he agreed, as a friend, to pay £500.[5]

The prospects of *Marlborough*'s second volume being published before the end of 1934 were already looking doubtful. There was not only the vast number of articles to which Churchill had committed, but political tensions in Europe were claiming a growing

---

* The Other Club is a cross-party political dining society founded in 1911 by Churchill and F. E. Smith. Both men were considered too controversial for election by members of its well-established precursor, The Club. The Other Club's founders 'elected' its members, which included 'distinguished outsiders', such as Camrose, in addition to politicians.

proportion of his time as he campaigned to reverse the British government's policy of disarmament.

In March 1934 a new distraction presented itself: the cinema. Ever since his visit to Hollywood in 1929 Churchill had kept an eye on this new industry as a possible channel for the extra earnings which he needed. Indeed, in 1933 Curtis Brown had almost clinched a deal for a film about Churchill's life, before Paramount Pictures pulled out, citing 'the banking situation, earthquakes in Hollywood, etc.'[6] By the time Randolph introduced his father to the film producer Alexander Korda* in 1934, the movie industry's prospects had been transformed by the invention of Technicolor.

Korda, a forty-year old Hungarian immigrant, was the managing director of his own London Film Productions. He well understood the publicity value of involving Churchill in a series of ten short, topical films that he was planning. Korda asked Churchill to name his price for helping to write and produce these movies. Churchill knew equally why he was wanted: 'It must be borne in mind that the main thing I am giving the company is the right to use my name and that, once this has been announced, a very valuable asset has been contributed by me,' Churchill told his lawyer. They decided he should ask for a salary of £400 a month for ten months, plus 25 per cent of the films' profits.[7]

Korda sent Churchill his first pay cheque at the end of March,[8] but there was to be no public announcement or substantive work until the autumn. This was just as well, because Churchill's political commitments now took up much of his time.** His campaign

---

* Alexander Korda (1893–1956), born in Hungary; founded London Film Productions 1932; British citizen 1936; produced 112 films, including *The Scarlet Pimpernel* (1935); knighted 1942.
** Randolph drafted replies to possible questions at the launch press conference: 'Mr Korda and Mr Myers will certainly be asked whether Mr Winston Churchill's contract involves his retirement from politics. They will register an emphatic negative. They will also be asked what salary Mr Churchill is being paid. [They] will say that it is not the policy of the Company to disclose the details of its interior finance. ' CHAR 8/495/54, 55–6.

against disarmament meant frequent speeches to the House of Commons, which required careful preparation. He also spent several days preparing a submission to the House of Commons Privileges Committee with the help of lawyers: Churchill had raised a complaint about possible tampering by the government with evidence put before the Joint Select Committee involved in the Government of India Bill.[9]

Still plugging away at the second volume of *Marlborough* when he could, Churchill dispatched eight chapters to Eddie Marsh for proofreading in May.[10] Meanwhile, he tried to keep Newman Flower satisfied that his *A History of the English-Speaking Peoples* was progressing. 'You will be glad to hear that I am making a great deal of progress in the preparatory work of this book,' he told Flower. Two days later, on the other hand, Churchill apologized to Oxford historian Keith Feiling, whom he had diverted from *Marlborough* to help prepare an outline for his *History,* that there had not been time to look over any of his work. 'I have been much burdened by politics,' he explained. These had now 'thrown *Marlborough* Volume III over to the spring of 1936'.[11]

Because he regarded *Collier's* and the *Daily Mail* as the mainstays of his income, Churchill had always written these articles himself. However, by the middle of 1934 the demands on his time made this impossible. In May Churchill was forced to ask William Blackwood to draft an outline of his next article for the *Sunday Dispatch*, but Blackwood went one better: he provided a finished text that needed no changes. It had been put together by Blackwood's jobbing journalist, Adam Marshall Diston. 'He is a splendid journalist, is Diston,' Blackwood enthused, 'and if you ever descend to having a "ghost" I could strongly recommend him.'[12] Churchill 'descended' a fortnight later, offering Diston £15 for each remaining article of his *Collier's* series, a fraction of his own fee of £350.[13] It was the start of a partnership that would flourish for the rest of the decade.

Every word, however, of Churchill's tribute in *The Times* of 2 July to his 'oldest and dearest friend', the 9th duke of Marlborough, was his own and intensely felt. His cousin's sudden death had evoked in Churchill sombre reflections on the changes in wealth and society that they had jointly witnessed bearing down on their family:

> During the forty-two years that he was Duke of Marlborough, the organism of English society underwent a complete revolution. The three or four hundred families which for three or four hundred years guided the fortunes of the nation from a small, struggling community to the headship of a vast and still unconquered Empire lost their authority and control. . . The class to which the Duke belonged were not only almost entirely relieved of their political responsibilities, but they were to a very large extent stripped of their property and in many cases driven from their homes.[14]

Churchill's growing commitments had not distracted him completely from the financial markets. The year had started inauspiciously when sterling weakened just before large forward dollar purchases matured, losing him £300.[15] His turnover of American shares was limited to $140,000 in the first half of 1934, much of it concentrated on 'BM'Is', as he kept checking with Baruch whether the long-awaited consolidation of New York's railway system was imminent. 'BMT oboy,' he cabled late in April, when the share price spiked just after he had sold most of his stake. 'Have still got some. Please advise.'[16]

By June Churchill had banked profits of $2,600, but his overdraft breached its £9,000 limit. As the long holiday season approached, Churchill realized that another encounter with the bank was inevitable. He forecast that his earnings would exceed expenditure by £5,000 for the rest of the year and so convinced Stanley Williams to let the breach of the bank's limit stand until the next *Marlborough* advances arrived.[17] As a result Grace Hamblin was able to use £650 to pay off selected tradesmen before Churchill set off for Cannes with Randolph.

Father and son found Maxine Elliott, their hostess, 'greatly impoverished by the American slump, & the $ exchange'. Her usual income of $150,000 a year had been reduced by a third,[18] but Clementine found it difficult from afar to sympathize with a single woman on £10,000 a year.

Even on holiday work continued to arrive. George Riddell cabled to say that he wanted a new series on Churchill's early life for the *News of the World*: 'Say – 30,000 words, price £2,500.' A follow-up letter sweetened the terms, although Riddell was adamant: 'Copy to be written by you personally, not too much politics.' Churchill immediately set his new ghost to work.[19] Diston would dig out old articles and books – in this case a copy of *My Early Life* that Churchill sent him – and then shuffle them and paste them together with linking passages, before returning them to Churchill to add an extra sentence or two. Confident that between them they would be able to stretch the word count, Churchill inked in an extra £3,500 to his forecast of income for the year. 'I hope to pay off a good many bills at the end of this year,' he told Clementine, '& next year we really ought to be able to save a substantial sum.'[20]

This hope came to an end when Churchill and Randolph visited Cannes's Palm Beach Casino to celebrate the dispatch of the final proofs of the second volume of *Marlborough: His Life and Times*. The newspaper gossip columns kept Clementine up to date:

> The Sunday papers are full of the Churchills & their works. Your instalments of *Marlborough*, Randolph's 'Searchlight', news that you & he are playing roulette (you did not tell your poor Pussy Cat!) you intensely, he in an 'effervescent manner'.[21]

Her letter prompted a confession from Churchill: 'I have indeed been playing at the Casino, though at Chemin de Fer, and have lost uniformly, but not on a large scale. Randolph too has lost and has stopped playing.'[22] Churchill had withdrawn 60,000 francs of cash for himself, but deposited only 1,250 on his return.[23]

Randolph's losses only emerged later, when the casino pressed him to honour cheques worth £1,900. That was just the tip of the iceberg. Randolph admitted to running up other debts of £4,350, all since his grandfather's trust's money had wiped the slate clean a year earlier. Churchill avoided strict censure, all too aware of his own brushes with 'Mephistopheles'. Instead he instructed Nicholl, Manisty & Co. to honour the cheques with money raised from his father's trust. Randolph was to repay £800 a year until he had reimbursed the full £6,100 now advanced to him.[24]

Churchill had promised Clementine that he would join her on an October cruise around the eastern Mediterranean, on board the *Rosaura*,* the private yacht of Walter Guinness. While on board he planned to work on Korda's film scripts. Just before he left, however, Korda came up with a new and even more lucrative assignment: he wanted Churchill to produce a screenplay for a film to mark George V's Silver Jubilee in 1935. 'I am going to begin this scenario immediately and side track all my other work', Churchill promised Korda, accepting the offer of a £10,000 guarantee and 25 per cent of the film's net profits.[25]

Churchill wrote his screenplay aboard the *Rosaura*, sailing between Athens, Beirut, Alexandria and Naples and handed it over to Korda on his return. While he was away George Harrap published the second volume of *Marlborough* in London,[26] but the disappearance of the maps at New York customs forced the postponement of the American edition – and (more significantly for Churchill) of Scribner's cheque on publication.

Churchill had promised his bank manager that his overdraft would reduce in size after the publication of the second volume of *Marlborough*. Instead, it finished October at a record level of £12,000.[27] Salvation came only when the *News of the World* agreed

---

* The 1,200-ton *Rosaura* had been converted from her former life as *Dieppe*, a cross-Channel steamer; she was requisitioned by the Royal Navy in 1939 and sank off Tobruk in 1941.

to send its cheque for Churchill's life story early: the bank was satisfied, although the cheque was post-dated to 1 January 1935. The
newspaper's general manager Major Percy Davies declared the
story (ghostwritten by Marshall Diston) to be 'brilliant and highly
entertaining', and happily agreed to Churchill's suggestion that his
fee for 44,000 words should be settled at £4,200.[28]

While struggling to contain his overdraft, Churchill kept up his
campaign against the National Socialists' treatment of Germany's
civilian population. He warned that the British would soon have to
choose whether or not to defend their way of life. Churchill's first
political victory came on disarmament, when the cabinet
announced the building of extra aircraft, a key concern of
Churchill's newspaper columns and House of Commons speeches.

The Churchill's preparation for a speech in the House involved days
of marshalling information from a network of informants, including his intelligence-linked neighbour, Desmond Morton, and a
senior Foreign Office diplomat, Roger Winant. The build-up to
parliamentary speeches became a familiar feature of Chartwell life,
but it meant that his books, films and personal business had to be
temporarily set aside.

The Garron Tower estate was certainly in need of Churchill's
attention. In theory it still generated £900 a year of rental income,
but large rent arrears were accumulating on the Carnlough slums
that passed for workers' cottages.[29] Churchill set his mind against
suing his tenants or turning them out of their homes. Instead, he
instructed his lawyers to hand the cottages over to their tenants for
one guinea each: 'The gift is conditional on this being done by all.
Let action be taken at once and the tenants be told by Christmas.'[30]

Disappointingly, the Silver Jubilee film project was making slow
progress. Korda had plenty of competitors and the king and the
government were trying to cajole them into forming a single, semi-
official consortium. Korda broke the news in mid-December that
his 'financial friends' wanted Churchill's guarantee halved to
£5,000.

Churchill complained that just two months earlier Korda had declared his screenplay 'a really splendid basis for preliminary work'; however, he had no alternative but to give way: Korda was his only good contact in an industry that he still regarded as central to his future finances. Churchill's only condition was that Korda's London Films should extend his monthly retainer on the original series, yet to be made. 'Toiling at film,' he cabled over Christmas, after Clementine left on a long cruise to the Dutch East Indies on a mission to bring back a Komodo dragon for London Zoo.[31]

In December 1934 Churchill presided at Chartwell over a meeting to revise the Silver Jubilee film scipt: 'We spent many hours jawing and seeking inspiration. Have no doubt that the film will be a commercial success and that I shall get at least my £10,000 out of it,' he reported to Clementine. He had paid off all but £1,500 of their outstanding bills, he proudly told her on New Year's Day: 'We have finished up the year better than we have ever done and the financial prospects of this coming year are very much more favourable than anything we have known. If we avoid all large capital expenditure and save money wherever we can, we ought to be in a good position by this time next year.'[32]

Churchill's New Year projections for his 1935 finances were characteristically optimistic. Thanks largely to London Films, he expected his income that year to exceed £25,000, well ahead of his spending, which he estimated at less than £11,000.[33] But in mid-January the sums started to go awry.

The new Silver Jubilee screenplay did not find favour. 'Korda dined with me last night at the flat,' Churchill wrote to Clementine, 'and said that while I had contributed a great quantity of material, he was not at all satisfied with the way it had been handled by the technical people. In other words, it would not do at all.'[34] Days later came another blow: 'It appears that an Act of Parliament says that a film which does not consist wholly or mainly of topical news reels, and which is longer than two reels, must be provisionally released six months before it can be finally released,' Churchill

explained.[35] Government lawyers had ruled that it could not, therefore, be released until November, far too late for the Silver Jubilee
in May. Two days later, he wrote sadly of the final cut:

> The film is busted and all my work and thought produced no
> result. I am to hear tonight from Korda what they propose
> about me. I have asked for either £5,000 or another film on the
> same terms as the Jubilee film, and also for the renewal of the
> £4,000 a year contract for another year for the short films. I
> hope to sell the articles based on the film in America for £1,000
> and have already sold the English counter-part to the *Evening
> Standard* for £1,000. So while all the large hopes have disap-
> peared for the time being there will still be enough to leave us
> comfortable this year.[36]

Korda opted for a second film, but there was to be no profit share
and no renewal of the 'short films' retainer. Churchill was to receive
£2,000 for their nominal 'supervision',[37] but he had to acknowledge
that his hoped-for breakthrough into the lucrative world of film
had failed for the time being.

By coincidence, he had reached the point in the next volume of
Marlborough when his ancestor had fallen out of favour at Queen
Anne's court, only to bounce back shortly afterwards. 'What a
downy bird he was,' Churchill told Clementine. 'He will always
stoop to conquer. His long apprenticeship as courtier had taught
him to bow and scrape and to put up with second or third best if
he could get no better.'[38]

It was an apt summary of his own approach. Inspired by his
ancestor's resilience, he tried to sell the Jubilee script first to the
Daily Mail, which passed, and then to Beaverbrook's *Evening
Standard*, whose editor, Percy Cudlipp, snapped up Churchill as
a new contributor without even bothering to quibble over his
£1,000 fee.[39]

The *Daily Mail* made amends by committing to take fifteen
articles in 1935, although it spiked the second of these, entitled

'The Grave Weakness of Britain's Defences'. Churchill was told that the centre pages were being kept 'as clear as possible of armaments and the more belligerent phases of international affairs'. Churchill's article appeared the next day, however, and a secretary at the *Mail* noted: 'Settled by Mr C. himself with Lord Rothermere 3.4.35.'[40]

In stark contrast, *The Strand* positively encouraged a 'frank' and 'outspoken' portrait of Hitler, though Churchill refused valuable offers to write in similar terms about his senior Tory colleagues. He remained at heart a politician keen to regain office and the Conservative Stanley Baldwin appeared close to succeeding the ailing Ramsay MacDonald as prime minister of the National Government. Now that Indian independence had finally receded into the political background, Churchill was rebuilding his credibility on the issue of German rearmament, helped by Hitler's recent announcement that Germany's air force already matched Britain's in strength. Among the many friends and contacts whom Churchill enlisted to assist his campaign was Brendan Bracken's co-owner of *The Economist* magazine, the austere Sir Henry Strakosch.* As chairman of Union Corporation, the South African mining business, Strakosch passed on confidential details of the raw materials which his company was supplying to the German armaments industry.

Soon Clementine would return from her cruise (with two 'dragons' for London Zoo, neither more than six feet in length), and Churchill looked forward at his financial prospects for the remainder of 1935 with renewed confidence. Discussions with London Films had reached a satisfactory conclusion, he told Clementine: 'In a nutshell, they pay me £2,000 a year for another year on account of the

---

* Henry Strakosch, (1871–1943), born in Austria; clerk, Anglo-Austrian Bank of South Africa, London 1891; assistant managing director Goerz & Co., South Africa 1895, chairman (renamed Union Corporation 1918) 1924–43; naturalized British citizen 1907; chairman, *The Economist* magazine 1929–43; adviser, central banking and reserves policy to the governments of South African and India; member, Council of India 1930–7; adviser, secretary of state for India 1937–42; knighted 1921.

short films, and £5,000 compensation for the failure of the Jubilee film.'[41] He promised Clementine that on her return she would find their bills almost up to date and underlined the point by enclosing a birthday cheque for 100 guineas. 'Everything has been paid up every month this year, and there are only three or four old stagers which exist.'[42]

In June 1935, shortly after Clementine's arrival, Stanley Baldwin became prime minister for the third time, but there was no cabinet post for Churchill. Baldwin did, however, invite him to join the Imperial Defence Committee's new air research sub-committee and, having sought assurances that this appointment was not intended to silence him on the issue of rearmament, Churchill accepted. So began a new round in his long-running battle with the Cabinet Office over his entitlement to keep cabinet papers.

A year earlier, just before Churchill set off on his Mediterranean cruise, he had received a letter telling all retired cabinet ministers of a decision by the cabinet to tighten up rules governing the custody and use of official papers. Lloyd George and Churchill had thwarted a similar move in 1919, but the more pliable cabinet of 1934 had accepted the need for change after a recent Labour cabinet minister's biography had quoted from official papers without prior clearance.[*] The new rules required all ministers to return their papers on leaving office, but the government could only request past ministers such as Churchill to do so. They would then have to visit the Cabinet Office in person to inspect their papers, which Churchill regarded as a serious threat to his literary livelihood.[43]

He replied to officials: 'The present Cabinet is no doubt entitled to make any arrangements which it chooses for the safe keeping of its documents. So far as concerns the past I am not aware of any facts which would lead me to accept your invitation to return any documents of the kind specified which I may have in my possession.'[45]

---

[*] *George Lansbury: My Father* (1934) by Edgar Lansbury, who was prosecuted under the Official Secrets Act. See D. Reynolds, *In Command of History*, p. 26.

Now, on Churchill's appointment to the air research sub-committee, the veteran cabinet secretary, Sir Maurice Hankey, visited Chartwell to make a personal appeal to Churchill for the return of official documents. He found himself entertained to an excellent lunch before Churchill re-asserted his legal ownership of the documents and letters which the Cabinet Office wanted back; Sir Maurice beat a judicious retreat.[45]

Churchill's confident financial forecasts for 1935 failed to allow for any investment or gambling losses, both of which were to feature during the summer. He had found it impossible to understand Vickers da Costa's share accounts for the first half of the year: 'What is so jolly about this is that it is absolutely impossible for me to learn the only thing that I want to know, namely, if everything were sold today at the present price, how much should I owe?' he complained to Jack. The answer was in the accounts, but it was not the one that he wanted to hear: even if he sent Vickers a cheque for £1,000 as requested, Churchill would still owe £800 on closing all his accounts.[46]

His response was to step up the pace of his dealing during the parliamentary recess. He asked his brokers to telephone every day with the New York prices, then he returned to trading his favourite names, including 'BMTs', moving in and out of each share according to its position within what he observed as its usual price range. Each day his secretary supplied him with a slip showing his gross and net balances.

August was not a success. Churchill started the month with net holdings of $42,000 and an accumulated loss of $4,500, but he finished it with positions of $62,000 and the loss more than doubled.[47] He carried on buying in September, until Jack and Cecil Vickers both gave warnings, after which Churchill made thirteen sales within a week to reduce his holdings by $50,000.[48] A week later, he was back asking Baruch: 'Do you advise buying BMT around 41?' 'Yes' came the reply.[49]

A young visitor to Chartwell recorded the picture that week in his diary: 'Found Churchill in blue overalls painting in his studio and in very grim mood. He was receiving frequent reports of Stock Exchange prices in London and New York – his secretary brought one in while we were at tea; said markets were very depressed owing to the political tension.'[50]

Churchill spent his summer holiday at Maxine Elliott's home in Cannes. The news was grim as Benito Mussolini tried to enlarge Italy's empire by invading Abyssinia. Churchill passed his days painting, rather than writing, and his evenings at the Cannes casino. Here he found the transport minister, Leslie Hore-Belisha, playing for stakes that Churchill judged much too high. His own losses had been 'nothing serious',[51] he told Clementine. But a success at baccarat persuaded him to stay one extra night, so as to treat his hostess to dinner at the casino. That evening Churchill drew 35,000 francs in cash. That made a total of 65,000 francs for the entire stay, but on his return he deposited only 10,100 francs.

His summer holiday had cost him at least £750.[52] Churchill had once again exceeded his overdraft limit and on his return to Britain Stanley Williams was lying in wait for him. Churchill blamed London Films for missing one of its payments, but this time Williams was not convinced. He refused Churchill's request for a grace period and enforced a sale of shares held by the bank as security to bring the overdraft below £8,000.[53]

17

'We can carry on for a year or two more'
Films, Columns and Debts, 1935–7

Exchange rate: $4 = £1
Inflation multiples: US x 17; UK x 60

MARLBOROUGH HAD FAILED to make any progress during the holidays and Churchill used the cover of a possible general election to warn George Harrap of further delays: 'If we have an election and I am forced to make a great many speeches, I doubt if it will be possible to complete the volume before the early autumn.'[1] Days later, Stanley Baldwin asked the voters to endorse the National Government's mandate, putting forward a platform of collective security that would be achieved through the League of Nations.

In the election that followed on 14 November 1935, the Conservatives won 432 seats in the House of Commons, dwarfing the Labour and Liberal parties' combined total of 175. At a post-election party, Lord Beaverbrook predicted that Churchill would not be asked to join the cabinet – and he was right. Wounded, Churchill 'set out with my paint-box for more genial climes',[2] but first there were business affairs to settle.

Adam Marshall Diston had already ghostwritten most of Churchill's *News of the World* series due to appear in January 1936. The paper's new chairman Sir Emsley Carr was so pleased with 'The Great Men I Have Known' (who included Lloyd George, Arthur Balfour and Joseph Chamberlain) that he signed Churchill up straightaway for another series in 1937.[3] William Chenery at

Collier's was less impressed and demanded changes to 'Rockefeller' and 'Charles Chaplin', declaring them 'written in a form better calculated to meet the requirements of English than American mass magazines'.[4]

More awkwardly for Churchill, Clementine insisted that before leaving for Paris, Majorca and Barcelona, they should make an impression on their pile of unpaid bills. Churchill's relations with Lloyds Bank were still strained, because he had used his London Films cheques to pay for election expenses rather than reduce his borrowings as promised. Armed with another post-dated cheque from the *News of the World*, however, he was able to persuade Stanley Williams to keep his overdraft limit at £8,000.[5] Even so, this left only £1,200 to allocate to the bills, which included one for more than £900 alone from the wine merchants Randolph Payne & Sons. Their bill particularly worried Clementine, because the company's chairman Lord Sandhurst had written to Churchill pointing out that he had promised three years earlier to pay any fresh bills straightaway, and also to reduce 'from time to time' his backlog of old accounts amounting to £660. Neither pledge, the chairman claimed, had been honoured.[6]

Before paying, Churchill asked his secretaries to analyse the household's alcohol consumption during the past year. The result was a cost of £920, including £268 spent on ten magnums, 185 bottles, 183 pints and 68 imperial pints of champagne.[7] Clementine sent Lord Sandhurst a cheque to clear the 'current account' only. By the time he wrote to ask for more, the Churchills had left.

Clementine and Mary returned for Christmas at Blenheim, followed by skiing in Austria, while Churchill and Randolph headed on to Africa. Christmas in Tangier was not a success, partly because of the rain and partly because of political events weighing on Churchill's mind. Sir Samuel Hoare, the foreign secretary, had misjudged the public mood by agreeing with his French counterpart that part of Abyssinia should be ceded to Italy following Mussolini's invasion of the country. Sir Samuel resigned and Churchill wondered if he should return to London. However, when Anthony Eden replaced Sir Samuel it seemed the matter was settled and Churchill and his son moved on to Marrakech, in the foothills of the Atlas Mountains. Churchill's spirits revived in the sunshine and in the company of Lloyd George and Lord Rothermere, who ensured a regular supply of London newspapers. Churchill told Clementine of a wager:

> Rothermere offered me 2 bets. First £2,000 if I went teetotal in 1936. I refused as I think life would not be worth living, but 2,000 free of tax is nearly 3,500 & then the saving of liquor, 500 = 4,000. It was a fine offer. I have however accepted his second bet of £600 not to drink any brandy or undiluted spirits in 1936.[8]

Lacking a casino, the Mamounia Hotel in Marrakech turned out to be an ideal base for Churchill.

> This is a wonderful place. In my opinion it is better than any of the hotels that I have stayed in on the Riviera. . . I spend the whole day painting and on *Marlborough* (apart from eating and drinking) but no neat spirits according to the bet.[9]

Churchill was preparing to leave after a stay of almost a month when news came through of the death of George V. The *News of the World* cabled, asking him for a tribute in time for the weekend's newspaper, at a fee of £400. Churchill dictated to Mrs Pearman while sitting among the party's suitcases and on the train to Tangier, where he left his tribute to the king for the *Daily Mail's* local correspondent to transmit to London.[10]

Two hundred pages of *Marlborough* had yet to be written, but Churchill was distracted by well-paid commissions as soon as he returned to London in January 1936. He accepted £250 from *The Strand* to write about the launch of Cunard's new transatlantic liner the *Queen Mary*. Although he fully intended to visit the ship in Glasgow, in the end he decided he could not afford the time and he sub-contracted the task to Marshall Diston for the usual fee of 15 guineas.[11]

For a long time Churchill had wanted higher fees for his fort-nightly political columns in the *Daily Mail*, but the paper would not pay more than £75. Churchill and his agent thought they should fetch £200 or even £250 if sold properly around the world.[12] Curtis Brown procured an offer from the editor of the *Evening Standard*, Percy Cudlipp, of £100 a column, to which Churchill could add any money which he raised from overseas syndication. Negotiations stalled until March when Cudlipp accepted Churchill's demand that he must be allowed to continue his lucrative non-political writing for the *News of the World*.[13] They were interrupted again almost immediately when Hitler's troops marched into the demilitarized Rhineland.

Prime Minister Baldwin was rumoured to be appointing a min-ister for the co-ordination of defence. Keen to take on the position, Churchill checked his instincts to make 'a telling speech' and remained on best behaviour while he dictated a trial article about the crisis for the *Evening Standard*. When Baldwin appointed Sir Thomas Inskip, a lawyer who had only ever held legal posts in government, Churchill came to the conclusion that Baldwin was never going to restore him to office and as a result, he felt at liberty to resume his criticism of government policy.

Churchill returned to the new arrangements for his political column. He only felt confident enough to give notice to the *Daily Mail* and to sign his contract with the *Evening Standard* once William Hearst personally agreed that his American newspapers would pay $500 for each article they used and Curtis Brown forecast at least £25 each time for European sales.[14] These new arrangements took effect in April, but hit an immediate difficulty: Churchill had offered Hearst the right to refuse up to a third of his columns if the subject matter was not interesting enough to American readers and his editors spiked his first two offerings. An exasperated Churchill sug-gested to Hearst that they abandon their arrangement. 'Mr Churchill is rather arbitrary,' Hearst reportedly told his staff, 'so perhaps we had better call it off before there is more grief.'[15] Shorn of its American outlets, the new series earned Churchill an average of £110 a column; it was half his initial target, but still an improvement.

Churchill could only turn his attention to the final section of *Marlborough* in Parliament's Easter recess during April. 'I am labouring to finish *Marlborough* in time for Autumn publication and I feel I have the measure of it in my mind,' he told the historian Keith Feiling.[16] However George Harrap's production manager, Charles Wood, was less confident of achieving this timetable, pointing out that an October publication would require the whole text to be ready by the end of July at the latest.

Churchill realized this was impossible. He suggested to Harrap that they split the book up again into yet another volume, so that he would have to write only fifty more pages to reach the next natural dividing point, the Battle of Malplaquet. Accustomed by now to Churchill's ways, Harrap agreed to the request for an extra £3,500 advance that accompanied Churchill's suggestion.[17] 'The inevitable has happened,' Churchill then told Charles Scribner and *The Sunday Times*, without daring to ask them for more money. '*Marlborough* must now extend to four volumes.'[18]

In August Newman Flower asked whether Churchill's *A History of the English-Speaking Peoples* would be ready for publication the following year, 1937 – the earliest date mentioned in their contract. Churchill broke the news that there was no hope of it being ready before the last contractual date allowed: 30 April 1939. 'I have been very much ridden in upon by politics owing to the need of urging this country to rearm,' he explained. 'However a great deal of work has been done upon the *English-Speaking Peoples*. Not only has the ground been surveyed, and the whole plan made out, but I have a very large mass of material which has been carefully collected under my supervision covering every chapter.'[19]

Suspicious, Flower asked to visit Chartwell to inspect this plan, but Churchill was too busy to fit him in. In fact, he was trying to finish the final fifty pages of the third volume of *Marlborough*, so that he could ask Harrap for his cheque before holidaying in France.[20]

Churchill left the last-minute publishing details to a new literary assistant, William Deakin,* while he returned to journalism at Maxine Elliott's Château de l'Horizon. 'I have just completed the first of my new articles for the *News of the World*,' he reported to Clementine. 'I mean to do at least three more before I leave. They are v[er]y lucrative.'[21] They needed to be, because Churchill was as usual losing money at the nearby casino. He withdrew 70,000 francs in cash during his stay, but only 3,400 found their way home, leaving his bank account the poorer by £870.[22]

Next came the most serious family crisis of the year. Diana's marriage had already ended in divorce, and Churchill had dealt with another episode of Randolph's gambling debts,[23] but now Sarah, their middle daughter, was in trouble.

A professional dancer, Sarah had fallen for her latest show's leading actor, Victor Samek,** and wished to marry him although he had already been married twice. Churchill considered Victor as 'common as dirt' when they met in February, as he wrote to Clementine: 'An Austrian citizen. . . twice divorced: 36 so he says. A horrible mouth: a foul Austro-Yankee drawl. I did not offer to shake hands: but put him through a long examination.'[24]

Churchill insisted Sarah and Victor should spend a year apart before making any decision on marriage, but they continued to see each other. Churchill commissioned a report from private investigators in America and confronted Sarah with its findings: Victor

---

* William Deakin (1913–2005), literary assistant to Churchill (paid £400 a year) 1936–40; fellow, Wadham College, Oxford 1936–50; military service including in the Special Operations Executive (SOE) 1940–5; literary assistant to Churchill 1945–55; warden, St Antony's College, Oxford 1950–68; author *The Brutal Friendship* (1962), *The Embattled Mountain* (1971); knighted 1975.
** Victor Samek (1898–1964), born in Austria; concert pianist in United States and Britain; stage name Vic Oliver; first interviewee of BBC Radio's *Desert Island Discs*.

13. Churchill, colonel of the 6th battalion of the Royal Scots Fusiliers, with his second-in-command, Major Sir Archibald Sinclair at Armentières on the Western Front, 1916.

14–17. Churchill's principal literary and film patrons: *(above left)* Thornton Butterworth, London; *(above right)* Charles Scribner III of Charles Scribner's Sons, New York; *(below left)* Newman Flower of Cassell & Co.; *(below right)* Alexander Korda, founding owner of London Film Productions.

1923		19,896	11	2
Jan. 11	J. Hunt	182	12	.
17	Pol. R. Leigh		15	.
12	Casino Cannes 7co 5,000 @68.30	73	4	2
10	— 7co 5000 @68.30	73	4	2
11	Triangle Motor Hire Co	14	3	3
23	Prem. Comt. Unc. H. Assur.			
	Pol. 147,521	6	6	.
17	Casino Cannes 7co 5,000 @71.80	69	12	9
19	— 7s. 10,000 @71.80	139	5	6
20	Thos. Cook	30	.	
20	Casino Cannes @ 7s 3,000 @72.15	41	11	7
19.	— 7s. 3,000 @72.15	41	11	7
25	Sandroyd School	73	15	.
27	J. A. Beckenham	50	.	
28	Turf Club.	5	.	
30	Subn: Eighty Club	1	1	
-	Knight, Frank, Rutley	150	.	
31	P. Tilden	400	.	
Feb 3	Ritz Hotel	110	.	
		21358	13	2

18. An extract from Churchill's bank statement, showing repeated cash withdrawals from the Casino de Cannes in France, January 1923.

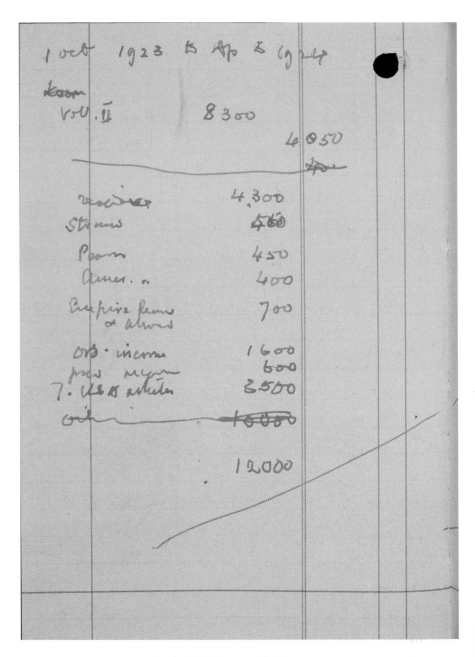

19. A characteristic Churchill 'forecast' of his income, covering the last quarter of 1923 and first half of 1924.

20. The Prince of Wales, later Edward VIII (*left*) with one of Churchill's financial mentors and benefactors, the mining financier Sir Abe Bailey (*right*), 1925.

21. Churchill boar-hunting in Normandy as a guest of the duke of Westminster, accompanied by his son Randolph (*left*) and Coco Chanel (*centre*), the duke's girlfriend at the time, January 1928.

22. Churchill with his son Randolph (*left*), nephew John (*centre left*) and brother Jack (*right*) during the family visit to Canada and the US, 1929.

23. During the same journey, Churchill with his nephew John (far left), son Randolph (second left), the earl of Feversham (centre) and Bernard Baruch, at Chicago, bound for New York, shortly before the Wall Street crash, October 1929.

Samek's first divorce had been granted on the grounds of his cruelty and there was no trace of a second divorce.[25] Three months later, Sarah eloped to New York to join Samek.

Churchill dispatched Randolph in hot pursuit. 'Don't communicate Samek or see him except with lawyer,' he instructed him. 'Matter turns on validity second divorce. No question friendly relations Samek whatever happens.'[26] But Churchill knew that if Samek's second divorce and American naturalization papers came through, there was little he could do.

In the meantime, he had his own problems to deal with. Churchill's fortnightly political column was still earning only half of what he thought it should. One way to boost his share of receipts would be to bypass his agent and renew his contract directly with the *Evening Standard*, and then to engage its syndication department to sell the articles overseas for him. He suggested the idea to the *Standard*'s Percy Cudlipp, but Cudlipp drove a hard bargain: he would only agree if Churchill accepted a reduction in the notice period that he could be given if the paper chose to cancel the arrangement, from Churchill's six months of notice to the newspaper's standard of one month; in addition Churchill was to bear the risk of syndication sales. The *Evening Standard* would advance him £120 for each article, but only guarantee £50 of the sum as its own fee; the remaining £70 would be clawed back if there were no sales.[27]

Curtis Brown reacted with predictable fury to being cut out of the deal and objected that it had introduced Churchill to the *Evening Standard*. 'You are mistaken in supposing that you "found this *Evening Standard* opening" for me,' Churchill coldly replied. 'I have been for some time in close relations with Mr Cudlipp. Now that a new contract is to be made on different terms and on a different basis, I do not feel justified in continuing that arrangement.'[28]

Churchill's political articles had become darker in tone during 1936 and attracted the interest of the Foreign Office. Rex Leeper, the head of the FO's news department, visited Churchill at

Chartwell to discuss how his popularity could be harnessed to counter public apathy towards the Nazis. A month later, Churchill spoke at the first private lunch at the Savoy Hotel of the self-styled Anti-Nazi Council. Sixteen guests debated how best to achieve their ends when the awkward question came up of how they might fund their future activities. Eugen Spier, a Jewish German banker resident in London since 1922, broke the long silence: he volunteered to take care of the next stage.

The group called itself the Focus in Defence of Freedom and Peace. It remained a secretive and unstructured organization, quietly supplying speakers and publicity material to anti-Nazi public meetings. Focus raised £20,000, mainly from members of the Jewish community, to fund its research and support for public meetings,[29] but there is no evidence in Churchill's bank statements of 1936 or 1937 to support any suggestion by historian David Irving that Focus or its leaders may have made undisclosed payments to Churchill.[30] What he did agree to do, in principle, for a fee of £5,000, was visit the United States at the end of 1936 or early in 1937 to launch a parallel American Focus group by giving speeches to prominent figures in New York, Philadelphia and Chicago.[31] Churchill had his long-established friendship with the prince of Wales, now Edward VIII, to thank for the fact that the trip never took place – and that the American arm of Focus never paid him.

Churchill's friendship with Edward had led a number of newspapers and magazines to commission him to write special articles to mark the King's Coronation which was expected in 1937.[32] However, during the autumn of 1936 events behind the scenes began to cast a doubt over whether the ceremony would proceed. Edward had formed a relationship two years earlier with an American divorcée, Wallis Simpson, who had recently separated from her second husband. He had given Wallis extravagant gifts of jewellery, as well as an annual expense allowance of £6,000.[33] Their relationship continued after Edward came to the throne, although it was not until late in October 1936 that the king discussed the possibility that they might marry with Prime Minister Stanley Baldwin. Baldwin was convinced that the British public would not accept the marriage of their king with a divorcee and urged a post-ponement of Wallis's divorce proceedings, to no avail. Edward was determined to marry Wallis as soon as she obtained a decree nisi.

The crisis broke at a difficult time for Churchill. After a period of relative calm in his finances, during which his literary earnings and small share sales had kept his overdraft just within its limit, the Inland Revenue had insisted at the end of October that he pay a large tax bill, long overdue, within days.[34] Only an appeal to the *News of the World* for another post-dated cheque convinced Lloyds Bank to provide temporary funds, but the incident convinced Churchill at the end of November that he had no alternative but to go through with his visit to New York in December to earn the £5,000 offered by Focus's American promoters.

'There is no less than £6,000 to pay in Income & super tax during 1937,' he explained to Clementine. 'This being so I feel it is necessary to take this US offer, & I am satisfied it is quite proper for me to do so.'[35] Bernard Baruch was not so sure: 'No committee yet formed nor cash raised,' Randolph reported after visiting his father's friend. 'Bernie advises against coming under Landau's* sole auspices since it merely representative Jewish Telegraph Agency.'[36]

The dilemma remained unresolved on 3 December, the day that Churchill publicly launched the British arm of Focus's Defence of Freedom and Peace movement at the Royal Albert Hall. It was also the day on which news broke publicly of the impasse over marriage plans between the king and the government of both Britain and its dominions.

Edward told the prime minister that Wallis was leaving Britain immediately. He then asked to meet his oldest political friend before deciding his own course of action. Churchill travelled to

---

* Jacob Landau (1892–1952), founder, Jewish Correpondence Bureau, The Hague, 1917; renamed Jewish Telegraph Agency (JTA) on move to London 1919; moved to New York, 1922; JTA distributed news affecting Jewish communities to more than 400 newspapers by 1925.

Windsor, where he advised an exhausted Edward to ask for a fort-night's grace and to give Baldwin an assurance that he would not marry against the advice of his ministers.

Churchill arrived late for the next session of Prime Minister's Questions at the House of Commons, unaware that Baldwin had already conceded more time to Edward although the king had refused to give an undertaking not to marry. When Churchill inter-vened to ask Baldwin to take 'no irrevocable step', MPs shouted him down, interpreting his words as yet another of his attacks on the prime minister that had featured in Churchill's House of Commons speeches on German rearmament. Churchill agreed with the diarist Harold Nicholson's verdict that he had spent two years rebuilding his reputation, yet undone the work in five minutes.[37]

Edward chose Wallis Simpson over the throne, but the damage to Churchill's position proved short-lived. He helped the king to craft a well-judged abdication speech and made a well-received contribution to the Commons debate that followed Edward's abdi-cation. He also turned down lucrative offers from American publications to write an insider's view of the abdication crisis.[38]

The duke of York took his brother's place on the throne, becom-ing George VI. A week later Churchill postponed his American visit, because Parliament was recalled to debate civil list payments for both the new king and the former king early in January. Churchill felt he must attend as he had taken part in these negotia-tions between the former king and the government.

Churchill acknowledged to Bernard Baruch that Baldwin had gained a new lease of political life as a result of his handling of the abdication crisis: 'This makes it easier for me to plan ahead. I have every hope that I shall be able to come over to the States in April and hope to inaugurate the Defence of Peace and Freedom move-ment about which Randolph consulted you.'[39]

The postponement meant that Churchill missed Sarah's New York marriage to Vic Oliver (Victor Samek's new name on becoming an American citizen). Early in January 1937 Churchill paused from dictating a long memorandum on German air strength to give his daughter and new son-in-law lunch at Morpeth Mansions on their return to London. Now that she was married, Churchill felt that they must treat Sarah in the same way as they had Diana. 'I told her what we proposed financially,' he wrote to Clementine afterwards:

> She seemed v[er]y pleased, & liked the idea of all except y[ou]r £100 pin money rolling up for a rainy day. "Vic" – I suppose we must call him that – is making about £200 a week for 8 to 10 weeks over here. They get special terms at the hotel. But what a life – hand to mouth, no home, no baby.[40]

Churchill felt strongly that while Vic was earning well, the capital of £4,500 that they would be settling on Sarah from either his father's trust or their own Elder Children's Settlement should be resettled in a new trust. He drew on his own experience in an attempt to persuade his daughter:

> Everyone knows how under pressures of circumstances, either tempting or adverse, funds which are not controlled by Trustees are almost invariably dissipated. General statements however sincere are no substitute for proper Trustees. These moneys have come down for several generations solely by virtue of the fact that they have been strictly tied up. But for this they would have been squandered long ago.[41]

But Sarah (who was known within the family as the 'Mule') continued to resist and, after taking advice from special counsel, Churchill finally gave way.

Although Churchill's overdraft was close to its limit of £8,000 at the end of 1936,[42] his letter to his bank manager about borrowing facilities for the new year was full of hope. Supported by £12,000-worth of literary contracts already in hand and £3,000 more income from his investments, director's fees and salary as an MP, he calculated that he should produce a comfortable surplus over spending. The only difficulty, as always, was timing: his income and expenditure being out of step. He asked to hold on to an overdraft limit of £7,000 and to all his longer-term loans.[43]

Privately, however, Churchill was less optimistic. He was sufficiently concerned to ask his farm accountant, James Wood* of Wood, Willey & Co., to help Mrs Pearman, his senior secretary at Chartwell, to devise more cuts in the Chartwell budget. Clementine's account at Harrods for expenditure during 1936 had run to over 80 pages and the household had additional accounts at such other leading London stores as Harvey Nichols, Peter Jones, John Lewis, Selfridge & Co. and Lillywhite.[44]

Wood and Mrs Pearman suggested losing three of the servants to save wages of £240 a year; reducing the swimming-pool temperature to halve heating costs; pruning the £240 annual laundry bill; and, boldest of all, recommended that expenditure on wine and cigars should be 'investigated'.[45]

Churchill summarized this new regime in a memorandum to his staff: he would continue to pay 'say £3,000' for the year's medical bills, bank and insurance payments, foreign travel, office salaries and Mary's school fees; all other household costs were to be kept below 'a maximum of £500 a month or £6,000 a year', not on any account to be exceeded.[46] Mrs Pearman kept up the pressure, submitting unpaid bills of £2,331, of which she labelled bills amounting to £642 as 'Most urgent'.[47]

For the second time, Knight Frank & Rutley was instructed to test demand for the purchase of Chartwell. 'Capon** said he would on no account mention any figure less than £30,000,' Churchill told Clementine. 'If I could see £25,000 I should close with it. If we do not get a good price, we can quite carry on for a year or two more. But no good offer should be refused, having regard to the fact that

---

* James Wood (1886–1972), son of a farmer; founder, Wood, Willey & Co. 1934.
** A partner of Knight Frank & Rutley.

our children are almost all flown, and my life is probably in its closing decade.'

If Churchill did not regain ministerial office on Stanley Baldwin's retirement, Frederick Leathers, managing director of the shipping and ports company William Cory & Son, gave him hope of 'important business administrative employment': 'Then I should be able to do my books more slowly and not have to face the truly stupendous task like *Marlborough* Vol. IV being finished in 4 or 5 months, simply for current expenses. For 1938–9 we have the *History of the English-Speaking Peoples*, worth £16,000, but entailing an immense amount of reading and solitary reflection if justice is to be done to so tremendous a topic.'[48]

Churchill hoped to start his *History* 'in earnest in the late Autumn', of 1937, he told Newman Flower,[49] but the truth was that he could not afford to turn down other offers, even if they distracted him from the books. He was now borrowing £22,500 from his bank and insurance companies and another £12,000 from his family trusts.[50] Still, austerity had its limits. His note on the new Chartwell economy drive ends: 'Wines, spirits etc. not included.'[51]

18

'I shall never forget'

Bracken and Partner to the Rescue, 1937–8

Exchange rate: $4 = £1
Inflation multiples: US x 17; UK x 60

CHURCHILL'S NEW *Evening Standard* contract had been in operation for only a matter of weeks at the start of 1937 when he was put in touch with Cooperation Press Service. A press agency founded by Dr Imre Revesz, a Hungarian Jew, it specialized in distributing articles written by European politicians across a network of 400 newspapers in seventy countries on the Continent. Cooperation had started in Berlin before Hitler's rise to power, then moved to Paris just before a raid on its offices by the Gestapo.

Cooperation wanted to do business with Churchill, but he ignored the agency's overtures until another client, Sir Austen Chamberlain, provided a positive endorsement. Revesz received an invitation to discuss matters at Morpeth Mansions, where he was greeted in the doorway by a naked Churchill, still drying himself after a bath. As best he could, Revesz explained how he could transform Churchill's European readership and influence, while at the same time beating the syndication fees of only £25 per article, which he understood Churchill earned from his four existing outlets in the region.

Churchill objected strongly to Cooperation's standard agency fee of 40 per cent, but nevertheless he picked up the telephone to check Revesz's figures with Lord Beaverbrook. In the owner's absence, the *Evening Standard*'s syndication manager, William Robertson, not only confirmed the figures, but told Churchill that none of his first three articles under the new arrangements had yet earned the break-even syndication fees of £70.[1]

Revesz then happened to let slip that Sir Austen Chamberlain was already easily out-earning him by using Cooperation. This settled the matter. Churchill agreed in principle with Revesz that the agency should take over his existing European contracts without any commission, and that it would earn 50 per cent on any new deals.[2] First, however, they had to sort out the problem of Dr Meyer, Curtis Brown's sub-agent in smaller European countries, whose contract had just been extended for six months.[3] Dr Meyer threatened to sue, but in the end Churchill ran out of patience with him and offered Revesz a three-month deal. Revesz, who had left on a sales trip to Scandinavia, changed the term to six months, while drafting the contract on a boat between Bergen and Trondheim.[4]

Churchill's new agent proved a hard taskmaster. Revesz first demanded the termination of a rival agent's* appointment to sell Churchill's less valuable articles for the *News of the World*. He then insisted upon changes in Churchill's writing schedule to allow almost simultaneous publication in London and Europe. Provided his articles reached Paris on a Wednesday evening, Cooperation staff would work throughout the night to translate and copy them, before dispatching them across Europe at dawn on Thursday. They would reach even the furthest-away cities in Europe by Saturday morning, only twelve hours behind the *Evening Standard* in London.

Twenty-one European newspapers bought Churchill's first Cooperation article in July, netting him £57, more than double his previous European fee.[5] His fourth article, 'Anglo-German Relations', proved too controversial for editors in Vienna and Belgrade to carry,[6] but nevertheless Cooperation's numbers kept

---

* Opera Mundi.

climbing, until journey times were disrupted by the arrival of winter snow.

In France over Easter, and before resuming work on *Marlborough*, Churchill looked over his finances for the rest of 1937. He still expected to earn £15,500, which he predicted would outstrip his spending by some £3,000 and lower his overdraft by the end of the year.[7]

He had, as usual, omitted to forecast any casino losses, which over Easter amounted to no more than a fairly modest £200.[8] However, a more serious flaw in his calculations became apparent on his return to Britain. His estimated income included £3,500 for *Marlborough*, but if the book was to catch the Christmas trade its proofs had to be ready by the end of May. Churchill realized that this was now impossible and left a sizeable gap in his finances.

Churchill decided to call in the reserve that he had established four years previously for just such an eventuality. He had con-tracted with Thornton Butterworth as long ago as September 1931 to publish his articles on 'eminent personages' in book form (now to be called *Great Contemporaries*). The book had been set in type in 1932 but Churchill had resisted several attempts by Butterworth to publish it in the intervening years, preferring to keep it in reserve in case 'ill-health or some other cause' left a gap in his publication schedule.[9] He now wrote to Butterworth: 'If you are still interested in it, I should be glad if you would make me a proposal.'[10]

Butterworth reminded Churchill that they already had a con-tract, signed six years earlier, which did not include a fixed advance. Instead, Churchill would earn an amount that would depend on orders at the publication date.[11]

Churchill waited another month before breaking the bad news to Harrap that *Marlborough* would not be ready in time for Christmas. Harrap knew Churchill well enough by now not to resist. However, he sounded a warning: 'Many booksellers have commented unfavourably on what they call "the long-drawn-out procession of the volumes", and the considerably diminished number of copies which we sold of Vol. III bear witness to the fact that readers do lose interest.'[12]

Churchill's postponement of *Marlborough* until the spring of 1938 required a parallel 'easement', as he called it, in the timetable for his *A History of the English-Speaking Peoples*, which was due to be finished only a year later in April 1939. Newman Flower and his publishing partners conceded an eight-month delay until 31 December, 'but not beyond it'.[13] Having rearranged his publishing commitments, Churchill dropped *Marlborough* again and turned all hands at Chartwell to working on *Great Contemporaries*.

The new book might ease Churchill's cash flow temporarily, but it could not repair the fatal flaw in his finances: his level of indebtedness. Unfortunately, his only valuable asset, Chartwell, had failed to find a buyer. There was a glimmer of hope, however. His Irish agent suggested that he might be able to sell the remaining ground rents on the Garron Tower estate for as much as £12,000, although there was no certainty and the process could take as long as a year.[14] Churchill enthusiastically gave it the go-ahead.

It was rumoured that Stanley Baldwin might step down as prime minister after George VI's coronation in May and if this were the case, Churchill reasoned, a new prime minister might conceivably recall him to office. Becoming a minister again had the added attraction of tax advantages: he could retire as an author for tax purposes, just as in 1925, and this would reduce his tax bills.

'It occurs to me that if a change should occur in my affairs in the near future (which I have no reason to expect),' he confided to his tax adviser at Lloyds Bank, Geoffrey Mason, 'it might be proper for me to change back to the basis of the current year, and if this change were proposed as a *bona fide* step in consequence of unforeseeable public events, the Treasury would raise no objection.'[15]

Stanley Baldwin did resign two weeks after the Coronation, but his successor Neville Chamberlain did not include Churchill in his cabinet. There was more bad news: Mason informed Churchill that he had not paid all of the tax due for the tax year that had just ended in April 1936, and he already owed more tax for 1937. Altogether he would have to pay £7,500 of tax in the next few months, two-thirds of which was already late.[16]

Chartwell went back on the market at a lower price of £25,000[17] and Churchill returned to his books and articles. He held back on publicly criticizing the new government's policy towards German rearmament, but he had gleaned enough information from private briefings by military experts to understand the threat posed by Hitler's government's rearmament. He made his feelings known in speeches, articles and private memoranda to ministers.

While the international scene darkened further following Japan's invasion of China in July 1937, Churchill told Clementine he was 'working night & day' at *Marlborough* and his columns.[18] By August he still had twelve *Marlborough* chapters to write, but he could not resist the promise of quick cash. For example, John Waddington offered 100 guineas for short written summaries of four battles, images of which were to feature on their jigsaw puzzles. Churchill accepted on condition that he could choose the battles.* Kathleen Hill, a new secretary, offers an insight into that summer's routine at Chartwell: 'When he was bricklaying we used to take our notebooks and mount the ladder – even there he would dictate but not at length. If it was a long letter he would come down.'[19]

Churchill avoided any difficulties with Lloyds Bank until April 1937, when the death of Freddie Guest removed the guarantor to one of his loans. Anxious that Lloyds might require a replacement guarantor or even a repayment, Churchill rather rashly mentioned

---

* Churchill selected the Battle of Blenheim (1704), the Battle of the Nile (1798), the Battle of Rorke's Drift (1879) and the Battle of Jutland (1916). He recognized the claims of the Battle of Waterloo (1815), but considered that the selection of both Blenheim and Waterloo would result in too much red, whereas Rorke's Drift offered a contrast in black. 25 May, 24 Jun 1937, CHAR 8/547/40, 61.

the sale of his Irish ground rents. His bank manager immediately extracted a promise that he would use enough of the proceeds to halve his loans from the bank by the end of the year.[20] Two days later, Churchill heard that only a single buyer had shown interest in the rents so far and that his surveyor had valued them at just £7,500.[21]

Meanwhile, Chartwell was attracting no interest, even at a reduced price of £20,000, and the pile of unpaid bills had risen above £3,000.[22] The storm clouds were gathering.

Churchill borrowed £1,700 – as much as his lawyers would let him – from Mary's trust (the only trust as yet untouched), before setting off for his August holiday in France.[23] There he convinced himself that he could get through to the end of the year if the bank took account of the £6,000 that he was expecting early in 1938 from his annual series of articles for the *News of the World* and on the publication of *Great Contemporaries*. However, as a precaution he began compiling monthly forecasts of his cash flow.[24]

The problem was that these forecasts took no account of his losses on the American stock market, which started to fall again in the middle of August. 'Grateful your opinion American prices now on basis no major war this year,'[25] he asked Bernard Baruch on 10 September, by which time prices had fallen by an average of one-sixth. Baruch replied only that he was not yet buying, but Churchill's problem was whether or not to sell to prevent further losses. 'Have small holdings and indisposed quit,' he cabled again a month later, puzzled at further falls in the market, which by now had doubled to an average fall of a third since August.* 'We cannot here conceive reason your collapse. No war Europe this year and immense production including armaments.'[26]

By now Churchill's losses had become serious enough for

---

* The Dow Jones Industrial Average share index stood at 190 on 14 August 1937; by 10 September (the date of Churchill's first letter to Baruch), it had fallen to 177; by 18 October (the date of Churchill's second letter) it had fallen to 125. *www.measuringworth.com.*

Vickers da Costa to demand regular repayments of the money he owed to them, but all he could offer was a legal commitment to pay them the proceeds from any sale of his Garron Tower rents, which he had already promised (less formally) to the bank.

Churchill cut costs more drastically at Chartwell, which had become the millstone around their necks that Clementine had feared it would fifteen years ago. The staff needed to run the place still included three gardeners and secretaries, a valet, lady's maid, chauffeur, housekeeper and other domestic staff.[27] A new 'Winter Scale', the fourth of Chartwell's economy regimes, was devised to halve monthly household running costs to £127:[28] secretaries were reduced to two, domestic staff to three. Champagne was restricted to a personal allowance for Churchill of five half-bottles a week, although cigars were declared exempt.[29] Clementine was less than wholly committed to the 'Winter Scale'. The £90 she spent re-draping her bedroom may just have pre-dated the new regime, but her purchase of gold kid shoes and an ermine coat, another expensive skiing holiday and a new brown whipped-stitch driving suit, alpaca coat, matching cap and cockade for the chauffeur certainly did not.[30]

Clementine's preferred remedy for their difficulties was to sell both Chartwell and Morpeth Mansions and to consolidate their property costs in a single, larger London home. She had found a suitable eight-bedroomed Victorian property on Porchester Terrace in Kensington,[31] which the Paddington Estate was ready to lease for £350 a year, provided the new tenants undertook to modernize the building.

An architect estimated the cost of repairs at £3,000[32] and Churchill warmed to the idea, but he lost heart when the estate's managers sent a seven-page list of mandatory repairs and the estimated cost of repairs almost doubled. 'I feel it would be imprudent to commit ourselves to so large an expenditure as £5,000 while we have the other two properties on our hands,' he told Clementine at Christmas, and that was effectively the end of the Porchester Terrace option.[33]

Churchill preferred to look for new sources of income, letting it be known discreetly that he was open to taking on more company directorships. There was only one tentative approach, on behalf of the Grosvenor House Hotel, and it came to nothing.[34] The film world beckoned briefly when London Films asked him to help with a project on Lawrence of Arabia, but Churchill overplayed his hand. He asked for a percentage of the profits and Alexander Korda's assistant had to explain that they had merely been thinking of three or four days work at a 'nominal' fee of £250.[35]

Louis Levy, his Chicago lawyer, suggested a paid speech to a conference of American manufacturers, but was told that a package of lectures and broadcasts netting at least $25,000 would be required if Churchill was to be tempted away from Britain. Nothing came of it.

One bright spot was the publication of *Great Contemporaries* in October. Sales were strong, reaching almost 20,000 copies by Christmas. Churchill received a steady stream of royalty cheques from both British and American publishers that eventually reached £7,000.[36]

In November Churchill delivered eight articles (on time and largely ghostwritten by Adam Marshall Diston) for the 1938 *News of the World* series. He hoped for a new contract for the following year: 'I have to try to parcel my work out as well as possible in the year and as you know it might in certain circumstances be a help to me to say "the contract is already made",[37] he told the newspaper's general manager. Colonel Percy Davies took the hint and signed him up for 1939. He also invited the Churchills to watch the newspapers coming off the presses on a Saturday evening three weeks later. At a dinner that followed, Churchill floated the idea of extending his contract to cover 1940 and 1941 to help him in his relations with his bank. Again, Davies obliged.[38]

Since the change of prime minister in the middle of 1937, Churchill had kept a lower profile in the House of Commons. At the year's close, however, he signalled a return to more active opposition. In the wake of the foreign secretary Lord Halifax's controversial meeting with Hitler in Germany, Churchill drew attention just before Christmas to the Nazis' persecution of German Jews and warned the British government against 'making terms' with Germany at the expense of the smaller European countries surrounding it – a prophetic reference to the fate that would befall Czechoslovakia within a year.

For the Christmas holiday, Churchill took the fourth volume of *Marlborough* with him to Blenheim. The text had already reached almost 800 pages and he told George Harrap that they had two options. Either he could cut 200 pages or he could write a bit more and they could split it again to produce a fifth volume.[39] This time, even Harrap had had enough: Churchill was going to have to prune his manuscript.

In the New Year, Churchill conducted his usual survey of his finances. With the help of the 'Winter Scale', he had managed to pay off his five-year-old wine bill, and he had kept 1937's spending to the same level as 1936, at just below £20,000.[40] He forecast that it could be cut further to £15,000 in 1938, but this was a case of hope triumphing over experience. For one thing, Churchill omitted all mention of tax; yet he needed to pay another £4,700 by March 1938, some of it already overdue.[41]

Churchill reluctantly concluded that another American lecture tour was inevitable. He received a visit from Harold Peat, who wanted to recruit more British lecturers after a successful tour by H. G. Wells. Late in December at Blenheim Palace the two men outlined a deal guaranteeing Churchill $23,500 net of expenses for twenty-five lectures to be delivered in autumn 1938.[42]

After that, Churchill left with *Marlborough* for a New Year holiday at Maxine Elliott's home in France. 'I am longing to get this book finished,' he told Clementine. 'I do not get up till luncheon time but work in bed and have a masseur.'[43] A week later he had still hardly left the house and told his wife that he had discovered a cheaper entertainment than the casino: 'I have not played bezique or been to the Rooms.* M[ah] J[ong] has been amusing and very inexpensive. I have lost about £2 after all these hours of harmless amusement.'[44]

While on holiday, Churchill authorized a large tax payment. However, he found on his return to Britain that he still owed £4,500.[45] Lloyds Bank had also sent him a formal letter recording its 'disappointment' at his failure to cut back his borrowings by the end of 1937 as promised. It now asked for a legal charge over the Irish ground rents until they were sold. This was impossible, because (without telling the bank) Churchill had already pledged them formally to his stockbrokers. He made some quick calculations and suggested instead that he repay the bank £2,000 the moment his next royalties arrived.[46]

He won a temporary reprieve, but the noose was tightening. In a private letter to Bernard Baruch sent while he was still in Cannes, Churchill had candidly set out his precarious position and asked Baruch again whether he should cut his losses on his American shares. But Baruch did not reply and Churchill began to lose hope. It coincided with Anthony Eden's resignation as foreign secretary in protest at Prime Minister Neville Chamberlain's frustration of Eden's attempts to take a firmer policy against Mussolini. 'My heart sank and for a while the dark waters of despair overwhelmed me,' Churchill wrote in his memoirs. 'I watched the daylight creep slowly in through the windows, and saw before me in mental gaze the vision of Death.'[47] This pessimism seeped into his personal affairs: he was not only unable to pay his tax bill but Vickers da Costa was pressing him to put up more cash against his American share losses.

Turning aside from preparing a speech to the House of Commons during a debate on British air defences, Churchill asked his solicitors at Nicholl, Manisty to raise an emergency loan of at least £5,000, which he would back by taking out a new life insurance policy. Nicholl, Manisty pointed out that his insurance

---

* A casino.

company borrowings alone would rise to £13,000, costing him £1,650 a year, but Churchill had nowhere else to turn.[48]

The next day, as Hitler ordered his troops to cross into Austria, Churchill made what the diarist and politician Harold Nicolson described as 'the speech of his life' to the House of Commons. He warned that Britain would soon have to choose between resisting Hitler's campaign of aggression or submitting to it.

Meanwhile there was still no reply from Baruch. It was too late anyway. Although the Commercial Union provided Churchill with emergency funds of £5,000 on 18 March,[49] a further fall in US share prices (which tumbled by a quarter in March)* caused Vickers da Costa to demand some immediate cash to plug the gap between the cost of Churchill's shares and their current value. This gap stood at £12,000 on 21 March,[50] but Churchill could only afford to write a cheque for £2,000. No buyer had come forward for Chartwell or Morpeth Mansions; he was already borrowing £35,000 from Lloyds Bank, from insurance companies and from his family trusts; and he had used up every scrap of security available. Churchill had simply come to the end of the road.[51]

Above all he wanted to avoid bankruptcy and be free enough to concentrate on Europe's worsening crisis. On the day that the cabinet's foreign policy committee decided that Britain must accommodate Hitler rather than fight over Czechoslovakia, Churchill gave his friend Brendan Bracken a handful of his stock market accounts. He asked him to mount a discreet rescue that could keep him afloat for a little longer. Bracken went straight to his co-owner at *The Economist*, Sir Henry Strakosch, one of the small group of experts who had been feeding Churchill confidential information about Germany's armaments expenditure.

Sir Henry, who was unmarried and had made his wealth at the helm of South Africa's Union Corporation, had been ill in Cannes just two months earlier when Bracken had asked Churchill to visit

---

* The Dow Jones Industrial Average share index stood at 130 on 1 March 1938; at 99 on 31 March. *www.measuringworth.com*

him on his sickbed, describing the sixty-eight-year-old as a 'lonely old bird'.[52] Sir Henry, for his part, regarded Churchill as the one politician in Europe with the vision, energy and courage required to resist the Nazi threat. He had no hesitation in agreeing to help out financially.

That evening of 18 March 1938, Bracken met Churchill to sketch out a face-saving plan: Sir Henry would meet Vickers da Costa's demand for cash, and for a period he would take over responsibility for any further gains or losses on Churchill's shares; no one else need know. He asked Churchill to produce a letter that he could show Sir Henry the following day, with a note setting out the figures. Churchill dictated both the next morning:

> I was profoundly touched and relieved by what you told me last night of the kindness of our friend. If it were not for public affairs and my evident duty I shd be able to manage all right. But it is unsuitable as well as harassing to have to watch an account from day to day when one's mind ought to be concentrated upon the great world issues now at stake. I shd indeed be grateful if I cd be liberated during those next few critical years from this particular worry, wh[ich] descended upon me so unexpectedly; to the chance of which I shall certainly never expose myself again. I cannot tell you what a relief it would be if I could put it out of my mind; and take the large decisions wh[ich] perhaps may be required of me without this distraction and anxiety. I send you a short note which explains the position; and perhaps you will show this to our friend.[53]

Churchill's note omits to mention his loans or tax liabilities and it puts an optimistic gloss on the liquidity of some of his assets:

> The following assets can, if desired, be immediately produced: Irish ground rents, not readily marketable, but valued at £7,500; Cash £2,500; Life policy for £6,000. . . In addition the present

holder, apart from the regular literary contracts on which he lives, has a contract for a book* on which some progress has been made, deliverable on December 31, 1939 for £15,000. He could accomplish this task within the specified time by laying everything aside; but how is he to do this while events run at this pitch, still less if he should be required to devote his whole energies to public work.

Churchill suggested that his rescuer should take over the shareholdings for the following three years 'with full discretion to sell or vary holdings at any time, but on the basis that no risk of greater liability to the present holder arises, thus removing altogether the speculative element'.[54] In the meantime, he expected to pay Sir Henry interest of £800 a year.

For Bracken's eyes only, he added an extra note: 'My dear B Enclosed is a letter wh[ich] you can show our friend. This is only to tell you that as Hitler said to Mussolini, on a recent and less worthy occasion, "I shall never forget this inestimable service."'

To save Churchill the cost of interest, Sir Henry paid Vickers da Costa the full original cost of the shares, £18,000. He chose to remain silent on what he expected to happen three years later,[55] although he added a legacy of £20,000 for Churchill to his will. Ironically, the shares almost doubled in value over the next seven months, cutting the 'cost' of Sir Henry's intervention to £8,500.[56]

Neither man ever spoke publicly about the rescue. Churchill kept knowledge of it to a very tight circle that did not include his bank or his lawyers. 'Owing to various arrangements', he told Nicholl, Manisty, he no longer needed all the recent Commercial Union loan money.[57] Realizing that he had found a new source of funds, Nicholl, Manisty asked for payment of its outstanding old bills amounting to £331. Churchill sent £81.[58]

On 1 April the *Daily Express* ran a headline: 'WINSTON PUTS HIS MANSION UP FOR SALE'. Churchill took Chartwell off the market

---

* *A History of the English-Speaking Peoples.*

and the next day *The Times* carried a clarification: the Churchills simply planned to retire to a cottage in the grounds.[59]

Sir Henry carried on providing Churchill with private briefing notes and within a week he was warning the House of Commons against a future crisis in Czechoslovakia, urging that a formal Anglo-French defence pact should be agreed. The following year, 1939, Churchill's dining society The Other Club elected Sir Henry Strakosch as a member, signifying this first-generation immigrant's reception into the bosom of the British establishment.[60] There was no other reward.

19

'The future opens its jaws upon us'
Struggling with *History*, 1938–9

Exchange rate \$4 = £1; francs 160 = £1
Inflation multiples: US x 17; UK x 60

T HE INK HAD barely dried on Sir Henry Strakosch's cheque, when on 24 March 1938 the *Evening Standard* abruptly terminated Churchill's fortnightly column, a mainstay of his income and an important political platform. Ever since Anthony Eden had resigned as foreign secretary in February, Churchill's columns had taken an increasingly anti-German, pro-Czechoslovakian viewpoint – and one not shared by the owner of the *Evening Standard*, Lord Beaverbrook.

Percy Cudlipp had given way to a new editor, Reginald Thompson,* whom Beaverbrook left to deliver the coup de grâce. 'As it is my duty to be completely frank,' Thompson explained, 'it has been evident your views on foreign affairs and the part which this country should play are entirely opposed to those held by us.'[1]

Churchill's secretary coldly informed Thompson that Churchill would write that week's column, 'after which he does not wish to write any further articles for the *Evening Standard*, and trusts that this will be convenient.'[2] Churchill urgently contacted his Other Club dining companion Lord Camrose and explained that his

---

* Reginald Thompson (1896–1956), served on the Western Front 1914–18; journalist, *Daily Express*, *Evening News*; editor *Evening Standard* 1938–9; editor and managing director, *Essex Chronicle*.

Evening Standard contract had been crucial, because it gave him access to a long list of other newspapers around the world that carried his column:

> As you will see it is a very fine platform, though as Nazi power advances, as in Vienna, planks are pulled out of it... The *Evening Standard* have now terminated the series so far as they are concerned, on the grounds that my views are not in accordance with the policy of the paper, and I should like to know whether the *Daily Telegraph* would care to carry on the series, and if so on what terms.[3]

Lord Camrose, who was personally closer to Chamberlain than to Churchill, would only commit to an experiment of six months, matching the *Evening Standard's* fee. He did, however, agree to move quickly so that the column did not miss a beat, re-appearing on 14 April.[4] 'It may interest you to know that I could have placed the articles in three, if not four, different quarters at the same fee,' Churchill enjoyed telling the *Evening Standard's* editor.

'Both the *News Chronicle* and the *Sunday Pictorial* were eager with offers,' he explained to Imre Revesz at Cooperation Press Service, 'but *The Daily Telegraph* is a far more powerful and suitable platform for me.'[5] Revesz was not so sure, because *The Daily Telegraph* was readily available across much of Europe; however, seventeen newspapers took Churchill's first *Telegraph* column and this rose to twenty-three, covering much of Europe and South America, by May when one article earned Churchill an extra £93.[6]

The *Telegraph* had no syndication department of its own, so Revesz took responsibility for the British dominions, shortening the gap before Churchill's columns could be published by transmitting them over the airwaves with the help of a Dutch radio company. 'It is a radio-telegraphic method by Morse-signs captured only by special apparatus,' he explained to a puzzled Churchill. 'This would give to our articles an unusual value as it will be for Australian and South African papers a sensational

achievement if they could publish the articles on the same day as
the London papers.'[7]

Churchill had finally completed the last volume of *Marlborough*,
but there were obstacles to clear before he could turn his attention to his long-delayed *A History of the English-Speaking Peoples*.
Another film, this time about Lord Kitchener of Khartoum,
briefly beckoned. Although 'rather stunned' by Churchill's
demand for a fee of 1,000 guineas to act as their 'official adviser',
the film's backers had paid their first instalment of one quarter
before the venture collapsed after failing to raise production
funds.[8]

Then another brush with gambling debts left Randolph in
need of funds. Churchill suggested to George Harrap a compilation in book form of his recent foreign policy speeches, to be
edited by Randolph.[9] Politically sympathetic, Harrap offered an
advance of £1,000 and even delayed the final *Marlborough* volume
to make way for *Arms and the Covenant*. 'I do not expect there
will be much profit,' Churchill told Randolph, 'but you shall have
half of whatever there is.'[10]

Harrap was also Churchill's first port of call when he returned
from France with a synopsis for his next book after *A History of
the English-Speaking Peoples*, which he was keen to parlay for a
signing advance. It was to be called *After Armageddon* and it
would tackle 'Europe since the Russian Revolution' over three
volumes, to be completed in 1940, 1941 and 1942. By April 1938
Harrap had put together a publishing group and – with the help of
George Newnes, which was to publish a 'parts' edition – he offered
a lump sum of £14,000, to be paid in phases. Churchill talked
them up to £15,500, securing an all-important cash advance on
signing of £2,000.[11]

The prospect of two books within three years, on top of almost
weekly newspaper articles, a crowded political diary and increasingly frequent parliamentary speeches, each of which needed
painstaking research, proved too much for Violet Pearman,

Churchill's senior personal secretary, who succumbed to exhaustion.[12] Her assistant, Grace Hamblin, took over the Churchills' personal affairs and accounts, while Kathleen Hill assumed the main responsibility for literary matters. Both were conscious that Churchill had reserved two months in his diary for an autumn lecture tour of America.

Harold Peat had already booked most of the programme, which was to start in Chicago on 25 October and finish on 14 December in New York.[13] After Louis Alber's experience, Peat had insisted on strict cancellation penalties and Churchill had finally agreed a climbing scale that reached $3,000 on 1 August.[14] With Europe in crisis and less than eighteen months left to write *A History of the English-Speaking Peoples*, Churchill decided during July that he could not afford the diversion of the lecture tour. After waiting until the day before the August deadline, he cabled his apologies. Peat reacted with fury:

> Cancellation is entirely out of the question. Not only will I be the loser by some $25,000. . . but my reputation would be ruined and, unfortunately, yours would be greatly impaired in this country and probably internationally. . . There is a distinct possibility that there will be fifteen to twenty law-suits on our hands from coast to coast. It is a very serious thing, sir.[15]

Churchill double-checked his legal position before telling his new American lawyer Arthur Leve (whose colleague Louis Levy was under suspension at the time) to hold the line: 'Peat must realize how extremely critical and dangerous the whole European situation is.' Leve restricted Churchill's penalty to $2,000.[16]

Churchill finally turned his attention to *A History of the English-Speaking Peoples*. He dispatched a 'first tentative and provisional instalment' to the publisher in mid-August, but Cassell's chairman Sir Newman Flower judged one chapter and a fragment of a second to be a slim payback for five years of advances.[17] Nor did he take kindly to Churchill's imperious request to be sent six sets of printed proofs by return. 'I am afraid we are not prepared to put this into type until we have the whole of the MS [manuscript],' Sir Newman wrote. 'So far, you have only delivered 30,000 words out of 400,000, and we fail to see how you are going to complete the other 370,000 words by the 31st December 1939, on which date the agreement falls in.'[18]

Puzzled, Churchill sent his other publisher Harrap a copy of the letter under 'Very Private' cover, asking for help with alternative printing arrangements and some advice on his next move with Sir Newman Flower. 'These are very unsatisfactory relations for an author to have with his publisher,' Churchill explained, 'and it is an entirely new experience for me.'[19] Harrap suggested asking Sir Newman's young son Desmond to lunch at Chartwell, following which an uneasy truce was declared. His father had not intended to be 'disagreeable', Desmond explained.

Churchill kept up a pace of 2,000 words a day, but had only reached the twelfth-century reign of Henry II early in September when he took over Randolph's duties on the *Evening Standard*'s 'Londoner's Diary' for a fortnight while he was on military training.

The launch of the last volume of *Marlborough* was overshadowed by the sudden crisis in relations between Germany and Czechoslovakia against which Churchill had been warning.[20] For some weeks Hitler had supported the claims for greater self-determination of the German-speaking residents of the Sudetenland region of Czechoslovakia. On 7 September a lead article in *The Times* suggested the Czech government should consider ceding this region to its neighbours, Germany, in order to make Czechoslovakia a more 'homogenous' state. Churchill was outraged. Taking time out from writing his *History*, he urged the foreign secretary Lord Halifax to warn Hitler that any aggression against Czech territory would result in war.

On 13 September the Czech government declared martial law; two days later Prime Minister Neville Chamberlain flew to meet

Hitler for the first time at the German chancellor's Berchtesgaden retreat. Churchill told a researcher: 'It has been a comfort to me in these anxious days to put a thousand years between my thoughts and the twentieth century.'[21] He abandoned his *History* again to travel to Paris to persuade friends in the French cabinet to stand by the Czech president, but without success. On his second visit to Germany within a week, Neville Chamberlain was confronted by a new demand from Hitler that those areas of the Sudetenland region where German-speaking residents were in the majority should be transferred to Germany without any need for a prior plebiscite.

Chamberlain urged the cabinet to accept Hitler's new terms on his return, but encountered some resistance, including for the first time from foreign secretary Lord Halifax. On the following day, 27 September, Chamberlain suggested to Hitler that the British, French, German and Italian leaders should hold a further meeting, while questioning during a radio broadcast whether Britain should fight over a quarrel 'in a faraway country between people of whom we know nothing'.

On the morning of 28 September Curtis Brown relayed to Churchill an American newspaper's offer for him to write a war diary for a fee of $1,000 per entry.[22] Churchill replied immediately that he did not expect war, a judgement that was vindicated by events in the House of Commons that afternoon. Chamberlain was speaking to a packed chamber when an aide passed him a note. Chamberlain absorbed it in silence before informing the House that Hitler had accepted his request for a third meeting in Germany. The rest of the House rose in acclaim – and the London Stock Exchange rallied sharply – but Churchill, Anthony Eden, Harold Macmillan and Leo Amery stayed in their seats.

In Munich the following day, the British, French, German and Italian leaders met, but without any Czechs present. Churchill attended a Focus Group lunch at the Savoy Hotel and returned that evening for a dinner at The Other Club. That night early copies of the next morning's newspapers arrived, bringing news of the Munich Agreement: Germany was to annexe all Sudetenland areas with a German-speaking majority within a fortnight, before a plebiscite elsewhere. Churchill experienced 'a towering rage and a deepening gloom', according to a fellow Other Club member.[23]

Chamberlain returned home to a hero's welcome and promised 'Peace in our time'. Just one cabinet minister (Alfred Duff Cooper) resigned and the thirty or so Conservative MPs who opposed appeasement still looked to Anthony Eden for leadership, rather than Churchill. He retreated to Chartwell, where he laid bricks and picked up once more the threads of his *History*. The House of Commons debated the Munich Agreement over three days in the following week, but Churchill delayed speaking until the final day. Those who read his *Daily Telegraph* column knew that he had already condemned the British and French leaders for applying 'unbearable pressure' on the Czech government.

By Christmas 1938 Churchill's History had reached the Wars of the Roses. He was ahead of his target, but not enjoying the experience. 'It is very laborious: & I resent it, & the pressure,' he told Clementine, who was once again cruising with Lord Moyne. 'If nothing intervenes, it will be done by June. . . My life has simply been cottage and book, (but sleep too before dinner).'[24] At least Churchill's bank account had finished 1938 just in credit, thanks to Sir Henry Strakosch's rescue, plus a second successful brandy bet with Lord Rothermere, and the *News of the World*'s agreement to let him cash its cheque early.[25] Chartwell's economy drive had kept costs steady and as he mapped out prospects for 1939 Churchill felt relatively optimistic about his finances. The delivery of the manuscript of his *History* accounted for a third of Churchill's projected income for the year of £22,000. This was well ahead of his estimate of spending, which was just £13,000.[26] (The eventual outcome of 1939 was to be almost the reverse of Churchill's estimates: he finished with receipts of £13,000, while he spent more than £20,000.)

On 7 January 1939, following a day of talks with French leaders in Paris, Churchill caught the night train to Cannes for a New Year break. He dictated his *Daily Telegraph* column over a dinner washed down with champagne.

Poor weather kept him mostly inside Maxine Elliott's home in Cannes, but this meant that his *History* made steady progress at 1,500 words a day. 'BEWARE CASINO,' Clementine warned him towards the end of his fortnight's stay,[27] but Churchill could not resist and found fortune to be on his side.

'Just as at Chartwell I divided my days between building and dictating, so now it is between dictating and gambling,' he told her. 'I have been playing very long but not foolishly, and up to date I have a substantial advantage. It amuses me very much to play, so long as it is with their money.'[28] Churchill had drawn 40,000 francs in cash, but had already deposited winnings of 60,000 at the Cannes branch of the Comptoir National de Paris.[29] On his way to the station for the journey home, he could not resist a final visit, as his secretary Mary Penman recalled:

> As we passed the Casino, he ordered the car to stop although we had little time to spare before catching the train. He jumped out and ran to the Casino entrance, his clothes flapping about him in the strong wind, looking a little shabby and untidy. He disappeared inside briefly and then came out still running, he waved his right hand triumphantly to me and grinned as he leapt into the car beside me. 'I have just won enough to pay for our fares home – what do you think of that?'[30]

'Safely home with forty-two thousand,' he cabled to Clementine.[31]

On the political front, Churchill anticipated another government reshuffle, but he told Clementine that he was happy to remain on the political sidelines until after an election. He was still confident that his *History* would be finished well ahead of its deadline:

> In the summer when I am sure the book will be finished, I think I will build a house on the ten acres. It will cost about three

thousand pounds to give a lovely dwelling for a man and his
wife, two children, one double and one single visiting bedroom,
and I expect we could sell it for five or six thousand with the bit
of land.[32]

By the end of January Churchill had reached 'Cromwell's Great
Rebellion' in his *History*, at which point his main researcher Bill
Deakin had to leave for military service. He was replaced by
George Young,* an older historian who had recently written about
Victorian England and was introduced by Eddie Marsh. 'I hope
you will not be vexed if I venture to suggest an *honorarium* of fifty
guineas,' Churchill proposed to Young, setting him to work on
the Stuarts.[33]

Meanwhile, Churchill was frustrated to find that after three
months in America Revesz had still not managed to sell his newspaper column to a newspaper; his agent seemed more interested
in pioneering the broadcast of the speeches of European politicians across the Atlantic. Revesz tried to explain his strategy
when he unveiled his 'greatest success to date' in February: the
New York Herald Tribune had agreed to carry Churchill's columns
at $80 each. There was no American tradition of paying politi-
cians for newspaper articles, Revesz explained, so he had
concentrated on setting up 'an entirely new wireless service of
international opinions'. Promising to pay the radio transmission
costs personally, he forecast that new buyers would soon double
or treble the *Herald Tribune*'s fee within months. 'It will mean
that all the subscribing newspapers will be able to pick up the
articles directly from Europe, and that they will receive everything you and the other European statesmen write within a few
hours and directly.' The next step, Revesz expected, would be an
opportunity for Churchill and other European politicians to earn

---

* George Young, ('G.M.', 1882–1959), fellow of All Souls College, Oxford
1905; civil servant 1908–20; author of an essay on Victorian Britain, *Portrait
of An Age* (1936).

additional fees by broadcasting recordings of their speeches to America over the radio.

Churchill reacted to his agent's long and excited letter with a single sentence, insisting that he would accept nothing less than $125 a column.[34] A less determined man than Revesz might have given up, but he immediately promised to pay the difference between $80 and $125 himself. His confidence was vindicated within a fortnight when he was able to cable: 'Further contracts already signed Washington Philadelphia Boston Buffalo Cleveland San Francisco Los Angeles Toronto.'[35]

Revesz returned to Amsterdam for the first radio transmission, after which he reported to Churchill: 'It is a very exciting procedure. After ten minutes came the message from New York that the reception was good and they speeded it up until 75 words per minute. About an hour later I received already the following message: ARTICLE FINE RECEPTION PERFECT THANKS.'

Cooperation started adding £50 'on account' for US sales to its payments, taking Churchill's earnings from each newspaper column close to £200.[36]

Three-quarters of Churchill's *History* was in print by the end of February, but he was facing mounting distractions. *Picture Post* magazine – only two years old, but already boasting a readership of one million – sent a crew to Chartwell to photograph Churchill writing and bricklaying.

Meanwhile, Randolph confessed to yet another set of debts that forced Churchill to release his son's final tranche of Lord Randolph's will trust, having first worked out that he could do so without having to repay any of his own loan from the same source.[37]

Most importantly, Chartwell remained the destination of choice for anyone who wanted to share private information about Hitler's military preparations, among them Sir Henry Strakosch. On 22 February he handed Churchill an unofficial estimate that Germany was spending 26 per cent of its national income on armaments, in contrast to Britain's 12 per cent.[38]

Three days later, Hitler's troops marched into Prague, Bohemia and Moravia, bringing an effective end to Czechoslovakia's existence as an independent state. It proved a pivotal moment for the British public, after which the word 'appeasement' began to carry a different meaning. Churchill called for Britain's air defences to be put on full alert.

He had only reached Queen Anne's reign in his *History* and Churchill realized that he was falling seriously behind schedule. Turning aside from a long memorandum to the prime minister on the use of sea power, Churchill asked the publishers of *Marlborough: His Life and Times* if he could reuse whole passages from the book to cover the reign of William and Mary in his *History*. 'I do of course paraphrase and alter as I go along, but still the identity of the two versions would be noticeable,' he admitted to George Harrap junior, who had taken over the running of Harrap with his younger brother Walter after the sudden death of their father. At the end of his letter Churchill offered them first refusal on a book of his *Evening Standard* and *Daily Telegraph* articles, which he described as 'a continuous survey of the darkening scene. . . Under some title such as *Step by Step*, I should think they would have a very good sale.'[39] The Harraps were not convinced: they allowed the reuse of the *Marlborough* material, but bid just £500 for *Step by Step*, thus allowing Thornton Butterworth a chance to take back his old author, by pledging £750 and promising to find buyers in Europe and America.[40]

Churchill's *History* fell further behind schedule in April. He put the book aside to prepare a speech to the House of Commons welcoming Chamberlain's surprise guarantee of the security of Poland, the country widely expected to be Hitler's next target. Churchill deprecated 'a sinister passage' in a leading article in *The Times* of 1 April which suggested that there was a distinction between guaranteeing Poland's 'independence' and guaranteeing its territorial 'integrity'. Churchill's suspicions were well founded – on 3 April Chamberlain confirmed privately that *The Times*'s interpretation of the government's intentions was correct.

On 7 April Mussolini's troops massed on the border before invading Albania. Harold Macmillan, who was visiting Chartwell at the time, recalled Churchill spreading maps all over his study, then sending Chamberlain unsolicited advice on how best to use the British fleet to seize Corfu and prevent a further Italian advance. On two further occasions in April Churchill had to put his *History* aside to prepare speeches in the House of Commons. He called for the establishment of a new ministry of supply (which Chamberlain did establish, but without appointing Churchill to head it) and urged as much co-operation with Russia as with France.

By May his *History* had already overrun its intended length, but Churchill had not yet reached the American Civil War. He dictated passages during car journeys to and from London, but he realized that he now needed literary reinforcements. John Wheldon* arrived at Chartwell to check the section on Henry VIII, while Maurice Ashley returned to inspect Cromwell and the Stuarts. 'It is very hard to transport oneself into the past when the future opens its jaws upon us,' Churchill told Ashley.[41] He also recalled Eddie Marsh to renewed proofreading duties. 'It has been a most educative ride for me,' he told his former private secretary. 'Though I have frequently had to dismount and talk politics to the wayfarers.'[42]

Churchill's fortnightly *Daily Telegraph* column was due to come to an end in mid-summer 1939. Cecil King, a friend of Randolph's and a young journalist at the *Daily Mirror*, suggested that his newspaper should take over. The editor Cecil Thomas offered 70 guineas a column, but for a period of only three months, until Revesz inspired a counter-bid by the *News Chronicle*, after which Thomas increased his bid to £100 and six months.[43]

---

* John Wheldon (b.1911), literary assistant to Churchill 1934–5, lecturer Balliol College, Oxford 1935–6, Courtaulds Ltd. 1936–9; war service including with the Special Operations Executive 1939–45; Courtaulds Ltd. 1945–60.

Churchill's relief at this new arrangement was short-lived when the *New York Herald Tribune* announced it was cutting its fee by a third at the end of its trial three months, even though the number of American newspapers now signed up to print Churchill's journalism had grown to fourteen.[44] Revesz set off immediately for America to take up the cudgels on Churchill's behalf, but once there he changed his priorities, preferring to concentrate on the other reason for his trip. He successfully concluded arrangements with the National Broadcasting Company for Churchill and other European politicians to make fortnightly broadcasts to America on 'international topics or events of worldwide interest'. Churchill's fee of £100 a broadcast, Revesz confided, was to be three times as much as any of his political colleagues.[45]

In Britain, there was a mounting press campaign for Churchill's restoration to the government, but he was locked in a race against time to finish the *History*. His bank overdraft had risen back above £7,000 and, if he did not complete his manuscript before the declaration of war (which he now regarded as inevitable), he would not only forfeit the £15,000 still due from the publisher, but have to reimburse the £5,000 he had already received – and long since spent.[46]

While Churchill continued writing, the Bank of England started secret shipments of its gold to Canada.[47] Nevertheless, life continued: debutantes danced in London beneath the Rembrandts and Gainsboroughs of Londonderry House; young men in striped blazers turned out for the rowing regatta at Henley; and at Blenheim the new duke and duchess of Marlborough threw open the palace's gates for a party in honour of their daughter. Powdered footmen in red velvet waited on guests in the library and chefs cooked lobster on the terrace beneath the palace's floodlit façade, but Churchill stayed in London to work on his *History*. 'I am staggering to the end of this job,' he told Marsh.

He promised his publisher in July that the work was almost done: 'I have had to work very hard, and many a night have sat up until two or three in the morning.'[48] Right up to the end, *A*

History of the English-Speaking Peoples had to compete for time with magazine articles for *Picture Post* or a *Daily Mirror* column or a last speech to the House of Commons before its summer recess or a first American radio broadcast. Then there was the 1940 series for the *News of the World* to consider. 'In view of the uncertainties which may affect me personally,' he told the newspaper's chairman, 'I should like to get the series for 1940 in an advanced condition, or at any rate on the stocks before the end of September.'[49]

In the middle of August Churchill made a short diversion to France to watch the French army on manoeuvres: the visit 'tore to shreds any illusion that it was not Germany's intention to wage war and to wage it soon', recalled his travelling companion General Spears.[50] Afterwards, Churchill painted in Normandy with his artist friend Paul Maze. 'Suddenly he turned to me,' Maze recalled, 'and said: "This is the last picture we shall paint in peace for a very long time."'[51]

With speculation mounting that Hitler's next move was imminent, Churchill flew back early to London, arriving as news broke that Germany and Russia had reached a non-aggression pact and that George VI had left his summer home at Balmoral to meet government ministers in London. The bank rate doubled to 4 per cent on 24 August. Churchill's *Daily Mirror* column that day was entitled 'At the Eleventh Hour'. The following day the British government advised Britons still living in Berlin and Germans living in Britain to return home.

On 29 August Churchill was still discussing passages in his *History* concerning the Seven Years' War with Bill Deakin. On 31 August, as some children began to leave London, Churchill wrote to his publisher Sir Newman Flower:

> I am, as you know, concentrating every minute of my spare life and strength upon completing our contract. These distractions are trying. However 530,000 words are now in print and there is only cutting and proof reading, together with a few special

points, now to be done.[52]

Churchill was still dictating at one o'clock on the morning of 1 September, as the first German tanks rolled into Poland.

20

'All my arrangements depend on this payment'
Early Burdens of War, 1939–41

Exchange rate: $4 = £1
Inflation multiples: US x 16; UK x 50

C HURCHILL TRAVELLED STRAIGHT to London when he heard the news. He was asked to call at 10 Downing Street, where the prime minister invited him to join a war cabinet as minister without portfolio. Pacing up and down at Morpeth Mansions, Churchill waited all that day for further word. It was not until the early evening of Saturday, 2 September, when Chamberlain summoned MPs to the House of Commons.

He surprised his cabinet colleagues by speaking of possible further negotiations with Hitler, rather than the ultimatum they had agreed to hours before. A group of rain-soaked ministers interrupted a private dinner between Chamberlain and Lord Halifax in 10 Downing Street to make their feelings known. Chamberlain backed down and an ultimatum was finally sent to Hitler: it would expire at eleven o'clock on Sunday morning.

When by a quarter past eleven on the next morning no official word had arrived from Berlin, Chamberlain announced on the radio that Britain was consequently at war against Germany. He made the same announcement to the House of Commons at noon; immediately afterwards he asked Churchill to serve as First Lord of the Admiralty with a seat in the war cabinet. Churchill accepted the very post he had filled at the outbreak of war twenty-five years earlier.

He lunched at the Savoy Grill before he joined the first meeting of the war cabinet. Shortly after France's declaration of war at 5 p.m., Churchill returned to the Admiralty – to the same desk in the same room that he had used a quarter of a century earlier. Behind the wooden panelling of his room hung the same charts on which he had then followed the tracks of the fleet.

The Churchills moved back into Admiralty House. They surrendered their Morpeth Mansions lease and closed Chartwell for the duration of the war. One cottage was kept open for family visits, but all of the staff had to leave, except for Kathleen Hill and Grace Hamblin, who moved to London to handle the Churchills' personal correspondence.*

On his first morning in office for ten years Churchill warned the *Daily Mirror* and Imre Revesz not to expect any more newspaper columns; within a week he had dropped his American broadcasts and *News of the World* column. It was not as if the First Lord's salary (still £5,000 a year, as it had been in 1912) meant that he could afford to stop writing, but Churchill remembered the tax advantages of retiring completely as an author, since any fees as yet unpaid would escape the Inland Revenue's grasp.

He knew, however, that he would have to find a way to boost his ministerial salary, since two-thirds of it would be swallowed up by tax and the interest on his loans, which still stood at £27,000. Fortunately, Churchill's 'retirement' did not prevent newspapers from paying him to rerun his old articles and books. The *Sunday Chronicle* offered £50 a week for extracts from *The World Crisis*,[1] to be topped shortly afterwards by Lord Rothermere's *Sunday Dispatch*, which bid 60 guineas each for excerpts from *My Early Life*; together, Churchill calculated, they would bring him in £6,000 a year, more than doubling his salary.

---

* Chartwell's wartime complement increased in only one department: Churchill agreed to the department store Harrods' request to transfer twenty-two varieties of rare fish into its lakes; in return, he could keep as many fish as he chose at the war's end.

But if he was to make any headway on reducing his debts, Churchill still needed the £15,000 due on completion of *A History of the English-Speaking Peoples*. Unfortunately, the manuscript was less finished than he had so recently claimed to Sir Newman Flower. Re-examining it, he came to the conclusion that only a little over half – up to the death of Queen Anne in 1714 – passed muster. The rest needed varying degrees of surgery. The task of carrying this out while officially 'retired' as an author and simultaneously serving as First Lord of the Admiralty at a time of war, would challenge even Churchill's ingenuity.

He interrupted a flow of memos to fellow ministers and admirals to brief George Young to use 'the fullest freedom of correction and improvement'[2] in reworking the more recent passages of his *History*. He also asked Bill Deakin, now attached to a Yeomanry regiment, to deal in his spare time with the early nineteenth century. Eddie Marsh was put on standby to proofread the results. Churchill would examine their collective efforts from time to time, before convening a plenary session during November. 'The matter is so important and the stress here is very great,' he impressed on Deakin.[3]

Shortly afterwards Desmond Flower, Newman's son, reminded Churchill of a promise he had made in 1937 to produce a special 20,000-word introduction for the parts edition of the *History*, the first version due to be published. Churchill summoned Young back to the Admiralty to add this extra piece to his brief. 'Apart from the introduction which I [in reality, G. M. Young] am doing and which will, I trust, soon be accomplished, and a few lacunae which require a paragraph or a page, the book is now finished,' he reassured his publisher.[4]

The last 'piecing together' of the *History* took place at the Admiralty over a weekend in November 1939.[5] While his team pored over the final draft, Churchill kept leaving the room to press forward plans to mine the Rhine river or to divert British trawlers to coastal mine-sweeping duties. Marsh finished proofreading in the middle of December, when Churchill paused in his drafting of a paper to the war cabinet (urging the interdiction of Norway's iron ore supply to Germany), so that he could attach a note to the final manuscript for the publisher: 'It has been a work of great interest but also of great labour to me to accomplish this task. I regard the delivery of this copy in full readiness for press as the fulfilment of my contract with you.'[6]

Flower graciously acknowledged receipt, but when he read the text over Christmas he was dismayed to find it incomplete. The *History* ended in 'an abrupt manner' at President Lincoln's assassination in 1865, he protested, rather than at the 1930s, as expected.[7] Before setting off to France for naval discussions, Churchill promised Flower a 10,000-word epilogue in compensation. Nevertheless, he failed to extract from Flower the all-important cheque for £7,500, on which he had been depending. He needed it to extinguish the overdraft on his bank account, which was now above £7,600.[8]

A letter from Flower soon confirmed that the non-arrival of the cheque was no oversight. 'We cannot regard the contract as having been filled and mature consideration convinces us that such fulfilment could not be brought about by the suggested epilogue,' he explained.[9]

Still in France, Churchill challenged Brendan Bracken to change Flower's mind. The telephone conversation that followed between Churchill's fixer and the younger Flower was described by Kathleen Hill as 'very frank'. Flower finally promised the cheque for the following morning, but only after Bracken had guaranteed that Churchill would 'round off the history' with extra words, although 'no new material could be expected of [him] until June 30, 1940'.[10]

Bracken tried to repair relations with Flower after the cheque had arrived: 'Forgive all my pertinacious telephone calls. You will, I think, understand that as I am Mr Churchill's honorary man of business, I am anxious to receive the cheque for £7,500, as all my arrangements depend on this payment.'[11] Churchill used the money to pay his literary team and meet £2,000 of overdue taxes; nevertheless, by the time he had paid some of his wine merchants' bills, his overdraft was back above £5,000.[12]

*

Bracken found a young historian, Alan Bullock, to draft the missing chapters and the team reassembled at the Admiralty to examine his work during another late-night session early in April. Bill Deakin recalled the occasion thirty years later:

> Naval signals awaited attention, Admirals tapped impatiently on the door of the First Lord's room, while on one occasion talk inside ranged round the spreading shadows of the Norman invasion and the figure of Edward the Confessor, who, as Churchill wrote, 'comes down to us faint, misty, frail'. I can still see the map on the wall, with the dispositions of the British fleet off Norway, and hear the voice of the First Lord as he grappled with his usual insight the strategic position in 1066.[13]

War had been declared, but life went on. London's fashionable res-taurants remained open; weekends still brought an exodus to the countryside; and the *Financial News*'s 30-share index stood higher than it had at the outbreak of war.[14] Everything changed on 9 April, when Germany invaded Denmark and British warships entered the Norwegian fjords. There could be no more work on the extra chapters, Churchill told Flower. He left his publisher to sort out the contractual consequences with Bracken,[15] while he turned to the debacle of Britain's Norwegian campaign, with its fateful echoes of the failed Dardanelles campaign in 1915.

Once again recriminations swirled around Westminster, but this time Churchill emerged unscathed. There was, however, growing dissatisfaction with Chamberlain's leadership. Encouraged by younger Tories, the opposition Labour Party tabled a motion of censure on the government in the Commons, at the end of which Chamberlain's majority fell to less than half its normal size.

Chamberlain knew that a National Coalition government was needed. Not expecting Labour MPs to agree to serve under him, Chamberlain met the most senior of his potential successors, the foreign secretary Lord Halifax, on the morning of Thursday 9 May to offer to serve in a broad-based government of which Halifax would be prime minister.

According to Halifax's diary, he expressed all the possible arguments against his appointment, including the difficulty of his leading the country from the House of Lords. His reticence may have reflected an instinct that Churchill was the more suitable wartime prime minister; and that Halifax could act as a more effective restraint against Churchill's impulsiveness if he was subordinate to Churchill, rather than nominally in control.

At a quarter past four in the afternoon, Chamberlain met both Halifax and Churchill, accompanied by the Conservative chief whip David Margesson. Chamberlain recapitulated his position, adding that he had made up his mind to resign because he expected the Labour leader and his deputy, Clement Attlee and Arthur Greenwood, to refuse to join a National Coalition which Chamberlain led. He therefore expected to recommend to George VI either Halifax or Churchill as his successor.

There are a number of differing accounts of what followed: Churchill's version tells of 'a talk about the situation in general', without any firm decisions made.[16] He places the meeting that sealed his succession as taking place on the morning of Friday 10 May, but his account was written seven years after the event. Those accounts which were committed to paper nearer the time all agree that the question of Chamberlain's successor was decided by the meeting on the afternoon of Thursday 9 May. Among them is a note written by Lord Camrose, the owner of *The Daily Telegraph*, whom Chamberlain briefed at six o'clock that evening. Ever a journalist, Camrose made a contemporaneous note of the outcome:

[Halifax] had said he would prefer not to be sent for as he felt the position would be too difficult and troublesome for him. He (Neville) would therefore advise the King to send for Winston. The latter [Churchill] had made it a condition that he

[Chamberlain] should remain in the Cabinet and be the Leader of the House. Winston would be the Prime Minister and also Minister of Defence.[17]

On the following morning, 10 May 1940, Hitler launched a sudden armoured attack through Belgium and Holland towards northern France. Chamberlain hesitated over whether he should still resign but cabinet colleagues made it clear that there could be no turning back. By evening the king had asked Churchill to form a government. Over the following two days Churchill constructed a coalition ministry in which each of the major politicial parties – Conservative, Labour and Liberal – was represented.

'Seldom can a Prime Minister have taken office with the Establishment. . . so dubious of the choice and so prepared to find its doubts so justified,' wrote one of Downing Street's private secretaries, Jock Colville.[18]

Within a week, the French prime minister Paul Reynaud had told Churchill that France's battle against Hitler was lost. German forces had successfully advanced into northern France, cutting off large numbers of French and British troops, who were left stranded on the French coast. The race was now on to evacuate them.

During this critical period, all that could be done by others for Churchill was, according to a young military aide, Ian Jacob: 'The whole of his energies were concentrated on this fight. Little or no effort had to be diverted to handling private business or to the machinery of living.'[19] Kathleen Hill proved herself capable of handling most of Churchill's literary negotiations, keeping him closely informed as he requested. If he or she thought that additional weight was needed, they brought in Brendan Bracken, who was now Churchill's parliamentary private secretary, to assist.

A large part of Britain's professional army was successfully evacuated from the beaches of Dunkirk in early June. However, Churchill was deeply immersed by the fate of France when Brendan Bracken had to ask for his personal intervention in the difficulties caused by the postponement of *A History of the English-Speaking Peoples*.

Cassell & Co. had agreed in principle to pay most of Churchill's outstanding advance, holding only £1,000 back against the book's completion after the war. The quid pro quo conceded by Bracken had been Cassell's right to publish immediately a compilation of Churchill's wartime speeches, a prize now made much more valuable by his elevation to the premiership. Sir Newman Flower wanted a watertight legal agreement which left no room for later argument about Churchill's royalties. Distracted by events across the Channel, Churchill agreed to forego his customary fixed advance. In exchange Cassell was to transfer immediately £2,500 of the remaining *History* payments to Churchill's bank.[20]

Churchill's salary as prime minister might have doubled to £10,000, but nine-tenths of it disappeared in tax payments; the remainder did not even meet the interest payments on his loans. Churchill knew that he faced large tax payments and interest bills at the end of June, but he had no means of paying them.

He came to the conclusion that his finances would never add up now that he could no longer supplement his salary by writing. Shuttling back and forth across the Channel in a last-bid attempt to encourage the French government to fight on, he asked for a special statement of his current account from Lloyds Bank, which showed an overdraft of £5,602 on 18 June.[21] Churchill had twelve days to find the money to pay his interest bill. He gave the statement to Brendan Bracken and asked him to arrange yet another private rescue.

Bracken called again on his business partner, Sir Henry Strakosch, who had responded to Churchill so generously two years earlier without demanding anything in return. Once again Sir Henry wrote out a cheque for £5,000, this time to Bracken himself in order to help disguise the identity of its true beneficiary. Bracken duly endorsed the cheque to Churchill, whose bank account it reached on 21 June, the day on which the Battle of France ended and the French government made it known that they wished to negotiate an armistice with Germany. Cassell's cheque arrived at

Lloyds Bank on the same day, making it possible for the prime minister to indulge in a flurry of bill-paying to wine merchants, shirt-makers and watch-repairers.

Churchill concentrated on marshalling defences against the invasion of Britain that was widely expected, but one cloud still hung over his finances. Since January he had left unpaid a bill for almost £1,000 from Harrap's printers. The firm had been pressed into printing *History*'s many sets of corrected author's proofs after Cassell had refused to indulge Churchill's expensive method of writing. He had expected Cassell to relent and pay the bill on the book's publication. Now that the book had been postponed until after the war, this was clearly not going to happen.

By July, as battle was joined with the Luftwaffe over England's skies, the bill had found its way into Brendan Bracken's in-tray. Misunderstandings abounded during the autumn between Bracken and George Harrap, representing the printers, until Harrap left a meeting at Downing Street in November convinced that the prime minister was at last about to pay the full amount outstanding. He was mistaken: it was a smaller cheque that Bracken instructed Kathleen Hill to put in front of Churchill to sign. 'You break a man's heart,' Walter Harrap told Bracken. 'We have just been blitzed out of our home so have mercy, my lord.'[22] There was none, a fact that the Harraps would not forget when the prime minister tried to cancel their contract for his next book before the war was out.

As the Battle of Britain raged in the skies early in September, Geoffrey Mason of Lloyds Banks alerted Mrs Hill to an important court case for authors and their tax:[*] it confirmed that an outright sale of a copyright for a lump sum, rather than royalties, could be treated as a 'capital' transaction, thereby escaping all taxation. Mason did not wish to disturb the prime minister at this time, but he wondered whether any of Churchill's newspaper contracts since the outbreak of war might qualify.

---

[*] *Beare v. Carter*, King's Bench Division 1940.

Despite the pressures of war, Churchill always had time for news about reducing his tax bill. He asked to meet Mason as soon as possible and focussed on his deal with the *Sunday Dispatch*: although the newspaper was paying him a fee for each extract used (normally the classic sign of a royalty) there was one factor which might help. 'I gathered from him that the matter was arranged verbally or possibly by letter and that no formal contract was entered into,' Mason confided to Mrs Hill. He began to assemble a case to put to the Inland Revenue.[23]

By then, a different literary problem was exercising Churchill: on 6 September Thornton Butterworth's publishing business collapsed. It owed Churchill almost £1,000 and six of his early copyrights (including *My Early Life* and *The World Crisis*) fell into the hands of a receiver.* Churchill's former secretary Violet Pearman returned from sick leave to document the missing royalties. She worked until the first half of October in Downing Street while the German Luftwaffe began its nighttime bomb attacks on London, known as the Blitz. On 14 October, the day that she finished, a bomb blew out the windows of 10 Downing Street, scattering papers inside.

Meanwhile Bracken looked for a friendly publisher who might buy the copyrights from the receiver, since Churchill had made it clear that he did not see why he should part with cash to do so. Bracken approached Lord Southwood, the owner of Odhams Press, as well as his own old firm, Eyre & Spottiswoode. Southwood was one of a growing number of publishers who had already expressed an interest in any future prime ministerial war memoirs, the groundwork for which Churchill had laid by instructing his private office to amass bundles of his official directives each month, carefully labelling them as 'Personal Minutes' in order to establish a claim to their ownership.**

---

* Mr Wingfield of Fairbairn, Wingfield & Wykes.
** Downing Street communications with Roosevelt were labelled 'My Personal Telegrams'.

Butterworth, Flower and Emery Reves[*] had each lodged approaches for the memoirs before Lord Southwood offered £40,000 on behalf of a syndicate, that included America's Houghton Mifflin, and he appeared to hint that more money might be available.[24] Bracken hoped that Southwood might divert some of his funds towards purchasing the old copyrights. However, he failed to do so before two bids for Butterworth's business landed on the receiver's desk during January 1941. The first was friendly, from Bracken's old firm of Eyre & Spottiswoode, and excluded Churchill's copyrights; the second was (from Churchill's viewpoint) a less welcome attempt by Butterworth to repurchase his business with the help of a friend, complete with Churchill's old copyrights.

The receiver chose the Eyre & Spottiswoode option so that he could pay Churchill the money owed for his outstanding royalties and then auction the copyrights separately to the highest bidder. 'Cd I not get these myself?'[25] Churchill asked Bracken late in March 1941, during the heaviest period of the Blitz. Surprised but delighted at this change of mind, Bracken swiftly struck a deal with the receiver at £1,500, in return for him abandoning the auction.[26] 'The Prime Minister has bought back his own copyrights,' Bracken firmly told his former colleagues at Eyre & Spottiswoode, 'and he does not intend to resell.'[27]

A disappointed Butterworth hazarded a final, emotional appeal to his old author:

> I have had blow upon blow during the last few months. The sudden death of my wife; the bombing of a valuable collection of Chinese and Japanese curios, and of Early Water Colour Masters; culminating with my business being sold to a higher bidder... Surely enough for one man. But the knowledge that

---

[*] In September 1939 Churchill helped Imre Revesz to obtain a post in the Ministry of Information and, early in 1940, to gain British citizenship under the anglicized name Emery Reves. Reves did not settle in the ministry; he moved instead to New York where in February 1941 he re-established his Cooperation agency as Cooperation Publishing Co. Inc.

you decided to place your Copyrights in other hands, and thereby terminate our connection of 18 years, during which time I hope I have been of some service to you, is particularly painful.[28]

Churchill did not reply.

Butterworth was so confident that he would re-acquire his old business that he confessed he had prematurely accepted £200 from the Reprint Society for permission to reissue *Great Contemporaries*.[29] A furious Bracken ordered the Reprint Society to rescind its arrangement with Butterworth and then asked them to make a higher offer. The Reprint Society paid up: it was Churchill's first dividend from ownership of his copyrights.[30] A second followed when Mrs Hill was able to provide the *Sunday Dispatch* with new copyright material for its weekly excerpts, almost doubling Churchill's fee in the process to 110 guineas a week.[31]

Chequers, the prime minister's official country residence, was put to good use by the Churchills. So much so that the Ministry of Food had to raise the food rations for Chequers to the level enjoyed by foreign embassies.* Seasonal pheasant and venison sent from Balmoral by George VI also helped to sustain morale. 'The luxury was heavenly, quantities of rare foods, fires, lights, drinks etc', Jack Churchill's daughter Clarissa recalled.[32]

However, use of the country house retreat came with a cost: the Chequers Trust provided prime ministers an allowance of £15 each weekend, but they were expected to meet the costs of food, heating, light, laundry, telephone and petrol.[33] When the Churchills' bills added up to twice the level of this allowance, their private staff argued that the government should at least pay half of all telephone costs.[34] Next they questioned the wine payments: at the Admiralty,

---

* Eggs were omitted from the list until late 1941, when the ministry agreed to deliver twelve a week, so long as they were 'for the specific purpose of providing eggs for diplomatic personnel who may be visiting'.

Churchill's personal consumption had cost £30 a month, but the wine bills at Chequers were often double this amount. The Government Hospitality Fund agreed to contribute on occasions when overseas visitors were present, a condition which posed no problem. Churchill was determined to enlist the military might of the United States on Britain's side on the war: American guests became frequent visitors to Chequers.*

In February 1941 Cassell & Co. published *Into Battle*, the first collection of Churchill's wartime speeches. It was a huge commercial success on both sides of the Atlantic and the first real evidence that Churchill's new international reputation had begun to transform the value of his work.

For the benefit of the tax authorities, the book's preamble pointed out that it had been 'compiled' by Randolph and that Churchill had played no editorial role; nevertheless, the contract entitled Churchill to 25 per cent of the sales proceeds, which reached more than £12,000 in Britain and America combined.[35] Together with his prime ministerial salary and his earnings from his Sunday newspaper articles, they took Churchill squarely into Britain's top wartime tax bracket of 97½ per cent.[36]

The Inland Revenue turned down Mason's attempt to argue that the *Sunday Dispatch*'s payments represented a series of capital receipts rather than royalties, because he had been unable to produce any proof that Churchill had sold the entire copyright in his works. An experienced politician, Churchill understood the sensitivity of fighting to remove his literary earnings from taxation at a time of war. However, the difference between no tax at all and a tax of 97½ per cent on earnings as high as £21,000 was too great to be ignored for a man as indebted as Churchill.

He was busy planning Operation Battleaxe to halt Rommel's

---

* This assistance brought extra bureaucracy: wine was only to be served with the fund's prior approval; for each bottle, the names of guests were to be logged in the cellar book and a separate form was to detail 'the nature of the entertainment'.

advance across the north African desert, when he asked Brendan Bracken to accompany Geoffrey Mason in the time-honoured ritual of a visit to the chairman of the Inland Revenue, Sir Gerald Canny. At the meeting, Bracken and Mason challenged the decision that Churchill must pay income tax on his Sunday newspaper earnings, and asked whether a sale of film rights to *My Early Life* would be taxed.[37] They added this item to their agenda at the last minute when Churchill received an offer out of the blue from Alexander Korda (backed by Warner Brothers). Bracken had managed to edge the studio's original offer of £5,000 up to £7,500, all payable on signature.

After consulting his colleagues, Sir Gerald told Mason that so far as the film was concerned, 'It is O.K.'[38] This decision raised an eyebrow or two within the Inland Revenue, but it was based on the acceptance that Churchill had retired as an author and sold all the film rights for a fixed capital sum. Churchill received his film payment by the end of June. This meant that his bank account ended the first half of the year in credit at almost £9,000, even after Churchill had repaid Sir Henry Strakosch's loan of June 1940.[39]

Sir Gerald took a different line on Churchill's Sunday newspaper articles. '[Mason] was unable to produce any evidence which could lead me to the view that these were not taxable,' he informed the chancellor of the exchequer Sir Kingsley Wood, who took an interest in the matter.[40] Neither Churchill nor his adviser was ready to concede, however. 'Mason wants to return to the charge,' Sir Gerald told one of his senior staff a week later. 'He wants to argue that each excerpt was a capital transaction in itself: but it seems to me a hopeless contention. However we must listen.'[41]

Mason cleared his submission with Churchill before sending it to the tax authority. Considering work had continued on *A History of the English-Speaking Peoples* until April 1940 it began by skating on thin ice:

> At the outbreak of the war, Mr Churchill was offered the post of First Lord of the Admiralty, the acceptance of which definitely precluded him from continuing his literary work. At this

stage Mr Churchill's capital consisted of his private investments, and the copyright of certain of his old articles. The
firms mentioned were anxious to purchase the right to publish
excerpts from these writings, but it was impossible at that time
to compute a fixed annual purchase price as it was not known
to what extent their right would be exercised. For convenience
it was arranged that payment should be made as and when
excerpts were published and these payments have been more or
less consistent each week for the past twenty months... It
appears to me that there can be no question but that each
payment received is a purchase of a portion of a capital asset.[42]

The Inland Revenue was unmoved. It would have to see more
evidence about Churchill's contract with the *Sunday Dispatch* if it
was to change its mind, it made clear. As there was none, Mason
suggested to Churchill that he should draft a letter retrospectively
confirming the terms from the owners of the paper, Associated
Newspapers. After taking legal advice on the wording (without
disclosing Churchill's identity), Mason had the final text cleared
by Churchill before the newspaper's managing director signed it.[43]
The letter admitted that Churchill's contract had been purely
verbal and involved neither a fixed sum nor the whole copyright.
This only hardened the Inland Revenue's position, so that its full
board 'adhered' to its earlier decision in November that the sums
should be taxed.[44] Churchill and his advisers would need to decide
whether or not to mount a formal appeal to the general commissioners of taxation, who are 'unpaid lay people of good standing'
appointed by the lord chancellor to hear appeals against tax assessments made by the Inland Revenue.[45]

Brendan Bracken's duties as Churchill's 'honorary man of business'
were not confined to the film world. In the summer of 1941 lawyers
asked who was to take urgently needed decisions about re-publishing
Churchill's early books, the copyright of which he now owned, but
which were all out of print. Churchill's one-word reply was

'Bracken'.[46] In fact, Bracken had already produced a typically trenchant recommendation on the subject:

> The earnings of Bernard Shaw and Kipling far exceeded those
> of any contemporary writer. They did not sell the copyright of
> their books to publishers. They made contracts with firms to
> publish their books on a commission of 10 per cent on all out-
> of-pocket expenses, such as manufacturing and advertising. . .
> and 15 per cent on nett [sic] proceeds of sales. And so the
> authors received most of the profits earned by their books.

The publishing firm of Macmillan & Co., Bracken told Churchill,
would handle his books on even better terms than Kipling or Shaw
had achieved. 'The position will be that you will continue to own
the copyright of your books, that you will take the major part of the
profits which they earn, and that you will have no responsibility for
the cost of producing and advertising the books. I think this is an
admirable arrangement.'[47]

Churchill approved the start of detailed negotiations, but he was
pre-occupied for most of June and July with the failure of Operation
Battleaxe, which required high-level changes in Britain's Middle
East command, and then came Germany's invasion of the Soviet
Union. Not until August – shortly before Churchill left for his first
summit with President Roosevelt off Newfoundland – did he find
time to examine the Macmillan agreement. To the horror of those
who had spent weeks negotiating each clause, Churchill put a line
straight through the section that authorized Macmillan to negotiate film, radio and serial exploitation of his copyrights. Daniel
Macmillan, however, kept a calm head: Churchill had not objected
to the third clause of the agreement, which committed all of his
future books to Macmillan. Effectively, the publisher believed, he
had secured the right to handle Churchill's war memoirs when the
time came, which almost everybody assumed it would.[48]

Once an Allied victory was assured, Churchill planned to retire
and avoid Lloyd George's mistake of staying on too long, he

confided to Lord Camrose in November 1941. 'His age precluded him from planning to be a big figure in the long and complicated negotiations which the peace would involve,' Lord Camrose told his son. 'He also has in mind the idea that he should make provision for his family. To do this he would have to be able to write.'[49]

For the time being, Churchill would have to be content with a second book of his war speeches. *Into Battle*'s success had encouraged Cassell to publish a sequel. In the absence of Randolph, who was on his way to fight in Egypt, Charles Eade, editor of *The Sunday Dispatch*, undertook to compile the book without payment. By October 1941 he had amassed 100,000 words, but Kathleen Hill found it impossible to pin Churchill down to discuss the publication. The demands of prime minister took precedence as British forces were besieged in Tobruk and the German army approached Moscow.

Churchill examined Cassell's standard royalty contract late in November. He was still pondering the tax advantages of an outright sale in early December, when the Japanese bombed the American fleet in Pearl Harbor. This brought the United States into the war and all thoughts of his book disappeared as Churchill sped towards Washington to discuss military plans with Britain's new ally.

21

***
'Taxed to the utmost'
Film Turns the Tide, 1942–5

Exchange rate: $4 = £1
Inflation multiples: US x 14; UK x 40

T HE PRIME MINISTER spent Christmas 1941 and the New
Year in Washington, then returned to find a House of
Commons and a public concerned about the British army's
retreat across northern Africa, together with naval losses in Asia.
Churchill turned a two-day debate on the conduct of the war into
a vote of confidence, at the end of which only one MP recorded a
vote of opposition.

Two weeks later, on 15 February 1942, Singapore fell to numer-
ically inferior Japanese forces, exposing the remaining Malayan
peninsular. If that fell, the enemy could threaten either India or
Australia and New Zealand. An increasing number of voices questioned the wisdom of one man being both minister of defence and
prime minister, so Churchill restructured his government. He held
on to his key positions, giving up only leadership of the House of
Commons, which he handed over to a senior Labour figure, Sir
Stafford Cripps. Sir Stafford also entered the war cabinet and was
to deputize for the prime minister in the House of Commons, so
that Churchill did not have to attend it so frequently.

Despite the numerous demands on Churchill's time, he still
wanted to settle the tax treatment of his regular Sunday newspaper
articles. His tax adviser Geoffrey Mason was in favour of a challenge to the Inland Revenue's ruling that these should be taxed as

royalties, although the challenge would require an appeal to a tribunal of general commissioners of taxation. Churchill's usual lawyers, Nicholl, Manisty & Co., had decided that such an appeal lay beyond their competence, so Mason had recruited help from a tax specialist, Anthony Moir, at Fladgate & Co., a firm of solicitors nearby in Pall Mall.

Soon after his return from the White House, and 'in strictest confidence', Churchill had authorized Mason and Moir to consult a barrister, Charles Graham-Dixon.* The hope was that the opinion of a well-respected tax barrister might persuade senior minds at the Inland Revenue to think again, but it failed to do so.[1]

Moir was therefore called to Downing Street in order to brief Churchill on the risks of mounting a formal appeal to a tax tribunal. Moir arrived for his first appointment on 19 May and expected the meeting would be short. Churchill was facing renewed criticism of his leadership, following the fall of the remainder of the Malayan peninsula, and the House of Commons was about to start a two-day debate on the conduct of the war. Years later Moir set down his recollection of the meeting:

> I was warned that [Churchill] would probably give me ten minutes, that I must be very brief and that I must tell him (if such was the case) that he had two or more courses open to him. Thereafter he would instantly make up his mind which course he would pursue. . . I was ushered into the Cabinet Room. . . and started off and said my piece which I had carefully prepared. [Churchill] after a short time got up and started walking around the table, talking as he did so, with the result that, when he arrived at each end he was completely out of earshot.. . . 'If I appeal, will it be entirely private; can anyone get to know about it?' I replied that it would be entirely private before the

---

* Leslie Charles Graham-Dixon is referred to as Leslie throughout Martin Gilbert's biography, *Winston Spencer Churchill*; however, his grandson assures the author that family, friends and colleagues called him Charles.

Commissioners, but if we won, they could appeal further and then the hearing would be in public.. . . And so it went on. My 'ten minutes' was eventually turned into one and a half hours, but when I left I came away with instructions to lodge an appeal. I remember walking down Whitehall and buying an evening paper, the headline of which was 'Why wasn't Churchill in the House Today?' and at least I felt that was a question which I could answer with some conviction![2]

Churchill's absence was part of a new policy that he should restrict his appearances in the House, but on this occasion it was criticized by many members. He was, however, exonerated by at least one his critics, Sir Edward Grigg, who concluded that Churchill had 'important preoccupations to keep him elsewhere'.[3] Little did he realize it was the prime minister's tax affairs.

Moir was asked to suggest more tax-saving ideas to Geoffrey Mason, while they waited for the appeal process to run its course. They came up with three. The first was that Churchill should share more of his earnings from *Into Battle* with Randolph, who paid a lower rate of tax. Mason calculated that if Churchill handed over half, father and son could save up to £1,500 of tax between them.[4]

At that time, in February 1942, filial relations were strained. Randolph's marriage had ended and he blamed his parents for taking his wife Pamela's side. However, he needed the money after losing £3,000 playing what a fellow officer, Evelyn Waugh, described as 'very high gambling, poker, roulette, chemin de fer' on the way to Egypt with his regiment.[5]

Two days after ordering the transfer of his earnings to Randolph, Churchill worried about the propriety of such an action, but he was assured that Mason had already sounded out the tax authorities.[6]

Another of Moir and Mason's suggestions was that Churchill should sell the second book of his wartime speeches for a capital sum rather than royalties. Early in February Aubrey Gentry, the Cassell director, obliged by offering £10,000, but Churchill was still undecided whether to accept the sum when the fall of Britain's Singapore garrison led the publishing firm to withdraw its offer on the grounds that the market for it had 'dulled'.[7] Kathleen Hill was quick to accept a revised offer of £8,000, but it was conditional on Cassell finding a buyer in America. This proved difficult because Churchill's stock was falling in tandem with the reputation of the British military. After three months of fruitless searching, Churchill met Gentry to agree a reduced price of £3,000 without American rights.[8]

Thirdly, Moir and Mason suggested that Churchill should resell the copyrights of his old books, because the money that he earned from exploiting them would always be subject to high rates of income tax; whereas he would pay no tax if he sold the copyrights on for a capital sum to Macmillan, the publisher who was due to produce and sell the books. Churchill approved Moir and Mason's plan, but it failed at the first hurdle when Daniel Macmillan was not prepared to name a price: he maintained that it was simply too early in the life of these new arrangements to know what a fair price would be.

Their first results emerged in the middle of the year, when Churchill was back in Washington, suffering the indignity of his forces surrendering control of Tobruk. They provided some cheer: the books had earned Churchill £4,000 in five months, thanks to an average publishing margin of 40 per cent, far above his old royalty rates.[9] Every copy of *My Early Life* had sold out by the time Mrs Hill told Daniel Macmillan in November: 'I know that Mr Churchill is very much pleased with the way in which you have been managing his affairs.'[10]

Churchill was equally pleased with his new solicitor Anthony Moir, who saved him the time and embarrassment of appearing personally as a witness before the general commissioners of taxation. Moir had persuaded the new chairman of the Inland Revenue, Sir Cornelius Gregg, that the two parties should produce an Agreed Statement of Facts on which their respective barristers would then simply make submissions to the tribunal.[11] The lay commissioners decided in Churchill's favour at the end of September 1942 and the Inland Revenue's solicitor advised his board that there was little prospect of reversing the decision without appealing all the way up to the House of Lords. He suspected, rightly, there would be little appetite for such a step. 'Acquiesce', Sir Cornelius instructed.[12]

This private victory over the Inland Revenue was soon matched by success on the battlefield. Within weeks Britain's Eighth Army broke out from its defensive positions at El Alamein, while American and British forces landed successfully in Algeria, and the Russian army began to turn the tide of battle against the Germans facing Stalingrad.

A more optimistic Churchill and Roosevelt met at Casablanca in January 1943 to settle the new year's military plans. They postponed a north European landing for another year and instead agreed on a summer invasion of Sicily. At home, Kathleen Hill suggested an early deal on a third volume of war speeches,* while military victories remained fresh in the public mind, but time was lost when Churchill wanted her to put Macmillan in competition with Cassell. After Daniel Macmillan declined to offer, Cassell reduced its price for a second year running, because it felt the formula was wearing thin.[13]

Before a new tax year started in April 1943, Mason persuaded Churchill that they should make another attempt to sell the copyrights of his early books. This time Macmillan offered a capital sum of £7,000, on condition that his firm retained the right to publish any new books by Churchill after the war. Horrified that he had missed this stipulation which would restrict his freedom of manoeuvre when dealing with his war memoirs, Churchill insisted

---

* Churchill initially chose the title *Onwards to Victory* from a list supplied by Charles Eade, but opted a few days later for the more prudent *The End of the Beginning*.

that Macmillan make a fresh bid without it. A disappointed Macmillan complied, keeping the same headline price, but back-dating the arrangement by a year to compensate his firm. The payment helped Churchill's bank balance at the end of June 1943 reach a record level of £21,500.[14]

Brendan Bracken, however, only heard of the sale in September. Furious that his his long-term strategy of Churchill owning his copyrights had been abandoned for short-term tax advantages, Bracken instructed Mrs Hill to reverse the sale – otherwise he would buy the rights back himself. Although Daniel Macmillan was bemused by the mixed signals from Downing Street, he agreed in principle to provide a refund. However, six months later, no documents had been signed. A chance conversation revealed the reason to Kathleen Hill: Daniel Macmillan was still insisting that a return to the original 1941 arrangement between Churchill and the publisher must include the clause that had given the firm the right to handle Churchill's books after the war.

The prospect of an Allied victory in the war was already pushing up the price of any potential Churchill war memoirs. Preparatory discussions with publishers took up an increasing amount of the prime minister's time from the summer of 1943 onwards because two earlier book contracts stood in the way. The first was the post-poned *A History of the English-Speaking Peoples* for Cassell & Co.; the second was the yet-to-be-started *After Armageddon* for George G. Harrap & Co. and its two publishing partners.*

Churchill had tried to terminate the *After Armageddon* con-tracts and to return the publishers' advances as early as 1940, but Harrap had insisted that the option to terminate lay with the pub-lishers, not the author. A desultory correspondence had continued,

---

* Churchill had signed three separate contracts: one with Harrap & Co., another with the British 'parts' publisher George Newnes, and a third with US publishers Harcourt Brace, under American law.

until Harrap revealed its hand in 1942 by offering Churchill a new contract at a higher price, 'if you feel you are able to write a different book' – in other words, his war memoirs.[15]

Churchill had ignored the firm at the time, but returned to the issue in 1943, now that more valuable offers were coming in from other publishers. In July he consulted privately with Sir Walter Monckton, a barrister he had befriended when they both worked on Edward VIII's abdication settlement. Churchill wanted to know how he might extricate himself from the Harrap contracts. Sir Walter suggested that he should build a case that his assumption of wartime duties as prime minister had led to the contracts' legal 'frustration'.

In early August Churchill drafted for his lawyers an impassioned memorandum to substantiate the argument:

> I have been called to fulfil public duties, which I could not have declined. These duties have absorbed every scrap of my time and strength since I assumed office. I have no leisure and take no holidays. I suppose I have not read a dozen books during the last five years. My full time and strength is taxed to the utmost. I cannot write any book while I am Prime Minister.

The idea of writing this particular book was now 'abhorrent', he wrote:

> The book is dead spiritually and in every dimension. I could not write about any of these countries as I had intended to write. The picture that I had in my mind has been effaced by subsequent events. . . I certainly would not be on speaking terms with Stalin if I wrote the things I would have written in time of peace.[16]

As the Italian government prepared to surrender, Churchill asked his personal solicitor Charles Nicholl to obtain a second barrister's opinion on this line of argument. They met early in October with

Charles Henderson KC to discuss the barrister's fourteen-page opinion. Its conclusions were not as clear-cut in Churchill's favour as he would have wished. Frustration could not be self-diagnosed, Henderson warned; it was a matter of legal fact, which could only occur if events outside either party's control 'rendered the performance of a contract indefinitely impossible'. If Churchill lost his case, any damages 'would in all likelihood be heavy'. Henderson therefore suggested redrafting Churchill's memorandum and aiming for arbitration if Churchill's claim of frustration was refused.[17]

Churchill's revised version, drafted by Henderson, was dispatched to Harrap on un-crested Downing Street paper. Noting that the book's completion date had already passed without any comment from Harrap, it suggested that the publishers' silence signalled an acceptance that 'supervening events beyond human control have rendered our contract impossible of performance and that I am accordingly discharged from liability'.[18]

The Harrap brothers, George and Walter, took a month to consult their partners before visiting Downing Street on 11 November. Churchill was busy putting the finishing touches to the Allied Expeditionary Force, which was due to land in France in 1944. When he met the Harraps (according to Kathleen Hill's minutes) they agreed that high office had prevented him from writing *After Armageddon* as it was originally conceived. Therefore, they had no intention of holding him to the contract. However, they felt 'entitled to the privilege of publishing another book, whenever that book might be written, but of course on Mr Churchill's own terms'. Churchill made clear his resentment at their stance; he agreed, however, to postpone applying for arbitration on condition that the Harraps put their undertaking not to sue in writing the next day.[19]

No letter came. Instead the Harraps asked Churchill for a draft that they could show their partners. Sent over Kathleen Hill's signature, it demanded from the Harraps an 'unequivocal admission' that their contract had lapsed, before hinting at 'favourable consideration' should Churchill ever write again after the war.[20]

By the time George Harrap responded, Churchill lay ill in Tunis, exhausted after a prolonged bout of travelling. He was annoyed not only because Harrap questioned the veracity of Mrs Hill's minutes, but also because he insisted once again that the option to terminate their contract lay with the publishers and not the author. Churchill added a specific objection to Harrap's 'manoeuvring' for his war memoirs to the draft reply which Charles Henderson prepared:

> The substance of your letter put into plain terms is that you are to be entitled to use the present circumstances as a bargaining lever in any future negotiations between us. Such a state of affairs does not commend itself to me. . . Disinclined as I am to occupy my time with my personal affairs at the present time, your letter leaves me no alternative but to call upon your Company to submit the dispute to arbitration.[21]

While the Harrap camp considered their response, another complication came to the fore. Just before Churchill attended the Quebec Conference of July 1943, Sir Alexander Korda had bid for the film rights to *Marlborough: His Life and Times*, this time backed by a different Hollywood studio, Metro Goldwyn Mayer.[22] Recalled from ministerial duties to negotiate on Churchill's behalf, Brendan Bracken pushed the bid up to £20,000, at which point Kathleen Hill suggested that they should obtain tax advice from Lloyds Bank.

It emerged that T. E. B. Harris, the manager of the Pall Mall branch of Lloyds, had an industry contact of his own: the larger-than-life Italian film producer Filippo Del Giudice. 'Mr Del', as the press called him, had arrived from Italy in 1932, 'alone, nigh penniless and lacking a word of English'; eleven years later, he now owned a flat in Park Lane and a country house near Beaconsfield.[23] It was Sir Alexander who had introduced 'Mr Del' to the film world before his protégé developed a more extravagant production philosophy through his own company Two Cities, backed by J. Arthur Rank. Two Cities proceeded to bid £30,000 for *Marlborough*, to which MGM responded by increasing its offer to £25,000, hoping that Sir Alexander's long personal relationship with Churchill would tip the balance in its favour.[24]

As soon as Churchill returned from the Quebec Conference in September he discussed both bids with Bracken on the train back to London. Kathleen Hill suggested they ask Two Cities for its 'best offer' before making a decision. It turned out to be a sharply increased £50,000, of which no less than £30,000 was to be paid immediately on signing.[25] Without waiting for tax advice, Churchill immediately accepted a contract worth twice as much as any he had previously been offered, and approved a press release prepared by Two Cities.[26] It was left to Brendan Bracken, more alert as minister of information to the damage that any talk of such a large sum might cause in the middle of war, to impose a news blackout.

To Sir Alexander Korda he offered a consolation prize: for a similar price, he could buy the film rights to A History of the English-Speaking Peoples. However, talks had to be broken off almost as soon as they began when the Daily Herald published a largely accurate story by its reporter Hannen Swaffer under the headline 'CHURCHILL'S BIG FEE':

> I heard yesterday the astounding statement that the film rights of Churchill's Life of Marlborough have been bought for no less than £55,000. If this is true, it means that the money has been paid for the use of the premier's name for publicity purposes, because any scenario writer of skill could adapt the life of the visitor of Blenheim from sources easily accessible in the history books and biographies.[27]

Negotiations remained stalled while Churchill first travelled to Cairo and Teheran and then fell ill at Tunis on the way home. Recuperating in Morocco afterwards, Churchill declared himself to be unconcerned by the publicity about his film fee and authorized negotiations with Sir Alexander Korda to restart. Sir Alexander and MGM accepted Bracken's price of £50,000 on condition that they were allowed to extract four films from different stages of English history;[28] Churchill was happy to accept, so long as they stayed away from *Marlborough*, which he had already sold. Sir Alexander shook hands with Bracken on 21 January 1944, the day that the Allies landed at Anzio on the Italian mainland.

Instinct then made Mrs Hill double-check that the film rights for *A History of the English-Speaking Peoples* still definitely belonged to Churchill. She found that it was unclear: the book's contract – drawn up in 1933, before the routine separation of book and film rights – simply gave Cassell 'the complete and entire copyright'.[29] Frustrated, Churchill called for a counsel's opinion:* he was advised to buy back the film rights just to be on the safe side.

Unwilling to part with cash for the purpose, Churchill preferred the idea of being given the film rights in exchange for granting Cassell & Co. first refusal on the British book rights to any memoirs that he wrote after the war. It must have seemed an attractive swap at the time – the film rights of *A History of the English-Speaking Peoples* were worth an immediate £50,000, whereas his post-war memoirs were still a distant prospect. Churchill asked Bracken to use Lord Camrose as his intermediary in the negotiations, as the newspaperman knew Cassell's chairman, Sir Newman Flower.**

At this point, February 1944, the Harrap brothers conceded that their contract for Churchill's next book, *After Armageddon*, would have to go to formal arbitration. Nevertheless Churchill decided to press on with the Cassell negotiations, authorizing two offers to be made to Sir Newman Flower: first, 'when the war is over and the author has some spare time he will write the introduction to the history [*of the English-Speaking Peoples*]'; second, 'subject to the decision of the arbitrator in Harrap's claim, Cassells and the

---

* Provided by a young barrister, Kenneth Diplock (1907–85), who later became a distinguished law lord.
** Camrose and his brother acquired Cassell & Co. as part of Amalgamated Press in 1927, but sold Cassell's books business to its managing director, Newman Flower, to help pay for their purchase.

Amalgamated Press will have priority in bidding for the right to buy any history of the War written by our friend'.[30] As a reward for acting as Churchill's emissary, Camrose and his business, The Amalgamated Press, won an equivalent priority in bidding for the rights to the memoirs' newspaper extracts.*

The talks went well, until Sir Newman asked for a legally binding agreement rather than a gentlemen's pact. This news came on the same day that Daniel Macmillan insisted on a written acknowledgement of his own firm's legal claim to publish any post-war book written by Churchill.

With D-Day less than two months away, Churchill now faced two competing legal claims to his post-war memoirs from Macmillan and Harrap, each potentially blocking the exchange he wanted to make with a third publisher, Cassell, so that he could sell Sir Alexander Korda the film rights to his *History*. Churchill convened a hurried series of meetings with his lawyers, to whom he had not previously mentioned these complications.

Nicholl and Henderson asked for a week to come up with a solution, but they were pre-empted by a direction from Churchill. In Macmillan's case, he told them, he was happy to let current arrangements stand, in which case 'it must be absolutely clear that. . . I am free in respect of any future work written'; alternatively he would return to their 1941 agreement and then give the firm notice 'a few days afterwards'. He remained determined to proceed with his Cassell exchange on one condition: if Sir Newman offered less than he thought the memoirs were worth when the time came, he must be free to go elsewhere; he would not, however, take a lower price from anyone else 'without returning to Cassell's'.[31]

Churchill's lawyers saw matters differently. He must press ahead with the Harrap arbitration, Charles Nicholl advised, and should acknowledge the validity of Macmillan's 1941 claim to handle his

---

* Camrose exercised this 'priority' through another of his newspapers, *The Daily Telegraph*, in 1946.

post-war book before he bought back the copyrights from
Macmillan. Churchill could then bring that arrangement to a
wholly legitimate, if brutal, end by giving the firm notice, as he
himself had suggested.

Meanwhile, Nicholl warned that Churchill should halt all correspondence with Cassell and Sir Alexander Korda, because he was
on much weaker legal ground than he realized. The 1938 synopsis
of *After Armageddon* had left the book's scope unclear. 'It might be
held to include the whole or part of the period of the present War,'
Nicholl even claimed. In addition, details of any option agreement
that Churchill reached with Cassell would have to be disclosed to
the Harrap arbitrator, handing his opponents a ready guide to
assessing damages.[32]

Churchill bowed to the advice. He signed the letter for Daniel
Macmillan that Nicholl put in front of him six weeks before the
D-Day landings. 'I notice the comment which you make upon
Clause 3 of the Memorandum of Agreement. It speaks for itself,' he
conceded, enclosing a cheque for £7,000.[33] Even after this had been
paid, Churchill's bank balance now stood above £50,000, helped by
a legacy of £20,000 from Sir Henry Strakosch, who had died in
October 1943, and whose final will had also cancelled the debt
owed by Churchill since his rescue in 1938.[34]

As D-Day came and went, the dispute between Churchill and the
Harraps advanced towards resolution as slowly as the Allied troops
across Normandy's *bocage*, then Harraps blinked first. They offered
to cancel Churchill's old contract if he promised to sign a new one
for his first post-war book. While visiting the invasion beaches,
Churchill turned them down flat.

A month later, as American forces finally fanned out across
northern France, Charles Nicholl allowed Churchill to give
Macmillan notice. 'It is incumbent upon me to put my affairs on a
solid basis when I am free to do so. Please do not think that I am
giving the notice because of other commitments as that is not the
case,' Churchill wrote, somewhat disingenuously, before flying off

to Algiers.[35] Daniel Macmillan gave way gracefully, but declined the suggestion that his firm should carry on handling the author's early books.[36]

The battle to liberate Paris was in full swing and Churchill was visiting the Italian frontline, when the Harraps made another attempt to settle in the fourth week of August: they would accept an informal letter giving them 'first refusal of any book on the War if such a book should be written by Mr Churchill, he being under no obligation to write any book and free if he did so to fix his own terms'.[37] Henderson and Nicholl urged Churchill to accept the Harrap offer before dealing with Sir Newman Flower by a small 'nuisance payment'.[38]

In the aftermath of the German surrender in Paris, Churchill was on the point of doing so when he changed his mind. He refused to give the Harraps

> any special consideration in respect of any book that I may write
> after the War is over about the War period. This is what they
> have been after all along, and they have been using this contract
> all this time as a blackmailing lever. The conduct of this firm,
> and particularly of Mr George Harrap, has been in my opinion
> so at variance with the usual conditions prevailing between
> author and publisher, that I do not wish to have any further
> dealings of any kind with them.[39]

There was a slight softening of this line when Bracken met the Harraps for informal talks on 4 September. As the Allied troops marched into Brussels, Churchill allowed him to discuss giving Harrap first refusal on a book 'exclusively, repeat exclusively, about the pre-War period'. Bracken returned with tentative agreement on 'say a biography of Napoleon or Hitler', but it was not enough for Churchill. Through Kathleen Hill, he relayed the fact that he had meant 'a book exclusively about the pre-War period, that is to say the period between the last war and this war'.[40] By the time the two parties met again that evening, Churchill's advisers had understood their master's intent and the meeting broke up without agreement despite another concession by the Harrap brothers.

Three days later, as V-2 rockets started to fall on London, a letter arrived at Downing Street from the younger Walter Harrap.

> We feel that a misunderstanding has crept into this matter in a way that is very regrettable, and to end all further discussion are willing that the Agreement shall be terminated forthwith. . . We are taking this course also because we greatly appreciate what you have done for us all through your courageous leadership in the world's greatest emergency, and it is distasteful to us, whether we are right or wrong, that we should be compelled to litigate the matter with a man to whom every one of us is indebted.[41]

As Churchill left to attend a second conference in Quebec, he dictated a magnanimous reply, declaring all misunderstandings overcome. A 'top secret' cable from Bracken pursued him, explaining that the letter could not be sent until the arbitration process had run its course, although it was a mere formality.[42]

Sir Alexander Korda was anxious for film negotiations to resume, but first a deal with Cassell had to be struck. On Churchill's return from Moscow, where he had travelled from Quebec for discussions with Stalin about the future of Poland and the Balkans, he set out the changed background for his emissary, Lord Camrose:

> Let me point out within what very small dimensions these difficulties have been confined. At the outside, Harraps could have claimed that one chapter out of the inter-wars book should deal with the opening of the present war. I am now entirely free from even this small tie. . . The way is therefore open for me to write a letter for you to give to Sir Newman Flower, as you so kindly offered to do, in which I will promise to give him the first refusal of any book I may write about this War, at a price to be mutually

agreed. Failing agreement, I should be free to look elsewhere, or return to him in case such quest failed.[43]

Camrose provided a first draft of the letter for Sir Newman, which Churchill amended before expressing the hope that it could be dispatched straightaway. In fact, it was to take another seven drafts and the lengthy involvement of Camrose, Henderson, Nicholl, Mason and Kathleen Hill – not to mention Churchill himself – before two separate letters left, four weeks later. The main stumbling block was how to engineer Cassell's option so that Churchill was not disadvantaged on the price. Churchill and Camrose discussed the problem together on 8 November, as recorded by Camrose:

> Had another discussion with W.S.C. about his book. He was anxious to get it settled so that he could sign the agreement for the film rights of the *English-Speaking Peoples*. With money from these, the £20,000 left to him by Strakosch and the sales of royalties of his other books, he would be quite independent and would be able to leave to his family a sum which he considered was quite adequate for them.[44]

They met again two days later, but questions remained in Churchill's mind. He wrote them down in a letter to Lord Camrose, while travelling to Paris for an Armistice Day visit:

> Is no offer to come from Sir Newman Flower? Am I to state my price and, if he thinks it too high, is that to be the end of the transaction with him? Am I to be entitled to go elsewhere and take a lower price if I cannot get my own figure, or am I thereafter to be inhibited from writing any book on the subject except at the original price asked for by me and the highest price which Sir Newman Flower is prepared to offer? This would seem to give him the entire power to fix the price.[45]

Lord Camrose produced a new formula, but Henderson and Nicholl found it fell short of the necessary legal detail. They drafted their own fifth version, but both Kathleen Hill and Churchill thought it too legalistic in tone. Churchill produced a sixth version, which the lawyers rejected. 'Mr Churchill may feel that we are being too pernickety,' Nicholl admitted to Kathleen Hill, 'but we really cannot advise him to write the letter in the form of the draft that you sent me this morning.'[46]

On the evening of 22 November, as French troops entered Strasbourg, Lord Camrose sat down with Churchill to hammer out a final version without lawyers present. After he had successfully warded off most of Churchill's last-minute changes, the two letters left Downing Street on 24 November.[47] 'I shall be very pleased to give your firm a first refusal, at the lowest price I am prepared to accept, in any work I might write on the present War once it is over,' Churchill's first letter read, detailing this option's mechanics over three pages.[48] The second, much briefer letter recorded their under-standings of 1940 about finishing *A History of the English-Speaking Peoples*; in place of extra chapters, Churchill was to write a 10,000-word epilogue within six months of leaving office.

Unaware of these letters, Albert Curtis Brown forwarded to Churchill the latest offer he had received for the memoirs, worth £250,000, to be added to the 'dossier': 'It is a letter of such importance that perhaps the Prime Minister would like to see it,' he told Kathleen Hill.[49] Alive to the sensitivity of the sum, however, Churchill wanted the correspondence brought to an immediate end. 'I do not want you to be under any misapprehension. The "dossier" to which you repeatedly refer has no existence,' his amended draft for Mrs Hill read. 'Would you please be good enough to let this correspondence end with the assurance that if Mr Churchill has need of your services at any time, he will not hesitate to ask you for them.'[50]

Once resumed, *History*'s film negotiations with MGM and Sir Alexander Korda proved more protracted than expected. MGM wanted control over radio and television rights as well as film and insisted that Churchill should share the cost of any US taxes. 'Offer Sir A <u>entire</u> film rights. No limit to number, and, if necessary, ½ American tax,' an emollient Churchill instructed his team. Nevertheless, there was still no detailed agreement in March 1945, when Churchill asked Bracken to 'get the matter settled'.[51] The following day, Sir Alexander called off his lawyers and substituted his own company in place of MGM as Churchill's paymaster. Kathleen Hill asked Lloyds Bank to put its receipt for the £50,000 cheque in a sealed envelope for delivery to her personally.[52] Churchill had begun the war with a large hole in his finances; as it drew to a close, his bank balance stood above £100,000.[53]

22

'A most profitable purdah'
Minting the Memoirs, 1945–6

Exchange rate: $4 = £1
Inflation multiples: US x 12.5; UK x 40

A S THE EUROPEAN war ended, the Labour Party's national executive opted for a summer general election, rather than extend the Coalition government's life until after the anticipated victory over Japan. Churchill resigned the office of prime minister on 23 May 1945, but stayed on at the head of a caretaker ministry formed of Conservative ministers. Although the general election was held on 5 July, the result was not announced until three weeks later after every soldier's vote was counted.

Churchill misread the public appetite for social reform during the campaign. While the Conservatives led on issues of international security, Clement Attlee and the Labour Party promised a new housing policy, nationalized healthcare, expanded state funding of education and national insurance. In a broadcast early in the campaign Churchill made the mistake of claiming that it would require 'some form of a Gestapo' to impose what he described as a form of socialism in Britain. The result was that the Labour Party's share of the vote increased by more than 11 per cent and it won an extra 239 seats in Parliament. The Conservative Party lost 190 seats, although Churchill's personal popularity remained high.

Clement Attlee became prime minister at the head of a new Labour government. Although bewildered by the outcome,

Churchill declined the knighthood which was offered to him and chose to continue in public life as leader of the Opposition. The post carried a salary of £2,000 a year, the same sum as the pension of a former prime minister which he could have claimed for the rest of his life if he had decided to retire.[1]

The Churchills could no longer live in Downing Street, but neither Chartwell nor the home at 28 Hyde Park Gate in Kensington that they had bought earlier in the year for £24,000 was ready to occupy.[2] They temporarily took a penthouse suite at Claridge's hotel.

Churchill's gloom following his shock defeat deepened as he thought about his post-war finances. For all his large deposit at the bank, it would last only for some five years if he returned to his pre-war level of spending, while tax rates of more than 90 per cent meant that he would keep very little of any future earnings if he resumed his writing.

Offers for his war memoirs started to flood in – the first (from an American newspaper syndicate, King Features) arriving at 6:36 p.m. on the day of his resignation. However, Churchill was in no mood to consider them unless his advisers could find a way around the tax problem. For the time being, their advice was to do nothing that might risk losing his tax status as a 'retired author', which at least meant that earnings from his past work escaped any tax.

Churchill asked Kathleen Hill to ignore the offers arriving from all over the world or to reply that he was 'not making any plans for writing books or articles at present'.[3] Emery Reves, who had recreated his press agency as Cooperation Publishing on reaching New York in 1941, was one of many who were ignored in July and August when he passed on book and magazine bids from all over the American continent. One was from *LIFE* magazine; another, from *Reader's Digest*, Reves deemed 'too sensitive to commit to paper'.[4]

Churchill took Lord Camrose into his confidence about his plans over a private lunch at *The Daily Telegraph*'s offices early in August 1945. 'At the moment he has decided that he will not publish his account of the war direction in his lifetime,' Camrose noted. 'He has voluminous detail inasmuch as every month his own tele-grams, decisions and instructions have been put into type by the Government printers, and he reckons that cach month's printing is equal to, say, two issues of a weekly review like *The Spectator*.'[5]

Although Churchill had kept all his papers – and carefully removed them to Chartwell after the war was over – he would need the new government's blessing to use them in any memoirs and he had advance knowledge this would be no mere formality. Before hostilities ended, a new cabinet secretary, Sir Edward Bridges, had advised him as prime minister that the rules on ministers and their official papers needed tightening up. Churchill had nevertheless insisted that the paper tabled to the cabinet a week before the Coalition came to an end should enshrine his three long-held tenets: (1) that ministers should be free to take with them copies of cabinet papers they themselves had authored; (2) that they should have access to all other cabinet documents of their time in office; but that (3) they must clear any proposed uses with the government of the day. That task still lay ahead, provided Churchill could find his way through the tax problem and summon the energy to write.

Churchill's early books had been left without an agency publisher since Macmillan had given up its role in February 1945. Brendan Bracken had asked the firm to reconsider in April, hinting that there might still be some role to play in connection with the memoirs, but the matter had simply become submerged under the fast-moving pace of events leading up to the end of the war, not least Hitler's suicide in his Berlin bunker and Germany's surrender.

Now, in August, a morose Churchill could not understand why Macmillan would not help him. Harold Macmillan was back in the family business after ministerial service during the war, and it was left to him to explain to his old chief that some 300 Macmillan titles were out of print due to paper shortages, and the firm could not give priority to Churchill. Churchill invited Macmillan to a 'man-to-man conversation', and warned him that there would be no role in the memoirs for his company and that the copyrights would soon be sold elsewhere. They were sold six weeks later, without film rights, to the persistent Lord Southwood's Odhams Press for £25,000.[6]

Casting around for other ways of earning money while he was forbidden to write, Churchill summoned the London representative of *TIME-LIFE* to his hotel suite.[7] A friend of Randolph's, Walter Graebner had been given one main task by his employers: to recruit Churchill as a contributor to *LIFE*, something that the magazine's managing editor, Daniel Longwell, had failed to achieve during the 1930s. As soon as the war was over, the magazine had offered Churchill $75,000 for three articles, but received no response. Now, ushered into the hotel suite before his host appeared, Graebner found Churchill's own paintings propped up on each chair. He recalled in his memoir how Churchill had finally entered and explained that he had found *LIFE*'s offer highly attractive, before adding:

> I am not in a position to write anything now. . . perhaps later. . . but not now. I have gone into the whole thing very carefully with my advisers and they tell me that if I come out of retirement. . . and write anything now I would have to pay taxes of nineteen and six in the pound, so what's the use? Then, gesturing toward the paintings, he concluded:
>
> But these are something else again. Do you think your people would like to publish *them* – that is, to take them in place of one of the articles? I would like such an arrangement better for the time being, as the income, I am advised, would be considered as capital gain and therefore nontaxable.[8]

Graebner settled a price of $20,000 with Randolph[9] after Churchill left for a painting holiday in Italy, ignoring warnings that the tax authorities might categorise him as 'carrying on the vocation of an artist'.[10]

*

Returning home via Monte Carlo, where he successfully avoided the 'very empty and dead-looking' but 'unsinkable' casino,[11] Churchill had a gloomy conversation about his finances late in September with Lord Camrose. During the war his personal spending had remained steady at £5,000 a year (wines, spirits and cigars accounting for a third),[12] but Churchill considered £12,000 each year a more realistic figure now that he was a private citizen again.[13]

Traditionally, generals and admirals had been handsomely rewarded financially for their famous military victories (Parliament had awarded £100,000 to the the army commander-in-chief Earl Haig at the end of the First World War). Although modern telecommunications now made the role of prime minister much more important to the success or otherwise of a military campaign, nobody in Parliament suggested the system be changed and Churchill be rewarded. Instead the House of Commons limited itself to considering whether the traditional prize money earned by sailors for seizing enemy merchant ships and cargo should now be shared with members of the Royal Air Force.[14]

Churchill's state of mind was such that he worried aloud to Lord Camrose about whether his finances might force him at some point to move out of Chartwell. Lord Camrose decided to talk privately to Churchill's solicitor, Charles Nicholl, with whom he hatched a scheme that would allow a group of Lord Camrose's business friends to buy Chartwell from Churchill. They would then donate it to the National Trust, on the understanding that the trust would rent the house back to the Churchills during their lifetime, before looking after it permanently.[15]

Willing to contribute £15,000 himself, Lord Camrose called the governor of the Bank of England, Lord Catto, who was in the middle of delicate negotiations with the Labour government over the central bank's nationalization.[16] Lord Catto offered £5,000, then persuaded Lord Bicester, the chairman of the merchant bankers Morgan Grenfell, to offer a similar sum. Emboldened by these early successes, Lord Camrose opened a 'Chartwell Account' at the Westminster Bank[17] and when the fund had reached £55,000

in November 1945 he gave his lawyers the go-ahead to start preparing documents.

Nicholl broached the scheme to a delighted Churchill over
Christmas, but it was to take another eight months before agreement was reached on a price for the Churchills of £50,000 – twice
the amount that they had unsuccessfully sought for the property in
1938 – together with an endowment of a further £35,000 to help
the National Trust look after the property. Churchill was to pay the
trust a rent of £350 a year and keep responsibility for the house's
insurance, rates, gardens and internal repairs or decoration, while
the National Trust took over the roof, walls, timbers, drains and
outside decoration.[18]

Before he learned about the Chartwell windfall, Churchill had
worried that his large coterie of tax advisers was showing worry-
ing signs of going soft on the subject. The Labour government's
budget of October 1945 had reduced the very top rate of income
tax to 92½ per cent,[19] but Churchill was concerned at some signs
that his advisers might be ready to re-submit to the Inland Revenue
some of the points that he had considered settled in his favour
during the war.

In 'A Note' dispatched to each of his advisers in October,
Churchill made it clear that they were to concede no ground over
the general commissioners' decision in 1942 that his newspaper
articles and the annual compilations of his speeches could be
treated as capital receipts by a retired author. 'The mere annual
repetition of these publications. . . in consequence of the duration
of the War in no way affects the facts of no marketable assets, no
emergence from retirement, and no physical or mental act on my
part,' he told them.

The fact that the authorities had agreed to treat *My Early Life*'s
film rights as a capital asset, he maintained, should also be good
enough to cover the larger, more recent film sales, which had raised
£100,000. A fourth sale was now also in prospect, because Sir
Alexander Korda had shown interest in the film rights to one of his

earliest books, about the Sudan campaign of 1898. 'The first decision of principle covers the other two,' Churchill asserted, 'and
would equally cover a further sale of film rights of, say, *The River
War*.'[20] His retirement, Churchill insisted, had been 'most strictly
maintained, even in the face of dazzling offers'.[21]

A more immediate threat to Churchill's status as a retired author
was his commitment with Cassell & Co. to complete *A History of
the English-Speaking Peoples* within six months of leaving office, in
other words by January 1946. Churchill asked Lord Camrose to
help by arranging a lunch with the chairman of Cassel, Sir Newman
Flower, whom he felt he did not know well. In October Churchill
explained to Sir Newman at the lunch that he wanted his *History* to
end no later than the year of his birth, 1874; he wondered whether
they should split the book into several volumes to 'afford both literary and financial prospects'; there was the sensitive question – for
both his literary reputation and tax status – of a Cambridge professor's recommendation that the sections dealing with the Georgians,
the American Revolution and Napoleon 'would benefit from
further polishing'; and finally there was the printing bill, which he
had paid during the war and still hoped that Cassell would reimburse.[22]

The lunch was a great success. The printing bill was paid the
following day and Sir Newman agreed that the book should end
at Churchill's birth. Better still, post-war paper shortages meant
that Cassell would not be able to publish the book before
December 1946, which removed the immediate threat to
Churchill's 'retirement'.

'Now that we have plenty of time you may rely upon me to bring
the book to a suitable conclusion by adding the ten years from 1864
to 1874 and by a general valedictory epilogue,' Churchill told Sir
Newman, in a new spirit of cordiality.[23] Nevertheless, he was sufficiently worried by the task of rewriting to want to clear it first
with the tax authorities. He carefully drafted the letter which he
wanted Geoffrey Mason of Lloyds Bank to send to the Inland
Revenue on his behalf. 'Mr Churchill delivered to Messrs Cassell &

Company the manuscript of his *A History of the English-Speaking Peoples* which he had completed at the beginning of the War,' it began carefully, skirting around the fact that work had continued for another six months. The crucial paragraph of the letter was saved until its end:

> Some portions suffered from the hurry caused by the approach of War and the rapid winding-up of Mr Churchill's affairs. He has done no work of any kind on it since his retirement. However on reading it through again, he sees it could be greatly improved in various ways. He has his past reputation as a man of letters to consider, and he would like to correct the proofs and recast certain portions of the work. He is under no obligation to do this, as the transaction is in every way completed. Any work he might do upon its proofs would be solely for his own personal satisfaction and without further payment of any kind or any consideration, direct or indirect, from Messrs. Cassell. The opinion which Mr Churchill wishes to ask is the following: Provided he receives no remuneration of any kind, would he be at liberty to correct the proofs and improve the text?[24]

The reply from the Inland Revenue was positive: Churchill was allowed to to tidy up a book already written without a loss of status as a retired author. However, it would require much greater ingenuity to avoid tax on the income received for writing a new set of memoirs, such as Churchill was contemplating to cover the events of the war. The seasoned lawyers Charles Nicholl and Charles Henderson had looked after Churchill's general affairs during the war; but for this more specialist challenge he chose younger men with a particular interest in the law of taxation: Anthony Moir and the barrister on whom he often called, Charles Graham-Dixon.

Offers to publish the memoirs had continued to flood in from as far afield as Greece, Palestine and Scandinavia.[25] However, it was an offer from the Eton-educated American newspaperman Marshall Field III* that gave Churchill's advisers the kernel of the idea which they eventually used to avoid a large measure of tax. While offering Churchill a five-year deal worth $1.25 million for newspaper articles, Field mentioned that his *Chicago Sun* would also be part of a consortium bidding at least $1 million for the memoirs. He then suggested that, before writing anything, Churchill should gift his personal papers to a trust for his children and grandchildren. The trust could then sell the book rights before employing him for a much lower sum to 'edit' the text – only this last link in the chain would attract tax.[26]

'They certainly disclose an interesting situation in America, if only it were possible for us to take advantage of it,' Churchill confided to Lord Camrose.[27] It was only a month since their gloomy conversation about Chartwell, yet Churchill was already feeling more confident about his finances. He had even summoned his bank manager, T. E. B. Harris, to discuss investing two-thirds of his money in longer-term instruments. Reluctant to admit that investment advice was not part of Lloyds' stock-in-trade, Harris consulted a friend,** who recommended investing £40,000 in government bonds and a much smaller sum in shares.[28]

Another opportunity to make money presented itself in November when Clement Attlee told Churchill that the government was minded to lift the ban on publishing speeches made to the House of Commons during its wartime 'secret sessions'. The wartime broadcasts of Churchill's public speeches had made a powerful impact across the world, but this set of six speeches had never been heard in public. Two days before the government was due to announce the lifting of the ban, Churchill summoned Walter Graebner from *LIFE* to his bedroom at Chartwell and, after melodramatically swearing his visitor to secrecy, read excerpts from his

---

* Marshall Field III (1893–1956), founder of the *Chicago Sun-Times*; purchased Simon & Schuster 1944.
** J. H. Keeling of 105, Grosvenor Square, who worked for London & Yorkshire Trust.

own speeches for an hour, asking at the end whether *LIFE* would like to publish them in America.[29]

Graebner cabled Churchill's asking price to his chairman. 'In my opinion $75,000 is Churchillian highbinding,' Henry Luce replied. 'I would offer $50,000 and mean it.'[30] Churchill tried splitting the difference, but Luce declined before Graebner sealed the deal with champagne and brandy over a convivial New Year's lunch at Chartwell.[31]

A long holiday in Florida was planned, before Churchill delivered a speech in early March 1946 at Fulton, Missouri, the home state of President Truman who taken office after the death of President Roosevelt in April 1945.

Before Churchill left, Emery Reves summarized his potential earnings in America: at least $2 million over five years for the memoirs; $500,000 from radio; $250,000 or more from newspaper articles; and $100,000 from magazines. Aware of the tax problem, Reves added that he could present 'certain suggestions as to the forms in which these transactions could be carried out over a period of years so that a large part of the yield would remain in your possession'.[32]

Churchill's baggage for the sea crossing to New York included nineteen different offers for his memoirs. He also had some early advice from his lawyers, Graham-Dixon and Moir, on how best to shield the income from tax. They made a bold assumption that the British government was unlikely to bring in a lifetime tax on capital transactions, even though many Labour Party supporters were urging an annual wealth or capital gains tax to help repair the country's finances. Graham-Dixon and Moir banked on the Inland Revenue mounting stiff resistance to any measure that would require taxpayers for the first time to volunteer information on their wealth, whereas taxes on income were now almost automatically collected through employers.[33]

Graham-Dixon and Moir therefore based their strategy on converting as many as possible of the payments for the memoirs into capital receipts, rather than royalties.* While they worked on a detailed scheme, they stressed that Churchill should do nothing to endanger his status as a 'retired author', which meant that his war papers still qualified as capital assets. He should wait patiently, they advised, before trying to emerge 'from a most profitable purdah'.[34]

That patience was immediately put to the test as Churchill approached the American coast with Clementine and Sarah on 14 January: a radio message arrived from Henry Luce offering him \$25,000 for a single broadcast, sponsored by *LIFE*. Churchill cabled Graham-Dixon to ask if he could accept the offer as a one-off 'thank you' for American hospitality, but his lawyer's advice was simple: 'Speak for love but not for money'.[35]

At a press conference on arrival in New York, Churchill stuck to the official line: he did not know whether he would write his memoirs, or whether they would be published during his lifetime if he did. In private, however, while he stayed in Miami Beach with Colonel Frank Clarke (his Canadian host at the Quebec wartime conferences), he became optimistic enough to begin their preparations.

Churchill had to be careful to rise above the cut and thrust of negotiations, but his team of Kathleen Hill and Brendan Bracken had moved on, to run Chequers and the merged *Financial News* and *Financial Times* newspapers respectively. Brendan Bracken, who now also chaired Sir Henry Strakosch's former company, Union Corporation, suggested that Lord Camrose should step into the breach, as *The Daily Telegraph* was already guaranteed a role in publishing the memoirs. Churchill agreed, but he also decided to call upon the more streetwise skills of his pre-war agent Emery Reves, whom he summoned from New York.

---

* The chancellor, Hugh Dalton, was to leave capital transactions untouched in his Budget of April 1946, but he increased the highest rate of sur-tax to 52.5 per cent, restoring a top marginal rate of tax of 97.5 per cent. In 1962 a Conservative government introduced a short-term capital gains tax which the Labour government of 1964 made a broader, permanent part of the British fiscal system. See M. Daunton, *Just Taxes*, pp. 189–211.

'Everyone wants me to write my memoirs,' Reves recalled
Churchill saying, 'which I may do if I have time. And, if I do, I have
not forgotten what you did for me before the war and I shall want
you to handle it.' Churchill then told him that 'for private reasons
and financial reasons he was going to carry out the transaction
through Lord Camrose because he had to make a capital deal'.[36] In
the meantime, Reves was to remain silent.

Still in Miami Beach, Churchill turned to the *Secret Session
Speeches*, which *LIFE* was about to publish, although it cut them
down to two excerpts. It chose not to cut its fee, however: a decision noted by Churchill. 'It was of course a pig in a poke,' Luce told
a colleague. 'I believe that *LIFE* has got to buy some such pigs in
order to keep a position in the meat market. . . Also, it can be worth
the space plus the money if, in some sense, Churchill becomes "our
author".'[37]

British reaction was distinctly frosty when Churchill's speeches
first appeared in an American magazine. One Labour MP called in
Parliament for the confiscation of half of all former ministers'
earnings from the publication of 'official documents collected
during their term of office'; a discomfited Churchill warned Nancy
Pearn, who he had appointed to handle the foreign sales of his
speeches against using the aggressive tactics of which he would
have approved in pre-war days. 'Do not make a great fuss to pick
up a few pounds here and there,' his revised guidance stated.[38]

By mid-February Charles Graham-Dixon had prepared a detailed
tax scheme for Churchill's memoirs. He had discounted the safest
option, the so-called 'tin-box' scheme that would delay publication
until after Churchill's death, on the assumption that Churchill or
his family would need the money during his lifetime. Instead, he
advised, Churchill should gift his papers to a family trust before he
started writing his memoirs; then the trustees should sell the copyright of the papers, for a lump sum, to a publishing group; finally
that group should make its own separate arrangements with
Churchill to write the memoirs for a lesser sum.

The effect of divorcing the documents' ownership from the memoir's authorship, he contended, would be to leave the publisher's money in the trustees' hands as capital, while only Churchill's fee as an author would attract any tax. He stressed two points: Churchill must gift the documents before writing a word; and the trustees, not Churchill, must settle the publishing contract. The prospects for success, Graham-Dixon thought, were 'reasonable'.[39]

Buoyed by this plan, Churchill played poker in the presidential train with Truman on the way to Fulton, Missouri. Here, at the small Presbyterian college of Westminster, he delivered the 'Iron Curtain' speech, warning of the shadow cast across the world by the Soviet Union's 'expansive and proselytising tendencies'.[40] His speech split opinion: for example, the *Chicago Sun* described it as 'poisonous', thereby damaging the owner Marshall Field's prospects of publishing Churchill's memoirs.

On his way home Churchill visited New York, where he met Reves four times, outlining the tax plans for the memoirs taking shape at home. Reves suggested that Cooperation Publishing could act as the main publishing contractor with the trust, controlling 'radio, press, magazine and book publication, drama and motion picture etc.' If chosen, Reves offered to hand over up to half of the equity to either Churchill or his trust, so that they could share in the publisher's as well as the author's profits. 'I believe that through such a set-up your literary properties extended over a period of five to ten years could bring into the family trust about a million pounds.'[41]

Arriving back in Britain in late March, Churchill continued to claim publicly that he had not made a final decision whether to publish his memoirs. Within a week, however, he had asked Bill Deakin to help him write them and his solicitor Anthony Moir to establish the trust for his papers.[42] Moir's first draft suggested that the trust should include all papers from Churchill's birth up to the end of the war; that Churchill should appoint the trustees; that they should be able to publish only with his permission; and that, at his death, the trust's capital should be divided equally among his children.[43] A firm believer in primogeniture, Churchill changed Randolph's share to a half.

The Chartwell Literary Trust came into being on 31 July 1946 with Clementine, Brendan Bracken and Professor Lindemann (now Lord Cherwell) as its first trustees.[44] Its official objective was to safeguard Churchill's papers for posterity, without any mention of the tax advantages: to this end, Churchill expressed his wish that the trustees should eventually pass the papers on to Randolph or Randolph's own son Winston, one of whom he hoped would write his official biography. Churchill was aware that the duke of Marlborough was considering selling Blenheim in the aftermath of war, so he wanted to make sure that the papers would 'remain intact at Chartwell and it may well be that my son or grandson will ultimately give them to the National Trust, should Chartwell itself be vested in that Body'.[45]

His papers safely gifted to the Chartwell Literary Trust, Churchill asked Lord Camrose to deal with Cassell's option, which he knew that Sir Newman Flower had agreed to assign to Camrose's *The Daily Telegraph*, as the larger and stronger organization with the trust to contract for the whole rights package. 'If you will settle matters with Cassell's,' Churchill told Lord Camrose, 'I am sure the trustees will be able at any time to enter into direct relations with you. This is what I desire.'[46]

Lord Camrose planned an autumn visit to the States to sell the all-important American rights. However, he knew as well as Churchill that they first had to obtain the British government's permission to use Churchill's sixty-eight bundles of war minutes and directives in the book. Churchill had already headed off another threat from the Cabinet Office that summer, when Prime Minister Attlee ordered yet another review of the rules. It was felt that Sir Robert (now Lord) Vansittart, the Foreign Office's senior pre-war civil servant, had taken undue advantage of the 'vindicator clause' to quote from official documents covering from the appeasement period. The cabinet secretary Sir Edward Bridges recommended a future distinction between the use of papers by civil servants and by ministers. However, he moved on to more threatening ground for Churchill's method of writing when he added another recommendation that ministers should only be allowed to quote from papers at length 'in very exceptional cases; and then only when the document is in some sense personal to the writer'.[47]

Attlee gave Sir Edward the unenviable task of securing Churchill's approval of his proposals. Over lunch at Chartwell, Churchill outlined his prolonged resistance to previous Cabinet Office assaults. However, in his formal response to Attlee he expressed 'general agreement' with the new proposals, before suggesting an 'exceptional consideration' for former prime ministers. To support his case, Churchill cited books recently published by General Eisenhower's naval aide Captain Butcher, and by *TIME*'s former publisher Ralph Ingersoll – both men had based their criticisms of Churchill's conduct on documents that had been made available under more liberal US rules.[48] For Churchill to put his own case, he felt he needed a greater freedom of movement than other ministers.

There matters rested during the holiday season, until Churchill sent Sir Edward a five-page letter on his return, to try to accelerate a decision. 'I am pressed from many quarters to give my account of the British war story,' he began, 'and, without at present making any definite plans, I have been getting my papers in order and considering the project.' He explained that he could not help quoting extensively from documents, because 'a great part of my work was done in writing'; but he would be happy 'to discuss the omission of any particular phrase, sentence or passage in memoranda otherwise unobjectionable'. Adding that publication was at least two or three years away, he proposed that the government should conduct a 'final revision of the text in detail. . . in case the foreign situation might be such as to make what is now harmless injurious'.

What he wanted to know, 'without necessarily accepting the view as final', was 'whether <u>in principle</u> there would be any objection' to his publishing three types of material: (1) papers he had written as First Lord of the Admiralty, prime minister or minister of defence; (2) extracts from his 'immense' series of minutes; and (3) 'Personal' telegrams to Roosevelt, Truman and other heads of government. He was seeking the prime minister's view, he concluded, but felt entitled to tell his side of the story: 'I am convinced it would be to the advantage of our country to have it told, as perhaps I alone can tell it.'[49]

Sir Edward Bridges interpreted Churchill's response as surprisingly supportive. He drafted a paper for the cabinet, 'tilted rather gently in favour of acceptance of Mr Churchill's proposal'.[50] Only the Foreign Office raised objections when the matter was debated on 10 October, but the foreign secretary Ernest Bevin missed the meeting. 'It is 100% acceptance, with no provisoes [*sic*], other than those which you yourself suggested,' Sir Edward told Churchill in a personal letter accompanying the formal approval. 'You know, I hope, that I and my colleagues in the Cabinet Office will always be ready to give you any help we can over these questions of documents and so forth. It will be our endeavour to be as helpful to you as you have been to us.'[51] It was a remarkable result, which Churchill expected would assist the sale of his memoirs in New York.

While he had waited for the official decision, Churchill made another of his periodic surveys of his finances, as he had done before the war. The picture was now transformed: even after repaying £20,000 of loans, he could still list personal assets of £187,500.[52] Film rights had made all the difference: he remembered selling three for £110,000 since the start of the war, although the correct numbers were four for £142,500, all tax-free.[53]

The only cloud on the horizon was that Churchill's personal expenditure was running at £15,000 a year, well above the estimate he had given a year earlier to Lord Camrose. However, his paintings and wartime speeches had paid unexpected dividends[54] and he felt confident enough to pass on the gift from a London hotelier of a substantial property in Sevenoaks to a charity for wounded servicemen.[55] The fruits of his war memoirs were yet to be harvested.

23

<hr>

'Agreeably impressed'
Selling the Memoirs, 1946–8

Exchange rate: $4 = £1
Inflation multiples: US x 11; UK x 35

L ORD CAMROSE LEFT for New York on the *Queen Elizabeth* in the middle of October 1946. He took with him a copy of the cabinet office's approval, some samples of Churchill's war minutes and a two-page synopsis of the memoirs which Churchill expected to take up five volumes.

Churchill balanced Lord Camrose's patrician diffidence with the silky sales skills of Emery Reves, who Churchill asked at the last minute to join Lord Camrose on the *Queen Elizabeth*. When Reves objected that the ship would be fully booked by now, Churchill telephoned Cunard's chairman and within twenty minutes Reves had 'a stateroom with a bath'.

Once on board, Reves found that Lord Camrose had no idea who he was or why he was there. They came to an agreement: Lord Camrose would deal with the newspapers, while Reves would concentrate on magazine and book publishers. Nevertheless, a cautious Lord Camrose insisted upon a formal exchange of letters. 'I think it desirable that it should be on record that 1. You are making this trip on your own account entirely; 2. Any conversation we may have does not commit either of us in any way whatsoever,'[1] he wrote to his new companion. Reves was happy to sign, confident that they could reach a figure of four or five million dollars if allowed a free hand. 'If you put such figures into the old man's head, it will be impossible to make any deal,' Lord Camrose warned him. Reves concluded that Lord Camrose, as the owner of *The Daily Telegraph*, was 'more experienced in buying copyright than selling it'.[2]

They arrived in New York on 21 October 1946 and stayed in different hotels on opposite sides of Madison Square, meeting each evening to compare notes. There was a natural tension between them – Camrose was already guaranteed a slice of the spoils, Reves none. *The Daily Telegraph*'s New York office warned of Reves's 'rather slippery' reputation, although it acknowledged that he was 'a very enterprising person' who knew the South American market well.[3]

Reves's first visit to *Collier's Weekly* did not go well. The magazine's editor, still William Chenery, questioned Reves's credentials to represent Churchill, with whom Chenery claimed to have just negotiated directly a $25,000 fee for an article based on a recent speech in Zürich. 'Please cable whether this is correct,' Reves asked Churchill that evening. 'Sincerely believe would be mistake offering *jus primae noctis* [right of the first night] before marriage for any price.'[4] Lord Camrose cabled Churchill to reassure him that he was in command: 'Reves acting under close control from me but have not allowed him to mention my name for reasons of security and strategy.'[5]

A visit to Daniel Longwell, *LIFE*'s managing editor, did not go well either. Reves never mentioned it to Churchill's biographer, his son Randolph, but Longwell recorded it in a taped interview for Time Inc.'s corporate history: 'A little fellow by the name of Reavis [*sic*], I think, who had been an agent of Churchill's, appeared and said he was representing Churchill on these memoirs,' he recalled, 'and that sort of threw me for a loop because I knew that he had said Camrose would be in charge. What Reves didn't tell me was that Camrose was in town.'[6]

Soon afterwards, Reves warned Churchill that Lord Camrose's style was ill-suited to the American market, which preferred raw competition to secrecy. What was needed, he claimed, was a single organization ready to shoulder all the risks of buying the entire rights package, but he claimed that Lord Camrose lacked the necessary appetite. Cooperation Publishing, on the other hand, was ready to act, funded by a wealthy Churchill admirer.

Camrose had told Reves to drop the scheme, but Reves wanted him overruled, while insisting that their relationship remained 'extremely cordial and satisfactory': 'I do hope you will understand my motive for going over the head of the Field Commander to the Commander-in-Chief,' he told Churchill. 'It is up to you to court martial or decorate me.'[7] Churchill's reply was terse: 'Pray be guided by C[amrose] in everything.'[8]

Despite their different styles, Camrose was glad to have Reves with him. 'He is a clever salesman with an abundance of ideas and many contacts,' he told Churchill. 'Where he is to figure in the ultimate picture I do not, at the moment, know but we can discuss this on my return.' Camrose's own approach had been characteristically British: 'It has been my policy to be careful not to show any eagerness and, above all, to avoid any action which might result in publicity,' he explained. 'Up to the moment, in this direction, I have been entirely successful and not a word of my doings has appeared in the papers.'[9]

During the pair's first three weeks in New York, many of their prime targets proved ill or absent – *The New York Times*'s Arthur Sulzberger in St Louis for a hand operation, the *Chicago Sun*'s Marshall Field III detained in his home city, *TIME-LIFE*'s Henry Luce travelling in China – but Camrose nevertheless asked for final bids on Churchill's memoirs by Friday 22 November.

According to Reves's account (widely accepted ever since),[10] *LIFE* failed to bid at all that day; *The New York Times* offered $750,000 on its own and the *Chicago Sun* syndicate (including the *New York Herald Tribune*) bid $1,100,000 for worldwide rights, bar those already reserved for *The Daily Telegraph* and Cassell. According to Reves, Lord Camrose favoured the *Chicago Sun* bid, but Reves suggested they try one more time to get a rival offer from *LIFE*; he claims to have persuaded Mrs Luce to rouse her husband from a jet-lagged sleep after returning from China and convinced him to meet them on the Monday.

In fact, *LIFE* did bid in the first round, *The New York Times* did not offer $750,000 and Henry Luce had returned from China two weeks earlier, on 8 November.[11] General Julius Adler, *The New York Times*'s general manager, had suggested to Luce that *LIFE* and *The New York Times* should work together. Luce and Longwell, *LIFE*'s managing editor, decided that the deal made sense: *The Times*'s footprint hardly ran 'further than Trenton [New Jersey] and probably New Haven [Connecticut], and a few copies to Washington', whereas *LIFE* sold five million copies nationwide.[12]

So Longwell did a deal with Adler: *LIFE* would run weekly excerpts of Churchill's memoirs, *The New York Times* would run daily excerpts, except at weekends. With a week to go before Camrose's deadline, Longwell asked his colleague Walter Graebner in London to find out what he could. Graebner met Churchill at Chartwell and reported back to Longwell:

> Camrose is reporting lengthily by mail to London. In latest letter he says he has appointment with Luce November 22 at which time apparently he intends to discuss proposition. He would welcome an offer from *LIFE* which I am convinced he prefers to all other publications, but he explained that he could neither feel committed to *LIFE* nor accept lower offers from us than he got elsewhere. Our friend [Churchill] asked that entire conversation be kept in strictest confidence so please give no indication whatever to Camrose that you possess foregoing information.[13]

Lord Camrose arranged to meet *LIFE* last on the day before the 22 November deadline. The magazine's offer of $1,250,000 included an allowance for book rights, said to be $200,000, but no named publisher. Camrose did not take Reves to the meeting and did not consult him before cabling the auction results to Churchill.

[Henry Luce] is working in conjunction with Adolph [sic].*
Adolph has made an independent offer of 300 [$300,000] for
serialization in his paper in event of Henry's combined offer not
being acceptable. Helen [Rogers Reid of the *New York Herald
Tribune*] offer 1100 not yet definitely confirmed. . . Offers for
American book rights from three firms all in neighbourhood of
200 but possibly final bid could be increased to 225. Possibly
Henry and Helen offers might be improved in final show-down
but not materially.

Camrose advised a quick closure, but spelled out his fellow-nego-
tiator's contrary view: 'Reves believes that with basis of 300 from
Adolph and individual nation-wide canvassing by him of all newspapers outside New York he could bring total from serial to much
larger figure. This would require two to three months' time and
substantial commission. Would also necessitate considerable
advance publicity.'[14]

Lord Camrose asked for guidance, but Churchill reminded him
that only the trust could decide, before conveying that he was 'personally agreeably impressed' at the result; he added that 'there
seemed to be advantages in the Luce offer on account of its simplicity', and that he had spoken to two trustees, 'C[lementine] and BB
[Brendan Bracken] who are favourable', and was sure the third 'CL
[Professor Lindemann] would agree'.[15]

Reves complained to Churchill that he had not been consulted. He tried again to carve out a role for Cooperation
Publishing: 'If situation can be created giving me authority to
dictate prices, I am convinced result can be greatly improved.
Perhaps purchase contract with trust can be signed leaving final
figure open for a few months. I realize this requires great confidence. Please do not mention C[amrose] this cable and do not

---

* Camrose appears to use the wrong name as a reference to the owner of *The
New York Times*. Its previous owner, Adolph Ochs, had died eleven years
earlier. After 1935, his son-in-law Arthur Sulzberger was the newspaper's
president and his nephew Julius Adler its general manager.

reveal its content.'[16] Churchill ignored him. However, Lord Camrose conceded that they could improve on the book bids. Before travelling to Montreal to sell the Canadian newspaper rights, he told *LIFE* to re-bid without the book rights and gave Reves the chance to put together a firm bid for them, so long as he beat the indicated price of $200,000.

Reves rushed down to Boston, where he lunched with Henry Laughlin and Paul Brooks, president and editor-in-chief of Houghton Mifflin. Reves had introduced a book* to the firm two years earlier in return for a share of the revenues and he wanted the same arrangement for bringing Churchill's memoirs. By the time lunch was over, Laughlin and Brooks had agreed to fund a bid of $250,000, paying Reves 15 per cent retail royalties once their outlay was recouped, plus an immediate 25 per cent, rising to 50 per cent, on sales to book clubs.

Back in New York Camrose arranged a second meeting with *LIFE* on the afternoon of Wednesday 27 November. He warned them in advance that they would have to raise their price, which worked out at $1,050,000 once the book rights were stripped out. Roy Larsen, the company's president, was ready to throw in an extra $100,000, but Longwell suggested asking *The New York Times* for more money too, so that they could together reach $1,250,000. Longwell later recalled:

> I called Adler at his home that night and said that if he really wanted this with us, he would have to pick up $400,000. He agreed. Next afternoon Camrose was to see us at 5 o'clock, and the *Herald Tribune* called me to have a final talk. I suddenly realized that the other syndicates were being sort of hard pressed to get up to the amount *LIFE* and *The Times* were bidding, so I got back here about twenty minutes before we met with Camrose

---

* Jan Karski's *Courier from Poland: The Story of a Secret State 1939–1944.* Reves received a commission of 2½ per cent of sales revenues on the first 50,000 copies sold to the retail trade and 20 per cent of sales to book clubs.

and told Larsen that we should be all right if we lowered our bid to $1,150,000, of which I expected *The Times* to pay $400,000.[17]

At the start of the meeting, Larsen spelled out the new price: 'Lord Camrose nodded a couple of times and – none of us understood what the nod meant, and we were very excited when he said, "That's fine," and we got it.'[18] Camrose's cable to England that evening was short and to the point: 'Please inform trust have closed with Henry for 1150. Book goes to Houghton Mifflin for 250. Total 1400.'[19]

He left New York the next evening, Thanksgiving Day, having raised an additional $110,000 from the *Montreal Standard* for the Canadian serial rights. 'Going on board tonight and delighted at prospect,' he told Churchill.[20]

The first press leak emerged within a fortnight. The North American Newspaper Alliance ran a story claiming that a $700,000 bid (its own) had failed. It predicted that Churchill would earn 'more than $1 million and probably about $1.25 million' from America alone, with more to come from the rest of the world.[21]

It took the American consortium a long time to find out what *The Daily Telegraph* and Cassell had paid for their rights: £75,000 and £40,000 respectively. On his return to Britain, Lord Camrose raised almost another £60,000 from Australia, South Africa and Ireland. After Reves had explained to him the complexities of selling to the less-familiar markets of continental Europe, Asia and South America, Lord Camrose asked him to name a price for purchasing the foreign language rights as a single package. Reves quoted £25,000 before testing the markets, but then returned with a price of £45,000, which Camrose pushed up to £47,500.[22] It was still to prove a bargain.

By the time the trustees had ratified the package in January 1947, the worldwide sale of rights for Churchill's memoirs had reached £550,000; it ended up at £600,000 or $2 ½ million. It was the world's largest-ever non-fiction publishing deal.[23] Just over half the money had come from America, but *TIME-LIFE* was content. Each volume of the memoirs would fill nearly ninety of *LIFE*'s editorial pages, Longwell calculated, equivalent to two whole issues, which would bring in $4 million of advertising revenue. Seen in that context, the magazine's fee to Churchill of $150,000 for each volume seemed modest. 'We always got credit for paying more than we really did,' he told his successor.[24]

Churchill was happy, too. His trust would clear at least £375,000 over the five volumes, while he earned £175,000 as the author – and *The Daily Telegraph* was to lend him an extra £15,000 on signature without charging interest.[25] Nevertheless, Reves told Houghton Mifflin in confidence that they had picked up the American book 'under most favourable conditions', judging from the prices the Europeans were bidding. Between them, Reves reported, French and Dutch publishers had paid him comfortably more than Houghton Mifflin had paid for the US rights, although the two European countries' combined market was one-tenth of America's size.[26]

While his memoirs were being sold, Churchill returned his attention to the world's stock markets. An economic recovery that had followed the war was making these more rewarding for investors than they had been during the Depression. On his own initiative, Churchill had sold all his bond holdings at a profit in April 1946 and asked his manager at Lloyds Bank to suggest shares to take their place. Without any advice on individual companies and their shares available inside the bank, Harris consulted a personal friend who made two suggestions: the Hong Kong and Shanghai Bank, and Imperial Continental Gas. By the time Churchill asked him for more information, Harris's friend had disappeared to a remote part of Yorkshire and could not be contacted. Lloyds Bank's role as a stock market adviser to Churchill came to an end.

Churchill turned instead to his brother. Although Jack had retired from Vickers da Costa at the start of the war, he nevertheless helped Churchill to spend £65,000 on buying eighteen new share-holdings through Vickers before the end of May.[27] There were faint echoes of the 1930s as contract notes from Vickers kept arriving in the post and the staff at Chartwell were once again tracking daily share prices; the big difference was that Churchill finished 1946 with modest profits of £1,350.[28]

By then, Lord Camrose's second syndicate of bankers and business friends had paid Churchill the agreed price of £50,000 to buy Chartwell on behalf of the National Trust. Churchill used the extra money to revive his farming ambitions, although Clementine was against the idea. 'He wants to have land girls and chickens & cows here,'[29] she had complained to their daughter Mary after the war, when to her relief Kent's chief agricultural officer Percy Cox had not been able to find any suitable land or cattle near Chartwell. Now, however, their neighbour offered first refusal on the 157 acres of Chartwell Farm. With the Camrose syndicate's money to hand, Churchill decided not to miss out. Knight Frank & Rutley helped Cox negotiate a price of £25,000 for the farmhouse and cottages, plus a year's use of the departing Major Marnham's dairy herd.[30] Two months later, Churchill spent £10,250 adding another 116 acres, 'practically adjoining Chartwell', at Parkside Farm, including heated greenhouses and a cold fruit store.[31] A proud Churchill instructed his bank, which had lent him £21,500 towards the purchases, to open a new Chartwell Farm account, through which he would channel 'the whole farming capacity of the 340 acre Chartwell estate'.[32]

Clementine's main concern was that there was nobody to run the farms. This problem was solved, however, when Mary's new husband Christopher Soames had a duodenal ulcer burst during their honeymoon. He had to leave the army and was engaged to look after the farms on a salary of £400 a year, living free in the farmhouse. 'My knowledge of farming is, to say the least, negligible,' Soames warned.[33] Two months later Churchill snapped up 94 more acres at Bardogs Farm for £8,700.[34] The estate had now grown to 450 acres, although it was to prove still too small for the wide

range of arable, dairy, pigs, poultry and market gardening under-
taken by Chartwell Farms.

Jack died from a heart attack in April 1947, as negotiation surrounding the contracts for Churchill's memoirs dragged on
throughout the spring. The interests of book publishers and newspaper editors often clashed and, as extra jurisdictions entered the
frame, copyright complications multiplied. Daniel Longwell at
LIFE was keen to protect his company against the risk of Churchill
producing extra volumes. 'I insisted on a clause in there that no
matter what the length of the book was – five volumes or six – we
paid one single price,' he recorded.[35]

His chairman Henry Luce was more worried that politics or ill
health would dog their seventy-two-year-old author or that he
might write for rival publications. Many at LIFE wanted Churchill
bound by contract not to write elsewhere, but Walter Graebner
argued that they should treat Churchill as a man of Edwardian
manners. Now a regular at Chartwell, Graebner showed his host a
copy of the cable that he planned to send to New York. It read:
'"Gentlemen's agreement, yes" [Churchill] said, "But binding contract no."' Churchill amended it to read: 'Moneywise, there would
be no point in writing articles because all the proceeds would dis-
appear in taxes.'[36]

This 'gentlemen's agreement' was put to the test at the end of
March when Churchill proposed to write an article on President
Truman's 'momentous' speech setting out a new foreign policy to
contain expansion of the Soviet Union. The consortium agreed to
treat the article as a 'dry run' and shared the cost, The New York
Times picking up 34.78 per cent of Churchill's $25,000 fee, the same
proportion of the American payments that it would shoulder for
the memoirs.[37]

By April Lord Camrose called all the parties to London to settle
a few outstanding points. LIFE was always to publish first, the
newspapers to serialize up to 40 per cent of each volume, and the
books to appear a week after the newspaper extracts had ended.[38]

'99 per cent set', Graebner cabled to New York at the end of the second day's talks.[39] All agreed that the deal should be announced on 15 May, the day after Lord Camrose signed the Houghton Mifflin contract.

'CHURCHILL MEMOIRS BRING A DOLLAR A WORD' ran *The New York Times*'s front-page headline, over a picture showing the author at work in his study.[40] Not shown was the supporting 'syndicate' that Churchill had already assembled: Bill Deakin, his pre-war literary assistant; General 'Pug' Ismay, his former chief of staff; General Sir Henry Pownall, who had experience of pre-war rearmament, the fall of France, Singapore's surrender and the secret 'Ultra' material which Britain had obtained by breaking German military codes (although this could not be mentioned in the memoirs); and Commodore Gordon Allen, a former naval officer, who had worked at Combined Operations HQ. The four were later joined by Denis Kelly, an Oxford history graduate and under-employed barrister.

By July 1947 the first volume of Churchill's memoirs was sufficiently presentable for Longwell at *LIFE* to spend a month in England working on the magazine's layout and illustrations. He was given access to the family scrapbook at Chartwell, where Churchill also posed for new colour photographs. Then Longwell did what Lord Camrose warned him no one in England would dare to do: he suggested changes to the text of the memoir, many of which Churchill accepted. Longwell was at first irritated by the way Lord Camrose kept referring to him in front of Churchill as a photographer; however, fences were mended when *LIFE* decided to share its pictures with other consortium members. Lord Camrose began addressing his letters 'My dear Longwell'.[41]

Meanwhile, Churchill was busy trying to establish some style rules with his veteran proofreader Eddie Marsh:

1. I am still balancing between 'Goering' and 'Göring' and 'Fuehrer' and 'Führer' etc. Curiously I like some some one way and some t'other. 2. On the whole I am <u>against</u> commas... On

the other hand I am very much in favour of the semi-colon; and think that blighter should have a good run for his money in the text. 3. We are both agreed that capitals should be reduced as much as possible. Will you think out the principle of capitals and talk to me about them. For instance, must the 'A' in 'Ally' always be cap?[42]

Political demands on the leader of the Opposition's time remained relatively modest while the Labour government enjoyed such a strong parliamentary majority. However, the rhythm of writing could still be disturbed by the lure of painting or the stock market. Churchill added £23,000 of government bonds to balance the shares in his portfolio in July,[43] but shortly afterwards the government's decision to restore the pound's free convertibility into the dollar* led to a run on the currency, causing bond prices to fall by 2 per cent and leading shares to fall by 10 per cent within a fortnight.

Alarmed, Churchill asked the newly ennobled Lord Bracken how he could invest more safely, yet still earn his rewards in the untaxed form of capital appreciation. Bracken directed him to the shares of Argentinian railways, which were quoted in London but had fallen sharply while they awaited the Argentinian government's nationalization terms; they were expected to rise almost 15 per cent before compensation was paid a year or two later, Bracken advised.[44] Within weeks, Churchill spent £65,000 buying shares in the Buenos Aires Great Southern Railway, Buenos Aires Western Railway and Central Argentine Railway.[45]

For its 1947 Summer Exhibition, which was open to the public, the Royal Academy of Arts had selected two paintings by Churchill (*Winter Sunshine* and *Loup River*) that he had submitted anonymously. To handle the public demand for their reproduction Churchill appointed advertising agents Walter Judd, who sent him

---

* Introduced on 15 July 1947, but abandoned by the government five weeks later on 20 August.

a first cheque for £20 in September. Its arrival prompted Churchill to ask his local Inland Revenue officer, known as an inspector, for an assurance that he would not be branded as a professional artist and subjected to income tax as a result.[46] The answer was not encouraging. The tax inspector not only refused to give such an assurance but threatened to reopen the file on Churchill's past earnings from his pictures. He settled for a limited barter arrangement with the Soho Gallery: the gallery arranged a free supply of Christmas cards using images of several of Churchill's paintings, in return for the right to reuse the images six months later on its own greetings cards.

Meanwhile the *LIFE* team had become concerned that Churchill's summer distractions had slowed progress on the proofs for the first volume of his memoirs, which had only advanced from 'Provisional Semi-final' to 'Provisional Final' by the time Parliament reassembled in October.[47] Walter Graebner did his best to nudge Churchill towards working on the text, supplying him with new pens and dealing with other potential distractions, such as finding a replacement for Rufus the poodle, who had been run over during the Tory Party's annual conference.[48] However, Graebner took the art of chivvying to a whole new level when he suggested to his superiors in New York that *TIME-LIFE* should pay for Churchill and his team to take a Christmas 'working holiday' in the Moroccan sunshine, well away from politics.

At the time each Briton was limited to taking £35 abroad to spend in the course of a foreign holiday, one of a series of measures introduced by Britain's post-war government to preserve its limited reserves of sterling. The sum was too small to allow Churchill to holiday in the style to which he was accustomed, so he had not enjoyed a holiday in the sun since his visit to Italy two years earlier. Walter Graebner was therefore able to report to New York an enthusiastic reception almost as soon as he was allowed to extend the invitation. 'Mr Churchill agrees with our suggestion that it would be in the interests of *LIFE* (and perhaps other members of the syndicate) to go to Marrakech this winter to work. He gladly accepts our proposal to pay his expenses and is leaving their arrangements to us,' Graebner relayed.[49] A few days later, he reported on more detailed arrangements:

> He plans to fly there on December 12 with his wife, Sarah, security, Greenfields and detective and stay about a month. The best procedure would be for us to deposit funds at a bank in Marrakesh. One point remains unsettled. Does our invitation include air passage to and from Marrakesh, regardless of whether it could be paid in sterling? I would like to be able to say we will pay all.[50]

LIFE was about to offer to pay for the flights when British Aviation Services authorized its Silver City Airways subsidiary to transport the party in both directions free of charge. So instead *LIFE* deposited $5,000 in Churchill's name, in order to pay his hotel bills, at the Banque d'État du Maroc.[51]

Meanwhile Longwell at *LIFE* tried to share the expense with his fellow American syndicate members. *The New York Times* agreed, but Houghton Mifflin declined, even though the first volume of Churchill's memoirs was sure to be a financial success, having just won the Book of the Month Club's coveted selection. The Club's 800,000 members had to choose six books a year from a monthly list of ten, but 'Book of the Month' selections normally guaranteed at least 200,000 orders.[52]

On the eve of his departure, Churchill sent the new cabinet secretary Sir Norman Brook a copy of the 'Provisional Final' text of the memoirs' first volume for his approval. Sir Norman shared his predecessor's view that Churchill's work was the closest Britain would come to an official war history. He read three successive proofs within a few weeks and offered the advice of an informal proofreader, becoming, in the words of David Reynolds's masterful account of the memoirs, almost 'an additional member of the Syndicate'.[53]

At the Mamounia hotel in Marrakech, Churchill, his daughter Sarah, Bill Deakin, two secretaries, a valet and detective took over seven bedrooms and bathrooms, a sitting room and studio at a fixed price of 16,150 francs (or £35 a day); this included one bottle of Moroccan wine for the secretaries, valet and detective to share at each meal.[54] When the first week's hotel bill came to £300, Churchill justified the arrangement to Clementine:

> When you recollect how much it means to all these publishers to get delivery of volume I by the end of February, and that they would perhaps lose many thousands of pounds and suffer immense inconvenience if I failed them, I feel fully justified in the course I have taken, which results only from the fact of our own currency regulations which prevent me from using my own money.[55]

However, the first week was by some margin the least expensive of the five weeks the party eventually spent at the hotel. 'The money here arn't arf going,' one of the secretaries reported home about halfway through the trip.[56] The second week cost £405, the third £458, and the fourth and fifth more than £600 each. The hotel had wisely excluded the cost of the drinks on Churchill's own table from the fixed price, so the list of extras came to 203,000 francs or £400 for the stay.[57]

Before Graebner joined the party, along with Lord Camrose, in mid-January, Churchill had already asked him for an extra $5,000. He greeted Graebner with a request for another $1,500.[58] They were still some $2,000 short when the party came to leave.[59] Deakin was not sure that the American publishers had received full value for the final bill of $13,600:[60] their guest had painted more than he had worked, he thought, but at least January's last proofs were now labelled 'Final' – even if Churchill spoiled the effect by adding, in his own hand, 'Subject to Full Freedom of Proof Correction'.[61]

24

'The unfolding of time, life and fortune'
Racing to the Finish, 1948–50

Exchange rate: $4 until August 1949; $2.80 = £1 thereafter;
francs 1,250 = £1 (1948)
Inflation multiples: US x 10; UK x 30

EMERY REVES SUGGESTED *The Second World War* as the simple but authoritative title for Churchill's war memoir and *The Gathering Storm* as the title for its opening volume. As the first extracts appeared in the newspapers early in April 1948, Soviet tanks were moving into Czechoslovakia. The repercussions of the Second World War were still being felt and Churchill had already warned his 'Syndicate' that a sixth volume might well be needed.[1]

The New York Times claimed an extra 25,000 sales a day and European newspapers saw circulation increases of between 15 and 25 per cent.[2] 'I am glad to have been proved right that your principal source of money-making would be your writing,' Bernard Baruch wrote; investment in the markets, he added, was simply 'too tough.'[3]

Churchill's success continued when *The Gathering Storm* appeared in book form in America during June and July 1948, while the Soviet Union began its blockade of Berlin. Between them, Houghton Mifflin and the Book of the Month Club sold 565,000 copies, earning the Boston publisher revenues of $600,000.[4]

In Britain Cassell & Co. could only look on in envy: strict paper rationing, still in force three years after the end of the war, had forced it to delay publication of *The Gathering Storm* until October. Nevertheless, the pre-publication orders were double the record for any previous non-fiction book, and when it was finally published the revenues from the first volume exceeded the amount that Cassell had paid for the entire copyright. *The Spectator* magazine speculated that Cassell must have earned a profit from the first volume alone of at least £100,000 – a figure that Churchill took to heart.[5]

Churchill's own finances remained sensitive territory: halfway through *LIFE*'s serialization of the first volume, Walter Graebner had to cable New York to put a halt to a companion piece the magazine had planned to print on this subject: 'It is most important that you omit the whole section on trusts, taxes and salary as publication of that kind would wreck our relations,' he told Daniel Longwell.[6]

Churchill's healthy bank balance at the end of the war had disappeared by the spring of 1948, because he had spent money on London properties, the Chartwell farms and new investments. But a second series of payments for his memoirs in May, followed by a batch of compensation awards for the Argentinian railway shares, restored his balance to a surplus.[7]

Despite the first volume's success, Churchill was making little progress with the second. He was even wondering if he had the will to go on writing. At a low ebb in June, he asked his solicitor Anthony Moir to look into his contract and see what would happen if he gave up writing the book altogether and found someone else to finish it; meanwhile, *The Daily Telegraph* could pay him something for the preparation he had already done on the later volumes.

This crisis passed, however, when Walter Graebner suggested another holiday paid for by *LIFE*: this time it was to be summer in the south of France. 'My own view is that it will be next to impossible for Mr Churchill to go to the south of France unless somebody makes an arrangement similar to that of last winter in Marrakesh,' Graebner told his chairman Henry Luce, promising it would be cheaper than Churchill's previous holiday.

Luce was not impressed: 'This business of supporting world figures gets a little beyond me,' he told his staff. 'I leave it to you.'[8]

Longwell at *LIFE* made another appeal for Houghton Mifflin's help in paying, but gave up as soon as he heard that Reves would have to be involved in the decision; he was still hesitating about *LIFE*'s contribution when he heard from Lord Camrose that *The New York Times* was considering picking up the whole bill itself. The two publications decided to share the cost in their normal syndicate proportions, as they did for each subsequent vacation.

'Tell our author both *Times* and ourselves would be delighted if he would have a good holiday in August,' Longwell cabled Graebner. 'I would like to keep budget around 8 or 9 thousand dollars if possible.'[9]

Clementine booked the Hôtel René-Roy in Aix-en-Provence, which quoted 400 francs a day for standard board or 680 francs for 'the more luxurious menu'. She checked with her husband: 'One table at the higher rate,' he decided.[10]

Before Churchill left for his holiday, Vickers da Costa provided him with a valuation of his investments. Economic controls imposed in the aftermath of war were gradually falling away as the Marshall Plan swung into action to stimulate recovery in Europe. Nevertheless, Churchill had managed to lose £7,000 buying and selling twenty-eight different shares during the first half of 1948. He responded by shaving £25,000 from the size of his shareholdings; his bank balance remained healthy, however, thanks to two more payments from Sir Alexander Korda for the film rights to *Savrola* and *My African Journey*.[11]

The Churchill party travelled to the south of France in a special carriage on Le Train Bleu, the luxury night express train. In Aix-en-Provence, Churchill's former parliamentary aide Robert Boothby joined them for lunch, as he recalled in his memoirs:

Langoustine mayonnaise, *soufflé*, a couple of bottles of Champagne on ice, and a bottle of Volnay, topped up with brandy. The bill was then demanded. Unthinkable said the proprietress. It was the greatest honour they had ever had. Perhaps Monsieur Churchill would sign his name in the book. Monsieur Churchill would; and did.[12]

While the Churchills were in France the last remnant of the Garron Tower inheritance – the lime works and harbour at Carnlough – were sold to the earl of Antrim for £8,000.[13] However, Winston and Clementine were more pre-occupied by the changes to their wills made necessary by the sale of Chartwell.

During the war, Churchill's solicitor Charles Nicholl had persuaded him to sign a new version of his will that confirmed the gift of his papers to Clementine; earmarked the final fifth of his father's will trust to Mary; and settled Chartwell on Randolph; all his other personal assets going into a trust, from which Clementine would draw the income until she died, when it would be divided among their children.[14]

Now the main house at Chartwell had gone to the National Trust and Clementine was horrified at her husband's plan to compensate Randolph by leaving him the farmhouse of Chartwell Farm – Randolph's 'propinquity' to the National Trust, she felt, was bound to become a source of embarrassment. Instead she suggested that Churchill Literary Trust should buy Randolph a small country house elsewhere and that the farms eventually should become Mary's property, as the Soameses were now living in the farmhouse and Mary was the only one of their children who really appreciated the countryside.

Churchill agreed that Clementine could take Randolph house-hunting well away from Chartwell, but the farms, he insisted, should go to young Winston, rather than Mary. The rest of Churchill's assets would now go to Clementine in her own right, rather than on a life interest, so that she could take the difficult decisions about how to divide them between their children.[15]

On their departure from France, the Hôtel René-Roy's final bill came to 2.2 million francs, but Churchill asked *LIFE* to transfer 3 million to his account.[16] He had lost some money on the way home in Monte Carlo, as explained in a passage of Walter Graebner's memoir:

> Churchill adored gambling and it was Mrs Churchill's constant worry that he would squander more money at the gaming tables than the family finances could stand. On his return one year from a visit to France. . . he asked me to come and see him immediately as there was something on his mind. 'I have a confession to make,' he said, 'and I don't know what I can do about the situation that has been created. . . I went to the Casino one or two nights, and ended up a little behind. I did very well at first, but then my luck changed. What *am* I to do about it?'[17]

LIFE paid up, but later that year Graebner had to kill a reference to the incident that was being planned in *TIME* magazine: 'Churchill did not repeat not go to casino and I know from previous discussions that he would be unhappy if casino were mentioned,' he cabled to New York.[18]

Bill Deakin had helped in France with the second volume of the *The Second World War*, a 'starred final' version of which reached the printers shortly after the holiday ended. However, so many changes were needed that Graebner found Churchill at a low ebb again during November. He suggested another holiday in the sunshine to Daniel Longwell:

> [Churchill] said several times 'I am not depressed about anything in particular – just depressed.' He then said he was a 'little fed up with our book'. I think that what troubles him is that he thinks Cassells, Houghton Mifflin and Reves are making much more on the deal than he is though he 'is doing most of the work'. Cassell, he calculated, had made about £100,000 from the first edition and he netted only £8,000 from that. He thinks Houghton got a fantastic bargain.[19]

Henry Luce authorized the expense. 'Okay Monte Carlo for $5,000,'[20] Longwell told Graebner, approving a booking at the Hôtel de Paris, which also housed the city's casino. Churchill set off with his bank balance comfortably above £60,000, fortified by more compensation payments for his Argentinian railway shares.[21] Only his losses at the Chartwell farms, to which he had already transferred £11,750 in cash that year,[22] were causing any immediate financial concern.

Meanwhile the Inland Revenue was on the point of deciding whether or not Churchill's complicated tax scheme to shelter the majority of the income earned by *The Second World War* was sound. On their decision rested a much greater sum of money than Churchill had lost through the farms. The local tax inspector, a Mr Boarland, had asked to see a copy of Churchill's contract with *The Daily Telegraph* and any other 'relevant' document, which Anthony Moir took to mean the parallel agreement between the newspaper and Churchill's Literary Trust. After consulting Churchill Moir decided against volunteering any extra documents, but instead he disclosed to Boarland:

> In July 1946, Mr Churchill created a Settlement of cash, a large number of personal records and memoranda covering his life both public and private during the period of approximately 1906 to 1945, papers formerly belonging to Lord Randolph Churchill and a casket containing letters from the First Duke of Marlborough, which are of considerable value and were given to him by the Queen of the Netherlands at the close of the War. Under this Settlement no benefit, whether pecuniary or otherwise was reserved to Mr Churchill and this document is not in his possession or under his control.

Churchill had sold his early copyrights after the war while 'retired' as an author, Moir added, but since resuming his writing career on 1 September 1946 Churchill had received twelve payments. Most of them, he contended, were 'capital moneys' for the *Secret Session*

Speeches. However, Moir ended his carefully worded letter by offering the tax inspector one small morsel: Odhams Press had paid
£500 to reproduce sixteen of Churchill's paintings in a new version
of *Painting as a Pastime*, which he admitted could possibly be construed as a royalty and therefore subject to tax. 'If the point is
pressed Mr Churchill will submit, without prejudice, to an assessment in respect of this sum,' he offered.[23]

There followed a 'very friendly' meeting at the tax inspector's
office, during which Moir insisted that Churchill's prime motive
for setting up the trust had naturally been to safeguard these 'vitally
important documents'.[24] For more than a month the most senior
minds at the Inland Revenue, including the chief inspector of
claims (Intelligence Section), pored over Moir's letter and the documents, but they could find no 'catch'.[25]

Churchill's solicitor was confident of the final outcome and in
February all five members of the Inland Revenue Board signed a
piece of paper that allowed Boarland to confirm that 'no liability to
Income tax arises under the present law in respect of the £375,000
payable by *The Daily Telegraph* to the Trustees – either on Mr
Churchill or on the trustees'.[26]

Churchill's team had won, but the Inland Revenue had not quite
finished. 'I should not imagine in view of the favourable decision
on the main contention that their claim to exclude sundry small
"pre-commencement" literary earnings is likely to be pressed but,
if it is, kindly re-submit,' ran the Board's instructions to Boarland.[27]
They had underestimated Churchill's aversion to paying tax.
Within a month, Boarland forwarded to his head office what its
chief inspector described to a technical colleague as 'this latest
attempt to minimize liability'.[28]

Churchill had accepted a speaking invitation at the Massachusetts
Institute of Technology ('MIT') in March 1949, shortly after *Their
Finest Hour*, the second volume of his memoirs, began to be serialized in newspapers all over the world. MIT offered to cover his
travel costs to Boston, but it blanched on hearing the price of the
first-class cabins that Churchill expected on the *Queen Elizabeth*.

At just the right time, the American Automobile Association provided a solution: it offered to sponsor an extra Churchill speech on
the trip at a fee of $25,000.[29] Churchill felt the sum should be
treated as an *honorarium* and escape tax. Before accepting the invitation, he asked his advisers to confirm his interpretation with the
Inland Revenue, but they took a less lofty view of the *honorarium*
and the speech was quietly dropped. Henry Luce stepped in to
meet the shortfall. He was still keen to keep *TIME-LIFE*'s brand
associated in the American mind with Churchill, so he authorized
Longwell to send a message to Graebner: 'You may tell [Churchill]
that we will take care of the difference somehow.'[30]

The Inland Revenue became even less co-operative when
Painting as a Pastime sold so many copies that Churchill's initial
payment of £500, which Moir had conceded might possibly be
construed as taxable, increased by a factor of ten to £5,000.[31]
Boarland refused to rule out taxing Churchill's earnings as the
professional income of an artist, prompting him to dictate a letter
for his solicitor to send to the inspector: 'Painting has never been
considered one of [Churchill's] professions and he has not sold any
pictures in the last twenty-five years. On the other hand his
expenses in making the pictures now reproduced in *Painting as a
Pastime* have been very heavy.'[32]

Boarland beat a retreat on the paintings, but he made a more
determined assault on Churchill's earnings of £3,000 from the
publication of *Secret Session Speeches*: he regarded the sum as
taxable and threatened to 'carry the matter into public litigation'
if Churchill appealed against his ruling and won.[33] Deciding not
to risk such a public airing of his tax affairs, Churchill again
dictated the reply which he wanted Moir to send: 'Mr Churchill
regrets the view taken by the Board of the Inland Revenue which
is of course contrary to the professional advice he has received.
In particular Mr Churchill regrets the contention of the Board
that, when he wrote the *Secret Session Speeches*, he had the idea
"at the back of his mind" that they would "subsequently be published for profit".'[34]

*

By the time he left for Boston in mid-March, Churchill was aware that the third volume of *The Second World War* would not be ready at the beginning of May, the deadline he had to meet to qualify for his next payment. He warned Michael Berry, then deputizing at *The Daily Telegraph* for his father, Lord Camrose. He would produce a manuscript by May, Churchill explained, but several months of 'polishing and improving' would be needed to bring it up to publication standard. Nevertheless, he wanted an assurance that he would still be paid on time: 'I am put to great expense by the staff I use, by the printing, and various other charges, and I need the instalment.'[35] The assurance was given.

Churchill used the time it took to cross the Atlantic to sketch out the case for a sixth volume of *The Second World War*. The fourth would reach only the Axis forces' surrender at Tunis in May 1943; it would be impossible to do justice to the remaining two years of the war in a single volume after that. Certain that his plan would be welcomed, Churchill asked Lord Camrose to find out what terms the syndicate would offer and suggested meeting the local members while in America. Lord Camrose thought it a good plan, but Churchill found a different reaction in New York.

Henry Luce welcomed Churchill by praising him at a dinner for 200 guests given by *TIME-LIFE* as 'the greatest war correspondent since Julius Caesar'.[36] However Daniel Longwell made it clear privately that *LIFE* would stick to the letter of its contract: the fifth payment would be for the final volume. He warned that *LIFE*'s partners would take the same line: 'They will say quite unanimously there should not be a sixth volume, that five is the limit the public will take, and the final volume should be the grand climax of the entire publishing scheme.'[37]

At first Laughlin at Houghton Mifflin supported *LIFE*'s line, but he changed his mind when Churchill visited him in Boston. Houghton Mifflin would pay the same price for a sixth book as for the first five, he told Longwell afterwards: 'We know of no other author we would rather go to with an advance payment of that size to secure a book for our list the following year.'[38] Reves then promised an extra £10,000 for the foreign language rights. 'It is my strongest conviction that you should write your War memoirs exactly as you think they should be written,' he told Churchill. Reves was convinced that Cassell would pay, too, producing an extra £50,000 for Churchill, even if *LIFE* and *The New York Times* stayed away.[39]

Churchill's bank balance still stood at £47,000, thanks to the payment for the third volume,[40] so there seemed little need for the extra money. Certainly, the champagne continued to flow at Chartwell: during April and May 1949, Churchill's staff recorded the consumption of 454 bottles, plus 311 bottles of wine, 58 bottles of brandy, 56 bottles of Black Label whisky, 58 bottles of sherry and 69 bottles of port.[41]

In the middle of 1949 Churchill decided to follow his father into the world of racing. The family expert, Christopher Soames, warned that a single filly would cost at least £1,000 to buy and £600 a year to train, taking into account the cost of vets, blacksmiths, race entries and jockey's fees. If he was lucky, Churchill would find himself with a solid investment 'which should bring you in a small tax-free income, and will always hold its value as a brood-mare'; if he was unlucky, he would 'lose about £800 on the original investment of £1,000, plus whatever expenses you might have incurred while it is being trained'.[42]

Clementine's 'horror' at this development was shared by Jo Sturdee, one of Churchill's secretaries, who warned him in writing against the risk of damage to his 'great reputation'.[43] Within two months, however, Churchill had re-registered his father's racing colours (pink with chocolate sleeves and cap) and assembled a stable of seven fully-fledged racehorses.

His first win arrived as early as August 1949. It came from Colonist II, a grey which a racing vet Major Arnold Carey Foster had spotted finishing second at a race in France while unfit. Carey

Foster had mentioned the horse to the trainer Walter Nightingall, who in turn recommended him to Christopher Soames, who persuaded Churchill to buy him for £1,500 from the exotically named Monsieur Theodore Cozzika.[44]

Colonist II won two more races in 1949 and six in 1950, a run during which Churchill's betting stakes on a single race grew from £325 in July to £675 in October.[45] By that time Colonist II had won £9,000 of prize money[46] and Churchill was telling Clementine: 'So far all this shows a quite substantial profit and the whole outfit could be sold for two or three times more than we gave for it.'[47] One of the sport's attractions to Churchill was that both prize money and bets escaped taxation: 'Don't forget, a thousand pounds made out of horses is equivalent to twenty thousand in normal business enterprise at today's rate of taxation,' he reminded Graebner.[48]

At the end of the 1950 season Colonist II was valued at up to £20,000 if he retired to stand at stud. Churchill decided to risk a drop in the horse's value to less than a half by keeping him in training for more demanding races in 1951.[49] Colonist II started with two early wins, but faded after coming second in Royal Ascot's top class Gold Cup field in June; he retired at the end of the season, after thirteen wins. Lord Derby's racing manager suggested a price tag of £20,000, but Colonist II failed to sell privately before falling under the auctioneer's hammer for 7,000 guineas at December's Newmarket sales.[50] Despite the disappointment, Churchill commissioned a special portrait of Colonist II to hang alongside his father's famous winner L'Abbesse de Jouarre.[51]

LIFE may not have offered any money for a sixth volume of *The Second World War*, but it was happy to fund another holiday in the summer of 1950. Churchill chose to spend it on the edge of Lake Garda in Italy.[52] He had planned to concentrate on the fourth volume, but strong criticism of his draft for the third volume, *The Grand Alliance*, forced a change of heart. In the eyes of Churchill's American publishers, the story was lingering for too long on

Britain's Mediterranean battlefields; they were openly impatient for him to reach America's entry into the war.

Reves sympathized with the American publishers, but put the case more tactfully. He urged Churchill to concentrate on the major political and strategic issues of the conflict and to leave minor events to others. 'In view of the fact that Roosevelt is dead and Stalin will never publish his documents,' he told Churchill, 'you are the only man who can reveal the decisive issues of the war.'[53] Now nearly seventy-five years old, Churchill was still absorbing this advice when he suffered a mild stroke at Max Beaverbrook's villa on the south coast of France and had to be flown home privately.[54]

In Britain a growing number of bankers had realized that the nation's war-damaged economy could no longer support a pre-war exchange rate of $4 to the pound. The storm broke in September 1949, when the chancellor, Sir Stafford Cripps, devalued Britain's currency by almost a third against the United States dollar.[55] Each pound became worth only $2.80. The public perception grew that the Labour government's stewardship of Britain's post-war economy was failing.

From this point onwards, Churchill's publishers exerted greater pressure on him to finish *The Second World War* before a general election, which might see him returned to office. Still recovering at home from his stroke, Churchill responded to Longwell in a reflective mood. Their joint enterprise faced 'astonishing uncertainties' in 'these gloomy and baffling years', he wrote. If 'the Socialists' won the election that he expected in early 1950, he would probably retire and complete the book, but the consequences of a Conservative victory were left unspoken. 'We can but await the unfolding of time, life and fortune!' he concluded.[56]

By the time Parliament re-assembled in October, Churchill had recovered physically and rekindled his appetite for Westminster politics. He managed only brief bouts of work on the fourth volume of *The Second World War* in the autumn, while he still revised its predecessor, *The Grand Alliance*. Another writing holiday was planned at Christmas, but in November Churchill began to doubt again whether he could really complete the task.[57] 'Keep adequate staff together. Somebody would have to be found to write it and also do what is necessary to polish vol. 4,' he noted after re-examining his contract and discussing with Lord Camrose whether Duff Cooper was a possible replacement.[58]

Meanwhile, the devaluation of the pound was causing Lord Camrose a different dilemma. *The Daily Telegraph*'s remaining payments from Churchill's American publishers would now be worth an extra third in pounds, but nothing in any of the contracts contemplated devaluation, let alone suggested that the newspaper should hand over the extra pounds to Churchill or his trustees. Privately, Lord Camrose indicated that he was willing to pay, but he needed his hand forced by Churchill if *The Daily Telegraph* was to be allowed to claim tax relief. Charles Graham-Dixon KC was called on to act as a formal arbitrator in the supposed dispute and duly awarded the extra amounts to Churchill and his trustees.[59]

Devaluation also brought interest from America in the commercial use of Churchill's paintings, which he had so far only licensed to the Soho Gallery in London. The Hall brothers of Kansas, Joyce and Raymond, relayed an offer of $5,000 a year to use five Churchill pictures annually for five years on the face of their Christmas cards.[60] Anthony Moir explained to the Halls the inequities of the British income tax system, as seen by Churchill, and they changed their offer to a single capital sum of $25,000, to last for three years. Moir thought that they might increase to $30,000,[61] but Churchill was less sure, cabling from France: 'Authorize you to try for thirty but do not lose contract. Pray act accordingly.'[62] Eventually the Halls raised their bid to $37,500,[63] earning Joyce Hall and his family a visit to Chartwell the following July. Moir warned Churchill that Hall was an 'unusual type for an American, very quiet and you will probably find very shy,'[64] but they became good friends until Churchill's death.

To settle the tax treatment of the Hall Brothers' payment, Moir arranged a quick meeting with Boarland the tax inspector, whom he knew was on the point of retiring. Boarland agreed that the Hall payment should be treated as a capital receipt, thereby earning himself a visit to Chartwell. He found the Hall Brothers' Christmas cards hanging in the house. 'I hear they have had a terrific success, selling over two million,' Churchill told the accompanying Moir. 'It is most important to me that this contract should be maintained.'[65]

By Christmas 1949 the Literary Trust had collected £173,500 in its bank. It was due to receive two more payments for the later volumes of *The Second World War* in May 1950 and 1951, but Moir had advised the trustees to keep a large reserve for death duties in case Churchill died before 31 July 1951, the fifth anniversary of his gift.

Churchill felt that the trustees' first decision to distribute only £35,000 to his children was much too cautious. They could expect £380,000 in their coffers by May 1951, so they should be investing much more – or buying his Chartwell farms.[66] Moir politely pointed out that the trustees might not find it an attractive prospect to invest in farmland which was still producing losses of almost £9,000 a year.[67] Nevertheless Clementine was careful to consult her husband before the next meeting, at which the trustees promised Randolph an income of £1,500 a year, and Sarah a lump sum of £10,000 to buy a London house with a studio for her new photographer husband.[68]

Meanwhile, Churchill's surplus in his own bank account had disappeared during 1949. The £60,000 with which he had started the year had turned into an overdraft by its end, largely because he had spent a net £50,000 buying shares.[69] Fortunately he 'earned' £80,000 in the 1949/50 tax year and had managed to shield all but £5,000 of it from tax. (He claimed almost half as capital receipts and deducted legitimate expenses incurred as an author or MP from the rest.)[70]

It was equally fortunate that *LIFE* and *The New York Times* continued to pay for Churchill's twice-yearly holidays. For the New Year of 1950 he chose the island of Madeira, at which he had briefly stopped fifty-one years earlier while travelling to and from the Boer War. Aided by Bill Deakin and Sir Henry Pownall, Churchill completed seventeen chapters of the fourth volume of *The Second World War*, to be called *The Hinge of Fate*, before news reached Madeira on 11 January that Clement Attlee had called a general election to be held on 23 February. *The Second World War* had to be put on hold again while Churchill returned to Britain by flying boat to join the campaign trail as leader of the Conservative opposition.

A month later the Conservative Party narrowly failed to dislodge Attlee's Labour government, which won 315 seats, compared to the opposition parties' combined tally of 307 (the Conservatives won 298 seats, the Liberals 9). It was a close enough result for talk of Churchill's retirement to be stilled and for his publishers to conclude that his time in which to finish *The Second World War* would be limited.

Nevertheless Churchill was confident *The Hinge of Fate* would be in good enough shape to meet the publishers' May 1950 deadline and to justify their payment. He was barely able to work on it before Parliament rose for Easter and, after a fortnight of furious writing during the holiday, he confessed to Clementine he was left feeling 'weighed down'.[71] The US publishers were equally unhappy because Daniel Longwell calculated only a quarter of its text was original writing.[72] Reves echoed their concerns and called Churchill's attention to a sharp fall-off in American sales, as much as 40 per cent down between the first volume and the third.[73] 'All your publishers are unanimous in pointing out the one and only cause of this reaction,' he wrote candidly. 'An overdose of documents, and too many details of military operations.'[74]

Churchill promised to make amendments when he had time, but a postscript to his reply, dictated but not sent, betrayed his deeper feelings: 'What is a miracle is what I have managed to produce in all the circumstances, and I am very glad that everyone has done so well out of it.'[75]

Churchill planned to return to *The Hinge of Fate* in September, during another holiday to be funded by *TIME-LIFE* in Biarritz. However, the Americans were starting to call the tune, as in the latter stages of the war itself. Laughlin at Houghton Mifflin decided that the only way to reverse the slide in sales was to launch the fourth volume in time for America's Christmas market. He lobbied the Book of the Month Club for a December selection, which would require his own firm to publish in November, the newspapers early in October and therefore Churchill to complete his manuscript by the end of August. Desmond Flower, now in day-to-day charge at Cassell, was appalled at the rush. 'I consider. . . the sweeping aside of all considerations of accuracy and the author's wishes for the sake of a Book Club are to be deplored,' he told Churchill,[76] but Laughlin would extend his deadline only to 11 September.

The timetable became an even greater challenge when North Korean forces invaded South Korea late in June. Parliament's summer recess was delayed to debate Britain's response and Churchill was forced to cancel his writing holiday. 'I have had to give up my holiday and cannot even squeeze a tube,' Churchill told his cousin Oswald Frewen on return. 'Volume IV is a worse tyrant than Attlee [who had kept Parliament in session].'[77]

In addition to the outbreak of the Korean War, British printers went on strike and a vital manuscript for the American edition of *The Hinge of Fate* disappeared in the transatlantic post. Reves complained that he had had to employ a staff of twenty, cutting and pasting stencilled sheets around the clock for three days, to make more than a thousand corrections to a version delivered three weeks earlier.[78]

The US State Department demanded last-minute deletions on security grounds, but extracts from *The Hinge of Fate* began running as planned on 10 October. On that day General MacArthur launched an amphibious landing behind North Korean lines. The coincidence gave the fourth volume of *The Second World War* a special resonance. *The New York Times* described the new conflict as a continuation of 'the same old fight for freedom and the democratic way of life that Churchill led'.[79]

25

'An insatiable need for money'

Post-war Prime Minister, 1951–5

Exchange rates: $2.80 = £1; francs 1,000 = £1
Inflation multiples: US x 9; UK x 25

THROUGHOUT NOVEMBER 1950 the pressure on Churchill's diary remained heavy. He briefed Prime Minister Attlee on the secret wartime accords reached with the Americans on use of the atom bomb; he led the Opposition attack in the House of Commons on the government's housing and foreign policy records; and he dealt with a stream of visitors and invitations from around the world.

Meanwhile, the question of a sixth volume of *The Second World War* remained unresolved. Emery Reves told Churchill that his Scandinavian publishers 'categorically' refused to pay anything extra for a sixth volume. But Churchill dismissed as 'quite impossible'[1] the suggestion that the fifth volume should end with Germany's surrender, and then he could write a separate book about the war's aftermath. Instead, Churchill dictated a synopsis for the sixth volume, before flying off for another Christmas writing holiday in Marrakech, again at the expense of *LIFE* and *The New York Times*.

When not painting, he worked at first on 'stringing together' documents and adding 'introductions and tail pieces' for this sixth volume, as he described the process to Clementine. 'Volume VI, though not yet a "literary masterpiece" at which we must always aim, is nevertheless an important commercial property,' he told her on Christmas Day.[2] He turned his attention back to the still incomplete volume five, *Closing the Ring*, only when Bill Deakin arrived to help: time was limited now and syndicate members no longer prepared research for the 'Master' to turn into his own prose; they drafted whole passages in the Churchillian style.

The writing party stayed in Marrakech until Parliament resumed on 23 January 1951. *LIFE*'s Walter Graebner expressed his relief to Daniel Longwell that the $8,000 hotel bill had come to 'less than I expected', but there was the usual sting in the tail: Churchill had chartered a plane to and from Marrakech at a cost of £2,000. 'Because of the political and military situation he thought he had to have a plane standing to rush him back to London in an emergency,' Graebner explained, asking Longwell to sanction payment. The wording of his request bore all the hallmarks of Churchill's own dictation: 'While he would like to have us pay the bill, and would be most grateful if we did, he does not want us to assume that this is a charge automatically to be borne by us.'[3]

This time, Longwell had reached his limit. 'I do think that this plane charge is excessive,' he told *The New York Times*, suggesting that they pay only the cost of a normal commercial flight. General Adler must have agreed, because Churchill's bank account records that a month later he paid just over half the cost himself.[4]

By Easter 1951 there were clear signs that the days of the Labour government were numbered. Its majority of votes in the House of Commons was only eight; two of its most senior figures, Sir Stafford Cripps and Ernest Bevin, had been forced by ill health to retire; and Prime Minister Attlee himself spent Easter in hospital as a result of illness.

Churchill was so close to becoming a peacetime prime minister that he worried at the risk of political embarrassment from the way the Literary Trust invested its surplus funds. Brendan Bracken had searched for assets that would escape high rates of death duty if Churchill died before the fifth anniversary of the trust's formation and had agreed a price of under £20,000 for the trust to buy 5,000 acres of the Biel estate in East Lothian, Scotland.

The value of the land was depressed by the number of sitting tenants, but would rise as these tenants died. So far as he could, Bracken was careful to hide the identity of Churchill's trust as the buyer. However, when the Biel estate's agent disclosed Churchill's name to reassure anxious tenants, *The Scotsman* carried a paragraph on the story. Having laid low for a fortnight, the trustees were about to sign on 6 April when the *Evening Standard* picked up the story in London. 'Every effort I made to persuade him [Churchill] that he was magnifying a small and transient matter was answered by peerless invective,' Bracken lamented to the newspaper's owner, Lord Beaverbrook. 'The reply was worse. "Do you want to drag my [*sic*] down in my last year?"' Bracken had 'sighed as a Trustee but obeyed as a friend'.[5]

Over Parliament's Easter recess in April 1951 Churchill and Deakin turned back to the fifth volume of *The Second World War* to meet the usual May deadline for a payment on its delivery. Neither *LIFE* nor *The New York Times* was legally bound to make its payment until the sixth volume was ready, but Churchill asked for at least a part-payment on delivery of the fifth volume, 'for personal reasons which include fact that he needs the money to run his huge establishment', Graebner explained.[6] His message persuaded Daniel Longwell and General Adler to make a long-delayed trip to Britain to explain their position: there would be no payment at all until the last book was ready, although both agreed that they would add up to $25,000 each to that payment as a gesture of goodwill.[7]

Churchill invited the two men to Chartwell, postponing any business talk until after a typically generous Sunday lunch. He then wrong-footed his visitors by producing 'almost finished' proofs, not just for the fifth but the sixth volume as well. Adler made notes of the conversation the following morning:

He then stated emphatically that, since the sixth volume was well along, we had nothing to worry about and that in the

event of his death it could be easily completed. Therefore he
would expect full payment less withholding of a 'token' amount
at the time of the delivery of Volume V, which would occur no
later than this present week. The token amount... he felt
should be in the neighbourhood of one fifth of the total amount
still due.

There was more to come from the master of negotiation, as Adler
noted:

Most adroitly Mr Churchill then reverted to the possibility of an
additional payment to be made only after the publication of
Volume VI. He reiterated that we owed him nothing for Volume
VI and that his association with Americans generally and with
ourselves specifically, had confirmed a lifelong impression over
our sense of fair-play. If, therefore, we felt disposed to pay him if
still alive an additional *honorarium* of whatever amount we
choose, it would be appreciated. If he were not alive, he was
confident that such an *honorarium* into the Trust, or to Mrs
Churchill, as a testimonial on our part to himself and his
memoirs, would be equally appreciated.

Churchill brushed aside the Americans' offer of an extra \$50,000
to fund more holidays, because it would be taxed. 'In concluding
the conference,' Adler recorded, 'he explained most patiently,
though I thought I could detect a twinkle in his eye, that he had no
right to make any arrangements because he was working for Lord
Camrose and any final decision on the matters we had been discussing would have to be concluded by "Bill".'[8]

Lord Camrose, it turned out, had received no warning of
Churchill's proposal. Two days later, after reading the draft, the two
men offered an immediate payment of \$150,000, with only \$80,000
held back until delivery of the sixth volume, expected on 31 July.[9]
Longwell was left to explain their capitulation to a sceptical *TIME-
LIFE* president in New York:

As you know, I came over here determined not to pay anything until we had V and VI in hand. Adler, however, wishes to be a little more generous; and since we have always dictated terms to the *Times*, I thought it tactful to go along with him. . . The Old Man refuses any further expenses – although I estimate there will probably be one more trip before VI is finished.[10]

Three months later the Literary Trust reached its fifth anniversary and thereby became exempt from death duty on Churchill's death: the duty could have been as high as 80 per cent.[11] 'Camrose came the other night to celebrate the five years consummation of our Literary Trust gift,' Churchill told Clementine. 'Randolph and Christopher were there too and all passed off jubilantly. . . This of course is the most important thing that could happen to our affairs, and relieves me of much anxiety on your account.'[12]

All the trust's funds could now be given either to his children and grandchildren or invested. According to Mary, her mother became 'ever ready to recommend to her fellow trustees that a child should be helped with some basic domestic improvement such as a new kitchen floor, or a service lift, or a modern boiler, or perhaps just a wonderful windfall towards furnishing, curtaining and carpeting our home-sweet-homes'.[13]

Henry Laughlin kept up his record by winning Churchill's fifth volume of *The Second World War* selection by the Book of the Month Club in America, just as he had for each of its predecessors. This time, however, the Club insisted on a November launch. While both men watched Colonist II run at Ascot in June, Laughlin gave Churchill a deadline to finish the book by 13 September. The Book Club had to be humoured, he explained, because it accounted for 80 per cent of American sales.[14] As soon as Parliament rose for the summer, Churchill 'plunged' into polishing his text, telling Clementine: 'You may imagine that I have little time for my other cares – the fish, indoors, and out-of-doors, the farm, the robin (who has absconded).'[15]

Longwell promised *LIFE*'s partners that Churchill's summer holiday at Annecy in France would be the last they paid for. This time, however, the only syndicate member able to travel was Charles Wood, the proofreader. Heavy rain limited Churchill's painting time, so he moved to Venice, from where the final chapters of *Closing the Ring* reached America only five days after Laughlin's deadline.

Looking back on these vacations for *TIME-LIFE*, Longwell felt that they had helped the company's cause: 'However, and this we must keep private, they were very lavish trips. Always some of the family went along to get their holiday. He had his cronies with him; he sent for various people from England. He had the best in food and hotels. We paid for his sort of state dinner to noteworthy folk, and the expedition to Marrakech presented an expense account I wouldn't want anyone to peer into too far.'[16] Briefing his successor a year later, Longwell was more positive: 'I find that the total amount we have spent on these vacations comes to $56,572.23. *The Times* paid 34.78 % of this amount, and we footed about $35,000 of the bills. I think it was a good investment. . . I have seen other great projects like this go to pieces.'[17]

Soon after Churchill returned to Britain in September, Prime Minister Attlee announced a general election. Churchill was alert to the tax advantages of 'retiring' as an author on taking political office, so he told the syndicate that he wanted 'a provisional version' of the final volume ready 'on or soon after 26 October', the day after the general election was to be held.[18] His writing staff worked flat out, but on 19 October Churchill countermanded the order, when it was obvious the book could not be completed in time.

A week later, a large crowd watching the general election results on a board outside the City's Royal Exchange building cheered as the Conservative Party reached 321 seats – sixteen more than the Labour and Liberal parties combined.

Churchill became prime minister again on 26 October 1951. He returned to 10 Downing Street with his finances in much better shape than they had been in May 1940: he had almost £50,000 in reserve, either at his bank or invested in government bonds. However, his spending had been running at close to £5,000 a month during 1951,[19] so he would clearly need to cut his costs or supplement his official salary.

A young British journalist, Malcolm Muggeridge, had travelled down to Chartwell with Emery Reves a year earlier, noting in his diary:

> Churchill has this characteristic 18th-century nobleman's atti-
> tude that he should have a Jew to look after his financial affairs
> and in this case there is no question but that the choice has
> turned out well. . . [Reves] said that Churchill had an insatiable
> need for money… His family costs him a lot, and though he
> doesn't live luxuriously, he lives amply and travels with a great
> suite, which is very expensive.[20]

On entering office at a time of difficulty for the British economy, Churchill asked his ministers to take a symbolic pay cut. As a result the prime minister's salary fell from £10,000 to £7,000 a year, although the impact on Churchill was cushioned by an agreement that he could treat £4,000 as a tax-free reimbursement of his expenses. (Churchill would pay tax of £1,425 a year on the £3,000 of taxable salary, equivalent to a rate of only 20 per cent tax on the full salary.)[21]

The main source of the extra earnings Churchill required was due to be the final volume of *The Second World War*, for which he signed a supplemental contract with *The Daily Telegraph* on 7 November, two weeks after taking office. The contract allowed him to choose how he wished to spread the £60,000 fee over the following three years, in whatever proportions best suited his tax position.[22] This flexibility became particularly valuable when Sir Norman Brook, still cabinet secretary, warned Churchill a fortnight later against trying to complete the book while he was prime minister; instead, he should announce that it had been 'submitted to the

appropriate authority for scrutiny on behalf of the Government'
and would require 'some revision' before publication.[23] At the time,
Churchill only expected to stay as prime minister for a year or so,
he told Jock Colville (who had returned as his private secretary).

As prime minister, Churchill aimed to re-establish a closer relationship with the United States and to reduce the tensions of the
Cold War, while he pruned government spending at home and rid
the economy of its post-war restrictions: 'houses and meat, without
being scuppered', as he put it to Colville.[24] He had only been back
in the post for three months when George VI died in February
1952 from a coronary thrombosis, which followed lung cancer.
Shortly afterwards Churchill experienced an arterial spasm. It
prompted the seventy-seven-year-old to look again at his will, this
time with Anthony Moir, Charles Nicholl having died in 1951.

Nicholl's 1947 version of Churchill's will had left almost everything to Clementine, so that she could decide the split between
family members. However, Moir pointed out how expensive this
could prove if Clementine were to die soon after him while death
duty rates were so high. Instead, Moir suggested that Churchill
should leave his wife a cash legacy of £25,000, but put everything
else into a trust, from which she could draw the income for the rest
of her life or be given more capital if she ever felt short of money;
then, on her death, the remainder would pass to their children.
This became the basic architecture of Churchill's will and it
remained in force at his death.

At the same time, Churchill had to decide whether he could
afford to continue paying his monthly family allowances or should
shift responsibility for paying them on to his Literary Trust. It was
a question closely linked to the choice of how much of his extra fee
for the last volume of *The Second World War* he should draw in
May 1952: the less he drew, the lower his tax rate for the year ahead,
yet he had to avoid running out of funds. His accountant James
Wood completed pages of calculations on the different permuta-
tions, before Churchill chose to draw only £15,000 for the book
and the Literary Trust took over responsibility for the family

allowances. The fee matched the amount *The Daily Telegraph* had been lending Churchill, interest-free, since 1947, but Lord Camrose had decided not to ask for its return until after Churchill's death.[25]

The American publishers were not so indulgent. *Closing the Ring* was already out in America* and they wanted a date for publication of the sixth and final volume, *Triumph and Tragedy*. While his government tried to counter Egypt's attempts to wrest control of the Suez Canal during Parliament's Easter holiday, Churchill polished the draft of the book sufficiently to win his May payment, but he then asked Lord Camrose to keep the manuscript under lock and key until after the American presidential elections in November.[26]

At *LIFE* Longwell despaired on hearing the news. 'The public gets further and further away from these events,' he told Graebner. 'Thus the project goes down in value all the time.'[27] Graebner raised the possibility of a final summer holiday paid for by *LIFE* to try to accelerate publication, but the idea did not survive scrutiny in New York or Downing Street.

Although Churchill was now living in official residences as prime minister, he was still spending at a rate of almost £40,000 a year during the summer of 1952, much of it on personal staff.[28] 'His *ménage* consists now of four Swiss maids and two Swiss men "all carefully vetted by M.I.5"', Lord Camrose noted after a private dinner in September 1952. He also found the premier 'at times a little bored with his present position and its too frequent frustrations'.[29] By September, there was nothing left in Churchill's bank account[30] and he was regretting not having drawn more of his fee for the book earlier in the year. He asked Lord Camrose if *The Daily Telegraph* would 'lend' him an extra £15,000, taking his borrowing from the newspaper up to £30,000. Lord Camrose obliged.[31]

Churchill spent his late summer holiday as the guest of Max Beaverbrook at his home in the south of France, where he gently

---

* Cassell did not publish in Britain until September 1952, as a result of paper rationing and printers' strikes.

polished the text of *Triumph and Tragedy*. Having practically completed the book before his return, he brought to an end the
employment of the syndicate of helpers to whom he was still paying
combined salaries of more than £5,000 a year. There was nothing
more to do until just before publication, he told them, and 'I cannot
at this stage say. . . whether indeed it will be published while I am
in office.'[32]

Three months passed before Churchill returned to *Triumph
and Tragedy* early in 1953, while he sailed across the Atlantic to
meet America's president-elect, Dwight Eisenhower. He toyed
briefly with the idea of releasing the first half of the book as a sop
to his publishers, while holding back the more politically sensitive
second part about the post-war settlement. Henry Laughlin put
him off the idea when they met: he wanted the whole manuscript
by May, to catch the Christmas market again. 'No hope', Churchill
told him.[33]

Back in England, Churchill had to decide how much income to
draw from his publishers in May to keep him going for the rest of
1953. Before making up his mind, he asked his doctor Lord Moran
the average life expectancy of a seventy-eight-year-old. The answer
was six years. 'I might go on for another eight years,' he told his
doctor. 'If I do it will be very tiresome for those who manage my
finances. You see, Charles, during the war I retired from business,
but by the end of the war I had become notorious; and all sorts of
things, such as film rights and the copyright of my books, gave me
quite a bit of capital. For the first time in my life I was quite a rich
man. But the income tax people take it all.'[34]

Churchill's growing losses on his farms – now almost £11,000 a
year – could hardly be laid at the door of the Inland Revenue.[35] In
fact, the ability to offset his farming losses against his other income,
to reduce the amount of tax he paid, was part of what persuaded
Churchill to persevere at farming for so long. Nevertheless he had
to raise more cash to meet the farms' losses in March 1953. Five
months earlier he had repaid £10,000 of his loan from *The Daily
Telegraph* and now he needed cash to last until his next literary

payment was due in May. He raised £25,000 by remortgaging the farms with Alliance Assurance.[36]

However, Wood finally convinced Churchill to sell the farms when he explained that the tax relief on their losses would cease the moment he died. Churchill accepted the advice of Percy Cox, whom he had re-engaged to take on the farms' management now that Christopher Soames had entered the world of politics, that they should sell the smaller farms first. Both Parkside and Bardogs farms seemed to find ready homes, until the buyer of Bardogs pulled out at the last minute and only Parkside went.[37]

Churchill's farming losses halved,[38] so that his spending reduced to £30,000 a year – nevertheless it was clear that his reserves would not last for more than two or three years after he received the final payment for *The Second World War*, due in May 1954. That calculation was struck, too, before taking into account the cost of horse racing, which, Wood reminded him, had somehow escaped the economy drive.

Christopher Soames had suggested cutting back his racing stable when Churchill became prime minister again, but five horses remained in training during the 1952 season, producing losses of £4,000.[39] 'On the present scale of Expenditure,' Wood wrote with uncharacteristic levity, 'the amount required from Capital will range from £7,000 to £13,000 according to the results from Racing (i.e. The faster the Horses run the less the Capital required!)'.[40]

Lord Camrose deflected from Churchill most of the pressure exerted by the American syndicate to publish the final volume of *Triumph and Tragedy*, the manuscript for which still lay in his safe. Stalin's death on 5 March 1953 introduced a new complication: Churchill did not want to damage his relationship with the Soviet Union's new leaders by publishing passages critical of their predecessor. On 25 March Churchill privately mentioned September to Camrose as a possible date for publication, but by the end of the month he had done nothing about clearing his use of quotations by past or present American presidents.

At a dinner of The Other Club in May, Churchill advanced his timetable: he told Camrose that June was a possibility if he had a good Whitsun – but he did not.[41] Anthony Eden's ill health forced Churchill to take over some of the duties of foreign secretary, while there was extra work to be done preparing for the young queen's coronation and a conference of Commonwealth government leaders. It left the seventy-eight-year-old Churchill exhausted.

'Pressure of public affairs over the Whitsun holiday weekend had prevented him from doing the amount of work that he had hoped,' Lord Camrose noted in mid-June. Churchill felt that he needed just three or four consecutive mornings to complete the book, but six days later, at an official Downing Street dinner, he suffered a serious stroke.

The paralysis spread down Churchill's left side the following day, a Wednesday, and his doctor, Lord Moran, doubted that he would survive the weekend. Lord Camrose was one of the few let in on the secret: 'The Prime Minister wants me to tell you for your most private information that he is far from well and may indeed have to resign shortly,' Colville wrote.[42]

Against the odds, Churchill himself telephoned Lord Camrose on the Saturday: he was being forced to rest, he said, which might turn out well for the book. Lord Camrose visited Chartwell for lunch on the Monday, when Churchill returned to the proofs with a shaky hand and forecast that they could be ready 'in tentative form' by mid-July.[43]

They were not and on 22 July Lord Camrose left Chartwell saddened by his visit. Churchill had walked in to lunch unaided and had managed a short tour of the garden before they sat on a bench until five o'clock, while Churchill reminisced, tearfully. He was unable to remember some of his favourite poems. As Lord Camrose left, Moran warned that another stroke was 'highly probable' and could prove 'fatal'.[44] Churchill's staff took Camrose aside to ask for another loan: the prime minister's current account was overdrawn, although there was more than £40,000 in his investment account.[45]

The Daily Telegraph discreetly lent another £12,000, taking its outstanding loans to the prime minister up to £32,000.[46]

Churchill defied his doctor's predictions during August. After tinkering with the proofs of *Triumph and Tragedy*, he presided over a cabinet meeting towards the end of the month and, two days later, he invited Walter Graebner to a lunch that lasted until nearly 5 p.m., helped along by two bottles of champagne.[47] Max Beaverbrook laid in four cases of Dom Pérignon 1929, before the Churchills and Soameses spent September at his French villa La Capponcina: 'It is the finest champagne I have ever tasted,' Beaverbrook observed. 'I hope you will use it.'[48]

Early in October Churchill gave a long speech to the Conservative Party's annual conference and reshuffled his cabinet, in defiance of growing calls for his retirement. A few days later he learned that he had been awarded the Nobel Prize for Literature, which, as he pointed out to Clementine, was worth £12,000 tax-free.[49]

The Nobel Prize was also the best possible publicity for the publication of *Triumph and Tragedy*. Like all the other volumes of *The Second World War*, it was selected by the American Book of the Month Club, this time for December publication. It sold more strongly than the fifth volume. 'The last is the best,' Brendan Bracken told Churchill. 'Your children and grandchildren have every reason to bless you for undertaking this herculean labour for them. I grieve beyond all telling that no benefit from it can come to Clemmie and you.'[50] In North America, the six volumes and the later abridged version of *The Second World War* sold nearly 2.2 million copies; in Britain and the Commonwealth, Cassell & Co. sold another two million.[51]

Churchill the Nobel Laureate at last turned back to the long-delayed *A History of the English-Speaking Peoples*. 'I've been living on *The Second World War*,' he told Lord Moran. 'Now I shall live on this history. I shall lay an egg a year – a volume every twelve months should not mean much work.'[52] He recognized that he must distance himself from the publishing negotiations, so asked his solicitor Anthony Moir to act on his behalf. Churchill had first settled terms with Cassell & Co. in 1933, then slightly revised them in 1945. Since then he had sold more than four million books. Now he wanted Moir to achieve a complete renegotiation of the book's terms with Cassell and its publishing partners, and to sell newspaper serialization rights around the world. Brendan Bracken recommended the editor of *History Today* magazine, Alan Hodge, to supervise the rewriting.

Thanks to *The Daily Telegraph*'s extra loan and the Nobel Prize money, Churchill left for 1954's New Year holiday with his combined bank balances standing at over £60,000.[53] They were even higher by the middle of the year, when Lord Camrose made the third and final payment for the final volume of *The Second World War* without asking for his emergency loan of the previous year to be repaid; it was Lord Camrose's final act of generosity before he died suddenly in June.[54]

As his eightieth birthday approached in November 1954, Churchill asked his solicitor to review his will again. Discounting any money still to come from *A History of the English-Speaking Peoples*, Churchill's personal assets amounted to £158,500, but they were offset by £84,500 of loans, bills and taxes. Moir estimated that death duties of £26,000 would leave a net estate of only £48,000, almost all of which would go to Clementine, who would collect half as much again from life insurance policies.[55]

Neither of them knew that these figures were about to be transformed. Without consulting Churchill, Lord Moynihan, the son of a prominent Leeds doctor, and Edward Martell, the editor of *The Recorder* magazine had set up the 'Winston Churchill 80th Birthday Presentation Fund'. By the middle of November, almost 100,000 members of the public had donated £150,000 to the Fund, despite some confusion over how the money would be spent. Lord Moran recorded Churchill's reaction to the Fund:

> If it's for me so that I can do what I want with it, I would like it very much. But I don't want them to raise a sum for charity just

to bring home some coloured gentleman from Jamaica to complete his education. I'd rather they did nothing. Of course, I might give some of the money subscribed to a charity that I was connected with. But I'm not a rich man. . . The four volumes of *History of the English-Speaking Peoples* will bring me a great income, but the Treasury will take it all.[56]

Shortly before Churchill's birthday, Moir pointed out that any money handed over to Churchill would become part of his estate, causing an extra tax bill should he die within five years, and for a year even if he gave it away. After urgent meetings with the Fund's legal team, Churchill's advisers decided that all the money raised so far would have to go to him, but they urged him to announce immediately that – his own needs now met – future donations would go towards a new Winston Churchill Birthday Charity that he was establishing forthwith.

The expected rush of City contributions never materialized, but donations reached £259,000; Churchill was presented with a first cheque for £150,000 on the day after his birthday, followed by another for £26,134 six months later. Both cheques went into a new 'Presentation Account' at his bank,[57] from which he transferred £25,000 as his personal contribution to his Birthday Trust.[58] Clementine received a cheque for £2,000 at Christmas and Churchill's bank accounts finished the year with more than £170,000 of cash.[59]

Throughout 1954 Churchill was encouraged by family and friends to retire. He dismissed any such suggestion, but early in 1955 he told a small circle of friends that he would leave halfway through the year. 'Our friend, under no pressure from Clemmie, Eden or other Ministers, intends to depart before July,' Bracken told Beaverbrook in the middle of January. 'His only wish now is to find a small villa in the South of France where he can spend the winter months in the years that remain to him.'[60] Just before he resigned in April 1955, Churchill invited Elizabeth II to dinner at

10 Downing Street. The young queen offered her prime minister a dukedom, but he declined. Without a great landed estate it would be an embarrassment, he decided.[61]

26

'I shall lay an egg a year'
A Third and Final Retirement, 1955–7

Exchange rates: $2.80 = £1; francs 1,000 = £1
Inflation multiples: US x 9; UK x 22

Afer retiring, Churchill took a fortnight's holiday with Clementine, painting and playing bezique in Sicily. While he was there, eighteen months of work by Churchill's solicitor Anthony Moir culminated in the announcement of publishing arrangements for *A History of the English-Speaking Peoples*.[1] Cassell & Co. had paid £20,000 for the worldwide rights in 1933, but acknowledged that much had changed since then. They suggested instead that their payment be treated as an advance on the new arrangements; Dodd, Mead and Co. and McClelland & Stewart – the American and Canadian publishers who had bought the book from Cassell before the war – took the same view: the book was too attractive a commercial property to lose to rivals.

Moir had set out the new contracts to ensure that Churchill was paid more and lost as little as possible to tax, because the book would almost certainly be Churchill's last and its earnings might have to last him for several more years. *The Second World War*'s tax scheme could not be used, because *A History of the English-Speaking Peoples* had been written before the Literary Trust came into being. However, Moir chose to arrange a series of fixed payments by the publishers, in the middle of which Churchill would retire as an author for the third and final time, thus converting all remaining payments into untaxed capital receipts.

Moir concentrated first on the American newspapers, agreeing four instalments of $50,000 each with *LIFE*.[2] Hearing that Henry Luce had been spotted leaving Downing Street with a sheaf of papers tucked under his arm, Emery Reves lobbied Churchill for the foreign language rights.[3] These rights had been part of *LIFE*'s package, but Churchill took up the cause of his old agent directly with Luce, cabling:

> I would like to have them handled by Emery Reves who had made a wonderful success abroad of the *War Memoirs* and who has worked with me since the anti-Hitler days before the War. Although I have made no personal profit by sale of the *War Memoirs* abroad it is a great pleasure to me to feel that these books are translated into 26 different languages and I am sure that no one could have done it except Reves who buzzed around the world for nearly a year making contacts.[4]

By Christmas 1955 the matter was 'settled': Reves paid £34,000 and *LIFE*'s price fell to $150,000, a fifth of the sum it had paid for The *Second World War*.[5] Although the baton had passed to a new generation at *The Daily Telegraph*, the Berry brothers followed family tradition by offering £40,000. They broke with their father's practice by asking for their loans to Churchill of £32,000 to be netted against their payments.[6]

Churchill's retirement from politics had encouraged him to expand his racing interests into breeding. In the spring of 1955 he had bought the Newchapel stud, close to Chartwell, for £6,500.[7] An *honorarium* of £1,000 a year secured the services of Major Arnold Carey Foster, the man who had spotted Colonist II, as a combined stud manager, racing manager and vet.[8] Within a year, the stud housed seven mares and four colts, with another four foals on the way.

After two victories by stud horses at the same Windsor race meeting in 1957, Churchill explained to Clementine that the stud was paying its way.[9] However, James Wood of Wood, Willey & Co. struggled to explain whether Churchill's 'equine activities' as a whole produced a profit. For tax purposes, racing and betting were considered a private hobby, which Wood calculated cost Churchill less than £1,000 in 1957. In contrast, the Inland Revenue treated the operations of the stud as a business, although Wood considered it an odd one. Most of the stud's theoretical 'income' depended on changes in the valuations of Churchill's horses as they moved between racing and breeding duties without any cash changing hands. The stud certainly cost £18,000 a year to run, but so far as Wood could tell the 'loss' was limited to £6,000 during its first year and this could all be offset against Churchill's other tax bill.[10]

Even after his retirement, Churchill still saw a selection of Foreign Office telegrams and had to deal with a constant stream of official visitors and correspondence. To help his office cope, the government provided the temporary assistance of a young civil servant, Anthony Montague Browne. He had joined Churchill's Downing Street office in 1952, but had returned to the Foreign Office on Churchill's resignation. Montague Browne was originally dispatched to help his former employer 'for a week' at Lord Beaverbrook's villa in the south of France, but the foreign secretary Harold Macmillan extended his appointment to two years during which Churchill reimbursed his salary to the Treasury.[11]

Macmillan's instructions to Montague Browne were to concentrate on Churchill's relations with other governments and his speeches on international affairs, and to keep away from his private affairs and finances, but that soon turned out to be impractical: 'For one so wise and far-sighted,' Montague Browne wrote in his memoirs, '[Churchill] was quite amazingly extravagant. . . There were only two ways of helping, either by making more money or by curbing expenditure.'[12] Wisely, Montague Browne concentrated on the former, conscious of the need to preserve his employer's reputation and avoid income tax.*

Churchill so enjoyed his two months painting, and polishing *A History of the English-Speaking Peoples* at La Capponcina in autumn 1955 that he asked his host whether he could stay for November and December. However, Beaverbrook's staff were due to move to his winter home in the Bahamas, so the Churchills were invited there.

Then another invitation came from Emery Reves and his partner Wendy Russell, who had just finished restoring La Pausa, their house on the French Riviera, overlooking Monte Carlo and the sea. It had been bought by Coco Chanel in 1928 and restored with money provided by her partner at the time, Churchill's friend the duke of Westminster. Now it was Reves's earnings from Churchill's *The Second World War* that had funded the restoration.

The Churchills chose La Pausa, so that they could search for a home of their own in the region, although Clementine was doubtful about this idea. They wanted a house set back in the hills, rather than on the coast, with at least ten bedrooms, four bathrooms and pleasant grounds.[13] On arrival at La Pausa early in 1958, however, Clementine was unwell, so Churchill had to house-hunt alone. He inspected properties priced between 26 and 65 million francs.[14] He even summoned his bank manager over from London to discuss how best to approach the Bank of England for the necessary licence to export £25,000 for a purchase.

'Sir Winston has been advised by his doctors that he should spend the winter months not in England but in the south of France', read the application, which the bank quickly rubber-stamped.[15] The Société des Bains de Mer de Monaco, which also owned Monte Carlo's casino, offered an alternative: in return for a rent of £1,500 a year, it would spend £50,000 on converting a villa overlooking the

---

* Among the many letter-drafting tricks that Montague Browne learned from Churchill was that, for gifts of under £500 in value, he would be 'indeed obliged'; above that level, he was 'most grateful'.

sea for Churchill's exclusive use for the rest of his life.[16] Over lunch
at La Pausa, Randolph had introduced his father to the Société's
main shareholder, the Greek ship owner Aristotle Onassis, and
Churchill had been favourably impressed. But Clementine was not
enthusiastic, as she told her husband:

> Somehow I don't want to be beholden to this rich and powerful
> man, & for the nest to be blazoned. Similarly, tho' to a lesser
> degree, I don't want to stay at La Pausa... Also I want this
> journey to last as long as possible and to get off at Marseilles &
> rattle along either by train or car to Monte Carlo, then stay with
> that unconventional and uneasy *ménage* does not allure me –
> Please forgive me; but you can't teach an old dog new tricks.[17]

The idea of a house where they could both spend months at a time
was dropped. Churchill stayed for four months at La Pausa, where
he was given the use of an entire floor, including office, bedroom
and rooms for his guests.

LIFE and *The Daily Telegraph* started running extracts from the
first volume of *A History of the English-Speaking Peoples* in the
spring of 1956. It was clear it would be a commercial success when
Paris Match bought an episode featuring Joan of Arc. It, too, was
chosen as Book of the Month in America, a decision worth 'at least
a quarter million dollars' to Churchill, according to Edward Dodd,
president of Dodd, Mead.[18]

With the publishers now able to forecast sales for the book's
later volumes, Moir asked Charles Graham-Dixon, QC, to plan
Churchill's retirement as an author, so that he escaped income tax
on any volumes published after his retirement date. It would not be
easy, the barrister advised: Churchill could not retire first and then
deliver a finished text later, so all the manuscript delivery dates
would have to be renegotiated with each publisher. Graham-Dixon
also warned that the Inland Revenue might anyway insist on taxing
some future income to match the literary expenses already claimed

by Churchill; for good measure, he advised that everything should be put in place over the following eight months, because he expected the budget of April 1957 to close some of the loopholes which they hoped to exploit.[19]

Churchill approved Moir's suggestion that he test the water informally with the Inland Revenue. Moir and James Wood left that meeting 'hopeful', but some of their optimism dissipated, however, when a new tax inspector, Mr Bullock, ruled that Churchill would have to match income and expenses for at least his last year as an author and possibly two.[20] This 'very disappointing' news would catch £56,000 of his remaining instalments due from LIFE and The Daily Telegraph, although any post-retirement payments for the later volumes of the book would be safe.

Moir and Graham-Dixon visited the headquarters of the Inland Revenue to challenge this decision.[21] Their first encounter was inconclusive, but their second, just before Christmas, ended in a classic compromise: the Inland Revenue agreed to apply a test that applied to The Daily Telegraph's payments, but not to LIFE's.[22] As a result, Wood estimated, £165,000 of Churchill's £276,000 earnings for A History would escape tax altogether. He would also be able to offset farming losses and literary expenses against the rest, leaving only a quarter to be taxed.[23]

Films were the second topic of discussion between Churchill and his lawyers. Bernard Baruch in America had weeded out most of the industry's offers before they reached Churchill, but he let one through on account of its size: the National Broadcasting Company was willing to pay $250,000 for six taped interviews of one hour each, to be filmed at a time and place of Churchill's choice.[24] The offer's one fatal flaw was that income tax could not be avoided. Churchill preferred to deal in any case with his old friend Sir Alexander Korda.

He wanted Sir Alexander to mediate between himself and the Ford Foundation, which was interested in sponsoring a television series for schools based on A History of the English-Speaking

Peoples. Sir Alexander mentioned tactfully that he suspected he had already bought the rights at the end of the war. However, Moir came up with a compromise under which each of Churchill and Korda contributed a small sum of capital to form a joint venture, M & P Investments.[*] It would buy the film rights to *A History* from Sir Alexander and 'live' television rights from Churchill, before selling its shares to the Ford Foundation for $350,000. Churchill's profits would remain untaxed because a sale of shares was treated as a capital transaction.[25]

M & P Investments duly took up its rights early in 1956, but when Sir Alexander Korda died suddenly of a heart attack, the Ford Foundation lost interest. Aware that historical films are expensive to make, Sir Alexander's partner, Sir David Cunynghame, was sceptical of finding a replacement sponsor. Churchill's team favoured using a New York agent, Charles Wicks, who was confident he could sell the rights for $1 million.[26] When he acknowledged failure three months later, Emery Reves tried to sell them at a reduced price of $100,000, but had to be relieved of his duties early in 1957 so that he could host Churchill at La Pausa.[27]

As hopes faded for the Ford project during 1956, an offer came out of the blue from Metro Goldwyn Meyer for the film rights to *My Early Life.* MGM's opening bid included a cash advance to Churchill of $100,000 on a half share of the film's profits, which the studio hinted might produce eventual earnings of $1 million or more.[28] New to Churchill's business affairs, Anthony Montague Browne checked the ownership of the rights with Moir, who gave the 'all clear' after checking in turn with Churchill's previous solicitors Nicholl, Manisty & Co.[29]

A senior MGM producer, Marjorie Thorson, flew to London and she had already raised the guarantee to $150,000 – and seemed prepared to go further – when the studio's own checks showed that Warner Brothers had bought the rights during the war for just

---

[*] Named after its first two directors, Anthony Moir and a fellow partner of Fladgate & Co., Ronald Plummer.

£7,500.[30] Churchill apologized profusely to MGM's owner Arthur Loew, while Brendan Bracken tried to buy the rights back from Jack Warner. Unwilling to release them to a rival, Warner tested whether he would be allowed to cover later episodes from Churchill's life if he went ahead and made a film.[31]

Moir felt Churchill had some bargaining power, as Warner's rights expired in two years' time if unused. So he asked Warner for the same terms that MGM had offered, with Churchill entitled to approve the film's cast and 'treatment'.[32] Warner professed interest, but caused consternation in the Churchill camp by putting his London lawyer in charge of negotiations: Dr Fletcher was not only a lawyer but 'a Socialist MP'.

By the time the two sides sat down to negotiations in January 1957, Churchill's final 'retirement', set for February, was fast approaching. Moir ruled out Warner's stipulation that the entire Churchill family would have to take part in filming at both Chartwell and Hyde Park Gate and the project was put on ice, pending a personal meeting between Churchill and Jack Warner.

Churchill returned to La Pausa for some last-minute work on *A History of the English-Speaking Peoples* before his retirement took effect on 18 February. Moir warned Churchill's staff that, once the date had passed, he would not be allowed to 'perform any act which would normally be carried out by an Author while continuing his profession': there could be no book prefaces or film or television appearances in connection with any books and no work on film scripts.[33]

With two weeks to go, Churchill was still trying to complete *A History*. He worked on on the epilogue himself, while Denis Kelly tackled the preface and Montague Browne added a chapter on nineteenth-century Germany. 'This was fun and I was rather proud of the result,' he recalled in his memoirs. 'WSC generously gave me £1,000 for my chapter, a large sum in those days, with the remark: "This is a present. It is not for the taxman." The taxman thought otherwise.'[34]

During the final week, both Kelly and Montague Browne helped

Churchill to earn an extra £20,000, provided by Reves, for a last-minute preface to an abridged version of *The Second World War*; to save time, Reves took the risk of selling the preface to the book's other publishers.[35]

Money poured into Churchill's bank once his retirement date passed. Only the Canadian publishers, McClelland Stewart, refused to commute royalties for the remaining three volumes into a lump sum; Cassell paid £70,000 for them after what Moir described as 'considerable but very friendly negotiation';[36] and Dodd added $250,000 for America, estimating that royalties would have reached $450,000.[37]

By April 1957 Churchill's bank accounts held nearly £300,000.[38] However, he was spending £30,000 a year, two-thirds of it on six secretaries, eight full-time and nine part-time staff, a complement that was only likely to grow as he and his wife needed more medical care.[39] At least he had staunched the steady stream of farming losses, which had required cheques of nearly £15,000 the previous year. A disappointing harvest and the Soames' imminent move to a home of their own had persuaded Churchill to give up his farming ambitions completely.[40] Auctioned in July 1957, the remaining land and livestock had fetched a combined sum of £50,000, more than enough to clear the farm overdraft and repay the mortgage.[41]

It was clear, however, that a wise investment strategy would be needed to ensure that the influx of money from *A History of the English-Speaking Peoples* saw the Churchills out to the end of their days.

Churchill told his bank manager Stanley Ball that he wanted very safe investments at one end of the scale, but speculative young oil and gas companies, preferably Canadian, at the other. Ball started at the safer end, investing £80,000 in a mixture of building society deposits and Victory Bonds that carried death duty advantages.[42] All and sundry were asked to suggest ideas for the shares of young Canadian companies. Max Beaverbrook's list was discarded because it contained too many 'blue chip' firms, so Churchill chose three of his own, Van-Tor Oils and Explorations, Permo Oil & Gas and Provo Oil & Gas.[43] Each was active in Alberta, where he had first invested and lost practically everything thirty years earlier. Anthony Montague Browne's friend Tom Hazlerigg, a Canadian specialist at Rea Brothers, a small merchant bank, was entrusted with investing a further £46,000.[44]

All went well at first. After asking for weekly valuations, Churchill watched his portfolio climb in value during July 1957 from £86,000 to £93,000, before it dropped to £77,000 in August.[45] Acknowledging some 'serious falls', Hazlerigg advised Churchill to sit tight while he spent five weeks in Canada investigating the reasons. Storm clouds were gathering over the British economy too, as inflation grew and sterling reserves drained away from London. The Treasury's announcement of a steep rise in interest rates was greeted by silence on the stock exchange floor in September. Uncharacteristically, Churchill continued to sit tight, advised to do so by his former private secretary Jock Colville, now the director of a City merchant bank. By early November his portfolio's value had fallen to £55,000 and the first six months of Churchill's complete retirement had seen his bank balances fall by nearly £50,000.[46]

27

'*Good business*'

Sunset, 1958–65

Exchange rate: $2.80 = £1
Inflation multiples: US x 8; UK x 20

NOW THAT HE had retired as an author and was not allowed to produce any new work, Churchill could only earn extra money by selling the rights to his old books or speeches for use in conjunction with modern technologies such as television, film or sound recording. These were industries in which both Churchill and his advisers lacked commercial expertise.

My Early Life's progress towards the big screen had already been stalled for almost a year, waiting for a face-to-face meeting between Churchill and Jack Warner. Just before that was due to take place in September 1957, internal opposition to the project within Warner Brothers forced Warner to call off the meeting and offer to sell back the film rights to Churchill for £15,000.

Throughout the delay, Churchill's team had kept in touch with Marjorie Thorson at Metro Goldwyn Meyer. Late in October she agreed to revive the project at MGM, but at the expense of cutting back Churchill's guaranteed advance and switching his share of proceeds from 'net profits' to 'distributor's gross receipts', which, she claimed, would pay more quickly, although not as much.[1]

Churchill's advisers' priority was that all his payments should escape tax by qualifying as capital receipts, even though they would not be fixed and would depend on box-office takings. Churchill was equally concerned himself to have some say over the screenplay and over the studio's choice of director or the actor who would play him. MGM undertook to avoid any known 'alcoholic or sex deviant or communist or man scandalously involved with women or having a criminal record'.[2] In the end, after much negotiation the only immediate payment that Churchill received from MGM on signature of the contract was $750; the rest of his guaranteed $150,000 would only be paid after he had approved the screenplay, written by the British dramatist Terence Rattigan. By agreeing to these terms, Churchill's still inexperienced team had unwittingly provided MGM with unlimited scope for delay.

The same innocence had allowed the television rights to *A History of the English-Speaking People* to lie dormant in M & P Investments for almost a year after the programme failed to sell in the American market. Early in 1958, however, a Harry Towers of Towers Films offered $100,000, the price that M & P's co-owner Sir David Cunynghame had always considered realistic.[3] Towers lined up Laurence Olivier as narrator and William Walton as composer, but nobody asked whether he had a buyer, or could afford to pay on his own if he did not.[4] The first payment from Towers arrived nine months late and only one of the four more due in 1959 was made before Churchill authorized the start of legal proceedings. Montague Browne began again the search for a new buyer.[5]

It had been a disappointing year for Churchill's film projects, and on the personal front 1958 proved no happier. Brendan Bracken died of throat cancer in August at the age of only fifty-seven;[6] Churchill's daughter Sarah had been arrested on charges of drunkenness in California after the break-up of her second marriage; and Churchill caught bronchial pneumonia while staying at La Pausa, thereafter needing care from two full-time nurses, which took his expenditure up to £50,000 a year.[7] The only bright spot was his golden wedding anniversary in September, which he marked by a gift to Clementine of £5,000[8] and by a joint celebratory cruise in the Mediterranean.

A year earlier the couple had been lent the use of the motor yacht *Aronia** in Monte Carlo, an experience that brought back fond memories of cruises on HMS *Enchantress*. The *Aronia*, however, was on the small side and smelt of fumes, so on their return to harbour one day the much larger and newer yacht *Christina* caught Churchill's eye. *Christina* belonged to none other than Aristotle Onassis, the Greek ship owner he had met previously and who had invited him to visit to the yacht.

Onassis readily agreed to host an anniversary cruise, during which the Churchills enjoyed the lavish hospitality of one of the world's richest men. Their bodyguard later catalogued *Christina*'s 'lapis lazuli baths, huge hand-carved images of jade, onyx tables, numerous valuable pictures, gold icons, and a bar with models of ships sailing around beneath a glass-topped counter';[9] equally she boasted a cinema, an operating theatre and eleven launches to carry her passengers on shore excursions.

The first cruise was such a success that Onassis offered a second early in 1959, this time from Morocco to the winter sun of the Canary Islands and back to Tangier. In advance of joining the *Christina* on the Moroccan coast, the Churchill party flew out to Marrakech on a plane provided by Onassis's Olympic Airways. There the local governor's car was put at their disposal to carry painting gear, food and the accompanying cases of Pol Roger champagne for picnics in the Atlas Mountains.

Churchill spent a month at La Pausa on his return from the Canary Islands, before a third voyage on *Christina* followed. This time the party sailed down the Italian coast and through the Greek islands to the city Churchill still called Constantinople, but which was now officially Istanbul.

*

* The 180-ton *Aronia* was owned by Jack Billmeir, who had built up his shipping business the Stanhope Line by blockade-running during the Spanish Civil War (1936–9). *Aronia* ran ball bearings from Sweden to Britain during the Second World War.

At home Churchill's staff continued to search for ways to exploit his past work, without undue risk to his reputation. *The Second World War* appeared in an abridged version, the preface carefully dated prior to Churchill's retirement and noting for the benefit of the tax authorities that Denis Kelly had edited the book, rather than the author. This one-volume edition was accompanied by a recording of Churchill's wartime speeches, which earned him a separate £20,000 payment from Decca Records.[10]

Meanwhile, the film version of *My Early Life* suffered another delay. Terence Rattigan had pulled out of writing the screenplay and MGM's chosen replacement, Nigel Balchin, had been so over-awed by his subject that the studio withdrew from the project after judging Balchin's script beyond rescue. Montague Browne tried to find a replacement from the British film industry, but *The Dam Busters*, its greatest post-war success, had earned only just over £500,000 from box-office takings and government subsidies com-bined, so it was far too small to match Hollywood.[11] Without any other avenue at hand, Montague Browne turned to a British-born agent in Beverly Hills, Hugh French. Although he had never pro-duced a film in his life, French saw in the Churchill project a chance of breaking into Hollywood's charmed circle.

While *My Early Life* floundered, Montague Browne decided to revisit screen rights to *The Second World War*, for which an American, Jack Le Vien, had made an approach in August 1958. One of Eisenhower's press officers during the war, Le Vien had met Churchill on several occasions while arranging news conferences at the front. After the war he had headed Pathé News until its col-lapse in 1956. Now he planned to make a television series about the war using the old newsreel material with which he was familiar. This idea conveniently by-passed any need for a personal appear-ance by Churchill (which his retirement ruled out for tax reasons), or for an actor to play his part, but Churchill cut short these discus-sions when his wartime American broadcasting friend Ed Murrow spoke disparagingly of Le Vien.[12]

In May 1959, when Churchill was invited to America by

President Eisenhower, Montague Browne decided to make up his own mind on Le Vien by meeting him in New York. He found that Le Vien had a detailed plan for thirty-nine thirty-minute episodes and had already raised the funding for production costs of up to $750,000 from Screen Gems, a subsidiary of Columbia Pictures. Once Le Vien raised Churchill's guarantee to $75,000 and promised him an extra 10 per cent of receipts once the series grossed $1 million, Churchill was persuaded to sign.[13]

Six months later a producer for America's ABC network (to whom Screen Gems had sold most of its stake) earned a rebuke from Montague Browne for saying to a British newspaper that Churchill was not appearing 'live' for tax reasons.[14] 'Sir Winston was disturbed that the tax question should have been made public,' Montague Browne wrote. 'Sir Winston not unnaturally does not want his personal financial position to be discussed in the Press.'[15]

Le Vien's television series *The Valiant Years* proved a financial and critical success when it appeared at the end of 1959. In contrast, Hugh French could still find no backer for *My Early Life*. Then, in the summer of 1960, a rival agent, Robert Morrell, put together a syndicate of American businessmen, including Fulbrights and Rockefellers, and won the backing of a prominent Hollywood producer, David O. Selznick. Morrell offered Montague Browne £3,000 to secure an option in July. He thought his offer had been accepted, but in fact his radio message had gone astray somewhere between Arkansas and the radio room of the *Christina*, on which Churchill was cruising at the time.[16]

Meanwhile Montague Browne had used the interest of Morrell's syndicate to present Hugh French with an ultimatum: he demanded from French a cash payment of £2,000 for his own option if he wanted to remain in the driving seat. French decided to pay himself and act as the film's producer, securing Churchill's signature in return for the promise of an advance of $175,000 on a 5 per cent share of receipts.[17] Annoyed at his syndicate's last-minute loss of its prize, Morrell wheeled out Senator Fulbright to protest, but Montague Browne stood his ground.

French finally rewarded Montague Browne's loyalty with the help of Jack Le Vien, who persuaded a senior producer friend from Paramount, Martin Rankin, to overcome his initial scepticism and take an interest in the rights to *My Early Life*. Rankin flew to London and, once there, he agreed to match almost every financial and editorial condition that Churchill's team had included in French's option. Paramount signed a contract in October 1960: *My Early Life* seemed to have found a new home at last.[18]

The Churchills had hesitated over their holiday plans at the beginning of 1960, before eventually accepting Aristotle Onassis's invitation of another *Christina* cruise, this time to the Caribbean. When they were allowed to choose guests of their choice, Clementine set her mind against including any of the 'South of France set', which ruled out Emery and Wendy Reves. Informed of this by Onassis, Reves felt excluded.

Later in the year, when Churchill asked if he could stay with Reves and Wendy at La Pausa in September, the reply was no. 'All kinds of intrigues' had been at work, Reves claimed, thereby 'destroying what was a happy and lovely companionship'.[19] Clementine wrote to try to mend bridges, but the friendship had been damaged. Thereafter the Churchills stayed in a penthouse suite at the Hôtel de Paris, which was put at their disposal by Onassis.

By early 1960, the Churchills' reserves had fallen to £150,000, including building society deposits of £35,000 and an investment portfolio of bonds and shares worth £73,000.[20] Concerned that his Canadian shares were still struggling, Churchill asked his new manager at Lloyds Bank, Cedric Watkins, to obtain a second opinion. The bank's stockbrokers, Simon & Coates, advised him to cut his losses, a painful process which took three months complete. Two of Churchill's own choices, Van-Tor Oils and Explorations and Permo Oil & Gas, had cost £10,000, but were now practically worthless and proved impossible to sell;[21] eight other shares, which had cost £46,000, fetched only £16,500. Hazlerigg's one success, the Philip Hill Investment Trust, joined

ICI as Churchill's only remaining shareholdings of any significance.[22]

These losses worried Churchill. His household spending was now running at more than £55,000 a year. His film and greetings card contracts had brought in less than this, £37,500, in the previous twelve months and their income was forecast to fall to £20,000 over the coming year.[23] However, help was to come from an unexpected quarter when Churchill chose this moment to anoint his son Randolph as his official biographer.

On establishing the Literary Trust in 1946, Churchill had told his trustees that he did not want anyone appointed as his biographer for five years after his death, when he hoped that they would consider Randolph for the role. No more had been said on the subject for almost a decade until he told Lord Camrose in 1953 that he thought Randolph had become 'a more serious writer'.[24] However, the real turning point was reached when Randolph undertook a biography of Lord Derby, the nineteenth-century Tory grandee, as suggested by his subject's grandson. Even with research help, the task had taken Randolph six years. On reading the proofs early in 1960, Churchill approved the 'remarkable' result and and indicated that he would be happy for his son to act as his biographer.

The decision to accelerate the appointment was made easier when Anthony Moir advised Churchill that he could exact a capital sum for giving copyright permission for the use of quotations taken from his post-war papers which he still owned – so long as the publishing contracts for the biography were settled while Churchill was still alive. The Literary Trust therefore funded Randolph to start his work on the book with a team of researchers in 1961. It formed a joint venture with *The Daily Telegraph*, called C & T Publications,* to reuse the template of negotiation that they had successfully forged while selling the rights to Churchill's *The*

---

* The name reflects its two shareholders, the Chartwell Literary Trust and *The Daily Telegraph*.

Second World War. The various rights fetched £535,000 worldwide when the syndicate was assembled in 1962: in Britain *The Daily Telegraph* paid £200,000 for newspaper extracts and William Heinemann £150,000 for the book – in each case a multiple of the sums paid for *The Second World War.* The American appetite was more restrained: Houghton Mifflin paid less than it had twenty years earlier for the book, while the newspaper and magazine rights went unsold.[25] Nevertheless a delighted Churchill collected his copyright fee of £50,000 and the sum went untaxed as a capital receipt in the hands of a retired author.[26]

By then, problems had resurfaced with the film of *My Early Life.* Terence Rattigan and Noël Coward had both declined Paramount's invitation to write a screenplay, so the task had fallen to one of Churchill's favourite authors: C. S. Forester of Captain Hornblower fame. His attempt also fell flat: 'It is like a devout Roman Catholic being asked to write the life story of the Pope,' was Hugh French's diagnosis.[27] The film's schedule (and Churchill's payment) was put back a year, while two more writers tried to find a convincing angle for the cinema. Even the mild-mannered Montague Browne was driven to declare the fifth attempt 'utterly useless, so full of impossibilities of taste, of fact and of dramatic construction that I can only regard it as a bad joke'.[28]

By the spring of 1961 the health and energy of both Churchill and Clementine were visibly declining. Clementine spent much of March being treated for depression in a London hospital. Churchill visited her between his own spells of sunshine in Monte Carlo and the Caribbean, where he sailed on *Christina,* calling on the way home at New York. He was not well enough to accept President Kennedy's invitation to visit Washington, D.C. but returned to Britain in time for the 1961 racing season.

The prize money from Churchill's stable had dipped in 1958 and 1959,[29] then recovered to £13,000 in 1960, when an early season victory by Vienna prompted her owner to remain in England rather than travel to the south of France. 'Owing to winning a £6,000 race yesterday I have moved into the Derby sphere which I cannot desert,' he explained to Lord Beaverbrook. 'Good fortune ties me by the legs.'[30] There was to be no Derby victory, but Churchill's five wins that season included one by High Hat, a newcomer to his string. High Hat went on to win £17,000 in 1961, coming first three times and rounding off the season with a fourth place at the Prix de l'Arc de Triomphe.[31] As a result, Major Carey Foster valued High Hat alone at £80,000, and the rest of the stud and racing string at a similar amount.[32] These were not fanciful sums. Another victory by High Hat brought a cash offer of exactly £80,000, with shares in the offering syndicate said to be worth an extra £5,000; Churchill, however, preferred a straight offer of £80,000 from a former aide-de-camp, Tim Rogers, who was now an Irish racehorse breeder.[33]

With High Hat sold, Christopher Soames made a second attempt to address the future of his Churchill's racing interests, which he was keen to take on, if he could afford them. They had enjoyed two wonderful seasons in 1960 and 1961, winning almost £40,000, largely thanks to High Hat and Vienna, he told his father-in-law; but £8,000 a year would be a more normal figure for the eight horses they had left in training.

Together, the costs of the stud and training expenses would amount to £25,000 a year; and only four or possibly five of the mares at his stud met the grade needed to make it a success. Soames suspected that the cost of replacing the other three or four with mares of the right quality would prove too high to be acceptable. The alternative was to reduce the stud's size, by selling the Newchapel site and the poorest mares for a combined £20,000 to £30,000; and then to transfer the good mares, with their foals and fillies, to Soames's new home at Hamsell Manor, where he would keep an eye on them at weekends and Carey Foster could still 'manage the set-up'. By this means, they could halve the stud's running costs, but Churchill would still be able to enjoy his racing for several more years.[34]

In fact, Carey Foster opposed the idea, rather than supporting it as Soames had assumed, and neither Montague Browne nor Moir thought that there was any hurry to break up the stud, which gave Churchill genuine pleasure.[35] Exercising his diplomatic talents, Montague Browne asked Carey Foster to report on the ground at Hamsell Manor, which the vet declared to be exposed, too much on a slope and requiring at least £10,000 spent on stabling and fencing. Moir finally killed off the idea by pointing out that relief from death duty on the Newchapel site would be lost if Churchill's stud moved to Hamsell Manor,[36] at which point Soames gracefully withdrew. Far from being wound down, the stud expanded and its losses increased, reaching almost £10,000 in 1962.[37]

Increasingly frail, the eighty-seven-year-old Churchill missed most of the 1962 racing season.[38] He was in London's Middlesex Hospital for six weeks after breaking his hip in Monaco. While he was convalescing, Montague Browne and Moir won an extra $30,000 guarantee from Le Vien for a new, full-length film of *The Second World War*.[39] The screenplay of *My Early Life*, however, remained stuck with Paramount.

In June 1962 the job of writing it passed from Ernest Gann, a protégé of Noël Coward, to Bryan Forbes, a Briton of whom Montague Browne approved as 'a rather unusual animal in the film world, holding agreeably right-wing views'.[40] Churchill's private secretary liked the result when Forbes finished it in March 1963, but Paramount did not. Exasperated, Hugh French spent the summer negotiating yet another switch of studio, this time to Columbia Pictures and to its producer Carl Foreman, who came to Churchill's story fresh from his triumphs with *The Bridge on the River Kwai* and *The Guns of Navarone*. Foreman insisted that Churchill's share of profits should not be triggered until Columbia had made money on the film, but he increased Churchill's guarantee to £100,000, all paid in cash on signature. Montague Browne resisted the temptation to ask whether Foreman had not meant dollars and immediately accepted.[41]

*

His powers clearly fading, Churchill returned to Monte Carlo for his eighth and last cruise on *Christina* at the end of 1963's summer. Montague Browne's bulletins to Lord Beaverbrook became sadder and sadder that autumn as Sarah's third husband died suddenly and Diana took her own life at the age of fifty-four. 'Sir Winston is depressed; Lady Churchill very depressed,' he wrote during October.[42]

At least there was some good news on the film front: Foreman had finally found a cinematic angle on *My Early Life*, as he concentrated on the strained relationship between father and son, which he described as a story 'of classical stature and almost biblical flavour'.[43] Negotiations on the film moved quickly when Montague Browne travelled to New York to settle a separate copyright action against Colepix, a record company. It turned out to be a subsidiary of Columbia Pictures, allowing the company's president to ease the settlement of the copyright dispute by increasing Churchill's profit share on their film from 5 to 6 per cent. Another nine years were to pass before *Young Winston* (1972) reached the silver screen, but Montague Browne returned from a second visit to New York in December 1963 clutching the largest single cheque that Churchill had ever earned, an occasion he recalled in his memoir, *Long Sunset*:

> I returned to London by air, went directly to Hyde Park Gate and found WSC dining with Violet Bonham Carter. I produced the cheque for £100,000 with the pride of a retriever emerging from a turbulent river with a particularly fine duck. WSC sent for his chequebook and said that he was going to give me £25,000. My mouth watered but this was totally impossible.[44]

A secretary relayed Churchill's final instructions to his bank: £30,000 was to go into his current account, £65,000 into his investment account, and £5,000 for Montague Browne.[45]

Le Vien's full-length film of *The Second World War* had also found a strong backer in Twentieth Century-Fox's Darryl F.

Zanuck, who paid Churchill an extra $35,000 for the rights.[46] Montague Browne struggled to keep the peace between Twentieth Century-Fox and Columbia Pictures as Foreman demanded late cuts in *The Finest Hours*, which he claimed had strayed on to the territory of *My Early Life*. Next Le Vien caused problems by releasing a recording of his film's soundtrack, just as Moir and Montague Browne were on the point of landing a new deal with Decca Records. The company was poised to pay £20,000 to release new recordings found of Churchill's wartime speeches to mark his ninetieth birthday. 'Good business,' Churchill noted to Moir and Montague Browne when they retrieved the situation.[47]

Churchill's ninetieth birthday also provided the pretext for Le Vien to propose making another documentary, this one based on Churchill's book *Painting as a Pastime*. Joyce Hall, who had used reproductions of Churchill's paintings on his company's greetings cards for more than a decade, paid $150,000 to buy the American rights for his company's own television channel.[48] Throughout, Moir and Montague Browne continued to defend Churchill's interests: Moir warned that they should limit the number of paintings used to prevent a final attempt by the Inland Revenue to brand Churchill as a professional artist, while Montague Browne removed a reference to Churchill's bodyguard allegedly signing his own paintings with Churchill's initials.

By the autumn of 1964 Churchill was too unwell to take any further interest in his business affairs. They were left to Clementine, guided by Moir and Montague Browne. She considered exiling a herd of Belted Galloways from Chartwell's fields 'in the interests of economy', but the cattle were reprieved when she was told that replacement mowers would probably cost more.[49] Clementine agreed that Christopher Soames should take over responsibility for her husband's racehorses in 1965, paying Churchill a sliding scale of any winnings.[50] Montague Browne issued a press statement explaining that the stud would carry on, but that Churchill was bringing his career as a racehorse owner to a close.[51] His racing account at Weatherby & Sons was closed at the end of October, before Sun Hat recorded a last victory in Paris early in December. The winner's purse brought Churchill's career winnings up to £90,000 and he had sold bloodstock worth £120,000.[52]

Churchill's final battle was fought with that most constant enemy of his long life: the taxman. This time he was American. The US Internal Revenue Service claimed in 1963 that for at least the four previous years (and possibly longer) Churchill should have been paying US tax on any earnings with an American connection.[53]

Moir had always assumed that the double tax treaty between Britain and America meant that no American tax had to be paid if none was owed in Britain. However, a successful tax avoidance scheme in one country does not automatically apply in another. In a letter running to twenty-two pages, Churchill's American lawyers at Davis Polk Wardwell & Co. estimated that Churchill owed at least $23,000 in US tax on Le Vien's film *The Valiant Years* and advised complete disclosure of all Churchill's past and future earnings that carried any American link.

Late in 1963, while still fit enough to do so, Churchill sent his own letter to the US authorities in the hope that they might be persuaded to desist in their claims, but all he achieved was additional time for his staff to reply in greater detail. They had still not managed to do so by the autumn of 1964, when Davis Polk Wardwell suggested sending a partner over to London to help expedite matters. Appalled at the likely cost, Moir suggested that Churchill's American lawyers should instead meet his private secretary while he was in New York on other business. Three Davis Polk Wardwell partners confronted Montague Browne to tell him that Churchill ought to disclose all his US-related earnings since 1941, including the £100,000 that he had just been paid by Columbia Pictures.

On his return to London, Montague Browne urged Moir to resist their advice, explaining that he had told the American lawyers that: 'Sir Winston's fortune was not on the scale that many people imagined. I felt that they might trim their sails appropriately if they were aware that they were not dealing with a millionaire.'[54]

Moir wrote before Christmas 1964 to tell his American colleagues that Churchill would not be disclosing the Columbia Pictures payment. He invited them to provide 'chapter and verse' if they disagreed with the decision.[55] Before they could do so, the ninety-year-old Churchill suffered a serious stroke at the beginning of 1965 and slipped into a coma from which he never awoke. He died on 24 January 1965, seventy years to the day after his father.

TIME-LIFE honoured its most famous contributor by sending a team of forty journalists and photographers to cover his state funeral, which took place six days later beneath the dome of St Paul's Cathedral in London. While Churchill was laid to rest in Bladon churchyard, just outside the walls of Blenheim Palace, the magazine's staff was already on the way home, preparing their story in a plane especially fitted out as a flying newsroom and photographic studio. As they did so, Madame Odette Pol-Roger in France instructed that a black band of mourning be placed around the label of her family's champagne.

EPILOGUE

Exchange rates: 1971 $2.40 = £1
1995 $1.60 = £1
Inflation multiples: 1971 US x 6, UK x 13
1995 US x 1.5, UK x 1.7

C HURCHILL HAD SIGNED the most recent version of his will in 1961, adding two short codicils before he died. It formed only a portion of the financial legacy which he left to his family since the Chartwell Literary Trust had already funnelled the major part of the income from *The Second World War* to his children and grandchildren and was contracted to do the same again with most of the revenue from the rights to his official biography.

The will itself left all Churchill's literary works and recordings to Clementine, together with his 'State and private' papers, which he hoped she would give on her death to the trust that owned his pre-war papers, if she had not 'disposed' of them beforehand. However, he was at pains to state that she should not 'feel in any way hindered or discouraged' from making up her own mind about their final destination.

He also gave her all of his many paintings at Chartwell, enjoining her once more 'to feel no reluctance or hesitation' about selling them. In contrast, he did not want his 'heirlooms' sold: on Clementine's death the medals, trophies and souvenirs were to pass to each successive generation's male heir 'according to seniority in tail male'. The remainder of the estate, after cash gifts for employees (including £10,000 for Anthony Montague Browne and £2,000 for Anthony Moir) was to be divided into two parts: one-third for

Clementine and two-thirds for his children in equal shares, without any larger portion now for Randolph.[1]

Within a month of his death the provisional value of Churchill's estate was published as £304,044 before tax.[2] During the four years that it took to settle all its affairs, the value must have risen appreciably, because even after all Churchill's papers and most of his paintings had been exempted from estate duty, the final amount of tax paid at a rate of 65 per cent reached £260,000.[3]

Churchill's late difficulty with the United States' Inland Revenue Service (IRS) fell to his executors – Clementine, her daughter Mary and the former private secretary Jock Colville – to resolve. Led by Colville, they tried to enlist the support of the British government, but were politely rebuffed and had to settle with the IRS. They used the more liquid funds in his estate to pay what was owed and to meet the first instalment of estate duty in Britain. However, they needed to find another £150,000 to pay the remaining duty owed.[4]

Rather than stay in Chartwell, Clementine chose to hand over the house to the National Trust straight after her husband's death. She was keen for it to be open to the public as soon as possible, with the appearance of the family home it had been during the 1930s. The paintings and furniture that had made it so had never formed part of Churchill's gift to the National Trust, so Clementine decided with her fellow executors to offer to sell these now to the National Land Fund. The Fund was a government body established to accept items of historic interest in lieu of estate duty, before it passed them to bodies such as the National Trust for public display. It operated by negotiating a market value with the executors of estates; it then deducted the estate duty theoretically due from the price it would pay, but added a *douceur*, or inducement, equivalent to one-quarter of the tax.[5] In Churchill's case, the Fund easily accepted the valuation of the executors' expert, just over £100,000, not least because the paintings included a work by Claude Monet, *Pont de Londres*. The Fund employed its usual formula to pay £56,000 of Churchill's estate duty bill, leaving the executors to find a final £95,000.[6]

was keen for the papers to end up at Churchill College, but that he had little money of his own as a result of his father's extravagant spending.[12] Colville had tried but failed to find a wealthy American prepared to buy the papers, then to deposit them in Cambridge; he therefore asked the government to step in and pay 'say £100,000 or perhaps £120,000'. He went on:

> Sotheby's, as very rough estimate, say that they might very well fetch something in the neighbourhood of £2 million, and even if one assumes that half of them, being state papers, could never be sold, the remaining half might well on this basis be worth £1 million.[13]

In reply, Sir Burke explained that – 'aside from any question of who actually "owns" the papers' – no public funds were available. The decision might lead to an eventual sale, Colville warned.[14]

There matters rested until seventeen years later in 1988 when Martin Gilbert finished writing the eighth and last volume of Churchill's official biography. The head of the Cabinet Office's Historical Section, Patricia Andrews, decided that the papers must be opened up to authorized access, as stipulated in the original estate duty exemption. However, she was shocked by the response received from Peregrine Churchill, the son of Churchill's brother Jack and by then a trustee. He explained that he had ordered the pre-war papers to be moved to Churchill College to improve their care on becoming a trustee in 1980, but he went on to register his concerns about the funding of both the college and its archive centre. As a result he hinted that the trustees were considering other plans for the papers' future.

The government's impression that a sale might be in the offing again was reinforced when young Winston stepped down as a trustee, to be replaced by a London solicitor, Ian Montrose, whose correspondence Andrews of the Cabinet Office soon described as 'hostile'. In 1989 the new trustees asked Sotheby's to conduct a fresh valuation of the Churchill papers and the Cabinet Office heard unofficially before the end of the year that the trustees hoped to sell to a public body such as the British Library to avoid estate duty; by May 1990 the government heard that the asking price could be as high as £15 million.[15]

There was a lull in 1990 while the trustees reorganized the trust to complete their tax preparations for a sale: young Winston now relinquished his direct interest in favour of a series of family discretionary trusts. In March 1991, when the trustees finally broke their cover, they did so from an unexpected quarter: they chose a recently retired senior minister, Norman Tebbit, to forward a memorandum to the prime minister of the day, John Major. It based their case for a sale on the trustees' concerns about the 'modest' scale of Churchill College's funding. It followed that, if they followed Clementine's lead in simply gifting the papers to the college, the college might one day sell them.

It would be better, they argued, if the government bought the papers and gifted them permanently to either the British Library or Churchill College. Norman Tebbit's covering letter told the prime minister that he understood the price would not be 'huge'.[16] However, at an unofficial lunch with the trustees soon afterwards, the cabinet secretary Sir Robin Butler heard that they were looking for a price of £12.5 million, based on Sotheby's valuation of the entire set at £20 million (less a deduction for estate duty, plus the addition of a *douceur*). They told Sir Robin that their preference was to sell to the government or to a private buyer, who would redeposit the papers with Churchill College, but if both possibilities failed they planned to auction the papers at Sotheby's.[17]

The government wished to keep all Churchill's papers together, whether pre- or post-war, public or private, but it remained unwilling to spend public money on buying the 'state' papers without testing the trustees' claim to ownership in the courts. It commissioned a legal opinion from two senior counsel which made uncomfortable reading: the disputed documents had certainly started life as 'state' papers, they said, and should never have been transferred by Churchill to the Chartwell Trust in 1946. However, the government had not lodged any objection then or since, so the case for starting now, some forty-five years later, was 'but weakly arguable'.[18]

In 1993 hopes briefly rose that Conrad Black, the owner of *The Daily Telegraph*, would step in as a private buyer, but this plan fell through. The government steeled itself to start legal proceedings, while at the same time it encouraged private negotiations between the trustees, Cambridge University and the National Heritage Memorial Fund. The Major government was introducing a new National Lottery from which the Fund was due to receive some of the money raised. By the end of 1994, after negotiations lasting almost a year, all parties agreed a provisional price of £12.5 million, expressed as covering Churchill's private papers only, while the 'state' papers were gifted separately without payment.

Officially, Cambridge University acquired the collection with the help of lottery money. It then passed the papers to a new Sir Winston Churchill Archives Trust, which reunited them with the post-war papers at Churchill College, Cambridge. There they remain in perpetuity, freely available to researchers. Churchill's contribution to his family's fortunes continues, however: the purchase price of £12.5 million did not include ownership of the copyright of the papers, which will continue to reward his heirs until it finally expires on 1 January 2039.

I have told the story of Churchill and his money without judgement. Clearly some of his actions or omissions would not survive scrutiny by the standards of transparency expected of today's politicians. During his early years as a minister, for example, Churchill accepted gifts of cash and kind from Sir Ernest Cassel; while responsible for South Africa's government as colonial secretary after the First World War, he held on to his South African mining shareholdings; and within a year of losing office in 1922 he earned a substantial fee from two oil companies in return for lobbying his former ministerial colleagues. After the Second World War, while leader of the Opposition and then prime minister, he accepted interest-free loans from a national newspaper, *The Daily Telegraph*.

A more interesting question is whether Churchill would have survived scrutiny by the standards of his own day if the details of his finances had become more public. Before the First World War, cartoonists lampooned Churchill for supporting the Liberal government's attacks through taxation on the wealth of the landed aristocracy, while he repaired regularly to Blenheim Palace for weekends of luxury. However, the press largely exempted Churchill from the charges of 'money corruption' which it pursued vigorously against other government members, notably Lloyd George.

The way in which Churchill dealt with the large, personal cheques sent to him before the First World War by his constituent James Caird tends to vindicate this judgement of the press. There is no sign, either, that Churchill ever lined his own pocket while controlling large amounts of public expenditure as First Lord of the Admiralty or minister of munitions, at the beginning or end of the First World War. The evidence of Churchill's bank accounts is that he did not take money from Jewish groups in return for his anti-Nazi campaigning during the 1930s, although there have been claims to the contrary. What might have caused him political trouble, had it been better known at the time, was his tax-paying record.

Until he was thirty years old Churchill was content to subscribe to the prevailing Victorian view that the recently introduced income tax was fairly set and collected: even for those at the top of the tree, the combined rates of direct and indirect taxation seldom exceeded 20 per cent until 1906, when the Liberal government came to power. Furthermore, Churchill fully supported its introduction in 1908 of a 'super-tax' for higher earners, possibly because it only added 2.5 per cent on top of income tax rates of less than 5 per cent – and he was not earning enough to fall within its bracket at the time.

His attitude to taxation changed when income and super-tax rates rose above 50 per cent during the First World War and, more importantly, when they stayed there afterwards. This coincided with a period when Churchill did not have the funds to pay his tax bills as they fell due, because he had already spent the money: it was during the 1920s that Churchill began a battle of wits with Britain's tax authorities that was to last for the rest of his life.

Most of his wealthy contemporaries played a similar game, but Churchill subtly added the power of his public position. Twice while chancellor of the exchequer, for example, Churchill summoned to his personal aid the chairman of the Inland Revenue, a government agency for which chancellor he was politically responsible. During the Second World War, Churchill was certainly economical with the truth when he declared to the Inland Revenue the date of his retirement as an author and the nature of his Sunday newspaper deals.

After the war, when taxes on income reached an eye-watering 97.5 per cent, Churchill rarely considered any business proposition unless his advisers assured him that he could present it to the Inland Revenue as a capital receipt, which would escape tax, rather than as income. The Inland Revenue had learned by experience during the war that, if Churchill exercised his right as a taxpayer to challenge its ruling in private before a tribunal of lay commissioners, he was likely to win the benefit of any doubt. It therefore tended to shy away from a direct challenge to the tax treatment which Churchill and his advisers submitted. Its real weapon was to threaten to appeal if it lost at the tribunal, because then the next stage of proceedings would be open to the public. On the one occasion after the war when the Inland Revenue threatened to take this step, Churchill retreated immediately, under protest, and paid the disputed amount of tax.

It was a rare victory. That Churchill emerged the winner from almost every other skirmish with the taxman over forty years is ruefully attested by a thick Inland Revenue file at the National Archives, which contains the records of its dealings with the greatest British leader of the twentieth century. The file was recently declassified; intriguingly, a second remains closed until 2040.

ACKNOWLEDGEMENTS

I am grateful to the following for permission to quote from letters or documents of which they own the copyright or which they have in their possession: Curtis Brown, London on behalf of the Beneficiaries of the Estate of Winston S. Churchill (copyright © The Beneficiaries of the Estate of Winston S. Churchill); the Master, Fellows and Scholars of Churchill College, Cambridge (copyright © The Master, Fellows and Scholars of Churchill College, Cambridge); the Sir Winston Churchill Archive Trust; the Churchill Centre; the Beaverbrook Foundation; the Henry W. and Albert A. Berg Collection of English and American Literature, the New York Public Library (Astor, Lenox and Tilden Foundations); Douglas and Valerie Boud; Harriet Bowes-Lyon; Elizabeth Buxton; the 140 Trustee Co. on behalf of Viscount Camrose; the earl of Dundee; ESI Media; Citibank NA, London Branch; the partners of Fladgate LLP; Andrew and Elizabeth Graham-Dixon; Ian Hamilton; the Houghton Mifflin Harcourt Publishing Co.; the partners of Knight Frank LLP; Stephen Knowles; Little, Brown Book Group Ltd.; the Hon. Richard Lloyd George; Lloyds Bank PLC; the Countess Mountbatten of Burma; Macmillan Publishers Ltd.; News UK & Ireland Ltd.; Orion Publishing Group; Princeton University Library; the Rothschild Archive; the Seven Pillars of Wisdom Trust; Simon & Schuster Inc.; Ian Thorton-Kemsley; and Time Inc. Crown copyright material is reproduced with the permission of the Controller of Her Majesty's Stationery Office and the Queen's Printer for Scotland.

*

Before her death in 2014, Lady Soames most kindly gave me permission to examine those statements of her father's bank account which do not survive in his own archive, but do survive in the Lloyds Banking Group Archives. I am also most appreciative of the encouragement given to me by Randolph Churchill (now Winston Churchill's senior direct male descendant) and of his help in securing my access to the papers of Fladgate LLP, the solicitors to his great-grandfather. In no sense do these acknowledgements of help from the Churchills mean that they have approved the contents of this book, because they have never sought such control. Lady Williams, née Jane Portal, who served as one of Churchill's private secretaries after the Second World War, was very kind to share her memories of the people who helped Churchill with his finances at the time.

I acknowledge my debt to several published works which I found invaluable when researching the financial world into which Churchill was born: notably Sir John Habakkuk's *Death, Marriage and Estates 1660–1880*; Sir David Cannadine's *Decline and Fall of the English Aristocracy*; David Kynaston's *The City of London;* and Martin Daunton's history of Britain's tax system, *Just Taxes*. I am also indebted to the authors of two works that impinge on important aspects of Churchill's finances: Stefan Buczacki's *Churchill and Chartwell* (which chronicles Churchill's dealing with all his many homes); and David Reynolds' *In Command of History: Churchill, Fighting and Writing The Second World War*.

No account of the works about Churchill to which I owe a debt could possibly be complete without the inclusion of Randolph Churchill and Martin Gilbert's official biography, *Winston Spencer Churchill*. It was their giant work, with its companion volumes of Churchill's documents, letters and speeches, which first sparked my love of history.

My chief thanks for help during the primary research required to write this book go to Dr Allen Packwood, the director, and all his staff at the Churchill Archives Centre of Churchill College, Cambridge. They have been unfailingly helpful and cheerful in dealing with my requests for literally hundreds of spools of micro-fiche material (as it then was before the archive's recent conversion to digital form); in addition, Allen Packwood has helped me to trace holders of private papers and, with Natalie Adams, their copyright owners.

Very few of Churchill's personal papers lodged in his archive remain restricted; the main exception is the working papers of his accountants Wood, Willey & Co. However, James Wood's lengthy reports to Churchill are open to researchers, so it is hard to conceive that there will be major revelations when these papers are opened on 1 January 2036.

The Churchill Archives Centre also houses the main papers of Churchill's mother, father, brother, private secretary Edward Marsh and (above all for this book) of his bank manager for nearly twenty years, William Bernau. Helpfully Bernau kept his personal notes of private meetings with Churchill and copies of the internal memos which he exchanged about Churchill's account with his superiors at the bank. Bernau's son later presented these papers to Churchill.

In Britain, I am also grateful to the staff of the following libraries for their help in researching papers among their collections: the National Archives at Kew; the British Library; the University of Southampton; the University of Reading; and the London Metropolitan Archive. The staff of the London Library has helped me to trace some of the more obscure published works which I have consulted and the library itself has afforded unequalled working space in the heart of St James's Square in London.

Turning to papers held in private hands, I am most grateful to the head of Lloyds Banking Group Archives, Karen Sampson, and to her assistant Silvia Gallotti: Lloyd's archive holds records of not only its dealings with Churchill after the Second World War, but its reluctant rescue of Churchill's private bank, Cox & Co., in 1923.

I am also grateful to Melanie Aspey, director of the Rothschild Archive, and her staff for help when I researched the banking records of Churchill's father, Lord Randolph: the Rothschild Archive is now rehoused in splendid quarters at the heart of the bank's new London building. I am obliged to the partners of Fladgate LLP, particularly Simon Ekins, for allowing me to see the records of Anthony Moir, Churchill's principal solicitor after the Second World War. I was also fortunate to be allowed to examine the Camrose papers which give a first-hand account of several important episodes in Churchill's financial life: I am grateful for the hospitality of Mr and Mrs Jeremy Deedes while I researched these papers and to Viscount Camrose for the right to quote from them. I am also grateful for the help of Anne Jensen while research-ing the management papers of *The Times*, held in the News UK & Ireland Archive in north London.

Churchill's life and finances were closely bound to the United States through ties of family, friendship, publishing, stockbroking, banking and lecturing. I am grateful to the staff of the following American libraries who helped me in my research: the Seeley G. Mudd Manuscript Library and Rare Books and Special Collections Library of Princeton University; the Rare Books and Manuscripts Library of Columbia University; the Houghton Library of Harvard University; the Beinecke Rare Book and Manuscript Library of Yale University; the Henry W. and Albert A. Berg Collection of the New York Public Library; and the Library of Congress, Washington, D.C. I am especially grateful to my Oxford history contemporary, Sir Peter Westmacott, to his wife Susie, Lady Westmacott, and their staff at the British Embassy in Washington for looking after me so well during two research visits.

Sadly some papers do not survive. Those of Churchill's main inter-war British publisher, Thornton Butterworth, fell victim to either the liquidator of his publishing business or to a German bomb; the pre-war papers of Cassell & Co. were definitely destroyed by fire after a bombing raid during the Blitz. Brendan Bracken ordered his chauffeur to burn his papers after his death – a great shame for historians as it robs us of the records kept by Churchill's self-styled 'honorary man of business'. I suspect the burned papers must include Churchill's stockbroking records for the months leading up to his financial rescue of March 1938, which Bracken arranged: it is the only small section of Churchill's investment records which is missing. In the same vein, I suspect that Bernard Baruch weeded out much of his private financial correspondence with Churchill from his otherwise immaculately ordered archive: many of Baruch's letters and cables appear in Churchill's papers, but not in his own.

As a new author I am particularly grateful for the early advice and encouragement I received from two friends in the literary world, Gill Leeming, née Coleridge, and Paul Langridge. Many others have helped me at some stage of the journey and I thank them all: James Bettley, Iain Butters, John Adam Fox, Tom Godfrey-Faussett, Anthony Greayer, John Harley, John Heskett, Jonathan Martin, Edward Paice, Jay Parini, Lee Pollock, Andrew Pomfret, David Reed, Sir Hew Strachan, Tim and Mary Seymour, Alan Warner, Andrew Whiffin, Margaret Willes and John Wilson.

I am especially grateful for the guidance and early confidence of my agent, Andrew Lownie. I have been lucky to benefit from the editing and copy-editing skills of Ian Pindar and Gill Paul respectively. I am grateful for the copyright help of Frederick Courtright and The Permissions Company and am indebted to the limitless patience and wise guidance of my publishers, Richard Milbank, assisted by Georgina Blackwell, at Head of Zeus and Stephen Morrison, assisted by Peter Horoszko, at Picador USA.

Last but not least I want to thank my family who have had to put up with a substantial extra presence in the Lough household for several years; nonetheless they have given me invaluable help in proofreading and de-contaminating my text of financial jargon, so far as is possible. This is especially true of my daughters Rosie and Kate, and above all of my wife Felicity, to whom I owe more than I can express in print. All remaining errors are of course my sole responsibility.

David Lough
Penshurst, April 2015

SOURCES

United Kingdom

The Churchill Archives Centre, Churchill College, University of Cambridge

Winston S. Churchill papers (Chartwell and Churchill Collections)

Lord Randolph Churchill papers

Lady Randolph Churchill papers

Lady Churchill (Clementine Spencer-Churchill) papers

John S. Churchill papers

W. H. Bernau papers

E. Marsh papers

The British Library, London

Macmillan & Co. papers

The Blenheim papers

Northcliffe papers

Fladgate LLP, London

Anthony Moir papers

Lloyds Banking Group Archives, London

Winston S. Churchill bank statements (by kind permission of the late Lady Soames)

Cox & Co. papers

Lloyds Bank papers

London Metropolitan Archives

GLC Architect's Department papers

Hodder & Stoughton papers

Times Newspapers Ltd. Archive, News UK and Ireland London
The Times management papers

Private collection, England
Lord Camrose papers

Reading University (Special Collections), Reading
Macmillan & Co. papers
Longmans, Green & Co. papers

Rothschild Archives, London
Lord Randolph Churchill bank ledgers and accounts

Southampton University, Southampton
Mountbatten papers (Sir Ernest Cassel)

United States

Princeton University, New Jersey (Department of Rare Books and Special Collections)
Bernard M. Baruch papers (Seeley G. Mudd Manuscripts Library)
The Scribner Archive (Firestone Library)

Columbia University, New York (Rare Books and Manuscripts Library)
Daniel Longwell papers
Paul R. Reynolds papers
Averell Harriman papers
Belmont Family papers
Pulitzer papers
Hodder & Stoughton papers
Curtis Brown papers

Harvard University, Massachusetts (Houghton Library)
Houghton Mifflin papers

Yale University, Connecticut (Beinecke Rare Book & Manuscript Library)

Lady St Helier papers

Library of Congress, Washington, D.C.

Henry & Clare Luce papers

Moreton Frewen papers

New York Public Library, New York

Sir Edward Marsh papers

A. P. Watt papers

BIBLIOGRAPHY

Alanbrooke, Lord (ed. Alex Danchev and Daniel Todman), *War Diaries 1939–1945* (Weidenfeld & Nicolson, 2001)

Ashley, Maurice, *Churchill as Historian* (Martin Secker & Warburg, 1968)

Atkinson, A. B., *Top Incomes in the United Kingdom over the Twentieth Century* (University of Oxford, Discussion Papers in Economic and Social History, Number 43, January 2002)

Attenborough, Wilfred, *Churchill and the 'Black Dog' of Depression* (Palgrave Macmillan, 2014)

Balsan, Consuelo Vanderbilt, *The Glitter and the Gold* (George Mann, 1973)

Baruch, Bernard, *My Own Story* (Henry Holt, 1957)

Birkenhead, earl of, *F. E.: The Life of F. E. Smith, First Earl of Birkenhead* (Eyre & Spottiswoode, 1959)

Blake, Robert and Luis, Roger (eds), *Churchill: A Major New Assessment of His Life in Peace and War* (Oxford University Press, 1993)

Blow, Michael, 'Churchill in Cuba', *Quarterly Journal of Military History*, 3:1, autumn 1990

Blunt, Wilfrid Scawen, *My Diaries: Being a Personal Narrative of Events 1888–1914* (Martin Secker, 1920)

Bonham Carter, Violet, *Winston Churchill as I Knew Him* (Eyre & Spottiswoode and Collins, 1965)

Boothby, Robert, *Recollections of a Rebel* (Hutchinson, 1979)

Brown, Jane, *Lutyens and the Edwardians* (Viking, 1996)

Buczacki, Stefan, *Churchill & Chartwell* (Frances Lincoln, 2007)

Butz, Arthur R, 'Was Churchill's Gold Bug Jewish?', *Journal of Historical Review*, January 2002

Cannadine, David, *The Decline and Fall of the British Aristocracy* (Yale University Press, 1990)

——, *In Churchill's Shadow: Confronting the Past in Modern Britain* (Allen Lane, 2002)

——, *The Aristocratic Adventurer* (Penguin, 2005)

Churchill, Randolph S., *Youth: Winston S. Churchill 1874–1900* (Heinemann, 1966)

——, *Young Statesman: Winston S. Churchill 1901–1914* (Heinemann, 1967)

——, *Companion Volume I, parts 1, 2 1874–1900* (Heinemann, 1967)

——, *Companion Volume II, parts 1, 2, 3 1901–1914* (Heinemann, 1969)

Churchill, Sarah, *A Thread in the Tapestry* (Andre Deutsch, 1967)

Churchill, Winston S., *The Story of the Malakand Field Force* (Longmans & Co., 1899)

——, *Lord Randolph Churchill* (Macmillan & Co., 1906)

——, *My African Journey* (Hodder & Stoughton, 1908)

——, *Liberalism and the Social Problem* (Hodder & Stoughton, 1909)

——, *The World Crisis* (Scribner's Sons, 1923–31)

——, *My Early Life* (Thornton Butterworth, 1930)

——, *Thoughts and Adventures* (Thornton Butterworth, 1932)

——, *Marlborough: His Life and Times Volumes I–IV* (G. G. Harrap & Co., 1933–8)

——, *Great Contemporaries* (Thornton Butterworth, 1938)

——, *Arms and the Convenant* (G.G. Harrap & Co., 1938)

——, *Into Battle* (Cassell & Co., 1941)

——, *The Unrelenting Struggle* (Cassell & Co., 1942)

——, *The End of the Beginning* (Cassell & Co., 1943

——, *Onwards to Victory* (Cassell & Co., 1944)

——, *The Dawn of Liberation* (Cassell & Co., 1945)

——, *Secret Session Speeches* (Simon & Schuster, 1946)

——, *The Second World War* (Houghton Mifflin Co., 1948–53)

——, *Painting as a Pastime* (Odhams, 1948)

——, *A History of the English-Speaking Peoples* (Cassell & Co., 1956–8)

Clarke, Peter, *Mr Churchill's Profession* (Bloomsbury, 2012)

Cohen, Ronald L., *Bibliography of the Writings of Sir Winston Churchill Volumes 1, 2* (Thoemmes Continuuum, 2006)

Colville, John, *The Churchillians* (Weidenfeld & Nicolson, 1981)

——, *The Fringes of Power: Downing Street Diaries 1939–1945* (Hodder & Stoughton, 1985)

Coombs, David, with Churchill, Minnie, *Sir Winston Churchill's Life through his Paintings* (Chaucer Press, 2003)

Cornwallis-West, George, *Edwardian Hey-Days* (Putnam, 1930)

Cornwallis-West, Mrs George, *The Reminiscences of Lady Randolph Churchill* (Edward Arnold, 1908)

Courcy, Anne de, *The Viceroy's Daughters: The Lives of the Curzon Sisters* (Orion, 2000)

Cox, Howard, *Mass Circulation Periodicals and the Harmsworth Legacy in the British Popular Press* (European History Association, 2008)

Crockett, Richard (ed.), *My Dear Max: The Letters of Brendan Bracken to Lord Beaverbrook 1925–1958* (Historians' Press, 1990)

Davis, Richard, *The English Rothschilds* (Collins, 1983)

Daunton, Martin, *Trusting Leviathan: the politics of taxation in Britain, 1799–1914* (Cambridge University Press, 2001)

——, *Just Taxes: the politics of taxation in Britain, 1914–1979* (Cambridge University Press, 2002)

Deedes, William, 'Churchill: Fortunes of War', lecture to International Churchill Society, July 1999

Eden, Clarissa, Haste, Cate (ed.), *A Memoir: From Churchill to Eden* (Orion, 2007)

Egremont, Max, *Balfour: A Life of Arthur James Balfour* (William Collins, 1980)

Elson, Robert T., *The World of Time Inc.* (Atheneum, 1973)

Ferguson, Niall, *The Ascent of Money* (Allen Lane, 2008)

——, *Rothschild: The World's Banker* (Weidenfeld & Nicolson, 1998)

——, *Civilization* (Allen Lane, 2011)

Field, Leslie, *Bendor: the Golden Duke of Westminster* (Weidenfeld & Nicolson, 1983)

Flower, Desmond, *Fellows in Foolscap: Memoirs of a Publisher* (Robert Hale, 1991)

Foster, R. F., *Lord Randolph Churchill* (Oxford University Press, 1981)

Ghaemi, Nassir, *A First-Rate Madness* (The Penguin Press, 2011)

Gilbert, Martin, *Companion Volume II, parts 1, 2, 3 1901–1914* (Heinemann, 1969)

——, *Companion Volume III, parts 1, 2 1914–1916* (Heinemann, 1972)

——, *Companion Volume IV parts 1, 2, 3 1917–1922* (Heinemann, 1977)

——, *Companion Volume V, parts 1, 2, 3 1922–1939* (Heinemann, 1979–1982)

——, *Winston S. Churchill III 1914–1916* (Heinemann, 1971)

——, *Winston S. Churchill IV 1917–1922* (Heinemann, 1975)

——, *Winston S. Churchill V 1922–1939* (Heinemann, 1976)

——, *Winston S. Churchill VI: Finest Hour 1939–1941* (Heinemann, 1983)

——, *Winston S. Churchil VII: Road to Victory 1941–1945* (Heinemann, 1986)

——, *Winston S. Churchill VIII: 'Never Despair' 1946–1965* (Heinemann, 1988)

——, *The Churchill War Papers parts 1, 2, 3 1939–1941* (Heinemann, 1993–2000)

——, *Winston Churchill: The Wilderness Years* (Macmillan, 1981)

——, *In Search of Churchill* (HarperCollins, 1994)

——, *Churchill: A Life* (Macmillan, 2001)

——, *Churchill and the Jews* (Simon & Schuster, 2007)

——, *The Churchill Documents, Volume 17, Testing Times, 1942* (Hillsdale College Press, 2014)

Gilbert, Martin (ed.), *Winston Churchill and Emery Reeves: Correspondence 1937–1964* (University of Texas Press, 1997)

Gilmour, David, *Curzon: Imperial Statesman* (John Murray, 1994)

Graebner, Walter, *My Dear Mr. Churchill* (Houghton Mifflin Co., 1965)

Grant, James, *Bernard Baruch: The Adventures of a Wall Street Legend* (Simon & Schuster, 1983)

Green, David, *The Churchills of Blenheim* (Constable, 1984)

Greville, Daisy, Countess of Warwick, *Life's Ebb and Flow* (W. Morrow, 1929)

Hamblin, Grace, 'Chartwell Memories', lecture to International Churchill Society, October 1987

Hamilton, Nigel, *The Full Monty: Montgomery of Alamein* (Allen Lane, 2001)

Harrod, R. R., *The Prof* (Macmillan, 1959)

Hart-Davis, Duff (ed.), *King's Counsellor: Abdication and War – the Diaries of Sir Alan Lascelles* (Weidenfeld & Nicolson, 2006)

Hartwell, Lord, *William Camrose: Giant of Fleet Street* (Weidenfeld & Nicolson, 1992)

Hassall, Christopher, *Edward Marsh: A Biography* (Longmans Green, 1959)

Hibbert, Christopher, *The Marlboroughs: John and Sarah Churchill 1650–1744* (Viking, Penguin, 2001)

Higham, Charles, *Dark Lady: Winston Churchill's Mother and Her World* (Virgin Books, 2006)

Hough, Richard, *Winston & Clementine* (Bantam Press, 1990)

House of Commons, *Ministerial Salaries*, House of Commons Information Office, July 2011

Hunter, Ian (ed.), *Winston & Archie: The Collected Correspondence of Winston Churchill and Archibald Sinclair 1915–1960* (Politico's, 2005)

Irving, David, *Churchill's War* (Veritas, 1987)

Jackson, Ashley, *Churchill* (Quercus, 2011)

James, Lawrence, *Churchill and Empire* (Weidenfeld & Nicolson, 2013)

James, Robert Rhodes, *Churchill: A Study in Failure 1900–1939* (Weidenfeld & Nicolson, 1970)

Jenkins, Roy, *Asquith: Portrait of a Man and of an Era* (William Collins, 1964)

———, *Churchill* (Macmillan, 2005)

John, Habakkuk, *Marriage, Debt, and the Estates System: English Landownership 1650–1950* (Clarendon Press, 1994)

Kapla, Justin, *When the Astors Owned New York: Blue Bloods and Grand Hotels in a Gilded Age* (Plume, 2006)

Keegan, John (ed.), *Churchill's Generals* (Weidenfeld & Nicolson, 1991)

Kehoe, Elizabeth, *Fortune's Daughters: The Extravagant Lives of the Jerome Sisters* (Atlantic Books, 2004)

Kynaston, David, *The City of London, Volume 1: A World of its Own 1815–1890* (Chatto & Windus, 1994)

——, *The City of London Volume II: Golden Years 1890–1914* (Chatto & Windus, 1995)

——, *The City of London, Volume III: Illusions of Gold 1914–1945* (Chatto & Windus, 1999)

Lee, Celia, *Jean, Lady Hamilton 1861–1941: A Soldier's Wife* (Celia Lee, 2001)

Lee, Celia and John, *Winston & Jack: the Churchill Brothers* (Celia Lee, 2007)

Leslie, Anita, *The Fabulous Leonard Jerome* (Hutchinson, 1954)

——, *Jennie: Life of Lady Randolph Churchill* (Hutchinson, 1969)

——, *Cousin Randolph: Life of Randolph Churchill* (Hutchinson, 1985)

Leslie, Shane, *Long Shadows* (John Murray, 1966)

Loelia, Duchess of Westminster, *Grace and Favour: The Memoirs of Loelia, Duchess of Westminster* (Weidenfeld & Nicolson, 1961)

Lovell, Mary S., *The Churchills: A Family at the Heart of History* (Little, Brown, 2011)

Lysaght, Charles, *Brendan Bracken* (Allen Lane, 1979)

Macdonald, James, *A Free Nation Deep in Debt* (Princeton University Press, 2006)

Mackenzie N. and J. (eds), *The Diary of Beatrice Webb* (Virago, 1984)

Macmillan, Harold, *The Past Masters: Politics and Politicians 1906–1939* (Macmillan, 1978)

Marsh, Edward, *A Number of People: A Book of Reminiscences* (Harper & Brothers, 1939)

Mather, John, MD, *Lord Randolph Churchill: Maladie et Mort*, Finest Hour 93, The Churchill Centre, 1993

Martin, John, *Downing Street: The War Years* (Bloomsbury, 1991)

Martin, Ralph, *Jennie: The Life of Lady Randolph Churchill* (Penticle Hall, 1969)

McGinty, Stephen, *Churchill's Cigar* (Macmillan, 2007)

McGowan, Norman, *My Years with Churchill* (Souvenir Press, 1958)

McLachlan, Donald, *In the Chair* (Weidenfeld & Nicolson, 1971)

Montague Browne, Anthony, *Long Sunset* (Cassell & Co., 1995)

Moran, Lord, *Churchill: The Struggle for Survival* (Constable, 1966)

Muggeridge, Malcolm, *Like It Was: The Diairies of Malcolm Muggeridge* (HarperCollins, 1981)

Murray, Edmund, *I was Churchill's Bodyguard* (W. H. Allen, 1987)

Naylor, John, *A Man and an Institution: Sir Maurice Hankey, the Cabinet Secretariat and the Custody of Cabinet Secrecy* (Cambridge University Press, 2009)

Nel (née Layton), Elizabeth, *Mr Churchill's Secretary* (Hodder & Stoughton, 1958)

Newfield, Dal, *A Lecture Tour to North America 1900–1901*, Finest Hour 17, The Churchill Centre, 1971

O'Keeke, Theodore, 'Irving on Churchill', *Journal of Historical Review*, spring 1986

Olson, Lynn, *Citizens of London* (Random House, 2010)

————, *Troublesome Young Men* (Farrar, Strauss & Giroux, 2007)

Owen, Dr David, *In Sickess and in Power* (Methuen, 2008)

Pearson, John, *The Private Lives of Winston Churchill* (Viking, 1991)

Pelling, Henry, *Winston Churchill* (Macmillan, 1974)

Pilpel, Robert E., *Churchill in America 1895–1961* (New English Library, 1977)

Porter, Richard, 'Puncturing the Churchill Balloon', Budapest lecture, www.spearhead.co.uk

Reynolds, David, *In Command of History: Churchill Fighting and Writing the Second World War* (Allen Lane, 2004)

Roberts, Andrew, *The Holy Fox: The Life of Lord Halifax* (Weidenfeld, 1991)

————, *Eminent Churchillians* (Simon & Schuster, 1995)

Roberts, Brian, *Churchills in Africa* (Hamish Hamilton, 1970)

Rose, Jonathan, *The Literary Churchill: Author, Reader, Actor* (Yale University Press, 2014)

Rose, Norman, *Churchill: An Unruly Life* (Simon & Schuster, 1994)

Rowse, A. L., *The Later Churchills* (Macmillan, 1958)

Ruffer, Jonathan Garnier, *The Big Shots: Edwardian Shooting Parties* (Quiller Press, 1977)

Sandys, Celia, *Chasing Churchill: The Travels of Winston Churchill* (HarperCollins, 2003)

Schneer, Jonathan, *London 1900: The Imperial Metropolis* (Yale Nota Bene, 2001)

Searle, G. R., *Corruption in British Politics, 1895–1930* (Clarendon Press, 1987)

Sebag-Montefiore, Simon, *Stalin: the Court of the Red Tsar* (Weidenfeld & Nicolson, 2003)

Sebba, Anne, *Jennie Churchill, Winston's American Mother* (John Murray, 2007)

Shutz, Frank, 'Emery and Wendy Reves "La Pausa" for sale for $56 million', *The Virginia Gazette*, September 2011

Soames, Mary, *Clementine Churchill* (Cassell, 1979)

——, *The Profligate Duke: George Spencer Churchill, Fifth Duke of Marlborough and His Duchess* (Collins, 1987)

——, *Winston Churchill: His Life as a Painter* (Collins, 1990)

——, *Speaking for Themselves: The Personal Letters of Winston and Clementine Churchill* (Doubleday, 1998)

——, *A Daughter's Tale* (Doubleday, 2011)

Spencer Churchill, John, *Crowded Canvas* (Odhams Press, 1961)

Spier, Eugene, *Focus: A Footnote to the History of the Thirties* (Oswald Wolff, 1963)

Storr, Anthony, *Churchill's Black Dog* (William Collins, 1965)

Thompson, R. W., *Churchill and Morton* (Hodder & Stoughton, 1976)

Thomson, Katharine, *Racing to Victory: Churchill & the Lure of the Turf*, Finest Hour 102, The Churchill Centre, 1999

Tilden, Philip, *True Remembrances: Memoirs of an Architect* (Country Life, 1954)

Toye, Richard, *Lloyd George & Churchill: Rivals for Greatness* (Macmillan, 2007)

Wardell, Michael, 'Churchill's Dagger: A Memoir of La Capponcina', *The Atlantic Advocate*, February 1965

Welsh, Peter, 'A Gentleman of History', *Cigar Aficionado*, autumn 1995

Wheeler-Bennett, J. (ed.), *Action This Day: Working with Churchill* (Macmillan, 1968)

Young, George M., *Stanley Baldwin*, (Hart-Davis, 1952)

Young, Kenneth, *Churchill and Beaverbrook: a study in friendship and politics* (Heinemann, 1966)

BIOGRAPHICAL NOTES

Asquith, Herbert (1852–1928), fellow of Balliol College, Oxford 1874–82; journalist, *The Spectator, The Economist* 1876–88; barrister, QC 1890; MP 1886–1918, 1920–4; home secretary 1892–5; barrister 1895–1905; chancellor of the exchequer 1905–08; prime minister 1908–16; leader of the Liberal Party 1916–26; earl of Oxford and Asquith, 1924.

Attlee, Clement (1883–1967), social worker, east London 1907–12; lecturer, London School of Economics 1912–14; war service in Gallipoli, Mesopotamia, France 1914–18; MP 1922–55; Chancellor of the Duchy of Lancaster 1930–1; leader of the Labour Party 1935–55; Lord Privy Seal 1940–2; deputy prime minister 1942–5; prime minister 1945–51; earl 1955.

Baldwin, Stanley (1867–1947), MP 1908–37; president of the Board of Trade 1921–2; chancellor of the exchequer 1922–3; leader of the Conservative Party 1923–7; prime minister 1923–January 1924, November 1924–9; Lord President of the Council 1931–5; prime minister 1935–7; earl 1937.

Balfour, Arthur J. (1848–1930), secretary for Scotland 1886–7; chief secretary for Ireland 1887–91; leader of the Conservative Party 1902–11; prime minister 1902–5; First Lord of the Admiralty 1915–16; foreign secretary 1916–19; Lord President of the Council 1925–9; earl of Balfour 1922.

Bridgeman, William (1864–1935), MP Oswestry 1906–29; secretary for mines 1920–2; home secretary 1922–4; First Lord of the Admiralty 1924–9; viscount 1929.

Bullock, Alan (1914–2004), journalist, BBC 1939–45; fellow, New College, Oxford 1945–52; author *Hitler: A Study in Tyranny* (1952); censor, St Catherine's Society, Oxford 1952–62, master, St. Catherine's College, Oxford 1962–80; Vice-chancellor, Oxford University 1969–73; knighted 1972, baron 1976.

Campbell-Bannerman, Henry (1836–1908), partner of family drapery business, Glasgow 1860; MP 1868–1908; financial secretary to the War Office 1871–4, 1880–2, to the Admiralty 1882–4; chief secretary for Ireland 1884–5; secretary of state for war 1886, 1892–5; leader of the Liberal Party 1899–1908; prime minister 1905–8; knighted 1895.

Cazalet, Victor (1893–1943), Military Cross, 1917; MP 1924–43; killed in the same air crash as General Sikorski, 1943.

Chamberlain, Austen (1863–1937), son of Joseph Chamberlain; postmaster general 1902–3; chancellor of the exchequer 1903–5, 1919–21; secretary of state for India 1915–17; leader of the Conservative Party 1921–2; Lord Privy Seal, leader of the House of Commons 1921–2; foreign secretary 1924–9; First Lord of the Admiralty 1931; winner, Nobel peace prize 1925; knighted 1925.

Chamberlain, Neville (1869–1940), son of Joseph Chamberlain, half-brother of Austen; minister of health 1923, 1924–9, 1931; chancellor of the exchequer 1923–4, 1931–7; prime minister 1937–40; Lord President of the Council 1940.

Curzon, George (1859–1925) MP 1886–98, under-secretary of state for India 1891–2, for foreign affairs 1895–8; viceroy of India 1899–1905; minister, Coalition Government 1915; leader of the House of Lords 1916; foreign secretary 1919–24; Lord President of the Council 1924–5; earl 1911, marquess 1921.

Eden, Anthony (1897–1940), King's Royal Rifle Corps 1915–9 (awarded Military Cross 1917); MP 1923–57; Lord Privy Seal

1934–5; minister for League of Nations affairs June–December 1935; foreign secretary 1935–8, 1940–5, 1951–5; secretary of state for dominion affairs 1939–40; secretary of state for war 1940; prime minister 1955–7; knighted 1954, earl of Avon 1961.

Edmonds, James (1861–1956), lieutenant Royal Engineers 1881, served in South Africa 1901–2, First World War 1914–18; brigadier general, head of the Military Branch, Historical Section of the Committee of Imperial Defence 1919–49; knighted 1928.

Eisenhower, Dwight (1890–1969), joined US Army, graduating from West Point 1915; service in the Philippines 1935–9; general 1943; supreme commander, Allied Forces Europe, 1944–5; governor, American Zone, Occupied Germany May–November 1945; chief of staff, US Army 1945–8; president, Columbia University 1948–50; NATO Supreme Allied Commander, Europe 1950–2; president of the United States of America 1953–61.

Elgin, 9th Earl of (1849–1917), born Victor Bruce; viceroy of India 1894–9; chairman, Second Boer War commission, 1902–3; colonial secretary 1905–8.

Fisher, John 'Jackie' (1841–1920), joined the Royal Navy 1854; rear admiral 1890, vice admiral 1896, admiral 1901; First Sea Lord (modernizing the fleet) 1904–10; Admiral of the Fleet 1905; First Sea Lord 1914–15; knighted 1894, baron 1909.

French, John (1852–1925), joined the Royal Navy 1866, army 1870; major-general, southern Africa (Boer war) 1899–1902; general, inspector-general of the forces 1907–12; chief of the Imperial General Staff 1912–14; field marshal 1913; commander-in-chief, British Expeditionary Force 1914–15; commander-in-chief, Home Forces 1915–18; lord lieutenant, Ireland 1918–21; knighted 1900, viscount 1915, earl of Ypres 1922.

Greenwood, Arthur (1880–1954) teacher and economics lecturer, Huddersfield 1903–14; secretary, Council for the Study of International Relations 1914; MP 1922–31, 1932–54; head, Labour Party research department 1927; minister of health 1929–31; deputy leader of the Labour Party 1935–45; minister without portfolio 1940–2; Lord Privy Seal 1945–7; paymaster-general 1946–7.

Grigg, Percy (1890–1964), principal private secretary to chancellors of the exchequer, HM Treasury 1921–30; chairman, Inland Revenue, 1930–9; permanent under-secretary of state for war 1939–42; MP 1942–5; secretary of state for war 1942–5; knighted 1932.

Haig, Douglas (1861–1928), joined the army 1884; service in Sudan, southern Africa 1898–1902; inspector general of cavalry, India 1903–6; staff duties, London 1906–9; chief of staff, India 1909–11; general, commander Aldershot 1911–14; commander 1st Army, British Expeditionary Force (BEF) 1914–15; commander-in-chief, BEF 1915–18; commander-in-chief, Home Forces 1918–21; knighted 1909, earl (and gift of £100,000) 1918.

Inskip, Thomas (1876–1947), barrister, KC 1914; MP 1918–29, 1931–9; solicitor general 1922–8, 1931–2; attorney general 1928–9, 1932–6; minister for co-ordination of defence 1936–9, secretary of state for dominion affairs January–September 1939, May–October 1940; lord chancellor 1939–40; lord chief justice 1940–6; knighted 1922, Viscount Caldecote 1939.

Ismay, Hastings ('Pug') (1887–1965), joined the Indian army, serving in India, Somaliland 1905–20; assistant secretary, Committee of Imperial Defence 1925–30; military secretary, viceroy of India 1930–2; intelligence officer, War Office 1933–6; deputy secretary, secretary (from 1938) Committee of Imperial Defence 1936–40; chief staff officer to prime minister and minister of defence 1940–5; general 1944; chief of staff, viceroy of India 1947–8; chairman, Festival of Britain 1948–51; secretary of state for Commonwealth relations 1951–2; literary assistant to Churchill 1948–53; secretary-general, NATO 1952–7; knighted 1946, baron 1947.

Kelly, Denis (1916–90), war service 1939–45; barrister 1942; literary assistant to Churchill 1947–57; deputy recorder, Bedford 1968.

Kennedy, John ('Jack') (1917–63), joined the US Navy 1940–4 (commanding motor torpedo boats in the South Pacific 1943); member from Massachusetts's 11th District, US House of Representatives 1947–53; senator from Missouri, US Senate 1953–60; president of the United States 1961–3; assassinated November 1963.

Kitchener, Horatio (1850–1916), joined the army 1871; governor general, eastern Sudan 1868–8; adjutant general, Egyptian army 1888–91, inspector general of police, Egypt 1889–91; commander, Sudan campaign 1896–8; governor general Sudan 1899; chief of staff, southern Africa (Boer war) 1900–2; commander-in-chief, India 1902–9; British agent and consul general, Egypt 1911; secretary of state for war 1914–16; drowned 1916; knighted 1894, baron (and prize of £30,000) 1898; viscount (and prize of £50,000) 1902.

Leathers, Frederick (1883–1965), joined Steamship Owners' Coal Association (later William Cory & Son) 1898; joint managing director 1917, deputy chairman 1928; minister of war transport 1941 (with special responsibility for shipping); secretary of state for the co-ordination of transport, fuel and power 1951–3; baron 1941,viscount 1954.

Lloyd George, David (1863–1945), solicitor 1884; MP 1890–1945; president of the Board of Trade 1906–8; chancellor of the exchequer 1908–15; minister of munitions 1915–16; secretary of state for war June–December 1916; prime minister 1916–22; leader of the Liberal Party 1926; Earl Lloyd-George of Dwyfor 1945.

Lytton, 2nd Earl of (1876–1947), born Victor Bulwer-Lytton (in India while his father was viceroy); Admiralty 1916–20; under-secretary of state for India 1920–2; governor of Bengal 1922–7.

MacDonald, Ramsay (1866–1937), a founder of the Labour Party; MP 1906–8, 1922–35, 1936–7; chairman of Labour MPs 1911–4, leader of the Labour Party 1922–31; prime minister 1924, 1929–35; Lord President of the Council 1935–7.

Macmillan, Frederick (1851–1936), New York branch of Macmillan publishers 1871–6, London partner 1876–1936; knighted 1909.

Macmillan, Harold (1894–1986), wounded at the Somme 1916; joined family publishing business, Macmillan & Co. 1919; MP 1924–9, 1931–July 1945, November 1945–64; minister of housing 1951–4; defence minister 1954–5; foreign secretary 1955; chancellor of the exchequer 1955–7; prime minister 1957–63; chairman, Macmillan & Co. 1964–74; earl of Stockton 1984.

Margesson, David (1890–1965), served on the Western Front (awarded Military Cross) 1914–18; MP 1922–3, 1924–42; chief whip 1931–40; secretary of state for war 1940–2; viscount 1942.

Maze, Paul (1887–1979) son of an art collector; artist; interpreter, military draughtsman with British army (meeting Churchill) 1914–8; naturalized British subject 1920; Home Guard 1939–45; official painter, Elizabeth II's Coronation 1953.

Monckton, Walter (1891–1965), Oxford University contemporary of Edward, prince of Wales, later Edward VIII; Military Cross, 1919; barrister 1919, KC 1930; attorney general to prince of Wales 1932–6, to duchy of Cornwall 1936–46, 1949–51; director general, ministry of information 1939–41; solicitor general 1945; MP 1951–7; minister of labour 1951–5, minister of defence 1955–6, paymaster general 1956–7; knighted 1937, viscount 1957.

24. American actress Maxine Elliott, pictured here circa 1920, who was a frequent hostess of Churchill at her château in the south of France in the 1930s.

25. Sir Henry Strakosch in 1931. The mining company chairman, part-owner of the *Economist* and informant on German rearmament, was also twice Churchill's financial saviour – in 1938 and 1940.

26. Churchill leaving for the House of Commons with Brendan Bracken (right), Churchill's 'honorary man of business', in which capacity he twice arranged Churchill's financial rescue, April 1939.

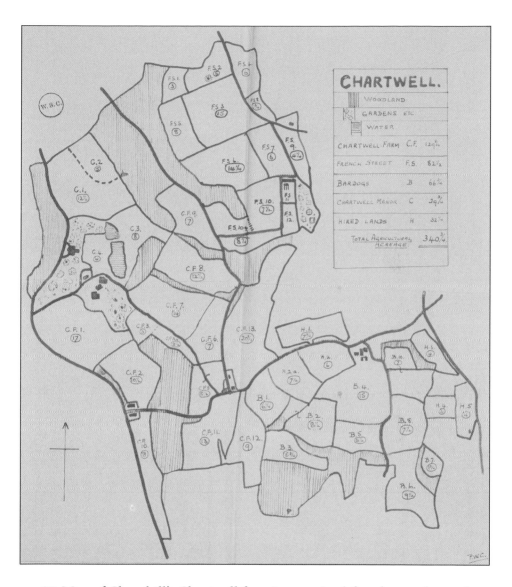

27. Map of Churchill's Chartwell farming empire (after the purchase of
Chartwell and Bardogs farms, but before the purchase of Parkside), 1947.
Chartwell itself stands at the centre left.

28. Emery Reves, Churchill's pre-war press agent and post-war
negotiator for the sale of his war memoirs; with his partner
Wendy, later his wife, Venice, circa 1950.

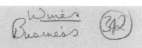

MR. CHURCHILL.

Herewith (at last!) the list of wines and spirits consumed during April and May at both London and Chartwell:-

	Chartwell April	May	London	April	May	Total
Whisky, black label	16	27	....	4	9	56
Brandy,martell)..........	17	25)	....	I)	0)	
" cherry)	I	I)		I)	I)	58
" liquer cointreau	2	2)	....	2)	5)	
Gin	3	5	....	2		10
Champagne,ponsorvin	36	36)				
" Pommery	80	80)				
" Pol: Rog:	48	74)	....	37)	21)	
" Roederer	10	10)	....	10)	12)	454
Sherry, amontill:	18	15	....	2	2	
" palsdar	8	7	....	3		
" old brown			....	2	I	58
Port, pipe line	12)	35)	....	3	3	
" special	12)	4)	....	0	0	69
Hock, (vire	24)	24)		0	0	
B - 33	14)	)	....	0	0	62
Vermouth	8	8	....	0	0	16
Claret, St.Julian).....	26	26	....	0	0	52
" Rothchild).....	12	12	....	0	0	24
White Wine,grosey grill	23	23				
Sauterne	10	8				
Moselle	9	9				
Malessart	15	15				
Cotes	8	14	....	8		
Hunt Nauchet	5	4				151
Burgundy		11	....	2	8	21

M.S.
21.6.49.

29. An analysis by Churchill's secretaries of his households' consumption of champagne, wine and spirits during April and May, 1949.

30. Churchill at Chartwell with Joyce Hall (*standing, right*) of Hallmark Cards, Mrs Hall (*seated, left*), their son (*standing, left*) and Anthony Moir (*standing, centre*), Churchill's solicitor and tax adviser, July 1950.

31. Churchill is helped off Aristotle Onassis' yacht *Christina* by Onassis (*left*) and Churchill's bodyguard, Edmund Murray (*right*), August 1959.

32. Churchill surveying his Chartwell domain, as captured by
photographer Phillippe Halsman, 1947.

Pakenham-Walsh, Ridley (1888–1966) joined the army 1908, serving in the Dardanelles, France 1914–18 (awarded Military Cross); School of Military Engineering 1923–6; major general, engineer-in-chief, British Expeditionary Force 1939–40; lieutenant general 1941; controller general, Army Provision 1943–6.

Rawlinson, Henry (1864–1925), joined the army 1884; Kitchener's staff, Omdurman 1898; commander Fourth Division, France 1914, Fourth Army 1916; general, commanding Second Army, 1917–18; commander-in-chief, India 1920–5; knighted 1918, baron 1919.

Roosevelt, Franklin (1882–1945), senator, New York State 1911–13; assistant secretary of the navy 1913–20; suffered from polio 1921; governor of New York State 1929–32; president of the United States 1933–45; in his first 100 days in office, introduced measures known as the New Deal to combat the Great Depression of the 1930s; died in his record fourth term of office.

Rothschild, Nathaniel ('Natty') (1840–1915), merchant banker; MP 1865–85; partner, N. M. Rothschild & Sons 1879; founder, The Exploration Company 1886; baron 1885.

Salisbury, Marquess of (1830–1903), born Robert Cecil; fellow of The College of All Souls, Oxford 1853; MP 1853–68; journalist *Saturday Review, Quarterly Review* 1856–68; chairman, Great Eastern Railway Company 1868–72; fellow of the Royal Society 1869; secretary of state for India 1874–8; leader of the Conservative Party 1881–1902; prime minister, foreign secretary 1885–January 1886, July 1886–92, 1895–1902; Viscount Cranborne 1865, marquess 1868.

Sassoon, Philip (1888–1939), cousin of Siegfried Sassoon; related by marriage to the Rothschild family; MP 1912–39; private secretary, Field Marshal Haig 1915–18; under-secretary of state for air 1924–9, 1931–7; first commissioner of works 1937–9; prominent social host and art collector at Port Lympne in Kent, Trent Park in Hertfordshire; succeeded to baronetcy 1912.

Smith, Frederick (*F. E.*) (1872–1930), barrister, KC 1908; MP 1906–18; solicitor general 1915; attorney general 1915–18; lord chancellor 1919–22; secretary of state for India 1924–28; knighted 1915, baron (as Lord Birkenhead) 1919, viscount 1921, earl 1922; co-founder with Churchill of The Other Club.

Spears (né Spiers), Edward (1886–1974), born in Paris; liaison officer with French army (meeting Churchill, Military Cross 1915) 1914–8; MP 1922–4, 1931–45; Churchill's representative to French government, May 1940, to Free French 1940–2; British minister, Syria and Lebanon 1942–4; chairman, Institute of Directors 1948–66; knighted 1942, baronet 1953.

Truman, Harry (1884–1972), farmer; served on the Western Front, 1917–18; senator from Missouri, US Senate 1935–45; vice-president January–April 1945; president of the United States April 1945–53.

Westminster, Duke of (1879–1953), born Hugh Grosvenor; land-owner; succeeded to dukedom 1899; Royal Horse Guards (Boer war) 1899–1900; Cheshire Yeomanry 1914–18 (developed Rolls-Royce armoured car as a prototype of the tank); partner, Coco Chanel 1925–35.

Wood, Edward (1881–1959), viceroy of India 1926–31; secretary of state for war 1935; Lord Privy Seal 1935–8; foreign secretary 1938–40; ambassador to the United States 1940–6; baron (as Lord Irwin) 1925, Viscount Halifax 1934, earl 1944.

REFERENCE NOTES

Abbreviations

References to the eight-volume official biography *Winston S. Churchill*, written by Randolph Churchill (vols 1 and 2) and Martin Gilbert (vols 3–8) (Heinemann, 1966–88), are shown by volume and page number, e.g., 5:101.

The volumes of companion documents (Heinemann, 1967–2000) are referenced by the volume number, followed by **C** (for Companion), part number and page number: e.g., 4C2:1123; or, in the case of the *The Churchill War Papers* volumes, by **CW**, part number and page number: e.g., CWP1:123.

References to letters written between Churchill and his wife sourced from the late Lady Soames' collection *Speaking for Themselves* (Doubleday, 1988) are shown as **SFT** followed by the page number: e.g., SFT:123.

References to Churchill's papers in the Churchill Archives Centre at Churchill College, Cambridge, are shown as either **CHAR** (for the Chartwell Papers, dated up to July 1945) or **CHUR** (for the Churchill Papers from July 1945 onwards), followed by their series, file and folio numbers: e.g., CHUR 1/25/123.

CHAR 28 includes the papers of Churchill's father, mother and brother; and also of W. H. Bernau, whose family donated his personal papers to Churchill. Bernau was his bank manager between 1918 and the early 1930s, first at Cox & Co. and then at Lloyds Bank.

Other libraries and collections of papers are abbreviated as follows:

BL	British Library
CAC	Churchill Archives Centre, Churchill College, Cambridge University
CURBMSL	Columbia University, Rare Books and Manuscripts Library
HLHU	Houghton Library, Harvard University
HMCO	Houghton Mifflin Company
LBGA	Lloyds Banking Group Archives, London
LoCW	Library of Congress, Washington, D.C.
NA	National Archives, Kew, London
NYPL	New York Public Library, New York
PUFL	Princeton University, Rare Books and Manuscripts Division, Firestone Library
PUMM	Princeton University, Rare Books and Manuscripts Division, Seeley G. Mudd Manuscript Library
RAL	Rothschild Archives, London
RULSC	Reading University Library, Special Collections
TNL Archive	Times Newspapers Ltd Archive, News UK and Ireland Ltd.
WSCDL	Winston Churchill Collection, Daniel Longwell Papers

Members of the Churchill family and other individuals or organizations frequently cited are abbreviated in the Notes as follows:

ACB	Albert Curtis Brown
AFM	Anthony Moir
AMB	Anthony Montague Browne
BL	British Library
BMB	Bernard Baruch
BRB	Brendan Bracken
CB	Curtis Brown Ltd
CS	Charles Scribner III

CSC	Clementine Churchill, née Hozier, Lady Churchill from 1953
DoM	Duke (or Duchess) of Marlborough
DoW	Duke of Westminster
EHM	Edward Marsh
ER	Imre Revesz, Emery Reves from 1940
JSC	John Spencer Churchill, known as Jack
KFR	Knight Frank & Rutley
LlBk	Lloyds Bank
LRC	Lord Randolph Spencer Churchill
LyRC	Lady Randolph Spencer Churchill, née Jennie Jerome, also Mrs George Cornwallis-West
MWB	Lord (Max) Beaverbrook, né Maxwell Aitken
NCBNY	National City Bank of New York
NM	Nicholl, Manisty & Co.
TB	Thornton Butterworth
VdaC	Vickers da Costa
WHB	W. H. Bernau
WSC	Winston Spencer Churchill

1. The Churchills and Jeromes

1. 20 Aug 1873 LRC letter to DoM, cited P. Churchill and J. Mitchell, *Jennie*, pp. 23–5.
2. 30 Apr 1937 WSC ltr to E. Marsh, Marsh papers, EMAR/2, CAC.
3. 5 Mar 1891 *The New York Times*, cited A. Sebba, *Jennie Churchill*, pp. 9–10.
4. E. Kehoe, *Fortune's Daughters*, p. 12.
5. M. Lovell, *The Churchills*, p. 25. Mrs Astor was born Caroline Schermerhorn before marrying William Astor.
6. A. Hays Sulzberger memorandum citing 1950s *New York Times* research, 'Meetings with WSC', box 1, WSCDL, CURBMSL.
7. A. Leslie, *The Fabulous Leonard Jerome*, pp. 90, 92.
8. A. Sebba, *Jennie Churchill*, pp. 18, 22.
9. S. Fiske, *Eminent New Yorkers* (1887), cited A. Leslie, *Fabulous Leonard Jerome*, p. 167.
10. WSC, *Marlborough*, p. 32.
11. C. Hibbert, *The Marlboroughs*, p. 91.

12. D. Cannadine, *The Decline and Fall of the British Aristocracy*, pp. 710–11. Data given is dated *c*.1880.

13. C. Hibbert, *The Marlboroughs*, pp. 336, 348.

14. M. Soames, *The Profligate Duke*, p. 115.

15. Feb 1820 Blenheim Papers, Add MS 61678 f.182–3, 184, BL.

16. *Journal of Mrs Arbuthnot* I, p. 304, cited A. Rowse, *The Later Churchills*, p. 201.

17. M. Lovell, *The Churchills*, p. 17.

18. Ibid.

19. R. Blake, *Disraeli*, p. 692.

20. A. Rowse, *The Later Churchills*, p. 232.

21. J. Bateman, *The Great Landowners of Britain and Ireland*, pp. 472–3, cited E. Kehoe, *Fortune's Daughters*, p. xi; 1873 *Return of Owners of Land*, cited A. Rowse, *The Later Churchills*, pp. 229–31; D. Cannadine, *The Aristocratic Adventurer*, p. 6.

22. 31 Aug 1873 DoM ltr to LRC, 1C1:12–13.

23. U/d Feb 1874 DoM ltr to LRC, 1C1:18.

24. 23 Jan 1874 Shipmond, Barlow, Sarocque, Macfarland ltr, 1C1:18–19.

25. 7 Oct 1873 L. Jerome ltr to J. Jerome, 1C1:17–18. Louisa Catherine, duchess of Leeds (1789–1874), was the third daughter of Richard Caton, a Baltimore merchant. She first married an English baronet and, after his death, the marquess of Clanricarde, later the duke of Leeds.

26. 25 Feb 1875 F. Capon ltr to RSC, 1C1:18–19.

27. 9 Apr 1874 L. Jerome ltr to DoM, 1C1:20.

28. M. Lovell, *The Churchills*, p. 41.

29. R. Martin, *Jennie: The Life of Lady Randolph Churchill*, I, p. 91.

2. Spendthrift Parents, 1875–94

1. WSC, *Lord Randolph Churchill Vol 1*, p. 72.

2. 14, 18 Jan 1876 LRC ltrs to LyRC, CHAR 28/5/13, 15.

3. C. Higham, *Dark Lady*, p. 61.

4. 29 Jan 1879 LRC ltr to LyRC, CHAR 28/6/65.

5. 12 Jul 1880 LyRC ltr to C. Jerome, cited A. Leslie, *Fabulous Leonard Jerome*, pp. 216–17.

6. Summary of the duke of Marlborough's will, CHAR 1/82/2.

7. D. Green, *The Churchills of Blenheim*, p. 116.

8. M. Lovell, *The Churchills*, p. 78.

9. S. Buczacki, *Churchill & Chartwell*, p. 11.

10. Wins in 1889 included the Prince of Wales Handicap (£1,000); Portland Plate (£775); Oaks (£2,600, at odds of 20 to 1). In 1890 Abbesse won the Manchester Cup (£2,200).

11. 5, 14 Aug 1890 LRC ltr to LyRC, CHAR 28/39/10, 28/9/17.

12. D. Kynaston, *The City of London* 2:13.

13. N. Ferguson, *Rothschild: The World's Banker*, p. 877.

14. D. Kynaston, *The City of London* 2:82.

15. 22 Mar 1891 Transcript, LRC ltr to N. Rothschild 101/22 T 15, RAL.

16. Rothschild 1891 ledger, I/8/13 account 178 LRC Syndicate Account, RAL. Contributions included £1,000 each from Lord Randolph's mother and sister, Lady Sarah Spencer-Churchill; £2,000 from Lord and Lady Wimborne (another sister, Cornelia); and £1,500 between them from two European friends of the Jeromes, the Marquis de Breteuil and Baron de Hirsch.

17. B. Roberts, *Churchills in Africa*, p. 14.

18. 30 May 1891 LRC ltr to LyC, CHAR 28/11/13.

19. Ibid.

20. 17 Jun 1891 LRC ltr to LyRC, CHAR 28/11/17.

21. 26 June 1891 LRC ltr to LyRC, CHAR 28/11/19.

22. Cited B. Roberts, *Churchills in Africa*, p. 38.

23. 13 Sep 1891 LRC ltr to LyRC, CHAR 28/11/36.

24. 29 Sep 1891 LRC ltr to LyRC, CHAR 28/11/39; B. Roberts, *Churchills in Africa*, p. 79.

25. U/d Jul 1891 LyRC ltr to C. Frewen, Moreton Frewen Papers, LoCW.

26. 23 Sep 1891 LyRC ltr to LRC, CHAR 1/2/9.

27. 13 Dec 1891 LRC ltr to LyRC, CHAR 28/11/49.

28. 1893 Rothschild ledger I/8/15 a/c 198 a/c no.4, RAL.

29. 28 Oct 1891 LyRC ltr to WSC, CHAR 1/8/27.

30. 4 Nov 1891 Mrs Everest ltr to WSC, CHAR 1/4/19.

31. 1 Jul 1890 LyRC letter to WSC, CHAR 1/8/4.

32. 29 Mar 1892 LRC ltr to WSC, CHAR 1/2/62.

33. U/d May 1892 LyRC ltr to WSC, 1C1:333.

34. U/d Sep 1892 LRC ltr to Frances, DoM, 1C1:338.

35. 9 Aug 1893 LRC ltr to WSC, CHAR 1/1/66.

36. 30 Aug 1893 WSC ltr to LRC, 1C1:402–3.

37. 3 Sep 1893 LRC ltr to Frances, DoM 1C1:404.

38. 17 Sep 1893 WSC ltr to LyRC 1C1:413–4.

39. 17 Jan 1894 N. M. Rothschild 1894 ledger, I/8/16 a/c 178, a/c no.4, RAL. Lord Randolph sold 500 Deep Levels shares at over £4 each in October 1893 to raise more than £2,000; and 200 for £5.12s each in February 1894, by which time the company had been renamed Rand Mines.

40. 24 Oct 1893 LRC ltr to Frances, DoM 1C1:423.

41. 21 Apr 1894 LRC ltr to LyRC, CHAR 1/2/78.

42. 22 Apr 1894 LyRC ltr to WSC, CHAR 1/8/59.

43. R. Martin, *Lady Randolph Churchill* 1, p. 297.

44. 24 Jun 1894 Rothschild 1894 ledger I/8/16 a/c 178 a/c no 4, RAL.

45. 24 Jun 1894 LRC ltr to WSC, CHAR 1/2/84.
46. WSC, *My Early Life*, p. 49.
47. 8 November 1894 LyRC ltr to C. Frewen, Tarka King Papers.
48. WSC, *My Early Life*, p. 195.
49. 5 March 1895 *The New York Times*, p. 5.
50. Rothschild 1894 ledger, I/8/16 a/c 178, RAL.
51. Rothschild 1895 ledger, I/8/17 a/c 178, RAL. Lord Randolph's executors were Lady Randolph Churchill, the duke of Marlborough and a brother-in-law Lord Curzon (later Earl Howe), who was married to Georgina Churchill. The Rothschilds' second, larger cheque was dispatched to the executors on 11 April 1895.
52. S. Van Oss, cited D. Kynaston, *The City of London* 2:110.
53. WSC, *My Early Life*, p. 195.
54. Epitome, full version of LRC Will, CHAR 1/79/2, 5.

3. Distant Army Duty, 1895–9

1. 21 Feb 1895 WSC ltr to JSC, CHAR 28/152/40.
2. 27 Apr 1895 WSC ltr to LyRC, 1C1: 569–70.
3. £2,000 a year came in rentals from the Manhattan property contributed by the Jeromes to the Churchill marriage settlement (the 'American settlement' in some documents); £2,000 in income from Lord Randolph's will trust's investments, worth approximately £50,000; and £700 in income from the Churchill family's contribution to the marriage settlement ('The English Settlement' in some documents).
4. In 1868, 2,166 people who recorded more than £5,000 of income were charged under schedule D of income tax. Report of the Inland Revenue, ii pp. 580–4, cited M. Daunton, *Trusting Leviathan*, p. 160.
5. WSC, *My Early Life*, p. 75.
6. 1 May 1896, WSC letter to LyRC, 1C1:671–2.
7. 4 August 1896 WSC letter to LyRC, 1C1:675–6.
8. WSC, *My Early Life*, pp. 101–3.
9. 19 Nov 1896 LyRC ltr to WSC, CHAR 1/8/73.
10. 11 Dec 1896 LyRC ltr to WSC, CHAR 1/8/77.
11. 26 Feb 1897 LyRC ltr to WSC, CHAR 1/8/91.
12. 5 Mar 1897 LyRC ltr to WSC, CHAR 1/8/94. Jennie's assessment of her annual income at £2,700 is puzzling since it was at least £5,000, as her sons discovered in 1914.
13. 17 Mar 1897 WSC ltr to LyRC, 1C2:741–2.
14. 17 Aug 1897 WSC ltr to LyRC, 1C2:778–9; 4 Nov 1897 CHAR 1/8/117. Lord William Beresford could not cash Churchill's cheque (repaying a loan made in July) for ten weeks.

15. 22 Aug 1897 B. Blood ltr to WSC, 1C2: 780.
16. 5 Sep 1897 WSC ltr to LyRC, 1C2:784–5.
17. 7 Oct 1897 LyRC ltr to WSC, 1C2:808–9.
18. 25 Oct 1897 WSC ltr to LyRC,1:355-7
19. 12 Sep 1897 WSC ltr to LyRC, 1:358–9.
20. 30 Sep 1897 LyRC letter to WSC, CHAR 1/8/109.
21. 25 Oct 1897 WSC ltr to LyRC, 1C2:811–2.
22. 17 Nov 1897 WSC ltr to LyRC, 1C2:827–8. Messrs A. F. Bernau, tailors; Messrs E. Tautz & Sons, tailors (owed £144.14s. for clothes supplied 1895–7, paid 1902); Sowter, saddler.
23. 11 Nov 1897 LyRC ltr to WSC, 1C2:832–3.
24. 31 Dec 1897 WSC ltr to LyRC, 1C2:840–1.
25. 7 Jan 1898 A. Watt ltr to LyRC, 1C2:852.
26. 20 Jan 1898 LyRC ltr to WSC, CHAR 1/8/125.
27. 27 Jan 1898 LyRC ltr to WSC, 1C2:880.
28. 26 Jan 1898 WSC ltr to LyRC, CHAR 28/24/26.
29. 18, 22 Mar 1898 WSC ltrs to LyRC, CHAR 28/24/49, 54. Longmans Statement Book, MS 1393/F1, pp. 169–71, RULSC. Churchill's first royalty cheque added £46 to his £50 advance; British sales were only 2,671 copies in fifteen months. Churchill had been expecting to earn £300.
30. 19 Jan 1898 WSC ltr to LyRC, CHAR 28/24/20.
31. 20 Jan 1898 LyRC ltr to WSC, CHAR 1/8/125.
32. 13 Jan 1898 LyRC ltr to WSC, CHAR 1/8/122.
33. 14 Jan 1898 LyRC ltr to WSC, CHAR 1/8/124. Neither the papers nor Lumley's accompanying letter survive, but the scheme's features are reconstructed from Churchill's subsequent correspondence with his mother and the duke of Marlborough.
34. 28 Jan 1898 WSC ltr to LyRC, 1C2:868–9.
35. This is the proportion which Churchill quoted, for example to his cousin Shane Leslie – see S. Leslie, *Long Shadows*, p.16.
36. 28 Feb 1915 E. Manisty account, as Receiver to Norwich Union Life Assurance Society, CHAR 28/124 1–4. Interest on the loan was 4¾ per cent a year (£807); the life insurance premium on Jennie's life cost £573 a year.
37. 30 Jan 1898 WSC ltr to LyRC, CHAR 28/24/33.
38. 30 January 1898 WSC letter to JSC, CHAR 28/152/144.

4. The World's Highest-Paid War Correspondent, 1899–1900

1. 16 Feb 1898 WSC ltr to JSC, CHAR 28/152/148.
2. 18 Mar 1898 WSC ltr to LyRC, CHAR 28/24/49.

3. 27 Mar 1898 WSC ltr to LyRC, CHAR 24/28/65.
4. WSC, *My Early Life*, p. 165.
5. 25 April 1898 WSC ltr to LyRC, 1C2:922.
6. 3 May 1898 WSC ltr to L. Leslie, CHUR 1/44/215–17.
7. 1 Jun 1898 WSC ltr to LyRC, 1C2:941–3.
8. 10 May 1898 WSC ltr to LyRC, CHAR 28/245/3.
9. D. Kynaston, *The City of London* 2:146, 248, 252–3, 270, 301.
10. WSC, *My Early Life*, p. 182.
11. 10 Aug 1898 WSC ltr to LyRC, CHAR 28/25/31.
12. U/d July 1898 WSC note to LyRC, CHAR 28/25/57.
13. 30 Jul 1898 WSC ltr to DoM, 28/25/27 enc. with WSC ltr to LyRC CHAR 28/25/30. Churchill's uncle John Leslie refused to give the second guarantee; one of Lord Randolph literary executors Ernest Beckett accepted instead.
14. 5 Aug 1898 WSC ltr to LyRC, CHAR 28/25/28–9.
15. 24, 26 Aug 1898 WSC ltrs to LyRC, CHAR 28/25/36.
16. 28 Oct 1898 WSC ltr to M. Frewen, CHUR 2/519/459.
17. 1899 Longmans' royalty ledger, MS 1393/E5/473, RULSC. As for *The River War*, there was no advance, but the British royalty was 20 per cent after sales of 1,000 copies, the US 15 per cent and 'colonial sales' earned Churchill 3d. per copy.
18. 1899 Longmans royalty ledger, MS 1393/E5/469, RULSC. If Churchill accepted an advance of £100, his royalty rate was 20 per cent after 1,500 copies.
19. 27 Oct 1898 WSC ltr to A. Watt, A. P. Watt Papers, NYPL.
20. Nov 1898 Cox & Co. statement, CHAR 1/21. Interest and life insurance premiums cost £300 a year. From March 1899 Churchill paid his brother £75 monthly (or almost monthly), but there are few other signs that the account was used for the purposes intended. Churchill sent £100 to King & Co. in Bombay; repaid £325 to his mother; and sent £50 to Palmer, his tailor, £12 to Hatchard, the booksellers, and £2 to Waterlow, his stationery supplier. There was nothing for Messrs Tautz, Bernau, Sowter or Day, still owed some £100 each. The Special Account was closed in October 1900, its balance of £292 transferred to Churchill's Private Account.
21. WSC, *My Early Life*, pp. 195–6.
22. 29 Dec 1898 WSC ltr to LyRC, CHAR 28/25/55.
23. 19 Jan 1899 WSC letter to LyRC, CHAR 28/26/3. Churchill was to record a profit (after expenses) of more than £8,000 when the book was published seven years later.
24. Mar 1899 WSC ltr to P. Plowden, cited the *Observer* (9 November 2003).
25. 17 Jul 1899 WSC ltr to A. Harmsworth, Northcliffe Papers, M/s Add 62156/1, BL.

26. Frances, Countess of Warwick, *Life's Ebb and Flow*, p. 141.

27. 22 Aug 1899 WSC ltr to LyRC, 1C2:1043–4.

28. Oct 1899 Longmans Group Papers, MS 1393/2/2371343/ii, RULSC. British royalties were set at 15 per cent on the first 3,000 copies; 20 per cent up to 10,000 copies; 25 per cent thereafter. Longmans, Green & Co. also published in the US and Canada at a royalty of 15 per cent.

29. M. Gilbert, *Churchill and the Jews*, p. 4. Lord Rothschild gave £150; Cassel £100.

30. 1907 Lumley & Lumley account, CHAR 1/58/1. The insurer was Norwich Union.

31. 1899 Randolph Payne & Sons account, 1C2:1052. Costing £27, the consignment included eighteen bottles of ten-year-old whisky, six bottles each of port, vermouth and *eau de vie*.

32. 24 Oct 1899 Longmans Book Notes, Impression Book, MS 1393/ H32/234, Royalty Ledger E5/469, RULSC. Longmans, Green & Co. printed 2,000 copies of the two volumes. It sold 1,306 copies in Britain before Christmas (earning Churchill £352 before agent's commission), and another 1,000 early in 1900.

33. 30 Oct WSC ltr to JSC, 1C2:1056.

34. WSC, *My Early Life*, p. 315.

35. L. Field, *Bendor*, pp. 12, 27, 29, 35.

36. 11 Apr 1900, CHAR 1/26/176. Generals Hamilton and Nicholson helped plead his cause.

37. WSC reminiscence, cited Lord Moran, *Churchill: The Struggle for Survival*, p. 189.

38. 25 Apr 1898 WSC ltr to LyRC, 1C2:922; 14 Mar 1898 Longmans Book Notes, MS 1393/L9, 15.42, RULSC. Longmans, Green & Co.'s sales notes summarize the plot: Laurania was an imaginary republic in the Mediterranean, ruled by an able despot Molaro, who was opposed by the rebel leader Savrola, 'a man of culture and a very persuasive orator'. When Molaro sent his beautiful wife to parley with and distract Savrola, she fell for him instead. 1898–1912 Longmans sales ledger, MS 1393/F1, pp. 169–171, RULSC. British sales were 4,704 up to the end of May 1900, but only 170 in the following year; 3,672 were sold in the colonies. *Savrola* earned Churchill royalties of £306 in its first accounting period.

39. 10 May 1900 WSC Introduction to *London to Ladysmith*, Longmans MS1393/2/72/398, RULSC.

40. 16 Feb 1900 A. Watt ltr to WSC, CHAR 8/10/1.

41. 21 Mar 1900 WSC ltr to LyRC, CHAR 28/26/52.

42. 1 May 1900 WSC ltr to LyRC, CHAR 28/26/54.

43. 22 May 1900 WSC ltr to LyRC, CHAR 28/26/53.

44. 12 May 1900 LyRC ltr to WSC, 1C2:1176.

45. Ibid.; 15 May 1900 Notes on Books, Longmans MS 1393/L9, RULSC.

46. Longmans royalty ledger and sales ledger MS 1393/E5/481–2 and F1/169–171, RULSC. Compiled from twenty-seven letters and telegrams despatched by Churchill to *The Morning Post* between 26 Oct 1899 and 10 Mar 1900, 7,571 copies sold within two weeks in Britain and a further 6,125 during the next year. Sales then slowed so sharply that they reached fewer than 15,000 before war broke out in 1914. In the US the book sold 1,850 copies. R. Cohen, *Bibliography of the Writings of Sir Winston Churchill*, pp. 92–3. Churchill's royalties failed to reach £1,000.

47. 9 Jun 1900 WSC ltr to LyRC, CHAR 28/26/59.

48. L. Amery, *Diaries*, p. 17.

5. Bachelor, Author, MP, 1900–5

1. G. Cornwallis-West in conversation with Shane Leslie, cited A. Leslie, *Jennie: Life of Lady Randolph Churchill*, p. 254.

2. Author's calculations, 24 May 1900 E. Cassel ltr to WSC, CHAR 1/23/134. Churchill had earned £2,050 from *The Morning Post*, £1,500 from his three recently published books and £500 from Sir Ernest Cassel's investments.

3. 31 Jul 1900 WSC ltr to JSC, CHAR 28/152/190–5.

4. 26 Jul 1900 Longmans Agreement with WSC, MS1393/2/237/1343 iii; Longmans Book Notes MS 1393/L9/p.254; Longmans statement ledger and royalty ledger, MS 1393/F1, E5/481–2; RULSC. Compiled from seventeen dispatches to *The Morning Post* between 31 March and 14 June 1900, with four unpublished letters added. British sales reached 6,216 over ten months after publication to 31 May 1901; then fewer than 200 in the following year. Churchill's first royalty was £339. In America, records are sparse but R. Cohen speculates fewer copies sold than the 3,000 for *London to Ladysmith*; 533 copies remained unsold in 1905.

5. Election result 1C2:1208.

6. Ibid.; 27 Oct 1900 WSC ltr to LyRC 1C2:1213–4. The duke was to pay £400 of Churchill's £1,450 expenses and meet his annual registration fee of £100.

7. 8 Sept 1900 WSC ltr to L. Leslie, 1C2: 1199. See also S. Buczacki, *Churchill & Chartwell*, p. 21.

8. 29 Oct 1900 The Lecture Agency Schedule, CHAR 1/27/13–15. Receipts totalled £3,782. Christie suggested a second tour in the spring of 1901, covering twelve more cities such as Nottingham and Derby, where Churchill could expect to earn £100. There was a further list of eighteen towns where he could expect £50–75 net. Churchill resumed the tour in March 1901, earning an extra £690. In the autumn of 1892 he made a

third tour of thirteen towns, grossing £479 (before agency commission and his travelling expenses). See 1/31/59, 90.

9. 22 Nov 1900 WSC schedule, CHAR 1/21. Churchill's cash at Cox & Co. totalled £1,033; he had £3,050 invested with Cassel; and £1,000 on its way by cheque from earlier lectures. Other amounts listed included £590 royalties due from Longmans and £1,200 to be earned from future lectures. A 'Prospective' category included the duke of Marlborough's £400 for Churchill's election expenses and £500 from his publisher.

10. 19 Nov 1900, CHAR 1/27/6. Including solicitor's fees, Churchill's debt to Thomas Briggs & Sons was £25.

11. The Oldham Deaf and Dumb Society, Oldham Evangelical Free Church Society, Lancashire and Cheshire Working Men's Association, The Boys' Brigade Oldham Branch, The Oldham Temperance Mission, Oldham Rifle Club and Oldham & District Ornithological Society pressed Churchill to offer subscriptions which varied from ten shillings to two guineas a year.

12. 21 Dec 1900 WSC to LyRC, 1C2:1222. Takings varied from £10 in Hartford to £120 in Philadelphia. The full list is at 1C2:1222.

13. 1 Jan 1901 WSC ltr to LyRC, CHAR 28/26/80. Door takings exceeded $2,000, but Pond had sold the evening for a flat fee of $500, of which Churchill's share was $350.

14. 1 Jan 1901 WSC to LyRC, CHAR 28/26/80.

15. WSC, *My Early Life*, p. 358.

16. E. Tautz & Sons Ltd. Account, CHAR 1/31/25: Tautz (breeches and trouser makers, military tailors) was paid the balance of his £144 account including 3 guineas for white cashmere racing breeches, 5 guineas for a chocolate satin racing jacket and matching racing cap, 6 guineas for a black angola dinner jacket with silk shirt, all supplied in 1895 or 1896; more recently eight jackets, nine vests and alterations to the waistline of fourteen pairs of trousers; A. F Bernau & Sons account 1/31/24: Bernau (tailor and habit maker) received £145 for items dating back to 1897, including two blue and brown jacket suits, each costing £7.10s.; a dress suit for 10 guineas; and a drab check Cheviot shooting suit for £7.15s.

17. 14 Feb 1900 WSC letter to LyRC, 2C1:27.

18. G. Cornwallis-West, *Edwardian Hey-Days*, p. 132.

19. U/d 1906 A.Anning Bills Paid in 1905, CHAR 1/55. Miss Anning lists spending items totalling £1,580, but she includes £500 sent to Sir E. Cassel for investment. The author has subtracted this amount, then added £275 for Churchill's annual rent and property taxes at 12 Bolton Street to which he moved in late 1905.

20. J. W. Allen (bag manufacturer) account, CHAR 1/47/25.

21. F. Smythson account, CHAR 1/31/14.

22. Ranelagh Club account, CHAR 1/31/58, 68, 79; J. Salter account,1/31/2.
23. 13 Mar 1901 WSC ltr to LyRC, CHAR 28/26/96. Jennie helped Churchill to hire a shorthand typist at a cost of 3s.6d. an hour.
24. U/d J. Brabazon ltr to J. Leslie 1C2:1209. Churchill and Pamela agreed to remain 'best friends' before he set off in unrequited pursuit of the American actress Ethel Barrymore, and later Muriel Wilson, heiress to a shipping fortune, to whom he proposed in early 1904. She turned Churchill down on the grounds of his poor financial prospects.
25. G. Cornwallis-West, *Edwardian Hey-Days*, pp. 119–20.
26. 12 Nov 1901 DoM ltr to WSC, CHAR 1/33/12
27. Lumley & Lumley 1906 account, CHAR 1/58/5. Five years later Lumley sent the account for payment to Churchill, not the duke.
28. Lumley & Lumley 1906 account, CHAR 1/58/1.
29. 15 Aug 1902 WSC letter to LyRC, CHAR 28/27/2.
30. Jul 1903 Andrew Stone account, CHAR 1/41/56.
31. M. Daunton, *Trusting Leviathan*, p. 336, citing L. Chiozza, *Money* (1907).
32. 19 Jun 1903 Lumley & Lumley ltr to WSC, CHAR 1/38/32; 1902/3 HM Inland Revenue account, 1/41/84.
33. R. Grenfell to C. Grenfell, cited D. Kynaston, *The City of London* 2:398.
34. 22 Aug 1904 WSC letter to LyRC, 2C1:450–1.
35. 22 Jan 1905 LyRC letter to WSC, CHAR 1/50/76.
36. 22 Aug WSC letter to LyRC, 2C1:450–1.
37. P. Clarke, *Mr Churchill's Profession*, p. 55, citing Delaney, *Literature, Money and the Marketplace*, pp. 107–15.
38. 29 May WSC ltr to Elibank, 2C2:393.
39. 27 May 1905 Lady Wimborne ltr to WSC, 2C1:393.
40. Feb 1905 Warner, Shepherd & Wade account, CHAR 1/52/3.
41. CHAR 1/52/11; 1/54/20, 45, 53. The first and second ponies, unnamed, cost 125 and 100 guineas; 'Redskin' and 'Sweep' cost £100 and £115.10s.
42. 7 Oct 1905 F. Harris ltr to WSC, 2C1:465–6.
43. 25 Oct 1905 F. Harris ltr to WSC, CHAR 8/21/88. Cassell & Co. bid £2,500, on account of a 30 per cent royalty; 24 Oct 1905 F. Harris ltr to WSC, 8/21/86.
44. 30 Oct 1905 F. Macmillan ltr to WSC, CHAR 8/21/92–3.
45. 30 Oct 1905 WSC ltr to F. Macmillan, Macmillan Archive, M/S Add 55245/2/91, BL.
46. 31 Oct 1905 Longmans letter to WSC, CHAR 8/22/1.
47. 2 Nov 1905 F. Macmillan letter to WSC, 2C1:480–1.
48. 3 Nov 1905 WSC ltr to F. Macmillan, Macmillan Archive, M/S Add 55245/2/98–100, BL.
49. 5 Nov 1905 Bangs ltr to C. Scribner, Scribner's Archive, Author Files I C0101 Box 31, M/S Div, BLPU.

50. 13 Nov 1905 WSC ltr to F. Macmillan, Macmillan Archive, M/s Add 55245/2/106–8, BL.

51. 15 Dec 1905 WSC ltr to F. Macmillan, Macmillan Archive, M/s Add 55245/2/118–9, BL.

52. Churchill polled 5,639 votes to his Conservative opponent's 4,398. Nationally, the Liberals won 377 seats compared to the Conservatives' total of 157.

53. 5 Feb 1906 F. Macmillan ltr to WSC, 2C1:492. Publication date was 3 January 1906. Macmilllan printed 6,250 copies in Britain, where the two volumes sold for a combined price of £1.18s. ($9 in the US).

54. 27, 30 Apr 1906 WSC corresp with F. Macmillan, Macmillan Archive, M/s Add 55245/2/138–9, BL; CHAR 8/24/153–5. Sales to the end of April totalled 5,777: a chart (8/24/39) shows their decline from an intial 2,300 a week to an average of 576 a week for five weeks, then 83 a week for the next five weeks and finally to 30 a week in April. American sales over the same period totalled 603 copies.

55. F. Macmillan, Mark Longman Library, RULSC.

56. 6 Jun 1906 WSC ltr to F. Macmillan, Macmillan Archive, M/s Add 55245/2/140, BL.

57. HM Inland Revenue recognized that authors' income was irregular, so allowed them to spread a book's profit for tax purposes over three years: Churchill's 1906/7 income tax return, submitted in February 1908, therefore included £2,417 of literary profits.

58. 12 Apr 1906 W. Turner Lord & Co account, CHAR 1/63/40, 91.

59. 31 Dec 1906 Hatchard Booksellers account, CHAR 1/69/15. For other booksellers' bills (and books bought), see 1/63–9. Hatchard's list ran to four pages; Churchill imported 4 cwt. of books from France.

60. 1906 Harrods account CHAR 1/63/104: Harrods' items cost £80; 1/69/2 Druce account: linen and soft furnishings from Druce cost £120.

61. 31 May 1906 J. Smith account, CHAR 1/63/71; Mar 1906 National Telephone, Westminister Electric Supply, Gas Light & Coke Co. accounts, 1/63/31, 26, 33.

62. May 1906 Mrs Thornley account January–April, CHAR 1/63/88.

6. Junior Minister and Marriage, 1906–8

1. 22 Mar 1906 Wickwar & Co. account, CHAR 1/63/38.

2. A. Anning Accounts Paid in 1906, CHAR 1/55; Ministerial Salaries factsheet M6 revised Sep 2011, House of Commons Information Office. The author has adjusted Miss Anning's record to exclude building works, but to include a full year of rent, income tax and amounts Churchill paid 'on account' for wine and cigars.

3. 21 Aug 1906 WSC ltr to EM, Marsh papers, EMAR 2, CAC.

4. 26 Aug 1906 WSC ltr to JSC, 2C1:573–4.

5. 14 Sep 1906 WSC ltr to JSC, CHAR 28/152/203.

6. 26 Aug 1906 WSC letter to JSC 2C2:573–4. In December 1906 James Shepherd & Co.'s list of stock exchange prices shows only five shares (of more than 200 quoted) to be those of British-based industrial companies. See D. Kynaston, *The City of London* 2:460–1, 468.

7. 1 Sep 1906 WSC ltr to LyRC, 2C2:578–9.

8. G. Cornwallis-West, *Edwardian Hey-Days*, pp. 158–9.

9. 19 Aug 1906 DoW ltr to WSC, CHAR 1/56/30.

10. 18 Sep 1906 LyRC ltr to WSC, CHAR 28/1/56.

11. 22 Jun, 6 Jul 1864 marchioness of Londonderry, epitome of will and probate valuation, CHAR 1/93/3–4.

12. 13 Nov 1906; 3 Jan, 7 Feb 1907; 16, 18 Feb 1921 T. Lumley ltrs to WSC, CHAR 1/57/19; 1/68/1–2, 4; 1/151/5–6, 7–8. Churchill's valuation, carried out by The Goldsmiths and Silversmiths Company, was £4,595, £170 higher: a compromise figure of £4,500 was agreed.

13. 9 Oct 1906 WSC ltr to H. G. Wells, H. G. Wells Papers, University of Illinois C-238-2, cited R. Toye, *Lloyd George and Churchill*, p. 56.

14. 11 Oct 1906 WSC speech St Andrew's Hall, Glasgow, reprinted 1909 WSC, *Liberalism and the Social Problem*, p. 78, 82–3.

15. G. Beare, *Index to the Strand Magazine 1891–1950* (Westport, CT: Greenwood Press), p. xviii. Churchill was to receive another £500 for a book collected from the articles and £30 for suitable photographs.

16. 21 Aug 1907 WSC to LyRC, CHAR 28/27/67.

17. 22 Aug 1907 LyRC ltr to WSC, 2C1:670–1.

18. 24 Sep 1907 JSC ltr to WSC, CHAR 1/66/30.

19. 27 Sep 1907 JSC ltr to WSC, CHAR 1/66/32. Scrivier had distinguished himself briefly in racing circles when he bought the filly Sceptre, which won four classic races before he sold her for £25,000. See CHAR 1/64/4–5.

20. 30 Sep 1907 JSC letter to WSC, CHAR 1/66/34.

21. 25 Oct 1907 JSC letter to WSC, CHAR 1/66/41.

22. 6 Nov 1907 WSC letter to LyRC, 2C2: 692–4.

23. 17 Nov 1907 WSC ltr to JSC, 2C2:699–700.

24. 17 Dec 1907 East Africa Protecorate account, CHAR 1/85/7. Churchill's share came to £38; the remainder was allocated to the governor's 'travelling account'.

25. 22 Apr 1908 British East African Protectorate ltr to EHM, CHAR 1/85/6; *Elgin Papers*, cited 2C2:797.

26. 14 Nov 1908 JSC ltr to WSC, CHAR 1/66/48.

27. 13 Jan 1908 WSC ltr to JSC, CHAR 28/152/214.

28. 21 Dec 1908 E. Manisty account as Receiver to Norwich Union, CHAR 28/124/1.

29. 13 Feb, 6 Apr 1908 NM ltrs to WSC, CHAR 1/80/14, 38.
30. 18 Jul 1908 Nelke Phillips Lord Randolph Churchill will trust schedule, CHAR 1/79/1. Bank rate had fallen to 3 per cent in March and 2½ per cent in May 1908.
31. M. Soames, *Clementine Churchill*, p. 31.
32. 12 Aug 1908 WSC ltr (unsent) to Hozier, 2C2:801.
33. In the absence of the bank statements that Churchill did not keep regularly until 1908, the author estimates that Churchill's income from 1900–8 totalled approximately £13,000 (from his father's biography, limited journalism, investment dividends and ministerial salary). His private expenditure and tax payments (documented by his secretary and tax adviser) over the period were of a similar order. In mid-1901, Churchill's investment balance with Sir Ernest Cassel was £6,000, but between 1901–5 he used the account to fund most of his living expenses. His net balance with Cassel was low by early 1906 when he topped it up by transferring to Sir Ernest £6,000 of his advance for *Lord Randolph Churchill*. Through other advisers, Churchill also bought shares worth £1,000–2,000 between 1901–6. He deposited most of them at Cox & Co. to act as security for his overdraft and loan of £1,000 from the bank.
34. M. Soames, *Clementine Churchill*, p. 71.
35. 17, 18 Aug 1908 NM ltrs to WSC, CHAR 1/80/47, 51.
36. 19 Aug 1908 WSC ltr to NM, CHAR 1/80/52.
37. 20 Aug 1908 NM ltr to WSC, CHAR 1/80/56.
38. 2 Sep 1908 NM ltr to WSC, CHAR 1/80/61; NM account 1/81/2.
39. 18 May 1909 NM summary, CHAR 1/89/38. Both policies were insured through Phoenix Assurance Company, the main policy costing £138 a year for five years, followed by £261 a year; the 'reverse annuity' policy cost £43 a year.
40. 29 Oct 1908 NM ltr to WSC, CHAR 1/81/6.
41. 12 Sep 1908 W. Blunt, *My Diaries*, p. 618.
42. Mackenzie N, & J, eds *The Diaries of Beatrice Webb*, 3:100.
43. Dec 1908 Catchpole & Williams account, CHAR 1/92/6. The ring cost £1.3s.6d. Churchill paid the account in 1911.

7. The HMS *Enchantress* Years, 1909–14

1. 14 Jan 1909 T. Lumley ltr to WSC, CHAR 1/89/1. The letter gave the annual income from the Garron Tower estate as at least £3,650 a year.
2. 1914 WSC schedule, CHAR 1/86/2; Randolph Payne & Sons. Ltd. accounts 1/86/3 *et seq*; in July 1914 the outstanding balance was £530 per 1/115/128.
3. J. Grunebaum & Sons account, CHAR 1/92/74.

4. 20 Sep 1908 WSC ltr to LyRC, 2C2:819–20.
5. 9 Mar 1909 T. Lumley ltr to WSC, CHAR 1/89/9.
6. 9 Mar 1909 Maple & Co. survey, CHAR 1/89/11.
7. 27 Apr 1909 CSC ltr to WSC, SFT:21. The establishment included a cook, two maids and a manservant.
8. Hodder & Stoughton Papers, CLC/B119/MS16318/001, London Metropolitan Archives; R. Cohen, *Bibliography of the Writings of Sir Winston Churchill.* 4,000 copies were printed: Churchill presented 350; 3,140 were sold in Britain; and 465 were sent to the US. Later in 1909 Hodder & Stoughton paid an advance of £100 for *The People's Rights Defended*, a collection of Churchill's speeches made in Lancashire. 30,000 copies sold at 1s. each alongside newspapers such as the *Yorkshire Observer* and *Liverpool Daily Post*.
9. Dec 1911 Carrington account, CHAR 1/106/14.
10. Jan 1909 N. Rothschild ltr to Rothschild Paris, cited D. Kynaston, *The City of London* 2:494.
11. 30 Jul 1909 D. Lloyd George speech, 2:325.
12. 4 May 1909 WSC speech Budget debate, House of Commons, printed in *Liberalism and the Social Problem*, pp. 290–1.
13. 22 Nov 1909 J. Baring, Lord Revelstoke speech to House of Lords, cited D. Kynaston, *The City of London* 2:498.
14. Cox & Co. statement, CHAR 1/94. Churchill was borrowing £1,000 through a twelve-month loan and £1,162 on overdraft. He had a £670 deposit balance on his 'Special Account' (for constituency expenses) and a £48 deposit on his 'C' Account.
15. 20 Dec 1909 *et seq* Cox & Co. passbook, CHAR 2/61/19–20.
16. 1 Apr 1911, ibid.
17. 16 Jan 1911 R. Davies ltr to R. Walden, CHAR 1/87/17–9.
18. 19 Dec 1910 WSC ltr to CSC, SFT:41–2.
19. 14 Oct 1910 W. Blunt, *My Diaries*, p. 735.
20. 19, 20 Dec 1910 WSC ltr to CSC, SFT:41–2.
21. 30 Apr, 5 May 1910 HM Inland Revenue ltr to EHM, CHAR 1/96/12, 13; A. Atkinson, *Top Incomes in the United Kingdom over the 20th Century* (University of Oxford Discussion Papers, Economic and Social History 43, Jan 2002), p. 6. The number of super-tax payers in 1911–12, the tax's third year of operation, was 11,554.
22. 1910 Cox & Co. statements, CHAR 1/94. In 1910 Churchill spent £6,145 from his main bank account, including £1,050 sent to his election agent (to whom he sent another cheque for £500 from his Special Account); he also transferred £980 to Clementine for household spending.
23. Feb, Mar, Nov 1911 Maple & Co., Bretell, Muntzer & Son, J. P. Lowter & Co., Randolph Payne & Sons and Grunebaum & Sons accounts, CHAR 1/101/15, 18, 53.

24. 20 Mar 1911 Cox & Co. ltr to WSC, CHAR 1/100/3.
25. 11 Aug 1911 S. F. Edge account, CHAR 1/101/49, 49, 54. The car was bought from S. F. Edge Ltd of New Burlington Street at a 10 per cent discount off the list price of £620; it cost over £600 after Churchill added extras.
26. 19 Jun 1912 *Punch*, p. 473, cited G. Searle, *Corruption in British Politics 1895–1930*.
27. 16 Dec 1911, 12 Jan 1912 Cox & Co. passbook, CHAR 2/61/19–20.
28. 14 Sep 1912 WSC ltr to A. Murray, CHAR 2/61/13. For a summary of the Marconi scandal, see note 33 below.
29. 21, 25 Sep WSC corresp with J. Caird, CHAR 2/61/18, 21–3.
30. 1 Nov 1912 P. Illingworth ltr to WSC, CHAR 2/61/24.
31. June 1915 Cox & Co. statement, CHAR 1/121/11.
32. 5 Aug 1916 Cox & Co statement, CHAR 1/126/11–2.
33. Two years earlier the British government had begun supposedly secret negotiations to build eighteen long-distance wireless stations at points around the empire with Britain's Marconi Wireless Telegraph Company. Marconi's managing director Godfrey Isaacs was the brother of Sir Rufus Isaacs, the government's senior legal official and a personal friend of David Lloyd George. By the time a successful outcome to the negotiations was announced on 7 March 1912, British Marconi's share price had doubled. A month later, on 19 April, London dealings were to begin in new shares issued by a separate but associated American Marconi Company, of which Geoffrey Isaacs was also a director. Isaacs had travelled to New York before the issue with a well-known London trader, Percy Heybourn, who obtained a supply of the new shares – he paid $1¼ each for most of these. Just before dealings began, American Marconi signed an attractive contract with Western Union and Canada's Great Northwestern Telegraph. Aware of these contracts, Isaacs' brother Sir Rufus bought 10,000 new American Marconi shares from Geoffrey and sold on 1,000 each of these to Lloyd George (chancellor of the exchequer) and to the the Master of Elibank (the government's chief whip). The shares started trading shortly afterwards at $3¼ each. Lloyd George sold and then bought back most of his batch of shares, finishing with a small loss. It was another two months before a journalist voiced suspicions of insider trading. W. R. Lawson wrote in *The Outlook*: 'The Marconi Company has from its birth been a child of darkness. Its finance has been of a most chequered and erratic sort. Its relations with certain Ministers have not always been purely official or political'. Forced to make a parliamentary statement, Sir Rufus denied any dealings in the shares of 'that company', meaning the British company, without disclosing his dealings in the American company. When they became aware at the end of 1912 that further revelations

were imminent, Sir Rufus and Lloyd George offered their resignations to Prime Minister Asquith, who refused to accept them. Leo Maxse, the proprietor of the right-wing *National Review*, drew a parliamentary investigatory committee's attention to the fact that neither Isaacs nor Lloyd George had denied owning American Marconi shares. When Paris's *Le Matin* reported his evidence, but inaccurately, Sir Rufus took the chance to sue for libel. See G. Searle, *Corruption in British Politics 1895–1930*, D. Kynaston, *The City of London* 2:552–5.

34. May, Jun 1913 WSC corresp with Lord Northcliffe, Northcliffe Papers, M/s Add 62156/40–53, BL.
35. 8 Jan 1913 D. Lloyd George ltr to CSC, CSCT 3/13/10, Spencer-Churchill Papers, CAC.
36. G. Cornwallis-West, *Edwardian Hey-Days*, pp. 264–5.
37. 13 Apr 1911 WSC ltr to G. Cornwallis-West, CHUR 2/519/456–7.
38. 16 Sep 1911 LyRC ltr to WSC, CHAR 1/392/4.
39. 17 Feb 1912 JSC ltr to WSC, CHAR 1/108/2.
40. 29 Nov 1913 WSC ltr to LyRC, CHAR 28/28/11.
41. 3 Dec 1913 LyRC ltr to WSC, CHAR 1/392/17.
42. 4 Apr 1914 LyRC ltr to G. Cornwallis-West, CHAR 28/39/19.
43. Mar 1914–Feb 1915 NM account 1914–5, CHAR 28/124/1; 1913 LyRC note, 28/79/136.
44. 10, 13 Feb 1914 T. Lumley corresp with WSC, CHAR 1/114/33–4, 35.
45. 14 Feb 1914 JSC letter to LyRC, CHAR 28/33/5.
46. 23 Apr 1914 WSC letter to CSC, SFT:85. The Churchills' Easter holiday in Madrid cost £51 for travel and £130 for their hotel, per April 1914 Cox & Co. statement, CHAR 1/111.
47. 27 Apr 1914 WSC ltr to CSC, SFT:86. During this period of financial strain, her daughter Mary suggests, Clementine took aunt Cornelia's wedding present, an 'exquisite' diamond necklace, to pawn at the jeweller's to raise money to pay household bills. According to the story, Churchill rushed out to try to reclaim it from the jeweller, but it was already too late. Ibid., p. 109.
48. 1 May 1914 R Cox ltr to WSC, CHAR 1/114/53.
49. 1 Jun 1914 WSC ltr to CSC, SFT:90.
50. 18 Jun 1914 High Court Judgement: *Churchill v. Churchill*, Justice Sargent, CHAR 28/79/18.
51. 9 Jul 1914 Cox & Co. ltr to WSC, CHAR 1/114/97. On commencement of his £7,000 loan, Churchill's £3,000 promissory note to Cox & Co. was cancelled; his Special Account was closed; and its balance was transferred to his main account, which then held £1,512.
52. 29 Sep 1914 Randolph Payne & Sons account, CHAR 1/115/128.

8. The Legacy of War, 1914–18

1. 6 Jul 1914 N. Rothschild ltr to Rothschild Paris, cited D. Kynaston *The City of London* 2:594.
2. 31 Jul 1914 WSC ltr to CSC, 2:714–5. The account for use of HMS *Enchantress* was £65.
3. 4 Aug 1914 WSC cable to British fleet, 2C3:1999.
4. D. Kynaston, *The City of London* 3:4.
5. 2, 9 Sep 1914 EHM ltrs to Phoenix Assurance Co., CHAR 28/142/23, 35.
6. 31 May, 19, 24 Jun 1915 F. Smith, Randolph Payne & Sons accounts, CHAR 1/122/21–2; 1/122/55, 58. Churchill ordered 1,600 cigars during the first six months of war.
7. 29 Mar 1915 A. P. Watt Archives 11036, folder 37.18 NYPL; R. Cohen, *Bibliography of the Writings of Sir Winston Churchill* A1.5, p.26. Churchill conceded 25 per cent of his fee to Longmans, Green & Co. which pointed out that it still owned the copyright. Sales of 6,449 copies over the next ten years failed to cover Churchill's advance.
8. 9 Jun 1915 WSC ltr to A. Sinclair, cited *Winston & Archie*, ed. I. Hunter, pp. 12–14.
9. 18 Jun, 17 Jul 1915 Cox & Co. ltr, E. Cassel account, WSC ltr to CSC, CHAR 1/121/11, 21, 42, *SFT*:111. Sir Ernest looked after two American bond holdings for Churchill; net of margin loans, their value to him was no more than £1,500. Churchill secured his bank overdraft through another £1,000-worth of shares, mainly in the Witbank Colliery; he overlooked another £1,000-worth of shares that he still owned in Pretoria Cement.
10. 19 Jun 1915 WSC ltr to JSC, 3C2:1041–3.
11. EHM, *A Number of People*, p. 248. Churchill spent £23 in August and September. D. Coombs with M. Churchill, *Sir Winston Churchill: Life through his Paintings*, p. 12.
12. 17 Jul 1915 WSC ltr to R. Cox, CHAR 1/142/71. Churchill accepted the quote of £147 from the Phoenix Assurance Society, on condition that it included 'risk from the fire of the enemy, so long as I do not serve as a soldier or take an active part in the hostilities'.
13. 17 Jul 1915 WSC ltr to CSC, SFT:111.
14. 20 July 1915 EHM ltr to R. Cox, CHAR 1/142/80.
15. 28 Sep 1915 WSC ltr to A. Sinclair, 4C:8–9.
16. 12 Oct, 22 Nov 1915 Cox & Co. promissory note, WSC Lloyds Bank statement, CHAR 1/120/64, 28/142/118; 1/123.
17. 19 Nov 1915 WSC letter to JSC, WSC LlBk statement, 3C2:1279–80, CHAR 1/123. Sir Ernest Cassell sent Churchill £125 a month for the next eight months, even after Churchill's net balance with him had been exhausted.

18. 11 Dec 1915 WSC ltr to CSC, SFT:124.

19. 21, 23 Nov 1915 WSC ltrs to CSC, SFT:115, 116–7.

20. Edward Hakewill Smith (later a Second World War general), who recounted the story to Churchill's official biographer – see Martin Gilbert, *Winston S. Churchill III 1914–1916*, p. 632.

21. 11 March 1916, *The Spectator*.

22. May 1916 Cox & Co. statement, CHAR 1/123.

23. 11 Jul 1916 H. Greenhaugh Smith, ltr to WSC, CHAR 8/30/4.

24. 15 Jul 1916 WSC ltr to JSC, CHAR 28/152/221, John Churchill Papers, CAC.

25. 16 Feb 1916 CSC ltr to WSC, SFT:211.

26. 15 Sep 1916 WSC ltr to A. Sinclair, cited *Winston & Archie*, ed. I. Hunter, p. 40.

27. 17 Oct 1916 Lumley & Lumley ltr to WSC, CHAR 1/126/21; 1 Dec 1916 NM ltr to WSC, CHAR 1/122/25; 8 Feb 1917 Cox & Co. statement, CHAR 1/123; loan schedule CHAR 1/130/41.

28. 11 Aug 1916 Cox & Co. ltr to WSC, CHAR 1/121/22. In 1917 Churchill had to pay £77 super-tax on his 1914–15 income of £4,778 (£4,500 salary as First Lord of the Admiralty, £282 dividend income). During the war the super-tax threshold had been reduced to £2,500 and the starting rate of tax increased to 9d. in the £. Churchill was allowed to deduct £349 of interest from his income, leaving £1,978 of qualifying income for super-tax.

29. 23 Mar, 15 Apr 1917 E. Wheater ltrs to WSC, CHAR 1/128/15, 17, 18; Cox & Co. schedule, 1/130/41. Churchill acquired 400 Barnsley Smokeless Fuel debentures, 400 British Coalite debentures plus extra share options and 375 Low Temperature Combustion shares. There is no evidence any of them produced a return.

30. 20 Jul 1917 Cox & Co. ltr to WSC, CHAR 1/130/22.

31. 5 Jan 1918 Cox & Co. schedule, CHAR 128/143/2; 14 Jan 1918 NM ltr to WSC, 1/130/1; Jan, Feb 1918 Cox & Co. corresp with WSC, 1/130/4, 6, 15.

32. 27 Feb 1918 Godstone District War Agricultural Committee report, CHAR 1/131/16. Churchill claimed to have tried three German prisoners, but found their work poor.

33. 25 Apr 1918 G. Partridge receipt, CHAR 1/131/55; June 1918 CSC note to EHM, 1/131/69.

34. 4 Apr 1918 WSC ltr to WHB, CHAR 1/130/28; Cox & Co. schedule, 1/130/41.

35. 9 Apr 1918 WHB ltr to WSC, CHAR 28/143/10; 10 Apr 1918 EHM ltr to WHB 28/143/12.

36. Jun 1918 WSC schedule, CHAR 1/130/43.

37. 13, 15 Jul 1918 WSC corresp with WHB, CHAR 28/143/53, 55.

38. 24 Sep 1918 WHB schedule, CHAR 28/143/77.
39. 27 Sep 1918 EHM ltr to R. Cox, CHAR 28/143/79.

9. A Timely Train Crash, 1918–21

1. Loelia, duchess of Westminster, *Grace and Favour*, p. 94.
2. 9 Jan 1919 D. Lloyd George ltr to WSC, 4C:450.
3. 27 Mar 1919 WHB schedule, WSC shareholdings at Cox & Co., CHAR 28/143/124. Churchill's share portfolio provided the security of *c*.50 per cent of his bank borrowings; the rest came from a mixture of inheritance prospects and life insurance policies.
4. 1923 LlBk statement, WSC receipts 1919–21, CHAR 1/130/118. In addition to his ministerial salary, Churchill earned £2,600 from journalism during 1919: £500 from the *Sunday Pictorial* (15 Jan), £500 from Associated Newspapers (7 Jul) and £1,600 from E. Hulton Co., owners of the *Daily Sketch* and *Evening Standard* (25 Nov, 24 Dec).
5. 27 Mar 1919 WHB note of mtg with WSC, CHAR 28/143/123. 'Marking the yellow strip' was an internal Cox & Co. procedure for formal authorization of banking facilities such as an overdraft.
6. 24 Mar 1919 WSC ltr to I. Hamilton, CHAR 1/133/7.
7. 13 Apr 1919 Lady Hamilton Diary, Hamilton Papers, cited C. Lee, *Jean, Lady Hamilton*, p. 206.
8. 21 May 1919 I. Hamilton ltr to WSC, CHAR 1/133/19.
9. 1923 LlBk statement, WSC receipts 1919–21, CHAR 1/130/118.
10. 15 Nov 1923 I. Hamilton ltr to Wood & Walford, Hamilton Papers.
11. 30 Jul 1919 NM ltr to WSC, CHAR 1/132/25. The trustees had paid capital costs of £6,978; the Churchills (technically Clementine as leaseholder) kept the profit of £3,022.
12. 15 Aug 1919 Lycett, Jepson & Co. ltr to NM, CHAR 1/134/30–31.
13. 19 Sep 1919 NM draft ltr to WSC, CHAR 1/134/40–43.
14. 10, 18, 21 Oct 1919 WSC corresp with Foster, NM, CHAR 1/134/50, 15, 61.
15. 7 Oct 1919 WSC schedule, CHAR 1/134/81. The largest rise in value had come from shares in Pretoria Cement (up from £2,125 on 1 Jul 1918 to £4,500 on 7 Oct 1919).
16. 15 Oct 1919 WHB schedules, ltrs to WSC, CHAR 28/143/55, 129–31, 139, 144. Churchill raised £2,100 by halving his holding of Pretoria Cement shares, but asked Bailey to reinvest £500 while sending Cox & Co. £1,600 to reduce his overdraft.
17. 25 Oct 1919 WHB ltr to WSC, CHAR 28/143/133. The payment of £5,497 for Lullenden was made up by £3,022 of profit on the property sale, approximately £2,000 for extra 'commodities' and an unexplained further component.

18. 8 Dec 1919 JSC ltr to WSC, CHAR 1/134/73; 19 Nov, 16 Dec 1919 B. Buckingham ltrs to WSC, 8/35/3, 4. Churchill bought £3,000-worth of shares through Bailey and committed to buy up to £2,000 through Vickers da Costa. By the time he was due to pay Vickers, he no longer had £2,000 left, so he asked for a £1,000 bridging loan until he received £1,500 for his recent newspaper articles.

19. 18 Dec 1919 NM ltr to WSC, CHAR 1/134/75.

20. 6 Jan 1920 E. Cassel ltr to WSC, CHAR 1/137/1; 6 Jan 1920 WSC letter to WHB, 28/143/156. 7 May 1920 NM letter to WSC, CHAR 1/137/49, 26 May 1923 LlBk statement of WSC 1920 receipts 1/130/118. In May 1920, after spending money on essential works, Churchill sold the lease to a former army friend Herbert Spender-Clay for £3,150. In the absence of Churchill's bank records between April 1919 and January 1921, it is unclear whether Churchill repaid Sir Ernest Cassel's loan of £2,300: no correspondence on the subject with either Sir Ernest or his executors (after his death in 1921) survives.

21. 20 Feb 1920 WSC schedule, CHAR 1/148/84.

22. 10 Feb 1920 WHB ltr to WSC, CHAR 28/143/166.

23. 20–21 Sep 1920 WHB note, CHAR 28/143/182.

24. 27 Apr, 28 May, 3 Jun 1920 WSC ltrs to NM, CHAR 1/137/44, 54, 58; 10 Jul, 23 Sep 1920 WSC ltrs to WHB, 28/143/181, 183.

25. 30 Jul, 1 Sep, 9, 28 Oct 1920 Oct A. Watt corresp with WSC, CHAR 8/38/8, 20, 23, 35. The reference is to a book to be collected from Churchill's recent newspaper articles, suggested by Watt on behalf of US publisher G. H. Doran, who was prepared to pay an advance of £100 for US rights. Watt was confident of obtaining £300–500 for British rights. Churchill gave up when Hodder & Stoughton made the highest offer, of only £200.

26. 22 Sept 1920 WSC ltr to WHB, CHAR 28/143/183.

27. 23 Sep 1920 R. Cox comment on WHB memo, CHAR 128/143/184.

28. 24 Mar 1920 F. Macmillan ltr to WSC, CHAR 8/38/4. Until December 1916 cabinet ministers enjoyed an unfettered right to retain and quote from their official papers. Prime Minister Lloyd George introduced a new cabinet secretariat led by Sir Maurice Hankey. After the war Sir Maurice drafted new instructions, specifying that minutes and papers 'were not the personal property of members and on the Minister leaving office it is the duty of the Secretary to recover from him. . . all cabinet papers issued to him.' Sir Maurice's proposal was omitted from the final version of the new rules debated in cabinet on 4 November 1919. Instead the cabinet agreed a rule in order to safeguard secrecy that 'no-one is entitled [to] make public use of cabinet documents without permission of the king'. See D. Reynolds, *In Command of History*, pp. 23–4, citing J. Naylor, *A Man and an*

Institution: Sir Maurice Hankey, the Cabinet Secretariat and the Custody of Cabinet Secrecy, pp. 67-9.

29. 1 Nov 1920 A. Dakers ltr to WSC, CHAR 8/38/37, 38-41.

30. 9 Nov 1920 TB ltr to WSC, CHAR 8/38/43.

31. 8 Dec 1920 WHB Note, CHAR 28/144/1. Signed on 28 November 1920, the contract included a royalty of 33⅓ per cent on the publication price of 1½ guineas. It also specified a length of 100,000 words; Churchill dictated 160,000, mostly to a ministerial private secretary H. A. Beckenham, whom he paid £350.

32. The contemporary model of publishing divided a work's rights into 'volume' (or book), 'first serial' and 'second serial' rights; and geographically between British Empire, America and other 'foreign' rights. 'First serial' rights were sold to a newspaper or magazine, allowing it to publish up to 40 per cent of the book's content in advance of the launch of the 'volume'. 'Second serial' rights were sold to less well-known newspapers or magazines and, if sold, usually preceded any 'cheap' or 'popular' book edition.

33. 14, 16, 17 Dec 1920 H. Wickham Steed corresp with WSC, CHAR 8/38/53-4, 55, 58; 21 Dec 1920 W. Lints Smith corresp with WSC 8/38/59; 29 Dec 1920 WSC ltr to CB; Christie's sale catalogue 28 November 2011, Malcolm Forbes Collection. *The Times* paid Churchill £2,000 on signature.

34. 8 Dec 1920 WHB note, CHAR 28/144/1.

35. 20 Dec 1920 C. Kingsley ltr to C. Scribner III, Scribner's Archive, Author Files 1 C0101, box 31/1, PUFL.

36. 7 Jan 1921 TB ltr to C. S. Scribner II, ibid.

37. 25 Jan 1921 C. Scribner II cable to TB, ibid.

38. 1 Feb 1921 ACB ltr to WSC, CHAR 8/40/10, 14 Mar 1921 Scribner's Archive Box Author Contracts Box 5/19, PUFL. Scribner's contract provided for a book of 150,000-200,000 words in two volumes, the first to cost $5. Churchill's royalty was set at 20 per cent, or 10 per cent on cheaper editions. His advance was split: $4,000 on signature; $5,000 on the first volume's delivery, $2,500 on its publication; $3,500 on the second volume's delivery and $3,500 on its publication.

39. Lord Hartwell, *William Camrose: Giant of Fleet Street*, pp. 95-6; D. Reynolds, *In Command of History*, p. 24, citing F. Owen, *Tempestuous Journey: Lloyd George and his Life and Times* (London, 1954), pp. 699-70; George W. Egerton, 'The Lloyd George *War Memoirs*: A Study in the Politics of Memory', *Journal of Modern History* 60 (1988), esp. pp. 57-61. Curtis Brown represented both Lloyd George and Churchill; the lead buyer for Lloyd George's rights package in both Britain and the United States was William Berry, later Lord Camrose.

40. U/d 1930s LlBk literary earnings 1920s, CHAR 1/185/26-8, u/d WSC

schedule Literary Profits War Book contracts, 1/148/55. Churchill paid £500 to a naval adviser, Admiral Jackson; £280 for printer's proofs and presentation copies.

41. The new post paid the same £5,000 a year salary as his old one. After an earned income allowance of £200, £4,800 a year was taxed. Income tax of 6s. per £ (30 per cent) was levied at source; if due, super-tax was assessed separately, one year in arrears.

42. 28 Jan 1921 WSC ltr to A. Chamberlain, CHAR 1/138/7.

43. 1 Feb 1921 A. Chamberlain ltr to WSC, CHAR 1/38/8.

44. 27 Jan 1921, WSC ltr to CSC, SFT:224.

45. 6 February 1921 WSC letter to CSC, Spencer–Churchill Papers, 4C2:1333–1334. The articles were to be reused in *Thoughts and Adventures* (1932) and *Painting as a Pastime* (1948).

46. J. Pringle, *Cambrian Railways Accident at Albemule 26 January 1922*, University of Leicester Library.

47. 3 Apr 1913, 24 Jun 1915, 16 Apr 1919 Lumley & Lumley ltrs to WSC, CHAR 1/108/10, 1/120/16, 1/134/17. Sales of houses to the tenants around Carnlough had raised £76,250, the Grosvenor Square property £4,440 and the fire-damaged Garron Tower Hotel £8,000.

48. 27 Jan 1921 T. Lumley ltr to WSC, CHAR 1/148/3.

49. 28 Jan 1921 Cox & Co. statements, CHAR 28/144/2, 1/156.

50. 7 February 1921 CSC ltr to WSC, CHAR 1/139/3.

51. 8 February 1921 CSC ltr to WSC, CHAR 1/39/10.

52. 9, 10, 24 Feb 1921 CSC corresp with WSC CHAR 1/139/11, 14, 45. 'Too good to miss,' was the reaction of Churchill, who hoped sell the articles to America for another £600. Ray Long's International Magazine Company, part of William Hearst's publishing empire, offered $1,000, equivalent to £200. Churchill held out for more, but Curtis Brown failed to place them at a price acceptable to Churchill – CHAR 8/40/71.

53. 28 Feb 1921 Lord Londonderry ltr to WSC, CHAR 1/151/15. The silver that Churchill inherited was valued by the goldsmiths Garrard & Co at £1,450.

54. 19 Feb 1921 WSC ltr to CSC, CHAR 1/151/5–6.

55. 19, 21 Feb 1921 WSC correspondence with CSC, CHAR 1/151/5–6, 1/139/35.

10. A Country Seat at Last, 1921–2

1. 7 May 1921 Lumley & Lumley ltr to WSC, CHAR 1/151/29.

2. Jun 1921 Cox & Co. schedule of investments, CHAR 28/144/51.

3. 12 Feb 1921 W. Hozier ltr to WSC, CHAR 1/138/14.

4. U/d 1917 NM schedule of LyRC liabilities, CHAR 1/128/31–4. Jennie

owed £40,000: £20,000 to Norwich Union and Phoenix Assurance; £10,000 to other official lenders, £4,200 to nine unofficial moneylenders and £3,750 to tradesmen, most of it for clothes. Churchill calculated that she had received an income of £70,000 from her trusts over the previous twenty years, but spent £45,000 of it on paying interest.

5. 6 Feb 1921 WSC ltr to CSC, 4C2:1333–4.
6. 4 Feb 1921 WSC ltr to CSC, CHAR 8/40/11; Mar 1921 H. Wodehouse LyRC account 1921, 8/124; Apr, May 1921 LyRC statement Banca Scaretti, Rome, 28/141/4–5.
7. Vittoria Sermonetta, *Sparkle Distant Worlds*, p. 11, cited A. Sebba, *Jennie Churchill*, p. 315.
8. 10 May 1922 H. Wodehouse ltr to W. Haynes, CHAR 1/1616/63; 27 Jan 1922 WSC ltr to CSC, SFT:248; 26 Jul 1922 EHM ltr to WHB, CHAR 28/144/156. The list of creditors included Sir Ernest Cassel's executors and the Enemy Debts Office, acting for Theodore Einstein & Co. Each eventually received half of what they were owed after Churchill family members waived their own claims.
9. 1921–3 WSC corresp with NM, Marshall & Co., Lincoln Trust, CHAR. 1/149/1, 2, 3, 7, 8, 10, 14, 15, 19, 21, 34, 36, 38, 42, 46, 51–2, 55, 56, 60, 61, 62; 1/161/33, 36–7; 1/169/6, 20. The dollar weakened to $4:£1 by November 1921, having stood at $3.70:£1 when Jennie died in June 1921. Churchill considered suing over the delays, but settled for a contribution of $5,000 by the Manhattan Club towards the brothers' legal expenses.
10. 21 Oct 1921 NM ltr to WSC, CHAR 1/150/43–4. Churchill's half-share of Lord Randolph's will trust was worth £16,500 (half of it already used to buy his Sussex Square lease). His marriage settlement was worth £37,500, after transfers from his parents' 'English' and 'American' settlements.
11. 5 Jul 1921 WHB note of mtg with WSC, R. Cox, CHAR 28/144/46.
12. 11 Aug 1921 WSC ltr to Cox & Co., CHAR 28/144/68, 1/148/36–7.
13. 17 Aug 1921 WHB note of mtg with WSC, CHAR 28/144/66.
14. For more background on Chartwell and its history, see S. Buczacki, *Churchill & Chartwell*, pp. 105–13.
15. 10 Jul 1921 CSC ltr to WSC, CHAR 1/139/58.
16. 11 Jul 1921 CSC ltr to WSC, CHAR 1/139/62.
17. 20 Jul 1921 CSC ltrs to WSC, CHAR 1/139/85, 86.
18. S. Buczacki, *Churchill & Chartwell*, p.101.
19. Jul 1921–Mar 1922 Nicholl Manisty account, CHAR 1/169/9.
20. 20, 28 Mar 1922 NM ltr to WSC, schedule, CHAR 1/161/19–21,22–3. For more information about the controversy over the use of trusts in 1921–2, see M. Daunton, *Just Taxes*, pp. 109–11.
21. 19, 22 Aug 1921 Barker & Co. (Coachbuilders) ltr & account, CHAR 1/153/24,27.

22. 18 Aug 1921 CSC ltr to WSC, CHAR 1/139/70.
23. WSC conversation with AMB, cited A. Montague Browne, *Long Sunset*, p. 147.
24. 23 Aug 1921 W. Blackburn & Son account, CHAR 1/153/38.
25. Nov 1922 Cox & Co. statement, CHAR 1/156.
26. 16 Dec 1921 WSC notes, CHAR 1/148/90. Churchill's personal assets comprised Garron Tower investments of £46,000, South African shares of £14,000, 'book money' and '[silver] plate' of £5,000.
27. 29 Dec 1921 WSC ltr to CSC, 4C3:1706–7.
28. See footnote, 4C3:1713.
29. 1 Jan 1922 WSC ltr to CSC, 4C3:1708–9.
30. Jan 1922 Cox & Co. statement, CHAR 1/156.
31. 4 Jan 1922 WSC ltr to CSC, SFT:247.
32. 30 Jan, 2 Jun 1922 VdaC contracts, accounts, CHAR 1/162/various, 28/144/109, 112. The Churchill brothers' investment approach was tactical: Victory Bonds bought on 30 January were sold ten weeks later for a profit of 7 per cent; Local Loans bought on 15 February were sold within a month for a profit of 8 per cent, re-bought in April and resold six weeks later.
33. Feb 1922 JSC schedule of WSC investments, CHAR 1/1/162/18. The value of Churchill's personal portfolio had risen to £60,000, of which three-quarters was invested in bonds, the balance almost all in South African mining shares.
34. 7 Feb 1922 WSC ltr to CSC, 4C3:1757.
35. Apr 1922 Cox & Co. statements, CHAR 1/156, 171.
36. See D. Reynolds, *In Command of History*, p. 25.
37. Jun 1922 Cox & Co. statement, CHAR 1/156. Churchill bought a mixture of Brazilian bonds and shares of British companies including Imperial Tobacco, Courtauld, Fine Cotton Spinners and J & P Coats.
38. 20 Jul 1922 WSC ltr to CSC, SFT:258.
39. 7, 9 Aug 1922 WSC ltrs to CSC, 4C3:1950.
40. 8 Aug 1922 CSC ltr to WSC, CHAR 1/158/44–5. The Frinton house cost £210 to rent for August.
41. 18 Aug 1922 WSC ltr to CSC, 4C3:1958–9.
42. 8 Aug 1922 CSC ltr to WSC, CHAR 1/158/44–5.
43. 14 Sep 1922 KFR ltr to WSC, CHAR 1/159/20.
44. 14, 15 Sep 1922 WSC corresp with KFR, CHAR 1/159/20/22.
45. Recollections of H. N. Harding, M. Gilbert, *In Search of Churchill*, p. 299.
46. S. Churchill, *A Thread in the Tapestry*, p. 22.
47. 22 Sep 1922 WSC ltr to WHB, CHAR 1/162/68; 28/144/61. £3,000 of the £25,000 was represented by a contract for American serial rights, which Churchill described as 'in view'. Curtis Brown had told Churchill nine

days earlier that, after struggling to sell these rights, they now had 'some hope' that the United Press Syndicate would pay $15,000 (£3,000). The sale did not materialize.

48. Ibid.
49. 13 Oct 1922 WSC ltr to DoM, CHAR 1/161/75–8.
50. 11, 13, 17 Oct 1922 DoM corresp with NM, WSC, CHAR 1/159/17, 1/161/75–8, 1/161/84.
51. *The Times* (17 Oct 1922).
52. 7 Nov 1922 WSC ltr to WHB, CHAR 1/162/79. Churchill sold his Brazilian government bonds for £11,250 to raise a net £1,250 after cutting back his bank loan by £10,000. He then borrowed a fresh £4,500 for a year from Cox & Co., using Chartwell as security. In addition, Lord Randolph Churchill's will trust lent Churchill £4,000 against a mortgage on Chartwell, after he and Jack had agreed how to divide the trust's assets between them – see Feb 1923 Nicholl Manisty account, 1/169/9
53. WSC, *Thoughts and Adventures*, p. 213.

11. Out of Office, 1923–4

1. 18 Nov 1922 T. E. Lawrence ltr to WSC, CHAR 1/157.
2. Dec 1922 LlBk statements, CHAR 1/171. The Rêve d'Or cost 15,400 francs (£243) to rent for three months; the Citroën cost 5,000 francs (£81).
3. R. James (ed), *Chips: The Diaries of Sir Henry Channon*, 29 Jan 1935, cited S. Buczacki, *Churchill & Chartwell*, p. 121.
4. 25 Aug 1926 T. Jones, *Whitehall Diary* 2:67, cited R. Toye, *Lloyd George & Churchill: Rivals for Greatness*, p. 232.
5. P. Tilden, *True Remembrances: The Memoirs of an Architect*, p. 115.
6. 6 Nov 1922 WSC ltr to CSC, 4C3:2118–9.
7. 28 Nov 1922 TB ltr to WSC, CHAR 8/41/112–3.
8. 27 Jan 1923 WSC ltr to CSC, 5C1:18.
9. 3 Mar 1923 WSC ltr to A. Bonar Law, 5C1:32–6.
10. 10 Jan 1923 WSC ltr to JSC, 5C1:15–6.
11. 4, 10, 30 Jan, 16 Feb 1923 WSC ltrs to JSC, CSC, CHAR 28/152/233, 234; 5C1:23–6, 28.
12. 10 Feb 1923 WSC ltr to JSC, CHAR 28/152/236.
13. 16 Feb 1923 WSC ltr to JSC, 5C1:27–8.
14. 7 Mar 1924 Price Waterhouse & Co. Report on Examination of Safe Custody Securities of Cox's Nominees Ltd. LBGA A56/2/b/3, pp. 34–52. Bank mergers, under way since the 1880s, had accelerated after the war: National Provincial Bank with Union of London & Smiths Bank;

London County Bank with Westminster Bank and Parr's; London City & Midland Bank with London Joint Stock Bank; Barclays Bank with London, Provincial & South Western Bank; Lloyds Bank with Capital & Counties Bank. See D. Kynaston, *The City of London*, 3:44.

15. 9 Jul–30 Oct 1918 B. Cockayne corresp with R. Cox, LBGA A56/B/104. A Royal Air Force contact had tipped off the Bank of England's deputy governor that a £30,000 loan to an aircraft company had taken Cox & Co. outside its area of expertise. The bank's main political contact was Andrew Bonar Law.

16. 3 Feb 1923 H. Bell ltr to Bank of England, LBGA A56/C/11; O. Hoare ltr to M. Baird LBGA 56/B/104; 9 Jul 1918 B. Cockayne ltr to R. Cox, ibid. Lloyds Bank demanded and received guarantees against loss: it was to treat Cox & Co. as a separate unit for four years, at the end of which it would share any surplus 50:50 with the Bank of England, but the central bank would guarantee losses up to £900,000. The Cox & Co. unit of Lloyds Bank lost £350,000 during 1923–4, then almost broke even in 1925. Lloyds Bank claimed £450,000 against its guarantees, but its payment was reduced to take account of Cox & Co.'s tax losses. Lloyds Bank kept Cox & Co.'s Gracechurch Street and Pall Mall offices (in the latter of which its Cox & Kings branch still trades). LBGA A/56/C/40, 11.

17. 17, 24 Feb 1923 WSC corresp with WHB, CHAR 28/144/183.

18. 4 Jan 1923 WSC ltr to JSC, 5C1:12; 5 Jan 1923 V. Cazalet diary, cited 5C1:13.

19. Jan–Mar 1923 LlBk statements, CHAR 1/171/various.

20. LlBk pass book, CHAR 1/155.

21. M. Soames, *Clementine Churchill*, p. 72.

22. 29 Mar, 16 May, 2 Aug 1923 TB ltrs to WSC, CHAR 8/50/1–3, 8,21–2; 22 Jun 1923 CSIII ltr to WSC, Scribner's Archive box 31/1, PUFL. Published in America at $6.50 per copy on 6 April (sales remained below 4,000 in February 1924); in Britain at 30s. on 10 April.

23. 26, 27, 29 Sep, 16 Oct 1923 WSC corresp with W. Lints Smith, TNL Archive Sir Winston Churchill Managerial File MAN/1; 1 Apr 1923 WSC ltr to CSIII, Scribner Archive box 31/2, PUFL; 2 Jun, 2 Aug 1923 TB ltrs to WSC, CHAR 8/5/20,21. Scribner agreed an advance of $6,000.

24. Mar 1923 WSC ltr to P. Tilden, Philip Tilden Papers, cited S. Buczacki, *Churchill & Chartwell*, p. 128.

25. 10 Jul 1923 P. Tilden ltr to WSC, CHAR 1/395/3–4.

26. 23, 30 Aug 1923 P. Tilden corresp with WSC, CHAR1/167/22,23; 1/395/13; 29 Aug 1923 WSC schedule 1/395/8. The Churchills also specified Gothic windows, wood panelling and other extras to increase the estimate by £320.

27. See M. McMenamin, 'Winston Churchill and the Litigious Lord', *Finest*

Hour 95, summer 1997 issue, The Churchill Centre; a summary of a longer article that first appeared in the publication *Litigation*, winter 1995.

28. 11 Oct 1923, Apr 1924 NM accounts, CHAR 1/169/36; 1/174/6.

29. See M. McMenamin, 'Winston Churchill and the Litigious Lord', ibid.

30. See H. Montgomery Hyde, *Lord Alfred Douglas*, and M. McMenamin, 'Winston Churchill and the Litigious Lord', ibid. Lord Douglas was convicted and sentenced to six months in prison.

31. 16 Aug 1923 WSC ltr to CSC, 5C1:54–5.

32. 2 Sep 1923 WSC ltr to CSC, 5C1:56–9.

33. 1 Oct 1923 R. Watson ltr to JSC, CHAR 2/128/18.

34. 5 Sep 1923 WSC ltr to CSC, 5C1:59–60; Sep 1923 LlBk statement, CHAR 1/171. Churchill's bank account confirms he made three cash withdrawals totalling 15,000 francs at the casino (and one other on the way home), then banked 59,000 French francs and 3,660 Spanish pesetas on return, a profit of more than 30,000 francs.

35. Sep 1923 LlBk statement, CHAR 1/171.

36. 2 Aug, 17, 23 Oct 1923 TB ltrs to WSC, CHAR 8/50/21, 32, 33. The second volume was published in October in time for the Christmas selling season on both sides of the Atlantic. By early 1924 British sales reached 9,587 (compared to the first volume's 11,848), at which point Churchill had earned British book royalties (for both volumes) of £9,424. US sales reached only 2,700 after three months. See R. Cohen, *Bibliography of the Writings of Sir Winston Churchill*, pp. 223, 238.

37. 15 Aug 1923 WSC ltr to CSC, 5C1:54–55.

38. A. Atkinson, *Top Incomes in the United Kingdom over the 20th Century*, p. 7, University of Oxford, Discussion Papers, Economic and Social History, 43, Jan 2002; u/d 1925 Cox & Co. schedule, CHAR 1/185/24.

39. 2 Sep 1923 WSC ltrs to CSC, 5C1:56–59; 20 Nov 1923 R. Waley-Cohen ltr to WSC, 5C1:68–9.

40. 22 Nov 1923 LlBk statement, CHAR 1/171.

41. Jan 1924 B. Bracken, 'Monthly Notes', *English Life*, cited C. Lysaght, *Brendan Bracken*, p. 60.

42. 16 Jan 1924 Tilden accounts, CHAR 1/395/48–9.

43. 22 Dec 1923, 16 Jan 1924 WSC corresp with P. Tilden, CHAR 1/395/19, 48; 12 Sep 1923 KFR ltr to WSC, 1/167/25. The finished property was due to comprise six reception rooms, twenty-two bedrooms and seven bathrooms.

44. 17 Feb 1924 WSC ltr to CSC, 5C1:105–7.

45. WSC, *Thoughts and Adventures*, p. 213.

46. 23 Apr 1924 WSC ltr to TB, CHAR 8/199/12; A. Curtis Brown ltr to CSIII, Scribner Archive 3A box 31, PUFL.

47. 12 Jun 1924 E. Nonweiler ltr to WSC, CHAR 1/176/5. Churchill's 1924/5

tax liability of £1,500 represented an effective tax rate of 26.5 per cent on £5,613 of literary and investment income. His 1925/6 liability of £3,400 worked out at 35 per cent on earnings of £9,713, triggering a greater super-tax liability.

48. 17 Apr 1924 WSC ltr to CSC, 5C1:144.
49. 8 May 1924 W. Bray schedule, CHAR 1/173/17–8;10 Apr, 4 May 1923 P. Tilden ltr to WSC, 1/395/21,23–5; u/d 1924 WSC draft notes, 1/395/6–12.
50. 16 Jun, 2, 4 Jul 1924 W. Bray, J. Leaning & Sons ltrs to WSC, CHAR 1/173/26, 35–6, 37–8; 10 Jul 1924 W. Bray ltr to P. Tilden, 1/395/44; 15 Jul 1924 WSC ltr to W. Bray, 1/395/51–2.
51. 22, 25 Nov, 1 Dec 1924 J. Leaning & Sons report and corresp with WSC, WSC correspond with NM, CHAR 1/173/46, 52, 55, 56; 1/174/30. The sum assured was £19,760.
52. G.M. Young, *Stanley Baldwin* p.88, cited H. Pelling *Winston Churchill*, p.296

12. Chancellor under Pressure, 1925–8

1. 8 Nov 1924 WSC ltr to WHB, CHAR 1/176/39.
2. Ibid. 9 Feb 1925 WSC ltr to NM, CHAR 1/184/6. Churchill borrowed an additional £1,150 from Lord Randolph's will trust.
3. 17 Jan 1925 WSC ltr to WHB, CHAR 28/144/243.
4. 15 Dec 1924 E. Nonweiler ltr to WSC, CHAR 1/176/40. Nonweiler forecast tax bills for Churchill of £4,480 in 1925/6, £5,933 in 1926/7 and £5,745 in 1927/8.
5. 6, 7 Nov 1924 WSC ltrs to W. Lints Smith, TB, CHAR 8/198, 8/199/18.
6. 4 Mar 1925 E. Nonweiler ltr to WSC, CHAR 1/185/6.
7. 15 Dec 1924 R. Hopkins ltr to WSC, CHAR 1/176/44.
8. 21 Oct 1924, 4 Mar 1925 E. Nonweiler ltrs to WSC, CHAR 1/148/56, 1/185/6.
9. 15 Mar 1925 WSC ltr to CSC, SFT:291. *Nash's Pall Mall* published one of these articles, *Hobbies – for Those Whose Work and Pleasure are One* (December 1925); it was reused as a chapter in *Thoughts and Adventures* (1932) and in *Painting as a Pastime* (1948). See R. Cohen, *Bibliography of the Writings of Sir Winston Churchill*, pp. 1348–9.
10. 2 Feb 1925 WSC corresp tr with Hope & Sons, P. Tilden, J. Leaning & Sons, CHAR 1/395/70–1, 72–4.
11. WSC draft memoirs, CHUR 4/76/13 cited R. Toye, *Lloyd George & Churchill*, p. 256.
12. 28 Apr 1925 WSC speech to House of Commons, Parliamentary Debates 5th ser. 183, 28 Apr 1925, cols 64–5, 85–6. Churchill increased death

duties on estates valued from £12,500 up to £1 million in order to cut the basic rate of income tax by 10 per cent, reduce the pension age from 70 to 65 and extend its payment to widows and orphans. See M. Daunton, *Just Taxes*, pp. 124, 132–7; 9 December 1924 WSC letter to Lord Salisbury, 5C1:297–8

13. May 1925 LlBk statement, CHAR 1/187.

14. 16 Aug 1925 WSC ltr to JSC, CHAR 1/184/62.

15. For more details of the first Chartwell economy drive, see CHAR 1/178/36, 1/182/54, 1/184/63, 66, 1/191/18; Oct 1925 E. Nonweiler schedule, CHAR 1/185/26–7.

16. 27, 28 Dec 1925, 23 Jan 1926 WSC ltrs to J. Leaning, CHAR 1/182/94, 95, 1/189/8.

17. 29 Jan 1926 P. Tilden ltr to Fleetwood, Eversden & King, Tilden Papers, cited S. Buczacki, *Churchill & Chartwell*, p. 145.

18. 4 Feb 1926 WSC ltr to CSC, 5C1:640–1

19. 25 Mar 1926 WSC ltr to W. Guinness CHAR 1/192/25. Walter Guinness had gifted the lamp to Churchill, who reported feeling 'decidedly more energetic' after two 'doses'.

20. May 1926 LlBk statement, CHAR 1/193.

21. 10 Jun 1926 JSC ltr to WSC, CHAR 1/190/15.

22. U/d 1926 R. Hopkins note, NA IR 40/12833

23. 9 Jun 1926 R. Hopkins note of meeting with WSC, ibid.

24. 30 Jun 1926 R. Hopkins draft ltr, CHAR 1/191/29; 20 Jul 1926 WSC amended ltr to R. Hopkins, 1/191/38. Churchill crossed out the words 'but not serially' in a sentence that Hopkins had drafted as: 'In these circumstances I am now proposing to complete the two books which I had in preparation & to publish them (but not serially) in the spring.'

25. 23 Jul 1926 J. Shaw note to R. Hopkins, NA IR 40/12833.

26. 30 Jul 1926 R. Hopkins ltr to WSC, CHAR 1/191/39.

27. 21 Jun 1926 C. Kingsley ltr to ACB, CHAR 8/207/40; 12 Jul 1926 Scribner contract, 8/205/10. Kingsley offered £700, later squeezed up to £800.

28. 13 May, 2 Jun 1926 TB ltrs to ACB, CHAR 8/207/30; 2 Jun 1926 LlBk guarantee, 8/205/2.

29. 31 Jul 1926 LlBk loan statement, CHAR 1/193, 196. The total includes: £6,500 overdraft; £2,000 bank loan; £12,000 mortgage from Lord Randolph's will trust; £11,600 loan from Churchill's Elder Children's Settlement. CHAR 1/196/1.

30. 27 Jul 1926 W. Lints Smith ltr to WSC, CHAR 8/205/11, 11 Sep 1926 WSC ltr to TB, CHAR 8/206/14, u/d W. Lints Smith internal memo, TNL Archive Sir Winston Churchill Managerial File, MAN/1.

31. Aug 1926 WSC memo to CSC, CSC Papers 3/24, CAC.

32. R. Boothby, *Recollections of a Rebel*, pp. 44, 46.

33. 11 Sep, 31 Oct 1926 WSC corresp with TB, CHAR 8/206/14, 30; 9 Nov, 7

Dec 1926, 7 Jan 1927 H. Bourne ltrs to WSC, 8/206/34, 42, 8/213/4. Churchill's final bill for corrections, deletions, errata slips, maps and index on the third volume of *The World Crisis* exceeded £600.

34. 6 Jan 1927 WSC ltr to CSC, 5C1:906–7.

35. 1 Feb 1927 LlBk statement, CHAR 1/193. Three separate cash withdrawals at Casino R. Ferrand that evening totalled 35,000 francs (£385); on return, Churchill deposited 1,020 francs (£8).

36. 28, 25 Jan 1927 WSC ltrs to CSC, 5C1: 922, 927–9.

37. 18 Mar, 25 Apr 1927 CSIII ltr, cbl to WSC, Scribner's Archive, Author files I, 3A Box 31/2, PUFL; 26, 27, 30 April 1927 TB ltrs to WSC, CHAR 8/213/15, 18,20; 22 Jul 1927 CSIII ltr to WSC, 8/214/67; 13 May, 2 Jun 1927 TB ltrs to WSC, 8/213/24, 28, 66. The book's extra length and many maps forced publication in a boxed set of two books, at a higher price. Scribner's printed 3,150 sets in America reporting sales of only 1,500 in the first six weeks; by late July 1927, they had picked up to 2,800.

38. 20 May 1925 LlBk statement, CHAR 1/193; 27 Mar, 30 Apr WSC ltrs to E. Nonweiler, 1/197, 40, 32.

39. 20 May 1927 WSC memo to O. Niemeyer, 5:238. Sir Otto Niemeyer (1883–1971) was Controller of Finance at the Treasury, 1922–7; he became a director of the Bank of International Settlements (1931–65) and of the Bank of England (1938–52).

40. 18, 23 Aug 1927 C. Fisher corresp with CB, CHAR 8/214/72, 76; 25 Aug, 29 Sep 1927 WHB ltrs to WSC, 1/197/16, 18; 22 Sep 1927 ACB ltr to WSC, 8/214/78; TB and CB statements, 8/214/81, 79.

41. 12 May 1927 Fleetwood, Eversden, King ltr to P Tilden, Tilden Papers, cited S. Buczacki, *Churchill & Chartwell*. Churchill had first expected the combined costs of purchase and alterations to amount to £13,500. Tilden's career went into decline; Churchill's carpenter, Wallace, left Westerham, bankrupt, two years later; the builders, electricians and surveyors disappeared from view, leaving only Henry Hope & Sons, the window and locks contractor, still trading.

42. 2, 4 Dec 1927 ACB corresp with WSC, CHAR 8/207/43, 44; 9 Dec 1927 with C. Kingsley, Scribner's Archive Author files I, 3A Box 31/2 PUFL; 28 Dec 1927, 16 Jan, 3 Feb 1928 CSIII ltr to ACB, ibid. Scribner first offered $3,000 before settling at $3,600 (£720).

43. 21 Nov 1927 W. Lints Smith ltr to WSC, TNL Archive Sir Winston Churchill Managerial File, MAN/1. *The Times* cut its fee from £2,500 to £2,000.

44. 29 Feb 1928 WSC contract, International Magazine Company, CHAR 8/219/5.

45. 26 Jan, 27 Feb 1928 WSC corresp with TB, CHAR 8/220/3, 9–10.

46. 1 Mar 1928 WSC ltr to TB, 5C1:1218–19; 2 Apr 1928 TB contract, CHAR

8/220/29; TNL Archive Sir Winston Churchill Managerial File, MAN/1. *The Times* lent Butterworth half the funding for the extra advance.

47. 6, 9 Dec 1927, 11 Jan, 6 Mar 1928 E. Nonweiler corresp with WSC, CHAR 1/197/24,23, 1/203/3, 9. Churchill introduced a single graduated scale, covering both income and the renamed sur-tax. See M. Daunton, *Just Taxes*, p. 111.
48. 8 Apr 1928 WSC ltr to CSC, 5C1:1253–4. For Scribner's contract, see CHAR 8/219/1.
49. Oct, Nov 1928 Hilda Neal account, Miss Bradford expenses, CHAR 8/219/16–18. Miss Bradford and a typewriter cost four guineas a week; she was put up at a hotel in Westerham and given a daily taxi to and from Chartwell.
50. 1 Aug 1928 S. Gaselee ltr to O. O'Malley, CHAR 8/217/41; 4 Aug 1928 C. Fisher letter to S. Gaselee, 8/217/43; 30 Nov 1928 S. Gaselee ltr to O. O'Malley, 8/218/147.
51. 7 Aug WSC ltr to CSC, 5C1:1321–2.
52. 21–3 Sep 1928 Diary of James Scrymgeour-Wedderburn, Dundee papers, cited 5C1:1340–47.
53. 22 Sep 1928 WSC ltr to TB, CHAR 8/220/44.
54. 27 Dec 1928 WSC ltr to W. Lints Smith, CHAR 8/219/40; 7 Jan 1929 WSC ltr to S. Baldwin, Baldwin papers cited 5C1:1411–3.
55. 25 Oct 1928 ACB ltr to WSC, CHAR 8/207/51.
56. 14 Nov 1928 WSC ltr to CSC, 5C1:1378–9.
57. 28 Dec 1928 TB ltr to WSC, CHAR 8/220/68.
58. 6 Mar 1929 R. Dingle ltr to WSC, CHAR 8/225/77.
59. 29 Mar 1929 F. Greenslet ltr to WSC, CHAR 8/225/81–5.
60. 10 May 1921 G. Harrap ltr to WSC, CHAR 8/225/95–6.
61. 23 May 1929 WSC cbl to TB, CHAR 8/226/54.

13. Making – and Losing – a New World Fortune, 1928–9

1. Jun 1929 WSC schedule, CHAR 1/211/6–7.
2. 5 Jul 1929 WSC ltr to W. Lints Smith, CHAR 8/225/162. When serialization began in June 1933, Lord Camrose decided to use *The Sunday Times* rather than *The Daily Telegraph*.
3. 30 Jan 1929 G. Blake ltr to EHM, CHAR 8/225/3717; 20 Feb 1929 WSC corresp with G. Blake, 8/225/60, 64.
4. 8 Jun 1929 J. Farquharson ltr to WSC, CHAR 8/228/4.
5. 1925 Dealing Profits and Losses, Baruch Papers, MC006/742, Mudd Manuscript Library, PUMM.
6. 29 Jun 1929 WSC ltr to C. Brown, CHAR 8/227/30.
7. 28 Jun 1929 WSC ltr to BMB, CHAR 1/205/29.

8. Jul 1929 BMB notes on WSC letter, Baruch Papers MC 006 Vol 64, PUMM.

9. 28 Jul 1929 WSC ltr to BMB, Baruch Papers, MC 006 Vol 64, PUMM.

10. 15 Jul 1929 BMB ltr to WSC, CHAR 1/206/17.

11. 30 Jun 1929 LlBk statement, CHAR 1/213. £872 income tax was already overdue for 1927/8; £880 income tax and £2,300 sur-tax was now due for 1928/9; Churchill would have to pay at least £1,200 income tax for 1929/30 in mid-1930.

12. 1, 22 Jul 1929 WSC ltrs to G. Harrap, CHAR 1/210/1–3; C. Scribner 5C2:23.

13. 30 July 1929 WSC ltr to WHB, CHAR 28/145/12.

14. 27 Jun, 16 Jul 1929 ACB ltrs to WSC, CHAR 8/227/31, 33.

15. 8 Aug 1929 WSC ltr to CSC, 2C:37–40.

16. 8 Aug 1929 WSC ltr to CSC, 5C2:37–40.

17. 12 Aug 1929 WSC ltr to CSC, 5C2:43–6.

18. 16 Aug 1929 E. Rich ltr to WSC, CHAR 8/227/2. *The Daily Telegraph* offered to take ten articles for a fee of £1,000; 29 Aug 1929 J. Wheeler ltr to E. Rich, 8/227/4; The Bell Syndicate guaranteed Churchill a minimum $500 each article for US sales; he was also to keep 60 per cent of Canadian sales. The articles were also sold to South Africa, Australia and Malaya (for a combined £225), and to Holland and France's *Le Figaro*. With a foresight to which he paid scant personal heed, Churchill suggested 'The Great Stock Market Craze' as an early subject.

19. 16 Aug 1929 WSC ltr to CSC, 5C2:51.

20. 20 Aug 1929 WSC ltr to TB, CHAR 8/226/71.

21. 27 Aug 1929 WSC ltr to CSC, 5C2:60–2. The article,'Trotsky – the Ogre of Europe', (fee £450) appeared in *Nash's Pall Mall* and *Cosmopolitan* (US) in December 1929. 'Lord Ypres' (formerly Sir John French) and 'Joseph Chamberlain' were despatched from New York on 10 October for the magazines' January and February 1930 editions. After retouching, both featured in 'Great Men of Our Time', the *News of the World* (1936).

22. 28 Aug 1929 J. Richardson ltr to WSC, CHAR 1/211/16. Together, the two stakes cost $6,271.

23. 25 Aug 1929 WSC ltr to CSC, 5C2:55–8.

24. 27 Aug 1929 WSC letter to CSC, 5C2:60–2.

25. 3 Sep 1929 F. Schultz ltr to WSC, CHAR 1/211/29.

26. 4 Sep 1929 WSC ltr to J. Richardson, CHAR 1/211/34. Churchill sold the shares three weeks later for a profit of $1,400.

27. 6 Sep 1929 RSC diary, 5C2:72.

28. 29 Sep 1929 WSC ltr to CSC, SFT:346–7.

29. 19 Sep 1929 WSC ltr to CSC, CHAR 1/207/81.

30. 7 Sep 1929 WSC schedule, CHAR 1/211/43.

31. 25 Sep 1929 WSC ltr to CSC, 5C2:93–6.
32. 30 Sep 1929 H. Vickers cbl to WSC, CHAR 1/211/54.
33. 29 Sep 1929 WSC ltr to CSC, 5C2:96–8.
34. 1 Oct 1929 W. Van Antwerp cbl to WSC, CHAR 1/211/62.
35. Oct 1929 Savoy Plaza Hotel account, Baruch Papers, MC 006 Vol 64, PUMM. For three weeks' stay, including theatre tickets and valet service, the bill was $1,250.
36. 9 Oct 1929 WSC cbl to W. Van Antwerp, CHAR 1/211/64.
37. 10 Oct 1929 WSC cbl to W. Van Antwerp, CHAR 1/211/67; 9 Oct 1929 Torge & Schiffer cbl to WSC, 1/208/9. The fee of $12,500 for a speech which Churchill gave at New York's Bond Club (arranged by Baruch and sponsored by McGowan) funded the first cheque – see 14 Oct 1929 E. F. Hutton Account, CHAR 1/211/57. Churchill sent a second cheque for $2,187.
38. 10 Oct 1929 WSC cbl to A. Bailey, CHAR 1/208/25.
39. 12 Oct 1929 WSC corresp with VdaC, CHAR 1/211/71, 75.
40. 10 Oct 1929 WSC cbl to VdaC, CHAR 1/211/69.
41. Dec 1929 VdaC schedule, E. F. Hutton dealings October 1929, CHAR 1/211/140–41.
42. Oct 1929 WSC schedule, CHAR 1/216/44.
43. 25 Oct 1929 Van Antwerp cbl to WSC, CHAR 1/211/92.
44. 25 Oct 1929 WSC cbl to H. McGowan, CHAR 1/208/108.
45. Cited C. Sandys, *Chasing Churchill*, p. 98.
46. 29 Oct 1929 WSC schedule, CHAR 1/211/98.
47. Averell Harriman Papers, General File, working file 2, CURBMSL.
48. 1929 Income tax computation, Baruch Papers, MC 006/742, PUMM.
49. 30 Oct 1929 BMB cbl to WSC, Baruch Papers, MC 006 Vol 64, PUMM.
50. 31 Oct 1929 B. Baruch cbl to WSC, CHAR 1/211/102. These transactions were the source of the story that Baruch reversed all of Churchill's New York losses (told in Sir John Colville's memoirs: J. Colville, *The Churchillians*, pp. 86–7): 'When Churchill arrived in New York, unhampered by his wife's sobering presence,' Colville wrote, 'he allowed his gambling instinct to take charge. He went to Baruch's office, sat down before the price indicator and played the markets. He knew nothing of what he was doing: to him it was like playing *roulette* at Monte Carlo. He plunged deeper and deeper. Finally he stopped, for he had lost more than he possessed. He realized that he must sell Chartwell and all that he owned. Baruch came into the room and Churchill told him that he was ruined. Baruch explained that, guessing what would happen, he had given instructions that every time Churchill bought Baruch would sell, and every time Churchill sold Baruch would buy. He was therefore all square. Presumably Baruch paid the commissions. Churchill never

forgot the debt he owed.' There is no evidence to back up this story in Baruch's Financial Records for 1927–36 [Baruch Papers, MC 006, box 742, PUMM]: these record Baruch's transactions with more than twenty brokers and identify the investments that he made for various third parties (his daughter *et al*). None of the sixty-seven deals recorded in his October 1929 accounts were originally carried out in Churchill's name. The deals consist of Baruch's customary mix of sales and purchases, undermining the legend that he was one of the few financiers to foresee the Crash.

51. 9 Dec 1929 WSC article, *Daily Telegraph*.

14. A Strategy for Survival, 1930–1

1. 12, 13 Nov 1929 WSC draft, WHB ltr to WSC, CHAR 1/211/106, 28/145/5.
2. 3, 7 Jan 1930 WSC corresp with G. Blake, CHAR 8/273/3, 13.
3. 20 Nov 1929 L Thornley ltr to WHB, CHAR 28/145/26–7; 28 Nov 1929 G. Allen ltr to WHB, 28/145/21; 11 Dec 1929 NM account, 1/211/135. The life insurance premium on Churchill's £6,000 policy (required to secure a £5,000 loan) cost £263 a year; loan interest at 5¼ per cent a further £262; a combined total of £525 a year.
4. 15 Nov 1929 BMB cbl to WSC, Baruch Papers, MC 006 Vol 64, PUMM.
5. 13, 16, 20 Nov, 3, 16 Dec 1929 WSC corresp with WHB, NM, CHAR 1/211/108, 111, 138; 28/145/26; 18 Nov WSC ltr to MWB, cited K. Young, *Churchill and Beaverbrook: a study in friendship and politics*, p. 110.
6. 23 Dec 1929 VdaC note, CHAR 1/211/143.
7. 12 Mar 1930 H. Vickers ltr to WSC, CHAR 1/217/75; 7, 10, 13, 27 Feb 1930 Churchill purchases of Simmons shares (aggregating 650 shares, at prices from $761/8 down to 65¾), 1/217/35, 41, 49, 59.
8. Author's calculations using VdaC contract notes and accounts, CHAR 1/211, 217, 218.
9. 16 Jan 1930 WSC ltr to G. Harrap, CHAR 8/271/7–8.
10. 12, 16 Jan 1930 WSC corresp with TB, CHAR 8/274/1, 5.
11. 28 Jan 1930 G. Dawson memo to W. Lints Smith, TNL Archive Sir Winston Churchill Managerial File, MAN/1.
12. 15 Jan 1930 CSIII ltr to WSC, CHAR 8/277/1–4.
13. 6, 30 Mar 1930 TB ltr to WSC, CSIII ltr to CB, Scribner's Archive, 3A box 31/3, PUFL.
14. 14 Feb 1930 WSC schedule, CHAR 1/216/41. Churchill forecast surpluses of £5,000 in the first half of 1930 and £7,400 in the following nine months.
15. 12 Mar 1930 H. Vickers ltr to WSC, CHAR 1/217/75.

16. 25 Mar 1930 VdaC ltr to WSC, CHAR 1/217/100.
17. 28 Jul 1930 M. Edwards Unpaid bills, CHAR 1/221/32. Of the total £2,813, Randolph Payne & Sons, wine merchants, accounted for £654. Bank interest would cost £800 for the quarter; life insurance premiums over £1,000.
18. 21 Jun 1930 WSC draft ltr to WHB, CHAR 1/216/13–16.
19. 1 Jul 1930 WHB note, CHAR 128/145/39–40; 12 Jul 1930 A. Bailey ltr to WSC, 1/218/90.
20. 11, 15 Aug, 2 Sep, 16 Oct, 10 Nov 1930 VdaC reports and corresp with WSC, CHAR 1/218/5, 24, 45, 64, 91, 93, 94, 105, 114; 1/219/2; 24 Oct 1930 BMB ltr to WSC, Baruch Papers, MC006 Vol 66, PUMM. Churchill's profit (before funding and transaction costs) was $2,600.
21. 25, 27, 30 Oct, 1 Nov 1930 *Sunday Chronicle* corresp with WSC and secretary, CHAR 8/276/315–6. Churchill accepted the newspaper's offer of £250, plus 25 per cent of any US sale; offered the subject of Moses, he asked whether anyone else was available. The *Sunday Chronicle* told him Joseph, Noah and David were free, but it thought Moses more fitting for Churchill, as a leader and lawgiver.
22. 16 Aug 1930 WSC ltr to TB, CHAR 8/274/142.
23. 23, 27 Jun 1930 WSC ltr to CSIII, *Daily Chronicle* ltr to WSC, CHAR 8/274/95, 8/809/1. The newspaper paid £1,500 for the rights, 'far beyond any price they have previously paid for serials', Churchill told Scribner.
24. 24 Sep 1930 WSC ltr to S. Baldwin, *Baldwin Papers* 5C2:186.
25. 5, 19 Dec 1930 CSIII ltrs to WSC, CHAR 8/277/128, 129; 17 Dec 1930 TB ltr to WSC, 8/275/126. Pre-publication orders were 4,830 in Britain; 811 in the US. By the end of 1930, 9,700 copies had sold in Britain and 4,700 in the US. Gross British royalties (£2,145) fell short of Churchill's £2,500 advance.
26. 9 Dec 1930 H. Vickers ltr to WSC, CHAR 1/218/87.
27. 17 Dec 1930 WSC ltr to NM, CHAR 1/215/62.
28. 14 Jan 1931 VdaC account, CHAR 1/225/17, 19, 20.
29. 12 Jan 1931 H. Frank ltr to WSC, CHAR 1/393/94.
30. 12, 14 Jan 1931 VdaC ltrs to WSC, CHAR 1/225/17, 19, 20. Churchill repaid the £2,000 loan on 15 September 1931.
31. 12 Jan 1931 H. Vickers ltr to WSC, CHAR 1/229/21.
32. 8 Jan 1931 WSC ltr to RSC, 5C2:242; 25 Feb 1931 WSC schedule, CHAR 8/292/19.
33. 22 Jan, 28 Apr 1931 CSIII ltrs to WSC, CHAR 8/296/5, 10; 20–26 Feb 1931 TB corresp with WSC, 8/294/8, 11, 14, 15, 17,20. During the first ten weeks after its publication, the abridged *World Crisis* sold 2,100 copies in the US and 3,500 in Britain (where – as Butterworth had predicted – the lending libraries shunned it).

34. 21 Mar 1931 WSC ltr to N. Pearn, CHAR 8/295/34. Pearn sold it to the *Sunday Pictorial*.
35. 17 Dec 1930 C. King opinion, NM brief, NA IR 40/12833.
36. 10, 15 April 1931 WSC corresp with P. Grigg, CHAR 1/224/1-2, 1/397/207.
37. 17 Jun 1931 R. Cave cbl to CSIII, Scribner's Archive, Author files I, 3A box 31/4, PUFL.
38. 19, 23 Jun 1931 CSIII corresp with J. Carter, ibid.; 19 Jun 1931 C. Scribner letter to WSC, CHAR 8/296/17-19.
39. 21 Aug 1931 BRB ltr to WSC, CHAR 8/816/20-1. The London General Press Agency (LGPA) paid £200, but terminated its remaining contract with Churchill after claiming Curtis Brown had previously hawked the material around the market. Churchill insisted on receiving a further £600, giving rise to lawsuits in both directions. The trial was delayed until late in 1932 by LGPA's insistence on a Special Jury, but financial difficulties prompted it to settle earlier by paying Churchill £750. LGPA survived, but did not handle any further Churchill material until 1935.
40. 24 Sep 1931 VdaC statement, CHAR 1/226/56; 30 Jun 1931 LlBk statement, 1/229/14. Churchill's receipts were £3,300; his expenditure before bank interest and investment losses £8,500. He paid £1,200 interest annually to his bankers; £700 of interest and life assurance charges to Commercial Union: £250 of interest to stockbrokers. (These figures exclude the additional interest that Churchill paid on the loans from his family trusts.)
41. 7 Aug 1931 WSC ltr to EHM, Marsh Papers, EMAR/2, CAC.
42. 16, 17 Jul 1931 TB ltr to WSC, cited in WSC reply, CHAR 8/294/99.
43. 16, 17 Jul, 11, 14 Aug 1931 WSC corresp with TB, WHB, CHAR 8/294/99; 28/145/55; LlBk statement 1/229/14.
44. 2, 3 Sep 1931 WHB corresp with E. Merrick-Taylor, LlBk statement, CHAR 28/145/53, 1/397/140, 1/229/21.
45. 3, 4, 5 Sep 1931 WSC corresp with WHB, LlBk statement, CHAR 28/145/64, 65, 68; 1/229/20.
46. Aug 1931 WSC schedule, CHAR 1/239.
47. The records of 1930s holidays during which Churchill drew money from his bank at French casinos suggest he incurred losses on eleven out of twelve occasions. From 1931-6, he averaged losses of approximately £900 a year; in 1937 and 1938 the loss was lower at an average of £125 a year. In January 1939 he won slightly over £100 – author's estimates from WSC LlBk statements (casino withdrawals, less deposits on return home and an allowance for expenses).
48. Aug, Sep 1931 LlBk statements, CHAR 1/229/18-20.
49. 3 Sep 1931 WSC ltr to G. Harrap, 5C2:355.
50. 10 Sep 1931 WSC ltr to TB, CHAR 8/294/108.

51. 21 Sep 1931 WSC ltr to CSIII, Scribner's Archive, Authors files I, 3A Box 31/4, PUFL; 9, 23 Oct 1931 CSIII ltrs and contracts to WSC, CHAR 8/296/29, Scribner's Archive, Authors files I, 3A box 31/4, PUFL. Over the following year, Churchill changed his mind several times about the order in which the two books should be published; in May 1932, he chose *Thoughts and Adventures* first – see 7 May 1932 5C2:426.
52. RSC memoirs, 5C2:384 footnote 1. RSC earned fees of $12,000.
53. 10, 12 Nov 1931 JSC ltr to WSC, LlBk statement, CHAR 1/226/70, 1/229/27.
54. 3 Nov 1931 WSC ltr to RSC, CHAR 1/226/74.
55. M. Ashley *Churchill as a Historian*, p. 122.
56. 20 Nov 1931 TB ltr to WSC, TB account, CHAR 8/294/138, 152; 16 Nov 1931 CSIII ltr to WSC, Scribner's Archive, Authors files I, 3A box 31/4, PUFL; 10 Dec 1931 J. Poli memo to CSIII, ibid. Pre-launch sales in Britain had reached only 3,852 and Churchill's cheque on publication was for £459. Published in America under the title *The Unknown War*, sales at publication were 1,500.

15. Trading Futures, 1932–3

1. 23 Dec 1931 WSC ltr to J. McCulloch, CHAR 1/399B/176. Churchill's hospital bill was $420.
2. U/d Phoenix Assurance ltr to WHB, CHAR 28/145/92.
3. 14 Dec 1931 WSC cbl to WHB, CHAR 28/145/91.
4. 16 Dec 1931 WSC cbl to E. Harmsworth, 5C2:383.
5. Randolph Churchill papers, 5C2:390–2.
6. 15 Jan 1932 WHB ltr to WSC, CHAR 28/145/105.
7. Mar 1932 WSC cbl to JSC, CHAR 1/398/118. On 28 December 1931 Churchill purchased an option to buy £6,000 at an exchange rate of $3.43, valid until the end of March 1932.
8. 12 Jan 1932 CSC ltr to RSC, 5C2:396.
9. WSC schedule, CHAR 1/224/18, 23. His revised forecast of his profits was £4,600.
10. 10 Feb 1932 WSC cbl to R. Boothby, CHAR 1/238/30.
11. 29 Feb 1932 WSC cbl to E. Harmsworth, CHAR 8/309/12.
12. 23 Feb 1932 WSC ltr to L. Levy, CHAR 1/399/142.
13. 9 Mar 1932 C. Vickers cbl to WSC, CHAR 1/398/114. For the first time since Britain left the gold standard London interest rates had fallen from 6 per cent; they reached 2 per cent in June, where they stayed until 24 August 1939.
14. 8 Mar, 8 Jul 1932 NCBNY note to WSC, CHAR 1/239/9, 49, 68; also Mar, Apr 1932 1/239/17, 27, 28, 58, 59. Churchill 'rolled over' his first contracts

at the end of March, but 'closed' them in the first week of April after a surge in sterling, netting $2,600 profit. His second foray, when he bought £4,000 sterling forward in May for July delivery, lost $667.

15. 9 Feb 1932 BRB ltr to WSC, CHAR 1/398/46. CHAR 1/231/2 Churchill's former girlfriend, Pamela Plowden (now Countess Lytton) could not afford to contribute: 'Alas that we cannot join the rich acquaintances, but must remain outside as affectionate friends.' Four press barons (Beaverbrook, Harmsworth, Camrose and Riddell) were contributors, as were Charlie Chaplin, John Maynard Keynes, the prince of Wales, the duke of Westminster, Sir Edwin Luytens and Harold Macmillan.

16. 21 Jun 1932 WSC ltr to H. Vickers, 5C2:435.

17. 22 Jun 1931 H. Vickers ltr to WSC, CHAR 1/235/59.

18. 28 Jul 1932 WSC ltr to JSC, CHAR 1/236/22.

19. 28, 29, 30 Jul 1932 VdaC contract notes, CHAR 1/235/82, 84; 2 Aug 1932 WSC ltr to FNB, 1/238/80.

20. 19 July 1974 K. Feiling ltr to M. Gilbert, 5:437.

21. 11 Aug 1932 VdaC ltr to WSC, CHAR 1/236/48.

22. Aug 1932 VdaC advice notes, CHAR 1/236/56, 85, 90, 91, 92, 96, 98, 102, 105. The sum covers London and New York commission costs.

23. 2 Sep 1932 H. Vickers ltr to WSC, CHAR 1/236/110, 116–17.

24. 16 May 1932 WSC ltr to TB, CHAR 8/312/41.

25. 30 Apr, 31 May 1932 WSC ltrs to EHM, Marsh papers EMAR/2 CAC, CHAR 8/306/40.

26. 5 Aug 1932 WSC ltr to E. Harmsworth, CHAR 8/309/28–9.

27. 26 May 1932 WSC article Daily Mail.

28. 30 Jul 1932 G. Riddell ltr to WSC, CHAR 8/311/2.

29. 2, 5 Aug 1932 WSC corresp with G. Riddell, CHAR 8/311/3–4, 9.

30. 5 Aug 1932 WSC ltr to EHM, CHAR 8/311/11–12.

31. 25, 28 July 1932 N. Pearn corresp with WSC, CHAR 8/313/65–66, 67.

32. 18 Jul 1932 WSC ltrs to G. Harrap, CHAR 8/315/6.

33. 23 Aug 1932 WSC ltr to R. Pakenham-Walsh, 5C2:469–70.

34. Sep 1932 LlBk statements, CHAR 1/229/50–53. Hotel and sanatorium expenses were £750.

35. U/d 1932 V. Pearman ltr to EHM, 5C2:444; C. Hassall, Eddie Marsh, p. 575; 29 Dec 1932 TB ltr to WSC, CHAR 8/312/159; 25 Nov, 20 Dec 1932 CSIII ltr and cbl to WSC, 8/314/42, 46. Thoughts and Adventures was published in Britain on 10 November 1932. Butterworth initially ordered the printing of 4,000 copies, but strong orders filtered through before launch and sales passed 7,000 before the end of the year. The US edition, Amid These Storms (published a fortnight later), sold 3,000 copies by the end of January 1933.

36. 17 Sep 1932 WSC ltr to EHM, CHAR 8/311/23.

37. 11 Nov 1932 WSC ltr to EHM, 5C2:489.

38. 3 Dec 1932 WSC ltr to EHM, CHAR 8/311/105. The *Chicago Tribune* did not renew.
39. 5 Dec 1932 WSC ltr to EHM, Marsh papers 5C2:501.
40. 30 Oct 1932 WSC ltr to N. Flower, CHAR 8/308/1–5.
41. 7 Oct 1932 WSC cbl to BMB, Baruch Papers MC006 Vol 70, PUMM.
42. 6, 8, 24 Oct 1932 WSC corresp with G. Duis, CHAR 1/239/73, 78b, 83.
43. 12 Nov 1931 NM ltr to WSC, CHAR 1/223/65–7. The Churchills took over the lease, costing £380 a year, from Frances Stevenson, Lloyd George's mistress.
44. 19 Oct 1932 A. Bailey ltr to WSC, CHAR 1/239/29.
45. 12 Nov, 14 Dec 1932 WSC corresp with H. Osborne, NM, CHAR 1/233/76, 87, 120; Dec 1932 NM ltr to WSC, 1/259/104. Churchill released seven-tenths of the Elder Children's Settlement's capital back to himself, reducing his loan from the trust to £3,358. Diana's marriage lasted only three years until 1935, when she remarried Duncan Sandys MP.
46. 1932 LlBk statements CHAR 1/241; LlBk schedule, 1/304/61; A. Atkinson, *Top Incomes in the United Kingdom over the Twentieth Century*, author's calculations using tables in Fig 4, 5, Table A1, pp. 36–40. Apart from investment losses, Churchill's other main spending headings in 1932 were: £5,700 tax, £2,800 transfers to Clementine (extra to her normal allowances); £1,200 staff (secretarial and literary); £215 club subscriptions; and £900 payments to Randolph and Diana.
47. Jan 1933 LlBk statement, CHAR 1/241/64.
48. 19 Feb 1933 WSC ltr to Arnold, CHAR 1/243/26.
49. 16, 18 Feb 1933 WSC cbls to Frazier Jelke, NCBNY, CHAR 1/246/32, 33; 1/249/36.
50. 16 May 1933 BRB ltr to BMB, Baruch Papers, MC006 Vol 73, PUMM.
51. 18, 21, 22 April 1933 WSC cbls to G. Duis, CHAR 1/251/21, CHAR 1/252/14, 15, 16; 24 Apr 1933 VdaC advice note, CHAR 1/247/78.
52. Apr–Jul 1933 WSC corresp with NCBNY, VdaC, LlBk, CHAR 1/251, 1/246, 1/249/various. On 6 July 1933, Churchill had sold 'forward' against sterling: US$50,000, C$40,000 and 200,000 francs.
53. May, Jun 1933 VdaC, Frazier Jelke advice notes; 29 Jun 1933 VdaC New York account, CHAR 1/246/91 *et seq.*, 138; 1/247/28. For example, Churchill judged Worthington Pump's trading range as between prices of $17 and $20: he twice switched in and out of the stock successfully, then kept 'shorting' it as it rose to $21, $23½ and $26. He finally cut his losses when the price had doubled to $35.
54. 10, 11 Jul 1933 H. Vickers ltr to WSC, VdaC summary, CHAR 1/247/21, 30.
55. 24 Jul, 10, 11 Aug 1933 VdaC ltrs to WSC, CHAR 1/247/54, 71, 73.

56. 11 Aug 1933 VdaC ltr to WSC, CHAR 1/247/76; 24 Oct 1933, LlBk advice note, 1/248/35.

57. 20, 28 Mar, 10 Apr 1933 N. Pearn corresp with WSC, V. Pearman, CHAR 8/336/40, 41, 45, 53.

58. 9 Mar 1933 G Riddell ltr to WSC, CHAR 8/332/63–5; 14 Mar 1933 G. Tingay ltr to WSC, 8/335/76–73; Oct 1933 V. Pearman note to WSC, 8/328/57.

59. 6, 12 Oct 1932 W. Harrap ltr to WSC, CHAR 8/324/66; V. Pearman note, 8/324/91; 28 Jul 1933 CSIII ltr to WSC, 8/337/16; 1/251/61. Churchill expected Harrap's advance to be £4,000, but their contract stated £3,000, which was reduced to £2,728 by bills for indexing, printers' corrections and presentation copies. The US edition was published on 10 November: Charles Scribner's warning that the book 'may prove to be a little too solid' for the American public was vindicated when the 4,000 copies printed took ten years to sell. Churchill received a cheque for $6,440 after Scribner deducted $560 US income tax from the $7,000 advance.

60. 7 Oct 1933 S. Baldwin ltr to WSC, 5C2:663.

61. 15 Oct 1933 WSC cbl to BMB, Baruch Papers MC006 Vol.73, PUMM.

62. Sep 1931 BMB schedule, Baruch Papers, MC006/742, PUMM.

63. 20 Sep 1933 WSC ltrs to LlBk, CHAR 1/250/39, 51.

64. 17, 18 Oct G. Mason corresp with WSC, CHAR 1/250/69, 73.

65. 28 Sep 1933 VdaC valuation, CHAR 1/248/4; 10 Jan 1935 NM ltr, 1/276/3.

66. 31 Dec 1933 LlBk statement, CHAR 1/241/ 98, VdaC accounts 1/230/8– 28. Stock market losses were £6,000; gambling losses approximately £1,000.

16. Summoning More Ghosts, 1934–5

1. 15, 18 Nov 1933 W. Blackwood corresp with WSC, CHAR 8/333/1–2, 13. Blackwood proposed £50 per article.

2. See 5C2:502. Publications included: *Pearson's Magazine*, *Pictorial Weekly*, the *Evening Standard* and the *Sunday Chronicle*.

3. 30 Oct 1987 *Chartwell Memories – Early Encounters*, G. Hamblin speech to International Churchill Society, Dallas, Texas.

4. 26 Dec 1933 WSC ltr to G. Harrap, CHAR 8/325/166–9.

5. 1, 5 Jan 1934 WSC corresp with Ld Camrose letter to WSC, 5C2:694–5, 697–8.

6. 23 Mar 1933 R. Crossett ltr to WSC, CHAR 8/36/44.

7. 1 Mar 1934 WSC ltr to H. Osborne, NM, CHAR 8/495/7–12.

8. 19 Mar 1934 LlBk statement, CHAR 1/241/109.

9. An informant had told Churchill that evidence originally given to the

India Select Committee by the Manchester Chamber of Commerce (representing Lancashire's important textile interests and hostile to the proposed reform) had been kept locked up in the India Office, while the secretary of state, Sir Samuel Hoare, and others persuaded the chamber to send a harmless replacement. Churchill raised the issue with the Speaker, who referred it to the Privileges Committee of senior parliamentarians. Churchill spent £500 of his own money obtaining legal advice before appearing in front of the committee late in April 1934. The committee refused Churchill's requests to question other witnesses or examine the correspondence between Sir Samuel and his alleged accomplices. It found unanimously against Churchill early in June, arguing that any 'pressure' applied to the Manchester Chamber was not illegitimate, since the committee was not a 'judicial body'. The India Bill passed into law in June 1935.

10. 22 Jun 1934 WSC ltr to EHM, Marsh Papers, Berg Collection, NYPL. 'One must regard the hyphen as a blemish to be avoided wherever possible,' Churchill told Marsh, whom he considered overfond of the device.

11. 11, 13 Apr 1934 WSC ltrs to N. Flower, K. Feiling, CHAR 8/506/8, 10.

12. 10 May 1934 W. Blackwood ltr to WSC, CHAR 8/492/60.

13. 13 May 1934 A. Marshall Diston ltr to WSC, CHAR 8/493/25.

14. 2 Jul 1934 *The Times*.

15. Jan 1934 LlBk contracts, statement, CHAR 1/63/various, 1/241/101.

16. 27, 30 Apr 1934 WSC cbl corresp with BMB, CHAR 1/255/6, 7. 'Reasonably priced around 40, cheap at 30,' Baruch replied. 5, 7, 10, 11 May VdaC contract notes, 1/261/5, 11, 15, 17.

17. 4 Jul 1934 LlBk ltr to WSC, statement CHAR 1/264/20, 1/241/116. 15 Sep 1934 WSC schedules, 1/264/77, 78.

18. 16 Aug 1934 WSC ltr to CSC, 5C2:847–9.

19. 20, 23 Aug 1934 G. Riddell cbl, ltr to WSC, CHAR 8/491/1, 3.

20. 25 Aug 1934 WSC ltr to CSC, 5C2:856.

21. 26 Aug 1934 CSC ltr to WSC, 5C2:861–2.

22. 27 Aug 1934 WSC ltr to CSC, 5C2:862–3.

23. Aug 1934 LlBk statement, CHAR 1/241/22.

24. 13 Sep, 11 Dec 1934 NM ltrs to WSC, CHAR 1/259/83, 121.

25. 23, 25 Sep 1934 WSC corresp with A. Korda, CHAR 8/495/64–5, 69.

26. 31 Oct, 5 Dec 1934 C. Wood ltrs to WSC, CHAR 8/486/201, 257. Sales were 9,500 in the first month, then slowed.

27. 30 Oct 1934 LlBk statement, CHAR 1/241/26,6. Churchill paid £2,383 of 1932/3 income tax and £1,730 of 1932/3 sur-tax. Scribner was due to pay $7,000 – he paid in February 1935 although he delayed the US launch until March 1935. R. Cohen, *Bibliography of the Writings of Sir Winston Churchill*, p. 429: 3,040 copies were printed; slow sales resulted

in the stock lasting until December 1941. 17 August 1935 WSC ltr to CSIII, 8/517/17; Churchill shared Scribner's disappointment: 'I am full of the deepest gloom at the ill success of all our joint projects. You are the only publisher I have ever dealt with who has not profited by our collaboration.'

28. 24 Oct 1934 P. Davies ltr to WSC, CHAR 4/491/30; 30 Oct 1934 V. Pearman ltr to P. Davies, 8/491/32; 19 Nov 1934 C. Everitt cbl to WSC, 8/493/93. Curtis Brown sold the series to the *Chicago Tribune* for $6,000, but the paper's insistence that all material must be 'first-run' meant Churchill had to re-employ Diston to paraphrase the material taken from *My Early Life*.
29. 10 Nov 1931 NM ltr to WSC, CHAR 1/223/59–60.
30. 18 Dec 1934 WSC ltr to NM, CHAR 1/259/13.
31. 21 Dec 1934 WSC cbl to CSC, 5C2:969.
32. 1 Jan 1935 WSC ltr to CSC, SFT:369–70; LlBk statements CHAR 1/241.
33. U/d Jan 1935 WSC schedule, CHAR 1/279/1. Churchill still based his spending estimates on household running costs of £500 a month; records show that the two households cost approximately £950 a month to run.
34. 18 Jan 1935 WSC ltr to CSC, SFT:373–4.
35. 21 Jan 1935 WSC ltr to CSC, 5C2:1037–40.
36. 23 Jan 1935 WSC ltr to CSC, 5C2:1044–6.
37. 23 Jan 1935 A. Korda ltr to WSC, CHAR 8/514/112–14.
38. 1 Jan 1935 WSC ltr to CSC, 5C2:979–83.
39. 11 Jan 1935 WSC ltr to P. Cudlipp, CHAR 8/508/4.
40. 2 Apr 1935 Secretary's note on A. Cranfield ltr to WSC, CHAR 8/509/15.
41. 13 Apr 1935 WSC ltr to CSC, 5C2:1137–41. It took three more months for lawyers to agree a final settlement: Churchill was to receive £7,000 in 1935 and the early part of 1936, of which £4,000 would be treated as compensation (exempt from tax).
42. Ibid. May 1935 LlBk statement, CHAR 1/269/46; SFT:299. The outstanding amounts, exceeding £1,000, were owed to Randolph Payne & Sons (wine merchants) and two tailors. According to her daughter, Clementine bought a pair of diamond earrings with the gift.
43. Cabinet Minute Cab.11 (34) 5, CAB 23/78; Cabinet Paper CP 69 (34), CAB 24/248, NA, cited D. Reynolds, *In Command of History*, pp. 26–8.
44. 19 Nov 1934 WSC ltr to R. Howorth, 5C2:925. Nine former ministers, including Lloyd George, held out.
45. 18, 27 Jun 1935 WSC corresp with M. Hankey, 5C2:1198–9, 1203–4. See D. Reynolds, *In Command of History*, pp. 26–8.
46. 6, 8 Jul 1935 WSC corresp with JSC, CHAR 1/277/90, 91; 27 Jun 1935 VdaC account, 1/277/92.
47. 1–28 Aug, 2–9 Sept 1935 VdaC reports and contract notes, CHAR

1/278/1, 3, 7, 10, 11, 13, 39–46, 50, 52, 54. At the end of August, Churchill's accumulated loss was $9,250.

48. 16–23 Sep 1935 VdaC contract notes, CHAR 1/278/67–82.

49. 5 Oct 1935 WSC cbl corresp with BMB, CHAR 1/272/19, 20. Churchill bought 100 shares at $423⅜ each.

50. 20 Sep 1935 C. Thornton-Kemsley, Sir Colin Thornton-Kemsley Diaries, 5C2:1262–4.

51. 11 Sep 1935 WSC ltr to CSC, 5C2:1257–9.

52. Sep 1935 LlBk statement, CHAR 1/269/58.

53. 14, 26 Sep 1935 WSC corresp with S. Williams, CHAR 1/279/152–3, 161.

17. Films, Columns and Debts, 1935–7

1. 3 Oct 1935 WSC ltr to G. Harrap, CHAR 8/504/56.

2. WSC, *The Second World War*, 1:141.

3. 12, 15, 23 Jul 1935 P. Davies corresp with WSC, CHAR 8/511/26, 25, 32; 12, 17 Oct 1935 A. Diston corresp with V. Pearman, WSC, 5/511/39, 40, 46, 49. Churchill received c.£350 for each article (before foreign sales or subsequent re-publication in book form); he paid Diston £15 for each draft (on Clemenceau, Balfour, French, Curzon, Morley, Chamberlain and Fisher).

4. 11 Sep 1935 W. Chenery ltr to C. Everitt, CHAR 8/512/85.

5. 2, 3 Dec 1935 WSC corresp with S. Williams, CHAR 1/279/197, 9. Churchill's £8,000 overdraft was secured by his holding in Sir Henry Strakosch's Union Corporation shares (worth £4,125), by gilt-edged stock (£1,750) and by the surrender value of his 1908 life insurance policy (valued by his bank at £3,500).

6. 9 Aug 1935 Randolph Payne & Sons ltr to WSC, CHAR 1/283/36; 11 Dec 1935 Lord Sandhurst ltr to V. Pearman, 1/275/150; Dec 1935 account, 1/283/39.

7. Dec 1935 Secretaries' analysis: 1935/6 Wines and spirits supplied, CHAR 1/318/4–12. In addition to the champagne, 1935's deliveries included £96 of brandy, £62 of whisky and £40 of port. Economy measures, including a switch to the less expensive 1926 Pol Roger vintage, reduced the cost in 1936 to £740.

8. 30 Dec 1935 WSC ltr to CSC, SFT:404–5.

9. 8 Jan 1936 WSC ltr to CSC, SFT:406–8.

10. 21, 29 Jan 1936 E. Carr cbl, ltr to WSC, CHAR 8/533/3, 13.

11. 31 Jan 1936 WSC corresp with R. Shaw, A. Diston, CHAR 8/535/1, 2, 6, 13.

12. 26 Nov 1935 WSC ltr to ACB, CHAR 8/516/71.

13. 28 Mar 1936 V. Pearman note re H. Long tel call, WSC ltr, CHAR 8/538/44, 43; 2 Apr 1936 WSC *Evening Standard* contract, 8/534/32–4.

14. 22, 27 Feb, 11, 19, 24 Mar, 2 Apr 1936 WSC corresp with W. Hearst, C. Everitt, H. Long, CHAR 8/813/78, 8/536/16, 8/538/32–4, 37, 38.
15. 3, 14 Apr 1936 WSC ltr to W. Hearst, H. Long ltrs to WSC, WSC cbl to Hyde, editor *Today*, 5C3:89, CHAR 8/538/56, 51, 8/536/31. Churchill and Curtis Brown lowered the price to interest other US buyers, but sold only two articles, one at a trial price of $100 and another at $250.
16. 18 Apr 1936 WSC ltr to K. Feiling, 5C3:104.
17. 18, 20 May 1936 WSC corresp with G. Harrap, CHAR 8/529/115–7, 122–3. The first volume of *Marlborough* had sold 13,000 copies, the second 9,500.
18. 23, 27 May 1936 WSC ltrs to CSIII, W. Hadley, CHAR 8/529/126, 8/528/195.
19. 6, 7, 11 Aug 1936 N. Flower corresp with WSC, CHAR 8/532/195, 196–7, 200.
20. 28 Aug, 7 Sep 1936 *The Sunday Times*, G. Harrap ltrs to WSC, CHAR 8/528/183, 8/530/112. *The Sunday Times* paid £500 at the end of August; Churchill's corrections, deletions and extra proof copies reduced Harrap's cheque to £2,624 (from £3,000).
21. 5 Sep 1936 WSC ltr to CSC, 5C3:336–8.
22. Sep 1936 LlBk statement, CHAR 1/269/90.
23. 29 Apr 1936 RSC ltr to WSC, CHAR 1/284/110; 13 May, 3 Sep 1936 NM ltrs to WSC, CHAR 1/290/31, 53; 3 Aug 1936 RSC cbl to WSC & CSC, 1/285/116. In April 1936 Randolph admitted to new debts (since his last rescue) of £1,180, mostly as a result of gambling losses. Churchill approved a fresh loan from Lord Randolph Churchill's will trust to Randolph, because bankruptcy would have ruined his hopes of a political career. By the time the trust completed formalities in September, it had advanced Randolph £7,200 and he declared himself 'definitely cured of casinoitis'.
24. 21 Feb 1936 WSC ltr to CSC, 5C3:52–4.
25. 5 Jun, 2 Jul 1936 Chadbourne, Stanchfield & Levy reports, CHAR 1/288/7, 21.
26. 20 Sep 1936 WSC cbl to RSC, CHAR 1/288/40.
27. 15, 17, 27 Oct 1936 P. Cudlipp corresp with WSC, CHAR 8/534/41–2, 39, 52.
28. 23 Oct 1936 WSC ltr to H. Long, CHAR 8/538/156.
29. 2 Oct 1936 Secretary note to WSC, CHAR 2/283/20.
30. D. Irving, *Churchill's War: The Struggle for Power* vol.i; E. Spier, *Focus*, pp. 20–2, pp. 160–2. Between 1936–9 Spier contributed £9,600 to Focus, which held several further lunches at The Savoy (29 October 1936, 19 April, 14 June, 16 December 1937, January 1938); public meetings at the Royal Albert Hall (3 December 1936), in Manchester and other cities (spring 1937); and in Manchester and Sheffield (May 1938).

31. 27 Sep 1936 J. Landau ltr to WSC, 5C3:251–2. The visit was planned by a group of friends led by Jacob Landau, an Austrian-born Jewish journalist, founder of the Jewish Telegraphic Agency in London and New York. Churchill marked Landau's letter 'Secret'.

32. 13, 15, 21 Oct, 26 Nov, 15 Dec 1936 R. Shaw corresp with WSC, CHAR 8/534/41–6; 13 Nov 1936 P. Cudlipp ltr to WSC, 8/534/57.

33. A. de Courcy, *The Viceroy's Daughters*, p. 229.

34. 21 Oct 1936 G. Mason ltr to WSC, CHAR 1/292/97. The amount claimed was £1,014.

35. 27 Nov 1936 WSC ltr to CSC, 5C3:438–9.

36. 28 Nov 1936 RSC cbl to WSC, 5C3:445.

37. 8 Dec 1936 H. Nicolson, *Diary*, Nicolson Papers.

38. 18 Dec 1936 H. Everitt ltr to WSC, CHAR 8/536/60. The offer was from the *Chicago Tribune*.

39. 1 Jan 1937 WSC ltr to BMB, CHAR 1/298/3.

40. 7 Jan 1937 WSC ltr to CSC, CHAR 1/303/2.

41. 2 Feb, 26 Mar 1937 WSC ltrs to S. Oliver, CHAR 1/330/21, 44.

42. 31 Dec 1936 LlBk statement, CHAR 1/297/102. Churchill's overdraft finished 1936 at £8,080.

43. 28 Dec 1936 WSC ltr to S. Williams, CHAR1/292/117–18. The long-term loans totalled £4,000.

44. December 1936 Harrods and other accounts, CHAR 1/311–2.

45. U/d 1936 V. Pearman memo, CHAR 1/310/1; 24 Mar 1937 Inventory of wine at Chartwell, 1/318/34–5. The inventory listed 180 bottles and thirty half-bottles of Pol Roger champagne, twenty bottles and nine half-bottles of other champagne, over a hundred bottles of claret, 117 bottles and 389 half-bottles of Barsac, thirteen bottles of brandy, five of champagne brandy and seven of liqueur whisky.

46. U/d WSC memo, CHAR 1/310/2–3.

47. 1 Mar 1937 Secretaries' schedule of accounts outstanding, CHAR 1/310/26–8.

48. 2 Feb 1937 WSC ltr to CSC, 5C3:572–6.

49. 2 Feb 1937 WSC letter to N. Flower, CHAR 8/550/1.

50. The loans included: £7,000 from Commercial Union, £5,000 from National Mutual, £4,000 from Lloyds Bank, where Churchill's overdraft stood at £6,500.

51. U/d WSC memo, CHAR 1/310/2–3.

18. Bracken and Partner to the Rescue, 1937–8

1. 24, 25 Feb 1937 W. Robertson memos to P. Cudlipp, CHAR 8/552/149–150, 152.

2. 1 Mar 1937 ER ltr to WSC, CHAR 8/561/10–11.
3. 26 Mar, 18 Apr 1937 V. Pearman note, ER ltr to WSC, CHAR 8/552/48, M. Gilbert (ed.), *Churchill and Emery Reves*, p. 33.
4. 13, 17, 30 Jun 1937 ER corresp with WSC, CHAR 8/561/19–22, 31–2.
5. 9 Jul 1937 Cooperation accounts, CHAR 8/561/36. The article's title was 'Arrest of British Socialism'.
6. 9, 20 Aug 1937 ER ltr to WSC, Cooperation accounts, M. Gilbert, *Churchill and Emery Reves*, p. 52, CHAR 8/561/81, 8/552/182.
7. 1 Apr 1937 WSC schedule, secretaries' schedule, CHAR 1/304/7, 1/310/35. Receipts included a £3,500 advance on *Marlborough*'s fourth volume, £4,200 from the *News of the World*, £2,100 from thirteen *Evening Standard* articles, £1,800 from six *Collier's* articles, £600 from a renewed brandy bet with Rothermere, and £2,550 from investment income, director's fees and MP's salary. Expenditure included £4,500 for nine months' household spending (at £500 a month), £3,000 tax, £2,000 for his office and old bills, and £1,000 for personal expenditure.
8. Apr 1937 LlBk statement, CHAR 1/297/114.
9. 18 April 1936 WSC ltr to TB, CHAR 8/357/11
10. 19 Apr 1937 WSC ltr to TB, CHAR 8/558/12.
11. 23, 27 Apr, 15 May 1937 TB corresp with WSC, contract, CHAR 8/558/14, 16, 29, 128–31.
12. 16 Jun 1937 G. Harrap ltr to WSC, CHAR 8/547/49.
13. 15 Jun 1937 N. Flower ltr to WSC, CHAR 8/550/11.
14. 7 Apr 1937 NM ltr to WSC, CHAR 1/303/48.
15. 13 May 1937 WSC ltr to G. Mason, CHAR 1/304/45.
16. 17 Jun 1937 G. Mason ltr, schedules to WSC, CHAR 1/304/65. 1935/6 income tax (£2,936) was due for payment in January and July 1936, but Churchill had paid only £1,760 by June 1937, leaving £1,176 to settle). 1935/6 sur-tax of £3,465 had been due in January 1937, but Churchill had paid only £1,465, leaving £2,000 to settle. By June 1937, 1936/7 income tax of £2,296 had also become due; Churchill had paid only £119, leaving £2,177 outstanding. 1936/7 sur-tax, estimated at £2,395, would become payable on 1 January 1938.
17. 5 Jun 1937 V. Pearman ltr to KFR, CHAR 1/393/178.
18. 3 Aug 1937 WSC ltr to CSC, 5C3:742–3.
19. K. Hill ltr to M. Gilbert, cited M. Gilbert, *In Search of Churchill*, p. 162.
20. 26, 27 May, 1 Jun WSC corresp with S. Williams, CHAR 1/304/47, 48, 56.
21. 16 Aug 1937 NM ltr to WSC, CHAR 1/303/114.
22. 1 Jul 1937 Secretaries' schedule, CHAR 1/303/100, 1/310/60.
23. 13 Aug 1937 NM ltr to WSC, CHAR 1/303/111. Churchill borrowed £1,700 against a mortgage on Wellstreet Cottage, which he had recently built on the edge of Chartwell's estate.

24. Late Aug or early Sep 1937 WSC schedule, CHAR 1/304/4.
25. 10, 13 Sep 1937 WSC corresp with BMB, CHAR 1/300/8, 16.
26. 18 Oct 1937 WSC cbl to BMB, CHAR 1/300/29.
27. U/d 1936 Male servant licence, CHAR 1/309/31.
28. U/d Nov 1937 Secretaries' schedule 'Chartwell Winter Scale', CHAR 1/332/2-4.
29. Ibid.
30. 29, 21 Oct, 15 Nov 1937 W. H. Haynes Ltd, H & M Rayne, Loufte & Co. accounts, CHAR 1/337/185, 118, 1/340/11.
31. 5 Nov 1937 Surveyor's report, CHAR 1/408/86. See S. Buczacki, *Churchill & Chartwell*, pp. 181–3.
32. Nov 1937 Mullett Booker & Co. ltr to CSC, CHAR 1/408/1; 2 Nov 1937, NM ltr to Ecclesiastical Commission, 1/408/3.
33. 31 Dec 1937 WSC note to CSC, CHAR 1/408/32-3. Neither Churchill nor Clementine wished to administer the *coup de grâce*; Clementine was still discussing plans for storing their silver with the architect in February 1938.
34. 22 Oct 1937 C. Hughes ltr to WSC, CHAR 1/306/10.
35. 22 Oct 1937 D. Cunnynghame ltr to WSC, CHAR 8/557/5.
36. 4 Oct, 24 Dec 1937 TB ltrs to WSC, CHAR 8/559/46, 8/668/108; 27 Jul 1938 TB sales report, K. Hill memo to WSC, 8/605/7, 62: British sales hit 14,000 in July 1938; CHAR 1/321/ 132–62 Churchill received £500 at publication, £248 (net of author's corrections) in October 1937, £455 in November, £608 in December, £750 in January 1938, £1,459 in February, £430 in May and £266 in June. 25 Dec 1937, 4 May 1938 G. Putnam cbls to WSC, CHAR 8/546/202, 8/605/33: US sales reached 8,000 in May 1938; Churchill received £500 on publication (on account of 15 per cent royalty on the first 7,500 volumes, 20 per cent thereafter). CHAR 8/598/75: Churchill received advances of £30–£75 on sales in France, Holland, Norway, Sweden and Germany (where the chapter on the Kaiser was omitted).
37. 6 Nov 1937 WSC ltr to P. Davies, CHAR 8/551/24-5.
38. 16 Dec 1937 P. Davies ltr to WSC, CHAR 8/551/33-4.
39. 23 Dec 1937 WSC ltr to G. Harrap, CHAR 8/547/218-20.
40. 31 Dec 1937 LlBk statement, CHAR 1/321/ 144; u/d early 1938 WSC schedule, CHAR 1/329/1.
41. 1 Dec 1937 G Mason ltr to WSC, CHAR 1/304/94. Liabilities included £2,364 of income tax and £2,345 of sur-tax.
42. 30 December 1937 H. Peat ltr to WSC, CHAR 1/407/62–4, 66.
43. 3, 10 Jan 1938 WSC ltrs to CSC, SFT:431, 433.
44. 10 Jan 1938 WSC ltr to CSC, 5C3:884–6. The casino lured Churchill before the end of his visit: per CHAR 1/321/147, his bank account shows the withdrawal of 50,000 francs (£330) over five visits at the end of the

month. Churchill brought 39,850 francs back to London (a net loss of £71).

45. 9, 11 Jan 1938 G. Mason ltr to WSC, LlBk statement, CHAR 1/329/13, 1/321/146. Two payments (£676 income tax and £1,000 sur-tax) had cleared the 1935/6 tax year, but left £2,177 of income tax and £2,345 of sur-tax owing for 1936/7.

46. 20, 22 Jan 1938, WSC schedule, ltr to S. Williams, CHAR 1/329/6, 18.

47. WSC, *The Second World War* 1:201.

48. 7, 10 Mar 1938 WSC ltr to S. Williams, NM schedule, CHAR 1/329/29, 1/327/33.

49. 18 Mar 1938 LlBk statement, CHAR 1/321/151. The payment allowed Churchill to pay £1,000 towards 1935/6 sur-tax, while leaving his bank account £1,204 in credit.

50. 21 Mar 1938 WSC schedule, CHAR 1/28/2; 10 Oct 1938 H. Strakosch schedule, 1/328/6. Churchill estimated the shares' cost at £17,600, but Sir Henry Strakosch's later schedule showed it to have been £18,162. Churchill estimated the shares' March value at £5,600; Sir Henry later showed it as £5,692. Original documents are not available, presumed burned with Bracken's other papers after his death.

51. 22 Mar 1938 LlBk statement, CHAR 1/321/152.

52. 18 Jan 1938 BRB ltr to WSC, CHAR 1/323/10.

53. 19 Mar 1938 WSC ltr to BRB, 5C3:950–1.

54. 19 Mar 1938 WSC draft, ltr to BRB CHAR 1/328/3, 4.

55. 24 Mar 1938 H. Strakosch ltr to WSC, 5C3:959. The shares which Sir Henry Strakosch took over were:
    400   Otis Elevator
    500   Worthington Pumps & Co.
    1000   Consolidated Paper
    400   Abitibi Paper Preference shares
    200   Abitibi Paper Common shares
    200   New York Central

56. 10 Oct 1938 H. Strakosch schedule, CHAR 1/328/6. The portfolio rose in value from £5,692 to £9,000.

57. 3 Apr 1938 WSC ltr to NM, CHAR 1/327/10. There is no sign that the loan was quickly repaid: on its first renewal date in March 1939, Churchill sent Nicholl Manisty a cheque for £1,630, almost certainly representing a £1,500 repayment plus a year's interest on the £5,000 loan.

58. 9 May 1938 NM account, LlBk statement CHAR 1/327/24, CHAR 1/321/160.

59. 1, 2 Apr 1938 RSC ltr to WSC, extract *The Times*, 5C3:970–2, *The Times* 2 April 1938.

60. Sir Henry Strakosch's membership of The Other Club was proposed

by Brendan Bracken, to whom Sir Henry left £2,500 in his will. He also marked out Bracken to succeed him as chairman of Union Corporation.

19. Struggling with *History*, 1938–9

1. 24 Mar 1938 R. Thompson ltr to WSC, CHAR 8/600/17. Beaverbrook had been giving Sir Samuel Hoare £2,000 a year, in the hope that he would succeed Neville Chamberlain and allow Beaverbrook to resume the influence which he had enjoyed while Bonar Law was prime minister: see R. Cockett (ed.), *My Dear Max: The Letters of Brendan Bracken to Lord Beaverbrook, 1925–1958*, p. 22.
2. 29 Mar 1938 Secretary ltr to R. Thompson, CHAR 8/600/20.
3. 4 Apr 1938 WSC ltr to Ld Camrose, CHAR 8/601/1–2.
4. 6 April 1938 Ld Camrose ltr to WSC, CHAR 8/601/3.
5. 11, 8 Apr 1938 WSC ltrs to R. Thompson, ER, CHAR 8/600/22–3, 8/607/29–30.
6. 28 Apr, 12, 26 May 1938 Cooperation accounts, CHAR 8/607/105–6, 108, 109.
7. 5, 6, 9 May 1938 ER corresp with WSC, CHAR 8/607/40–42.
8. 9 Jun 1938 WSC ltr to ACB, CHAR 2/353/12; 16 Jun, 1 Jul 1938 H. Hilton ltrs to WSC, 2/353/13, 23.
9. 2 April 1938 WSC letter to G. Harrap, CHAR 8/547/1.
10. 3 Apr 1938 WSC ltr to RSC, CHAR 8/598/1. *Arms and the Covenant*, consisting of forty-one speeches made by Churchill between October 1928–March 1938, was published in Britain on 24 June and in America (as *While England Slept*) on 30 September, by G. P. Putnam's Sons. 12, 18 Sep 1938 C. Wood ltrs to WSC, LlBk statement, CHAR 8/594/54, 63, 1/321/164. £100 of Churchill's advance was clawed back in September when sales in Britain reached only 2,484; the American print run of 5,000 was sold by the end of 1938.
11. 29 Apr 1938 WSC draft agreement with G. Harrap re 'Europe since the Russian Revolution', The Winston S. Churchill Collection of Malcom Forbes, Jr., sold at Christie's 15 Nov 2011.
12. 1 Nov 1938 WSC ltr to V. Pearman, CHAR 8/594/174. Churchill spoke to Mrs Pearman's doctor before telling her that he would continue to pay her monthly salary of £12 while she was away. When Mrs Pearman died in 1941 (at the age of forty), Churchill continued to pay her salary to her seven-year-old daughter Rosemary. From 1943 he covenanted £100 a year towards Rosemary's education. See M. Gilbert, *In Search of Churchill*, pp. 157, 159.
13. 18 Apr, 20 Jun 1938 H. Peat ltrs to WSC, 5C3:997–8, CHAR 1/407/138.

14. 26 Jan, 15 Apr 1938 H. Peat ltrs to WSC, Memorandum of Agreement, CHAR 1/407/102, 22–6.
15. 30 Jul 1938 H. Peat cbl to WSC, CHAR 1/407/146.
16. 17 Aug 1938 WSC ltr to A. Leve, 5C3:118–19; 19 Dec 1938, 10 Jul 1940 WSC ltr to G. Mason, G. Mason ltr to secretary, CHAR 1/329/52, 1/356, 58. Churchill wanted to claim the $2,000 penalty as a tax-deductible expense, but Mason omitted the item on his tax return. Churchill spotted the omission after checking his return during the Battle of Britain in 1940. Through a secretary, Mason reminded Churchill that he had visited him to advise against making the claim because 'money paid in default could not be said to be money earned'.
17. 12 Aug 1938 WSC ltr to N. Flower, 5C3:1116.
18. 2 Sep 1938 N. Flower ltr to WSC, CHAR 8/597/34.
19. 14 Sep 1938 WSC ltr to GSH, CHAR 8/597/25.
20. 12 Sep, 10 Nov 1938 C. Wood ltrs to WSC, Harrap account, CHAR 8/598/59, 188; 8/608/56; 13 Oct 1938 CSIII ltr to WSC, 8/595/188. Harrap deducted £309 for author's corrections from its advance of £3,500. Despite critical acclaim, the book sold only 5,410 copies in the first ten weeks after publication in Britain.
21. 19 Sep 1938 WSC ltr to R. Mortimer Wheeler, 5C3:1166. Sir Robert Mortimer Wheeler CH (1890–1976) was later director of the National Museum of Wales, keeper of the London Museum and director-general of the Archaeological Survey of India.
22. 28 Sep 1938, CB corresp with WSC, CHAR 8/604/79, 80.
23. Recollection of Colin Coote, see 5:988.
24. 19, 29 Dec 1938 WSC ltrs to CSC, 5C3:1316–7, 1327–31. Churchill helped to build Orchard Cottage at Chartwell.
25. 31 Dec 1938 LlBk statement, CHAR 1/321/185, 186. The *News of the World* cheque was for £4,200.
26. 1 Jan 1939 WSC schedules, CHAR 1/347/1, 1/345/38–39; 1939 LlBk statements, 1/354/187–234.
27. P. Clarke, *Mr Churchill's Profession*, p. 219.
28. 18 Jan 1939, WSC ltr to CSC, 5C3:1346–9.
29. Jan 1939 LlBk statement, CHAR 1/321/188.
30. 23 Jan 1939 M. Penman, *Penman Papers*, 5C3:1352.
31. 31 Jan 1939 WSC cbl to CSC, CHAR 1/344/20.
32. 18 Jan 1939 WSC ltr to CSC, 5C3:1346–9.
33. 28 Jan 1939 Literary account 1939, CHAR 8/639/77; 24 Mar, 2 May 1939 WSC ltrs to G. Young, 8/626, 5C3:1487. Churchill converted Young's *honorarium* to a salary within two months.
34. 10 Feb 1939 ER ltr to WSC, CHAR 8/638/19–22.
35. 17, 18, 20 Feb, 2 Mar 1939 WSC cbl corresp with ER, CHAR 8/638/26, 30, 34.

36. 9, 11 Mar 1939 Cooperation accounts, ER ltr to WSC, CHAR 8/638/159, 41.
37. Jan, 8 Mar 1939 RSC, WSC schedules, CHAR 1/345/49, 38; 1/321/ 220. Randolph's new debts amounted to £4,000; his remaining share of the trust was £1,630. Churchill's loan from the trust was still £12,000, secured on a mortgage over Chartwell.
38. 22 Feb 1939 H. Strakosch ltr to WSC, CHAR 2/374.
39. 28 Mar 1993 WSC ltr to G. Harrap, CHAR 8/626/135–7.
40. 4, 6, 15, 18 Apr G. Harrap, TB corresp with WSC, CHAR 8/636/28, 31–2, 42, 44, 47. Butterworth sold *Step by Step*'s US rights to G. Putnam's Sons for £300. Churchill received cheques for £644 (net of author's corrections) on publication in Britain (27 June) and £202 in September. It was published in New York on 25 August 1939 and translated into five European languages.
41. 24, 30 Mar 1939 WSC ltrs to M. Ashley, J. Wheldon, 5C3:1404, 5.
42. 6, 22, 24 Jun 1939 WSC ltrs to E. Marsh, G. Young, Chartwell Literary Account, 5C3:1513, 1532–3, 1541. Marsh received £20 per 100,000 words.
43. 27 Apr 1939 C. Thomas ltr to WSC, CHAR 8/633/7.
44. 2 Jun 1939 ER ltr to WSC, CHAR 8/638/79–80.
45. 20 Jun, 11 Jul 1939 ER cbl, agreement with WSC, CHAR 8/638/98, 103–4. Churchill's first talk (eight minutes long) was aired on 8 August. War broke out and Churchill had taken office before the second could take place (scheduled for 5 September).
46. Jul 1939 LlBk statement, CHAR 1/354/215.
47. D. Kynaston, *The City of London* 3:458.
48. 20, 9 Jul 1939 WSC ltrs to EHM, N. Flower, CHAR 8/626/58, 5C3:1558.
49. 8 Jul 1939 WSC ltr to E. Carr, 5C3:1557.
50. M. Gilbert, *Winston Churchill: The Wilderness Years*, p. 260.
51. 20 Aug 1939 P. Maze diary, Maze papers, 5C3:1591.
52. 31 Aug 1939 WSC ltr to N. Flower, CHAR 8/624/205.

20. Early Burdens of War, 1939–41

1. 28 Sep 1939 J. Drawbell corresp with WSC, CHAR 8/631/20, 11–13.
2. 10 Sep 1939 WSC ltr to G. Young, CHAR 8/626/190–3.
3. 6 Oct 1939 WSC ltr to W. Deakin, CWP1:215–6.
4. 10 Nov 1939 WSC ltr to D. Flower, CWP1:355.
5. 19 Nov 1939 WSC ltr to W. Deakin, CWP1:392.
6. 16 Dec 1939 WSC ltr to D. Flower, CHAR 8/626/247.
7. 27 Dec 1939 D. Flower ltr to WSC, CHAR 8/626/245.
8. 31 Dec 1939 LlBk statement, CHAR 1/354/236.

9. 4 Jan 1940 D. Flower ltr to WSC, CHAR 8/658/55.
10. 4 Jan 1940 K. Hill cbl to WSC, CHAR 8//658/52.
11. 4 Jan 1940 BRB ltr to D. Flower, CHAR 8/658/51.
12. Jan 1940 LlBk statement, CHAR 1/354/236, 237, 238.
13. Jan 1969 W. Deakin lecture, University of Basel, published as supplement 'Churchill the historian' to *Schweizer Monatshefte* 1970; CWP1:1152. Although Deakin gives 27 April 1940 as the date of the working session, this is unlikely. By 19 April, Bullock had stood down and Churchill had approved an agreement between Bracken and Flower to postpone *History*'s publication until after the war. The more likely date is late March or early April 1940.
14. A. de Courcy *The Viceroy's Daughters* pp.314–5, D. Kynaston, *The City of London* 3:471.
15. D. Flower, *Fellows in Foolscap*, p. 171.
16. WSC, *The Second World War Vol. 1 The Gathering Storm*, p.522.
17. 9 May 1940 Ld Camrose notes of conversation with Mr Neville Chamberlain, Camrose Papers.
18. J. Wheeler-Bennett (ed.), *Action this Day: Working with Churchill*, pp. 48–51.
19. Ibid., p.175.
20. 16 Apr 1940 D. Flower ltr to BRB, CHAR 8/658/47; 26 Jun 1940 BRB note to WSC, 8/803/168.
21. 18 Jun 1940 LlBk statement, CHAR 1/354/252.
22. 14 Jan 1941 W. Harrap ltr to BRB, CHAR 8/681/11.
23. 23 Oct 1940 G. Mason ltr to K Hill, CHAR 1/356/66.
24. 31 Jul 1940 ACB ltr to WSC, CHAR 8/663/8–9.
25. 25 Mar 1941 WSC annotation on K. Hill memo, CHAR 8/685/38.
26. 13 Jun 1941 NM ltr to K. Hill, CHAR 8/685/48. Churchill paid £1,515 (including £15 stamp duty).
27. 21 Apr 1941 BRB ltr to D. Jarrold, CHAR 8/685/27.
28. 1 May 1941 TB ltr to WSC, CHAR 8/685/42–3.
29. 7 May 1941 A. Bott letter to K. Hill, CHAR 8/685/40–1.
30. 3 Mar, 16 Jun 1942, D. Macmillan, L. Dickson ltrs to K Hill, CHAR 8/700/5, 38. Churchill earned £1,800 from 95,000 copies sold by the Reprint Society.
31. 15 Oct 1941 S. Bell ltr to K. Hill, CHAR 1/363/42.
32. C. Eden, C.Haste (ed.) *A Memoir: From Churchill to Eden*, p. 57.
33. 14 Sep 1940 K. Hill ltr to G. Penrudock, CHAR 1/35/3.
34. 14 Sep 1941 Chequers Trust accounts, CHAR 1/365/3. Twelve weekends in May–July 1941 cost Churchill £198, of which telephone calls cost £38.
35. 26 Nov 1940 WSC contract with Cassell & Co., *Into Battle*, CHAR 8/803/2–3; 16 Dec 1940 A. Gentry ltr to WSC, 8/803/20: G. Putnam's

Sons paid an advance of £650 against a royalty of 15 per cent, while Cassell bought other foreign rights for £600. 28 January 1941, CHAR 8/803/119: Publication in America as *Blood, Sweat and Tears* was postponed until April 1941 to clinch selection by the Book of the Month Club, which Putnam estimated to be worth an extra 120,000 copies or $15,000 in royalties.

36. 1941 LlBk statements, CHAR 1/354/273–304. The April 1941 budget raised the basic rate of income tax to 50 per cent. A top rate of 47.5 per cent sur-tax applied to marginal extra income as high as Churchill's.
37. June 1941 Draft WSC contract with Warner Bros, NA 40/12833.
38. 13 Jun 1940 G. Canny ltr to G. Mason, CHAR 1/363/15.
39. 23 Jun 1941 K. Hill letter to G. Mason, CHAR 1/363/17; 17 June 1941 LlBk statement, CHAR 1/354/291.
40. 6 Jun 1941 G. Canny memo to Tucker, NA IR 40/12833.
41. 16 Jun 1941 G. Canny memo to F. Slee, ibid.
42. 9 Jun 1941 G. Mason ltr to G. Canny, copied WSC, CHAR 1/363/22–3.
43. 5 Sep, 15 Sep 1941 K. Hill memo to WSC, S. Ball ltr to K. Hill, CHAR 1/363/33, 42.
44. 8 Nov 1941 F. Slee memo, NA IR 40/12833.
45. Her Majesty's Revenue and Customs, Capital Gains and Other Taxes Manual, app.37.
46. 13 Jun 1941 WSC annotation on NM ltr to K. Hill, CHAR 8/685/48.
47. 30 May 1941, BRB ltr to WSC, CHAR 8/686/28–30.
48. 3 Aug 1941 WSC–Macmillan agreement, CHAR 8/685/13–15; 28 Aug 1941 Macmillian Archive, M/s Add 55245/2/197-8, BL. Daniel Macmillan declined Mrs Hill's request to handle the deleted rights informally. He diplomatically suggested that a side-letter should be used to reinstate the appointment; Mrs Hill slipped such a letter into Churchill's signing folder at the end of August.
49. 14 Nov 1941 Ld Camrose letter to S. Berry, Camrose Papers.

21. Film Turns the Tide, 1942–5

1. 21 Jan 1942 C. Graham-Dixon opinion, NA IR 40/12833.
2. U/d, post 1953 A. Moir reminiscence, Fladgate LLP papers. Moir places his meeting with Churchill on 18 May 1942, but the House of Commons did not sit that day; it began its debate on 19 May.
3. 19 May 1942 E. Grigg, MP for Altrincham, House of Commons speech, Hansard c90.
4. 18 Feb 1942 G. Mason ltr to WSC, CHAR 1/370/8. Churchill had paid Randolph £700; Mason suggested he now transfer an extra £4,200.
5. E. Waugh, *Letters*, p.151. Randolph joined no. 8 Commando Regiment,

a unit trained for special operations by Colonel David Stirling, later the founder of the Special Air Service (SAS).

6. 18 Feb 1942 T. Harris ltr to K. Hill, CHAR 1/370/8. The payment was made on 30 March 1942, the day before Churchill paid his own reduced tax bill of £3,500 (which would otherwise have been approximately £9,000) – see 30 Mar 1942 LlBk statement, 1/354/309.

7. 17 Mar 1942 A. Gentry ltr to K. Hill, CHAR 8/804/107.

8. 20 May 1942 A. Gentry ltr to K. Hill, CHAR 1/804/90.

9. 30 Jun 1942 Macmillan & Co. accounts, CHAR 8/700/58.

10. 9 Nov 1942 K. Hill ltr to D. Macmillan, CHAR 8/700/45.

11. 9, 12 Jun 1942 W. Blatch note of meeting with A. Moir, G. Mason, note to C. Gregg, NA IR 40/12833.

12. 29 Sep, 1 Oct 1942 general commmissioners of taxation decision, C. Gregg note, NA IR 40/12833.

13. 27 Jan, 18 Feb 1943 CHAR 8/805/76, 71, 63. Cassell bid £3,000 for the worldwide rights: Little, Brown cut its contribution by half to $4,000.

14. 22, 30 Jun 1943 LlBk statement, CHUR 1/1/15/329. The balance was £21,464.

15. 6 Sep 1943 C. Nicholl brief to Counsel, CHAR 8/710/13–14.

16. 4 Aug 1943 WSC note, CHAR 8/710/3–6.

17. U/d Oct 1943 C. Henderson KC Opinion, CHAR 8/710/15–21.

18. 13 Oct 1943 WSC ltr to W. Harrap, CHAR 8/710/26–7.

19. 11 Nov 1943 KH note, CHAR 8/710/32.

20. 16, 17 Nov 1943 C. Henderson draft, K. Hill ltr to W. Harrap, CHAR 8/710/35, 39, 41.

21. 18 Dec 1943 WSC ltr to G. Harrap, C. Henderson draft, CHAR 8/710/48, 54.

22. 27 Jul 1943 K. Hill note, CHAR 8/709/3.

23. 20 Dec 1943 William Hickey column, the *Daily Express*.

24. 13, 23 Aug 1943 K. Hill note to H. Osborne, Two Cities ltr to H. Osborne, CHAR 8/709/5, 10.

25. 19 Sep 1943 K. Hill note, CHAR 8/709/16. The remaining £20,000 was to be paid nine months later, or on completion of the shooting script, whichever occurred earlier.

26. 19 & u/d Sep, 6 Oct 1943, 18 July 1944 K. Hill notes, contract, CHAR 8/709/16, 32, 40, 61; 4 Oct 1943 LlBk statement CHUR 1/1/19/333. The first payment of £30,000 (lodged on 4 October 1943) increased Churchill's bank account balance to almost £46,000; the other £20,000 followed on 18 July 1944. The film was never made.

27. 16 Nov 1943 *Daily Herald*, CHAR 8/709/44.

28. 28 Jan 1944 K. Hill note, memo to WSC, CHAR 18/713/3, 1.

29. 5, 8 Feb 1944 Agreement WSC and Cassell & Co., K. Hill ltr to C. Nicholl, CHAR 8/713/5, 4.

30. 7 Mar 1944 BRB ltr to Ld Camrose, CHAR 8/713/14.
31. 13 April 1944 WSC note, CHAR 8/713/21.
32. 18 Apr 1944 C. Nicholl, C. Henderson memo, CHAR 8/713/23.
33. 27 Apr 1944 WSC ltr to D. Macmillan CHAR 8/714/32.
34. 15 Mar 1944 LlBk ltr to WSC, statement, CHAR 1/382/18, CHUR 1/1/338. Sir Henry Strakosh died in September 1943. On payment of his legacy in March 1944, Churchill's bank balance reached a record £56,806.
35. 10 Aug 1944 WSC ltr to D. Macmillan, CHAR 8/714/50, Macmillan Archive, M/s Add 55245/2/202, 203, BL.
36. 11 Aug, 9 Oct 1944 D. Macmillan ltrs to WSC, CHAR 8/714/51, 57. Macmillan & Co.'s accounts for Churchill's book earnings for year to 30 June 1944 showed profits (£3,714) double the previous year. *My Early Life* contributed over £2,000 (selling 5,200 copies through bookshops and 79,785 through the World Book Club); *Great Contemporaries* took second place with £857 (selling 3,000 copies) – see 17 Oct 1944 CHAR 8/714/59–60.
37. 23 Aug 1944 C. Nicholl ltr to K. Hill, CHAR 8/710/106.
38. Ibid.
39. 4 Sep 1944 WSC note to BRB, CHAR 8/710/112–13.
40. 4 Sep 1944 K. Hill note, CHAR 8/710/114–15.
41. 7 Sep 1944 W. Harrap ltr to WSC, CHAR 8/710/117.
42. U/d Sep, 23 Dec 1944 BRB cbl to WSC, WSC corresp with C. Nicholl, CHAR 8/710/123, 168, 169. Each side paid its own legal costs. The arbitrator, Sir William Raeburn, decided not to charge. Churchill wanted to send him an *honorarium* of 100 guineas but Nicholl persuaded him to send 25 guineas (which Raeburn donated to the Overseas Tobacco League for Soldiers Abroad).
43. 24 Oct 1944 WSC ltr to Ld Camrose, CHAR 8/713/32.
44. 8 Nov 1944 Ld Camrose note, Camrose Papers.
45. 10 Nov 1944 WSC ltr to Ld Camrose, CHAR 8/713/61.
46. 21 Nov 1944 C. Nicholl ltr to K Hill, CHAR 8/713/71; 26 Apr, 2 Aug 1945 C. Nicholl ltr to K. Hill, WSC letter to C. Nicholl, 8/720/16, 20. In April 1945, Colonel Charles Nicholl raised the question of Churchill's legal fees with some diffidence. Both he and Charles Henderson KC had spent hundreds of hours during the war on Churchill's affairs, but neither wished to charge their normal rates. They felt Churchill's unique responsibilities had left him short of time and exposed to serious public damage from any mis-step. Each suggested a token fee of 250 guineas. Churchill paid and thanked them after he left office ('I think these charges are indeed moderate and I thank you'). 30 Dec 1960 CHUR 1/117/115–6: there was a codicil fifteen years later, after Nicholl's death, when the two remaining

partners of Nicholl, Manisty Co. merged with Withers & Co., its larger neighbour. One of the partners, J. W. Roome, explained to Churchill that, while he was clearing up loose ends before the merger, he had noticed the firm had never charged Churchill for any post-war work. 'I understand it was Colonel Nicholl's wish and intention that the Firm should not make any charge for the work involved,' Roome wrote. While he proposed to 'treat the bills... as having been discharged', he asked Churchill to reimburse cash payments (such as stamp duty) made by the firm on his behalf. Churchill obliged with a cheque for £200.18s.7d.

47. 19, 20, 21 Nov 1944 C. Henderson draft of WSC ltr to N. Flower, K. Hill note to WSC, WSC ltr to Ld Camrose, C. Henderson advice, C. Nicholl ltr to K. Hill, CHAR 8/713/68–70, 65, 81–3, 84–6, 72, 71.

48. 24 Nov 1944 WSC ltr to N. Flower, CHAR 8/713/97–99. The second letter is ibid./100.

49. 30 Nov 1944 ACB ltr to K. Hill, CHAR 8/715/12; Lord Southwood's letter of 23 November is at CHAR 8/715/13.

50. 21, 22 Dec 1944 C. Henderson draft for K. Hill ltr to ACB, amended by WSC, signed version, CHAR 8/715/17, 19.

51. 5 Dec 1944, 13 Mar 1945 K. Hill notes to BRB, CHAR 8/713/105, 8/720/8.

52. 14, 26 Mar, 6 Apr 1945 K. Hill note to WSC, C. Nicholl ltr to K. Hill, K. Hill note CHAR 8/720/10, 11, 14.

53. 1 Dec 1944 LlBk statement, CHUR 1/1/33; 2, 17, 19 Nov 1945 LlBk ltrs to WSC, 1/11/23, 25, 29; 1 Jan 1946 8:25; Scribner Archives C0101, Author files III, box 12, folder 9, PUFL. Churchill's 1945 bank statements do not survive, but these receipts, taken together with Korda's £50,000 April 1945 payment for *History*'s film rights added at least £86,450 to Churchill's last known balance (December 1944) of £52,000. Churchill's major outlay during the first half of 1945 was £24,696 for the purchase of 28 Hyde Park Gate. In August 1945, he told Lord Camrose that he had 'between £110,00 and £120,000 in the bank'.

22. Minting the Memoirs, 1945–6

1. 29 Sep 1945 Treasury Chambers letter to WSC, CHUR 1/16/112.

2. 28 Jan 1945 CSC ltr to M. Soames, cited M. Soames, *Clementine Churchill*, p. 418; 13 Dec 1945 KFR account, CHAR 1/389/36. The Churchills later leased the first and second floors of the adjoining 27 Hyde Park Gate for seven years at £350 per annum, until they bought the property for £7,000 in February 1946 – see 18 Feb, 22 Aug, 17 Oct 1946, WSC cbl to KFR, NM ltrs to WSC, CHUR 1/17/116, 164, 172.

3. 26, 27, 31 Jul, 2 Aug 1945 ER cbls & ltrs to WSC, K. Hill reply, CHAR 8/721/2, 4, 5, 7
4. 8 Aug 1945 ER ltr to WSC, CHAR 8/721/8–9.
5. 7 Aug 1945 Ld Camrose note, Camrose Papers; Ld Hartwell, *William Camrose, Giant of Fleet Street*, pp. 333–4.
6. 30 Nov 1945 WSC ltr to H. Macmillan, CHAR 8/722/60.
7. 1 Aug 1945 W. Graebner ltr to WSC, CHUR 4/15/572. *LIFE* (a weekly pictorial news magazine), *TIME* and *Fortune* formed the core of a publishing empire founded by Henry Luce. Luce was brought up in China, before he made his way to England, aged fourteen, and then to Yale University. He founded *LIFE* in 1936. Ten years later it enjoyed a readership of five million and contributed two-thirds of the group's $96 million annual revenue – see R. Elson, *The World of Time Inc.*, pp. 182–3.
8. W. Graebner, *My Dear Mr Churchill*, p. 2.
9. 17 Nov 1945 *TIME-LIFE* ltr to WSC, CHUR 4/15/555. *LIFE*'s January 1946 edition pp. 44–52 carried pictures of eighteen paintings under the heading 'The Paintings of Winston Churchill', pp. 44–52. Mrs Hill negotiated a further fee of £1,000 for *The Strand*'s use of seventeen paintings in spring 1946.
10. 10 Oct 1945 A. Moir ltr to G. Mason, CHUR 4/15/570.
11. 24 Sep 1945 WSC ltr to CSC, SFT:540–1.
12. 12 Feb 1946 J. Wood ltr to WSC, CHUR 1/17/367–8, schedules 369–ff.
13. Lord Hartwell, *William Camrose, Giant of Fleet Street*, p. 336.
14. 19 Dec 1945 House of Commons, Hansard vol 417 cc13124.
15. U/d Sep 1945 Ld Camrose note, Chartwell file, Camrose papers.
16. NM account, Camrose Papers, Chartwell file.
17. 25 Oct 1945 Westminster Bank, Temple Bar branch statement, Camrose papers.
18. 1946 Country House file, Camrose papers; 13 Dec 1954 A Moir ltr to J. Colville, CHUR 1/28/290, A. Moir ltr to WSC, 7 Oct 1958, 1/37/43–4;13 Dec 1954 1/28/290. Camrose finally raised £95,000 from seventeen names, interest raising the total to £95,343. Churchill was paid £50,000 on 4 October 1946, before the purchase completed formally on 29 November; the National Trust received its endowment on 2 December. After lawyers were paid, £8,931 remained in the Chartwell subscription account, so £8,728 was added to the National Trust's endowment in March and April 1947, taking the endowment to £43,728; investment gains and accumulated income raised the endowment's value to £60,000 at the end of 1954. Lord Camrose's son, Lord Hartwell, made the list of donors public in 1989. Apart from Lord Camrose's £15,000, each donor subscribed £5,000: Viscount Bearsted (art collector and philanthropist), Lord Bicester (merchant banker at Morgan Grenfell), Sir James Caird

(ship owner), Sir Hugo Cunliffe-Owen (businessman, British American Tobacco), Lord Catto (governor of the Bank of England), Lord Glendyne (stockbroker), Lord Kenilworth (motor manufacturer), Lord Leathers (shipping), Sir James Lithgow (ship builder), Sir Edward Mountain (underwriter), Viscount Nuffield (motor manufacturer and philanthropist), Sir Edward Peacock (merchant banker), Viscount Portal of Laverstoke (paper manufacturer), J. Arthur Rank (flour miller and film-maker), James de Rothschild (Liberal politician and philanthropist) and Sir Frederick Stewart (engineer).

19. M. Daunton, *Just Taxes*, pp. 198–9. The budget reduced the standard rate of income tax from 50 to 45 per cent, while the top rate of sur-tax remained 47.5 per cent. The combined top rate was restored to 97.5 per cent six months later.

20. 5 Oct 1945 K. Hill note to WSC, CHAR 8/716/61. Sir Alexander Korda bought the film rights to *The River War* for £35,000 (paying a first instalment of £25,000 in August 1946). The film was never made.

21. U/d, c16 Oct 1945 WSC note, CHUR 1/15/9–13.

22. 17, 24 Oct 1945 WSC ltr, memo to Ld Camrose, CHAR 8/718/4, 5–9, 8/713/38–42. The Cambridge professor was Denis Brogan.

23. 1 Nov 1945 WSC ltr to N. Flower, CHAR 8/718/14.

24. 12 Dec 1945 WSC draft for G. Mason, CHAR 1/388/30.

25. 17 Sep 1945 ACB ltr to K. Hill, CHUR 4/6/107–9.

26. 19 Nov 1945 M. Field III ltr to WSC, CHUR 4/6/165–6; 17 October 1945 S. Curtis Brown ltr to WSC, 4/6/104–5. Curtis Brown's estimate of the US rights' value was $1.1 million, close to the figure achieved a year later.

27. 15 Oct 1945 WSC ltr to Ld Camrose, CHUR 4/6/157.

28. 8 Nov, 10 Dec 1945 T. Harris ltrs to WSC, CHUR 1/9/3, 12. Churchill bought £10,000 of 2½ per cent Consols, £20,000 of 3 per cent Local Loans, £10,000 of 3 per cent Savings Bonds 1965/75, £2,000 of railway preferences shares and £1,000 of Bolsover Colliery shares (despite the the threat of nationalization). 8 Jan, 18 Feb 1946 WSC ltrs to T. Harris, CHUR 8/1/46; 1/9/14, 87; 1/41/194. The day before he left for New York, Churchill gave Lloyds Bank authority to invest a further £20,000 for him, using a pre-agreed list of shares (including Union Corporation, Allied Bakeries and two investment trusts, Select Trust and African & European).

29. 17 Dec 1945 W. Graebner, *My Dear Mr. Churchill*, p. 4.

30. 17 Dec 1946 H. Luce comment on W. Graebner cable, box 1, WSCDL, CURBSML.

31. 8, 15 Jan 1946 W. Graebner ltr to WSC, WSC ltr to H. Luce, CHUR 4/5/263, 254–7.

32. 19 Dec 1946 ER ltr to WSC, CHAR 8/721/16–17.

33. The advance had been made in 1944 by the introduction of a 'Pay As You Earn' or PAYE system, through which employers deducted income tax at source before they paid salaries to their employees.

34. 8 Jan 1946 C. Graham-Dixon Opinion, CHUR 4/41/17–18.

35. 24 Jan 1946 G. Mason cbl to WSC, citing C. Graham-Dixon, CHUR 1/7/77.

36. ER conversation with RSC, cited M. Gilbert WSC 8:187–8.

37. R. Elson, *The World of Time Inc.*, p. 157.

38. 18, 24 Apr, 7 Jun, 25 Jul 1946 N. Pearn corresp with WSC, N. Sturdee, CHUR 4/29/200, 218, 221, 227, 8–10, 114. Pearn, Hollinger & Higham raised almost £5,000 for outright sales: 60,000 French francs from *Le Figaro*, £300 for Spanish rights, £100 for Scandinavian and Dutch rights.

39. 18 Feb 1946 Fladgate & Co., Schemes, C. Graham-Dixon Opinion, CHUR 4/41/13–18, 11–14.

40. 5 Mar 1946 WSC speech, Westminster College, Missouri.

41. 20 Mar 1946 ER ltr to WSC, CHUR 4/12/321–2.

42. 11 Apr 1946 WSC memo to A. Moir, CHUR 4/41/127–31; May 1952 E. Sturdee note, 4/41/289–90. Omitted from the list were the 1939–45 Prime Minister's office files, known as the 'Premier' files, which had been moved to the Cabinet Office basement, but to which Churchill could have laid claim under war cabinet guidelines. Moir only heard of their existence in 1952, when it was too late to include them in the trust.

43. May 1946 A. Moir Draft Chartwell Literary Settlement deed, CHUR 4/41/20–7.

44. 19 May, 31 Jul 1946 WSC ltr to A. Moir, Chartwell Literary trust deed, CHUR 4/41/29, 59–6. The trust's final form gave half to Randolph on winding-up and half to his other children. It excluded Churchill and Clementine as beneficiaries.

45. 31 Jul 1946 Fladgate & Co. Chartwell Literary Settlement Trust deed, CHUR 4/41/51, 52.

46. 4 Aug 1946 WSC letter to Camrose, CHUR 4/42/124–5.

47. 10 May 1946 CP (46) 188, NA CAB 129/9.

48. 29 May 1946 WSC to C. Attlee, NA CAB 21/3740.

49. 23 Sep 1946 WSC ltr to E. Bridges, Camrose Papers.

50. 27 Sep 1946 E. Bridges memo WSC, NA CAB 21/3747.

51. 10 Oct 1946 E. Bridges ltr to WSC, Camrose Papers.

52. 25 Sep 1946 WSC schedules, CHUR 1/8/129–31; 13 Sep 1945 VdaC list of WSC securities, 1/16/226–7.

53. 1941 *My Early Life* £7,500, London Film Productions (A. Korda)/Warner Bros.; 1944 *Marlborough: His Life and Times* £50,000, Two Cities Films (del Giudice)/J. Arthur Rank; 1945 *A History of the English-Speaking*

Peoples £50,000, London Film Productions (A. Korda)/MGM; 1946 *Savrola* £35,000 London Film Productions (A. Korda).

54. 5 Apr, 23 May 1946 Wood, Willey & Co. schedules, CHUR 1/7/97–104, 1/17/61. Before his tax was computed, Churchill could deduct £1,039 of life assurance payments on policies with Phoenix Assurance, National Mutual Life and Commercial Union, £668 interest on loans from Lord Randolph's will trust (£12,000) and his settlement for Mary (£1,700). There were also large deductions for his covenanted payments to Pamela Churchill, Sarah Oliver, Randolph and Mary (his £500 a year covenant for Randolph cost a net £180 each year after Churchill made deductions against both his income tax and sur-tax assessments).

55. 14 Oct 1946 www.britishpathe.com/video/winston-churchill-gives-away-a-house/query/sevenoaks. The gift came from C. A. Hopkins. Churchill gave Kippington Court, now Churchill Court, to the British Legion 'for the comfort of the wounded and the sick'.

23. Selling the Memoirs, 1946–8

1. 17, 19 Oct 1946 Ld Camrose corresp with ER, Camrose papers.
2. 1966 ER recollections to RSC, M. Gilbert, *Winston Churchill and Emery Reves*, pp. 264–71.
3. Oct 1946 *Daily Telegraph* New York office memo to Ld Camrose, Camrose papers.
4. 24 Oct 1946 ER cbl to WSC, CHUR 4/31/1.
5. 25 Oct 1946 Ld Camrose cbl corresp with WSC, CHUR 4/31/4, 5, Camrose Papers. Written in early November, the *Collier's* article appeared in January 1947 as 'High Road of the Future'. Churchill donated $4,000 of his $25,000 fee to the British Handling Group of the project for a United States of Europe (his son-in-law Duncan Sandys was treasurer). 7 Nov 1946, 13 Feb 1947 CHUR 4/31/28, 51, 68, 85, 100: *The Daily Telegraph* paid £400 for British rights; Australian, French, Belgian and Swiss rights fetched £450 and *Reader's Digest* paid $1,100 for reprint rights.
6. 22 Aug 1957 D. Longwell interview transcript, *TIME-LIFE* file A–M, WSCDL, CURBSML.
7. 4 Nov 1946 ER ltr to WSC, CHUR 4/12/284–6.
8. 10 Nov 1946 WSC cbl to ER, CHUR 4/12/282.
9. 15 Nov 1946 Ld Camrose ltr to WSC, Camrose papers.
10. See, e.g., M. Gilbert, *Winston Churchill and Emery Reves*, pp. 264–71.
11. Appointments Calendars 1945, 1946, Clare Booth Luce papers, box 744, LoCW.
12. 22 Aug 1957 D. Longwell interview, 3:5–13, *TIME-LIFE* file A–M; memo to E. Thompson, box 4 WSCDL, CURBSML.

13. 20 Nov 1946 W. Graebner cbl to H. Luce, box 2, WSCDL, CURBSML.
14. 0900 23 Nov 1946 Ld Camrose cbl to S. Berry, for passing to WSC, Camrose papers.
15. 24 Nov 1946 WSC cbl to Ld Camrose, Camrose papers.
16. 24 Nov 1946 ER cbl to WSC, CHUR 4/12/265–6.
17. D Longwell memo to E. Thompson, box 4, WSCDL, CURBMSL.
18. D Longwell interview transcript, *TIME-LIFE* File A–M, WSCDL, CURBMSL.
19. 27 Nov 1946 Ld Cam cbl to WSC, Camrose papers.
20. 28 Nov 1946 Ld Camrose cbl to N. Sturdee, Camrose papers.
21. 11 Dec 1946 North American Newspaper Alliance cutting, Camrose papers.
22. 9 Dec 1946 ER ltr to Ld Camrose, CHUR 4/12/280–1.
23. 6 Jan 1947 A. Moir schedule, CHUR 4/41/119; Ld Hartwell, *William Camrose, Giant of Fleet Street*, p. 334; author's estimates. The main amounts were:

LIFE / New York Times	$1,150,000	£ 287,500
Montreal Standard	$ 110,000	£ 27,500
Houghton Mifflin	$ 250,000	£ 62,500
The Daily Telegraph		£ 75,000
Cassell & Co.		£ 40,000
Australia serials		£ 20,000
Australia book		£ 20,000
South Africa serials		£ 16,500
Ireland serials		£ 2,500
Reves for foreign rights		£ 47,500

24. 22 Sep 1946 D. Longwell memo to E. Thompson, box 4 WSCDL, CURBSML.
25. 6 Jan 1947 A. Moir ltr to WSC, CHUR 4/41/117–18; u/d probably 7 Jan 1947 WSC ltr to Ld Camrose, 4/41/118.
26. 6 Jan 1947 ER ltr to P. Brooks, H. J. Frank file, box 318/1 HMCo HLHU. France and Holland paid the equivalent of $300,000.
27. 17, 23 May 1946 JSC schedules, CHUR 1/9/75, 282. Churchill added to existing holdings in Selection Trust and Africa & European, and started new investments in British Oxygen, British American Tobacco and Imperial Tobacco.
28. 15 Dec 1946 VdaC valuation, CHUR 1/9/282. Gains of £3,250, all on bonds, were offset by losses on shares of £1,900.
29. 26 Aug 1945 CSC ltr to M. Churchill, M. Soames, *A Daughter's Tale*, p. 363, *Clementine Churchill*, p. 301.
30. U/d 1946 J. D. Wood particulars, CHUR 1/32/312; 20, 22 Oct WSC corresp with R. Marnham, 1/32/293, 292. Major Marnham's dairy herd was expected to produce £2,000 of milk during the year.

31. 6, 9, 19 Dec 1946 Fox & Mainwaring ltrs to WSC, CHUR 1/35/16, 6, 18; 1/34/27. The asking price had been £12,500. Contracts were exchanged on 18 March 1947.

32. 13 Nov 1946 T. Harris ltr to WSC, CHUR 1/32/284; 3 Jan 1947 WSC ltr to G. Mason, 1/11/132. The loan of £21,500 carried an interest rate of 3½ per cent.

33. 8 Mar 1947 C. Soames ltr to WSC, CHUR 1/42/295–7.

34. 16, 24 May 1947 Fox & Mainwaring particulars, ltr to WSC, CHUR 1/34/9, 13.

35. 19 Dec 1946 D. Longwell interview transcript, box 4 WSCDL, CURBMSL.

36. 24 Jan 1947 W. Graebner cbl to D. Longwell, box 2 WSCDL, CURBMSL. Churchill crossed out the word 'nearly' in front of 'all'.

37. 1 Apr 1947 D. Longwell ltr to E. James, NYT, box 3, WSCDL, CURBMSL. *The Daily Telegraph* paid £600; *LIFE* recouped $5,000 by selling secondary US rights to *Reader's Digest*, which also paid Churchill $2,451 (its usual author's fee of $200 per page plus $1 per word) for use in its international edition. May, Jun 1947 Reves accounts, CHUR 4/43/14, 17, 37: Reves raised £2,530 from other foreign sales, Churchill's 60 per cent share amounting to £1,518.

38. 5 Feb 1947 Draft agreement, Time Inc., *New York Times* box 2, WSCDL, CURMSL. *LIFE*, published weekly on Fridays, *The New York Times* (read mainly in America's north-east corridor) daily.

39. 15 Apr 1946 W. Graebner cbl to D. Longwell, box 2 WSCDL, CURBMSL.

40. 3 Jun 1947 Agreement *The Daily Telegraph*, Time Inc. box 2 WSCDL, CURBMSL, CHUR 4/41/66–74: *The Daily Telegraph*'s copyright purchase and side agreements with Time Inc. and *The New York Times* were signed on 23 June and completed on 3 July. Their provisions were relatively simple: *The Daily Telegraph* bought from the Chartwell Literary Settlement the entire copyright in the records and memoranda of Winston Churchill, employing Churchill to write his memoirs which would 'relate to the period following the Treaty of Versailles, including the rise to power of Adolf Hitler, as well as the actual period of the said war, and will include a substantial portion of new writing by Mr Churchill in addition to extracts from the documents hereinafter mentioned'. The first volume was to be delivered by 15 October 1947, the second and third during 1948 and the fourth and fifth during 1949 without Churchill being bound to the number of volumes or dates. Outside the US, Churchill retained performing, dramatic, film, radio, television and other mechanical rights. Within the US, Churchill assigned all rights but *The Daily Telegraph* undertook to use its best endeavours to return them to Churchill as soon as it could. *The Daily Telegraph* was to pay Churchill £175,000: £35,000 on signature; £35,000

on 1 May 1948 and each of the following three years (providing each volume was delivered on time) with a last payment on 1 May following delivery of the final volume, whichever number volume it might turn out to be (at the insistence of *LIFE*). *The Daily Telegraph* was to loan Churchill a further £15,000 without interest, to be repaid by him on delivery of the last volume. The possibility of delays as a result of Churchill resuming office or being incapacitated was addressed: if there was gap of more than eighteen months between instalments, *The Daily Telegraph* had the right to cancel the agreement or, in certain circumstances, appoint another author (approved by Churchill or his executors) without further payment to Churchill. Churchill and *The Daily Telegraph* agreed to split in half the risk of unforeseen tax demands by countries outside Britain.

23 June 1947 Agreement *The Daily Telegraph*, trustees of the Chartwell Literary Settlement CHUR 4/41/75–80: To the Chartwell Literary Trustees, *The Daily Telegraph* was to pay £375,000: £49,000 on signature, then three instalments of £69,000 on 1 June 1948, 1949 and 1950; and finally £119,000 on 1 June 1951 (or on the dates of delivery if later). The same tax arrangements were to apply as in Churchill's contract: the trustees and *The Daily Telegraph* shouldered half of the risk each. The trustees' agreement included a clause providing for an arbitrator to settle disputes between the two parties if 'the value or prospects of the said rights of copyright shall be materially affected by war, pestilence, famine, currency trouble, or any other national or international change or chance beyond the control of the vendors or Purchaser'. On behalf of *The New York Times* as well as itself, Time Inc. was to pay *The Daily Telegraph* $1,150,000 by five instalments of $230,000, the first on signing and the remainder on delivery of each volume.

4, 5 July 1947 H. Laughlin ltr to D. Flower, Houghton Mifflin agreements with Cooperation Publishing Corporation and *The Daily Telegraph*, Churchill: Contract and Copyright for memoirs file, 1947 box 318/1, HMCo HLHU: on 4 July Desmond Flower and Henry Laughlin agreed that Cassell & Co. would enjoy exclusivity for English language sales in Europe while Houghton Miflin controlled the 'Western Hemisphere', except for Britain's Caribbean dependencies. On 5 July Houghton Mifflin signed both its agreement with *The Daily Telegraph* and its side-agreement with Reves.

41. 30 Oct 1947 Ld Camrose ltr to D. Longwell, WSCDL, CURBMSL. Dan, as his American correspondents called Longwell, picked up the signal and replied 'My dear Lord Camrose'.
42. 30 Aug 1947 WSC ltr to EHM, Marsh Papers, Berg Collection, NYPL.
43. 2, 28 July 1947 LlBk ltrs to WSC, CHUR 1/9/222. Churchill bought 2½

per cent Treasury Stock at a price of 91½. He lost 2¼ per cent of his investment on sale.

44. 31 Jul 1947 BRB ltrs to WSC, CHUR 1/9/232, 235.

45. 5, 7, 11, 22 Aug, 23 Sep 1947 VdaC contracts, CHUR 1/9/248, 256, 258, 261, 262, 269.

46. 24 Sep 1947 W. Judd ltr to WSC, CHUR 1/23/361.

47. D. Reynolds, *In Command of History*, p. 83.

48. W. Graebner, *My Dear Mr. Churchill*, pp. 99–102; 22 Oct 1947 D. Longwell memo to W. Graebner, boxes 2, 4 Payments, WSCDL, CURBMSL. Graebner suggested *LIFE* should fund Rufus's replacement, but Longwell insisted that he and Graebner meet the cost personally. Rufus II cost $159, but was not a success as he contracted 'St Vitus's dance' after an inoculation against distemper.

49. 11 Oct 1947 W. Graebner cbl to D. Longwell, box 2, ibid.

50. 23 Oct 1947 W. Graebner cbl to D. Longwell, box 2, ibid.

51. 28 Nov 1947 D. Longwell cbl to W. Graebner, box 2, ibid.

52. 13 Nov 1947 P. Brooks memo to H. Laughlin, Book of the Month Club 1948 and 1949 file, box 318/1 HMCo, HMHU.

53. 10 Dec 1947 D. Reynolds, *In Command of History*, p. 86–7.

54. 24 Nov 1947 T. Cook ltr to WSC, CHUR 1/68/205.

55. 24 Dec 1947 WSC ltr to CSC, CHUR1/44/33–8.

56. 7 Jan 1948 N. Sturdee ltr to L. Marston, CHUR 1/18/42.

57. Dec 1947–Jan 1948 Summary of Mamounia Hotel bills; CHUR 1/69/77, 85, 90–2.

58. 10 Jan 1948 D. Longwell cbl to W. Graebner, box 2, WSCDL, CURBMSL.

59. 18 Jan 1948 N. Sturdee ltr to Banque d'État du Maroc, CHUR 1/68/240; WSC cbl to D. Longwell, box 2, WSCDL, CURBMSL.

60. Jan 1948 Box 4 Vacation Payments to Winston Churchill, WSCDL, CURBMSL.

61. D. Reynolds, *In Command of History*, p. 90, 131–2.

24. Racing to the Finish, 1948–50

1. 25 Mar 1948 WSC note to Ld Ismay, Ismay papers 2/3/45, cited D. Reynolds *In Command of History*, p. 68.

2. 28 Apr 1948 A. Sulzberger ltr to WSC, CHUR 4/17/206; 3 Jun 1948 E. Reves ltr to WSC, 4/12/179. See D. Reynolds, *In Command of History*, pp. 129–33.

3. 21 Apr 1948, BMB ltr to WSC, Baruch Papers, MC006 Book 125, PUMM.

4. Mar 1948 H. Laughlin ltr to ER, WSC ER 1948–51 file, box 318/1, HMCo, HLHU; 28 Jun 1948 ER ltr to WSC, CHUR 4/12/177; U/d HM

Co Trade Sales 'Showings' 1919–76 file, box 319/7, HMCo, HLHU. The Book of the Month Club accounted for 412,000 sales, Canada 27,700. *The Second World War*, including the final boxed set and abridged version, grossed Houghton Mifflin $2,240,000 and produced approximately $800,000 contribution to its profits, after it had paid $500,000 profit share to Emery Reves.

5. 4 Feb 1949 *Spectator*, p. 141, CHUR 4/24/334, cited D. Reynolds, *In Command of History*, p. 139. Cassell & Co.'s revenue from the first volume reached £275,000.

6. 2 May 1948 W. Graebner cbl to D. Longwell, box 3 WSCDL, CURBMSL.

7. Apr 1948 LlBk statement, CHUR 1/1/35.

8. 26 Jun 1948 W. Graebner ltr to H. Luce, H. Luce note to D. Longwell, box 2, WSCDL, CURBMSL.

9. 1, 2 Jul 1948 W. Graebner cbl corresp with D. Longwell, box 2 WSCDL, CURBMSL.

10. 29 Jul 1948, CSC note to WSC, CHUR 1/71/178.

11. 12 Aug 1948 LlBk statement, CHUR 1/1/58. The payments were of £10,000 each; neither film was ever made.

12. R. Boothby, *Reminiscences of a Rebel*, p. 60, 63.

13. 25, 26 Aug, 1 Sep 1948 NM corresp with WSC, LlBk statements, CHUR 1/18/141, 168; 1/1/61, 62.

14. 12 Apr 1944 C. Nicholl ltr to WSC, CHUR 1/40/1–6. Churchill's daughters were only to be entitled to the income, not the capital, from their shares.

15. 17 Feb 1949 NM ltr to WSC, CHUR 1/40/19–29.

16. Aug, Sep 1948 Hôtel René-Roy accounts, Snedaker, *TIME-LIFE* ltrs to L. Marston, CHUR 1/70/8, 96, 114, 130; CHUR 1/70/143–6.

17. W. Graebner, *My Dear Mr Churchill*, p. 34.

18. 11 Dec 1948 W. Graebner cbl to Babington-Smith, *TIME*, box 3, WSCDL, CURBMSL.

19. 12 Nov 1948 W. Graebner ltr to D. Longwell, box 2, WSCDL, CURBMSL.

20. 14 Dec 1948 D. Longwell cbl to W. Graebner, box 3, WSCDL, CURBMSL.

21. 31 Dec 1948 LlBk statement, CHUR 1/1/82.

22. 1948 LlBk statements, CHUR 1/1/37, 40, 46, 61, 73, 81; 24 April 1948 WSC note to C. Soames, CHUR 1/32/416.

23. 30 Nov 1948 A. Moir ltr to H. Boarland, CHUR 4/41/255–6; 5 Nov 1947, 18 Nov, 16 Dec 1948, 24 May 1949 Odhams Press letters, agreement with WSC, 4/40/130, 97, 146–7, 29–30; 12, 22 May 1949 E. Warner ltrs to WSC, 4/40/17, 19; July 1951 CHUR 4/40/85. The £500 payment at issue was small compared with the tax at risk on *The Second World War*, but Churchill initially refused to accept Charles Graham-Dixon's view that he should disclose the payment to the Inland Revenue, and offer 'without prejudice' to pay tax. Churchill asked Odhams Press to convert

his future royalties to a single lump sum: Odhams set the sum at £5,000, provided Churchill's paintings did not appear elsewhere in book form for five years.

As confidence in sales grew in the run-up to publication in November 1948, the publishers raised their initial print run to 25,000 copies. These sold out; two more print runs followed in 1949 and sales reached 57,000 copies. McGraw Hill published in the US during May 1950: sales were 20,000 after ten days and still running at 1,000 per week. A Japanese edition followed in 1951.

24. 10 Dec 1948 A. Moir ltr to WSC, CHUR 4/41/253–4.
25. 10 Jan–9 Feb 1949 HM Inland Revenue internal correspondence, NA IR 40/12833.
26. 9 Feb 1949 HM Inland Revenue Board minute, NA IR 40/12833; 24 Feb 1949 A. Moir ltr to WSC, CHUR 4/41/252.
27. 21 Feb 1949 V. Timbrell memo to H. Boarland, NA IR 40/12833.
28. 28 Mar 1949 V. Timbrell memo to J. Snellgrove, ibid.
29. 19 Feb 1949 W. Graebner cbl to D. Longwell, box 2, WSCDL, CURBMSL.
30. 25 Feb 1949 D. Longwell ltr to W. Graebner, ibid.
31. 8 Mar 1949 A. Moir ltr to WSC, CHUR 1/28/301.
32. Mar 1949, WSC ltr to A. Moir (drafted but not sent), CHUR 1/28/298–300.
33. 21 Apr 1949 H. Boarland ltr to A. Moir, CHUR 4/41/249.
34. 30 Jun 1949 WSC draft ltr for A. Moir, CHUR 4/41/236–8.
35. 2 Mar 1949 WSC ltr to M. Berry, CHUR 4/13/144.
36. Mar 1949 H. Luce Speech Churchill Dinner 1949 file, box OV2, Clare Booth Luce Papers, LoCW.
37. 1 Apr 1949 D. Longwell ltr to WSC, box 2, WSCDL, CURBMSL.
38. 15 Apr 1949 H. Laughlin ltr to D. Longwell, WSC: *LIFE* magazine 1950 & 1951 file, box 318/1 HMCo, HLHU.
39. 1 Apr 1949 ER ltr to WSC, M. Gilbert, *Winston Churchill and Emery Reves*, p. 295.
40. 2, 3, 31 May 1949 WSC ltr to Ld Camrose, LlBk ltrs to WSC, CHUR 4/13/9;1/12/47, 8.
41. 21 Jun 1949 Secretaries' memo to WSC, CHUR 1/21/342.
42. 3 Jun 1949 C. Soames memo to WSC, CHUR 1/92/128–9.
43. J. Colville, *The Churchilians*, p. 27; 30 Jun 1949 J. Sturdee memo to WSC, CHUR 1/92/328.
44. 23 Jul 1949 C. Soames memo to WSC, CHUR 1/92/125.
45. 14 Jul, 15, 23 Sep, 12, 26 Oct 1950 Betting records, WSC cbl to Ld Camrose, CHUR 1/92/65, 63, 59, 58, 51. Camrose was part of Churchill's betting circle.
46. U/d Schedule, Races won by Colonist II, Prize money 1949–60, CHUR 1//92/115, 1/158/136.

47. 29 Apr 1950, WSC ltr to CSC, SFT:555.

48. W. Graebner, *My Dear Mr. Churchill*, p. 84.; J. Wood, Racing Profit & Loss account, CHUR 1/92/3. Wood's accounts records show Churchill's betting between August 1949–June 1950 netted profits of £1,000.

49. 15 Oct 1950 C. Soames memo to WSC, CHUR 1/92/120–3.

50. 6 Dec 1951 *The Times*, 23 Dec 1951 LlBk advice to WSC, CHUR 1/14/16. Churchill netted £6,493 after expenses.

51. 29 Nov 1951 WSC ltr to R. Millais, CHUR 1/92/69. The artist was Raoul Millais.

52. 21 Apr, 7, 9 Jul 1949 D. Longwell cbl corresp with W. Graebner, WSC Holiday expenses 1947–9, box 2, WSCDL, CURBMS. The holiday cost $8,300.

53. 22 Aug 1949 ER ltr to WSC, M. Gilbert, *Winston Churchill and Emery Reves*, p. 297–300.

54. The question of whether and how Churchill should pay his physician, Lord Moran, after the war proved sensitive. It was common ground that Moran's flights and other expenses should be reimbursed, but Moran himself had refused more direct reward. The tax advantages of a seven-year covenant provided the solution. Churchill began paying Lady Moran £500 a year, officially net of tax, thus allowing her to reclaim the tax notionally deducted before Churchill's payment, so that she ended up with £900 a year. Churchill was allowed to deduct this notional £900 from his income before calculating his tax, reducing his net cost to just over £100 a year. As an ageing Churchill's demands on his doctor grew, similar arrangements were established for the Morans' sons, Geoffrey and John.

55. 18 Sep 1949 Sir Stafford Cripps announced that the official exchange rate between the pound and the US dollar would fall from $4.03 to $2.80 = £1 (a reduction of 30.5 per cent) with effect from the following day.

56. 23 Sep 1949 WSC ltr to D. Longwell, box 2, WSCDL, CURBMSL.

57. 11 Nov 1949 H. Scherman ltr to H. Laughlin, Churchill Book of the Month Club 1948 and 1949 File, box 318/1 HMCo, HLHU. By 11 November 1949, the club had despatched 247,500 of the second volume compared to 366,000 of the first volume.

58. 3 Nov 1949 WSC note, CHUR 4/13/33.

59. 12 May 1950 C. Graham-Dixon Opinion, CHUR 4/41/200.

60. 17 Sep 1949 R. Lewenthal ltr to WSC, CHUR 1/26/34. The royalty rate proposed was 5 per cent.

61. 18 Nov 1949 A. Moir ltr to N. Sturdee, CHUR 1/26/70.

62. 10 Jan 1950 E. Gilliatt cbl to A. Moir, CHUR 1/26/106.

63. 24, 25, 26 Jan 1950 A. Moir ltrs to N. Sturdee, WSC, draft to Odhams, CHUR 1/26/116–7, 118, 120. 8 Jan 1950 (backdated) WSC agreement

with Hall Bros, 1/26/97–105. Permitted uses of the paintings included calendars, greeting and playing cards as well as Christmas cards. The Halls' first cheque for $12,500 arrived on 13 February 1950.

64. 19 Jul 1950 E. Gilliatt note to WSC, CHUR 1/26/196.

65. 23 Dec 1950 WSC ltr to A. Moir, CHUR 1/26/235.

66. 5, 15 Oct 1949 D. Kelly Chartwell Literary Trust Minutes, WSC note, CHUR 4/41/178, 175–7.

67. 15 Aug 1950 C. Soames note to WSC, CHUR 1/46/301–2. Losses were £8,607 (1948), £8,707 (1949), £8,751 (1950) and £8,414 (1951).

68. 4 Nov 1949 NM ltr to WSC, CHUR 1/27/103. Papers for the meeting showed £21,063 already gifted: £10,213 to Randolph, £10,000 to Diana and £400 each to Sarah (now married to Anthony Beauchamp) and Mary.

69. 1 Jan, 31 Dec 1949 LlBk statements, CHUR 1/1/83, LBGA B/1034/b/51. Churchill's current account finished 1949 with a credit balance of £1,347 but was £307 overdrawn after New Year payments.

70. LlBk schedules 1949/50 taxation, CHUR 1/7/160, 161–70. £37,000 of the £80,000 was treated as 'capital receipts'. The potentially taxable £43,000 remaining was reduced to £5,000 when Churchill claimed £38,000 of expenses: £20,000 literary expenses, £8,900 farming losses (and the balance mainly family allowances). The Churchills' joint investment income was £4,800 (£2,800 of dividends, interest and underwriting fees on Churchill's account; £900 from Lord Randolph's will trust and marriage settlements; £336 in Clementine's name; and £700 from her marriage settlement).

71. 15, 29 Apr 1950 WSC ltr to CSC, CHUR 1/47/104, 136.

72. 26 May 1950 D. Longwell ltr to H. Laughlin, WSC: *LIFE* magazine 1950 and 1951 file box 318/1, HMCo, HLHU.

73. 15, 20 Jul 1950 ER ltrs to H. Laughlin, WSC; Houghton Mifflin schedule of sales, Churchill: Emery Reves 1948–51, box 318/1, HMCo, HLHU; CHUR 4/12/74.

74. 5 Jul 1950 ER ltrs to WSC, CHUR 4/12/74–6, 96–9. French sales fell from 85,000 (first volume) to 45,000 (second volume) and then to 28,000 (third volume).

75. 11 Jul 1950 WSC ltr to ER, CHUR 4/12/86–7.

76. 2 Aug 1950 D. Flower ltr to WSC, CHUR 4/24/433.

77. 22 Aug 1950 WSC ltr to O. Frewen, CHUR 2/167 cited 8:548.

78. 2 Sep 1950 ER ltr to H. Laughlin, WSC: Emery Reves 1949–51 file, box 318/1, HMCo, HLHU.

79. 10 Oct 1950 *New York Times*, pp. 1, 22, 30, 33, cited D. Reynolds, *In Command of History*, p. 349. Houghton Mifflin met its publication date in November 1950; in Britain a strike by printers and shortages of paper forced Cassell & Co. to wait until August 1951 to publish.

25. Post-war Prime Minister, 1951–5

1. 3, 8 Nov 1950 ER corresp with WSC, M. Gilbert, *Winston Churchill and Emery Reves*, pp. 311–14, CHUR 4/63C/744–5.
2. 25 Dec 1950 WSC ltr to CSC, 8:580.
3. 26 Jan 1951 W. Graebner ltr to D. Longwell, CHUR 4/15/427.
4. 31 Jan 1951 D. Longwell ltr to J. Adler, *New York Times* file, box 3, WSCDl, CURBMSL; 6 Mar 1951 LlBk statement, LGBA B/1034/b/51. Churchill paid £1,126.
5. C. Lysaght, *Brendan Bracken*, p. 288.
6. 15 Feb 1951 W. Graebner cbl to E. Thomson, box 2, WSCDL, CURBMSL. Thomson was Daniel Longwell's assistant; he looked after the Churchill series when Longwell became ill.
7. 29 Apr 1951 J. Adler Memorandum, box 3, WSCDL, CURBMSL.
8. 29 Apr 1951 J. Adler Memorandum, box 3, WSCDL, CURBMSL.
9. 3 May, 30 Mar 1951 D. Longwell cbl, ltr to J. Adler, *New York Times* file box 3, WSCDL, CURBMSL.
10. 1, 10 May 1951 D. Longwell cbl to H. Luce, ltr to R. Heiskell, box 3, WSCDL, CURBMSL.
11. M. Daunton, *Just Taxes*, p.229.
12. 3 Aug 1951 WSC ltr to CSC, 8:627–9.
13. M. Soames, *Clementine Churchill*, p. 459; 17 Dec 1951, 4 Feb 1952 N. Sturdee note to WSC, Λ. Moir ltr to N. Sturdee, CHUR 4/41/214, 221, 223. Relieved of the death duty threat, the trustees made the long-term investments for which Churchill had long pressed, committing £128,000 to the purchase of shares in leading British companies, such as Associated Electrical Industries, Babcock & Wilcox, The Distillers Company, Metal Box & Printing Industries, The Peninsular and Oriental Steamship Company (P&O), The 'Shell' Transport and Trading Company, and Tube Investments.
14. 26 Jul 1951 H. Laughlin ltr to WSC, CHUR 4/14/113. The Book of the Month Club accounted for 1,118,750 of 1,491,051 sales.
15. 3 Aug 1951 WSC ltr to CSC, 8:627–9.
16. 10 Dec 1952 D. Longwell memo to R. Heiskell, box 3, WSCDL, CURBMSL.
17. 22 Sep 1953 D. Longwell memo to E. Thompson, box 3, WSCDL, CURBMSL. Longwell estimated excerpts from *The Second World War* attracted $4 million of advertising revenue to *LIFE* – see also 22 Sep 1946 D. Longwell memo to E. Thompson, box 4, WSCDL, CURBSML.
18. 20 Sep 1951 WSC memo to syndicate, CHUR 4/25/38.
19. Oct 1951 J. Wood schedules, CHUR 1/8/10–11. Churchill's taxable income between 5 April–5 October 1951 totalled £37,852, nearly all from his books. 5 Oct 1952 J. Wood, Wood, Willey & Co. Financial Statement, 1/8/27–9.

20. 23 Aug 1950 M. Muggeridge diary, *Like It Was*, p. 408, cited M. Gilbert, *Winston Churchill and Emery Reves*, p. 311.

21. 1952 J. Wood schedule, CHUR 1/8/137.

22. 25 Oct, 7 Nov 1951, March 1953 Slaughter & May ltrs to A. Moir, WSC contract with *The Daily Telegraph*, CHUR 1/7/189, 1/28/116, 126. Churchill was to receive [1] £35,000 (or such lesser sum as he chose for his tax-planning purposes) on 1 May 1952; [2] £25,000 (or, again, such lesser amount as he chose) on 1 May 1953; [3] any balance remaining on 1 May 1954. Houghton Mifflin contributed the largest sum of £17,826; *The Daily Telegraph* £15,000. After adjustments for falls in the pound's value against the dollar, Churchill finally received £63,726 for the sixth volume.

23. 16, 28 Nov 1951 N. Brook memo to WSC, 'Note for the Record', CAB 21/2181 (NA), cited D. Reynolds, *In Command of History*, p. 432.

24. J. Colville diary 23 March 1952, *The Fringes of Power*, pp. 643–4.

25. 31 Oct 1951, A. Moir letter to N. Sturdee, CHUR 1/7/187. Camrose asked for a gentleman's agreement that *The Daily Telegraph* should be able to ask Churchill to pay the tax reclaim it had expected, if the amount was not allowed to be deducted against the newspaper's tax bill.

26. 1 May 1952 Secretary ltr to Ld Camrose secretary, CHUR 4/13/70.

27. 28 May 1952 D. Longwell memo to W. Graebner, box 2, WSCDL CURBMSL.

28. Sep 1952 Wood, Willey & Co. schedule, CHUR 1/8/21–2.

29. 8 Sep 1952 Ld Camrose note, Political memoranda, Dinner with WSC, Camrose Papers.

30. Sep 1952 LlBk statement, LBGA B/1034/b/5.1.

31. 12, 20 Sep 1952 *The Daily Telegraph* ltr to WSC, LlBk statement, CHUR 1/14/86, 1/2/232. £10,000 of the loan was repaid on 5 December 1952.

32. Ibid.; 25 Oct 1952 WSC ltrs to G. Allen, W. Deakin, H. Pownall CHUR 4/24/24, 25, 281–2, 4/25/374–5.

33. 6 Jan 1953 H. Laughlin corresp with WSC, CHUR 4/14/25, 26–7.

34. 24 Feb 1953 Ld Moran WSC, *Struggle for Survival*, p. 401.

35. 30 Sep 1952 Wood, Willey & Co. Farm Accounts, CHUR 1/8/2. £5,000 was invested in machinery and £12,250 in live and dead stock. Losses during the year to 30 September 1952 were £10,860.

36. 29 Nov 1952 WSC letter to Ld Camrose, Camrose papers; 3 Dec 1952, 24 Nov 1953 E. Carden ltr to A. Moir, A. Moir letter to WSC, CHUR 1/28/18, 96. The professional valuation of the farmland was £37,500 (Chartwell farm £20,000; Parkside farm and market garden £9,780; Bardogs £7,050; woodlands £3,060; less allowances for tithe and land tax £1,850). The loan was completed in March 1953; its interest rate was 5 per cent.

37. 30 Nov, 22 Dec 1953 A. Moir ltrs to WSC, CHUR 1/28/34,293. Parkside's

price was £10,000 plus £2,035 for its livestock. Its sale to Lord Cromer released £5,286 cash to Churchill and reduced his loan by £6,750. Sir Arthur Garret, a friend of Korda, originally agreed to pay £10,250 for Bardogs.

38. 14 Jan 1955 J. Wood Farm & Stud accounts, CHUR 1/8/118.

39. 15 Jun 1952, 8 Mar 1953 C. Soames notes to WSC, CHUR 1/92/56–7, 1/94/283. The five racehorses with which Churchill started the 1952 season were: Pol Roger, Non-Stop, Gibraltar, Prince Arthur and Loving Cup.

40. 15 Feb 1953, J. Wood ltr to WSC, CHUR 1/8/30–2.

41. 7 May 1953, Ld Camrose note, The Other Club file, Camrose papers; u/d May 1953 Supplemental Agreement, WSC and *The Daily Telegraph*, CHUR 1/28/119–20. Churchill was to receive payments of £15,000 in each of May 1954 and 1955.

42. 25 Jun 1953 J. Colville ltr to Ld Camrose, Camrose Papers.

43. 29 Jun 1953 Ld Camrose note, Political Memoranda, Camrose papers.

44. 22 Jul 1953 Ld Camrose note, Lunch at Chartwell – Wednesday 22 July 1953, Camrose Papers.

45. 25 Jul 1953 LlBk investment account statement, CHUR 1/4/2226.

46. 30 Jun, 25 Jul 1953 LlBk statements, CHUR 1/2/195, LGA B/1034/b/5.1.

47. 4 Sep 1953 W. Graebner ltr to D. Longwell, box 2, WSCDL, CURBMSL.

48. 29 Aug 1953 MWB ltr to WSC, CHUR 2/211/20.

49. 16 Oct, 11 Dec 1953 WSC ltr to CSC, 8:901, LlBk statement, CHUR 1/4/206. £12,093 was credited to Churchill's bank account on 11 December.

50. 3 May 1954 BRB ltr to WSC, CHUR 2/212/12. In May 1954, the trust gave Christopher and Mary Soames £20,000 towards the cost of buying, 'converting and reconditioning' Hamsell Manor, on the border between Kent and Sussex.

51. Houghton Mifflin & Co. Trade Sales Showings, A–F 1919–76, HMCo, HLHU; 25 April 1954 H.O.Ward *Reynolds News*, cited D. Reynolds *In Command of History*, p.489.

52. 19 Aug 1953 Ld Moran, *Winston Churchill, Struggle for Survival*, p. 457.

53. 30, 31 Dec 1953 LlBk statements, CHUR 1/2/116 (current a/c), 1/4/206 (investment a/c).

54. 4 May 1954 LlBk ltr, statement, CHUR 1/14/269, 1/2/97.

55. 10 Nov 1954 A. Moir ltr, schedule to WSC, CHUR 1/28/150–2. Life assurance benefits would total £27,500, free of tax.

56. Oct 1954 Ld Moran, *Struggle for Survival*, p. 607.

57. 1 Dec 1954, 12 April 1955 WSC announcement, A. Ball ltr to WSC, WSC LlBk Presentation account, J. Colville memo to WSC, CHUR 2/431/77, 47, 48; 1/5/72, 77; 2/430/2–3.

58. 8 Dec 1954 Trust particulars, LBA B/1034/B/12. The trustees were

Viscount Leathers, Baron Moynihan, J. Colville, E. D. Martell and A. Moir. 17 Feb 1956, 1958 A. Moir ltr to WSC, CHUR 4/41/386, SFT; 621 f/n. In February 1956, the trustees made grants of £36,750 (including £10,000 each to the Churchill Homes, Bristol University, Harrow School and £5,000 to the Professional Classes Aid Council). In 1958 they contributed £25,000 towards the £3,500,000 appeal for the foundation of Churchill College, Cambridge.

59. 31 Dec 1954 LlBk statements, CHUR 1/2/62; 1/4/149, 1/5/72; 25 Dec 1954, 4 Jan 1955 WSC ltrs to CSC, SFT:589, LlBk statement, CHUR 1/2/174.

60. 17 Jan 1955 BRB ltr to MWB, cited K. Young, *Churchill & Beaverbrook*, p. 305.

61. A. Montague Browne, *Long Sunset*, p. 182.

26. A Third and Final Retirement, 1955–7

1. 16 Jul, 12 Sep 1955 A. Moir ltrs and schedules to WSC, McClelland & Stewart, CHUR 1/28/127–40, 136–7, 159. In Britain, Cassell paid a royalty of 20 per cent (10 per cent on Book Society or export copies), keeping the first £3,400 of royalties for each volume in recognition of the advances it had paid Churchill in the 1930s. In the US, the royalty was 10 per cent on the first 2,500 copies, 12½ per cent on the next 2,500, and 15 per cent thereafter. Dodd kept the first $7,070 of Churchill's royalties (then the equivalent of the £2,525 it had paid Cassell in 1939); in Canada, McClelland & Stewart paid a 10 per cent royalty on the first 5,000 copies and 15 per cent thereafter (deducting C$2,950 to offset the £1,075 paid to Cassell in 1939).

2. 11 Nov 1954 A. Moir ltr to WSC enc Wood, Willey & Co. memo, CHUR 1/8/159, 160.

3. 31 Mar 1954 M. Gilbert, *Winston Churchill and Emery Reves*, p. 341.

4. 21 Nov 1954 WSC cbl to H. Luce, M. Gilbert, *Winston Churchill and Emery Reves*, pp. 344–5.

5. 28 Dec 1954 WSC note to E. Gilliatt, 16 Jul 1955, A. Moir notes to WSC, CHUR 1/28/132–3, 138, 140. M. Gilbert, *Winston Churchill and Emery Reves*, p. 344. Reves' payment was spread over five instalments of £8,500 each; *LIFE* bought US, Canadian and Spanish serial rights, spreading payment across four instalments of $37,5000 each on 1 May of 1956, 7, 8, 9.

6. U/d post-May (probably Sep) 1955, 10 Nov 1954 A. Moir, schedule, CHUR 1/28/134–5, 152.

7. 13 Jun 1955 Fladgate & Co. ltr to secretary, CHUR 1/37/80.

8. 12 May 1955 WSC ltr to A. Carey Foster, CHUR 1/93/40–1.

9. 1 Jun 1957 WSC to CSC, SFT:617–8.

10. 5 Apr 1957, 15 Apr 1958 Wood, Willey & Co. accounts re Racing, Stud 1956/7, CHUR 1/113/58, 68.

11. 1956–7 LlBk statements, CHUR 1/2/4, 35. Churchill reimbursed Montague Browne's salary by paying HM Treasury £172 per month in 1956 (rising to £175 in 1957).

12. A. Montague Browne, *Long Sunset*, p. 233.

13. 31 Dec 1955 CSC & WSC ltr to J. Taylor & Sons, CHUR 1/29/82.

14. 12, 20 Jan 1956 J. Taylor & Sons ltrs to WSC, CHUR 1/29/82, 83.

15. 7, 8 Mar 1956 E. Woolgar ltr to L. Menzies, A. Ball ltr to WSC, LBGA, HO/O/Off/19, CHUR 1/105/26.

16. 17 Jan 1956 WSC ltr to CSC, SFT:601–2.

17. 19 Feb 1956 CSC ltr to WSC, SFT:603–4.

18. 9 Mar 1956 E. Dodd ltr to WSC, CHUR 1/7/8.

19. U/d May, 4 Jun 1956 A. Moir Instruction to Counsel; C. Graham-Dixon QC Opinion, CHUR 1/7/8–9, 11–13.

20. 14 Sep, 12 Oct 1956 J. Wood ltr to WSC, V. Bullock ltr to A. Moir, CHUR 1/7/26, 30.

21. 16 Oct 1956 A. Moir ltr to WSC, CHUR 1/7/32–3. £175,000-worth of publishers' payments escaped tax – £75,000 from Cassell and £100,000 from Dodd, Mead and McClelland & Stewart.

22. 24 Dec 1956 A. Moir ltr to WSC, CHUR 1/7/42.

23. 31 Dec 1956 J. Wood ltr to WSC, CHUR 1/113/33–4; 1 May 1957 J. Wood ltr to WSC, CHUR 1/113/73, 76. When Wood completed the tax return for 1956/7, Churchill paid £27,000 of tax, not £50,000 as expected, because Wood explained, with evident satisfaction, he had taken advantage of a technique called a 'spread back', which allowed authors to spread expense claims back over three years, if works had taken more than twenty years to complete: *History*'s contract had been signed in 1933.

24. 24 Aug 1955 BMB ltrs to WSC, CHUR 4/446/1–2.

25. 13, 21 Oct, 1 Nov 1955 A. Moir ltrs to WSC, A. Korda ltr to WSC, CHUR 4/446/7–8, 9–10, 14, 17. Per 18 July 1958 A. Moir ltr to WSC, CHUR 4/446/121: Churchill's fellow shareholders were Randolph and Christopher Soames, who each subscribed £200 alongside Churchill's £2,098 (and the two nominee directors £1 each).

26. 1 May 1956, 28 Apr 1958 A. Moir ltrs to WSC, CHUR 4/446/29, 95.

27. 12 Jul, 14 Dec 1956 C. Wick ltr to A. Moir, WSC cbl to ER, CHUR 4/46/37, M. Gilbert, *Winston Churchill and Emery Reves*, p. 362.

28. 23 May 156 D. Schery ltr to WSC, CHUR 4/447/1–3.

29. 22 Jun 1956 AMB memo to A. Moir, CHUR 4/447/11, 13.

30. U/d Aug 1956 A. Moir memo, CHUR 4/447/38–9.

31. 3 Jan 1957 A. Moir ltr to AMB, CHUR 4/447/72.

32. 15 Dec 1956 AMB memo, A. Moir note, CHUR 4/447/41–2, 35–6.

33. 21 Jan 1957 A. Moir memo, CHUR 1/7/43–4.

34. 5 Apr 1957 Wood, Willey & Co. accounts, CHUR 1/113/58, A. Montague Browne, *Long Sunset*, p. 192. Churchill paid £2,000 each to Denis Kelly and Alan Hodge and £1,000 to Anthony Montague Browne for *History*'s 'early completion'.

35. 29 Jan 1957 ER ltr to WSC, M. Gilbert, *Winston Churchill and Emery Reves*, p. 363–4.

36. 14, 20 Feb 1957 LlBk ltr to WSC, A. Moir ltr to WSC, CHUR 1/105/72, 1/111/195–6. Cassell's accountants had suggested only £35,000, but Desmond Flower offered £50,000. Moir countered with £75,000, but Flower pointed out that their experience with *The Second World War* showed sales tailed off after the first volume. (The first volume grossed £377,250, the last £210,150: these figures imply average sales of £250,000 per volume, or £1.5 million for the series. If Churchill had earned a royalty of 20 per cent, Cassell would have paid £300,000 instead of the £40,000 Churchill and Cassell had agreed.)

37. 4 Jan, 20 Mar, 4 Apr 1957 E. Dodd ltr to A. Moir, A. Moir ltr to WSC, LlBk ltr to WSC, CHUR 1/111/179, 199; 1/5/88. On 4 April, Dodd, Mead paid $274,675 (worth £98,851), made up of the $250,000 lump sum plus $24,675 royalties outstanding for the first volume (which had earned Churchill $60,432). In Britain, *A History*'s first print order was 100,000 copies, increased for later volumes to 150,0000. R. Cohen, *Bibliography of the Writings of Sir Winston Churchill*, A267.3(i) pp.938–9.

38. 9 Apr 1957 S. Ball ltr to WSC, CHUR 1/105/92, 93. Churchill's credit balances at Lloyds Bank totalled £292,862, offset by an overdraft of £18,409 on his farm account. He held $14,500 at Morgan Guaranty of New York, 20,604 francs in his French bank account and owned securities worth £20,000 kept at Lloyds Bank.

39. 5 Apr 1957 Wood, Willey & Co. accounts, CHUR 1/113/58. Churchill's secretaries cost £2,402 a year; other domestic staff £17,170; food just under £4,000; motoring £2,000; telephones and telegrams £750. Transfers to Lady Churchill, 'so far as identified', were £5,430.

40. 30 Apr, 12 Oct 1956 P. Cox ltrs to WSC, CHUR 1/37/63, 64–6; 30 Sep 1956 Wood, Willey & Co. schedule, 1/113/46; 1936 LlBk statements 1/4/81, 65; 1/2/19, 12, 32.

41. 25 Oct, 1 Nov 1957 Fladgate & Co. ltr to WSC, Statement of Receipts and Purchases, CHUR 1/37/96, 102, 105. Chartwell farm (and farmhouse) fetched £37,500, livestock £13,400. Churchill repaid £16,250 to Alliance Assurance; Knight Frank & Rutley charged commission of £1,626, Fladgate a fee of £503.

42. 11, 12 April, 20 Jun 1957 S. Ball letters to WSC, CHUR 1/105/94, 97, 153, 140. £25,000 was invested in Treasury Bills; £35,000 spread across seven

building societies; and £25,000 in 4 per cent Victory Bonds, which cost 94⅛ each but were accepted at par value of 100 after six months' ownership for death duty payment. Churchill sold them after ten weeks at 92¾.

43. 18, 21 May 1957 WSC corresp with S. Ball, CHUR 1/105/126, 128–30.

44. 12, 13, 20 Jun 1957 T. Hazlerigg ltrs to WSC, CHUR 1/108/13, 19, 25, 26, 27. Hazlerigg spent £10,000 on shares and £5,000 on debentures in Quebec Natural Gas; £21,000 on four investment trusts, including the Philip Hill Investment Trust (Churchill's major post-retirement investment success); £4,600 on West Coast Transmission; and £9,650 on Steep Rock Mines (a small iron-ore producer).

45. 5, 27 Jul 1957 D. Pugh notes to WSC, CHUR 1/110/3, 6.

46. 25, 28 Oct, 1 Nov 1957, 3 Jan 1958 WSC corresp with S. Ball, CHUR. 1/105/183,184; CHUR1/110/26, 37. In January 1958, Churchill's current account held £15,068, the investment deposit account £124,487. The combined value of his bond and share investments was £116,300.

27. Sunset, 1958–65

1. 5, 16 Sep, 30 Oct 1957 A. Moir, M. Thorson ltrs to AMB, CHUR 4/447/116, 93, 99–101. Churchill was offered 35 per cent of 'distributor gross receipts' instead of 50 per cent of 'net profits'.

2. 28 Aug, 4 Sep 1958 M. Thorson cbls to A. Moir, CHUR 4/448/124, 150.

3. 5 Feb, 5 Mar, 10, 16 May 1957 A. Moir corresp with AMB, WSC, CHUR 4/446/79, 85, 101, 102.

4. 1, 18 Jul 1958 A. Moir ltrs to WSC, CHUR 4/446/114, 121. Towers Films was to buy M & P's shares over five instalments, so that Churchill received his £21,000, and Randolph and Christopher Soames £2,000 each for their shares, without liability to tax. M & P's shareholders formed a new company, S & M Investments, to take over any remaining rights after Towers had made his programmes.

5. Jan, 11 Feb, 22 Apr, 16 May 1959, 16 Feb 1961, 22 Sep 1964, A. Moir ltrs to WSC, AMB, CHUR 4/446/143–4, 173–182–3, 188, 209, 295. Towers Films paid £20,000 in February and £7,500 in October 1959; then an extra £5,000 early in 1960, when it set out a programme for paying the outstanding £20,000 with the help of Associated British Pictures Corporation. Complications followed when Sir David Cunynghame put London Film into liquidation during April 1959 to help sort out Sir Alexander Korda's complex estate, suggesting (unsuccessfully) that Churchill bought out the liquidator's share of M & P. Towers paid one more instalment, taking his total to £35,000, but made no more and *History*'s film rights remained unexploited at Churchill's death.

6. C. Lysaght, *Brendan Bracken*, pp. 327–8. Bracken left an estate of £145,000, mainly to Churchill College, Cambridge. 12, 19 November 1958 WSC ltrs to J. Colville, LlBk, CHUR 1/212/105, 1/3/32: Churchill subscribed £1,000 towards Bracken's memorial fund.

7. 23 Sep 1958 J. Wood ltr & accounts, CHUR 1/113/80–8.

8. Sep 1958 LlBk statement, CHUR 1/3/43.

9. E. Murray, *I was Churchill's Bodyguard*, p. 216.

10. A. Montague Browne, *Long Sunset*, p. 237; Cassell Papers, SWW Abridgement, cited Reynolds, *In Command of History*, p. 508.

11. 7 Feb 1959 AMB note to WSC, CHUR 4/448/245–6.

12. 17, 23 Sep 1958 J. Le Vien corresp with AMB, A. Moir, CHUR 4/452/34, 36.

13. 15, 20 May, 29 July 1959 AMB correspondence with J. Le Vien, A. Moir letter to WSC, CHUR 4/452/63, 68, 131. Churchill's bank account was credited with the first instalment of £17,783 on 30 July 1959. LlBk statement, CHUR 1/106/124.

14. 21 May 1960 *Daily Sketch*.

15. 26 May 1960 AMB ltr to E. Peterson, CHUR 4/453/64.

16. 4 Jul 1960 AMB memo to WSC, CHUR 4/451/64.

17. 5, 17, 19 Aug 1960 AMB ltr to A. Moir, memo to WSC, H. French ltr to AMB, CHUR 4/449/89, 111; 4/451/88.

18. 21 Oct 1960 A. Moir ltrs to G. Brownell, A. Moir, CHUR 4/449/266, 277.

19. 21 Aug 1960 ER ltr to WSC, M. Gilbert WSC & ER pp. 385–7.

20. 5 Feb 1960 D. Pugh note, CHUR 1/110/147.

21. 16, 18, 29 June 1960 Simon & Coates ltr to LlBk, WSC ltr to Rea Bros, LlBk schedule, CHUR 1/109/9–10, 15, 95.

22. 29 Jun 1960 LlBk schedule, CHUR 1/109/95. The Philip Hill Investment Trust holding was worth £20,000, ICI £15,000.

23. 16 May 1960, 9 Jan 1961 A. Moir ltr to WSC, J. Wood accounts, CHUR 1/111/127, 1/114/13. The previous year's total of £37,504 included $50,000 or £17,783 from Le Vien for *The Second World War* rights, £4,200 from M & P for *History of the English-Speaking Peoples* and £5,498 from Hallmark Cards; the next year's estimate of £20,000 was made up by another £4,500 from Hallmark Cards, the final £9,000 from *The Second World War* and £6,300 for *A History of the English-Speaking Peoples*.

24. 10 Feb 1953 Lord Camrose note, Political Memoranda, Lunch at 10 Downing Street, Camrose Papers.

25. C & T Publications Ltd. 1985 Accounts, Companies House. C & T Publications paid Randolph £9,000 a year (to include the costs of his researchers ands secretaries) but he completed only two volumes before his death in 1968. The task of writing the further six volumes required, each with its own companion volume of documents, fell to one of his

researchers Martin Gilbert. Gilbert earned £133,000 from C&T for twenty years of work, mostly funded by the Chartwell Literary Trust.

26. 22 Oct 1961 A. Moir ltr to WSC, CHUR 1/111/90; 22 Jan, 4 Feb 1963, 13 Jan 1964 AMB memo to WSC, ltr to LlBk, Fladgate & Co. account, CHUR 1/107/88, 95; 1/112/138–40. C & T Publications Ltd 1985 Annual Accounts, Companies House. After commission, Churchill received £47,500, spread over two instalments. C & T publications earned revenue of £530,000 from the publishing syndicate.

27. 3 May 1961 H. French ltr to AMB, CHUR 4/450/14.

28. 23 Oct 1961 AMB ltr to H. French, CHUR 4/450/52.

29. 11, 18 Dec 1958, 30 Sep, 8 Dec 1959 W. Nightingall, A. Carey Foster ltrs to WSC, CHUR 1/158/131–3, 143, 1/156/86; 12 Jul, 4 Oct 1959 C. Soames ltrs to WSC, CHUR. 1/160/151, 156; J. Wood, Profit and loss account for Stud, CHUR 1/158/143, 1/114/4.

30. 20 Apr 1960 WSC ltr to MWB, CHUR 2/519/387.

31. U/d 1960, 1961 Racing Wins, CHUR 1/155/3, 5, 1/158/218. The stable won £13,000 of prize money in 1960 and £20,900 in 1961.

32. 14 Jul 1961 AMB memo to WSC, CHUR 1/133/62. Carey Foster's valuation of bloodstock and stud together came to £168,500.

33. 14, 18 Jul 1961 A. Carey Foster ltr to C. Soames, K. Freeman ltr to WSC, CHUR 1/157/21, 23, 24.

34. 4 Dec 1961 C. Soames ltr to WSC, CHUR 1/133/47–9.

35. 7, 11 Dec 1961 AMB corresp with A. Moir, CHUR 1/133/51, 60.

36. 11 December 1961 A. Moir ltr to AMB, CHUR 1/133/60.

37. 30 Sep 1962, 21 Jun 1963 P. Cox, J. Wood ltrs to WSC, CHUR 1/158/62, 1/114/47.

38. U/d Racing Wins, CHUR 1/155/7, 11; 22, 24 May 1962 WSC ltr to T. Rogers, A. Carey Foster ltr to WSC, CHUR 1/160/56, 1/156/106; 3 Nov 1962 LlBk ltr to WSC, CHUR 1/107/76. Six horses remained in training, winning £12,900 of prize money, led by Vienna, who won twice before being sold at the end of the season for £16,000, again to Tim Rogers.

39. 27 Mar 1962 A. Moir corresp with AMB, CHUR 4/454/132, 133. Signing was delayed until 28 September, in Paris, while Le Vien struggled to find larger studio backers. Churchill received further payments from Twentieth Century-Fox in 1964, but no payments under his share of gross receipts.

40. 9 Aug 1963 AMB ltr to MWB, CHUR 2/519/232.

41. 27, 30 Sept 1963 AMB corresp with A. Moir, CHUR 4/450/289,292.

42. 3 Sep, 2 Oct 1963 AMB ltr to MWB, CHUR 2/519/195.

43. 3 Oct 1963 C. Foreman ltr to AMB, CHUR 4/450/301.

44. Anthony Montague Browne, *Long Sunset*, p. 236.

45. 9 Dec 1963 D. Pugh ltr to LlBk, CHUR 1/107/140.

46. 3, 18 Dec 1963, 18 Jan 1964 J. Le Vien ltr to AMB, AMB memo to WSC,

The Finest Hours Agreement, CHUR 4/454/215,217,223. Churchill received a first cheque for $2,000 on January 1964 when the contract was signed in Paris and was due another $18,000 due as soon as shooting began in July.

47. 15, 24 Apr, 29 Jun 1964 AMB memo to WSC, A. Moir ltr to AMB, AMB ltr to LlBk, CHUR 4/445/255,268; 4/456/104–7; 1/107/165. The £20,000 advance was against a royalty rate of 15 per cent.

48. 23 Mar 1964 A. Moir ltr to AMB, CHUR 4/457/1.

49. 24 Sep 1964 AMB ltr to J. Wood, CHUR 1/133/197.

50. 15 Oct 1964 A. Moir ltr to AMB, CHUR 1/111/259. Soames was to pay 10 per cent of winnings up to £1,500; 33 per cent up to £3,000 and 50 per cent above.

51. 21, 27 May 1964 AMB notes to WSC, CHUR 1/133/136–7, 152. The stud had been expanded in 1964 by the purchase of the neighbouring Leylands farm, complete with a bungalow for a future stud manager, for £16,000. 10 Sep 1964 A. Carey Foster ltr to WSC, CHUR 1/133/182, 186. Churchill's final property deal was the September 1964 purchase of 4½ acres' grazing next to the stud for £900.

52. U/d Dec 1964 C. Soames note to WSC, CHUR 1/133/218.

53. 19 Aug 1963 A. Moir ltr to AMB, CHUR 1/115/6.

54. 16 Nov 1964 AMB ltr to A. Moir, CHUR 1/115/63–67.

55. 21 Dec 1964 A. Moir ltr to Davis Polk, CHUR 1/115/102–106.

Epilogue

1. 20 Oct, 27 Oct 1961, 12 December 1963 WSC last will and testament, subsequent codicils, www.gov.uk.

2. 9 Feb 1965 Grant of Probate, www.gov.uk.

3. 11 Jun 1968 J. Petrie, Estate Duty Office, NA T227/2810.

4. 9 Feb 1965 Grant of Probate, www.gov.uk; Jan–Feb 1965 LBA B/1034/B/12. Shares sold by Churchill's executors raised £45,000: 9,000 ICI shares raised £19,240; 6,850 BRINCO [The British Newfoundland Development Corporation] shares £11,815; 15,000 Philip Hill Investment Trust shares £14,063. Also sold, without any recorded sums raised, were shares in East African Estates, Van-Tor Oils and Explorations and Permo Oil & Gas. Churchill's other assets at his death included local authority loans, £40,423 raised by the sale of government bonds, bank deposit accounts, properties at 27 and 28 Hyde Park Gate, personal chattels and paintings. Churchill's executors' accounts will remain closed until 31 December 2035.

5. M. Soames, *Clementine Churchill*, pp. 555–9.

6. Feb 1967 valuation schedules, NA T22/2809.

7. 7 May 1968 R. Alley ltr to Estate Duty Office, NA T 227/2810.
8. 31 Oct 1968 J. Colville ltr to R. Jenkins, NA T227/3933.
9. www.nationaltrust.org.uk/chartwell/prices; the Association of Leading Visitor Attractions. Chartwell's admission price for adults in 2015 is £14.30 (143 times the 1966 price). It recorded 226,582 visitors in 2014.
10. 4 Mar 1977 UPI press release. *Mimizan*, painted in 1924, fetched £29,000; *The Pope's Palace at Avignon* nearly £16,000. The other paintings were a portrait of Clementine and Sarah by Sir John Lavery and *Nesting Swan* and *Black Swans at Chartwell* by William Nicholson. 14 Jul 2007 www.telegraph.co.uk: in 2007, Churchill's *Chartwell Landscape with Sheep*, originally presented to Henry Luce, became the first of his paintings to sell for £1 million. In December 2014 a buyer paid £1.8 million for *The Goldfish Pond at Chartwell*, one of the paintings from the estate of Lady Soames sold at auction by Sotheby's.
11. 27 Jun 1952 N. Brook memo to J. Colville, memo of conversation with A. Moir, CHUR 4/41/316, 317–9.
12. 24 Sep 1968 Calendars of The Grants of Probate & Letters of Administration, OxfordDNB.com. Randolph left £70,000 before estate duty.
13. 28 May 1971 J. Colville ltr to B. Trend, NA LCO 67/50.
14. 19 Jul, 8 Sep 1971 B. Trend corresp with J. Colville, ibid.
15. 17 May 1990 P. Andrews ltr to M. Phippard, NA TS 27/1584.
16. 27 Mar 1991, N. Tebbit ltr and enclosure to J. Major, NA LCO 67/50.
17. 13 May, 12 Aug 1991 R. Butler memo to J. Major, P. Andrews ltr to Y. Woodbridge, ibid.
18. 25 Jul 1991 M. Hart QC and W. Charles opinion, NA LCO 67/50.

INDEX

14	To purchase 200 Goldfields.	
	" " 200 East Rands	
	" " 100 Rand Mines	
24	" interest @ 4% to 31st May	
15	" payment	
1	" purchase 100 Atchison Pref. shares	
	" " 100 " Ordy. "	
	" " $10,000 " 4% Adjt Bonds	
	" " 100 Cent London Ordy shares	
28	" " $5000 Atchison Adjustt Bonds	
25	" " Lire 55,000 4% Obl. Ital. Médit Ry	
31	" " £1000 Mex. Cent. Ry. Sec. Co. A Deb Stk	
25	" Cash	
12	" "	
22	" Applicn £10000 New Consols.	
7	" Call £10,000 do.	
2	" Applicn 500 Agr. Bk of Egypt Ord. Shs.	
17	" Cash	
28	" do.	
3	" do.	
8	" Applicn £10000 Japan 5% Bonds.	
15	" payment Cox & Co.	
11	" Call 500 Ordy Agric Bank of Egypt.	